ANTIGUA CALIFORNIA

FOR MURIEL STANDEVEN-FOSTER

Harry W. Crosby

Antigua California

MISSION AND COLONY ON THE

PENINSULAR FRONTIER, 1697–1768

Harry W. Crosby

Published in cooperation with
The University of Arizona Southwest Center
and the Southwest Mission Research Center

University of New Mexico Press Albuquerque

The watercolor facsimiles of original art by Padre Ignacio Tirsch are the work of Joanne Crosby. Tirsch was the only eyewitness to leave pictures of life in Jesuit California. With only minor alterations, the captions are those written on the paintings by Tirsch.

Library of Congress Cataloging-in-Publication Data
Crosby, Harry W. 1926–
Antigua California: Mission and Colony on the Peninsular Frontier,
1697–1768 / Harry W. Crosby.
p. cm.
Published in cooperation with the University of Arizona Southwest
Center and the Southwest Mission Research Center.
Includes bibliographical references and index.
Contents: Pt. 1. Colonial California's first half-century — Pt.
2. The organization and operation of Jesuit California — Pt. 3. The
decline and fall of Jesuit California — Epilogue. The aftermath.
ISBN 0–8263–1495–3.
1. California — History — To 1846.   2. Spaniards — California —
History — 18th century.   3. Jesuits — Missions — California.
4. Indians of North America — California — History — 18th century.
5. Baja California (Mexico) — History.   6. Jesuits — Missions — Mexico —
Baja California.   7. Indians of Mexico — Mexico — Baja California —
History.   I. Title.
F864.C924   1994
972'.202 — dc20   93–38946
CIP

Book design: Kristina Kachele

To Joanne Haskell Crosby

Sole keeper of the hearth and single parent while I did extended fieldwork and archival research off and on for thirty years. Thanks to her love and generosity, I was always able to return to a home and a family. My warmest thanks for that, and much more.

Contents

CONTENTS

Illustrations

Maps

Figures

Tables

Preface

Until 1769, the name California meant only the peninsula known today as Baja California. When a new frontier area was opened to the north, its pioneers dubbed it *Nueva California*, and began to call the peninsula *Antigua California*, partly from nostalgia, partly to eliminate confusion in the minds of those who were receiving reports from the region. By 1800, both names were discarded; the two areas were divided administratively and renamed Baja and Alta California. Today, Alta California is the most populous of the United States. Its history has been written many times over, but little attention has been paid to the modest peninsular settlement from which the giant sprang. This work looks back three hundred years to the individuals and events that created the first permanent California colony and influenced everything that happened thereafter in both Californias.

Antigua California remains a peculiarly apt title for the peninsula in the time of which I write. It retains a sense of prior history, the two hundred years of Spanish explorations, labors, dreams, and disappointments that led up to the colony's founding. It captures the poignant vision of two groups that left the peninsula at the time this work ends. In 1768, California's Jesuit missionaries, the founders of the colony, were ousted and exiled to Europe. The term *Antigua California* recalled for them the field in which they had labored for up to thirty years and in which sixteen of their fellows were buried. Meanwhile, men — and before long, women — who were born in peninsular California or had worked there for years, were pressed into service to take and hold Nueva California, far to the north. For them, *Antigua California* summoned up visions of home, family, and traditional life. This book is largely the story of these two groups; its title recognizes their feelings for the land they had claimed as their own.

Because of Antigua California's unique origin and development, its documentation had an unusual bias. Only Jesuits wrote its history and, to a great extent, Jesuit missionaries made its reports and kept its records. Their agenda limited their candor in reporting their own activities and in describing the people they had come to evangelize. They seldom had reason to report on the roles of their paid Hispanic help and had no interest in giving accounts of their private lives. When the Jesuits were forcibly uprooted and banished from the New World, their archives were commandeered and divided, some preserved for the government's bureaucratic purposes, some discarded, some salvaged by sympathetic churchmen or scholars. Jesuit California's records were diminished along with the rest; they were left, at best, dispersed and fragmentary. Wherever possible, I have tried to supplement the written record with personal examinations of the geography and the sites, the physical remains of buildings, roads, trails, waterworks, and other agricultural developments. In this pursuit, I received the indispensable assistance of several peninsular ranchers who guided and informed me. I have grateful and affectionate memories of my late friend, the remarkably observant and discerning Eustacio Arce. In the course of a decade, I spent more than a year with him and his son Ramón finding and photographing historic and pre-historic sites in the sierras of Guadalupe, San Francisco, San Juan, and San Borja. I also appreciate the excellent assistance that I had from Narciso Villavicencio of Rancho San Martín and Mulegé and from several members of his family.

I am deeply indebted to many people who helped me in my search for Antigua California's sparse and scattered documentation. I particularly wish to recognize Alan K. Brown, Ernest J. Burrus, Miguel León-Portilla, Doyce Nunis, Charles W. Polzer, and W. Michael Mathes — scholars who have transcribed, edited, and published key documents and taken the trouble to discuss them with me. W. Michael Mathes introduced me to several archives and their people, discussed my project, and assisted me with his encyclopedic knowledge of printed materials. Vivian Fisher has given me years of patient attention and expert advice on pursuing the incredible resources of The Bancroft Library. I thank Jorge Amao, director of the Archivo Histórico de Baja California Sur, Steve Coy of the Mandeville Special Collections at the University of California at San Diego, Rudecinda LoBuglio of Los Californianos, and Fritz Jandrey of Documentary Research of the Southwest for repeatedly digging up data at my request. I am grateful to Nadine Vázquez for sharing her finds in the Archivo de la Sagrada Mitra de Guadalajara. I thank Cristina Gil and Elisa Villalpando for directed research in the Archivo General de la Nación and the Biblioteca Nacional de México, respectively, and particularly Pedro Franco for keeping my interests in mind as he searched through the Archivo de Instrumentos Públicos de Guadalajara. I send my thanks afar to Dr. Peter Rivas of London, England, for sharing family research on the post-California careers of his ancestors, Pedro de la Riva and Cristóbal Gutiérrez de Góngora. I also owe a debt to Edwin Carpenter, Christon I. Archer, and Susan M. Deeds who read the manuscript and called my attention to errors and neglected opportunities.

Bernard L. Fontana of Southwestern Mission Research Center marshalled his organization and enlisted Joseph Wilder of The Southwest Center in the cause of this work's publication. I am most beholden to them and to all that were involved in their successful efforts.

People close to me made major contributions to the form and content of *Antigua California*. I am proud to be the recipient of their generosity and their skills. My daughter, Bronle Crosby Barba, helped to shape and prune every page of the text. My wife, Joanne, created the facsimiles of Padre Tirsch's paintings which supply our only visual evidence of California life in the Jesuit years. Paul Ganster, partner in my first peninsular adventures twenty-five years ago, undertook a general critique of this work, advised me at length and in depth on its historical context, and lent me many of the background works cited herein. Finally, I want to recognize the inspiration provided by my great-aunt, Frances Helen Relf, Ph.D., chronicler of the Parliaments of Oliver Cromwell, and by her grandmother, Gertrudis María Quiñones, my corporal link to the Hispanic world.

I

Colonial California's
First Half-Century

*The California peninsula was visited by Spaniards as early as 1533.
During the next century and a half, the Spanish crown repeatedly financed efforts to explore and colonize, but all failed. In the last years of the
seventeenth century, the Society of Jesus was authorized to occupy California in the name of the crown, but at its own expense. A Jesuit enclave was
established and produced an unusual frontier area. For half a century
thereafter, missionaries dominated most religious, military, economic, and
social endeavors.*

*Such concentration of power in religious hands was opposed by impor-
tant people in both Spain and New Spain. And even as it expanded, the
mission lost the support of many converted natives and failed to attract
others that the Jesuits hoped to convert. As the years passed, the Jesuit
monopoly in California weakened in the face of internal and external
challenges.*

ONE

The Road to California

 In October 1697, a small ship named *Santa Elvira* left an open anchorage near the mouth of the Yaqui River in Sonora, sailed to the peninsula that lay a hundred miles to the west, and landed ten men. California had already met Hernán Cortés, Juan Rodríguez Cabrillo, Thomas Cavendish, Sebastián Vizcaíno, Pedro de Porter y Casanate, Isidro de Atondo y Antillón, and Eusebio Francisco Kino. These names were familiar to kings and queens and included a conquistador, a viceroy, navigators, and a scientist. Cortés claimed the peninsula for Spain in 1535, yet in all the years since his time, no Europeans had established a lasting presence. After numerous visits and two extended, costly attempts at colonization, the native people were unsubdued and unconverted.

The *Santa Elvira* anchored off a gulf shore of California, lowered its long-boat, and landed these pioneers:

Padre Juan María de Salvatierra — the leader, a Jesuit missionary
Luis de Tortolero y Torres — a Spanish soldier
Esteban Rodríguez Lorenzo — a Portuguese ranch foreman
Nicolás Márquez — a Sicilian cannoneer and seaman
Bartolomé de Robles — a creole miner and muleteer
Juan Caravana — a Maltese artilleryman
Andrés from Cuzco — a Peruvian mulatto sailor
Marcos from Guázabas — a Yaqui warrior
Alonso from Tepahui — a Mayo herder
Sebastián from Ventitán — an Indian boy, the padre's page[1]

This least impressive of armies had come to stay. It was the vanguard of a small group destined to conquer California. The story that lay behind them stretched back over one hundred and fifty years.

How California Frustrated Spain

Shortly after the expeditions of Christopher Columbus, a Spaniard, Garcí Ordóñez de Montalvo, wrote a romantic adventure, *The Exploits of Esplandián*. Part of the work was set in the New World, the topic of the age. The author described a fabulous island replete with gold, pearls, and Amazons — standard ingredients in such literature, including the journals of Columbus himself. However, in fateful decisions, Ordóñez de Montalvo called his island California and placed it "on the right hand of the Indies." That ambiguous phrase seemed to describe a location just west of the North American continent since many Europeans believed that "the Indies" of Marco Polo lay not far beyond. By coincidence, an apparent island was soon found in just such a place.[2]

Hernán Cortés conquered Mexico in 1521, beginning the subjugation of the larger territory that he called New Spain. Within three years, the conquistador had reports of another land lying offshore to the northwest. In 1535, Cortés crossed the water to establish a base for exploring the new terrain and exploiting its resources. The discovery was soon called "California" because it was thought to be an island that answered Ordóñez de Montalvo's description. Of the supposed riches, however, Cortés found only a few pearls. He soon returned to the mainland to face other challenges.

Cortés's California settlement withered for lack of every necessity. The colonists had never dreamed of such an inhospitable place — hot, dry, sterile, and without readily exploitable resources. Worst of all, it lay far from any center of Hispanic population, supplies, or shipping. Many died before the colony was abandoned in 1536.[3]

By 1740, Francisco de Ulloa and Hernando de Alarcón, in separate sea explorations, had penetrated the Gulf of California sufficiently to be convinced that the new land mass was a peninsula — but their conclusions were rejected by European geographers. During the century that followed, navigators such as Juan Rodríguez Cabrillo and Sebastián Vizcaíno sailed around the southern tip of the supposed "Island of California" and far up the Pacific shore of North America. Strangely, neither they nor others who sailed those waters were able to present convincing evidence of California's peninsularity. In fact, navigators' reports were interpreted in ways that led to the perception that there might be two or more California islands, and *las Californias* became a popular and persistent form of the name. That and the firmly planted "island" concept would be perpetuated for over two hundred years.[4] However, if early seamen's charts and accounts could not clear up this sort of confusion, they did extend the concept of California far beyond the small area explored by Cortés. As navigators pushed northward, the name California came to include Spanish claims from the tip of the peninsula to Puget Sound.[5]

Sailing off the shores of the new land was one thing, but occupying it proved to be quite another. Inducements abounded. Cortés had returned from California with pearls. Gold was promised by the same romantic book that gave the land its name; that work also reinforced the medieval idea that great mineral wealth lay in hot and barren lands. Moreover, almost annually after 1565, Spanish merchants sent one or more of their trading ships, the *naos de Filipinas*, or Manila galleons, on an epic trans-Pacific round trip. These armed merchantmen sailed from Acapulco southwest to the Philippines where they traded Mexican silver for Asian goods and materials. The galleons returned by sailing north to the latitude of Japan, east to the shores of North America, then southeast along the coast to return to Acapulco. California was a Manila ship's first landfall after a voyage of more than three months. The personnel of these rich cargo carriers reached the California coast prostrate from malnutrition and with imperative needs for fresh food, rest, and water. In their weakened condition, they were easy prey for pirates who occasionally lurked around Cabo de San Lucas. The Spanish government planned endlessly to create a proper base for the protection and relief of the galleon crews and their ambitious sponsors, the speculating merchants who were so vital to Spain's trade. But even with strong incentives, this problem of the Manila trade was not solved — money was short, men were few, distances immense, and winds adverse.[6] During the seventeenth century, several public and private attempts failed to colonize California.[7]

The history of the peninsula suffers from a side effect of these failures. With no observers or chroniclers on the ground, little can be known about the size or condition of the population at the time of European contact or the subsequent cultural and epidemiological impact of a century and a half of occasional interactions between indigenous people and pearlers, explorers, and would-be colonists.

Spaniards Occupy Lands Adjacent to California

The conquistadors gained no permanent foothold in California, but they did extend their presence and control on the mainland east of the Gulf of California. Only a decade after Cortés's conquest of Mexico, Spaniards in search of gold and other immediate wealth stumbled upon an ancient trade route that linked the Guadalajara area in the south to the pueblos of New Mexico in the north. As fortune hunters and slave raiders pushed north along this "Road to Cíbola," they encountered a succession of agricultural peoples who occupied large, well-built adobe or wooden villages. Spanish leaders were disappointed by the lack of golden treasure, but some continued to dream of carving out personal empires in what is now Nayarit and Sinaloa. They called on the crown for conquerors' spoils, perquisites that had become customary, first in the Caribbean islands, then in New Spain. Some were granted the right to use vast tracts of land; some were given access to labor through *encomiendas*, patronage over a designated number of the natives.[8] Humbler conquistadors, underlings in the conquest, were granted minor parcels of land and restricted access to Indian labor. Frontier forts — *presidios* — were established and manned. A small but growing Hispanic population soon raised cattle in the environs of protective presidios and provided the basis for an effective Spanish occupation.

The conversion of native Americans, both to the Catholic faith and to a settled Hispanic way of life, was basic to the Spanish colonial plan. Explorers and conquerors on the west coast frontier of New Spain were accompanied by Franciscan missionaries and other clerics, all of whom had difficulty in converting the indigenous people. In 1591, the crown awarded the religious responsibilities to the Society of Jesus, a new, vigorously evangelical order.

The Jesuits had arrived in the New World half a century after the conquest began. Their first evangelical efforts in North America were impractical and short lived attempts, between 1566 and 1572, to settle and preach among Indians around Chesapeake Bay and in Florida. With idealistic fervor, they undertook the ventures without the protection of soldiers and paid the price by the loss of ten or more of their members. Meanwhile, plans were afoot to send Jesuits to New Spain, and the first arrived in 1572. By then, the populous regions with highly organized societies had been relegated to other missionary orders for conversion to Christianity and Europeanized village life. The Society of Jesus turned to available tasks, created a school system, and soon offered New Spain's foremost teachers and operated its best and most prestigious colleges. This function brought the order into close contact with the colonial elite class. However, the Jesuits soon became involved in the crown's renewed interest in adding lands and peoples to the holdings of Spain. The strongly-backed Royal Orders for New Discoveries of 1573 placed missionaries in the forefront of forces directed to find, occupy, and evangelize new lands. The active Jesuits made themselves available and, as noted, in 1591 accepted the challenge of New Spain's remote and inhospitable northwest frontier.[9]

By the late sixteenth century, the Society of Jesus was well established on the coastal plain that forms the eastern shore of the Gulf of California, then called the Mar de Cortés or the Mar Bermejo (Sea of Cortés or the Vermillion Sea).[10] Before a century had passed, Jesuits had created a series of missions in Sinaloa and Sonora that gathered thousands of converts. These neophytes learned not only the rudiments of Christianity but also the skills to propagate thriving agriculture and large herds of domestic animals, particularly cattle.[11] However, the Spanish government's ideal plan — which asked the military and the religious to perform different roles and to share power — seldom worked harmoniously. Missions occupied land and sequestered convert laborers. These same assets were coveted by local ranchers and miners, some of whom were soldiers as well.[12] Conflicts over authority and economic advantage were common in New Spain, but they reached unusual heights of acrimony in Sinaloa and Sonora, a circumstance that was to color the history of nearby California.[13]

The Society of Jesus

Jesuits came to the New World at a perfect time to infuse new life into a flagging system. The Society of Jesus had not been present during the conquest period; it arrived late and had its greatest growth at exactly the time when populations, economies, and the zeal and morale of other religious orders were declining. Moreover, the mendicant orders, of which the Dominicans, Franciscans, and Augustinians were conspicuous in New Spain, were creations of medieval impulses; their philosophies and their organizations were old. The Society of Jesus, founded in 1540, was an outgrowth of Spain's crusading zeal and the Counter Reformation, an age as secular and commercial as the former had been religious.[14]

The founder of the order was Saint Ignatius of Loyola, Spaniard and former military man, who conceived an efficient and in many ways modern organization. Jesuits knew their chain of command and obeyed the orders that emanated from it. One *padre general*[15] ruled them from Rome; a *padre provincial* headed each major geographical area in which the Society was represented. Within the walls of the order, members communicated with relative freedom and honesty. Rules covered most aspects of life, especially procedures by which the Society operated. Most observers of those or later times agree that Jesuits more scrupulously obeyed their rules than did members of other orders. All this constructive discipline gave Jesuits a sense of calm and security. They could take pride in the honor and respect accorded their organization. They could feel usefully and honorably employed. They were relieved of many individual responsibilities. They did not have to deal personally with the many levels of government or compete economically for a livelihood.

The Society was popular with young intellectuals all over the Catholic world. It drew on men of many nationalities, gave them excellent higher educations, and deployed them wherever the order needed them. This open policy contrasted with that of other religious orders that operated in Spain's possessions—most limited their local membership to Spaniards or their descendants. From its broader base, the Society found outstanding men; morale was very high; dedication and achievements reached levels that would have attracted attention in any time or place. All of this contrasted sharply with the slower and less-directed pace of other aspects of colonial life, encumbered with inefficient traditions and a government characterized by divided authority and endless bureaucracy.

Jesuit achievements worldwide attracted the attention of prominent people. Jesuit morality was viewed as superior. Jesuits conducted their internal affairs so privately that the public had little sense of discord. Despite being closely watched, the Jesuits inspired deepening awe and admiration. The Society's growing domination of higher education increased its advantages. Its students, the children of the influential and wealthy, appreciated their educations and, as they matured, rewarded their mentors with political favors and financial endowments. The Jesuits in turn cultivated those who favored them; they saw to it that their benefactors received public recognition from men at the top of their order and from the crown itself. In a country characterized by complex, overlapping jurisdictions in civil and religious affairs, the cohesive network of Jesuits and their supporters generated substantial power to further the work of the order. Hapsburg rulers of Spain favored the Jesuits because they made themselves available, volunteered for difficult duties, and achieved results. At all levels of the royal bureaucracy, officials turned to them for advice and assistance. Jesuits inspired confidence.

Not surprisingly, Jesuit success and influence provoked distrust and envy in many quarters. Other religious orders were jealous of the patronage and perquisites that the Jesuits seemed to have reaped at the former's expense. The secular church — the local cathedral and parish clergy under regional bishops — resented sharing religious authority and duties with missionaries as well as foregoing income from the lands and peoples that composed missions. Parish priests tended to be New World born; they and many nationalistic Spaniards resented the foreign religious brought in by the Society of Jesus. When the Jesuits invested their money wisely in land and animals — and ran their businesses with unusual efficiency — economic and religious rivals became bitter and made a common cause of anti-Jesuit muttering. Jesuit accomplishments were attributed to every sort of scheming, consorting, and covenanting that the jealous minds of competitors could devise.[16]

In seventeenth-century New Spain, no religious organization was as prestigious as the Society of Jesus or had the ear of more powerful people. Nevertheless, the corresponding increase in detractors and enemies helped to create a climate of opinion that resulted in the order's expulsion from the entire Spanish world that took place in 1767 and forms the end of this study of Antigua California.

The Jesuits Encounter California

During the seventeenth century, the Jesuits' mission chain was extended northward in Sonora until it flanked unconquered California and reduced its isolation.[17] Missionaries did more than dream about a harvest of souls across the gulf waters. In 1643, Pedro Porter y Casanate was in Sinaloa outfitting an expedition royally licensed to explore California. Padre Provincial Luis de Bonifaz, the head of New Spain's Jesuits, made a prophetic statement. He asked the superior of the Sinaloan missions to offer appropriate assistance to the explorers "because that other coast is to be ours to settle; the two missions will be sisters that help each other greatly."[18] He knew that Sonoran missions in the rich agricultural valleys of the Mayo and Yaqui rivers raised surpluses of livestock and foodstuffs and could help to supply a new mission venture.

In late 1681, Padre Eusebio Francisco Kino,[19] a Jesuit just arrived in New Spain, was assigned as geographer and mapmaker as well as missionary in a costly, government-backed effort to evaluate and colonize the California peninsula. From 1683 to 1685, *Almirante* (Admiral) Isidro de Atondo y Antillón led a group of soldiers, sailors, servants, colonists, and missionaries who tried to establish themselves, first at the harbor of La Paz and then at a site they called San Bruno on the mid-peninsular gulf coast. However, the expedition suffered

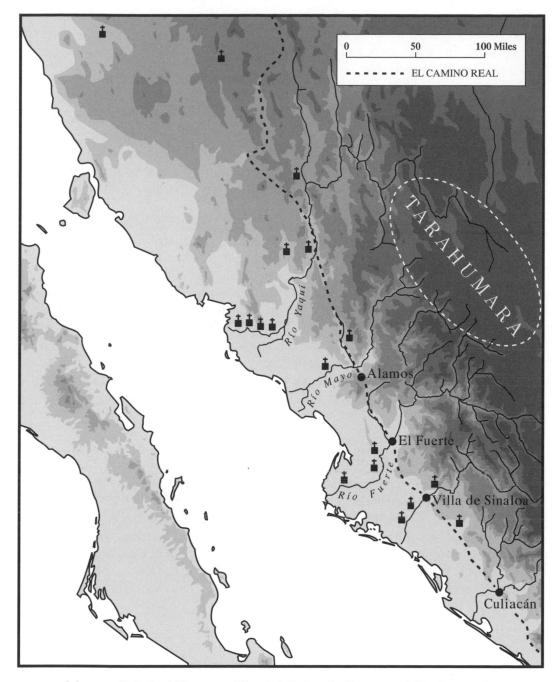

Map 1.1 Principal Towns and Jesuit Missions in Sonora and Sinaloa c. 1690

from an accumulation of problems and was withdrawn to a mainland port to regroup. Before it could be outfitted for a return, Spain experienced one of its periodic financial crises and the monies for California were preempted for more pressing imperial needs. Almirante Atondo had spent nearly a quarter of a million pesos and he blamed the new land's sterility and lack of usable resources for much of the cost. He helped to create a perception of California that dealt a severe blow not only to the continuation of his own venture, but also to the prospects of anyone who might later try to raise money for an occupation of the peninsula. After royal funding was withdrawn from the Atondo-Kino operation, the Society of Jesus declined to finance the activities that would be needed to reopen and sustain their suspended mission.[20] For the time, California was abandoned by all Spanish interests.

While Kino was with Atondo, necessity forced him on two occasions to leave the peninsula, sail to Sonora, and beg for large quantities of food at the Yaqui missions.[21] After his California mission was suspended and during the time he was waiting to return to it, Kino became convinced that a Jesuit California would need to have a close relationship with its prosperous sister missions across the gulf. Even the royal decision to abandon California did not end Kino's aspirations. When he received the news, he immediately wrote to his provincial to ask to be sent to the missions of Sonora; they were closest to California and from them he could pursue his return to the peninsula. When he was installed in Sonora, Kino wrote to a legal advisor of the Council of the Indies in Madrid to point out the prosperity of Sonora's missions and to ask for permission to plan a California campaign which those missions would help to supply.[22]

Kino sustained an active correspondence with benefactors to stimulate support for his ideas.[23] He initiated a campaign of letters and personal visits to fellow Jesuits in northwest New Spain. As a result, Padre Francisco María Piccolo, a missionary in the Tarahumara, became the first to petition the Jesuit general for a post with Kino in California.[24] As years passed, Kino regularly interrupted his routine missionary chores to carry out explorations that led ever closer to the head of the Gulf of California and a possible land route to the peninsula. Even as he established new missions among the Pimas, he initiated cattle herds that might some day assist a Jesuit expansion to California.

Kino and Salvatierra Plan a Mission to California

In midwinter of 1691, in the heart of the Sonoran desert, a pair of Italian missionaries rode from mission to mission. Far into each night on the trail, they sat before hardwood campfires and planned a religious conquest in the name of their chosen patroness, Our Lady of Loreto.[25] One of these men was Eusebio Francisco Kino. His companion was Padre Juan María de Salvatierra, recently appointed to be *visitador general*, the inspector of all Jesuit missions in northwest New Spain.[26] Despite the posts these men held, neither New Spain nor the Pimería occupied their minds. A California crusade was being born. Six years after his agonizing withdrawal from that storied land, Kino was enlisting for a new campaign.[27]

Salvatierra and Kino had much in common. Salvatierra was forty-two and Kino forty-five. Both were born into affluent, influential families in northern Italy. Both had university educations and had turned their backs on cultured, intellectual circles to undertake careers among people that their European peers regarded as savages. Salvatierra had worked for a decade as a missionary in the Tarahumara, the wild region of high mountains and vast gorges that forms a barrier between the Meseta Central of New Spain and Sonora on the coast. He was smarting from the setbacks suffered by Tarahumara missions during recent revolts by their neophytes. He felt that the natives had rebelled against abuses by Spanish military and civil authorities, but that his missions had suffered the consequences. He was more than receptive to plans for a fresh start in a new land.[28]

Eusebio Kino was already a considerable figure in the greater world. He had published research in the field of astronomy. He was respected for his role in Atondo's aborted California effort. His letters to influential people had stirred new interest in the mainland missionary frontier and the fabled "island" lying beyond. His subsequent labors were well on their way toward establishing an extensive network of missions in the Pimería Alta; yet Kino was restless. He had not willingly substituted service at mainland missions for the pursuit of his California dreams. He saw the two areas as a continuum, with rich Sonora provided by God to support the spiritual conquest of poor California.[29] Kino's determination was galvanized by the enthusiasm of his visitor general. Throughout Salvatierra's official visit to the Pimería, the two refined a plan to go together to take the prize that lay across the Sea of Cortés.[30] The particulars of their deliberations are not known, but much may be inferred from their later writings and the pattern apparent in their subsequent actions. Salvatierra and Kino reviewed California's history; in particular, they analyzed the failures of past expeditions. Padre Kino had experienced the rise and fall of a major campaign to establish a California colony and mission. He came away from it with strong opinions. He deplored the divided objectives and divided authority that resulted from an amalgam of secular and religious leadership. He had chafed under military rule and been appalled by some of its actions. At La Paz, Almirante Atondo overreacted to threats by a band of natives and ordered a cannon fired into their midst, killing or maiming a dozen men. That cost the Spaniards all contact with local inhabitants. They were forced to leave and make a fresh start far to the north.[31] Many expedition members had been primarily interested in harvesting pearls. A bonanza would have made them wealthy and gone far to justify private and government investments. However, efforts at pearling produced only discouraging results while occupying much time, manpower, and equipment. Colonists, too, were a burden. They became discouraged by harsh conditions and the short rations that resulted from long, insecure supply lines. They lost heart and clamored to be returned to New Spain.

All considered, Kino and his fellow Jesuits could not fault the admiral's decision to withdraw from California. They blamed the failure primarily on soldiers and colonists, but they also realized that the practical side of the religious effort had been inadequately prepared. In order to survive, a mission would need more capital, a better supply organization, and a nearby source of food. Kino hammered these points home—as well as his conviction that Sonoran missions could be tapped for much material aid.[32]

Salvatierra had not experienced the anguish of total defeat and the abandonment of neophytes whose instruction had begun; but he had felt the frustration of divided authority during his missionary years in the Tarahumara. Traditionally, church and military had gone together to effect the subjugation and conversion of a new region. Royal guidelines made their roles complementary: each worked in its own way to add people and lands to royal holdings.[33] Military leaders and their men undertook conquests, protected the missions, created routes and conditions favorable to trade and colonization, governed civilians, and performed other services for viceroys, audiencias, or the governors of their regions. Missionaries were assigned the responsibility of attracting native Americans to mission life, then holding and governing them while they were taught Hispanic ways and citizenship. The missionaries viewed this as service to God and felt rewarded by saving souls through conversion and baptism, but they and their missions were ruled and treated as instruments of the state.[34]

During the initial stages of religious conversion, frontier presidios provided military protection for the missionaries. Later, they helped to shield the missions and their converts from heathen foes. Despite the apparent harmony of the roles assigned to mission and presidio, there was dissatisfaction on both sides. Soldiers and padres had different viewpoints and different ambitions. Treatment of native people that soldiers thought just and natural often was viewed by missionaries as exploitation and rape. Even where soldiers' official conduct was adequately controlled, they were allowed, in their own circles, to practice "vices" that neophytes were taught to abhor.

During the seventeenth and eighteenth centuries, populations of civilians grew up around presidios to house families of soldiers and hangers-on. Soldiers engaged in activities aside from their military chores. Some soldiers worked fields of their own or grazed herds on broad tracts of land. In either event, they needed Indian labor. In many cases, the neophytes of a nearby mission formed the only potential pool of workers. Efforts to use this resource brought soldier-entrepreneurs into conflict with missionaries who resisted just such exploitation of their charges. Many soldiers chafed under restraints imposed by the religious.

Secular communities posed other problems for missionaries. Establishment of a presidio usually opened a region to trade and other forms of economic development. Commercial ventures attracted more colonists and created more distractions and more demand for labor from neophytes. Growing economic and social activity diverted the converts' attention from the desired religious focus of mission life. Silver ore was discovered in the Tarahumara during the latter half of the seventeenth century. The demand for Indian laborers grew intense and had the tacit support of a government that was principally financed by New World silver. When missionaries continued their efforts to isolate their converts and deny their labor to miners, they increased the outcry against missions and stimulated growing demands that they be secularized into parishes served by curates appointed by a bishop.[35]

Salvatierra and Kino were convinced that they could gain and hold the proper influence over neophyte Christians if they could achieve two goals. First, they needed effective control over the soldiers required to secure the desired territory.[36] Second, they needed permission to exclude colonists — people that, in their minds, would have a disruptive and degrading influence on mission converts. They knew these objectives would be difficult to realize. Colonization, commerce, and mining were cornerstones of royal policy. Keeping colonists at bay would require dogged persistence and exquisite diplomacy. The right to control soldiers was also a touchy issue. Soldiers served under a captain whose authority stemmed from the viceroy, the highest royal official in New Spain. Missions were nominally under viceregal control as well; but presidios and missions had prerogatives, in practice and by tradition, that were not easily rearranged to suit even so powerful a figure as the viceroy. In consequence, disputes between the two entities could not readily be settled; they tended to persist — to the particular detriment of missionary programs. As a practical necessity, the superior of a mission area often had to establish a satisfactory personal relationship with the captain in his region.

Jesuit missionaries found concessions to the military especially distasteful. The highly educated, upright, and righteous Jesuits had little in common with soldiers, sometimes reporting that even officers were too ignorant, coarse, self-interested, and proud to make satisfactory associates. The thought of deferring to such people, bargaining with them perhaps, was repugnant in the extreme.

As Kino and Salvatierra mulled over their grand plans for California, they struck on the concept of a single authority in the field. They worked out details for a different sort of *conquista*, religious to the core. The large, isolated Sonoran missions to the Yaqui and Mayo had provided them with more than an inkling of the advantages of relative independence,[37] but they aspired to more. In the fashion of the famous Jesuit institutions in Paraguay, their plan foresaw missionaries as the governors of an entire area and sole supervisors of all tasks required by both church and state.[38] They anticipated costs, problems of supply, and a host of other concerns.[39] When their arguments were thoroughly prepared, the two experienced missionaries felt ready for new careers in California. Salvatierra submitted a report of his Sonoran visitation to the provincial and added a letter in which he asked, as Padre Piccolo had done earlier, to be assigned to work with Kino for the religious conquest of California.

Although Padres Kino and Salvatierra were known and respected even in Europe, the provincial rejected the new proposal outright. He knew the bitterness of royal officials who had authorized the expenditures for Atondo's attempt to open California. The crown helped to fund all the existing Jesuit missions; the provincial refused to associate his order with requests for large sums of new money. Salvatierra then tried to go to the top; he appealed to the king and the Council of the Indies. When these letters were met with silence, the California conspirators realized that they would have to enlist broader support within both the Jesuit system and the government bureaucracy.[40]

Permission for the Conquest of California

Kino and Salvatierra's quest for a license ultimately became separate campaigns to two very different organizations: the government of Spain and the Society of Jesus. The former was as convoluted and declining as the latter was direct and vital.[41]

Because her New World possessions were so far away, Spain soon learned that she needed new methods of government for the colonies. As early as 1524, the crown had established a body to preside over American affairs; appointees were chosen from a wide range of disciplines that were judged useful for governing new lands and people: lawyers, churchmen, geographers, mathematicians, historians, and economists, each with an entourage suited to his area of expertise. This body was called *el Consejo Real de Indias*, the Council of the Indies.[42] Because cycles of reports and replies from and to the New World required months, deputy kings, called viceroys, were appointed and sent to rule each important territory. A viceroy was the most powerful authority in his territory. When the Council of the Indies wrote laws, it was usually the viceroy who interpreted them and translated them into political, social, and economic reality. He was responsible for defense, civil order, revenue collection, and the appointment of governmental subordinates within his area.

No viceroy could have dealt with all the myriad detail inherent in Spanish bureaucracy. Moreover, the crown desired checks and balances to the power that each viceroy exercised far beyond the royal view. Thus, regional tribunals, called *audiencias*, were installed in major colonial population and administrative centers. Audiencias were given legislative powers in some municipal and regional matters. They acted as advisory councils and as courts of appeal for some viceregal decisions. An audiencia was subordinate to its viceroy and to the Council of the Indies but advised the parent council if its findings differed from decisions made by its viceroy. When a viceroy died, was incapacitated, or when the office was temporarily vacant, the pertinent audiencia ruled in his stead.[43]

At its best, Spain's system of government for the New World produced satisfactory results, although it was always slow and cumbersome. However, by the latter half of the seventeenth century, government in the motherland was at a low ebb. The king was Carlos II, a mentally and physically incompetent product of centuries of Hapsburg inbreeding.[44] Carlos came to the throne as a small child. His authority was used by his mother and her entourage in a series of capricious intrigues that weakened the central government. As Spain drifted, many factions wrestled to gain control of their pathetic king. The struggle for power at the country's center led to greater freedom for wealthy nobles whose self-interested actions were more devastating to the government than even the numerous corrupt councilors and ministers. All aspects of Spanish life suffered and lagged. Hunger was widespread, and the population declined. Industry died; trade was wrested away by foreigners, chiefly Spain's traditional enemies, England and Holland. This erosion of infrastructure and power, combined with a series of costly military campaigns and defeats, virtually bankrupted the government.[45]

Spain's overseas governments declined as well. Positions on the Council of the Indies became prizes for the highest bidders rather than appointive offices held by qualified and respected professionals. Favorites of the powerful, rather than effective administrators, were appointed as viceroys. By the latter years of the century, seats on audiencias were also for sale — and were in great demand.[46] In this and other ways, de facto regional power and autonomy grew as the central government weakened.

Individuals or organizations in the New World could sometimes sidestep their viceroys by dealing with their audiencias and, through that body, reach higher councils. If they had access to higher authorities or courtiers in Spain, so much the better. The Jesuits created an effective network of official and unofficial contacts with all levels of Spanish government and society, but before Salvatierra and Kino could exploit this asset, they had to overcome the resistance within their own order. Individuals, even those as popular and respected as Kino and Salvatierra, could not simply declare their own crusades.[47] Any major undertaking had to be endorsed by a succession of superiors that ended with the general in Rome. Only with his support could a plan of such scope be brought before the civil government.[48] However, the hierarchy of the Society of Jesus remained conspicuously cool to the California proposal. The crown had been thoroughly disillusioned by the great amounts of royal money squandered on previous California ventures.[49] Jesuit leadership was understandably reluctant to associate itself with past failures and request additional outlays from a bankrupt royal treasury.[50]

Early in 1693, probably with help from influential friends, Salvatierra was made rector of the Jesuit college in Guadalajara. The energetic Jesuit found himself with more available time than he had had as a missionary and in a perfect position to promote interest in the California mission. Guadalajara was the seat of a bishopric, and its bishop, then Fray Felipe Galindo, had ecclesiastical authority over California and most of the intermediate lands. Salvatierra sought and received from Galindo the authority to administer the holy sacraments and to perform other ecclesiastical functions controlled by a bishop.[51] The Audiencia of Guadalajara had civil jurisdiction over the peninsula and had previously taken a stand like that of the Council of the Indies, opposed to spending more royal funds in California where Atondo had seen so little promise. Nevertheless, members of this audiencia, and other members of the elite class in Nueva Galicia, were susceptible to any plan to develop an area over which they had jurisdiction and from which they might derive profit by commerce or other means. They were all too aware of Guadalajara's secondary status after Mexico City, and they were always on the lookout for opportunities to develop business in their more remote and less-favored part of the Spanish world. A Jesuit mission would not lead directly to economic development, but it would be the necessary first step to establish the Spanish presence and open the peninsula to exploration. It was a simple task for the diplomatic Salvatierra to lobby effectively among Guadalajara's civil authorities and influential citizens.[52]

Salvatierra's most useful and best-placed ally was José de Miranda y Villayzán,[53] *fiscal* (attorney) for the crown seated on the Audiencia of Guadalajara.[54] Don José held a doctorate in liberal arts and had previous ties to the Jesuits as a teacher at their local college. In the spring of 1691, Miranda y Villayzán made a successful secret bid of eight thousand pesos to the Council of the Indies for an alternate's seat on the Audiencia of Guadalajara. The crown, however, had an ambivalent attitude toward the outright sale of influence; a royal order of the same year removed Miranda y Villayzán from the audiencia, precisely because his post had been purchased. Nevertheless, when he claimed the perquisites guaranteed with his purchase, he was put in a special waiting position and within a year or two received a full seat on the audiencia. By 1704, he advanced from fiscal to *oidor* (judge), a post he held until his retirement in 1718.[55] José de Miranda y Villayzán was an especially effective Jesuit advocate because of his connections. His brother Antonio was the influential dean of the Guadalajara cathedral chapter, and no doubt a confidant of the bishop.[56]

During 1696, Salvatierra sent a number of letters to Fiscal Miranda y Villayzán to explain his arguments for returning to California. With these ideas, Miranda y Villayzán persuaded his reluctant colleagues that opening California would serve the economic interests of the province of Nueva Galicia. He also forwarded his position paper to the Conde de Galve, viceroy of New Spain since 1688. The audiencia withdrew its opposition and sent the viceroy a formal request to grant Salvatierra's petition. Although the viceroy rejected these appeals, the incident marked a notable change in the attitude of some civil authorities.[57]

Kino and Salvatierra expanded the scope and frequency of their correspondence within the Jesuit chain of command. Kino, in particular, had the ear of Padre Tirso González, the general in Rome, a sympathetic ex-missionary under whom he had studied in Sevilla. By 1695, the provincial in Mexico City, Padre Diego de Almonacir, not only felt the pressure of the missionaries' petition but also learned that it was supported by the general.[58] While Salvatierra sought backing among the Society's prominent benefactors, Kino enlisted the assistance of his fellow missionaries in Sonora and the Pimería Alta, some of whom began to accumulate herds and stores to contribute to California.[59]

Funding was the crucial factor in gaining approval from both the Jesuit hierarchy and royal officials. Part of the blueprint that Kino and Salvatierra drew up with so much care depended on freedom from the regulations and interference that would inevitably accompany funding that they did not control. To overcome that obstacle, Salvatierra and his advisors worked out an ingenious proposal. They recalled that back in 1671 Alonso Fernández de la Torre — a citizen of Compostela, a town on the road between Guadalajara and Sinaloa — left an endowment for the establishment of missions in Sinaloa and California.[60] Kino had used income from this bequest to finance his 1683–1685 efforts to establish a California mission. This gift from Fernández de la Torre gave the enthusiasts the idea of financing the entire venture through donations that would establish an adequate endowment. This solution would disarm the opposition. The viceroy would feel less like a watchdog for royal coffers. Jesuit leaders would not feel called upon to share money earmarked for other missions. Outside the immediate California organization, the Society of Jesus would be relieved of any future financial responsibility. Nevertheless, a newly installed Jesuit provincial, Padre Juan de Palacios, was convinced that it was impolitic to defy *Virrey* (viceroy) Galve's stated opposition. Salvatierra overcame Palacios's resistance to the California project by spiritual blackmail; he suggested to the seriously ill provincial that his malady was the outcome of hindering a work dedicated to Our Lady of Loreto. When Palacios promised support for California, Padre Juan María took his novices to pray for the Virgin's intervention; the provincial recovered, and the score was settled.[61]

At the end of 1696, there were other promising developments. José Sarmiento Valladares, the Count of Moctezuma and Tula, was made viceroy of New Spain. He proved more sympathetic to the California proposal than either of his immediate predecessors. Padre Provincial Palacios was induced to present Moctezuma with a petition that spelled out pertinent arguments for the Kino-Salvatierra plan: the Society of Jesus was prepared to reoccupy California at no cost to the king. There were, Palacios emphasized, "pious persons who would assist us with alms" and ships promised at no cost to the royal treasury; all this largesse could be lost by delay or through the death of willing benefactors.[62]

Salvatierra and Kino played on long-standing royal interests. Many of Spain's woes had roots in the relatively easily acquired riches of the New World. Gold and silver had paid for goods and wars and luxuries while trade and industry were neglected; but now that Spain was desperate, no one in power wished to close the door on possible California riches. While making no promises, Salvatierra reminded the crown of the advantages of thriving industries in pearl fishing and mining, both paying royal taxes, and a port in California to assist the profitable but troubled Manila galleon trade with Asia. In the fashion of the time, a few other arguments were advanced that may have weighed little in serious councils but could be cited publicly for pious effect. The Atondo expedition had come away with three California natives whose people had been promised their return; Spanish honor was at stake in making good that promise. Moreover, Eusebio Kino and the other Jesuits, Padres Juan Bautista Copart and Matías Goñi, had begun the religious instruction of many natives. Further neglect of these converts would encourage them to relapse into their former heathen state, a blow to the faith and to the king to whom they had promised allegiance.[63] At the same time, Virrey Moctezuma was made the object of a private campaign carried out by Salvatierra in his typically thorough and pragmatic Jesuit fashion: the persuasive missionary obtained an audience with the viceroy's wife, Doña Andrea de Guzmán, and won her over as a most effective advocate.[64]

The proposal now had the ear of the viceroy and the Audiencia of Mexico. Stated simply, a responsible group of churchmen was proposing to give the crown a long-sought domain without expense to the royal treasury. Under these terms, there were no reasonable grounds for refusal. On 5 February 1697, Virrey Moctezuma granted Salvatierra and Kino a license to establish their mission in California. This license was exceedingly explicit about the powers and responsibilities that it conferred. On the paramount issue of funding, the viceroy wrote, "I concede the license which they request with the condition that nothing from the royal treasury can be drawn nor spent on this conquest without his Majesty's order."[65]

Salvatierra had been too shrewd to volunteer the services of his order or to undertake to pay all costs without receiving concessions in exchange. He boldly asked for and got control over matters normally administered by secular authority. His license broke with tradition and set precedents: Jesuits were given military powers. The superior of the mission to California was allowed to retain any armed men whose salaries he could pay. He had the power to choose and dismiss officers and, by inference, common soldiers; the viceroy merely had to be informed of changes. In the same manner, the missionary leader could appoint and remove civil authorities from office.[66] In exchange, the holders of the new license gave the easy promise that all conversions would be made in the name of the king, and the difficult promise to pay every peso of California costs.

Provisions of this license crop up many times in the following pages. The unusual concessions made by Virrey Moctezuma were to become as important as geographical isolation in determining the special character of California culture.

The Pious Fund

As soon as signs were favorable, even before the license was granted, a campaign was launched to obtain endowments. Salvatierra and Kino, patricians both, had networks of friends in high places to suggest who could be courted, how, and by whom. However, the problems of distance and slow communications remained. Kino, at work in the Pimería, was at the farthest extremity of New Spain; Salvatierra was in Guadalajara; most benefactors and royal officials were in or near Mexico City. Influence was exerted within the order and, in January 1696, Salvatierra was transferred to be rector and master of novices at the Jesuit college of Tepotzotlán, near the capital city. As soon as he was granted the license to open California, he was released from other duties and freed to go in person to solicit donations. At about this time, Padre Juan de Ugarte enlisted proudly as a third beggar for California. This prominent Jesuit, then a professor of philosophy at the Colegio Máximo in Mexico City, threw himself into the fund raising with the same energy and dispatch that would characterize his later missionary endeavors.[67]

The upper classes in the Spanish colonial world had accepted the evangelical and charitable enterprises of the church as part of their responsibility. They applauded and esteemed people who gave generously to pious works. In the late seventeenth century, Jesuit missions were a popular cause, and the Society of Jesus courted donors actively. Jesuit missionaries were assiduous in writing to benefactors about the spiritual progress that resulted from their gifts. Glowing letters contained verbal pictures of the happy faces of people rescued by Christ and Mary from benighted heathendom. They described little children baptized with benefactors' names. Some of these had died and stood now as "candles in heaven." This baroque religiosity had enjoyed a long vogue and did not strike the recipients of the letters as extravagant in any way. European or creole patrons did not live on the frontier in contact with non-Christians; they had no idea of their actual states of mind. The popular reports of the time led them to imagine the heathen as existing without purpose in the darkness of a moral void, hidden from the light of Christian doctrine. The unconverted were commonly thought to be in a sort of joyless limbo, dumbly awaiting a salvation they would embrace if only the Word could be brought to them. In an atmosphere of such beliefs, benefactors who made missions possible were admired by all classes of society and at times vied with each other to endow the likeliest missionaries. Not until the latter part of the eighteenth century did Jean Jacques Rousseau, with his "noble savages," help to create a romantic regard for primitive cultures and to initiate an anti-missionary point of view.[68]

But, at first, California did not appeal to the wealthy who engaged in fashionable philanthropy. Past failures had been well publicized. The skepticism of leaders in both church and government was well known. Many viewed Salvatierra and Ugarte as madmen because they proposed to do with private alms what immense sums from the royal treasury had failed to accomplish.[69] One affluent churchman showed his irritation by dismissing Juan de Ugarte by putting one peso in his doffed hat. The tide finally was turned by unexpected gifts from two men reputed to be practical and tight fisted. Alonso Dávalos y Bracamonte, the Conde de Miravalle, and Mateo Fernández de la Santa Cruz, the Marqués de Buenavista, each gave one thousand pesos — with striking public effect. The accounting soon showed eight patrons, five thousand pesos in hand, and ten thousand more promised.[70] It was a good beginning, but Salvatierra knew that the endowment for a new mission area would cost several tens of thousands of pesos, and ten thousand pesos was the cost of an elegant home, a year's income for a very rich man, or the dowries for two of his daughters.

However, the California cause was alive; circles of interest widened and soon included the first major contributor. In July 1696, Juan de Caballero y Ocio, a wealthy secular priest in Querétaro, donated twenty thousand pesos for the permanent support of two missions.[71] Another benefactor, Pedro Gil de la Sierpe, treasurer of His Majesty's royal exchequer at Acapulco, had wealth and a position from which he could make invaluable contributions. In October of the same year, he arranged to have the *Santa Elvira*, an old ship belonging to the king, made fit for service and then offered it for Salvatierra's use. Don Pedro later donated a larger vessel, the *San Fermín*, a large launch named *San Javier*, and a small launch called *El Rosario*. Both launches would serve long and well in California. The cost of the three vessels, plus Gil de la Sierpe's other contributions, represented more than twenty-five thousand pesos; in addition, he paid to maintain one soldier in California. He gave all this with enthusiasm and fervor as may be inferred from a passage in one of his letters to Salvatierra:

> I do not forget what I said to your Reverence, when I gave you the last embrace, namely, that I would beg alms for this work. And so I do nothing but talk about California, and about its conversion and the support for it, and I possess nothing that is not for this purpose. If your Reverence suggests it, I will sell my shirt. I cannot answer to my conscience if I do less.[72]

With such examples of pious generosity, more of the wealthy contributed. Skeptics were stilled as an endowment grew that might actually finance the quixotic venture. All money and property promised to Salvatierra, Kino, or Ugarte was pooled to form a single financial entity, a trust fund in support of California missions. A major new post was created — *padre procurador de Californias* — administrator of finances to oversee all monetary activity and record keeping for the new adventure. Salvatierra chose Juan de Ugarte, who had performed admirably in similar positions with Jesuit schools, to assume this vital responsibility.[73] Ugarte installed a central bookkeeping system and used the donated funds to buy *haciendas*, rural properties that were profitably devoted to raising sheep or cattle.[74] These investments formed the basis of the Pious Fund for the Californias, an entity that eventually grew to a value of several million pesos and endured for over two centuries.[75]

The Road to California

Juan María de Salvatierra displayed his typical optimism and self-confidence in the months that preceded the permit to open California. While he was still at Tepotzotlán, Salvatierra enlisted his first recruit for the new venture, Esteban Rodríguez Lorenzo, a Portuguese overseer at an hacienda owned by the Jesuit college. The choice of Rodríguez was to prove fortunate, like many of the padre's inspirations.[76] When the permit was rumored to be imminent, Salvatierra completed so many arrangements and gathered together so many necessities that he was able to leave Mexico City on 7 February 1697, only two

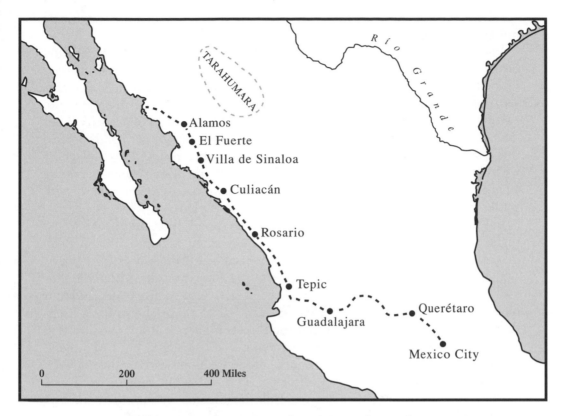

Map 1.2 Padre Salvatierra's Route from Mexico City to Sonora, 1697

days after receiving the viceroy's authorization. Before he left the capital, he arranged with Pedro Gil de la Sierpe to dispatch the promised ships from Acapulco at the proper time. Don Pedro also offered to find sailors who would stay to serve in California and said that he would try to send some soldiers. Salvatierra also visited Padre Juan Bautista Copart—who had accompanied Atondo and Kino—to borrow his glossary of the language spoken at San Bruno, the final site occupied during the earlier California venture.[77]

Juan María de Salvatierra set out on the principal roadway, or *camino real*, that would take him to Guadalajara and then on to Compostela and Rosario in the coastal province of Sinaloa. His duties as visitor general of Jesuit missions had taken him over this route several times. Because he knew the country and the people, Salvatierra counted on making most of the necessary arrangements for manpower and supplies along the way rather than in Mexico City. At Querétaro, he visited his benefactor Juan de Caballero y Ocio. In Guadalajara, he conferred with José de Miranda y Villayzán, his ally within the Audiencia of Guadalajara, and left carrying a letter of support from that body.[78] Salvatierra and Rodríguez arrived in Villa de Sinaloa during Easter week of 1697.[79] In the midst of the services and fiestas, they visited Martín de Verráztegui, who had served as a lieutenant under Atondo in California and was now a local official on good terms with the Jesuits.[80] Here was Salvatierra's opportunity to discuss military preparations with a veteran.

Just then an unforeseen obstacle blocked the path to California: a rebellion broke out at a mission in the remote Tarahumara. Sparks from the uprising ignited disorder all along the frontier of northwest New Spain.[81] Soldiers, ships, and supplies were diverted to fight the revolt; promises long-made to Salvatierra were set aside. A slighter spirit than his might have despaired; but the padre never doubted the divine inspiration of his mission; he had promised this conquest to Our Lady of Loreto and, in her name, responded to adversity with characteristic energy and fervor. While visiting the Tarahumara and doing what he could to calm the uprising, he continued to correspond regularly with actual and prospective supporters of his California plans.[82]

In four months, the crisis passed and Salvatierra and Rodríguez began to put together the pieces of their expedition. They visited Sonoran and Sinaloan missions and towns where priests and colonists had promised gear or provisions; these they packed on mules for the journey northward. At Rosario, they assembled a little collection of livestock: a horse, ten sheep, five goats, and four pigs bought or donated during their travels. While there, the padre was approached by a man named Bartolomé de Robles Figueroa. Robles was born in the town of Magdalena a few miles northwest of Guadalajara, but had gone to Sinaloa with a little money to try his luck at mining. Now destitute, he hoped to turn his hand to soldiering in California. The padre put him to work as a herder, and the caravan headed for Villa de Sinaloa in the north of that province, site of a presidio and a Jesuit college. Toiling doggedly in summer heat, Salvatierra and his growing entourage continued to gather necessities and moved north to rendezvous with other members of the expedition.[83]

On 14 August 1697, at about the time Padre Salvatierra was leaving the troubled Tarahumara to return to the coast, two vessels promised by Gil de la Sierpe finally arrived at Puerto Yaqui, a minor shelter at the mouth of the Yaqui River that was to serve as port and staging area for the expedition to California. The larger ship, the *Santa Elvira*, was a galliot, a slim, shallow-draft, partially decked craft intended to be rowed with sweeps as well as sailed. Juan Antonio Romero Gil de la Sierpe, a cousin of the benefactor, captained the craft. The sailing launch, *El Rosario*, destined to stay in California as the mission's own, was piloted by Juan de León.

The season of July through October is a traditional time of storms along the west coast of New Spain and that year they occurred repeatedly. Both galliot and launch had been badly buffeted during a slow and terrifying voyage from Acapulco. Although the crews came safely through their ordeals, much of the cargo did not. All the corn—several hundred bushels—was soaked by the storms and lost to subsequent spoilage. Fresh supplies had to be obtained from missions along the Yaqui, and that required time. The sailing craft were anchored in quiet water cut off from the river mouth by a great sand bar. Ships' crews had abilities as repairmen; those at Puerto Yaqui built temporary shelters on the beach and worked on the battered ships as well as shortages of equipment and materials allowed. They also contended with the heat, humidity, and insects of the season.

Gradually, the bare essentials were gathered at Puerto Yaqui. Padres at the nearby missions of Ráhum, Tórim, and Bácum generously donated thirty head of cattle. Those were slaughtered and the meat dried and delivered to the camp. The flour Salvatierra had ordered in Guadalajara finally arrived. Corrals and pens were built for the animals brought from Rosario.[84]

When most of the supplies were in and repairs effected, the expedition waited for two vital elements: more soldiers and Padre Eusebio Francisco Kino. As time dragged on, it became apparent that presidios on the frontier feared additional uprisings and were unwilling to release men who had volunteered for California.[85] At the end of September, a letter from Kino shocked Salvatierra. The great pioneer of the Pimería Alta had received the permits from his provincial, Juan de Palacios, and from Virrey Moctezuma freeing him to go to California. He sent them to Padre Horacio Polisi, superior of the Sonoran missions, and took the trail to Guaymas to join Salvatierra. However, Padre Polisi immediately wrote to the provincial to protest that in those troubled times only Kino could control and placate the disturbed neophytes of the huge area he had evangelized. Moreover, Polisi informed the governor of Sonora and New Mexico, Domingo Jironza Petriz de Cruzate, of Kino's release. The governor importuned the viceroy in the strongest terms, insisting that Padre Kino was worth more than a presidio in an area that threatened revolt. Both the provincial and the viceroy gave in to the arguments. Kino became the victim of his own success as he was ordered back to his mission. Padre Francisco María Piccolo was released from his mission in the Tarahumara to take Kino's place. For the second time, Spanish officialdom had denied Kino a return to California.[86]

Salvatierra now faced a major decision. His collection of food and stores would not keep indefinitely and could not be transported in one load. The *Santa Elvira* would have to make two crossings before it returned to Acapulco. If all the money and effort spent so far were not to be lost, he would have to go to California at once, shorthanded as he was.[87] The decision must have been agonizing. As his period of opportunity was coming to an end, the padre took inventory of the men at his disposal.

Ironically, after all the years of work and all the important people that had been involved in preparing this project, Salvatierra now had little choice in the men who would decide its fate. Nonetheless, Padre Juan María had received some help; the influence of his backers was evident even in the apparently haphazard group crew at hand. Religious and secular benefactors had done more than give money. They had used their prestige, their economic power, and at times their own poorer relatives to provide manpower for the new conquest. The indispensable patron, Pedro Gil de la Sierpe, for example, had not only dedicated money and ships to California, but he had also recruited his cousin as captain and found a crew that could be useful.

After assessing the men available, Salvatierra enlisted four who impressed him. One was Luis de Tortolero y Torres, a veteran soldier who had fought in

1694 as a volunteer in resisting the Moslem siege of Ceuta, the Spanish enclave in Morocco. Another was Nicolás Márquez, a Sicilian who had served many years as a sailor and, fortunately for the new conquest, as a cannoneer in the royal navy. Both men had had some education and must have seemed unusual in that out-of-the-way place. A third, Juan Caravana, like Márquez, was an old sea dog, a Maltese who had been a bombardier in the merchant fleet. The fourth, a young Peruvian mulatto named Andrés, was recommended by *Capitán* (Captain) Romero, who had had a chance to evaluate his predominantly Peruvian crew during the perils and exertions of the stormy voyage northwest from Acapulco. Without Gil de la Sierpe's help, Juan María de Salvatierra would have found it difficult to recruit such able men along the northwest coast of New Spain.[88]

Salvatierra's own religious order had helped him to obtain other recruits. He found Esteban Rodríguez at work at a Jesuit hacienda. Marcos de Guázabas[89] and Alonso de Tepahui were Indians raised in Sonoran missions, doubtless accompanying Salvatierra on the recommendation of their Jesuit missionaries. Sebastián de Ventitán, the missionary's own page, probably was obtained through contacts with brother Jesuits in Jalisco.[90] Such Indian auxiliaries regularly accompanied expeditions into new areas during Spanish expansion in the New World. They were able to serve several purposes, acting as low-cost servants and additional fighters during emergencies. Those now with Salvatierra were significantly Hispanicized. When taken out of their own cultural context, they would have little in common with the indigenous people of new areas and would be natural allies of the more familiar Spaniards. Thus, they could also serve by providing unconverted people with examples of native Americans operating in harmony with Spanish forces.

For the time being, Padre Juan María would have no fellow Jesuit to share his burdens; Padre Piccolo was not expected for days and would have to await another sailing.[91] Under intense pressure, Salvatierra considered his crew—nine men and a boy—and consulted his conscience. He prayed fervently and then ordered that the boats be loaded. The various containers of goods and provisions were carried down to skiffs and rowed out to the *Santa Elvira* and the sailing launch. Since the galliot would carry the livestock and passengers, the launch was loaded with sacks of grain, meat, and other delicate or perishable materials that might be trampled or jostled. At last everything was ready. The animals were loaded, and anchors were weighed. Late on 11 October, after two months of inactivity, the sails were unfurled. The ships moved out of their little harbor and into the quiet water near the river's mouth.

In less than a mile's sailing, trouble began. The *Santa Elvira*, heavily loaded, would not work to windward in the light air. The craft drifted onto a sand bar and it took the skill of Antonio Justo,[92] an Italian boatswain, and strenuous efforts by all the crew and soldiers to get it off. Some pushed with oars and poles, others manned boats, hooked up towlines, and rowed in an attempt to break it free. At last the galliot moved away from the bar. Once again the crew hoisted sails. As the *Santa Elvira* cleared the land and evening fell on the Sea of

Cortés, the air turned cool — a marvelous relief from the sweltering marshlands of the Yaqui delta. Padre Salvatierra, launched for California at last, had reason to offer up a prayer of thanks.[93]

Trials and frustrations soon intervened. Adverse winds blew the two vessels northwest of their destination. They became separated, and *El Rosario*, missing for days and then weeks, was feared lost altogether. The *Santa Elvira* put into Bahía de la Concepción for shelter (see Map 3.1). Here Salvatierra touched California soil and ate the fruit of a *pitahaya* (organ-pipe) cactus — his first California harvest — but he found no California people. When winds were favorable, the pioneers sailed the galliot ninety miles to the southeast to a beach near San Bruno in the vicinity of Kino's failed mission. During the days of sailing and delay, the padre chose Luis de Tortolero, on the basis of his experience and valor, to command his tiny, makeshift army.[94] He awarded Tortolero the rank of *alférez*,[95] the lowest grade of officer in presidial military usage at that time. (The modest rank reflected Jesuit thrift and the tiny command rather than depreciation of the new leader.) Alférez Tortolero's first official act was to lead a detachment put ashore near San Bruno.[96]

The landing party was greeted by a few Californians, Cochimí, some of whom had known Kino's mission twelve years before. The Cochimí led the newcomers over a difficult trail to the former mission site, and there the party spent the night. The experience was dispiriting. Water was scarce and brackish, and no arable land could be found. The shore party returned to the galliot for a conference. Capitán Juan Antonio Romero had sailed the coast two years before — probably in quest of pearls — in company with Francisco de Itamarra who had been one of Atondo's crew a decade earlier.[97] Romero recommended a bay some twenty miles to the south that had a landing place with more and better water close to the beach. Salvatierra was inclined to stay at San Bruno. The link with Kino and the past seemed important, and as he later admitted, he was tired and wished to avoid a move.[98] After inconclusive discussions, lots were drawn in the belief that Our Lady of Loreto would influence the decision. The slip selected bore the name San Dionisio, the place remembered by Romero.

On 18 October the *Santa Elvira* anchored near the strand of an open bay. Salvatierra and the captain went ashore.[99] A short time later the padre described his first encounter with the place that the natives called Conchó.

> Quite a few Indians with their women and children came to greet us.[100] They knelt to kiss the Crucifix and the Virgin. The group was camped about half an harquebus shot from the sea. [Harquebus: a swivel-supported musket with a range of perhaps a hundred and fifty yards] We went with them to see the water holes. We came upon them in an open gully flanked on the southside by a level mesa, elevated ten or fifteen feet above the water, and continuing to become a high mesa on the west.
>
> A spot on this mesa, about a gunshot from the sea, seems a great place for us to dig ourselves in. We would be protected on the north side by both the

height of our hill and the depth of the gully. The lower part of that water-course forms a small lake, somewhat brackish but suitable for our animals. Beyond that, on the other side of the valley, is a great stand of carrizo; arrows shot at us from that distance would lose their force, whereas our firearms could reach the carrizo. Our herds can graze within our sight.[101]

Salvatierra spent the next day searching for a better site and then made his decision. Conchó was to become Loreto, named in honor of the patroness to whom he had committed his life and work. He dedicated the place to her in a ceremony performed on 19 October 1697.[102]

So it was that this tiny band began the long-awaited Hispanic occupation of California. By design, it was to be a purely mission venture and for two-thirds of a century it retained that focus; but from the beginning, missions were not the whole story. Hispanic soldiers and servants helped Salvatierra and subsequent missionaries to found and expand his California colony. Jesuit chroniclers largely ignored the impact of these humble assistants; they were seen as incidental necessities in the religious conquest; but however unacknowledged and little reported, these ordinary men and their families had come to stay. From their stock, which was neither missionary nor convert, arose an Hispanic population that would supplant the Indians and outlast the missions.

TWO

The Pioneer Period, 1697–1701

Native Californians

When Padre Juan María de Salvatierra landed at Conchó, he needed all his Tarahumara mission experience and all of Kino's information and advice to gain a foothold among California's people.[1] Each band, tribe, or nation in the New World was distinct, but not many were as unusual as the groups on this isolated peninsula.[2] Despite three distinct linguistic stocks, and therefore three somewhat different cultures, the material attainments of all the peninsular peoples were strikingly similar.[3] Few cultures north of Tierra del Fuego had such rudimentary technology; Salvatierra found himself among people who had no agriculture, no fixed places of residence, no permanent or portable shelters, and little clothing—none on men, and only grass skirts on women. They had no boats, no pottery, and no domestic animals—not even the dog. The list of what they lacked seems more impressive than a tally of their possessions and attainments. However, that tally is based on sources of information that are few, fragmentary, and biased. Very little archaeology has been done and reported; and by the time formal ethnography began to develop, all the cultures of the central and southern peninsula were extinct. The few seventeenth- and eighteenth-century accounts of native Californians suffer from the limitations of their authors' European perspectives. In the cases of Jesuit observers, missionary needs and objectives also influenced what was and was not reported.

The Californians' material culture was not as impoverished as it was proclaimed to be. Europeans placed high value on structured societies, fixed communities, large permanent constructions, durable implements, elaborate clothing, and realistic art. Visitors to California found none of these. Peninsular people apparently had rather egalitarian societies, lightly ruled by headmen and informal councils of elders. They moved about constantly, so they manufactured for long-term use only objects small enough and light enough to transport readily. They used fibers from agaves and yuccas to make strong, light cordage and various nets, some for fishing, others for containers. The same fibers were the basic material of women's skirts; short segments of fine cane, *carrizo*, were strung on them like beads to fall in two broad bands centered front and rear. The Californians also worked fibers and leaves into fine basketry. They pierced their ears and noses and wore decorations of shell or bone. They tattooed designs into their skin. They created elaborate hairstyles enhanced by inclusive ornaments of pearls, mother of pearl, or seeds. They worked wood to form bows, arrows, lances, bowls, and ceremonial objects, the last elaborately and expertly painted. They ground colored minerals to very fine powders to be used as pigments for ritual rock paintings, typically located on walls or ceilings of large, open caves and rock shelters. They painted different subjects in different areas: in the north and south, abstract figures; in the mid-peninsula, larger-than-life, stylized men, animals, birds, and fish. They engraved the soft rock found in caves and the hard, desert-varnished surfaces of basalt boulders, usually with abstract figures, but occasionally with representations of life forms like those in the paintings.

The natives were divided into semi-autonomous bands — Spaniards called them *rancherías* — fifty to eighty people who had to move about in an annual cycle to strip their living from the natural resources in different areas. Despite the fact that the land had to support only about one person per square mile, existence was precarious. People gathered edible roots, stems, seeds, and fruits — eating some as they were found, and grinding, roasting, or boiling others. They caught grubs, insects, rodents, bats, snakes, lizards, and occasionally larger game such as deer, mountain sheep, or antelope. They combed seashores for shellfish and built simple rafts from bundles of cane-like grasses or from the light, pithy trunks of a local tree. From these, they caught fish with either spears or nets. All their activities were, however, limited and controlled by the constant scarcity of water. People foraged around a known source, then were forced by necessity to move quickly to another.[4] A Jesuit later wrote of them:

> God alone, who has numbered our steps even before we were born, knows how many thousands of miles a native eighty years of age has wandered about until he has found his grave, from which he was all his life separated only by a finger's length. I am certainly not greatly mistaken when I say that many of them change their sleeping quarters more than a hundred times a year.[5]

The Californians' struggle for existence was the most laborious and unrelieved that Kino, with all his frontier experience, had ever witnessed. He and Salvatierra had discussed its implications for their new mission and adopted a simple but powerful plan that had been used repeatedly by missionaries in northern New Spain. Food would attract the scattered heathen to the mission and hold them during indoctrination. In the Orient, people drawn to missions in this way have been called "rice Christians," but the Jesuits expressed no misgivings over this visceral lure to a spiritual goal.[6]

The Battle for Loreto Conchó

Padre Salvatierra's party remained armed and alert as it took up a position on a hillock above the beach at Conchó. Kino had reported that natives in the area possessed weapons, were accustomed to their use, and were capable of turning against neighbors and strangers alike. The size and makeup of Salvatierra's "army" reflected his difficulties in recruiting and the depth of his faith more than it did his common sense. His lone officer, Alférez Luis de Tortolero y Torres, was an experienced soldier, but the unit of nine men and a boy was tiny when compared to the military forces employed in the times of Cortés or Atondo. But this group did have some advantages over its predecessors. It was not encumbered with colonists or entrepreneurs; it had no need to expend time and supplies in seeking and developing local sources of wealth. It was armed with Kino's experience and so did not expect to be self-sufficient. It was well supplied for the immediate future and had relatively nearby support from Sonoran missions with large food resources. Finally, the lexicon that Padre Copart developed in 1685 allowed the newcomers to communicate with local people.[7]

When the camp site was cleared, the *Santa Elvira*'s longboat was used to transfer cargo to the beach. Domestic animals were landed first, then the sacks, bales, barrels, and boxes that contained equipment and supplies. The mission party then began to move its goods to the clearing and arrange them into an open square.[8] The ship disgorged supplies, its crew labored to bring them ashore, and the landing party struggled to carry them up from the beach. At first, the local people watched the landing activities with simple curiosity. When a few offered to help, the experienced missionary reinforced the positive impulse by ordering his men to unpack a cauldron, support it over a fire, and fill it with a mixture of water and grains, ingredients of a staple mission food called *atole*. When the volunteers were fed along with the crew, many more stepped forward, and the tempo of work increased.

However, as the greater body of native Californians realized that food was stored in the camp, they began to press toward it, and the missionary party felt threatened. The newcomers dug a trench around their goods and made a barrier of thorny mesquite branches. Seeing this, the local people became angry and menacing. The padre's men landed a *pedrero* (a mortar designed to fire a charge of stones) from the galliot, dragged it up to the fortress square, and anchored it to the trunk of a mesquite tree cut for the purpose. The unloading continued in this uncongenial atmosphere for three days. On the fourth night, rain drenched the area. The following morning, an effigy of Our Lady of Loreto was landed and greeted with salvos of gunfire. Her church was a tent raised next to a large wooden cross erected in the compound two days earlier.

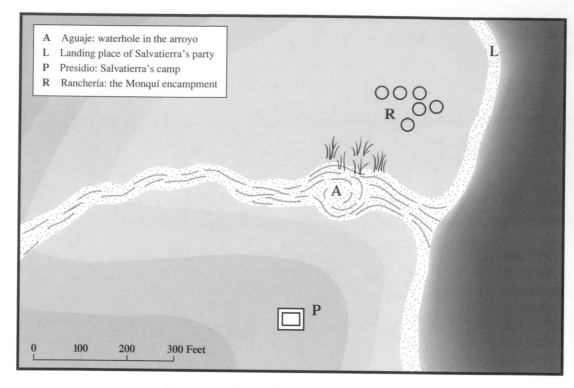

A Aguaje: waterhole in the arroyo
L Landing place of Salvatierra's party
P Presidio: Salvatierra's camp
R Ranchería: the Monquí encampment

Figure 2.1 Loreto Conchó, November 1697

On the seventh day, the ship departed to search for the launch lost during the gulf crossing. The ten pioneers were left to cope with hundreds of curious Californians who had been attracted by their presence at Conchó.

From the first, the missionary party suffered a measure of pilfering but took no punitive action. Some of the Californians in the encampment had cooperated with the Atondo-Kino expedition, and Salvatierra did not want to overreact to trivialities. As time passed, however, there were more ominous developments. More natives appeared daily, and all became less cooperative. They did little work and paid less attention to the padre's attempts at religious instruction. They continued to demand food and, by early November, some were attempting to drive off and slaughter the small herd of livestock brought from Sonora.

For three weeks, the Californians' attitude became increasingly threatening. Finally, an aged chief who had known Kino left his deathbed to warn Salvatierra that his fellows were planning an attack. A few natives continued to come to the camp for religious instruction and the gruel that followed it, but the majority remained aloof and their ranks grew daily. Men from four different bands, about two hundred strong, congregated around the tiny enclave on the mesa above the beach. On Wednesday, 13 November, they called out to their fellows in the missionary camp and warned them to leave. The Battle of Conchó was begun.

Salvatierra's first report from California, written two weeks later, makes clear that the fate of the expedition and the years of preparation by many devoted people came to depend on a handful of employees who now doubled as soldiers.[9]

We heard some shouting in the area of the reeds; Alonso, the Christian Indian from Tepahui bravely drove the few escaped sheep and goats to the little corral within the compound. Inasmuch as the pigs were not far away, the lieutenant, a soldier, and another Sonoran Indian, went out and brought them in. . . .

Arrows began striking our compound. . . . We were under attack from all sides. From the wash of the watercourse below, one of the groups charged, protected by a rearguard that came down the arroyo, and they in turn protected by a contingent on the heights of the mesa. Thus they had us walled in on two sides [with forces] in the valley and on the mesa that looks down on it.

Our little group also took up its position. Our leader, Don Luis Tortolero, and Bartolomé de Robles Figueroa defended the most dangerous spot — at the juncture of the valley below and the mesa closest to the sea. At the center of the beach side was Marcos, a very courageous Sonoran Indian from Guazabas who labored mightily in the battle. To the rear of Don Luis stood another Indian, Alonso from Tepahui; and in the center below him, Andrés, a mulatto soldier from Cuzco in Peru. Along the strongest trench, at the least dangerous spot, on the last side of the mesa, the Portuguese, Esteban Rodríguez, took his place. Stationed near the gate, at the corner of the compound, was the Maltese bombardier, Juan Caravana, who had served on the Manila Galleon. He was in charge of the mortar defending the entrance. On the other side, facing the beach, was the Sicilian, Nicolás Márquez, who had served our king for many years as bombardier.

I was also along the trench and tried to go from one place to another wherever the danger seemed greatest. My helper was an Indian lad [Sebastián Martín] from Ventitán near Guadalajara.

The four groups of hostile Indians were from as many different tribes. . . . On the two sides above us were the Laymón from beyond the Giganta. The Monquí occupied the southern side. The Didiú and the Edú held the heights and low areas towards the beach.[10] All four groups made a concerted assault on our position. Besides shooting arrows, they began hurling rocks from the heights on two sides.

The barrage of rocks continued for two hours, then ceased, but arrows continued to fly. After a half-hour rest, the original attackers, with reinforcements, made a second and more determined assault. Salvatierra described the perilous events that ensued:

No use had yet been made of the mortar, reserved for the final and desperate stand, many of the men having the greatest confidence in it. From time to time they would pretend to be on the point of firing it; each time the groups of natives would withdraw in fright from the junction or valley above.

Finally, our leader, compelled by this second charge, resolved that the Maltese bombardier should fire off the mortar. The most holy Madonna worked a veritable miracle in preserving from death me, the bombardier, and the two soldiers standing nearby, because the mortar burst with such violence that the surrounding wall was smashed to pieces, hurling part of it some six paces away; even the iron wedge was split into three pieces, each one flying off into a different direction. The mortar's magazine was hurled some nine paces with such force that it sailed almost directly above me. I did not notice it until I saw it lying several yards beyond me. The bombardier was knocked over by the mighty rush of air when the mortar exploded. He fell from his position to the ground below with such violence that he remained unconscious. . . . Two blows brought him back to his senses, and we realized that he was not seriously injured. He snatched up his weapons and again took part in the battle.

We all regained courage to fight until death. The enemy also grew more insolent. Word was quickly passed to all the groups that, since the mortar caused no casualties, much less would the two little harquebuses. By virtue of this conviction, they closed ranks, coming from every direction, for the final assault, certain now of finishing us off and seizing the booty. They now approached with such insolence that I felt obliged to accost them on the side where the mortar was; and, standing before them, I warned them that, unless they withdrew, they might be slain. Their reply was to shoot simultaneously three arrows at me.

In this desperate strait, God inspired me with the conviction that it would be wiser to lend the men a hand. From the moment when the natives no longer obeyed the voice of their Padre, they were struck down from every side — some were injured and others were killed outright. Disheartened and terrified at our valor, they all withdrew simultaneously at about sunset.

The most absolute silence ensued. After some fifteen minutes, we saw the sick chief emerge from the reeds facing our trench and come through the valley below. Because of his illness, he walked very slowly toward our compound. . . . We received him with great happiness . . . for he came as a harbinger of peace, weeping, tears flowing freely as he entered. Sobbing, he told us that three of the attackers died. He was amazed to find us so cheerful and unharmed. Both Alférez Luis and Bartolomé de Robles, a soldier, were hit by arrows, but, since the injuries were not serious, they said nothing about it, and not even the rest of us knew about it until late at night; nor did any of the Indians ever learn about it.[11]

The principal weapons used to defend the makeshift fort were a pair of harquebuses, or swivelguns. These were not much more than oversized muskets mounted atop stout tripods and suspended in devices which, like oarlocks, allowed them to swivel 360 degrees and tilt up or down. Juan Caravana and

Nicolás Márquez, the experienced cannoneers, probably manned the harquebuses. The mainland Indians used bows and arrows; everyone else fired muskets since the enemy was never close enough for the use of lances or swords.

Salvatierra did not describe his exact role in this drama. In his letters, he modestly gave credit to his "army," and, in any event, would not have been so impolitic as to emphasize unpriestly behavior. But his various reports leave no doubts about his active role. He progressed from such circumspect references as, "I tried to assist at whatever place danger most threatened," and, "God inspired me . . . to lend the men a hand . . . ,"[12] to the more revealing "in the midst of seven pieces of bronze and iron that flew past our very hair from the burst mortar, we encouraged each other with rapid reloading of the guns."[13] Nor is it unlikely that the Jesuit took an occasional shot himself. His proficiency with arms is revealed in another passage relating not to battle but to exercises intended to impress and educate Californians: ". . . every effort was made to have the natives realize the might of our weapons . . . a board was set up as a target at a considerable distance. All took turns at hitting it to show that they knew how to shoot. I also took a shot—one of the best of them all."[14] Every missionary sent to a heathen frontier anticipated martyrdom as a possible end to his service, and dozens of letters show that Jesuits were well prepared to pay this price. However, there are few reports of fighting padres, and one of the Society's regulations, promulgated in 1662, forbade the use of firearms by its members.[15] Salvatierra's role in the defense of the compound reveals his pragmatism, the degree of his commitment to the conversion of California, and a partial explanation for his considerable success.

Salvatierra's improbable army had established a base and, though greatly outnumbered, successfully fought off the Californians' concerted attack. The missionary gave his troops generous notice and praise for the skills, valor, and determination that saved his enterprise. He knew, too, that public praise and tangible rewards could help in recruiting—and more men were sorely needed at Loreto. These considerations were reflected in the report that he wrote to Virrey Moctezuma two weeks after the battle.

> All of these poorly equipped soldiers, so few in numbers, fought like lions under the command of Don Luis Tortolero y Torres. [Elsewhere,] I have recorded their names to serve as an example to their successors. I find verified in them what I said to Your Excellency "a few determined Spaniards suffice to effect an extensive conquest." I should like to encourage these poor pioneer conquistadores. If it could be arranged, some reward or supplementary pay given by the king in recognition of their victory would be most effective. I leave all to your wisdom and decision. After the victorious battle, and in your name, I appointed Don Luis Tortolero y Torres to be captain of this garrison as a reward for his competency and valor.[16]

This dramatic battlefield promotion demonstrated Salvatierra's foresight in appointing Tortolero initially with the modest rank of alférez. He was thus able to reward the officer promptly for his valor by raising him to the rank of *capitán* that the leader of a presidio was expected to hold.

Constructing a Base for the Mission

The long overdue launch, *El Rosario*, arrived to a heartfelt welcome two days after the battle. The men in the beleaguered enclave recovered not only lost comrades but also dried beef, their best grain, and the vessel itself. They counted on skipper Juan de León and his crew to make this little craft — variously called sloop or launch — their contact with the outside world.

In another week, the galliot returned with more supplies and men, including the second Jesuit, Padre Francisco María Piccolo.[17] The new man was more than just another missionary. In addition to experience, energy, and dedication, the tall, fair, blue-eyed Piccolo made a striking figure to impress the Californians.[18] Like Salvatierra, he brought a young neophyte to be his servant. Piccolo's man, a Tarahumar named Ignacio Javier, would accompany his master on all his expeditions and journeys for many years.[19]

Padre Juan María described the work done by his enlarged party to strengthen the defenses around his headquarters.

> We began immediately to build our stronghold on the height, near the pond and the water holes. The fortification is strong, consisting of two rows of stakes driven into the earth. These stakes are united by reeds, making a continuous barrier. The two rows of stakes are banked up with earth on both sides; this bank is about a yard in thickness. We did this that we might resist not only the Indians but even an enemy ship. Within the fort we built the Holy House of the blessed Virgin and the House of Loreto. Joined to the church, on one side, there is a large room, and on the other side another room for the captain and the fathers.
>
> The heathen Indians, both men and women, helped us very much in building the fortification. A great deal of labor was involved in raising the bank of earth which comes to the height of a man's neck. We left many gates in it through which the Indians could go and come at their pleasure before we took up our residence within. We did this in order that the heathen might not understand how we were going to use this fort. For in the meantime our men were lodged in the old fortified compound built of boxes, bundles, and crates, and overlooking the new fortification, which as yet was not finished. On the outside we completely surrounded this new stronghold with the sharp spines and thorns that grow in this country, to serve as a defense against any persons who might try to leap the breastwork.
>
> The new fort is practically triangular in shape. It is defended by a small field-gun and by two swivel-guns. But one of the latter will not be good for more than a shot or two; for on November 13th, the day of the general attack, it broke, and we have tied it together as best we could. In addition, with the

assent of all our soldiers, our gunner employed a ruse, by which he has deceived some of the Indians. He loaded two iron pipes with stones and shot. He set them up on the fortification on either side of the church. Then he signaled one of the California Indians, a friend of his, bidding him bring him a firebrand, so that he might fire the guns. But the Indian entreated him not to fire, because it terrified him. We have profited well by this ruse. From a distance, these "cannons" look convincing and strike terror into the Indians.

And so, when everything was done in the new fortification, one very chilly afternoon, when the Indians had withdrawn because of the cold, our men worked tirelessly, dismantled the old fortification, and took all our supplies to the new. Before it was time to sleep, we were securely settled within our new fort. The following morning, the California Indians were surprised when they saw that the gates had been closed and that, within this short time, we had settled ourselves inside a new stronghold. On the eve of the Feast of the Nativity, Padre Piccolo consecrated the new cross and the church, both made of the wood of a white tree, [palo blanco (*Lysiloma candida*)] which resembles that which on the mainland is called dragon's blood. This luxuriant and showy tree grows in great abundance in this valley. We have been able to build all structures within the fortification with these trees.[20]

Supplies and Reinforcements

More help arrived in February 1698. Juan de León and a crew of four had taken the launch to the mainland. They returned during a violent storm that León decided to ride out in the lee of Isla del Carmen, an ordeal that lasted for two anxious days. Salvatierra reported the outcome of Loreto's vigil of fear and prayers:

> During the night the sea became quiet, and with dawn on Saturday — Saturdays are fortunate days for this conquest — there was a profound calm. Therefore, early in the morning, it was easy to land the reinforcements brought by the launch. Six persons arrived: four of them Spaniards — all experienced soldiers — one mestizo, and a Yaqui Indian.
>
> The Spanish soldiers had been comfortably placed in New Spain. They come to us impelled purely by zeal for the Faith and by a desire to establish the Holy Cross in this new kingdom. They endured many sarcastic remarks from their friends and spent whole months near the shore, waiting for the launch. Finally, they embarked in this small vessel and endured many discomforts and hardships.
>
> One is Isidro [Grumeque] de Figueroa from Sevilla, now made alférez of this company. He is a soldier highly recommended for skills in handling arms. The second is Antonio [García] de Mendoza from La Rioja in Old Castile.[21] He has been alférez and adjutant and held other positions in the presidios of Spain — at San Sebastián and on other coasts. He is a master wood-worker.

The third is Joseph Murguía, a Basque. He is a brave soldier and has participated in many skirmishes with the Indians at the presidios where he has
served both as soldier and surgeon. Now, without regard for his own interests,
and moved purely by zeal, he has come to serve in both these capacities. The
fourth is named Juan de Arce, an Englishman brought up from boyhood in
New Spain, who has served in the presidios of Sinaloa. The mestizo is named
Francisco de Quiroga. The Indian boy, Marcos, belongs to the Yaqui tribe; he
is very strong and a good fighter. These reinforcements, so entirely unexpected, overwhelmed all of us with joy. We encouraged one another, and were
ready to do battle with the whole of Hell.[22]

Salvatierra was putting the best possible face on the matter. He needed
manpower badly, especially skilled men, but these recruits were different from
the initial nine; these European volunteers had no ties to Jesuit well-wishers.
Probably, some were adventurers, men with an eye out for worlds to conquer
and resources to exploit. The word had spread on the mainland: California had
been opened once again. Entrepreneurial eyes were doubtless alight, and those
willing or needing to gamble were on the move. Of the new recruits, only
Marcos, the young Yaqui warrior, fitted into a familiar category. He came from
a Sonoran mission — doubtless at the suggestion of a Jesuit — as had Alonso and
the other Marcos in Salvatierra's original crew.

Loreto's garrison now numbered fifteen: nine Europeans, a *criollo* (a creole, or
person of European descent born in the New World), a mestizo, a mulatto, and
three mainland mission neophytes. Despite their widely different backgrounds,
these men shared aspects of a common culture and religion. Throughout the
eighteenth century, Hispanic frontiersmen employed a collective term — *gente
de razón* — to distinguish themselves from the heathen or the new converts. The
words literally meant "people with the capacity to reason" but in fact signified
people born into Christianity and Europeanized culture.[23]

A Second Wave of Resistance

In the months that followed, the padres and their helpers busily added to the
Real Presidio de Loreto, as the compound of the tiny fort was grandly called. The
Californians formed a large labor pool whose allegiance and aid could be
bought with missionary gruel, but they needed constant instruction and supervision. A pattern emerged that was characteristic in frontier military service:
soldiers set aside their arms and practiced and taught their civilian skills.
Soldiers and some of the new converts felled, stripped, and carried in the trunks
of mesquite and palo blanco. From these they fashioned the furnishings needed
in the pioneer establishment. They built stout corrals for the livestock. Gente
de razón with farming experience supervised the clearing of fields, the removal
and piling of stones, and the preparation of soil. Others dug shallow, open wells
and lined them with heavy pieces of stone. Some laid out and dug irrigation

ditches. Some set aside rocks to clear paths to water sources, animal pens, and the landing place on the beach below the fort.

The hundred or more Indians in attendance were ill at ease during all this activity. Some helped with the building chores and were receptive to Salvatierra and Piccolo's religious instruction. Others were present, but remained detached and uncooperative. Still more seemed to lurk in the neighborhood, resisting the blandishments of both food and the new faith. Those uncommitted to the mission were a disturbing influence for all but the most dedicated neophytes. Salvatierra saw and reported the situation in black and white terms; those who came to instruction regularly, worked, and took food were "good children." Those who resisted were "bad" and would have to be coaxed or, ultimately, forced to cooperate.[24]

Actually, the missionary had injected himself into more complicated circumstances than he perceived. He was not dealing with an otherwise homogeneous people that happened to be divided into elements that cooperated or did not cooperate with him. Conchó was an uneasy meeting place of groups that represented two different cultures and linguistic stocks. The Monquí lived on the narrow coastal plain that runs from around Conchó to a point twenty miles to the south. They were an isolated splinter of a larger group, living farther south, that spoke a language called Guaycura.[25] The Monquí were surrounded geographically by bands that spoke dialects of Cochimí, the language of the people who inhabited the northern two-thirds of the peninsula. Moreover, beside confronting two different cultures, Salvatierra was addressing several distinct bands of each, rancherías composed of people related by kinship. Each had a different home area but often competed with other rancherías for the same food supply. Any of the four or five bands that assembled to visit Salvatierra's mission had pre-existing ally or enemy relationships with each of the other bands.

Similar situations developed in many places during the Spanish conquest of the Americas: smaller, weaker groups, or those temporarily at a disadvantage in local politics and diplomacy, more readily embraced Christianity. They saw the missionaries and their soldiers as allies against their traditional enemies. More powerful groups, with more to lose, held back, but they soon saw their adversaries under the strong protection of the aliens and perhaps preparing to turn the new power against them. Spanish intruders, religious or military, were concerned with their own motives and evaluated the internal problems of native American societies largely with an eye to using them to their own advantage.[26] By chance, Kino and Atondo had landed at San Bruno and established themselves among people they called the Didiú, a Cochimí subgroup. Some of the Monquí,[27] inhabitants of the Conchó area, were able to visit San Bruno during the Spanish occupation of 1683–1685.[28] Thus, many of the people Salvatierra met in 1697 had memories of the Atondo expedition. At San Bruno, the Spaniards found it convenient to favor some bands — and the enemies of those bands therefore resisted the missionaries' overtures. When Atondo and Kino left, their erstwhile protégés were abandoned and probably suffered at the hands of their enemies.[29] Salvatierra's mission once again split the people of the area, but this time the Spanish camp was in Monquí territory and the Cochimí were the visitors.

All California natives must have been troubled by previous contacts with white men. They knew from personal experience — or from reports or legends — that these strangers came, stayed for a short time, and disappeared. There had been no long-range benefits from dealing with them, and some contacts with pearlers, pirates, and even such well-intentioned groups as that headed by Atondo, produced tragic consequences.[30] Furthermore, the shamans of California bands traditionally commanded respect as priests and healers; they were often the most powerful figures in their loosely structured societies. However, a shaman's authority declined or ceased when his band accepted mission life. Most shamans in California and elsewhere did everything in their power to dissuade their groups from giving up their old customs.

Nevertheless, Salvatierra's inducements did prove effective. Some bands came to the mission seeking protection from enemies. Many people were drawn simply by curiosity; the strangers had fascinating livestock, tools, and trinkets — things that local people had never seen or imagined. Most were compelled by hunger; women, especially, gravitated to the padres' magic kettle with its daily bounty of whole-grained gruel. The lives of peninsular Californians depended on naturally occurring foods, and finding the scant natural produce demanded constant movement with the changing harvests. Unless times were desperate, men had some free time to spend in groups, gaming and exchanging stories, but women worked hard most of their waking hours at gathering and preparing food. They were attracted by what they saw of mission life, and were more than willing to escape the endless moving about and life-or-death searches for food.[31] Thus, the mission had a divisive impact, even within families. Part of the Californians were drawn to it and took part in its activities; part remained opposed and urged that the alien interlopers be killed or driven off.

While the newcomers were distracted by their rites on Easter Sunday of 1698, a rumor spread amongst the assembled converts and soon reached the soldiers.[32] Salvatierra recounted the ensuing events:

> About three o'clock in the afternoon we learned that the canoe had been stolen. When the news reached the fort, the soldiers determined to humble the pride of the wrongdoers. Captain Don Luis Tortolero y Torres and Lieutenant Isidro [Grumeque] de Figueroa[33] set forth, accompanied by Antonio [García] de Mendoza, Joseph Murguía, Juan de Arce, the skipper of the launch, Juan de León, three other sailors, and Marcos, the Yaqui Indian. Seven were armed with muskets, two with halberds, and one with bow and arrows; all were protected by stout shields.[34]

The captain and his soldiers went down to the shore, then followed the thieves' tracks up the coast. Two miles from the fort, they found the canoe broken into pieces and soon after encountered a few warriors who dared them to fight but retreated at the same time. The captain suspected an ambush and divided his force. He continued up the beach with some of his men but ordered Alférez Grumeque de Figueroa, García de Mendoza, León, and the Yaqui archer to strike off to the east behind the dunes to flush out the enemy. The latter group did find a party of warriors lying in wait. The three soldiers and the Yaqui defended themselves stoutly and wounded several of their opponents. Just as they were running low on gunpowder, their companions came to their aid.

All the soldiers were now encouraged, but the Californians fought on vigorously. Then the mission party moved to a better position and, as the sun was setting, the Californians sounded a retreat on their pipes.[35] Some six of them had fallen, either killed or badly wounded. Not one of our men was killed. Alférez Isidro de Figueroa had been wounded by a stone which struck him on the lip, and Juan de Arce had two slight wounds, where arrows had struck him obliquely. But these wounds were in no way serious, and the men were not confined to their beds.

The battle was fought about three leagues from the fort and on lower ground so, when the sun had set, we could see the flash of firearms. Our men returned to the *real* at ten o'clock at night, and then, with due solemnity, the Litany was chanted in honor of the conquering Virgin.

In this way the pride and arrogance of the Indians was humbled. They learned that our men knew how to fight, even in an open field, away from their fortification. And so, this victory, small though it was, was of great importance to us.[36]

The aftermath of this second victory justified the missionary's optimism. The local people offered little more armed resistance anywhere on the narrow coastal lowlands north or south of Loreto. The triumph weakened anti-mission leaders; the mission was better accepted and received more support from the people who clustered around. Such allegiance was crucial to the next steps planned by the missionaries — a series of explorations to reach new people and find sites with sufficient natural resources to support additional missions.

Exploring the New Land

The shortage of water severely limited the California mission's ability to grow food, so its dependency on sister missions in Sonora and Sinaloa continued. Loreto's launch carried most cross-gulf shipments and was sent over to the Río Yaqui whenever weather permitted (see Map 3.1). In June of 1698, it was long overdue and spirits drooped at Loreto Conchó. Provisions were reduced to three sacks of moldy flour and three more of wormy corn. Since the converts could be fed no longer, and since the season for harvesting pitahaya fruit was at hand, the mission was nearly deserted.[37] Gente de razón joined neophytes in fishing, hunting, or gathering. Their venture was near failure. Even the usually high-spirited, optimistic Salvatierra struck a lugubrious note in writing to his cohort, Juan de Ugarte:

> As I write this account, I do not know that I shall be able to finish it. We find ourselves with many needs, and our situation grows worse every day. I am the oldest man in this Real of Nuestra Señora de Loreto. If we are forced to pay the ultimate tribute, I, the weakest, will fall first into the grave.[38]

As the padre's ink dried, an excited commotion was heard at the gate of the fort. A neophyte had reported the arrival of a large ship, but with no sail in view, doubt set in and the fellow was thought to be lying. However, four men were soon seen in the distance, but coming from the wrong direction, down the arroyo rather than up from the beach. Although clothed, they were taken from a distance to be local converts who had been given shirts and pants, but Salvatierra cast that idea aside, remembering that " . . . the California Indians, even when they have clothes, take them off and bundle them when they go and come on trails."[39] All doubts vanished when one of the newcomers discharged a musket; he was enthusiastically answered by a volley from the presidio. In minutes, the hungry garrison at Loreto heard that the long wait was over. The schooner, *San José y las Animas*, had mistakenly touched at a point several miles south and sent a party ashore; its men were guided to the fort by a Californian. The ship was owned by its captain, José Manuel Ganduzo, who had been hired by a Jesuit agent to cross the gulf with supplies sent by pack train from Guadalajara, through Compostela, and embarked at the port of Chacala (see Map 5.1).[40]

In addition to the crucial food and stores, the *San José* brought seven young volunteer soldiers. Two were relatives of the Conde de Miravalle, the first contributor to the Pious Fund. Capitán Ganduzo, like the count, lived in Compostela.[41] The recruits were issued arms, and the presidio at Loreto held its first military review; the flags, clothing, and equipment of the newly arrived stood in sharp contrast to that of the ragged veterans. Salvatierra now commanded a garrison of twenty-seven men. His storehouse bulged with cheeses and several hundred bushels of wheat and corn, his corrals held forty-eight young cattle.

In August, other gifts and purchases arrived: horses, cows, supplies, and provisions, and, most welcome of all, the bark *San Fermín*, dedicated to mission service. Pedro Gil de la Sierpe of Acapulco also sent the padres a new launch, the *San Javier*.[42] This generous support allowed the missionaries to consider expanding their mission. Their first steps would be *entradas*, cautious excursions by a missionary, an armed escort, and selected neophytes to reconnoiter the land and meet the people. By late October 1698, such a group set out to re-establish contact with a ranchería at Londó, a water hole near San Bruno. Kino had named the place San Isidro, and there Atondo's party kept its domestic animals.[43] Salvatierra wrote a lively account of his impressions as his soldiers and neophytes explored northward in the new land.[44]

> On November first, the captain and I and six soldiers set out on horseback, well equipped with provisions. We had not been able to ascertain whether there was water on the road so each of the Indians had been given a blanket on condition that he should carry a little maize and a small keg of fresh water. To give ourselves more time, we set out a little before daybreak. There was a great deal of work in clearing the way through thorny shrubs and long spike-studded arms of the pitahaya. We traveled about three leagues very laboriously, for we were in a very forest of cactus, and the trails had never been trodden before by horses.[45]

The explorers labored to climb steep ridges and work their way down difficult descents. Nine miles into the journey, they found a side-canyon with water and trees and shrubs on which the horses could browse. In another three miles, the terrain became more challenging. Salvatierra recorded graphic details.

> . . . the canyon narrowed between the hills and we found ourselves shut in between two cliffs through which the Indian trail continued; it was impossible to make it wide enough for horses. We all dismounted to explore the summit of the hill, a summit covered with very rough stones and crowned with a cornice which was not easy to climb even on foot, and much more difficult on horseback. Juan de Arce had a terrible fall, and so we called the grade La Cuesta de Juan de Arce.[46] Invoking the aid of the Madonna of Loreto and perspiring profusely, all of us tried to find a path. We finally surmounted the grade, and not a single animal was lost. Later, traveling along the slopes, we came to a descent consisting entirely of sterile earth and small loose stones. It was so steep that we could not go down even on foot, and so we had to let ourselves slide, and it was to our great good fortune that the animals were willing to try it. The Indians were amazed when they saw the courage and good spirits of our men.

Although lessons were learned in travel techniques, the excursion proved to be an evangelical failure. Salvatierra's party arrived at Londó to discover that a portion of the ranchería had gone to the sea to fish, while the others had gone to gather fruit on the slopes of La Giganta. The explorers could find no trace of Atondo's old settlement, and when none of the Cochimí had appeared by the morning of the second day, they headed back to Loreto.

On the return trip, they stopped to rest at a water hole discovered on their outbound journey.

> It was here that we set about teaching Californians to carry letters so as to establish communication between various parts of the country. I wrote a note

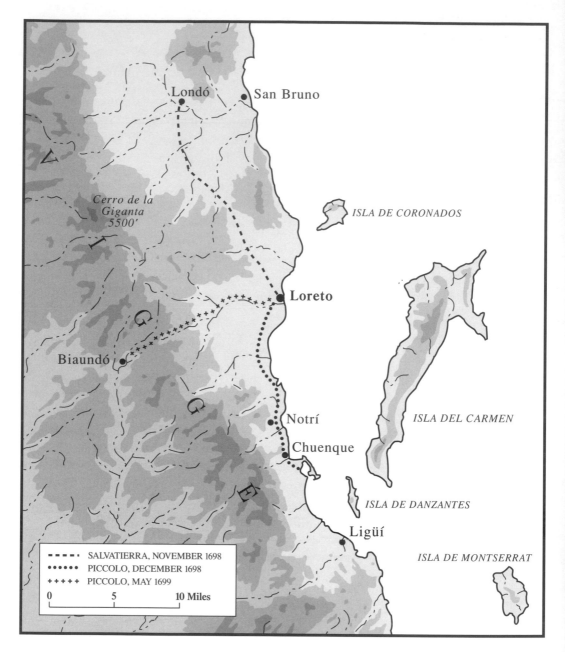

Map 2.1 *Routes of Explorations from Loreto Conchó*

to Father Francisco María Piccolo in the Monquí language. When I had finished writing it, I called together all the Californians who had accompanied us. I read the note aloud to them; but they had no idea of its purpose. The Indian who offered to carry it was a chief. He reached Loreto at four o'clock in the afternoon, and the father and the Spanish soldiers were delighted to see letters instituted in California. The father read the letter aloud in the presence of Chief Pablo, the bearer. When he heard the padre, paper in hand, repeating what I had previously said, he was amazed. And thus all the Indians became aware of the power of letters.

When he returned to Loreto, Padre Juan María discovered that his first overland exploration had been educational for the Californians in another way:

> The Indians were astonished to learn that we had gone on horseback through their mountains and found passage where they had not pointed out the trail. They realized that if it were necessary, a Spaniard could go in pursuit of them through the sierra.

Preparations for a Second Mission

The astute missionaries came to California confident that food was the key to attracting scattered peoples to fixed places to receive the Christian message. They knew that Indians drawn in would cluster around as long as food was offered, but during a year of frustrating experiences, the padres learned the difficulties of providing food, imported or domestic. Loreto, by then, had proved its value as a base and its worthlessness as a breadbasket. Padre Piccolo yearned to found a second mission, but knew he would have to find a site with solid promise for agriculture. With that in mind, he, Capitán Tortolero, and eight soldiers headed southward on the Monday following Christmas of 1698. They reached Chuenque, then a rush-filled marsh back of the beach, and visited nearby Puerto de Danzantes (soon to be named Puerto Escondido).[47] That exploration, coupled with information from local guides, convinced the missionary that the low, open land east of the mountains and along the gulf had little water and a small population. He decided to climb and cross the intimidating mountains to the west on an entrada to seek a more promising mission site and greater numbers of people. That jagged wall, seen from the gulf and even from the mainland, had for more than a century been called *La Giganta* in honor of Queen Calafia, ruler of the California amazons in Ordóñez de Montalvo's romance.

Cochimí from these highlands — which they called Viggé[48] — had come down to visit Loreto since the first days of the conquest. Some wintered in the Conchó area to escape the cold at higher elevations, and some of their children had already been baptized. Missionary interest in the uplands was further piqued by reports of agricultural potential, reports that came to Loreto by curious means. From the mission's inception, Salvatierra had sent California converts on supply voyages to *la otra banda*, then and now the peninsular term for the mainland coast.[49] He hoped to expose the new converts to life at mature missions. He presumed that they would bring back detailed accounts and be effective propagandists for evangelism. Some of these first native Californian travelers were impressed by fields of grain at Sonoran missions. On their return to Loreto, they insisted that there were similar fields up in Viggé.[50] This surprising possibility spurred Piccolo to explore the mountain valleys and the plains reported to lie farther to the west.

In crossing the peninsula in 1684, Almirante Atondo had worked around the north end of the Giganta range.[51] Padre Piccolo now planned to approach it just west of Loreto. Although this was one of its higher points, he chose the route because it was the avenue to Conchó used by the inhabitants of Viggé. Piccolo, the captain, and nine soldiers mounted their horses and set out on Sunday, 10 May 1699. A headman from the high country and a dozen or more of his men acted as guides, and each shouldered about fifteen pounds of provisions.

An ancient foot trail led into the mouth of a watercourse that was soon called Arroyo de las Parras for its tangles of wild grapevines. About seven miles from Loreto, the trail led out of the wash and began to ascend steep slopes covered with loose, sliding rock. Soon it was apparent that no horse could make the climb. Piccolo intended to continue on foot, but found the soldiers reluctant. Capitán Tortolero y Torres and one or two others argued that the party should abandon the ascent. The padre countered with the announcement that he would continue with the Cochimí. Shamed, the soldiers dismounted and joined him. Horses and saddles were left in the care of a few trusted converts. That night, the padre felt obliged to encourage his soldier escort. In the chronicler's words, "he explained to them the reward awaiting them from God as they went forward protected by the Blessed Virgin, La Conquistadora, and sheltered by her Royal House of Loreto." Piccolo's listeners were said to have been so moved that they promised not to turn back until their objective was reached.

The next day, the weary party reached the pass and crossed over into a broad watercourse that the natives called Biaundó.[52] There they found level ground that might be suitable for planting. Piccolo was enchanted to be greeted by a large group of receptive gentiles. He baptized thirty children and marked that day as the founding of San Francisco Javier, second mission of the conquest.[53] After four days in Biaundó, the group returned to Loreto in a single day, testimony to their growing experience and to the advantage of traveling downhill.[54]

The Resignation of Capitán Luis de Tortolero y Torres

In reporting this arduous crossing of the mountains, Padre Francisco María Piccolo introduced two threads that became inextricably woven into the fabric of the Jesuits' seventy-year California adventure: soldiers depicted as unwilling and faint-hearted participants, and agricultural prospects heralded in glowing terms. Piccolo described the heretofore valiant Capitán Luis de Tortolero as lacking in courage and resolve and reported that his party had found in Biaundó "a valley extensive and delightful to behold, with groves and streams . . . we scanned broad pasture lands with great contentment. . . ."[55]

Juan María de Salvatierra was the sole reporter of California affairs during the first year and a half of his mission. His occasional mention of soldiers and their attitudes was positive and grateful. Now Piccolo found Capitán Tortolero contrary, reluctant to have his nine-man detachment dismount and climb a very steep canyon. Two or three of the men also were said to have been opposed to the venture, and after the soldiers agreed to proceed on foot, Piccolo complained that one of them had such a negative attitude that it would have been better if he had been sent back to Loreto.

Piccolo's account can be filled out with a few additional facts. The padre implied that the captain was disheartened by what he encountered on the trail, but elsewhere he revealed that Tortolero had voiced concerns before the trip began. Piccolo planned to enter an unexplored area reported to have a large population. Its people's disposition toward the newcomers had not been tested, and Tortolero had vivid memories of his battle with warlike Cochimí only months before. Despite the captain's cautions — or because of them — Piccolo decided in advance that, if necessary, he would make the trip with no escort but his Cochimí guides.[56] The padre and soldiers did go together, but when they discovered that they would be without pack animals, the captain must have felt that it was his responsibility to reiterate his concern about the risks. A week after the trip to Biaundó, Tortolero resigned, reportedly because he suffered from a chronic infirmity and a troublesome inflammation of the eyes. However, the captain's reservations about sending small groups of soldiers into unknown conditions should be kept in mind because they recur notably in the history of his successor.[57]

The first mention of Tortolero's infirmities accompanied the announcement of his resignation, but had they been serious everyone would have been aware of them and they would have limited his activities. However, the padres decided that his usefulness was past only when he proved less than eager to make the important entrada on Padre Piccolo's terms. Salvatierra's subsequent letters do not refer to illness but do stress the need for tight control over soldiers. In writing to his friend and colleague, Juan de Ugarte, procurador de Californias in Mexico City, Salvatierra used the incident to reinforce the arguments for the Jesuit-ruled presidio.

> . . . unless this exploration had been made with complete independence of admirals and others, we would have turned back; we would never have found other good lands to enter but only to leave. . . . Those whose vision is not cleared by the pure air of heaven, but are induced to act only by base and earthly motives, are not inspired by the blessing of heaven. . . .[58]

Here Salvatierra referred to Kino's problems with Almirante Atondo in 1683–1685; Salvatierra claimed that only because he was the ultimate military authority did the soldiers carry out the search for Biaundó. This version of recent events gave Ugarte ammunition with which to defend Loreto's unorthodox presidio.[59]

Even if Capitán Tortolero was not sufficiently cooperative and had to be relieved of his command, his case required careful and diplomatic handling. Don Luis had come to California at the behest of an indispensable benefactor. He had been the subject of several good reports in connection with the crucial early defenses of the new mission. In a sense, the missionary order had invested in him as a symbol in their elaborate public relations campaign. Any attempt to give Tortolero a new, negative image would raise questions and doubts about their judgment. Nor would it help their cause or their recruiting to have an embittered ex-employee abroad in the very land from which they obtained volunteers. Although Tortolero was replaced in May, he did not leave Loreto until late October. With him on the galliot went Salvatierra's letter to his staunch supporter and benefactor, José de Miranda y Villayzán, *fiscal* to the Audiencia of Guadalajara. The padre wrote, in part:

> Captain Don Luis Tortolero is setting out on the galliot to begin a journey to Mexico City. I presume that he will be going by way of Guadalajara. If so, I ask you to receive him with all kindness in recompense for his pioneer service in this forsaken enterprise. I beseech that you do this so that Don Luis will be consoled on seeing that all he has done for us is appreciated.[60]

On the basis of this recommendation, and perhaps because of his previous career as well, the audiencia named Tortolero as *alcalde mayor* of the Nueva Galician mining town of Santa María del Oro de Tequepexpa.[61] The post of *alcalde mayor* combined judicial, political, and tax-collecting duties. In New Spain, these positions were coveted both for the prestige they conferred and the lucrative, often extra-legal uses that could be made of their power. Since the post was usually sold to a qualified bidder, it may be that some Jesuit money accompanied the better-documented pulling of strings; whatever the case, the post constituted a reward for Tortolero.[62]

Padre Piccolo was one source of ongoing misconceptions about California's agricultural potential. Two years after Tortolero left, Piccolo went back to New Spain to raise fervor and money for the support of California. To further his cause, he published a tract that has come to be called Piccolo's *Informe of 1702*.[63] In it, he described the economic potential of peninsular California in terms that would make a modern real estate swindler blush. Ironically, this work was so widely read and believed that it conditioned the attitudes and expectations of influential people for more than half a century. With this stroke, Piccolo achieved the dubious distinction of making others jealous of Jesuit prospects in California at the same time that his missionary order had to justify extraordinary expenses to combat the stubborn sterility of the same land.[64]

During 1701, a new king of Spain asked for information about current conditions in California. In February of 1702, Don Luis de Tortolero y Torres was called before the Audiencia of Guadalajara to help its members make a report to His Majesty. He answered questions and offered testimony about conditions in California. This was Tortolero's final contribution to the California cause — one well appreciated and recorded by Jesuits. In an ironic twist of fate, the tribunal was investigating Piccolo's *Informe*, a work hauntingly reminiscent of the same author's unrealistically glowing picture of Biaundó — written at the same sitting as his report of Tortolero's poor performance.[65] The transcript of the ex-captain's declaration suggests a forthright, honest witness whose factual report neither contradicts nor amplifies what is known from other sources. His testimony was favorable to the Jesuits but not hyperbolic. Nevertheless, two appreciative notices in an official Jesuit history suggest that the order felt repaid for the favors Tortolero had received upon retirement.[66]

Loreto's Second Captain

Padre Salvatierra accepted Luis de Tortolero's resignation and simultaneously appointed a replacement. The second-in-command under Tortolero, Alférez Don Isidro Grumeque de Figueroa, was not considered for advancement. Instead, by 23 May 1699, Don Antonio García de Mendoza was picked to command the garrison.[67] He was a true volunteer, one who had arrived unbidden and at a time when the tiny camp at Loreto badly needed help. The new captain had an impressive background. He was born in the region of La Rioja in Old Castile. He enlisted in one of Spain's regional armies and served in various places — Fuenterrabía, the fortified town near the French border, was listed among his posts. He came to the New World, served as an army adjutant in San Luis Potosí, then struck out on his own to open and operate mines in the wild Tarahumara area (see Map 1.1) near the Jesuit mission of Nuestra Señora de Montserrat de Huric (modern Urique in the Mexican state of Chihuahua). This last activity should have concerned Salvatierra and Piccolo. They were dedicated to keeping entrepreneurs away from the peninsular people. They might have reasoned that a man would not abandon a successful business and that if his first venture had failed, he might be seeking another opportunity.[68]

García de Mendoza was typical of many Spaniards who came to the New World seeking their fortunes. Some were troublesome adventurers, others brought the skills and energy needed to develop the new land. For the Jesuits' immediate purposes, the soldier was a prized asset; with energy and dispatch, he tackled problems that faced the mission. He proved adept at trail building, not a surprising skill in a veteran of the wicked slopes of the Barranca del Cobre in the Tarahumara. He volunteered to undertake the seemingly impossible task of constructing a *cuesta herradura* (a graded switchback trail for riding and pack animals) from Loreto, up the Arroyo de las Parras, and over the 1,800-foot pass to Biaundó. The new captain surveyed the terrain, gathered his men, exhorted them, and bade them to swear they would persist in their task until they could ride from Loreto to San Javier. Padre Piccolo was shocked and would not allow the men to make a solemn promise lest it prove impossible to fulfill. Nevertheless, beginning on 1 June 1699, García de Mendoza supervised and motivated soldiers and neophytes to work so hard that all wore out their shoes and had to resort to scraps of leather. The soldiers amazed the natives by prying out huge boulders and sending them crashing down the slopes and precipices. They dug into a bank here and piled high retaining walls of fractured basalt there. On Friday, 12 June, the soldiers were able to ride over the pass and down to San Javier without once having to dismount.[69]

The captain accepted another challenge at Biaundó on the very day the trail was completed. He eyed a high peak nearby and decided that it might be a vantage point from which he could get a view of *la contracosta*, the peninsula's Pacific shore. He hoped to see some indication of a harbor that could become a haven for Manila ships. Early the next day, he, Esteban Rodríguez, and another soldier started out to scale the peak; Rodríguez was first to the top. The three could see both the gulf and the Pacific, and they imagined that they could make out the famous Magdalena Bay.[70] They estimated that the contracosta was two days distant over apparently smooth terrain. In fact, what looked to them like a long, simple slope to the sea was a rugged mesa of basaltic rubble cut by deep arroyos invisible from their angle of view.

This overview of the country to the west led Don Antonio to think seriously about additional explorations. Two weeks after his mountain climb, García de Mendoza was back in Loreto penning a diplomatic letter introducing himself to Juan de Ugarte, procurador de Californias in Mexico City.[71] With ceremonial modesty, García de Mendoza reported his appointment to the captaincy, his unworthiness, and his determination to serve his two selfless and deserving superiors. He urged the procurador to convince Salvatierra and Piccolo to rely on him, García de Mendoza, to lighten the enormous burdens they had undertaken. He promised to instruct the troops in military skills, a matter that he felt had been neglected. He asked Ugarte to intercede for him in obtaining an official appointment from the viceroy.[72] After the traditional complimentary closing, he signed. Then, as if struck by an afterthought, he added a naive postscript that betrayed his anticipation of a search for the long-desired Pacific port that could offer relief to ships in the Manila trade.

> This past night I dreamed that I was traveling to the Pacific shore when suddenly I was engaged by a great troop of Indians. Then a bugle sounded and they were all struck with fear. At that moment I awoke. I found myself with no bugle and nothing with which to buy one. Possibly there may be some benefactor who has had such a dream, who knows how the sounding of a trumpet can serve to give courage to our people and to dismay the enemy.[73]

A Church is Built at Biaundó

Francisco María Piccolo had promised the natives around Biaundó that he would return, establish a permanent presence, and build a church — but he had to be patient. The mother mission in Loreto had pressing needs; the number of participants at Padre Salvatierra's religious services were limited by the tiny size of the chapel in the presidio compound. Food shortages delayed progress, but in June 1699 an overdue supply ship arrived. With bountiful foodstuffs, local people were induced to provide labor and the construction of a proper mission church at Loreto was begun.[74] After a chosen area was marked off and cleared, García de Mendoza and Piccolo staked out sites for a church and outbuildings. While converts worked to excavate for foundations and for the earth and clay to make adobe building blocks, the soldiers were finally free to assist Piccolo in the heights of Viggé.[75]

On 7 October 1699, Piccolo, García de Mendoza, fourteen soldiers, five Yaqui,[76] and several of Loreto's converts headed west leading a string of pack animals loaded with provisions and tools. Upon reaching Biaundó, the missionary assembled the local Cochimí and announced that he had come to live among them and teach them, and that he had enough food so that they could remain with him for several days. He told them that the men in his escort would build three structures: a place of worship, a public meeting place, and a house for the padre. He also explained ways in which they could help to create the mission. Piccolo then exhorted the soldiers to act as benefactors of the new mission, to roll up their sleeves and exercise the skills that only they could provide. The captain stood up and reminded them that their labors would be not only an offering to God and the Blessed Virgin but also a service to the king in securing his newest territory.

Then everyone went to work. Stakes were driven and cords drawn to outline foundations — presumably by García de Mendoza and Piccolo, the pair who had laid out the foundations in Loreto. The planned chapel would face onto a large level area where neophytes could stand when there were too many to fit within; the front door would be large to give those outside a sense of participation in services. A second rectangular building would be the padre's bedroom and storehouse. The third, the *sala* (sitting room; Piccolo called it "la salitta") would serve as a place where the missionary could meet with people, write letters, and keep his record books. The inside dimensions of San Javier's chapel were twenty by twelve feet; Piccolo's house and his "salitta" might have been about half that size. Soldiers and Cochimí volunteers dug foundation trenches and filled them with large stones until they were a few inches above the original ground level. These would form the base for adobe walls, and would enable them to withstand runoff water during the deluges brought by *chubascos*, the violent summer storms common to the area.[77]

The preparation of adobe began the next day. Soldiers were divided into two teams of seven men each. The captain headed one group and an unnamed soldier the other. In the morning, some of García de Mendoza's men supervised the Cochimí and worked at digging and carrying soil to the construction site. Others brought water and any plant materials that approximated straw. These ingredients were mixed and trampled into a uniform, thick mud. The captain and one helper laid out the dozens of wooden forms they had brought from Loreto. These they filled with the mud mixture and after appropriate intervals raised, leaving free-standing bricks, still very damp but capable of retaining their shape as they dried. They laid out and filled the forms again and again. The admiring padre reported that the captain and his helpers made five hundred adobes during the morning. In the afternoon, the other team — apparently headed by Esteban Rodríguez[78] — produced six hundred. In two days, these crews made twenty-five hundred adobes. When the first-made adobes had dried sufficiently, all hands turned to erecting walls using the new bricks and the same mud mixture as a mortar. Adobes were laid in the traditional pattern, two blocks wide, with the joints staggered between side-by-side rows and successive vertical rows.

When the soldiers and their local helpers had raised the walls to their full height, they needed to pause for several days to allow the mortar to cure before applying the additional load of a roof.[79] This wait gave the padre and the captain time to pursue their second objective. García de Mendoza's mountain-top view of the distant contracosta had initiated a plan to search for a port. The construction crew had brought extra provisions for this venture, and both captain and padre were eager to fulfill this long-time wish of royal authorities.

The Quest for a Port to Aid the Manila Trade

Throughout the seventeenth century, Spain, and New Spain as well, profited from trade with the Orient through the annual sailings of Manila galleons. But the participants and beneficiaries of that trade wished to make it less onerous and more profitable. As the century progressed, so did their clamor for a secure, manned port along the vast northern coast of Spain's California claim. Royal councils felt the pressure of these demands and coveted the revenues from increased trade. Failures of royally funded ventures like that of Atondo frustrated all the interested parties and left an old and nagging item on governmental agendas. Salvatierra played on this interest in New Spain's northwest coast during the long negotiations over his California license; he repeatedly stressed the possibility of finding a port for Manila ships. Two years after landing on the peninsula, he was mindful of his unfulfilled promise to the crown. Although he was short of men and supplies, Padre Juan María reasoned that the discovery of a useful harbor would create interest on all sides and stimulate support for his missions.

Padre Piccolo and Capitán García de Mendoza shared high hopes as they made ready for their first visit to the Pacific shore. The padre sought glory and favor for his order; the captain anticipated personal advancement and retirement benefits. When he returned from this exploration, Padre Piccolo was so moved by his experiences that he sat down and wrote a full and lively account.[80]

The explorers had prepared well; they brought provisions and a wide range of equipment and *bestia de carga* and *bestia de silla*, the necessary pack and riding animals. Their herd included live goats, animals that could feed off the country, provide milk, and serve as an emergency source of meat. A pair of dogs was brought along to reduce the time and trouble devoted to driving and rounding up the goats and also as to act as guards at nighttime encampments. García de Mendoza was an experienced wilderness traveler and knew the importance of having a knowledgeable man to dole out food as needed and keep a close tally on supply. He chose Esteban Rodríguez, a veteran hacienda mayordomo, to perform this duty and also that of pack master, in charge of loading and unloading. In various letters, Piccolo mentioned two pieces of pack equipment the explorers used. One was the classic Spanish *aparejo*, or pack saddle, a one-piece leather contraption that draped over the back of each of the bestia de

Figure 2.2 Burro with Cacastles

carga. It provided very little padding at the animal's spine but, on either side, the aparejo covered the beast's vulnerable ribs with a large pouch made from two thicknesses of leather and stuffed with straw or other resilient plant material to act as padding. *Cacastles* were crates to hold gear or provisions that were tied in pairs on top of aparejos. Soldiers made cacastles locally from the straight stems of an arroyo plant called guatamote (*Baccharis glutinosa*). These they fashioned in many sizes by cutting the straight, tough plant stems to suitable lengths for sides, bottoms, and ends, then slightly notching them so that the corners could interlock like those of a log cabin. They laced the joints of these open boxes tightly with wet rawhide, and they became very rigid and

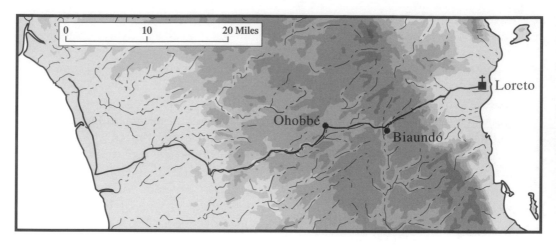

Map 2.2 The 1699 Exploration to California's Pacific Coast

strong when the leather dried and shrank.[81] Most of the soldiers from north-west New Spain were experienced *arrieros*, mule drivers, familiar with such equipment and adept at packing and unpacking and keeping an eye on the status of the loaded animals as they lurched over the broken ground.

On 24 October 1699, at seven in the morning, García de Mendoza and Piccolo set out, leading their troop of soldiers and Cochimí down arroyos and across the mesas west of Biaundó. After ten miles, they came to a place named Ohobbé, the principal encampment of a ranchería that had been represented at the founding of Misión de San Javier. Piccolo was delighted to find over a hundred receptive people. He baptized a couple of children and gave the site the Christian name of Santa Rosalía, the patron saint of his native Palermo.[82] The party went on into rough country, and during some difficult descents, someone discovered that several of the horses needed to be reshod. The expedition had extra horseshoes in its stores, but no man with experience as a farrier. Fortunately, García de Mendoza was enough of a craftsman to do the job, and, according to Piccolo, to do it well. The pitahaya season was at hand, and the guides took advantage of the break to pick cactus fruit, which they shared with the captain and the padre.

The party came down from the hills and traversed a level plain criss-crossed with well-worn trails; they crossed a few dunes, and at the end of the second day stood on the wave-washed shore. There was no fresh water for the animals, but the guides showed the soldiers where they could dig *batequis*, temporary water holes, in the sandy soil back of the dunes. Since horses often balked at drinking from unfamiliar excavations, the travelers had brought along a large copper cauldron, familiar to their mounts, that could be filled from the batequis.[83]

The explorers reconnoitered the shoreline northward during the third day and found an abundance of abalone shells, the famous blue seashells that were used as a trade item among Indians as distant as the Pimería Alta. However, there was no harbor. From their mountain-top vantage point at Biaundó, Mendoza and Rodríguez may have seen the sheltered water just south of Punta Pequeña, later the site of the village of San Juanico. But at the end of the fourth day, before they could reach even that open anchorage, Rodríguez announced that they had gone as far as their food permitted.

On the backtrack to Biaundó, the disappointed García de Mendoza had to hope that his efforts would yet bring him some favor when reported to royal authorities, but Padre Piccolo obtained immediate rewards. On the return trip, he preached to the band of gentiles at Santa Rosalía, baptized eleven children, and persuaded the whole group to come to San Javier to begin religious instruction. Then the padre ordered a goat slaughtered and given to his potential converts, hoping that news of his generosity would spread throughout the sierra. The captain, too, sent a convincing message — about Spanish might. He dispatched the goat with a pistol shot in the head at the very feet of the ranchería's leaders.

Back at Biaundó, the erstwhile construction crew found that during their week of absence the natives had plastered the walls of the new buildings by imitating demonstrations made by the soldiers before they left. All hands now turned to roofing. First they put up rafters, no doubt of palo blanco or split palm trunks, then they laid palo blanco branches across them for a ceiling and topped that with a thatch that could support a layer of adobe mud.[84]

Salvatierra Asks for Royal Funds

On 1 March 1700, Juan María de Salvatierra signed a long report and petition addressed to the Audiencia of Mexico. It is the most informative and revealing document that survives from the first years of the California colony.[85] As an introduction, the padre outlined the history of his conquest: the battles, the explorations, and the establishments. He included extravagant compliments for his captain, citing "the manifest valor, zeal, and wisdom of Capitán Antonio García de Mendoza, and likewise the protection he has given to the poor natives . . . and the perseverance he has shown in carrying forward the conquest for God and for the King." Salvatierra enumerated his forces on land, men and families: "sixty Christian souls from New Spain," and on sea: "thirty sailors." He emphasized the great gains for the crown, the great costs in money and effort, and the fact that private donations had paid the bills, including salaries that added up to sixteen thousand pesos annually. Eventually Salvatierra came to the point of his communication; it was, in fact, a petition for royal funds. He had to admit that his mission could not survive on private support alone; he could no longer pay his soldiers and soon they would be forced to leave his poor mission defenseless. He reminded the audiencia of the immense sums expended on the failed efforts of Almirante Atondo fifteen years earlier, no doubt hoping they would feel some gratitude for what he had contributed, gratis, to that date. By asking that the case for royal funding be re-opened, Salvatierra tacitly reneged on the promise that persuaded the viceroy to grant him the permit to open California.

His appeals to the king's representatives were really intended for His Majesty's ears; he implied rewards that would gratify the king's patriotism, piety, greed, and vanity. Salvatierra offered not only new lands and the salvation of untold souls, he dangled the promise of pearls almost within royal reach. Finally, he argued, that unfortunate name, "California," should it not be changed to something more august and all-conquering? Audaciously implying that he could personally assume custody of two centuries of California letters, maps, usages, and legends, Salvatierra proposed to rename the land "Carolina" to reflect the grandness of Carlos II, the benefactor he was wooing.[86]

Padre Salvatierra went on to sketch out dire consequences in the event of royal neglect. His dramatization of the aftermath was incarnate melodrama: defenseless missionaries slaughtered, Mary's church defiled, the flag disgraced. Surely, no self-respecting audiencia could contemplate such a scene, but in fact, Salvatierra's petition was made moot by the financial demands of other royal projects. Virrey Moctezuma refused to act on any part of Salvatierra's memorial when it was referred to him by the audiencia. He had already committed hundreds of thousands of pesos to military reoccupations of Florida and Texas.[87] Moctezuma had other reasons for ignoring pleas for money from California. He well remembered Salvatierra's promises to provide all the funds for his venture. The memorial, addressed to the Audiencia of Mexico City, was the first public break with those vows, but the viceroy had been receiving letters from Salvatierra and personal visits from Ugarte — both petitioning for money — since the second month of the conquest. Moreover, letters from the California Jesuits to José de Miranda y Villayzán, their contact on the Audiencia of Guadalajara, had resulted in private appeals to the viceroy.[88] In 1698 and 1699, Moctezuma reported the progress of the California conquest to the king, but he did not endorse or even report Jesuit requests for money.[89] Ultimately, the viceroy responded to all the Jesuit pressure by declaring that he would forward the whole matter to the Council of the Indies and to His Majesty. Apparently, however, neither he nor his successor carried out this promise.[90]

Patrons and the Presidio

At the end of Salvatierra's report and petition of 1700 was the statement that all the soldiers of the presidio had added their signatures to those of Padres Salvatierra and Piccolo.[91] In fact, one group did actually sign:

Antonio García de Mendoza	Esteban Rodríguez	Diego de Yepes
Isidro Grumeque de Figueroa	Juan de Arce y Conde	José Dávila y Guzmán
Nicolás Márquez	Juan de León	Juan de Guillón
Diego José de Yepes	Francisco Javier de Lima	Nicolás Rodríguez de Pina

Juan González [de Tuñán][92]	Domingo Manfredo	Antonio Zamudio
Juan Alejo [de Robles][93]	Diego Carrasco[94]	Cristóbal Rochón
Andrés Romero	Juan Antonio Romero	

A second group was signed "by another's hand, since they do not know how to write":

Juan Caravana	Matheo Romero
Juan Bautista Gómez	Antonio Solis
Pedro Rodríguez	Martín Bernal
Cristóbal Gutiérrez de Góngora[95]	Francisco Rubio
Felipe del Valle	Francisco de Saucedo
Antonio de Rueda	

In the text, Salvatierra boasted:

> These soldiers are few in number, but all of them are, so to speak, picked men, chosen from Spain and Europe as well as from New Spain. Among them there is a discharged captain of infantry, and likewise there are other discharged officers, as will be apparent from their signatures, and all of these are assisting steadfastly, joyfully, and disinterestedly in the conquest of this realm.

Several of these men can be shown to have been "picked" by wealthy benefactors of California. Pedro Gil de la Sierpe sent his cousin Juan Antonio Romero, one of the signers, as captain of his galliot. Either Gil de la Sierpe or Romero had recruited Nicolás Márquez and Juan Caravana.[96] Some of the soldiers were badly needed volunteers rather than hand-picked men, but the presence of Francisco Rubio and Cristóbal Gutiérrez de Góngora provides solid evidence of support from another benefactor. Both men had come from Compostela, the market center of an area dominated socially and economically by a Salvatierra patron, the Conde de Miravalle. Francisco Rubio came as a volunteer in early 1698 and served in California until 1704 when he returned to Compostela with his family, several of whom later enjoyed employment or patronage from Miravalle. Rubio had two sons who returned to serve in California.

The exact connections between Miravalle and men serving at Loreto are not known, but much is suggested by events in the ensuing years that involved Cristóbal Gutiérrez de Góngora. By 1703, he held the prestigious post of alcalde mayor of neighboring towns of Compostela and Tepic, to which he had returned after two years of service in California.[97] By 1712, he was captain of the local regional militia. When a daughter was born to him and his wife, Rosa de la Torre y Redondo, her baptism was celebrated in the private chapel of the Conde de Miravalle. The godparents were the count's younger son, Don José Antonio Dávalos y Espinosa, Caballero of the Order of Santiago, and Doña Isabel de la Torre y Redondo, who was not only a sister-in-law of Gutiérrez de Góngora, but also the wife of Loreto's ex-captain, Don Luis de Tortolero y Torres. Also identified as witnesses to the baptism were Don Juan Antonio

Romero, captain of the *Santa Elvira* when it brought Salvatierra's pioneer group to California in 1697, and, by 1712, mayor of Compostela, and Don Cristóbal de Rivera y Mendoza whose son Fernando Javier would one day be captain at Loreto.[98] A son of Gutiérrez de Góngora, his namesake, Cristóbal, would later serve in California and marry a daughter of Esteban Rodríguez.

The appearance of these men on Loreto's muster rolls demonstrates that the Conde de Miravalle, the largest holder of land and slaves northwest of Guadalajara, was determined to help in California and that he exerted his formidable influence and rewarded those who cooperated. The records emphasize the fact that people who supported and manned Jesuit California moved in very small circles.[99] If all the men who signed the Report and Petition of 1700 could be traced, it is likely that few would prove to have been simply "assisting . . . joyfully and disinterestedly in the conquest of this realm."

Dissension in the Ranks

At about the time of Salvatierra's "state-of-the-conquest" message and open petition for royal funds, strong winds blew Loreto's best bark, the *San Fermín*, onto a sand bar near the mouth of the Río Fuerte (see Map 1.1). The heavily laden craft broke up and was lost. Heroic efforts saved the crew and cargo, including many cattle, but the beleaguered mission was crippled without its last serviceable link to the opposite shore.[100] Salvatierra composed a second petition with a strong appeal that California be granted the use of a Peruvian ship that had been confiscated at Acapulco for illegal activities. The response to that request reveals the building resentment of the Jesuit monopoly in California. According to Venegas, the Jesuit chronicler, a flood of rumors spread through Mexico City: the loss of the *San Fermín* was a hoax; Salvatierra was engaged in a fraud to obtain royal funds. Affidavits were quickly submitted to show that the loss was very real, but an ugly backwash remained. For the first time there were tales of secret Jesuit profits in pearls.[101] The Jesuits, in turn, saw to it that the viceroy was accused of obstructing Jesuit access to another ship, one that had belonged to their recently deceased benefactor, Pedro Gil de la Sierpe. It was said that the pearler who got the craft had offered to split his take of pearls with his excellency, the viceroy.[102]

The viceroy submitted Salvatierra's request for the Peruvian craft to his fiscal, who demanded that the Jesuits exhibit their license to open California. To the Jesuits' chagrin, this was a ruse to read into the record once again Salvatierra's original promise to bear all costs—and to prove to all interested officials that the Jesuit license contained that promise.[103]

Meanwhile, Jesuit Provincial Francisco de Arteaga decided to circumvent the constant shipping problems and ordered Salvatierra to look for a land route to California. In January 1701, Padre Juan María crossed the gulf, then traveled to the mission of Caborca to join his ally, Padre Eusebio Francisco Kino, in an exploration to the northwest. At their farthest excursion, Kino and Salvatierra climbed Cerro Santa Clara, the nearly four-thousand-foot central cinder cone in the Pinacate outcropping. From there, they saw the mountains of California beyond the gulf and the Colorado delta, and though they were unable to go closer, both men were satisfied that they had found a land route. Salvatierra returned to the Sonoran coast and established a "California" mission, San José de la Laguna — popularly called San José de Guaymas — just north of Guaymas, whose great natural harbor could be used as a shelter for the ships and an embarkation point for the supplies headed toward the peninsular missions (see Map 3.1).[104]

While Salvatierra was away in Sonora, his mission gained the third and last of the pioneer missionaries who would become Jesuit legends. Padre Juan de Ugarte turned over his post as procurador to Padre Alejandro Romano, and left Mexico City on 3 December 1700 to take on a greater challenge. Knowing Loreto's desperate need for food, he devoted three months, with meager success, to obtaining funds, supplies, and a boat to serve California. His itinerary ran through Querétaro, Guadalajara, Compostela, Villa de Sinaloa, Ahome, and Puerto Yaqui (see Map 1.2). He arrived in Loreto on 19 March 1701 in a nearly derelict *lancha*.[105] He brought no greater gift than his own presence, which was sorely needed and soon put to use. Salvatierra was openly discouraged. He had returned from Sonora to find conditions at Loreto worse than when he left, the food problem still critical, and no new ship in the offing.

At this inopportune time, a discordant voice from the distant peninsula was heard in Mexico City. In the fall of 1700, the captain of the Real Presidio de Loreto, Don Antonio García de Mendoza, began to send the viceroy and other influential people a succession of letters that contained serious complaints and charges against Salvatierra, Piccolo, and Jesuit policy in California.[106] The Jesuits professed to be caught off-guard by García de Mendoza's change of heart, but they had created the conditions that underlay it. The special character of the Jesuit license to open California was not published, and even if it had been, the state of literacy and communication would have concealed some of its implications from men recruited for California service. The captain was experienced, literate, and intelligent — a considerable figure in that out-of-the-way place. Jesuit reports of his performance had been flattering and appreciative. Moreover, after nearly a year as captain, he had led his men in signing Padre Salvatierra's petition to the Audiencia of Mexico. However, García de Mendoza came to California from the Tarahumara where Jesuits governed mission and other religious affairs, but did not direct the military; he and many other soldiers were surprised when they encountered California's unique balance of secular and religious power. Revelation and disillusionment were inevitable.

On other frontiers in northwest New Spain, missionaries had little control over economic activity outside their missions. An ambitious captain could use his authority and positioning to claim mineral rights, ranchlands, and trading privileges. He was usually well placed to exploit Indians as an inexpensive source of labor, a near-necessity if one were to profit from holdings on the frontier.

The economic activities of soldiers and their families could be detrimental to any nearby mission communities, but the government's religious and secular interests were so intertwined that a degree of compromise and cooperation was imperative. Kino and Salvatierra had worked long and hard to obtain the power to dominate their military escort and thus free the missionaries from such compromise.

The initial California recruitment took place in 1697, during the Tarahumar Rebellion. Neither Salvatierra nor his benefactors emphasized the disadvantages of California employment. When good and experienced men could be found, they were enlisted with few formalities. In 1697, in telling of the ship and crew destined to work for his mission colony, Salvatierra noted that they left Acapulco, encountered a violent storm, and were nearly lost. "Out of danger," he reported, "they continued on to Chacala. Here, on learning that the purpose of the expedition was not pearl fishing, the crew came close to mutiny against the captain."[107]

Soldiers like García de Mendoza came to California with their share of the hopes and dreams that had expanded Spanish colonial frontiers and developed the hinterlands. Service along a new frontier was hazardous and unpleasant. Men were drawn by its potential for profit or advancement. Their labor added value to mineral and agricultural resources by bringing them under royal control. They expected to profit from that development. Government was usually cooperative. Certain rights of exploitation cost the crown nothing to grant and might yield a profit in taxes thereafter.

The excitement of the first uncertain days in California soon gave way to the drudgery of routine. Men nominally hired as soldiers were expected to act as teachers, farmers, manual laborers, herders, artisans, and overseers. They suffered an extreme degree of social isolation. They faced resentment and danger from reluctant and disaffected converts who were virtual inmates at mission communities. They had to oversee the work done, punish offenders, and enter hostile territory while chasing runaways. Meanwhile, they were denied many of the diversions and pleasures normally allowed to men of their calling.[108] The reverend fathers were satisfied with converts and the rewards of heaven, but poor men with families toiled in the new land with dwindling hopes. After being hired for California service, soldiers discovered that they were forbidden to search for pearls or precious metals or to use natives of the region for their own gain. Soldiers wondered how and where they might retire when their service ended; the missionaries laid claim to every potential pasture or garden plot.

After Antonio García de Mendoza achieved the captaincy, he became privy to the extent of Jesuit authority and realized the absolute limitations on personal gain. His first reaction was to resign his commission. He offered as a reason his despair of finding royal favor after the viceroy failed to recognize his efforts to find a harbor for the Manila ship.[109] The captain also referred to his age and accumulated infirmities.[110] Salvatierra refused the resignation. He needed the captain and had a government-approved contract to which he could be held.[111] After that, García de Mendoza began his letter-writing campaign with its criticisms of the missionaries, in which he included charges that they lacked concern for their soldiers' safety.[112]

A general sense of disillusion overtook the presidio. The captain probably reflected the convictions of most of his men when he was reluctant to send small detachments into difficult terrain to face untested populations. Most of the soldiers were veterans of mainland military actions and their experiences may have made them more cautious than California dangers warranted. In time, they would come to know that the Cochimí were the least dangerous people on the peninsula — and that any of the peninsular Californians waged less effective battles than the natives of Sonora or the Tarahumara — but in the beginning, the men of the presidio at Loreto were justifiably cautious.

No one questioned the selflessness and bravery of the California missionaries, but their displays of these virtues were not always prudent. Their letters show that the prospect of sacrificing their lives was not unwelcome. It was true that they were not to seek martyrdom or to provoke its consummation, but in their minds it was an ever-present possibility that could convert a disaster into a personal and sanctified triumph. The soldiers were religious, but they were born into the faith rather than dedicated to it. They did not regard their positions in California as heroic or sacrificial; they considered them jobs. They evinced a willingness to face unavoidable obstacles with courage, but also to sidestep as much trouble as possible. They understood the practical end of missionaries' objectives — the mechanics of creating and maintaining missions — but they knew that their own business was to make those objectives possible. They occasionally cautioned a missionary who was determined to face danger, but rarely did a padre show gratitude to those who urged him to curb his zeal.[113]

García de Mendoza Released from the Captaincy

When Salvatierra petitioned for royal funds, he created an inconsistency that rankled Antonio García de Mendoza. The California missionaries could not always meet their payroll and they were attempting to renege on their promise to fund the conquest, yet they held fast to other provisions of their cherished license. García de Mendoza wrote to the viceroy and poured out complaints: the presidial captain at Loreto was subservient to the Jesuits, he was a mere errand boy. The Jesuits showed no concern for royal coffers; they permitted no development of resources in the new land. Padres coddled their converts and chastised them little, even for gross misbehavior. This made tribes outside the mission influence especially insolent, yet Salvatierra and Piccolo were accustomed to sending small groups of soldiers on perilous expeditions among them. García de Mendoza's exasperation led him to this outburst:

> In order to stop these rash acts, I am not able to find any remedy other than to give the story to the Most Reverend Father Provincial of the Sacred

Company of Jesus, asking that he remove from here the two *religiosos* and put them where they will receive the punishment they merit, and he may put me in a tower with a strong chain [as an example] so that my successors will not allow themselves to be led into similar fates.[114]

Jesuit historians writing a generation or more after these events painted García de Mendoza as a man gone wrong, an ingrate who could not accept a subordinate position and whose avarice overcame his judgment and debased him into bearing false witness,[115] but at the time, Salvatierra and Piccolo pointedly refrained from public censure of their captain. They endured his complaints for nearly a year, until late 1701, when they sent the viceroy a conciliatory statement:

> Captain Don Antonio García de Mendoza, captain on land and sea of this troop of soldiers of Nuestra Señora de Loreto and of the royal presidio, presented to me, Juan María de Salvatierra, superior of this mission of Nuestra Señora de Loreto, and to my companion, Father Francisco María Piccolo, a petition in which he asked us to accept his resignation of the office of commander because of his chronic malady and because he is well advanced in years. And we did accept it, for such a malady is incompatible with the burden of this office in a country where a new conquest is in progress.[116]

The language of this report is remarkably similar to the one that accompanied the resignation of Capitán Tortolero two years earlier. Once again, the padres did not want to aggravate a delicate situation. Recently, they had praised García de Mendoza in extravagant terms. If they now castigated him, their judgment would be called into question. Once García de Mendoza was released, it became apparent that he had been a spokesman for wider disaffection. When he left, seventeen soldiers went with him. The presidio on the distant strand was reduced to a muster of twelve.[117]

THREE

California Accommodates Bourbon Rule

A Change of Imperial Dynasties

For California, the year 1700 was marked by two significant events: the public admission by the Jesuits that private financing could not sustain their mission, and the open disaffection of their military chief accompanied by embarrassing charges against the missionary leadership. Padre Juan María de Salvatierra appealed to the highest powers in New Spain for assistance with both problems. In previous years, the prospects would have been favorable; the Jesuits had a long record of success in dealing with the entrenched governmental bureaucracy. They might have had an inside track to some funding and little trouble in dealing with a challenge from a soldier-employee. However, 1700 was more than the last year of the seventeenth century; it was the last year of Spain's Hapsburg dynasty. Carlos II died childless on the first day of November. His designated heir was the eighteen-year-old Bourbon prince, Philip of Anjou, grandson of Louis XIV.

News of the king's death and the change of royal houses reached New Spain early in 1701. A period of inactivity followed as colonial leaders waited for signals from a new ruler and speculated about changes that might be made. France was Spain's most-watched neighbor; Bourbon objectives were well known. Everyone whose wealth or position depended on royal favor searched for ways to defend his perquisites or to take advantage of anticipated changes in governmental practices and demands, but changes came slowly and were slower still to arrive in the colonies. Virrey Moctezuma was not replaced until the end of 1701 and then by the archbishop of Mexico, Juan de Ortega y Montañez, serving on an interim basis for the second time.[1] Not until the end of 1702 did a truly Bourbon appointee, Francisco Fernández de la Cueva, *Duque* (Duke) de Alburquerque, arrive and assume the office of viceroy.

The last Hapsburg passed the problems of a profoundly sick nation to his

Bourbon heir. When the young prince was installed as Felipe V, he brought a group of French councilors; under his aegis, they began to reshape the Hapsburg chaos into a characteristically Bourbon regime. During the next three years, the first, halting steps were taken toward more efficient administration, better revenue collection, an effective defense, and the reduction of contraband trade. The new regime initiated a campaign to return scattered authority to Madrid by reducing the influence of provincial nobles and cutting back on special privileges that ran counter to royal financial and political interests, particularly privileges that had been retained by or granted to particular regions of Spain. Felipe V appointed secretaries of state with powers and responsibilities that reduced those previously delegated to councils, including the Council of the Indies.[2] All of these predictably Bourbon moves were reported in the New World and became part of the planning and intrigue carried on by those who had to deal with government. Groups like the Jesuits, who had long operated under carefully crafted older arrangements, now tried to keep abreast of changes and make successful accommodations.

At the same time that Bourbon reforms were being introduced, foreign Hapsburg interests challenged the Bourbon claim to the Spanish throne. Both the threat of a greater Bourbon weight in Europe's balance of power and the lure of New World riches impelled England, Holland, and Portugal to back the claims of a legitimate Hapsburg contender, Archduke Charles of Austria. Within Spain's borders, the provinces of Catalonia and Valencia opposed Bourbon rule as a challenge to their limited autonomy, and a considerable part of the Castilian aristocracy resented moves by the new dynasty to strip them of powers to which they had become accustomed. Thus began the Wars of Spanish Succession. In 1705, Archduke Charles invaded Spain. Armed strife on Spanish soil lasted until 1709, and the issue remained in doubt until 1711. The Bourbons prevailed, but at high cost in territorial and economic concessions.

Throughout, Felipe's ministers were hard pressed to raise money to support armies. Newly installed or contemplated reforms were sidetracked for lack of attention and funds. Civil war and foreign invasion provided both the necessity and the excuse to abridge many aspects of traditional justice and administration. This climate allowed the Bourbon ruler and his sophisticated advisors exactly the emergency powers they needed to move rapidly toward an absolutist state. Renegade Catalonia and Valencia were stripped of special privileges. Aragon's separate financial system was incorporated into the common fiscal program. Royally appointed ministers in Madrid took precedence over councils that represented the broader interests of nobles, the church, and captains of commerce.[3]

In New Spain, Bourbon objectives were manifested in a change of the relative power of audiencias and the viceroy. Audiencias still reported and appealed to the once-powerful Council of the Indies, but under Felipe V, the council was more subservient, and the lines from king and councilors to viceroys became more direct. Suddenly, groups like the Jesuits found that their influence with audiencias was more difficult to translate into advantageous grants, concessions, or even into maintenance of the status quo. However, just as Bourbon philosophies and practices began to take hold, the Wars of Spanish Succession intervened. A decade passed in which all of Spain's energies and income were devoted to Bourbon survival. This hectic period provided the New World with an interlude during which ideas of Bourbon reform circulated and were discussed and pondered.

Changes were subtle; the factions with wealth and influence remained the same, as did their interests, but some perceived that Bourbon influence could create new opportunities as it altered established relationships and privileges. The history of Bourbon France suggested that government would favor economic interests over the religious. That prospect gave hope to rivals of the Jesuits, but it was accompanied by the discouraging fact that the young king had brought his Jesuit confessor from France.[4]

Some competitors of the Jesuits were churchmen. Franciscans and Dominicans were jealous of Jesuit influence and prestige; they hoped for further shares of the mission field. The secular clergy also had reasons to be dissatisfied. The original mission concept, as codified in the Laws of the Indies, had visualized missions as brief way stations in the process of creating towns and parishes. During this developmental period, missions and all their people were exempt from paying tithes, the tenth part of all agricultural produce to which the diocese was otherwise entitled. However, missionaries on heathen frontiers showed little desire to give up their hold on mission lands and peoples. The interested prelates of the Diocese of Guadalajara, within whose jurisdiction California lay, could argue that Jesuit practices, by then tested in the northwest for over a century, might never lead to a secular life in which the ordinary clergy could share and from which the diocese might profit.

Men engaged in regional commerce and the exploitation of natural resources suspected that the Jesuits intended to run California as a church state for an indefinite period. These influential people saw that Jesuit policy not only excluded their activities but prevented any firsthand assessment of California's resources. In the absence of real knowledge, they imagined the Society of Jesus enjoying profits from immense mineral deposits and fabulous beds of pearl oysters.[5] They despaired of trade because they saw that Jesuits resisted civilian colonization. Guadalajara already saw its commerce limited by virtual monopolies held by Mexico City merchants; now it saw the expansion of its frontier trade curtailed by Jesuit interests. Smaller businessmen — miners, traders, and ranchers — close to Jesuit missions felt keenly that Jesuits hindered their progress and profits by denying access to so much Indian labor.[6] California was a useful target for accusations because it was so tightly controlled by missionaries and so little known by higher authorities. Stories began to circulate that purported to unmask clandestine Jesuit commerce, such as trading their presumed hidden treasures with the annual Manila galleon or, worse by far, with the English enemy, which was constantly rumored to have a flotilla off California shores.[7]

Royal councilors were impatient with the situation in California. The always over-committed royal treasury was further depleted by war. Officials who were not openly sympathetic to the Society's aims came to regard California as a venture that merely consumed money. Jesuit reports from California over-flowed with rich harvests of souls, but no bounty from which the *real quinto*, or royal fifth, could be exacted.[8] This balance of expenditure and income was accepted in pious Hapsburg times, but it was unacceptable to a Bourbon regime that hungered for economic development. A barrage of letters from California missionaries explained away some disappointments and managed to placate some critics on some scores, but it was never enough to relieve the pressure from Madrid. California was also a sore subject in Mexico City. Since 1584, successive viceroys smarted from a notable failure: there had been many ex-pressed wishes, and several direct royal orders, but there was still no port where the Manila galleon could be relieved and resupplied after its man-killing trans-Pacific journey.

Given all these factors, it is no surprise that men at the upper levels of government, the military, and the church formed shifting, informal alliances while attempting to loosen the Jesuits' paternalistic grip on California.

California Jesuits Defend their Position

Jesuits were tough and well-organized, as a small group of dedicated, like-minded people can be, and they needed those strengths to defend their the-ocratic control of a place that had excited such speculation. Royal councils, viceroys, and audiencias were sympathetic to religious aspirations and believed that the religious orders were important parts of the coalitions needed to open and develop new areas, but no element of government was prepared to accept religious control of large areas as an end in itself. Ministers and councils did not wish to preclude other results of conquest — colonization and economic devel-opment — that firmly established royal claims to the land and created profits for the treasury. Thus, a covert conflict was built into the California adventure from its start. Salvatierra the diplomat, had agreed to certain conditions and paid lip service to certain principles that Salvatierra the missionary did not support in the field. Perhaps he and royal officials alike envisioned a new Christian community capable of developing the land and holding it against Spain's enemies while making it pay into Spanish coffers. But if there were common elements in their goals, there was little agreement about how those goals should be reached or which of them had priority.

Spain's rulers had learned from experience that they could derive profit from native Americans only when they were induced to work and pay taxes. Those who lived in their traditional ways outside Spanish control made little contribu-tion to the Spanish economy. Even worse, warlike groups along frontiers impeded royal ambitions. The government therefore decreed that native Americans be converted and brought into Spanish society. Kings and councils regarded missionaries as appropriate agents for this change, but they expected converted peoples to become participants in Hispanic affairs. Civil authorities might pay lip service to missionary plans for long, slow conversions, and they might cooperate with missionary orders during periods when the crown lacked funds or men to take an active part in a conquest. But most civil officials, publicly or privately, held that a new area should be opened to colonists and commerce as soon as possible and that it should rapidly become an extension of Spanish colonial society. As always, the native people were tacitly expected to occupy society's lowest level and serve as a pool of inexpensive labor.[9]

Missionary orders agreed with civil authorities on the first point; they too intended to divorce native Americans from their ancestral ways. However, the alternative prescribed by the religious was mission life, an existence that they imagined was far more humane and beneficial than that endured by Indians attached to colonial Hispanic society as its lowest and most exploited class. In the missionaries' plan, neophytes would be instilled with a pure devotion to God; converts would be shielded from the corrupting influences of profit, possessions, and pleasures of the flesh.[10] The churchmen believed that the lot of their mission inhabitants would stand in glorious contrast to the fate of converts left to be used and degraded by New Spain's unruly and exploitive frontier folk.[11]

The Jesuits insisted that their version of the civilizing process required a great deal of time; in Sonora, for example, their missions still ministered to "neophytes" three or four generations removed from conversion. The crown's gain during that long procedure was limited to the addition of new Christian subjects and the establishment of a physical presence, a few missionaries and soldiers who represented the king. Jesuits defended the isolation of their converts and their vast mission enclaves. In their plans, the coming of colonists, the exploitation of natural resources, and the establishment of commerce were perpetually limited to some vague future time.[12]

In California, the Jesuits had realized a long-term ambition of the crown; their presence established Spanish claims better than any earlier forays or empires merely mapped on paper. Salvatierra never tired of reminding viceroys and royal councils that this conquest, this prize, was laid in the king's lap virtually as a gift. However, the Jesuits now had to renege on their promise to support California themselves; royal funding had become vital. This change of direction required delicate diplomacy. The missionaries were determined to maintain the powers granted in their license and thus maintain California's treasured isolation, but to appeal for support, the Jesuits had to reveal at least some of the difficulties and shortcomings of the land, the people, and the chosen mode of conquest. That tack, however, could not be carried too far. If the truth were more fully known, perhaps the great gift would appear small in royal eyes and unworthy of further expenditures. Jesuit ingenuity was taxed to produce a series of reports, like Piccolo's *Informe of 1702*, which promised much at some future time in return for present investments of money and effort. Such promotions, properly timed and placed, contributed to Jesuit political success, but they also created problems. Unrealistically glowing reports aroused economic interests and jealousies that threatened California's isolation. This dilemma continued throughout the Jesuit occupation.

The Society of Jesus had powerful friends in court; Jesuits were the preferred educators and confessors for many of the elite, including, at times, the royal family,[13] and the Society did not hesitate to invoke the favors that special relationships could command. Through diplomacy, it was possible to gain approval of a Jesuit plan and sometimes to have funding ordered by royal decree. On the face of it, this outcome might seem to be a coup, but it often produced little result. The royal hand that signed such orders piecemeal did not submit them as a group to the rigors of a budget.[14] Impoverished Spain simply could not fund all the projects so grandly decreed. Royal councils had tacit understandings with lower officials that many expenditures ordered by royal proclamation would be delayed or curtailed. The viceroy of New Spain had to consider all the expenditures ordered for his region and trim them down to the money at hand. Meanwhile, he had to pretend that all royal wishes not immediately acted upon were in the offing.[15] It is no wonder that viceroys publicized as few as possible of the decrees they were ordered to execute.

In their reports and histories of such dealings, the Society of Jesus portrayed a faultless monarch, pious and determined to provide handsome support for high-minded Jesuit ventures. They placed the blame for failures to execute the royal will on lesser authorities like viceroys.[16] They intrigued to know of favors that had been granted to them by high councils and then suppressed within the system. Records of unfulfilled royal commands were kept as bargaining points should a viceroy place unacceptable demands on the Society.

Whatever Jesuit leaders may have understood privately, they were unwilling to admit publicly that officials often did not cooperate simply because they could not accommodate all legitimate claims to royal funds.[17] This was particularly true in Jesuit dealings with viceroys of New Spain between 1702 and 1715. In its singleness of purpose, the Society of Jesus was intolerant of opposition and unsympathetic to the predicaments of bureaucrats who had to cope with the manifold economic problems and pressures of a long war.[18]

Padre Piccolo Courts Favor and Funds

Felipe V's advisors displayed an early interest in California, though they had no more official information than the progress reports that Virrey Moctezuma had submitted in 1698 and 1699. More current news, including California's urgent need for funds, came to them through the network of private Jesuit supporters.[19] The first Bourbon recommendations appeared to be favorable to California Jesuits. A *real cédula* (royal decree) of 17 July 1701 awarded six thousand pesos annually to support the California mission and ordered Virrey Moctezuma to further the enterprise and encourage private benefactors.[20] Related cédulas were sent to the audiencia and bishop of Guadalajara asking that they resolve an old dispute so that the bequest given earlier by Alonso Fernández de la Torre could be used to benefit California missions.[21]

In June 1701, missionaries in California had no knowledge of these activities in Madrid. They labored to alleviate critical local shortages of food. Padre Salvatierra met with his cohorts and proposed to abandon California. The younger, more vigorous Padre Juan de Ugarte was opposed, and his argument carried the day. The group decided that Padre Francisco María Piccolo should go to Guadalajara and Mexico City to plead the California cause, but his first two attempts to sail were thwarted by storms; California's envoy could not get under way until the end of December.[22] By then, news about the royal funds granted to California had reached New Spain. Piccolo heard of it soon after landing at the port of Matanchel on the coast of Sinaloa.[23]

Padre Piccolo's arrival in Guadalajara was well timed. The local audiencia had received a cédula from the king asking for more information on California; the missionary had come prepared to plead his case and answer questions. He appeared before the tribunal attended by Francisco Javier, a neophyte from Misión de San Javier, and a Tarahumar, Ignacio Javier, who had been the padre's page since his days in the missions of that region. Piccolo also brought along three young Cochimí boys from San Javier to show as fruits of California labors. The audiencia took testimony to send to the king from everyone in Piccolo's party.[24] At the audiencia's request, Piccolo wrote his influential *Informe*.[25] California was still a golden legend wherever its name was known, and this striking man with his eyewitness account was lionized. The glowing *Informe* was printed in Mexico and later published in English, French, and German. The immediate results were as Piccolo had hoped and planned. Beside making the land seem promising, he had appended a list of recommendations that appeared open and reasonable and were calculated to counteract rumors that California missionaries resisted observation, or were engaged in dubious practices. He proposed, for example, that the king appoint a civil functionary to supervise the business affairs of the colony—supplies, storage, shipping, and distribution—and that some Spanish artisans live there with their families and teach their skills to converts.[26]

In March 1701, Piccolo went on to Mexico City to confer with Padre Alejandro Romano, Juan de Ugarte's successor as *procurador de Californias*. Romano had received reports of the colony's perilous condition and passed them along to a new viceroy, *Arzobispo Virrey* (Archbishop Viceroy) Ortega y Montañez, who had replaced Moctezuma in November 1701. Romano and Piccolo personally urged the viceroy to execute the outstanding royal orders that awarded money to California. The Jesuits were abetted by the fiscal of the Audiencia of Mexico whose written opinions favored most of their requests.[27] These negotiations continued while Piccolo supervised the printing of his *Informe* and made the rounds of actual and potential donors, drumming up enthusiasm for his cause. The impressive and enthusiastic Sicilian gave heart to benefactors who had withheld their support when dismayed by rumors and criticisms. All were reassured. The Marqués de Villapuente stepped forward to offer endowments for three missions.[28] Don Nicolás de Arteaga and his wife endowed another.[29]

Finally, after months of petitions, sub rosa pressure, and public pronouncements, Arzobispo Virrey Ortega y Montañez agreed to deliver the initial six thousand pesos called for in the royal decree of 17 July 1701. Piccolo left Mexico City in September 1702 to return to California. Prospects were joyful. The mission's survival seemed assured by new private donations as well as royal funds and sympathy. However, Salvatierra and Piccolo soon became aware of strings attached to their royal grant. By November, the viceroy's seat was filled by the Duke of Alburquerque, representing the new Bourbon regime that aimed to enhance the power of the state at the cost of ecclesiastical privileges.[30]

The First Captaincy of Esteban Rodríguez Lorenzo

The 1701 exodus of ex-captain Antonio García de Mendoza and other volunteer soldiers left Loreto a very small and sober colony. The military unit, recently over thirty men, was reduced to twelve, and these few were left with the same labors to perform and the same discipline to enforce. Alférez Isidro Grumeque de Figueroa, the second-in-command, was elevated to *teniente* (lieutenant) and made interim commander of the presidio, but when called into action to punish a group of heathen Cochimí who had despoiled San Javier, he was so cautious, or faint-hearted, that even the soldiers were dissatisfied, or so says the missionary report.[31]

Grumeque de Figueroa was not cut out for this command — one that he had never sought and that came to him by default. He soon attempted to resign from the presidio. Salvatierra, mindful of his shortage of men and Grumeque de Figueroa's good record as alférez, excused him from the command but retained him in his former role. The padre then gathered his dozen soldiers and told them that the choice of a leader was theirs to make. A secret ballot was taken, and a majority chose Esteban Rodríguez Lorenzo.[32]

Their choice must have pleased Juan María de Salvatierra. Rodríguez was the padre's first recruit and had been more than faithful to his promises. Rodríguez had been assigned only the modest rank of corporal in the initial conquest because he had no military experience, but the Portuguese proved brave and resourceful and was now recognized by his peers. Salvatierra and Piccolo immediately drafted a document to notify the viceroy of Rodríguez's nomination. The padres praised Rodríguez and recounted his achievements. In addition to his exploits as a soldier and explorer, the candidate was said to have served, without title or extra pay, as Loreto's supply officer, overseeing the procurement, delivery, and distribution of food and equipment. The padres emphasized the difficulties of this job in so remote a place, across the water from all sources. They described Rodríguez's devotion to the sick, his indefatigable labors as a nurse and attendant. Salvatierra and Piccolo closed by asking the viceroy to issue his own confirmation — which would allow Rodríguez to assume the captain's duties — and then to submit a formal application for a royal appointment. When Padre Procurador Romano received the news of the nomination in Mexico City, he wrote a letter to the viceroy, seconding the motion and asking that Rodríguez be exempted from paying the usual fee for such an appointment "because he is a poor man."[33] On 6 December 1701, Arzobispo Virrey Ortega y Montañez acceded to their request and named Rodríguez as captain at Loreto.[34]

Esteban Rodríguez assumed his new position at a time when his employers and the recently installed Bourbon government had just begun a round of political infighting. The Jesuits hailed the king's decision to support their cause with royal funds, but for as long as possible they tried to ignore the fact that his orders also called for changes in California that would thwart or profoundly alter the Jesuit modus operandi. The Council of the Indies raised four points repeatedly as they attempted to rewrite Jesuit privileges. First, the Bourbons opposed religious control of a military troop. Second, the crown was disturbed that nothing had been done to succor the Manila galleon. Third, governmental bodies charged with raising money resented the Jesuits' stifling of private economic development, a potential source of tax revenues. The fourth bone of contention was related to the second and third: Jesuit opposition to the civilian colonization that both a naval base and economic development would require. Capitán Rodríguez was soon deeply involved in arguments and resentments that would characterize a long test of strength and will between the Jesuits and royal officials.

One of Rodríguez's earliest letters to a viceroy plunged the new captain into controversy. On 18 April 1702, he wrote to Arzobispo Virrey Ortega y Montañez to ask for clarification of his role as supervisor of pearling in the gulf. Two boatloads of pearlers had already appeared and claimed to have licenses but refused to show them. The new captain wished to know his duties and powers. He asked if he should send a reliable soldier with the pearlers to see that they reported their take honestly and that they "practice no extortion and do no injury to the heathen of these coasts, thereby leaving them in a state of resentment." Rodríguez reported that the unconverted Californians did not distinguish between mission craft and those of pearlers. The misdeeds of the crews of the latter would confer a stigma on those of the former.

However, it was another issue, raised in the same letter, that touched off a round of controversy. After inquiries about his new office, Rodríguez made an apparently ingenuous observation about pearling: "and whereas we [soldiers] have not engaged in this business, but have been serving his majesty without pay from his royal treasury, these ships come from afar to reap the profits of a venture which might later bring some comfort to the men who have been, and even now are risking their lives." The captain closed his fateful letter after reporting that he had not received royal confirmation of his appointment to the captaincy despite having applied many months earlier. "The distance," he wrote, "perhaps has caused the delay and prevented me from receiving it."[35]

It is difficult to believe that Rodríguez surprised his employers with this implicit plea for pearling rights for California soldiers. The captain probably intended this as a gambit toward obtaining future privileges to take the place of the lands or mineral concessions granted to retired soldiers in other places. He remembered the García de Mendoza furor, during which it was made plain to the soldiers who remained in California that they would receive no such concessions. Rodríguez had been Salvatierra's companion since the early days of organizing the mission to California. He had an excellent sense of his superior's desires and would not have opposed them. His incredibly long California career (1697–1744) bears ample witness to his sensitivity and fidelity to the missionaries and their cause. Rodríguez probably consulted Salvatierra before he wrote this letter; at the least, he shared its contents, as will later be seen. It may be that Salvatierra did not then object to the "pearls-for-soldiers" suggestion because his operation was already under fire for its captive presidio. Rodríguez's apparently independent request for soldiers' benefits was similar to those made by presidial captains elsewhere; Salvatierra may have thought it would counteract the image of a kept military. He probably encouraged his captain to paint a negative picture of the influence of pearlers on the conversion process; that passage in Rodríguez's letter echoed the view that Jesuits consistently urged on anyone sympathetic to their cause. Nonetheless, in the face of new Bourbon policies that favored economic development, it was a view the missionaries themselves did not wish to trumpet publicly.

A Subtle Struggle over Pearling

Pearling in the Sea of Cortés was an old enterprise.[36] Between 1632 and 1694, a dozen licensed pearling operations had worked the oyster beds off the gulf shores of California and Sonora. According to reports made to the interested authorities, none of these forays made enough profit to amortize its costs, but pearlers may have submitted just such reports to discourage competition and justify smaller payments of the royal fifth. Apart from these visible, properly licensed ventures, smaller flotillas — some illicit — were often at work in the gulf.[37] By 1702, the presidio of Loreto had contacts with pearling operators from Colima, Compostela, and Villa de Sinaloa.[38] The pearler from Sinaloa was no less than the provincial governor, General Andrés de Rezábal. Throughout his governorship, which began in 1696 and ended with his death in 1723, he continued to operate a bark and several small craft. When Salvatierra was having difficulty gathering forces and supplies for the conquest of California, the governor made several gifts. He was the colony's most frequent visitor, and he continued to make donations and to lend his craft to the missionaries when they were most needed.[39]

The whole pearling issue put the superior of California missions in an awkward position. In various propositions to the viceroy, he had committed himself to promoting the industry. Pearling was, after all, the only known

California resource from which the crown could hope to collect the quinto, but to encourage pearling wholeheartedly would be contrary to immediate Jesuit interests. Moreover, Governor Rezábal would feel rebuffed if Salvatierra encouraged competitors.

Pearlers had boats and crews, but they depended on local Indians to find oyster beds and to do the actual diving. The missionaries opposed these contacts, regardless of the pearlers' intentions or success in dealing with the natives. If the Californians were treated badly, exploited physically or economically, they would be suspicious and resentful of all who came to their land. If the local people were treated well and received food, clothing, and other material things from the pearlers, they would be less open to mission influence. That would set a bad precedent and be a divisive element in the theocracy planned for California. For these reasons, Salvatierra encouraged highly placed Jesuits and friendly government officials to oppose the liberal granting of licenses to would-be pearlers. The governor of Sinaloa was established in the area as a representative of the crown and would have little trouble maintaining his pearling license. Jesuit influence might help him by reducing the numbers of his competitors.

Capitán Rodríguez's straightforward and innocent letter opened to debate what had been a tacit conflict. He touched off a contest of philosophy and influence. Rodríguez had not suggested that pearling be prohibited, although he did indicate some of the problems it created; he did not ask directly that pearling be made the province of Loreto's soldiers, but he stressed the possibility of such a benefit. His points were soon sharpened by others.

Arzobispo Ortega y Montañez was replaced as viceroy by the time Rodríguez's letter arrived in Mexico City, and the Audiencia of Mexico ruled New Spain until the next appointee should arrive. Rodríguez's communication was first reviewed by the audiencia's fiscal, a man sympathetic to the Jesuits. In his hands, and probably with Jesuit advice, interpretation of the letter strayed from its literal content. The fiscal read so much into it, indeed, that his commentary became an endorsement of the Jesuit position that pearling endangered missionary progress.[40] This change in emphasis is evident in a resolution drawn up and released by the Junta General in Mexico City. That body's opinion, ostensibly in response to Rodríguez's letter, actually was a reaction to the stronger recommendations of the fiscal.

> With regard to pearl fishing, it is impossible to forbid such persons as have licenses, offer proper security, and pay the royal fifth, from engaging in this business. But in order to prevent, at least in part, the damage which may follow from the action of all others not so licensed, it is recommended that the aforesaid captain be directed to demand licenses of all ships coming to the island of California, and — in the case of those that can not present them — to draw up depositions, while laying an embargo upon the ships and the merchandise that they carry. And the captain shall report such cases to his Excellency, in order that such persons may be punished. Furthermore, the

reverend Fathers Juan María de Salvatierra and Francisco María Piccolo are to be requested and enjoined to inform his Excellency, in full detail and with the utmost clarity, of the annoyances, damages, and losses which may befall those missions and conversions in consequence of the aforesaid pearl fishing. For though bearing in mind the benefit to the Royal Treasury, and the expense to which the latter is put in the matter of the six thousand pesos which his Majesty gives as annual alms [to support California missions], it may be that this pearl fishing can not be allowed even for the sake of the Royal Treasury, although experience has shown what great advantage can be derived from the commercial profits of the aforesaid vessels. . . .[41]

The implicit message in this decision seems modern, though read between lines written nearly three hundred years ago. In the mercantilistic view, the main aim of the government was to produce income and enhance authority; the rights of enterprise were not to be set lightly aside, particularly where potential tax revenues for the royal treasury were involved.[42] These politicians openly encouraged the reverend fathers in their good works, but they also charged them to be more explicit in their complaints about the consequences of pearl fishing, and not to leap to gloomy conclusions before the law had a chance to cope with any problems.

On 27 November 1702, Francisco Fernández de la Cueva, Duque de Alburquerque, arrived in New Spain as the first viceroy imbued with the Bourbon point of view. As he saw it, California missionaries were now recipients of royal funds; they could expect to answer directly to the interests and authority of royal councils, the viceroy, audiencias, and all the rest of the government machinery. In short, they were not about to receive six thousand pesos a year without having their precious autonomy challenged and subjected to more royal scrutiny.[43]

Although his efforts to curb pearling had proved disappointing, Salvatierra had handled the affair as a skillful politician. He and his associates in the Jesuit apparatus had contrived to sound out the new government on a touchy issue. They learned what they needed to know about government policy and the viceroy's position, but it was their employee, not they, who made the unpopular proposal. Indeed, at this juncture, Salvatierra wrote to Alburquerque to remind him that he had supported pearling as far back as his original application for the California license. The missionary went on at great length to detail the advantages that would result from the plan developed by the junta and the viceroy. Salvatierra commented unfavorably on Rodríguez's supposed plea for presidial pearling concessions, saying that he had known about it from its inception but had not had the heart to oppose the soldiers at a time when he could not even pay their back wages.[44]

From that moment, the California Jesuits accepted the government position on pearlers as a condition of their lives. However, they continued to oppose the use of their converts by pearlers and to forbid any involvement with pearling by their soldiers or members of their families, and Salvatierra was vigilant in trying to prevent pearling ships or the Manila galleons from leaving strangers in California. Those who sought such refuge were believed to be criminals trying to hide in the remote missions. Experience had taught that they would encourage drunkenness and "many other vices."[45] From time to time, pearlers lost ships or ran out of supplies and became a burden on California; at other times, they and their sailing craft provided useful or even vital services to the missions.[46]

Contention over Larger Issues

Government interest in California affairs soon extended beyond pearling and emanated from higher circles than Mexico City. In June 1703, the royal council in Madrid issued a resolution that reflected the recent change from Hapsburg to Bourbon rule in its attitude toward the religious and the priorities of the royal treasury. The advisory group urged that the Jesuits be denied control over the captain of the presidio at Loreto. The council opined that the power to hire and fire the king's only secular representative could lead to abuses. As a compromise, they suggested that the civil authorities in Guadalajara be ordered to appoint men to this position who could work harmoniously with the padres.[47] The council advised that pearling be controlled, not halted, and concluded the resolution with a revealing passage. The viceroy of New Spain was instructed to see that "poor families who of their own volition wish to settle in these provinces [of California] not be prevented from doing so or have difficulties put in their way."[48] Although two years had passed, these recommendations suggest that the complaints of Antonio García de Mendoza had finally reverberated in Madrid.

In late September 1703, a royal decree incorporated part of the Council's recommendations. In a grand gesture, this cédula ordered continued royal support for the missions but also the establishment of a second California presidio, with its own captain and thirty to forty soldiers, located at Cabo de San Lucas or on the western shore of the peninsula where it could provide a way station for Manila ships. The cédula directed royal authorities to purchase an additional supply ship to expedite the development of California. Echoing one of the matters raised by the council, it decreed that this ship transport families of would-be colonists and that the proper authorities actively promote colonization. The royal order did not change the method of appointing the captain at Loreto; proponents of the Society of Jesus had succeeded in sidetracking that sensitive issue.[49] However, Virrey Alburquerque continued to disapprove of military authority in religious hands. His short-term predecessor had not found time to act on Esteban Rodríguez's application for royal confirmation of his captaincy.[50] Alburquerque dragged his feet on the matter for eight years, forced Rodríguez into the humiliation of repeated requests, and established a precedent for successor viceroys who also turned deaf ears.

On the face of it, the decree represented a major blow to Jesuit plans.

Maritime trade, a new presidio, and a growing civil population would make short work of the insulated mission theocracy, but the threat was only on paper; the grandness of the order was its undoing. New Spain, already heavily taxed and drained by the continuing Wars of Spanish Succession, had more pressing demands for available money than catering to such peripheral royal whims. The cédula was not overtly disobeyed; it was discreetly placed in abeyance for more than a dozen years. Its expensive provisions could not be implemented, so no effort was made to enforce the others. In short, Virrey Alburquerque and the Society played a game. During his tenure (1702–1711) and that of his successor, the Duque de Linares (1711–1716), no colonization schemes were carried out, and no presidio was built. In return, the Jesuits took their six thousand pesos per year and made no complaint about the crown's failure to provide the much-needed supply ship.[51] However, this stalemate neither reconciled the contestants nor resolved the questions of authority. Though shelved, the cédula authorized steps that could be ruinous to Jesuit plans, and it would remain technically in effect as a command. The Jesuits were not allowed to forget its existence throughout the years of their California regime.[52]

Searching for Mission Sites

At the beginning of 1703, when Padre Piccolo returned from his successful fund-raising journey, Padre Salvatierra was armed with the endowments for four new missions and had high hopes for royal funds. Missionary Padres Juan Manuel de Basaldúa and Geronimo Minutili had been sent to assist him. As shorthanded as he was, Salvatierra felt that the time had come to expand his venture. He ordered Capitán Rodríguez to prepare an expedition to search for mission sites and new concentrations of gentiles. In late February, Padres Piccolo and Basaldúa, Capitán Rodríguez, and squads of soldiers and neophytes passed through Misión de San Javier and its visiting station of Santa Rosalía, then pressed southwest to the contracosta. The 1699 explorers had turned northward, searching for a port. Rodríguez led his party to the south, looking for arable land with water resources or local people who might act as guides, but the few natives that they saw fled at their approach and, although the explorers found signs of bountiful fish and shellfish, they accomplished little else. When the party came to the mouth of the arroyo of San Javier, they turned inland and followed the watercourse back to the mission.[53]

By the time the searchers returned to Loreto, Salvatierra had planned an exploration northward to investigate a fascinating report. During the previous year, the mission's supply launch had been blown off-course and forced to land just north of Bahía de la Concepción. The skipper told the father visitor that local Cochimí showed him a place that they called Mulegé where he could take on water. To his amazement, it proved to be a river flowing into the gulf, the first permanently flowing water to be found in the mid-peninsula.[54]

The explorers paused to celebrate Lent and Easter at Loreto and to allow their horses to recover. In early May 1703, a relatively grand expedition was led by Rodríguez: Padres Salvatierra, Ugarte, and Minutili,[55] ten soldiers, and a large group of converts who were familiar with part of the terrain to be crossed. The party went overland as far as the southern reaches of Bahía de la Concepción, but there they found that rugged mountains plunged precipitously into the sea. This coastal barrier proved to be waterless and exceedingly difficult to traverse. The trailblazers retreated to Loreto determined to return by sea at the earliest opportunity.[56]

In late August, a complicated plan was put into action. Padres Piccolo and Basaldúa took ship with Rodríguez and an unspecified number of soldiers, probably piloted by the same skipper who discovered the watercourse. They returned with no problem to Mulegé and its coveted "river," a slow-flowing stream at the foot of a large alluvial plain. Piccolo and Basaldúa confirmed its potential as a mission site, but their immediate plan was not yet completed. They again took ship and sailed for Guaymas, where they obtained ten horses and two mules from Jesuit Padre Andrés de Cervantes whose mission lay nearby on the banks of the Río Yaqui.[57] They loaded up, sailed back to Mulegé, and disembarked soldiers and animals. Rodríguez intended to seek again for a land route from Mulegé to Loreto, but because of the previous difficulties, he took a shrewd precaution. He told the pilot of the mission ship to wait for his party for three days before sailing.

The captain's foresight was rewarded. During the three days, his party searched the steep walls of the vast amphitheater that surrounds Mulegé from the southeast to the northwest. They found no trail suitable for their mounts, so they returned to the waiting ship and sailed back to the south end of La Concepción from whence they could follow their previous route to Loreto. Padre Piccolo then sailed to Sonora to continue his quest for supplies.[58]

The Conquest at its Lowest Ebb

Capitán Rodríguez encountered a crisis when he returned to Loreto. On 20 September 1703, the day after his party landed at Bahía de la Concepción, a chubasco drove two pearling craft onshore at Loreto; the boats were heavily damaged, but all hands survived. Loreto's own supply launch, its only available craft, was similarly maltreated by the storm, so Rodríguez had no way to send for help or to return the pearlers to the opposite shore. Seventy extra men were added to the drain on Loreto's already short supplies. The problem was compounded a few days later. A third pearling craft operating farther to the south had sunk outright, and its fourteen starving survivors paddled two canoes into Loreto. The needy colony now had eighty-four extra mouths to feed.[59]

Piccolo, on leaving Mulegé, encountered the same storm and saw his little ship sustain heavy damage to its foremast and rudder. However, his crew was able to jury rig the vessel and reach the calm waters of landlocked Guaymas bay, where some repairs could be made. Meanwhile, the padre busied himself with

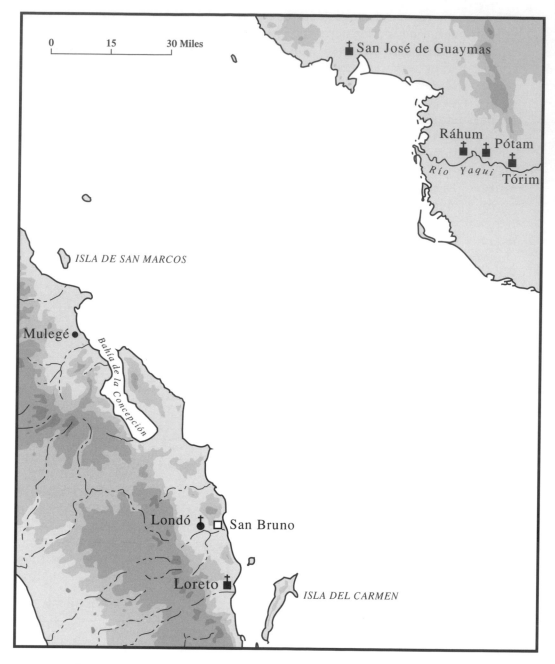

0   15   30 Miles

✝ San José de Guaymas

Ráhum
✝
Pótam
✝
Río   Yaqui
✝
Tórim

ISLA DE SAN MARCOS

Mulegé ●

Bahía de la Concepción

Londó ● ✝   □ San Bruno

Loreto ✝

ISLA DEL CARMEN

Map 3.1 Loreto's Relationship to the Río Yaqui, Guaymas, and Mulegé

obtaining supplies from brother missionaries in Sonora. Along the way, he hired carpenters and caulkers to go with him to California to repair his craft properly. Piccolo's arrival at Loreto in mid-October was a godsend. Not only were the foodstuffs aboard his ship sorely needed, but the workers he brought to repair the California ship could also repair the launch and the pearling craft sufficiently to send them and their crews back to New Spain. This was done in two months, and the unwelcome guests were sent off.[60]

Salvatierra realized that his whole undertaking was in serious jeopardy for lack of ships and supplies. He wrote the strongest possible pleas to royal officials and friends of his cause. He sent Piccolo back to Sonora to inform all missionaries of California's plight and to beseech their support. Piccolo arrived to find that he had been appointed *padre visitador* (superior) of the Sonoran missions. He was soon using his power to enlist aid for California and continued to do so while serving more than four years in the new post.[61] Meanwhile, Salvatierra dispatched Padre Juan Manuel Basaldúa as his personal representative to Virrey Alburquerque and as solicitor of alms from potential benefactors. Basaldúa left Loreto on 12 February 1704, made good time on sea and land, and arrived in Mexico City as promptly as the primitive travel conditions permitted, but his hopes were soon dashed.

Most benefactors' wealth was linked in some measure to the lucrative wholesale trade in European goods. A great fleet of merchantmen, carrying commodities in which the benefactors and their associates had large investments, recently had been sunk by a storm off the Spanish port of Vigo. Everyone Basaldúa approached had suffered such a loss that he was forced either to give nothing or to scale down his gift. The viceroy had no better news. He pleaded government losses at Vigo and cited the huge expenses of recent military occupations in Florida and Texas. He would not sanction any part of current or back payments promised by the crown to support California. Padre Basaldúa had a sorrowful report to carry back to his hungry companions at Loreto.[62]

Another disappointment followed. A crew aboard the newly repaired launch had been sent from Loreto to Sonora to beg for food. Five months later, they returned with the astonishing news that contrary winds had prevented them from ever crossing the gulf. They had put into one shelter after another and were now more starved than those they had gone to help.[63] Juan María de Salvatierra saw his people emaciated and losing hope. He called them together and offered to send them back to the mainland, even the baptized converts and their families. However, he announced that he would stay at Loreto because he had sworn never to abandon the conquest. Faced with that courage, the other padres, Rodríguez, and his men promised to remain.[64]

The fall and winter of 1703–1704 had been extremely dry in California. Padre Juan de Ugarte and his neophytes had expended huge efforts to prepare the ground and plant corn at San Javier, but little of it matured. Ugarte and the soldiers joined the neophytes in digging edible roots and collecting and roasting mezcal hearts. Ugarte began a program of fishing from canoes at night; the report of this confirms that the gente de razón at Loreto were landlubbers and did not ordinarily practice fishing. Local Monquí must have done so; Salvatierra had already noted that, in calm weather, both *canoas* (dugout canoes) and *balsas* (rafts of bundled reeds) went to and from Isla del Carmen, nine miles offshore from Loreto. It is unlikely that all that activity was involved only in collecting salt from the island's natural salt pan.[65]

By the fall of 1704, the Society of Jesus had marshalled its forces in Madrid to press for all that king and councils had promised — and that the viceroy had not delivered. This Jesuit pressure resulted in instructions to Virrey Alburquerque that he could not conveniently ignore. He proposed to discuss the matter with the Jesuits in Mexico City. Padre Provincial Manuel Pineiro, in turn, sent word to Salvatierra to come from California to help in the negotiations. Loreto had no ship at that time, but while the padre visitador awaited passage with a pearler, he delegated the responsibilities for running the colony during his protracted absence. Fortunately, Padre Pedro de Ugarte, Juan's brother and look-alike, had accompanied Padre Basaldúa on his return and could now substitute for Salvatierra by directing the colony's affairs from Loreto.[66]

When Padre Juan María de Salvatierra finally arrived in Mexico City in November 1704, he faced two rude surprises. Two weeks earlier, Padre Provincial Pineiro had died, and when sealed instructions from the padre general were opened, they named Salvatierra as the successor provincial of New Spain. The missionary was far less moved by this honor than by the blow it delivered to his plans. He made strenuous efforts to convince a council of Jesuit elders that his place was in California, but they invoked the order's discipline and ordered him to serve.[67] The power of the office emboldened Salvatierra to seek a settlement of the issue of royal funds for California. After a few months of inconclusive sparring with Alburquerque, he wrote out the California position in a new memorial.[68] When that produced only promises and no funds, Padre Juan María went before a council of Jesuit elders for advice — or perhaps to request its approval of a plan already made. On the basis of its findings, he offered the viceroy what amounted to an ultimatum. He must pay the funds ordered for California or accept the renunciation of all the Jesuit missions of the northwest.[69] Virrey Alburquerque assumed that this was a bluff, but Salvatierra wrote to padres visitadores of all the Jesuit mission areas to notify them of the coming renunciation. The viceroy was forced into action because by then even the governors and military commanders in the field were writing to him with their fears of events that would follow a Jesuit departure.[70] Finally, Salvatierra accepted a compromise; Alburquerque paid the sum ordered for the year — thirteen thousand pesos — but he paid out none of the backlog that had accrued since the original cédula of 1703.[71]

Esteban Rodríguez's Resignation and Reinstatement

Esteban Rodríguez chose the moment when Salvatierra was planning his trip to Mexico City to resign his captaincy and leave California. By all accounts, this pioneer of the conquest had been a cornerstone of the support called for and needed by the padres. According to the Jesuit chronicler Miguel Venegas, "an ambitious rival, wishing to succeed to his post, had so filled him with reports, stories, and lies that he felt compelled to resign." Venegas tells us that this unnamed cohort convinced Rodríguez that the padres were planning to replace him with another, and that he would find no justice in their court; ". . . he advised the captain to look to his honor by resigning, because, being entirely deserving, it was a disgraceful thing to be put aside, labelled as a delinquent, and banished for his transgressions."[72]

Venegas wrote that Salvatierra regretted this development, that he had the warmest feelings for the captain and appreciated his talents. The padre is said to have reasoned with his officer, pointed out the false basis of his fears, and assured him that no other had been appointed in his place and that no change was planned. However, Rodríguez is represented as being convinced that "once Padre Juan María had left, his rivals and detractors would join in a cabal to dishonor him. To escape this specter, he pleaded with tears in his eyes that he be allowed to accompany his employer to Mexico City, where Salvatierra could help him to obtain his official release from the appointment he had received from the viceroy."[73]

Simultaneously, Alférez Isidro Grumeque de Figueroa offered his resignation and requested the same assistance in dealing with the viceroy. On 29 September 1704, Salvatierra accepted the resignations and wrote out certificates of honorable service.[74] To provide direction for the soldiers on an interim basis, the father visitor appointed Nicolás Márquez, a pioneer like Rodríguez, to be acting captain.[75]

Salvatierra arrived in Mexico City in company with Rodríguez and Grumeque de Figueroa, and he acted promptly to secure the releases they needed from the viceroy. These were granted by early December 1704.[76] Five months later, as negotiations between the viceroy and the Jesuits were nearing their end, Padre Provincial Salvatierra received a letter from Padre Juan de Ugarte reporting that a Capitán Escalante, hired to succeed Rodríguez, had proved to be a detriment and should be replaced. Salvatierra thought the matter over and decided to pay a visit to Esteban Rodríguez, who happened to be in Mexico City. The provincial explained his problems and asked his ex-captain to return to California as a favor to him, to the other padres, and to the presidio. "With humble generosity, Don Esteban accepted this offer," said Venegas. By 23 May 1705, only eight months after his resignation had been accepted by Salvatierra, Esteban Rodríguez's appointment as captain was reinstated by the viceroy.[77]

Most of the facts and interpretations relating to the hiatus in Esteban Rodríguez's captaincy were preserved only in Miguel Venegas's great chronicle of California's first forty years. A study of events surrounding the affair suggests that Venegas offered a somewhat disingenuous reading of his sources or was led into just the skewed interpretation that their authors intended. Venegas's explanations of causes and motivations seem designed to gloss over some politically inconvenient controversy within the California Jesuit apparatus.

Rodríguez had established a reputation for sound judgment, good works, and devotion, and he went on to become a legend of the Jesuits' own making, but he seems totally out of character in Venegas's version of this episode. Not only was he represented as easily misled and easily disheartened, but the individual said to have caused the problems was a soldier in his own command. Moreover, Salvatierra, who held the ultimate power to hire and fire, knew of the whole affair.

It is likely that Esteban Rodríguez was discouraged by his lack of prospects in California. Across the waters of the gulf, captains held vast tracts of land on which they ran thousands of cattle; one Sonoran captain had recently helped Salvatierra with a gift of over a ton of dried beef.[78] Jesuit policy denied Rodríguez any hope for such personal holdings. After three years as captain, he had received no royal appointment and therefore could not even count on military retirement benefits. He may have learned how he was used and condescended to by his superior in the contentious aftermath of his pivotal "pearling letter" to the viceroy. With pearling also closed to him, he may have become disillusioned about a career that promised so little beyond hard work and unquestioning subservience in so lonely and isolated a place. He was in his thirties, unmarried, and had virtually no hope of finding a suitable wife on the peninsula.[79]

Rodríguez's relinquishment of the captaincy could not have been the surprise that Venegas reported. Nor was the captain mistaken in his belief that a replacement was being sought. Salvatierra accepted Rodríguez's resignation on 29 September 1704. Salvatierra chose this date because the pearling craft that was to start him on his journey to Mexico City had arrived in Loreto and, two days later, would leave to carry him to Matanchel. By then, Salvatierra was expecting the imminent arrival of a replacement for Rodríguez. He had long since written to the military officer who headed the escort protecting the mission at Guaymas.[80] On 13 October Padre Piccolo, in Guaymas to obtain food, reported that "Alférez Juan Bautista de Escalante yesterday left this port for California, called by Padre Juan María de Salvatierra to be head or captain of that presidio."[81]

Either this appointment had indeed been set in motion before the captain's resignation—as Rodríguez believed—or that resignation had been tendered earlier than Venegas suggests. All presidial soldiers were nominal employees of the crown. All officers' appointments had been accorded formal recognition by a viceroy, and many of these were confirmed by the central government. (As noted above, Rodríguez felt that he must appear personally before the viceroy to expedite his release from the captaincy.) Even in the relatively loosely organized frontier presidios, a junior officer like Escalante did not have the power to leave his post to accept another position. Surely his commanding officer was consulted and the usual Spanish formality of paperwork was not by-passed.

Salvatierra had known Escalante for years. He had served in the presidios of Sonora since 1690 and had taken active roles in difficult and bloody actions.

Escalante had been posted in the Pimería Alta while Padre Kino founded a series of missions. He had served under Juan Mateo Manje, often Kino's military escort during his entradas.[82] No doubt, it was Padre Eusebio who introduced Escalante to Salvatierra.[83] By 1700, Escalante was assigned to lead the soldiers protecting Guaymas and was there in 1701 when Salvatierra founded San José de Guaymas as a mission in support of California.[84] Venegas described Escalante as "a famed soldier, and very valorous." He told of his arrival at Loreto in these terse terms: "The new captain of the presidio arrived in California on the 22nd day of October and that same day Padre Juan de Ugarte put him in command, ordering him to . . . institute no innovations but rather to follow the practices of his predecessor."[85]

Venegas reported that Escalante, in turn, was replaced by Rodríguez because of his mismanagement and misconduct as captain, but nowhere does the Jesuit chronicler describe any action, good or bad, taken by Escalante. His name next appears in a description of events that occurred five or six months after his arrival. "Worse than the hunger emergency was the suffering from the bad conduct and management by new captain Escalante, for he did not perform as had been expected. He caused trouble and uneasiness. Although he received several admonitions, he did not change his ways. Finally, Padre Ugarte had to write to the absent Padre Juan María to give an account of what had happened and to ask him to give command of the presidio to a captain more attuned to his duties." Salvatierra then took the aforementioned steps to re-enlist Esteban Rodríguez and get him confirmed.[86]

Venegas's description of the change of power at the presidio seems to cover more than it reveals. "Padre Juan María made [this transfer] with such delicacy and discretion that the deposed captain was happy in leaving the command, feeling that he had held it on an interim basis as a substitute." Padre Juan de Ugarte facilitated this impressive feat of diplomacy with a clever idea. Before he informed Escalante that he was to be replaced, he told him that the much-valued previous captain had lost all his money in an unwise investment in a general store. He said that Rodríguez had gone to Salvatierra and pleaded with him to let him recoup in a place and job that he knew. Out of gratitude for his pioneer services, the father visitor promised to restore his position. Escalante was said to have accepted this fabrication and not only stepped down graciously but stayed on in California as a mere soldier for over a year. By then, the assiduous Ugarte had arranged through brother Jesuits in Sonora that Escalante be made second-in-command at his previous presidio of Nacozari.[87]

Most probably, Escalante did no real wrong in California, but also did not match Rodríguez's performance, and was so moved aside. His alleged wrongdoing was fabricated to serve Salvatierra's purposes; just then he was engaged in a furious dispute with Virrey Alburquerque who proposed to remove the Jesuits' right to hire and fire the captain of the California presidio. Padre Juan María's strongest argument lay in his claim that an independent soldiery would destroy the mission. The decision to remove Escalante provided a convenient opportunity to drive this point home. There was nothing personal in this, and obviously neither Salvatierra nor Ugarte intended that he should actually suffer as a result of charges that he probably never heard.[88]

Many facts refute Venegas's depiction of Juan Bautista Escalante as a badly behaved captain who was deplored by the missionaries. Escalante served as a godfather at Loreto twice during the period in which he was said to have been stationed there. The padres were unlikely to have encouraged Escalante if he and they were truly at odds. He also acted as godfather at Loreto once during each of three subsequent years. Each time, he was described in the baptismal record book as "el Capitán Juan Bautista Escalante."[89] Even more interesting is the last paragraph of a letter that Padre Piccolo wrote to Salvatierra from Mulegé in 1709 to report on a recent exploration. After wishing each of California's current padres good health, he appended, "to them I commend myself sincerely, and likewise to Capitán Rodríguez, Alférez Escalante, and all other good companions."[90] Finally, as late as 1712, Escalante stood as godfather at Misión de San Javier to a baby girl from the ranchería of Santa Rosalía. The baptism was performed and the entry signed by Juan de Ugarte, the padre supposedly most dissatisfied with Escalante's performance as captain.[91]

These documented events belie the spirit of Venegas's account—an important point since that historian is the unique source of much early Californiana. Every mention of Escalante in later California histories draws on Venegas's harsh judgment, but the documented facts paint a kinder picture and suggest that the deposed officer was not only forgiven—if indeed there was anything to forgive—but prove that he was welcomed into the ceremonial and social life of the peninsular missions.[92] They also suggest that he remained in California beyond the reported year, though he may have been stationed at Guaymas, had sailing capabilities, and, on occasion, brought supplies to California himself. In later years, Loreto would have officers, and even soldiers, who regularly performed such services.[93]

The whole story of Esteban Rodríguez's resignation and reinstatement will never be known. It is likely that both he and the Jesuits miscalculated: he, that life on the mainland would prove fulfilling and profitable, and his employers, that the capable Portuguese could be readily replaced. Both sides learned and took steps that cemented a close relationship for the remaining forty years of Rodríguez's life. This incident also highlights and illustrates the conflicting motives of some of the human elements in the dramatic conquest of California. It reveals that even a few people on a distant frontier could create controversy and intrigue in the viceregal capital. It would be the forerunner of decades of greater contests that would reach all the way to Spain.

Missions at Mulegé and Ligüí

Since the Jesuit provincial was expected to visit the headquarters of the various mission areas of New Spain, Salvatierra decided to return to California with his newly reinstated captain and to take with them a Jesuit *hermano* (brother),

Jaime Bravo, as an assistant.[94] The three men landed at Loreto late in August 1705 with a load of supplies, bought in part with the newly delivered royal funds.

Hermano Bravo soon expressed a strong desire to work in California. Salvatierra agreed but with an unusual condition: Bravo should try the job, and if it proved too much for his health or energies, he should write to Salvatierra and he would be replaced.[95] Bravo apparently suffered from tuberculosis, and this shows his superior's awareness and concern. Bravo finally wasted away and died of his ailment but not before serving forty active and useful years in California.[96]

Bravo's enlistment facilitated plans to open new missions at Mulegé and Ligüí. He was installed as Loreto's business manager, responsible for bookkeeping and ordering and distributing supplies; that freed Padre Pedro de Ugarte to be reassigned. Salvatierra stayed on for nearly three months readying Ugarte and Basaldúa to open and operate the new missions. By late October 1705, he was satisfied with his preparations and returned to resume his duties as provincial in New Spain.

An unusual event took place at Loreto on 5 November 1705: two pack trains were prepared, and two bands of soldiers and neophytes assembled and left the presidio. One, led by Padre Basaldúa, headed north; the other, led by Padre Pedro de Ugarte, headed south. A few days later, the number of California missions was doubled from two to four by the addition of Santa Rosalía de Mulegé[97] and San Juan Bautista de Ligüí.[98]

Salvatierra's Final Decade

Padre Juan María de Salvatierra was miserable away from California. He performed the duties of provincial of the Society of Jesus in New Spain with his usual fervor and thoroughness, but at the same time he was writing to Rome with appeals to Padre General Tirso González to allow him to return to his unfulfilled responsibilities at his own mission. González died in October 1705 without taking action and was succeeded by Michaelangelo Tamburini. The new general was impressed that Salvatierra profoundly desired to give up a post to which most Jesuits would aspire. In mid-1706, he appointed Padre Bernardo Rolandegui to take Salvatierra's place as provincial of New Spain.

Delighted, Padre Juan María began the long trek west that would be punctuated with stops to visit benefactors and to buy and arrange to ship goods and provisions needed in California, but the trip proved to be difficult and sad. Salvatierra's party was hampered by bad weather and the illness, in particular, of the padre's "sons" from Loreto. When he journeyed to Mexico City in 1704, he brought several of his neophytes to show off their knowledge of Spanish and Christian doctrine and to stimulate interest in his distant mission. When he visited the peninsula in 1705, he brought them back safely and took six different men with him on his return to central New Spain. Now, while homeward bound, all the native Californians fell ill. Finally, after repeated bouts, one died in Salvatierra's arms. The gulf crossing was an additional great trial and near disaster with days of raging north winds and high waves. Everyone was terrified and exhausted by the time the little ship was able to take cover behind Isla de San José.[99]

When the shaken Californians recovered, they had wonderful tales to tell, wonderful not only for their fellow neophytes, but even for most of Loreto's gente de razón — who had never had the opportunity to visit the capital city or appear before representatives of government, church, and society. One repeated image stood out in their stories: their many sightings of Our Lady of Loreto, alive in the streets of Mexico City. They had mistaken society women, dressed in their finery and riding in glass-enclosed, decorated carriages or sedan chairs, for the elegantly dressed effigy of the Virgin within her glassed-sided tabernacle in their mission church.[100]

Salvatierra's return freed Padre Juan de Ugarte from his duties at Loreto and allowed him to make important changes at Misión de San Javier. Cattle had been introduced to browse around the mission as soon as it had a resident padre. Under Ugarte's supervision, neophytes learned to appreciate the advantages of sizeable herds and to tend them rather than view them as objects for clandestine slaughter. In the ensuing decade, San Javier's cattle herd advanced from dozens to hundreds.[101] However, even as the animals multiplied on the barren land, agriculture in general lagged. Since 1702, rainfall in the area had been scant or absent. The mission's fields, once described in such admiring terms by Padre Piccolo,[102] were particularly vulnerable to drought. Biaundó, as the vicinity was called, lay in a broad valley, open to winds, at an elevation over 1,500 feet and very near the top of the water catchment on which it depended. However, water continued to surface at San Pablo, an open area five miles south in the same watercourse and at an elevation two hundred feet lower than San Javier. Here the arroyo was sheltered from winds by high walls and received water from additional canyons that drained catchments in the heights to the east. Ugarte had discovered San Pablo in 1706 while returning from an otherwise fruitless search to the south for a port at which to welcome Manila trading ships. That expedition had been provided with forty "volunteer" neophyte warriors from missions on the Río Yaqui, and the ever-provident Ugarte did not waste the manpower thus put in his hands. He had these workers build flumes of stone and mortar to carry water from the best spring to various small fields that they cleared of stones; these stones and others were rolled into place to form dikes to protect against floods.[103] Ugarte thereby introduced the form of agriculture that is still used in the area. Early in 1707, Ugarte sent many of San Javier's neophytes to live in this better-favored spot. His plan was so successful that, by 1710, San Pablo's agriculture was instrumental in feeding the people of San Javier and those of Loreto. Moreover, grapevines were among Ugarte's many experimental plantings; they prospered notably and soon led to production of the first California wine.[104]

Ugarte then directed the construction of a stone-and-mortar church at San

Pablo. The *cal*, or natural cement, had to be dug on Isla de Coronados, taken by canoa to Loreto, fired in a kiln, packed up from the beach twenty-three miles, and ground to powder at the construction site. Beams for the new church were imported from forests in the mountains above Matanchel, which by this time had become the principal port of embarkation for California's supplies (see Map 5.1).[105] About 1710, when the church and a padre's house were completed, Misión de San Javier was moved. The name moved with it and obliterated that of San Pablo. The former mission site was then called San Javier Antiguo—today Rancho Viejo.[106]

In 1708, the first of the endowments obtained six years earlier from the Marqués de Villapuente was used as the financial basis of a new mission, San José de Comondú, located over thirty miles north-northwest of San Javier. (The story of its founding and the history of its Jesuit years comprise Chapter 8 of this work.)

In 1709, Padre Piccolo returned from his assignment as padre visitador of the Jesuit missions in Sonora. He immediately took over as missionary at Santa Rosalía de Mulegé, a post vacated months before when Padre Juan Manuel de Basaldúa was transferred to a mission on the Río Yaqui in Sonora. Basaldúa's soldier-escort, Juan Bautista Mugazábal, literally ran the mission in the long interim between missionaries. Piccolo was happily surprised to find that the neophytes were not only working industriously, but that their instruction had proceeded and that the soldier had conducted all the services that a layman might appropriately direct. Mugazábal confessed that he hoped to become a Jesuit himself. The impressed padre began Mugazábal's instruction and later turned him over to Padre Juan de Ugarte who asked permission from the provincial to administer the necessary tests and receive the vows that would allow the soldier to enter the order as a brother. The request was most unusual, but it was granted because of the high esteem in which Ugarte was held, and the time, great distance, and inconvenience involved in sending the man for years of instruction at a conventional center for novices. Mugazábal was initiated as a brother in the Jesuit order in 1718 just as Hermano Jaime Bravo became a full-fledged padre. As Hermano Juan Bautista, he took over Bravo's long-time post of bookkeeper and storekeeper in Loreto, a position he then held for an incredible forty-one years.[107]

When Francisco María Piccolo came to Mulegé, he discovered that leaders of Cochimí bands in the nearby sierra were requesting that a padre visit and talk to them. On 11 June 1709, Piccolo left Santa Rosalía with a party made up of Mugazábal, Bartolomé de Robles—one of Salvatierra's pioneer soldiers—several neophytes, and some guides from the sierra. This exploration lasted only eight days but must have been hard work; the party ascended 2,000 feet to the peninsular divide, then traveled fifty miles through the mountains, along the arroyo of San Miguel, to reach the Pacific shore. In 1712, Piccolo was escorted by Capitán Esteban Rodríguez and a squad of soldiers when he made a more difficult crossing of the sierra, climbing almost due south out of the arroyo of Mulegé, up a precipitous grade to a 2,600-foot pass, and into the

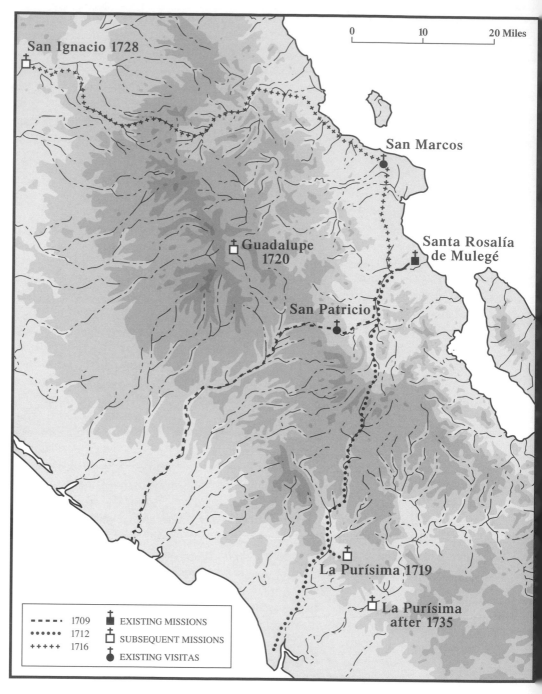

0   10   20 Miles

San Ignacio 1728

San Marcos

Santa Rosalía
de Mulegé

Guadalupe
1720

San Patricio

La Purísima 1719

La Purísima
after 1735

- - - -   1709   ■ EXISTING MISSIONS
••••••   1712   □ SUBSEQUENT MISSIONS
+ + + + +   1716   ● EXISTING VISITAS

Map 3.2 Padre Piccolo's Explorations from Mulegé

headwaters of Arroyo de Guajademí which led them down to the Pacific. As a result of these explorations, Piccolo was the first to recognize the potential of the arroyos in which, a decade later, the Jesuits developed the missions of Nuestra Señora de Guadalupe de Huasinapí and La Purísima Concepción de Cadegomó.[108] During the earlier exploration, Piccolo recorded some ethnographic notes and descriptions of activities on the trail. The Cochimí who accompanied him "carried their seeds with them and, everywhere they stopped, hunted for *metates* (flat rocks on which to grind the seeds)." They collected fruit of the pitahaya for his party and used their basins (open, pitch-lined baskets or large dishes hollowed from wood) to bring water to the mules. They treated the mules as if they were gente de razón, possibly because they heard Bartolomé de Robles scolding them from time to time; it was his habit to talk to them "now with words of affection, and again angrily, as is the habit of muleteers."[109]

Another devastating five-year drought cycle began in 1709 and that year also saw the most lethal epidemic of smallpox known to have visited the peninsula. In a little over a year, half of the California converts died.[110] From 1710 to 1715, the missionaries made little material or spiritual progress. Everyone was engaged in tending the sick, burying the dead, collecting food, or working at the difficult problems of getting food from Sonora and Sinaloa in small, poorly maintained craft.[111] Moreover, age had begun to impede California's intrepid pioneer padres. In 1715, Salvatierra was sixty-seven and suffering with kidney stones. Piccolo was sixty-one, and Ugarte was fifty-five. Nevertheless, explorations were resumed when good rains returned in 1715 and 1716. Two expeditions in the latter year achieved markedly different results.

By 1716, Spain's colonies were receiving greater attention from the central government as a result of the end of the Wars of the Spanish Succession. California Jesuits learned that their requests for assistance were being considered again and that some long-standing demands on them were about to be reinstated. They expected to be reproached again for failing to find a California port to sustain the Manila galleon. To counter this criticism, Salvatierra, ailing as he was, took ship in May with Rodríguez and an unspecified number of soldiers and converts from Loreto to sail to La Paz. The padre visitador hoped to establish a base in the cape region from which missions and a port installation finally could be developed. To assist that effort, the expedition returned three Guaycura men from the La Paz area who had been prisoners in Loreto. These men had been well treated, and the missionary hoped they would act as ambassadors and interpreters to establish contact between missionaries and the people alienated by Admiral Atondo's "massacre" in 1683.

The venture was doomed. As the ship landed, the local people beat a hasty retreat. While the captain and soldiers were delayed in the travail of disembarking their horses, the Loretan neophytes took off in hot pursuit of the fleeing Guaycura. The local men easily outdistanced their pursuers, but many women did not. When cornered, they fought with stones, but the rampaging Loretans overpowered them, injuring and killing many. The soldiers arrived too late to prevent the killings. The missionary party had no recourse but to give up the entrada and sail home, having only added to the damage done by Atondo three decades earlier.[112]

In late 1716, Padre Piccolo mounted his last exploration. He had reports of numerous large bands of Cochimí, much fresh water, and broad fields located four or five days' ride northwest of Mulegé. This time he was accompanied by soldiers José Altamirano, Juan de Villalobos, and Sebastián Martín, Salvatierra's page in 1697, but an employee of the presidio since 1701.[113] The party left Mulegé on 13 November 1716 and in three weeks visited a magnificent site at the focus of one of the peninsula's largest water-catchment basins. Piccolo called the place San Vicente, but a few years later it became Misión de San Ignacio, one of the peninsula's most successful from the standpoint of food production. The padre was greeted by hundreds of people, whom he commenced to evangelize, and by so much water that two of his horses drowned trying to cross the pools in the great arroyo.[114]

At the beginning of 1717, Salvatierra had a message from his provincial, Padre Gaspar Rodero: a new viceroy had arrived and was prepared to reopen the whole issue of royal support for California. The new man wished to confer with Salvatierra himself. Could the venerable father make his way to Mexico City? By this time Padre Juan María was tired. He was sixty-eight years old and weakened by his kidney problem. Nevertheless, in March 1717, he pulled himself together for the long trek. He appointed Juan de Ugarte to serve in his place, and he asked Hermano Jaime Bravo, his right hand, to accompany him. The brave old soldier of Jesus got as far as Tepic before he collapsed. He was carried a hundred miles on a litter to Guadalajara. There, on 19 July 1717, he died in the Jesuit College that he had governed a quarter of a century before.[115] The last weeks of his life were spent in preparing Jaime Bravo for conferences with the viceroy.[116] Through that medium, Juan María de Salvatierra posthumously achieved his long-sought goal of substantial royal support for his cherished California missions.

FOUR

Missions Create Turmoil in the South

California Gains Royal Funding

A new viceroy came to Mexico City in 1716, Baltasar de Zúñiga y Guzmán, the Marqués de Valero, an experienced diplomat and bureaucrat. Valero's briefings in Madrid had made him acutely aware, on one hand, of Jesuit influence in high places, and, on the other, of his superiors' impatience for the fulfillment of long-standing royal wishes. The new man soon announced plans for California. He would finally disburse some of the royal money allotted to the missions years before, but he would also insist on the creation of a Pacific port supported by a new presidio and mission. To remind the Jesuits of the history of these matters, he resurrected the cédula that first spelled them out — and also called for a colony of españoles who could develop California resources in keeping with imperial interests.[1] Valero was armed with a new royal decree that chided the California missionaries and previous viceroys for dragging their feet on all these issues. However, as a diplomat, Valero did not present the matter in a negative light. On the contrary, he presented it to the interested Jesuits in Mexico City — Padre Provincial Gaspar Rodero and Padre Procurador de Californias Alejandro Romano — as great news for their California enterprise. He painted a glowing picture of an additional presidio that would support expansion of their mission program, and he reminded them of the advantages that a greater volume of shipping would have in ensuring the flow of supplies to California.

Rodero and Romano were shocked. Romano, recipient of all reports and requisitions from California, was delegated by his superior to begin the new viceroy's education. Romano opened the file on California and deluged Valero with selected truths: a colony could not support itself — there simply was no land with sufficient water to grow food; many ships would be required to bring supplies from the mainland; costs to the royal treasury would be disastrous;

there were no resources that could be developed to offset the losses.[2] Valero was not dissuaded. He replied that it was in his power at least to found the new presidio and that he wished to confer with Padre Salvatierra in the capital before he made decisions on the other points. Padre Provincial Rodero reluctantly relayed the unwelcome news to California. So it was that Padre Juan María and Hermano Jaime Bravo set out for Mexico City, though they had traveled only as far as Guadalajara when Salvatierra died in mid-July of 1717.

After a month, an appropriate interval of mourning, Jaime Bravo left Guadalajara to meet with Valero, Rodero, and Romano. In the interim since his own arrival, the viceroy had consulted with many people and he now knew better the character, interests, and abilities of those who pushed and pulled at him in his new position. He discovered that in California affairs he had no alternative but to deal with Jesuits. Even if they were adamant in resisting his orders, there was no other group that could take their place and be expected to perform as well, so Valero called on Jaime Bravo to outline his ideas for improving and speeding the conquest. Bravo's response was an intricate document in twelve parts with all sorts of requests, great and small, for money and concessions.[3]

Most of Bravo's proposals reflected the perennial desires and needs of the California Jesuits, but two were exceptions. First, Bravo abandoned a long-held Jesuit position when he acceded to Valero by calling for a new presidio with its own muster of twenty-five men. The Jesuits appear to have concluded that further opposition to the development of a port and presidio would be counterproductive. Doubtless they realized that since they alone occupied California, whatever plans the crown might make would be immensely costly and problematic without their participation. In short, it was an issue on which the Jesuits could bide their time.

Bravo's other surprise was included in his request for a large ship to transport major supply shipments. Despite Kino and Salvatierra's exploration in 1701 and the resulting conviction that California was a peninsula, Bravo added fuel to an old fire by suggesting that California might well be an island, separated from the mainland by a narrow strait. If the Jesuits had a ship suitable for explorations, that passage might be found and the Manila galleon could sail directly into the secure gulf at its north end and avoid the long and perilous voyage down the Pacific shore of California. Bravo's tantalizingly simple solution to an old problem must have been designed more to attract funds for a ship than to reflect a consensus of Jesuit thought.[4]

The Marqués de Valero's response to Bravo's petition was polite and encouraging. He had his advisory junta go over the entire bill of particulars, though he had reservations about its more expensive requests. He knew that the crown's immediate interest was not so much in hastening California's spiritual conquest as in making it a useful and safe place for Spanish shipping. Englishmen had been lurking off Cabo San Lucas to prey on the Manila ship. As recently as 1709, Captain Woodes Rogers had captured the Philippine ship's smaller companion, and the booty he seized was valued at seven hundred thousand pesos.[5] The junta convened by Valero brought in recommendations favorable to most of Bravo's requests, but the viceroy made no move to order their fulfillment. Instead, he gave the California mission eighteen thousand pesos and his pledge to continue to support twenty-five soldiers.

In less than two years, Virrey Valero convinced Jesuits of the post-Salvatierra era that the government apparatus from top to bottom was determined to gain its long-sought goals in California. A royal cédula of 1719 called for the occupation of California as far north as San Diego and Monterey. It is likely that this peremptory and impractical order was elicited by the viceroy as part of his campaign to direct Jesuit efforts toward exploration. Padre Juan de Ugarte, Salvatierra's successor, responded to Valero's stimulus by launching an era in which the Jesuits made substantive efforts to accommodate some of the royal desires.[6]

Delays and Difficulties in Seeking a Galleon Port

Juan María de Salvatierra had been the grand architect of the California conquest; he formulated the early plans, supervised their execution, and then orchestrated drives for additional funding and supplies, exerting his considerable social, economic, and political power in the process. His accomplishments contributed to the self-assured independence he displayed when dealing with governmental demands that did not complement his plans. This attitude was responsible in part for the Jesuits' long delay in finding a haven for the Manila ship. The concept of annual dealings with the galleon did not appeal to California's padres. They were aware that its port would become — in season — a bustling, noisome place whose commerce and incidental intercourse would upset the even tenor of their ideal for mission life. They knew that gente de razón and California natives attracted to the port would stay and seek other business. The necessary civil government would become large and far-reaching and would encroach on Jesuit authority.

If a harbor had to be found and developed, the California missionaries believed it should be close to a mission and as near as possible to Loreto. Such an arrangement would put them in a strong position to offer their own presidio to protect the port and the produce of their missions to resupply the ships. If the galleon must land in California, Jesuit interests would best be served if, instead of letting another authority into their land, they remained the sole providers of goods and services.

When Virrey Valero made plain his determination to develop a base for the galleon, the Jesuits broadened their port-seeking efforts. All indications pointed south. Explorers and pearlers had given La Paz a reputation as California's finest harbor. Manila ships had already made emergency landings at the tip of the peninsula. The Jesuits had not pressed their conquest toward the cape, however, because past experience had persuaded them that their own interests were better served in the north.

Salvatierra's mentor, Padre Kino, had spent several weeks among the Guay-

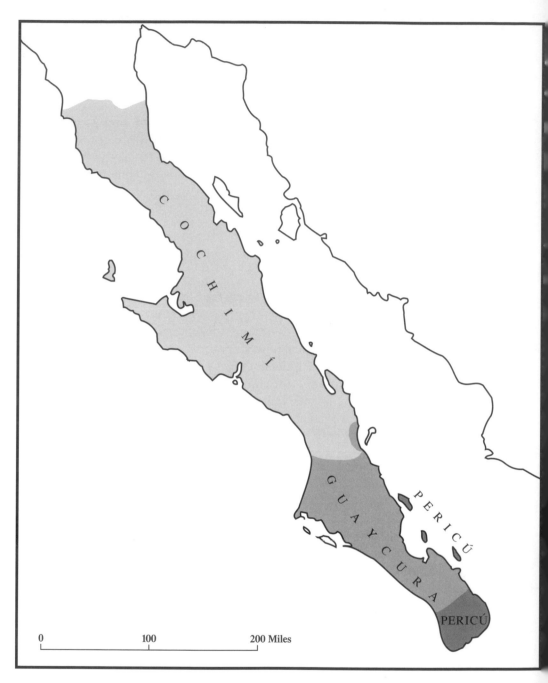

Map 4.1 The Geography of Peninsular Languages

cura at La Paz in 1683 as a member of Atondo's expedition. From there, Kino had gone two hundred miles north and made a longer, more successful contact with the Cochimí. Salvatierra could say that he chose Loreto because Almirante Atondo had ordered a broadside of mortar fire at La Paz that slaughtered ten Guaycura. Kino and Salvatierra averred that people of that region would never again welcome missionaries. In fact, Salvatierra picked the more northerly base because the people there had been more receptive to Kino's mission. Once established in California, the Jesuits found that the farther north they traveled, the more amenable the people seemed to conversion and the less rebellious in subsequent relations. Furthermore, the Yuman language that the Jesuits had learned to communicate with peoples just northwest of Loreto continued to be useful as they pushed a hundred miles beyond.

In contrast, prospects for missionary activity in the south were discouraging. A few contacts had been friendly, particularly during early entradas when missionaries offered gifts and made no demands. However, as the Jesuits gained experience with the southern people, they noted more and more negative elements. The natives were broken into many warring bands that spoke several different languages. They had a long history of disturbing encounters with Europeans, quite apart from the disasters created by Atondo in 1683 and Salvatierra in 1716. For almost two centuries, the peoples of the greater cape region had occasional contact with ships that put in for water and wood, usually pearling expeditions or pirates stalking a Manila ship or laid up for rest and repairs. The intruders used native labor when it could be arranged, paid with trinkets, and left, but their diseases and probably some descendants remained. In that time, several men — some white, some mulatto — who had deserted from ships or been marooned or shipwrecked, stayed on the peninsula, made peace with the natives, and added to the cultures and bloodlines near the cape.[7] Contact with outsiders influenced local cultures. Most of these aliens were, by Spanish definition, outlaws or runaways; they had reasons to instill in the local people their own fear of any representative of Spanish authority.

Ugarte Begins to Redeem Jesuit Promises

Juan de Ugarte was the logical successor to Salvatierra as leader of the California mission. Ugarte had held every other post in the organization. He had been an energetic and resourceful builder and organizer. He had directed important agricultural development around his mission at San Javier by impressive personal effort and through his ability to inspire and direct his servants and neophytes. As visitador, he became responsible for the Jesuit promises made as part of Hermano Jaime Bravo's accord with Virrey Valero. Ugarte's concerted actions during the ensuing decade give evidence of a sincere and sustained effort to fulfill those promises.[8] The new padre visitador turned his own and his people's energies toward establishing missions for the conversion of the cape peoples and the assistance of the galleons. California's foremost benefactor, the

Marqués de Villapuente, made Ugarte's campaign possible by endowing the proposed series of southern missions.[9]

In February 1719, Ugarte came down to Loreto to meet with Capitán Esteban Rodríguez, Alférez Francisco Cortés de Monroy, and Padre Clemente Guillén, then the missionary at San Juan Bautista de Malibat, previously known as Ligüí.[10] Ugarte asked this group to rediscover and reconnoiter Magdalena Bay, a great port on the Pacific shore first found and explored from the sea over a century earlier by Sebastián Vizcaíno. Atondo and Kino had tried and failed to approach it by land in 1684. Ugarte was determined to send the viceroy hard facts about the nature of the land route from Loreto to the Magdalena region, the availability of water and wood by the bay, the sorts of people in the area, and the prospects for a mission.

In early March, Guillén, Rodríguez, and Monroy left Loreto at the head of a column of twelve soldiers, half the presidio's muster, fifteen trusted California and Sonora neophytes, and two Guaycura guide-interpreters who knew the first part of the terrain to be crossed. The party passed the outpost mission at Malibat and crossed the spine of the Sierra de La Giganta on the route followed today by the trans-peninsular highway. They climbed the narrow, steep ridges that rise directly from the sea. After turning from their last view of the indigo gulf and its jagged isles, they climbed over the relatively low passes that lead to the headwaters of Arroyo Guatamote; they followed that arroyo through the mountains to a vast plain that slopes down to the southwest.

Padre Guillén kept a diary and recorded salient discoveries and events of the trip. Both the title, "Expedition to the Guaycura Nation in California and Discovery by Land of the Large Bay of Santa María Magdalena on the Pacific Ocean by the Señor Capitán Don Esteban Rodríguez Lorenzo, Its First Conqueror," and much of the contents seem to have been conceived to honor Esteban Rodríguez. Perhaps the captain's employers were seeking to bolster his reputation as a commander and explorer and to dispel his image as a mere tool of the missionaries, a recurrent theme in their detractors' jibes. Guillén's daybook describes the terrain and records encounters with roving bands of Guaycura as the explorers pushed southward down the plain. He noted dozens of indigenous placenames; two of these, Quepo and Tiguana, became the names of private ranches on the same sites more than half a century later.

After three weeks, the explorers came to the head of an estuary, but it led to the open sea, not a great bay. Local Guaycura told them that they must go northwest, so Rodríguez took a scouting party in that direction and on 24 March 1719 finally saw the expanse of Bahía de Magdalena beyond a marshy beach. After several days of reconnoitering potential approaches to the bay, Rodríguez and Guillén abandoned the search. Their own explorations plus information from transient Guaycura indicated that the bay region had no good source of water and no wood—the same findings that Vizcaíno had recorded in 1602.[11] The great bay, as capacious and landlocked as it was, could serve neither as a base for the galleon nor as a mission site. The members of that party must have made the long ride back to Loreto with regrets that so promising a harbor had proved so useless. However, the trip served as an entrada for Clemente Guillén. He would spend most of his evangelical years among the Guaycura, and these first contacts eventually led to the establishment of missions Los Dolores and San Luis Gonzaga.

Ugarte Builds a Ship

Dynamic Juan de Ugarte next addressed the task of providing California with a dependable sailing vessel to transport supplies and fulfill the Jesuit obligation to explore by sea. Ships purchased in New Spain had failed to provide long or good service in California. Those built to order in west coast shipyards had been exorbitantly expensive and had served no better. Ugarte decided to attack the problem in a new way, to build his ship in California where he could supervise the work, and he decided to obtain and use native wood for its construction.

During the early years of the California conquest, the padres and their employees found no trees that could yield planks or long timbers, nor did they suspect that such trees existed. Mesquite trees (*Prosopis* species) were common and produced hard, durable wood suitable for door- and window-frames, lintels, small cabinetry and various wooden fittings. Typically, however, trunks of mesquite in California were no more than ten feet in height and a foot or so in diameter, and they were seldom straight. They yielded bent or curved timbers that were useful for ribs in ship construction but never planks.

Padre Piccolo was the first explorer to discover real timber. During one of his penetrations into the Sierra de Guadalupe west of Mulegé, he came across, or was taken to, a stand of *güéribos* (*Populus brandegeei*). This white-barked giant poplar is the largest tree that grows in the central and southern parts of the peninsula. It is found in company with the *zalate* or wild fig (*Ficus palmeri*), also with whitish bark, the second largest plant in the region. These trees share deep canyons at higher elevations of Guadalupe and the other sierras that range southward to the Cape. The güéribo is erect in habit and reaches heights in excess of sixty feet and diameters of over six feet. The wood has medium density but is fine-grained and strong.

Concentrations of güéribos were rare, even at the time of their discovery, but as soon as Juan de Ugarte knew the quality of their wood and had reports of a number of trees, he set out to secure timbers. In September 1719, he, a shipwright, two soldiers, and a number of selected neophytes left Loreto Conchó and headed northward to Mulegé, the base for their sierra venture. There he was joined by Sebastián de Sistiaga, the local missionary. In his detailed letter to Piccolo, Ugarte did not name his soldier escorts, but he made familiar references to his shipbuilder: Capitán Guillermo ("Captain William"). Guillermo Strafford, an Englishman, was active on and around the Vermillion Sea for decades. He was skilled as a ship's captain, navigator, and pilot, as well as carpenter and shipwright. He served Ugarte as a pilot on a memorable voyage in 1721 and in the 1740s, after nearly thirty years of experience on the gulf, wrote an *informe* describing its islands, reefs, currents, winds, and tides as well as the locations of pearl oyster beds and fresh water supplies.[12]

Two months after leaving Loreto, Juan de Ugarte and his companions completed the first phase of their lumbering operation and returned to Mulegé. Ugarte's report to Piccolo, who was holding the fort at Loreto Conchó, was dictated to Padre Sebastián de Sistiaga and vividly recreates some of the adventures and the spirit of the undertaking.[13]

> This is written by the father secretary, both in order to save your Reverence the trouble of reading my poor handwriting and also because I do not know where my eyes, feet, hands, and head are. For with feet, hands, and head, we have been rolling about all over the Sierra, where we did not have the good fortune which others have had in finding bread and timber. For all the timber has consisted of güéribos, (which can not be mentioned to the father secretary even in a letter), and there was not so much as a scrap of bread. There were days when we did not have a crumb of it. This is a theme which would provide wordy employment for the father secretary's pen, except that he hopes to give an account with his own mouth when, by God's grace, we shall see one another. But now it is necessary to give a report of all that has happened since we left Conchó, down to the present hour.

Ugarte tells how they traveled to Londó, slaughtered two of twenty head of cattle recently arrived from Sonora, and went on to Mulegé, in all a journey of three or four days. They then spent two days in preparations and in waiting for the correspondence that had to be answered before the father visitor's prolonged absence.

> On the day following the arrival of the letters we set out for the sierra, accompanied by Father Sebastián. We went by way of Hiatael, took our siesta at San Patricio el Viejo, and spent the night at a place very near Los Angeles. Only because we had all the angels with us were we able to get out of the labyrinth which we had entered, looking for pasturage and for the trail.

The location of Hiatael, a Cochimí name for a place somewhere in the vast arroyo of Mulegé, may be irretrievably lost, but Old San Patricio and the region of Los Angeles can be identified from other early accounts, the survival of the names, and the ruins of a chapel.[14] The lumbering party rode up the huge wash of Arroyo Mulegé to a point near present-day Rancho Trinidad, then climbed out of that bowl-shaped watercourse and crossed a high ridge to the west. The padre's "labyrinth" is easily recognized in the twisting, barren canyon through which the trail between the old visita of San Patricio and Los Angeles still passes. Today, local residents call the convoluted maze *El Caracol*, the spiral or snailshell.

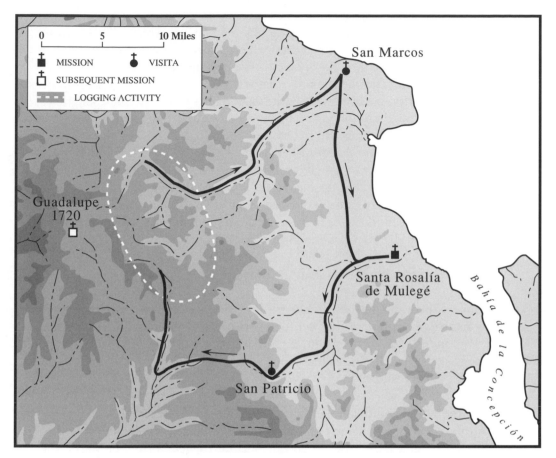

Map 4.2 Padre Ugarte's Lumbering Expedition, 1719

The next day we came to the first canyon where the timber grows, and that very afternoon the men began to fell the trees, and continued for another cycle of the moon in the great labor of shaping the wood. We made the keel, the keelson, the stern-posts, the transom, the wales, and other great timbers. In the meantime the men began to clear the ground and open a road, to get the keel down, for it was now finished. Since the other oxen were useless — one of them was blind in one eye, and the white one belonging to Father Kappus[15] was either weak, or was terrified because it was new to the work of hauling timber — we tried to use the ox Angel, which they also called Santo Tomás. Father Sebastián made the first attempt. Perhaps to save his shoes, which were now as worn out as my own and, just as other men put on their shoes in order not to work, so that father took his off in order to pull out the timber. He worked at it until he had the log free, lying on a small tract of level ground where it was intended to put the other timbers which had been trimmed where they fell. Now the men began to move these, trying all possible means. We tried pulling the timbers with the oxen, but gave it up, for all the animals were bulls, and there was only one ox which was broken to work. (If I had had the trained oxen which I keep at San Javier, the timber would already have been down below.) We tried using the strength of men's arms. Christians, heathen, soldiers, fathers, and carpenter, all joined in the work, and by using wooden rollers, we made a little progress. But at length we gave up this method too; for we had no food to give the heathen who were serving as oxen, and this had to be taken into account.

We were now somewhat dismayed; for we had tried very hard. But we made another attempt. We mounted our horses and settled ourselves firmly in the stirrups. We took a cable, doubled it, and attached the horses to the middle of it; three pairs of men came in the rear, using poles as levers; and so, with two rollers, all the timbers were brought down and the other methods were consequently abandoned. I think that this is the way in which the work will have to be done, until one or two yokes of trained oxen are sent to us to serve as leaders for the bulls. Then all the timber may be gotten down.

Once the first-felled timbers were in a place from which neophytes and unconverted Cochimí recruits could drag them to the beach, Ugarte, Strafford, Sistiaga and the soldiers began to explore for other stands of güéribo in canyons 2,000 to 2,500 feet above sea level. The rough Sierra de Guadalupe did not give up its treasure easily.

After examining the timber in a canyon, we decided to reconnoiter to the north. We went up on horseback not without difficulty, as far as we could, and then dismounted in order to go on. But the ruggedness of the sierra, the obstacles that lay in our way, and the ravines which were dangerous, even for men on foot, obliged us to go back. We had reached a spot where Padre Sebastián and Capitán Guillermo not only saw the sea of the Contra Costa, but also this sea of the Strait and the mainland on the other coast.

Here we were, then, on a knife-edge, without water, and without a trail by which we could go back; and yet to go back was necessary. The day was too far gone to allow us to reach a place of safety by daylight. We decided to do what is ordinarily done in such desperate circumstances, that is, to try to go down to an arroyo which, as we knew, led to the plains of Guezenopí [Huasinapí]. Since the Indians assured us that there was no trail, and that the arroyo had steep sides, each of us endeavored to find a path for himself. We separated, and some of us found güéribos, others found damp slopes where wheat could be sown, others found loose rocks which rolled under them, and all of us became greatly exhausted. But eventually we reached the arroyo, and instead of lamenting and grieving — for we had had nothing to eat or drink — we rejoiced over the fact that we were all together again.

We had come to a broad stretch of ground, and we thought that we were now free of precipices like the preceding, and that we would be able to go downstream without further difficulty. But presently we came to a dropoff, at the sight of which sheer terror sent the blood down to our heels. Again we dismounted. We took off our spurs, in order to descend the several levels of the fall, to see if there was any place where we could bring the horses down without danger. And one of us, carrying his spurs, went over the edge, leaving the animals and the other men up above. He did not know where the arroyo ended, but he was not turning his back on the danger, for he had made up his mind to find the path. (I do not say that this was the father secretary, for I do not want him to drop his pen in consternation.) By God's will, he found a path, and the animals came through without danger, and in a little while we all reached the plains.

Ugarte's determination to build a ship had come during one of the frequent periods when California missions suffered from shortages of all necessities. The entire venture had been carried out with minimal supplies, particularly food. Now the explorers had none at all and were eating hearts of mezcal after the fashion of the natives, but they were alert to the possibility of hunting for deer.

We arrived at a water hole. There were many tracks around it. We had sent the Indians ahead on foot, and with them the soldier who accompanied them; but they found no game. However, we had a stroke of good luck. For while we were taking our siesta at this water hole, we noticed some vultures, and knew that there must be something dead in the neighborhood. We sent men to look for it, and it was a deer which had been killed by a lion. It stank so vilely that when it was put on the pack animal, which was carrying only the blankets, the men who came behind drew back because of the stench, and laughed at the idea that they were going to eat that. But when we reached San Marcos, where not an Indian remained in the ranchería, hunger, which masters appetite, caused us to wash the meat and to put part of it on a spit and the rest of it in a kettle, to see which of the two would smell less. We had no snuff, for we had used it all on the journey, and hence there was nothing to distract our sense of smell, and to counteract the stench. But I assure your Reverence that it tasted better to us than the fish of Kahelopú, and that no stew in the whole world was ever eaten with more enthusiasm, and, although we laughed at one another, not a fragment of the venison was left.

And so the great woodcutting adventure ended. Padres and pilot returned to Mulegé, hungry but safe; soldiers, Cochimí helpers, and oxen followed with the precious logs. In all, it took four months to collect the required wood at the impromptu shipyard; construction consumed another six.

Under Ugarte's direction, Guillermo Strafford supervised shipbuilding operations on the beach at Mulegé. Carpenters and iron workers were brought from the other coast and were kept working at a pace dictated by the colony's great need. For want of a ship, Loreto had not received its annual supplies from Acapulco; other means had to be found to feed and supply the shipworkers.

Ugarte dedicated nearly all of San Javier's supplies to this cause. His neophytes joined in the privations as two hundred head of their mission's cattle were slaughtered and the meat taken to Mulegé. To further sustain and inspire the workers, the padre visitador brought them much of the entire colony's store of chocolate, wine, and brandy.[16]

On 16 July 1720, the day of the Holy Cross, Padre Piccolo, who had come for the occasion from Loreto, blessed the hull crudely propped up on the beach. He christened the new craft *El Triunfo de la Cruz*, as Ugarte had planned since his first inspiration for the project. On 14 September 1720, the ship was launched. Within six weeks it was fitted out and under sail.[17]

Little is known about that first native Californian vessel. Jesuit annals are full of praise for the craft and its builders, and it did serve for many years,[18] but Padre Jaime Bravo provided the only clue to its dimensions. He gave a keel length of twenty-seven cubits (just over fifty feet). Bravo said of the ship's height and breadth only that they were "in proportion."[19]

Ugarte Explores to the Head of the Gulf

Juan de Ugarte's four years of energetic leadership as visitador produced Jesuit California's most dramatic burst of expansion. Between 1719 and 1721, four missions were founded, entradas were prepared for two more, and major explorations were carried out on land and sea. Misión de la Purísima Concepción de Cadegomó was founded by Padre Nicolás Tamaral in the first week of 1720.[20] In November, Ugarte escorted Jaime Bravo — newly elevated from brother to padre — to La Paz where Bravo was to found a mission and remain as its missionary.[21] That same fall, German Padre Everardo Helen founded Misión de Nuestra Señora de Guadalupe at Huasinapí, 2,300 feet in elevation and near Ugarte's ship-timber groves.[22] In August 1721, Padre Clemente Guillén founded Misión de Nuestra Señora de los Dolores near the gulf coast between Loreto and La Paz.[23] In November of that year, Capitán Rodríguez and Padres Helen and Sistiaga renewed the search for a harbor on the contracosta. For two weeks, they explored the coast from a point nearly west of Guadalupe southward to the latitude of Comondú. By coincidence, Padre Nicolás Tamaral had set out to explore from La Purísima and covered some of the same ground in the same season.[24] The round of explorations was not confined to land. Juan de Ugarte wished to put an old controversy to rest by proving that California was a peninsula. On 15 May 1721, he left Loreto with *El Triunfo de la Cruz* and the open sailboat *Santa Bárbara* and headed north to reconnoiter the still-mysterious northern end of the gulf. Ugarte wrote that the *Triunfo*'s crew included six Europeans. He identified four by name: Guillermo Strafford, English, who acted as his pilot; Juan Sevilla de Torres, an Estremaduran Spaniard; Don Antonio de la Campa Monanes, presumably a Spaniard; and José Morfie [Joseph Murphy], Irish. Ugarte listed some of the previous experiences of his European shipmates; unfortunately, he did not connect them with the names of the men involved. One had made a voyage to Newfoundland. Two had sailed the Straits of Magellan. The most-traveled of the lot had crossed the Atlantic to New Spain, made a voyage to Manila from Acapulco, and, while returning, had been captured by the English off Cabo de San Lucas and taken by them to Holland.[25] Other than the Europeans, Ugarte's crew included Juan Miguel Montaño, a native of Peru, and thirteen Filipinos.[26] Ugarte listed the crew on the *Santa Bárbara*, his smaller companion craft, simply as five California converts, two Filipinos, and a Yaqui.

The expedition visited the Sonoran coast and the island of Tiburón, then sailed to the mouth of the Río Colorado. Ugarte and Strafford wrote reports that prove they understood that they had arrived at gulf's end and were in the mouth of a river. They had shown once again what Ulloa and Alarcón had reported in 1539 and 1540 and what Kino had observed in 1700: California was a peninsula. Nevertheless, their reports fell largely on deaf ears. A quarter of a century later, another Jesuit would repeat Ugarte's labors and still fail to convince the skeptics in New Spain and Europe.[27]

Missions in the Region of Cabo de San Lucas

Juan de Ugarte had committed himself and his California organization to evangelizing the cape region and establishing a presence that could offer help to Manila ships, but neither royal interest nor the best missionary intentions could assure that missions in the cape region would avoid a problem that the Jesuits had foreseen and feared. Missions in the cape region would have to bring together peoples of several independent and antagonistic linguistic groups. Padre Clemente Guillén had already begun to contact the largest, the Guaycura, who occupied most of the area between Loreto and La Paz, but the Guaycura were fragmented into half a dozen linguistically distinctive subgroups; those, in turn, were divided into widely scattered and competitive rancherías.[28] South of all the Guaycurans, in a three-thousand-square-mile area that terminated at Cabo de San Lucas and included the gulf islands from Isla de San José south, lived a second distinct group, the Pericú, whose language was unrelated to Guaycura or Cochimí.[29]

The Guaycura were particularly difficult to attract and retain by conventional missionary methods.[30] Most of the lands they occupied were among the peninsula's poorest in water and food resources. Their bands were small, highly mobile, and unusually antagonistic. The northernmost Guaycura traded raids with the Cochimí along an uneasy frontier. Those of the south regularly attacked or defended against the Pericú, and the splinter groups of the southern Guaycura spoke substantially variant dialects and incessantly warred or skirmished with each other. In all, the Guaycuran groups may have totaled five thousand people, but none was large enough to justify its own mission. Any mission in Guaycura territory was assured of a poor economic base and the necessity to reconcile age-old enemies.

The Pericú differed in many ways from the Guaycura but also presented missionaries with difficult problems. Their numbers totaled about three thousand[31], they spoke a common Pericú language, and their bands were less antagonistic, but the Pericú were accustomed to a great deal of personal, family, and small-group autonomy. Even when they consented to being concentrated at a mission, they retained their independent nature, resisted the authority of the missionary — and the mission governor he had selected from their ranks — and continued to come and go as their spirits moved them. Their independence was enhanced by mobility: their skills as boatmen and swimmers were unmatched by other peninsular people.[32] All missionaries who tried to cope with the problems of Pericú conversion commented at length on this independence — although it was usually called by some other name: stubbornness, fickleness, impertinence, or ingratitude.[33]

Misión de Nuestra Señora del Pilar de la Paz, 1720

On 1 November 1720, *El Triunfo de la Cruz* sailed from Mulegé to Loreto and in two days was loaded and manned for a voyage to La Paz. Jaime Bravo had been chosen to found a mission at the old port, his reward for fifteen years of hard work as procurador at Loreto and for being Salvatierra's substitute and an effective advocate for California with Virrey Valero. Juan de Ugarte sailed to La Paz with Bravo. Padre Clemente Guillén from Misión de San Juan Bautista de Malibat came by land with soldiers and some of his neophytes. When all were met, a great fiesta was held to celebrate the dedication of a new mission and Bravo's recent elevation from brother to padre. Ugarte's new ship stood at anchor off the beach as its people on shore entertained the local Guaycura and Isleño Pericú with bonfires, games, and salvos from their guns.[34]

Padre Bravo took advantage of this rare concentration of men, animals, and supplies to explore areas adjacent to La Paz. On 20 December 1720, he and a party headed to the south over open ground and spent the night at the foot of hills some thirty miles from the port. During the following day, *Soldado* (soldier) Ignacio de Rojas discovered a showing of silver ore, the precursor to California's first mines, founded three decades later.[35] Bravo's group also discovered stands of oaks and yucca, the latter useful for their fruit, seeds, and fiber. More important, they encountered groups of natives, probably Uchití, who seemed to welcome them. Bravo read that as a good augury.

The leaders of this Spanish party wrote accounts suggesting that they felt successfully launched on an undertaking which Cortés, Vizcaíno, and Atondo before them had tried and failed. The land to the south attracted them more than anything they had seen in California. Beside the traces of silver, there were springs and arable ground that promised agriculture, and pasture land that suggested cattle ranching. The men of this entrada carried away tales of all these things and the cape region soon had its own name, *el Sur* (the South), which would persist longer than Spanish rule.[36]

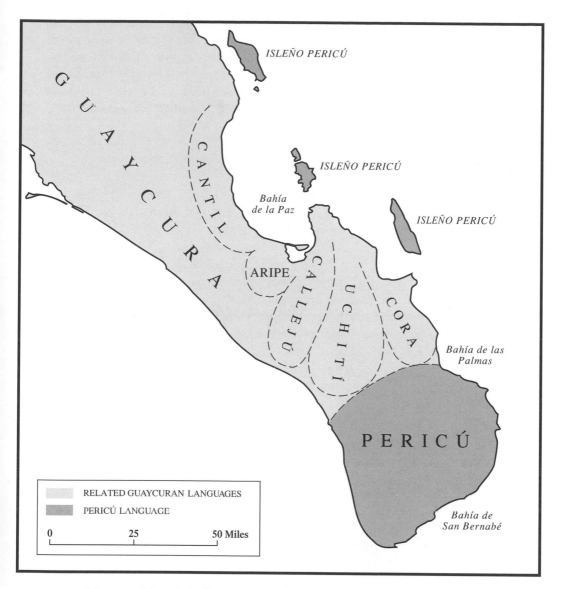

Map 4.3 Linguistic Groups in the Cape Region of California c. 1730

However, at La Paz, Padre Bravo and his party faced greater problems than they had anticipated. La Paz lacked accessible water and was home to no particular people.[37] The missionary newcomers thought they were dealing with just two cultural groups: Guaycura and Cora. The Spaniards imagined that the latter were the only group living between La Paz and the cape.[38] In fact, the great bay of La Paz, with its teeming seafood, attracted diverse and competitive people from every direction: Cantil[39] to the north, Callejú and Aripe to the west,[40] Uchití to the south,[41] Cora to the southeast,[42] and Isleño Pericú from the Islands of San José, Espíritu Santo, and Cerralvo.[43] None claimed La Paz as its own, and all were intermittently at war.[44] To succeed, or to operate at all, the new mission would need to bring diverse groups together and effectively instill new ways. It was not to be. After less than thirty years of a very fitful existence, Misión de Nuestra Señora del Pilar de la Paz would be closed. During that time, the ill-fated mission was to serve more as a base for the unintentional destruction of the region's peoples than as a center for their evangelization.

Misión de Nuestra Señora de los Dolores, 1721

Misión de San Juan Bautista de Ligüí (later Malibat) was opened in 1705 but occupied only sporadically in the ensuing fifteen years. Soon after the founding, its endowment was lost through the bankruptcy of its guarantor,[45] and its location proved impractical as well. Agriculture was impossible with the little water available, and, at certain seasons, its people had to go afield to find water to drink. The mission's original neophytes were Monquí, like those at Conchó, a splinter of the greater Guaycuran linguistic group. The islands just offshore and those nearby to the southeast were inhabited by fierce and unconverted Isleño Pericú who made destructive raids on the mission's stores and possessions.[46] During San Juan Bautista's first years, its Monquí neophytes diminished notably, either through deaths or moving to join their fellows at Loreto. Their places were taken by a few dozen Cochimí who came from the Pacific slopes of the mountains to the west. In fact, the change in the mission's name reflected its new constituency; Ligüí was the Monquí name for the place that the Cochimí called Malibat.[47]

When the Marqués de Villapuente agreed to underwrite new missions in the South, Ugarte decided to relocate San Juan Bautista's Monquí neophytes to Loreto and send their missionary, Padre Clemente Guillén, south to open a mission closer to the center of the large area occupied by the Guaycura. In 1720, Guillén scouted for suitable mission sites while he and a party rode south to support Jaime Bravo in opening his mission at La Paz. Guillén discovered several watered places along his route and later chose one, called Apaté, two miles from the gulf shore and at an elevation of 150 feet. Here, in August 1721, he relocated the Guaycura neophytes from Malibat in a new mission named Nuestra Señora de los Dolores, in keeping with donor Villapuente's wishes.[48] Misión de los Dolores proved to be an important step in opening and holding the South; it provided a way station for land trips between Loreto and La Paz, and it helped to pacify some of the troublesome Guaycura by introducing them to mission life.

Misión de Santiago el Apóstol, 1724

Meanwhile, Padre Ignacio María Nápoli—like Piccolo, a Jesuit from Palermo, Sicily—arrived in California and was sent to open a new mission some fifty miles southeast of La Paz. No site had been selected, but the target area lay near the shores of Bahía de las Palmas, a region that pearlers knew for its good water resources. In July 1721, Nápoli boarded Loreto's supply ship along with Esteban Rodríguez and four soldiers. The party reached La Paz after two weeks of dangerously strong headwinds, triple the time normally required for the trip. The delay cost them the further use of the supply vessel; it was overdue to run to the mainland and Loreto badly needed provisions.[49]

Once again, and for the last time, an old Jesuit ally came to the rescue. General Andrés de Rezábal's pearling schooner was in port at La Paz, and its skipper gave Nápoli the use of two canoes to carry supplies and gear. Meanwhile, Padres Nápoli and Bravo, the captain and soldiers, and a troop of La Paz converts followed a land route to Bahía de las Palmas. They saw no people along the way, although they moved through an area normally occupied by the Cora, a small Guaycuran linguistic group. Scouting and building a trail proved difficult in the rough, confusing terrain. The trek consumed eight days, partly because of poorly chosen routes. Esteban Rodríguez, now in his mid-fifties, came near to tragedy. Twice he survived falls on steep inclines when his horse went over and pinned him beneath it. The padres regarded his escapes as near-miraculous signs of the power of their protectress.

Nápoli and his party arrived at Bahía de las Palmas to find that their approach had sent the Cora into hiding. Cora scouts had noted that the Spaniards were accompanied by men from a rival Guaycura band, probably Callejú. It took the party ten days to gain the Cora's confidence sufficiently that they would allow women and children to visit the padres' camp. Gradually, with gifts of cloth, ribbon, ornaments, and servings of pozole, the missionaries coaxed the Cora to attend meetings and offer their children for baptism. Nápoli performed these rites and handed out new rounds of gifts to the women. The Cora replied with offerings of freshly gathered fruits and seeds.[50] The padres then withdrew to La Paz, feeling that they had accomplished the purposes of their entrada. Nápoli studied the Cora language while he awaited the supplies he would need to found a mission. Rodríguez required some time for punitive expeditions against the Isleño Pericú from Isla de Cerralvo. These allies of the Cora,[51] perhaps having been told that the padres and soldiers were absent, had attacked La Paz and killed several Guaycura converts.

By early 1722, Nápoli was ready to establish his mission. However, his previous experiences with the long, difficult trail had convinced him to locate his first mission as a way station between La Paz and Bahía de las Palmas. He chose a place near the spot where Ignacio de Rojas discovered silver ore in 1720, and he named it Santa Ana. Two small adobe structures were erected: one to house the padre, and another to serve as a chapel until a real church could be built. Nápoli began to learn the Cora dialect from his neophytes and to practice his language skills with the oratory of evangelization.

By 1723, the padre had assembled enough food to sustain the workforce needed to build a larger church. It was to be roofed over but open-sided so that its services could be observed by crowds too large to enter the building.

Convert workers and soldiers erected tree trunks to form the corners and sustain the ridgepole, then raised rafters and began thatching. Just then, a violent rain and wind storm arose, and the converts took refuge under their construction. The cross bracing must have been inadequate; the whole structure collapsed. The heavy logs and the mass of roofing materials crushed several people and injured many others. By chance, neither the padre nor the soldiers were involved in the ruin, though they were near enough to hear the crash and rush to aid the injured. The padre hastily baptized the dying and tried to console the rest. Relatives of the dead and wounded blamed Nápoli for the tragedy, and although he reasoned with them as best he could, he also wrote to Bravo for more soldiers to protect him and bring food and medicine to the incapacitated. Finally, the missionary was so shaken that he resolved to quit Santa Ana and seek a new site. He left his flock and went off to Loreto to confer with Ugarte about his plans. At that time, Padre Everardo Helen at Misión de Guadalupe was seriously ill and had to be brought to Loreto. The padre visitador packed Nápoli off to substitute at Guadalupe while the German recovered his health.[52]

Meanwhile, trouble persisted at Santa Ana. Beginning in 1722, intermittent plagues of locusts destroyed much of the native vegetation on which men and animals depended for food. At the same time, and probably not coincidentally, epidemic diseases—smallpox and measles, and perhaps typhoid fever and typhus—ravaged the indigenous people. Shamans of unconverted bands declared these misfortunes to be omens prophesying disaster for all who consorted with the foreigners. Moreover, local people held their grudge against the Spaniards for the deaths and injuries caused by the church collapse. Early in 1725, a disgruntled group raided the settlement, burned the remaining buildings, and terrorized the converts. Esteban Rodríguez was summoned. He and his men pursued and arrested some of the raiders, punished them with floggings, and put the rest to flight. No sooner had they done this than the captain received news of Uchití attacks on the new Christians at La Paz. While giving chase, Rodríguez was ambushed and wounded in the back by an arrow that pierced his *cuera*, the long leather coat that shielded frontier soldiers.[53] The wound was nearly three inches deep, but fortunately oblique. His soldiers killed all but one of the small group of Uchití; the survivor managed to escape, although he was horribly wounded by a sword chop across the ear and upper jaw. Rodríguez needed two months at La Paz to heal and recoup his strength. During that time, his wound was kept secret from even the mission converts so that he would retain his image of power.[54]

While Nápoli's Misión de Santiago project was stalled and Esteban Rodríguez recovered, Padre Jaime Bravo worked at developing the area assigned to his mission at La Paz. During 1724, he had heard about a ranchería of people related to the Uchití who lived fifty miles to the south, near the Pacific shore. He visited them and found their location promising, two miles from the sea in a floodplain with a permanent flow of sub-surface water. Bravo named the place Todos Santos and planned to create a farm and ranch to support the local people and provide crops and herds for water-poor La Paz. Now he used Rodríguez's otherwise unemployed soldiers and some willing neophytes to clear fifty miles of trail over largely level ground to connect his mission with the new site. When the work was done, Bravo founded the visita of Nuestra Señora del Pilar at Todos Santos.[55]

After a four-month absence, Ignacio María Nápoli returned to the South and chose an entirely new location, a site southwest of Bahía de las Palmas known locally as Aiñiní. There he re-established Misión de Santiago el Santo Apóstol at an elevation of 450 feet in a broad, well-watered valley. The move had two objectives, both more practical than evangelical. Nápoli had explored and coped with the area long enough to recognize the geographic characteristics needed to support a mission,[56] and he realized that it was more promising to start afresh, with Pericú to convert, than to try to reconcile the Cora in the aftermath of the church collapse.

At the same time, at Todos Santos, Padre Bravo was working a crew of neophyte laborers sent to him from Jesuit missions in Sinaloa. They burned off stands of brush along the banks of the humid arroyo and planted patches of corn, squash, melons, and unspecified vegetables. Bravo decided to visit Nápoli by following as direct a route as possible from Todos Santos to Santiago. The passage was made over a shoulder of the great sierra then called *El Enfado*, the troublesome or discouraging. The journey required two and a half days and much labor, but it proved useful and portended the future of the area. The padre and his soldier noted stands of useful trees, güéribos, oaks, and madrones. They recognized useful pasture lands and springs. Jaime Bravo could not resist reporting cool, shady stopping places, virtually unknown in arid, hot California. When he got to Santiago, Bravo sent out his page and a local soldier for a further reconnaissance of the area he had just crossed. His team returned with word that the sierra consisted of decomposing granite, an easy material in which to build trails. Unwittingly, the padre had introduced gente de razón to lands on which they would be tempted to run cattle, farm, and live more comfortably. Shortly thereafter, Padre Nápoli returned the visit by traversing much the same trail.[57]

After two years spent developing Misión de Santiago, Nápoli was transferred in 1726 to the Jesuits' Sonoran mission system, where he served until 1745.[58] His place at Santiago was taken by Padre Lorenzo José Carranco, a young missionary born in Cholula in the province of Puebla, New Spain.

"Santiago de los Coras"

Padre Nápoli apparently entered the cape region mistakenly believing, as had Padre Bravo, that all the people living south of La Paz were Coras, and Nápoli's first efforts were indeed among the Cora.[59] When Nápoli founded his mission at Santa Ana in the country of the Cora and the Uchití, he and others were justified in calling it Santiago de los Coras. However, when that effort failed,

Nápoli moved Misión de Santiago from Santa Ana and re-established it at Aiñiní in the territory of a different people, the Pericú, and that aspect of the move was poorly reported and led to confusion. "Entrada a la nación Cora," Nápoli's 1721 report of his first attempt to found Santiago, was sent to the provincial, to the mission's benefactor, the Marqués de Villapuente, and to a wider audience of people, thus popularizing the name "Santiago de los Coras." As a result, later historians — and even a few California Jesuits — misnamed the mission and misreported the population that it served.[60] However, all later references to the Cora show that they were assigned to share the mission at La Paz with other Guaycuran speakers. Venegas, who never visited California, was unaware that Misión de Santiago became Pericú when it was moved.[61] The printed edition of his history perpetuated "Santiago de los Coras," and it has appeared here and there, inappropriately, in many subsequent accounts and histories. That inaccuracy did not escape the sharp eye of Padre Miguel del Barco, a thirty-year veteran California missionary: "This was never a mission to the Cora, but rather to the Pericú. . . . In California, it is simply called *Misión de Santiago*, with no additive title. . . . To call it *Santiago de los Coras* is like calling the [Castilian] city of Burgos, in Spain, *Burgos de los Catalanes*."[62] Barco's work should have set the record straight in the 1770s, but it was not published or circulated until 1973. Misión de Santiago was peopled by Pericú from the time of its second founding until 1795, when it was closed because virtually all its neophytes had died.

Misión de San José del Cabo, 1730

In the fall of 1729, Padre Visitador General José de Echeverría arrived at Loreto to begin his inspection tour of California. For seven weeks he visited the missions north of Loreto, traveling on the camino real and guarded and assisted by two soldiers and a few neophytes.[63] Echeverría was energetic, enthusiastic, and filled with admiration for the accomplishments of his California brothers. His letters and reports contain some of the rosiest views of peninsular life that survive from Jesuit times.

While serving as procurador in Mexico City, part of Echeverría's duty was to inform California benefactors about the progress of missions they had helped to found and to solicit more funds. The most generous and attentive patron was the Marqués de Villapuente, who had recently been persuaded to give an additional ten thousand pesos to pay the costs of opening the long-desired mission at the tip of the peninsula. Villapuente asked that the patron saint be San José, as he had specified earlier when he endowed the mission at Comondú. Misión de San José del Cabo would be the second, after Misión de Santiago, to evangelize the Pericú. Padre Echeverría was determined to see the mission established while he was in California and to make a personal report to the donor.

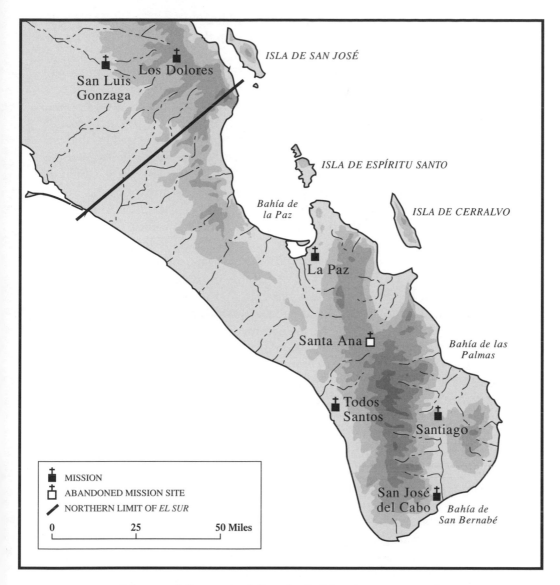

ISLA DE SAN JOSÉ

San Luis Gonzaga

Los Dolores

ISLA DE ESPÍRITU SANTO

Bahía de la Paz

ISLA DE CERRALVO

La Paz

Santa Ana

Bahía de las Palmas

Todos Santos

Santiago

San José del Cabo

Bahía de San Bernabé

† MISSION
☐ ABANDONED MISSION SITE
／ NORTHERN LIMIT OF *EL SUR*

0   25   50 Miles

Map 4.4 Missions in el Sur de California, *1734–1748*

After visiting all the California missions and missionaries, Echeverría selected Padre Nicolás Tamaral, the experienced founder of Misión de la Purísima, to develop the mission that would be called San José del Cabo. Sigismundo Taraval, a newly arrived Italian missionary, was assigned to La Purísima to free Tamaral for his new duties. On 10 March 1730, Echeverría, Tamaral, Capitán Rodríguez, and a few soldiers sailed from Loreto and arrived at La Paz after a wind-buffeted nine days. They were greeted by the Scottish Jesuit, Guillermo Gordon, who had taken Jaime Bravo's place as missionary at La Paz.[64] After Visitador General Echeverría performed his inspections of Todos

Santos and Santiago, the party went south and chose a location for Misión de San José del Cabo, a site two and a half miles from the sea located in the broad watercourse that leads down to the beach and lagoon of San Bernabé.

The party stayed with Tamaral for two weeks. His mission began slowly since few of the local people came forth. At first, those who could be found claimed that most of their kin had died in a recent epidemic. It soon became clear, however, that most of the Pericú were frightened away by the presence of soldiers. Some neophyte men at Santiago had recently been flogged by soldiers after being charged with resisting the padre's authority. Nevertheless, people gradually did come into camp at San José del Cabo. Tamaral began the difficult processes of learning their language and training them in the mysteries of the church. Rodríguez and his men used the time to build a basic chapel and a small house for the padre. Then the party broke up. Echeverría went back to La Paz with an escort and took ship for Loreto. Rodríguez assigned a small guard to Tamaral, then took his remaining soldiers to visit, successively, Santiago, Todos Santos, and La Paz to discipline groups of rebellious neophytes who were reported to be disturbing those missions.[65]

The impatient visitor general had been so anxious to see San José del Cabo established in his presence that he pushed for what proved to be a premature choice of locations. Padre Tamaral soon discovered that the area to be developed as the mission's garden was tainted with alkali, and the soil in the approaches was so sandy that irrigation ditches absorbed most of the precious water before it could reach the fields. Poor air movement and standing water doomed the spot to heat and bothersome insects. Tamaral moved downstream to a place the Pericú called Añuití, the site that the mission occupied for its remaining existence and which determined the location of the pueblo—now the town—of San José del Cabo.[66]

However, the move did not solve all of Tamaral's troubles. A few years earlier, Padre Nápoli had been fascinated by what he took to be evidence of European visitors to the region. "I have never seen people taller than these; their bodies are well-proportioned and filled out, their skin pale and ruddy. Youths particularly resemble Englishmen or Flemings in fairness and high color."[67] Tamaral echoed these observations, but also noted a dark-skinned element. He reported that the population included foreigners—men marooned, castaway, or runaway—whose presence disturbed the natives of the cape region. He complained of "a number of *coyotes*, *lobos*, and others of mixed background[68] left by the English or Dutch ships that had long frequented those coasts. These people of vile, mixed blood are the ones who disturb and agitate the local people. They are the ones who domineer the populace and lead them astray."[69] Tamaral described the Pericú as conniving, secretive, vengeful, traitorous, and given to falsehoods and the creation of rumors—all traits that could have been induced or intensified by disturbing and manipulative intruders. The missionary hoped to overcome these faults through teaching and conversion. He believed that soldiers could help significantly by taking punitive action against troublemakers.[70]

The way a California soldier and his daughter are dressed.
(Watercolor facsimiles by Joanne Crosby.
Original art and captions by Ignacio Tirsch, S. J.)

San José del Cabo, a Mission in the Foothills of [Cabo de] San Lucas which was nearly completed by me. The mission is depicted with the Philippine ship arriving to be supplied with food.

How the wife of the mule-driver, sitting on a mule, delivers red cloth to the mission.

How . . . California Indians kill a deer with arrows, skin it in the field and prepare it for roasting. A California Indian woman carries green seed pulp.

Here you see how a Spanish lady from California walks in her garden,
served by a Moorish woman and an Indian woman. They wear this
kind of clothing when it is a bit cool. Then they cover themselves with
this kind of coat, which is called a Manga [poncho].

The Governor, with his wife. . . . His outfit is depicted as when he appears on public occasion. The man with the gun is a common California soldier.

Young Güéribos (Populus brandegeei), *the Tree That Padre Juan de Ugarte Felled for Timbers to Be Used in California's First Homebuilt Ship.*

Native Palms (Brahea brandegeei) *in the Arroyo of Todos Santos Signal Its All-year, Underground Flow of water.*

Alamos, Sonora

Matanchel, California's Principal Port of Supply and Communication during the Jesuit Period (1697–1767).

Chacala, Homeport for Many California Pearlers and Explorers in the Seventeenth and Eighteenth Centuries.

The Old Walled Town of Villa de Sinaloa on the Sinaloa River, Birthplace of Many of California's Pioneer Hispanic Settlers.

Misión de San Luis Gonzaga, Built in the 1750s by a German Jesuit,
Padre Jacobo Baegert.

El Camino Real Near Rosarito, Midway between the Missions of San Ignacio and Santa Gertrudis.

Grapevines at Misión de San Ignacio, Long the Most Prolific Wine Producer among the Peninsula's Missions.

Agriculture in the Arroyo of Misión de San José de Comondú

Peoples of the Cape Resist Change

Tragically, even as the missions of *el Sur* were established, their constituencies were disintegrating under the burden of alien diseases and attacks on the basic cultures. Pestilences had ravaged every band of the cape's people. The missionaries, with whom these people had ever-increasing contact, worked ceaselessly to undermine their ancestral customs and beliefs. In 1733, for example, the southern missionaries stepped up their campaign against polygamy. This attack seems to have created a rallying point among the Pericú, an issue that stimulated organized resistance to mission life. Jesuit reports made much of this practice and its influence on the events that followed. They depicted natives as childish, the willing dupes of immoral leaders who coveted multiple wives.

The subject of women was particularly sensitive among the Pericú at that time. Diseases, most notably imported syphilis, were disproportionately reducing the female population. Neophytes in the South were deeply disturbed by a growing lack of mates. In any of the native peninsular groups, women traditionally gathered most of the food. Chiefs, shamans, and other important men among the Pericú had long been accustomed to acquiring extra wives as practical status symbols. Sensing an opportunity to challenge these local leaders, the padres redoubled their efforts to attract young women as converts, a conscious campaign to frustrate the influence of shamans and chiefs. Nicolás Tamaral was explicit about the attack on polygamy and the motives behind it.[71] Headmen and shamans, on the verge of being superseded, fought back with all available weapons. They appealed to ancient traditions, tribal pride, the sense of lost freedom, and any other argument, however extreme, to restore some semblance of the old order. Fear gripped nearly everyone as emotions were battered by sickness, the death of kinsmen, and the ideological battle between medicine men and missionaries. Meanwhile, soldiers continued to patrol the area as a threat to anyone who resisted conversion to the mission society.

In 1731, an incident occurred that illustrates Padre Tamaral's conflict with local leaders. A mulatto named Chicori was the captain of a ranchería called Yenecá that pertained to the mission of Santiago. Like most men of power, Chicori kept a string of women, including a girl who wished to become a Christian. She took instruction from Tamaral at San José del Cabo, but when the time came for her baptism, she was detained at Yenecá by Chicori. Tamaral confronted the captain, who was unmoved by the padre's arguments. Tamaral quoted his adversary as saying, "What harm is caused by my having many women, or that this girl is among them?" It was claimed that Chicori later conspired with Domingo Botón, the governor of the converts at Santiago, to kill Tamaral when he left that mission to return to his own. The padre somehow was warned, and he sent for a band of his own neophytes to march north and escort him back to San José. Later, both ringleaders were said to have confessed to the plot and repented (though Venegas, in hindsight, added "God alone knows" to the latter allegation).[72]

The pacification of the South never went well. The size of California's presidio remained the same: just twenty-five soldiers to patrol a growing area, a growing number of missions, and people far more belligerent than the more familiar Cochimí of the north. As early as September 1725, Padre Clemente Guillén wrote to Virrey Casafuerte to describe the situation as perilous. He told of Esteban Rodríguez's labors and the wound he had received. Incidents of unrest and violence multiplied:

> On August 24, several Indians were seized in the mountains of Chillá who had slain natives of other settlements. On the 25th . . . other Indians were arrested . . . guilty of similar crimes. Letters have just arrived from Misión de Santiago [from Padre Nápoli] reporting various incidents of Indian disrespect for Spanish soldiers. Because of this, Corporal Ignacio Acevedo, after shooting down an Indian as he was about to loose a dart at another Spaniard, ordered the native's head cut off and placed on a stake within sight of the numerous Indians of his and other rancherías.[73]

The fierce and defiant Uchití continued to harass all those around them. Capitán Rodríguez and some eight to ten soldiers spent six months, from March to September of 1729 trying to pacify the Uchití and protect the neophytes of La Paz, Todos Santos, and Santiago.[74] Despite Padre Visitador General Echeverría's cheerful description of the situation at San José del Cabo, the missions in *el Sur* were threatened at every turn. After Rodríguez and his soldiers left the newborn mission at the cape, they spent the rest of 1730 putting down revolts and rounding up runaways in the area. In the following year, the Uchití, from their homeland south and west of La Paz, attacked some of the Guaycura from Misión de los Dolores after feigning to welcome them at a festival. With much travail and in difficult terrain, Alférez Francisco Cortés de Monroy and a detachment of fourteen soldiers and fifty neophyte warriors from Loreto and Dolores managed to capture some of the Uchití leaders. He brought them to Loreto to administer punishment but not death.[75]

By March 1731, Capitán Rodríguez felt compelled to write to Visitador General Echeverría, now in Sinaloa, to press the point that an additional presidio with twenty-five soldiers was crucial to maintaining California in Spanish hands. He noted that, of his own twenty-five men at Loreto, eighteen were assigned as mission guards. Missionaries who previously had no soldiers—Julián de Mayorga at Comondú, Agustín María de Luyando at San Javier, and Lorenzo Carranco at Santiago—now required guards because of Indian unrest. Rodríguez made the obvious case that with the seven remaining men, he could not carry out his other duties safely, particularly escorting the padre visitador over five hundred miles of trail every six months.[76]

A few days after he wrote to Echeverría, Esteban Rodríguez received a passionate letter from Padre Sebastián de Sistiaga, then the visitador of the peninsular missionaries. Sistiaga echoed his captain's fears in the most dramatic terms. He worried over the isolated character of missions in *el Sur* and the possibilities, even probabilities, of a revolt. He made the gloomy prediction that all could be lost, "the padres killed, the soldiers killed, the servants killed, the Catholic faith wiped out—the worst loss of all. The Devil would be thereby returned to his throne." He concurred with the captain that the only potential remedy would a sub-presidio; he recognized that the troops in Loreto had barely sufficed before *el Sur* was opened, and that they were now stretched much too far to be effective. He repeated the common Jesuit opinion of the natives of the South: "they have turbulent dispositions." He reminded Rodríguez of the wound he had received from one of their arrows, calling it plain evidence of their insubordinate nature. Sistiaga believed that they needed a "godmother," and that godmother was a squad of soldiers. He urged Rodríguez to lay the facts before the viceroy and to press for help.[77]

Misión de Santa Rosa, 1733

By mid-1731, Padre Guillermo Gordon at La Paz was weighed down with yet other problems. The Guaycura converts living around his mission's visita at Todos Santos had been nearly exterminated, either by diseases or by their interminable fighting with neighboring Uchití and Pericú,[78] but Todos Santos had become too important a producer of food to abandon. Gordon described three functioning *trapiches*, arrangements of presses, cauldrons, and fireplaces used to extract juice from sugarcane and boil it down to produce *panocha*, cakes of crude brown sugar that were the staple sweet of New Spain's northwest frontier. Todos Santos could produce two hundred pack-animal loads of panocha each year. Gordon listed vineyards and plantings of figs, oranges, and pomegranates. To provide the labor for this desirable cultivation, Pericú from farther south were gradually being resettled at Todos Santos.

Gordon not only had the difficult task of supervising mission centers fifty miles apart, but he also had to cope with a new language in order to teach and deal with the newly arrived Pericú.[79] By 1732, the decision was made to relieve Gordon of his distant visita but to continue its agricultural development. In early 1733, Padre Visitador Clemente Guillén employed a recent endowment and sent Padre Sigismundo Taraval to found the new mission of Santa Rosa among the Pericú at Todos Santos.[80] In theory, missionaries at Santa Rosa, Santiago, and San José del Cabo would direct the Pericú, while those at La Paz and Los Dolores were to manage the various Guaycuran splinter groups.

A Haven at Last for Manila Galleons

January 1734 seemed to mark the successful culmination of thirty years of royal and viceregal demands and a great deal of hard work and sacrifice by California Jesuits and their helpers. *Nuestra Señora del Pilar de Zaragoza* became the first Manila ship to put in at the cape since the establishment of local missions.[81] Crew and passengers were suffering the usual scurvy and shortages of food and water when they put into San Bernabé hoping to find relief at Misión de San José del Cabo. Padre Tamaral rounded up and delivered the needed aid in a very short time. Most of the afflicted were soon cured by eating pitahaya fruit and fresh meat.

Don José Francisco de Baitos, the ship's captain, and Fray Domingo de Horbigoso, who was returning to Mexico City after a term as head of the Augustinian missionaries in the Philippines, were seriously ill. They remained under Tamaral's care for two months after the galleon sailed for Acapulco. The peninsular Jesuits did not waste this opportunity to demonstrate the importance of their efforts to develop the cape region. In addition to resupplying the galleon, they provided well for their important visitors. Padre Jaime Bravo was by then the missionary at Loreto and director of the colony's sailing craft and supplies. When the stranded travelers were well enough, he sent a ship to carry them to Matanchel. Padre Tamaral assigned his soldier escort, Santiago Villalobos, to accompany and assist these influential guests all the way to Mexico City. There, they and others who had been on the ship gave grateful testimony to a newly installed viceroy, Arzobispo Juan Antonio de Vizarrón y Eguiarreta.[82]

Jesuits in Mexico City watched these proceedings with interest. As archbishop of New Spain, Vizarrón y Eguiarreta had disagreed with the Jesuits when they argued that they should not pay tithes to the bishops in whose areas they operated haciendas and missions.[83] However, the archbishop-viceroy's reaction to reports by the galleon's passengers was reassuring. He sent orders by the next departure for Manila that all returning ships should regard San Bernabé as a port of refuge after their debilitating Pacific crossings.[84] It then appeared that Padre Juan de Ugarte's campaign to settle the South had borne fruit, and that one of Kino and Salvatierra's original pledges had been fulfilled at last.

A Rebellion against Rule by Missionaries and Soldiers[85]

By mid-1734, the widespread dissatisfaction among converts at the three southernmost missions had coalesced into an active conspiracy. The missionaries in the area tended to blame unrest on the Devil's work, or on the scheming of a few rebellious shamans, or on the machinations of mixed-blood interlopers, or on the native men's desire to retain the luxuries of polygamy—all familiar themes long cited by frontier missionaries threatened with revolts.[86] Mission life had not captured the hearts and minds of most neophytes in the cape region sufficiently to overrule the accompanying confusion and fear. Their cultural traditions were challenged, belittled, and eventually denied to them. Epidemics had reduced their population by half in a single generation. The ringleaders of the rebellion, deposed chiefs and shamans like Domingo Botón, the mulatto ex-governor of Santiago, and Bruno, shaman of the Aripe, played on all these doubts and fears. They must have found it relatively simple to convince their traumatized people to resist and cast off the alien power that had loosed incomprehensible killers among them.

In the late summer of 1734, the southern cauldron came to a boil. Plots of every sort had been reported or were evidenced by mutinous behavior, but few precautions were taken. Perhaps conditions had been so bad during the brief local mission period that the padres did not differentiate the symptoms of a final crisis. In any case, pathetically few soldiers were stationed in the area. Nicolás Tamaral at San José del Cabo had none. His man Villalobos had not returned from the mainland and, in any event, the padre was sensitive to his flock's resentment of soldiers and hoped to make greater progress without them.[87] The soldier normally stationed at Misión de Santiago had retired to Loreto because of illness; Padre Lorenzo Carranco was accompanied only by servants, two retired mestizo soldiers.[88] The mission at La Paz stood empty and was guarded by one soldier, Don Manuel Andrés Romero. La Paz's padre, Guillermo Gordon, had been away from that post since July of the previous year, reassigned to supervise Misión de San Javier's important visiting station at San Miguel.[89] His neophytes had been sent to Misión de Santa Rosa at Todos Santos to be under the care of Padre Sigismundo Taraval. Only Taraval had any real protection: two capable soldiers, armed, and quite aware of the threat implicit in the behavior of the neophytes in the greater area.[90]

The missionaries in the South recognized the general unrest. They were also accustomed to taking advantage of rivalries between different rancherías attached to the same mission. If one was sullen or mutinous, the padres made use of spies or informers to learn what was happening, but by now the neophytes knew of the padres' intertribal or even intratribal espionage, and they turned it to their own advantage. The padres were fed such a stream of conflicting reports and rumors, some frightening and some reassuring, that they were unable to distinguish truth from falsehood and lacked the means to interpret the evidence before them.

During August 1734, the rebels succeeded in luring many neophytes away from the missions. Some of these uncertain converts continued to drift in and out, telling stories that further confused and frightened the padres, their servants, and the faithful neophytes. The missionaries constantly sent letters to each other to keep abreast of events, but these missives only fed the fears of their recipients with the doubts of their senders.

By October 1734, Padre Nicolás Tamaral at San José del Cabo, Padre Lorenzo Carranco and his two servants at Santiago, and Don Manuel Andrés Romero, the guard at La Paz, had been killed by rebels. Loyal neophytes who fled these rampages brought stories to Todos Santos of the padres' deaths by clubbing, and of the mutilating and burning of their bodies. Padre Sigismundo Taraval narrowly escaped the same fate when three soldiers virtually dragged him away from his mission. The presidio was mobilized, but California missionaries and soldiers soon realized that the entire South was involved in the uprising. Traditional enemies had unified in opposition to Jesuit rule. The insurrection included too many people and covered too great an area to be dominated and pacified by Loreto's few soldiers.

News of the uprising and calls for assistance were hurriedly circulated on the other side of the Gulf of California, both in Jesuit missions and in civilian towns. Sonoran missions quickly sent a hundred armed Yaqui volunteers.[91] Francisco Cortés de Monroy, earlier an officer at Loreto, left his mining activities in Sonora and brought a few men that he had recruited. Among mainland gente de razón, the most notable response came from the colony clustered around Compostela, relatives and erstwhile neighbors of ten men in California's little garrison. Manuel Andrés Romero, slain at the age of twenty-two, was a native of that city, and a son of Don Juan Antonio Romero, a prominent citizen and a California pioneer. Of thirty white men who answered the Jesuits' plea, fifteen were from Compostela.[92]

A call was also sent for recruits from the trusted Cochimí of the more northerly California missions. By the spring of 1735, several dozen arrived at Misión de los Dolores after marching that long way led by a few soldiers.[93] The force hastily assembled at Los Dolores was made up of odd lots; the California neophytes joined familiar officers and soldiers from Loreto but also met over a hundred total strangers from the mainland: gente de razón, and Yaqui and Mayo volunteers.

The strained atmosphere at Los Dolores involved more than the polyglot encampment of new arrivals. The people of the place, neophytes of the mission, were secretly divided in their loyalties. Some supported the Jesuits, some conspired with rebels. Spies were felt to be everywhere, and rumors flew. After some months, most of the nearby renegades were rounded up. Eight were sentenced by Capitán Rodríguez and put to death by firing squad. But the soldiers' occasional forays over great distances to rebel territory produced little action or even contact. Bands of people who had never converted and those who had rebelled roamed freely all over *el Sur* as the situation stagnated.

Shortly after the first reports of the loss of the southern missions and two padres' deaths, Padre Visitador Clemente Guillén sent an urgent message to the viceroy asking that he provide men, supplies, and ships. As time passed, there were growing expectations that such help would come, but the arch-bishop-viceroy's only acts were to plead a lack of authority to order troops to California and to refer the matter to Madrid, which guaranteed a long delay as messages crossed and recrossed the Atlantic.[94]

A different light was cast on the whole situation in January 1735. The Manila galleon put in at San Bernabé in its usual stricken state. Pursuant to the viceroy's instructions, a detachment in a longboat was sent to the shore to seek help at the mission. By then, rebel Pericú were in control of the region. Out of sight of the anchored vessel, they intercepted the landing party and killed all thirteen men. Before those on the ship suspected trouble, many Pericú paddled or swam out and were taken aboard, feigning friendship as they attempted to capture the galleon itself. Their plot was discovered and thwarted, and four were captured. The Manila ship sailed on to Acapulco where the captain had quite a tale to tell, and where the captive Pericú talked freely, even boasted, of their deeds and intents.[95]

Manuel Bernal de Huidobro

Four missions had been destroyed, two Jesuits and three local gente de razón killed, and a longboat full of sailors ambushed and slain. The peninsular mission system was thrown into a profound upheaval, but the single incident involving the galleon brought more attention to California affairs than all that had gone before. The Audiencia of Guadalajara convened a board of inquiry. The captain and his crew told their stories. Officers and passengers who had received assistance the previous year at San José del Cabo praised the missions and missionaries. The Jesuit procurador described conditions before and after the disastrous uprisings and blamed the lack of subsequent action on Arzobispo Virrey Vizarrón. Moreover, the Jesuit provincial took his case directly to the crown in a comprehensive report that accused the viceroy of specific derelictions of duty.[96]

Vizarrón was aware that matters had taken a new turn. As long as the rebellion had discomfited only the Jesuits, he could play a waiting game, but the Manila galleon affair involved powerful business interests as well as public opinion. The viceroy solved his problem with a decision which for public consumption seemed simple and efficient — and privately served notice to the Jesuits that he had not appreciated their attempt to circumvent his authority. Vizarrón ignored the Jesuits' plea that Capitán Juan Bautista de Anza, their military ally in Sonora, be sent to their rescue.[97] Instead, the viceroy delegated the governor of Sinaloa to go to California with a suitable force to quell the uprising.

The logic was impeccable. Sinaloa's governor, Manuel Bernal de Huidobro, was the military commander nearest the scene; he had troops, access to ships, and could move more quickly than any other candidate, but he was also a leader who was engaged in serious disputes with Sonoran Jesuits over their methods of governing their neophytes and their right to monopolize Indian labor. Vizarrón could scarcely have conjured up a man more likely to confound and frustrate the beleaguered California Jesuits. A glance at Gobernador Bernal de Huidobro's own province may suggest why this was so.

In southern and central Sinaloa, power was primarily in the hands of civilians and the military. That area had largely passed from being a frontier — where the Jesuits and their missions were needed to convert Indians — to a more settled state where the secular church could take over. The church was put into the hands of diocesan clergy and organized into parishes under the jurisdiction of the Diocese of Guadalajara. Parish priests received low salaries, which they augmented with income from extra services performed, such as weddings and burials. These curates usually cooperated with local civil and military officials.

Indeed, they were often members of important families in the regions where they served and part of the local elite power structure. Unlike the members of religious orders, with their vows of poverty and service, parish priests could openly involve themselves in entrepreneurial activities such as trade, cattle ranching, interests in mines, or whatever commerce their regions offered. Their families and connections, in turn, were the primary source of ecclesiastical tithes to the diocese and frequently had recourse to the church for capital in the form of mortgages on rural and urban property. Thus, in older, settled areas, the diocesan church was deeply rooted in local society.[98]

In Sonora, frontier presidios protected missions, mining camps, and ranches against bands of unconverted Indians. Military men had more power and more conspicuous and active roles than did those of Sinaloa, but they also had a more formidable religious contingent with which to share regional authority. In Sonora, the typical religious institution was not a parish with a cooperative curate, but a mission with a Jesuit who was determined to protect and retain the lands and rights of his mission and especially to protect his neophytes from exploitation. The immovable stance of Sonoran missionaries put them into direct conflict with every ambitious miner, rancher, trader, or military authority in the area—in other words, the coalition that dominated the private economic sector.[99] That coalition desired access to resources controlled by the Jesuits: Indian labor and the best range and agricultural land. Local businessmen wanted relief from competition with Jesuits in supplying military and mining establishments with food and beasts of burden. The goals of these frontiersmen coincided with many stated royal aims: the secularization of missions, payment in money to Indian laborers, and the exactment of tribute from them as full-fledged vassals of the king. Opponents of the Jesuits harped on the fact that missions were conceived as stepping stones to the full citizenship of native people, yet a century or more after establishing some of their missions the Jesuits showed no inclination to give them up or to agree to changes in the status of their neophytes.[100]

A presidial captain in any part of New Spain—other than California—had rights and perquisites that could make him a relatively powerful and independent figure. In addition, certain self-aggrandizing practices of these officers were widely tolerated, practices that included the purchase and sale of supplies, investment of funds (including soldiers' retirement pay), money lending, nepotism in appointments and promotions, and the use of soldiers' labor for private purposes.[101] Since pueblos of colonists tended to grow up around presidios, the captains often achieved civil authority as either appointed or de facto governors. Frequently they became privileged, even exclusive traders as well. If a captain were shrewd, he could become relatively wealthy. If not, he could bankrupt not only himself but his entire garrison or community.[102]

The common presidial soldier was not entirely left out of this socio-economic system. Although he was often misused and his pay extorted in various ways, a soldier who gave good service had reason to anticipate some rewards, the most important of which was land. He could be given a parcel for his own use and be allowed to raise crops and domestic animals. Such little ranchos were a potential source of income and, of particular importance, gave independent work to soldiers' sons. Thus, both officers and soldiers had potential conflicts with Jesuit missionaries over access to local resources, labor, and markets.[103]

Andrés de Rezábal, governor of Sinaloa, operated a pearl fishing fleet along the coasts of Sonora and California but was a friend of Jesuit missionaries in the greater area. He shielded those of the mainland from the full impact of early Bourbon policies that encouraged economic development and promoted civil authority at the expense of the religious, but with Rezábal's death in 1723, the new era finally came to the region. Capitán Manuel Bernal de Huidobro was appointed as his successor and lost no time in obtaining for himself the advantages enjoyed by military men in frontier provinces.[104] His coterie of friends and relatives controlled broad lands, mining interests, commerce, and commanded the loyalty of many local Hispanic people.

Bernal de Huidobro became an open adversary of the Jesuits when his area of jurisdiction was expanded to include Sonora in 1732.[105] The governor was under strict orders to keep the peace in the area and he read his appointment as a mandate to govern Indians as well as castas and españoles. He patrolled the area annually[106] and called on the Sonoran Jesuits to provide neophytes to help in tracking and repelling hostile marauders from the north. When the missionaries demurred, the governor retaliated by holding hearings at which Yaqui and Mayo neophytes were encouraged to air their complaints against the mission system.[107] Soon, he was proposing that the padres no longer choose the men who held office in neophyte communities. He openly sided with miners and ranchers who sought regular access to Yaqui labor.[108] The California missionaries must have been shocked when they learned late in 1735 that Virrey Vizarrón had ordered Manuel Bernal de Huidobro to undertake the pacification of the rebels in *el Sur*. Vizarrón and his representative became a thorn as painful to the California Jesuits as their strayed converts.

Recent changes in governmental regulations had made governors more dependent on the viceroy. A governorship was a post which, in those times, was virtually bought. For a long time governors and the presidial captains who served under them on the remote frontier had had a practical autonomy in matters of local civil and economic power. In 1729, however, a new directive introduced curbs on the powers of governors and captains. A governor now had to obtain viceregal confirmation for any individuals he appointed. A governor's involvement in the commodity trade was subject to new regulations. The key to making a personal fortune from the potentially lucrative governor's post now depended more than ever on good relations with the viceroy.[109] Bernal de Huidobro's career was linked to that of Vizarrón, and he lost the governorship shortly after Vizarrón was replaced as viceroy in 1740, but prior to that, the two carried on a considerable correspondence and the governor basked in the archbishop-viceroy's favor for at least the first three or four years of the latter's term in office.[110]

The call for help from the California missionaries had actually presented Arzobispo Virrey Vizarrón with an unprecedented opportunity. In nearly forty years of Jesuit development, no authority outside their order had visited their California installations or the interior of the isolated peninsula. Indeed, only a few pearlers and supply vessels had put in at its lonely ports. These circumstances had created an aura of mystery comparable to that which had existed before the conquest. Interest and speculation ran deep and far; California was a topic in Mexico City, Madrid, and other capitals of Europe. The masters of California had called for help; when it came it would have probing eyes and ears.

The viceroy seized the opportunity. His orders to Bernal de Huidobro stated that the governor was acting on behalf of the viceroy and was not in any way subject to the authority of the padres. His instructions contained other provisions that must have aroused misgivings when read by the Jesuits: the governor was to proceed against the rebels "with propriety" and, if possible, effect his ends "without offensive warfare, punitive expeditions," and so forth. Vizarrón must also have charged Bernal de Huidobro to observe California, evaluate the Jesuit effort, and assess the country's prospects. To bear out such an assumption, the governor's actions from the outset of his campaign suggest that he was primarily collecting intelligence to be forwarded to the viceroy.

The month before the governor was to sail for California, he dispatched his lieutenant and a small squad of soldiers as an advance party. Shortly after their arrival in Loreto, this group, with a few California soldiers to guide and escort them, made a long tour of the northern missions. Because of the revolt, Padre Visitador Clemente Guillén had withdrawn the padres from these missions during the year. The Jesuits claimed at the time that this necessity threatened the loss of hard-won establishments. Now Bernal de Huidobro's lieutenant toured the north, found the missionaries returned to their stations, and those missions quiet and orderly—surprisingly so in light of the recent alarming reports. Only a squabble over a supposed neophyte plot to murder the missionary at San Ignacio required the attention of the visiting troops, and no basis was found for that suspicion. In January 1736, the lieutenant reported all of this to the governor who was by then at Loreto. Bernal de Huidobro spent long hours conferring with Capitán Rodríguez and his men but sought little contact with the padres and asked for none of their advice. Fathers Guillén and Bravo remarked on this in a guarded fashion, but Sigismundo Taraval characteristically suspected a plot. He was scandalized by the governor's failure to consult the real authorities, the missionaries themselves.

If Manuel Bernal de Huidobro disapproved of Jesuit powers in Sonora, his attitude toward the state of affairs in California can be imagined. Within a few months of his arrival, he was submitting to the viceroy reports that criticized all aspects of the peninsula's government. The low estate of the presidio was especially distasteful to him, contrasting as it did with the greater independence and opportunities for the military in his own territory.[111] The presidio of Loreto was ruled by the religious. Neither the captain nor his men had the economic power or advantages enjoyed by the personnel of other presidios. With the exception of Esteban Rodríguez's right to his own cattle, gente de razón were forbidden lands, the working of mines or pearl fisheries, even the running of herds of privately owned domestic animals. If Padre Taraval can be accepted as a truthful reporter, Bernal de Huidobro was disdainful of Rodríguez and his men. Rather than dealing with the captain in the fashion to which his rank and length of service entitled him, the governor accorded him the treatment of a subaltern qualified to run errands but not to command. By the same token, he found fault with California troops, claiming that they were poorly disciplined and lacking in courage. Whatever the pretexts, he attacked the system by trying to drive a wedge between its missionaries and soldiers. By belittling Rodríguez, he sought converts among the soldiers. He tried to reduce their confidence in their leaders and in the way their interests had been represented.[112]

Bernal de Huidobro's Campaign against the Rebels

In February 1736, the Governor of Sinaloa left Loreto and took his forty men south to La Paz. There they joined the California forces and the governor assumed command of the campaign. After sending his lieutenant on a fruitless hunt for rebels in the Uchití region, Bernal de Huidobro embarked on a non-violent campaign to win over the insurgents. He made friendly overtures, invited rebel leaders to his camp, then, during a very leisurely series of contacts, offered them concessions and gifts in exchange for their submission. The natives' response was slow, incredulous, and frequently derisive. Padre Taraval was witness to these events and soon lost his composure, writing that the governor came "with the intention of waging war on the padres, and to offer, extend, and even implore peace of the rebels."[113] Taraval responded in private by writing page after page of the bitterest scorn. He had expected and longed for the direst punishment of his one-time tormenters. In his view, an army of the dimensions commanded by Bernal de Huidobro should have gone out, hounded the rebels to earth, executed the ringleaders and returned the humiliated rank-and-file to mission folds. Instead he still heard the "jibes, scorn, derision, and torture inflicted by the enemy who in every possible way ridiculed, insulted and triumphed over us."[114] It is questionable whether all the taunts of the unsophisticated natives could have topped the invective that the disappointed padre heaped on the governor while keeping his journal.

Bernal de Huidobro was acting on orders, a fact that Taraval either did not know or chose to ignore. Furthermore, by precedent, a field commander on the frontier was entitled to alter orders or to put them into abeyance as he saw fit. Here, the governor was satisfied to progress at a slow pace. He was not disturbed by vocal abuse from the native Californians. Were it not for the underlying tragedies, this scene would be comic: the governor issuing proclamations and invitations and conferring occasionally with insurgent chiefs or their ambassadors; the greater bands of rebels milling around just beyond gunshot range, curious about Spanish intentions and boastful in their liberty; the padre raging in his tent and unwittingly preparing the last laugh as he wrote what has been the affair's only history.[115]

There were several reasons why Bernal de Huidobro pursued such a deliberate and low-pressure campaign. The padres, in correspondence and conference, had expressed their opinions about how the matter should be handled. In all likelihood, the governor ignored this advice to demonstrate to all concerned that he was, as he had been ordered to be, independent of Jesuit control. In addition, the rebellion represented a failure of the Jesuit missions. Bernal de Huidobro and Vizarrón wished to hear out the plaintiffs and to gather evidence of Jesuit miscalculations and missteps rather than simply to destroy the evidence by force of arms. Finally, the visitors wanted to know more about California. An extended campaign provided opportunities for a wider and more effective reconnaissance. The last assumption is bolstered by Bernal de Huidobro's swift action when the need arose. After a year and a half in California, the governor received news of an incipient rebellion in his own territory. He immediately changed his tactics and conducted a few vigorous military actions against the rebels. His forces captured bands of Aripe, Uchití, and Cora, and he exiled twenty-six of their most effective leaders to the mainland to await a decision by the viceroy as to their punishment.[116] After that, most of the rebels sued for peace.[117]

Missionary Versus Soldier in the South

Manuel Bernal de Huidobro was criticized in the strongest terms by Jesuits in Sonora and California. Their opinions, committed to paper, became the standard sources for histories of that troubled time, histories in which the governor usually was presented as a bungler and an obstructionist. However, this was not the contemporary view outside Jesuit circles. Thanks to the patronage of the viceroy, the low loss of life in his campaign, and the relative peace that followed, his actions were viewed in a favorable light by most authorities. His opinion was sought and respected on several matters pertaining to California. His influence was most evident in the post-rebellion resolution of two old problems: the placement of a presidio in the South and decisions about the status of its captain and troops. The governor began by opposing the establishment of an additional military force, both because it was favored by the Jesuits and because he had been praised for reducing the size of his own presidio in Sinaloa. However, he acquiesced to Vizarrón's decision and proposed to locate a new presidio at San José del Cabo. Before he left the peninsula, Bernal de Huidobro carried out Virrey Vizarrón's order of 1736 and installed the long-discussed new military force in *el Sur.* By the terms of the new presidio's charter, its captain and troops were not subject to Jesuit control.[118]

Bernal de Huidobro appointed Bernardo Rodríguez, a son of Esteban, as the first captain of the Royal Presidio of the Frontier of the South of the Californias, usually shortened to "The Presidio of the South." Rodríguez's tenure lasted only a few months. He divided his thirty men into sub-presidios of ten men each at La Paz, Santiago, and San José del Cabo, a plan known to be favored by missionaries who felt the need for protection at newly re-established missions. This deference to the Jesuits did not please either the governor or the viceroy. It is quite possible, however, that the real reason the viceroy replaced Rodríguez was his desire to have a cohort in California who would continue to observe its affairs and make intimate reports. Bernardo Rodríguez was replaced by Pedro Antonio Alvarez de Acevedo, a protege of Bernal de Huidobro.[119] Alvarez de Acevedo was, like the governor himself, a choice that seemed designed to disturb and affront the Jesuits. He had been a militia captain and miner in Sonora and one of the most vociferous petitioners for Yaqui labor from Jesuit missions.[120]

Jesuits penned the surviving descriptions of the southern presidio, and they painted Capitán Alvarez de Acevedo an unrelieved black. He was accused of being the creature of Gobernador Bernal de Huidobro, placed in California to bear false witness against the missionaries. He was said to have alienated soldiers and padres to a degree never before seen in California. He was blamed for the continuing difficulties with the natives of the cape region. Alvarez de Acevedo's methods of dealing with them were held to have been too harsh, and it was claimed that a near rebellion resulted from his practices. By 1739, the wrangling between the new captain and his missionary neighbors at Santiago and Todos Santos had become so acrimonious that Padre Visitador Sebastián de Sistiaga went so far as to have the officer excommunicated.[121]

In retrospect, the Jesuit charges seem partisan and predictable. It would scarcely have been possible for the captain to maintain independence — as envisioned by a Sinaloan soldier — without displeasing a California missionary. Neither his reports to his superior nor his dealings with his men were likely to please Jesuits who until recently had controlled all such matters themselves. California Jesuits had accused the governor of Sinaloa of indulgence and laxity in his handling of the rebellion; now his handpicked captain was accused of cruelty and overzealousness in dealing with similar problems. The real basis for Jesuit dissatisfaction was the independence of the southern presidio and the connection between its captain and the detested governor of Sinaloa. A small but detailed correspondence survives to substantiate that view.

In 1740, a dispute arose between Capitán Alvarez de Acevedo, as commandant of his presidio, and Padre Antonio Tempis, the missionary at Santiago.[122] Alvarez de Acevedo complained in a deposition that the neophytes of Santiago had used rocks and bows and arrows to attack grazing horses and mules that belonged to his command. The padre justified the acts on the grounds that the herd had trampled and destroyed mission crops. The captain replied with complaints that Padre Tempis condoned an extreme reaction to a minor provocation. He noted that he had had little cooperation from any of the padres; everyone from Padre Visitador Lamberto Hostell on down treated him in a cold and distant fashion. Alvarez de Acevedo related that he had found a spring and a small plot of grazing land at a place called El Salto de San Antonio about midway between the missions of Santiago and San José del Cabo. He removed his herd to that place and began the construction of some buildings to accommodate two soldiers and six servants. Tempis heard about this development and either inspected the place or sent someone to do so. He explained in a letter to the captain that Misión de Santiago was poor in lands and water. The mission must have this valuable spring to guarantee a livelihood to its people. Alvarez de Acevedo responded that he had to have pasturage or he could not do the king's work to which he was assigned. Regulations were on the captain's side. The Laws of the Indies prohibited presidios from pasturing animals within three leagues of missions; El Salto was distant by ten.

Despite the captain's seemingly reasonable position, Padre Tempis appealed to higher authorities in Mexico City to block the soldiers' use of El Salto. His case might have seemed plausible to the viceroy or his advisors, far away in Mexico City, but its factual basis was contradicted by other Jesuit reports. Before and after this incident, the immediate lands and water of Misión de Santiago were described by various missionaries as some of the best in California. An inspection of the place today bears out that view.

Before the viceroy could make a ruling, neophytes from Santiago, under Tempis's orders, destroyed the structures at El Salto, a move that the padre justified in another letter to Alvarez de Acevedo. The subsequent exchange produced a vignette of Jesuit sophistry pitted against mundane interests. The Jesuit employed a Latin phrase in his defense of the action; in reply, the captain stated bluntly that the destruction of his buildings was self-evidently wanton and against royal or even mission interests, no matter the meaning of the Latin — the phrase being lost on him since he had never studied that language.

Alvarez de Acevedo raised an important point for the first time in California: just what were the limits on mission lands and jurisdiction? The Jesuits obviously felt they were in a strong enough position to fight any concession. The monolithic Jesuit organization would not concede even a minor point to a man they considered an enemy. This stand reflected more than the usual Spanish love of litigation and contention. Conceding one point would imply a general weakness on the part of the Society of Jesus. A rule from "Regulations for the Missions" compiled by Jesuit Padre Provincial Alonso de Arrivillaga in 1715 was applied in this case: if anyone came to discredit the missionaries "the door was to be shut on him."[123] The reported coldness of the California Jesuits and the implacable opposition of Tempis can be interpreted in this light. In his final letter to Alvarez de Acevedo, Tempis indicated that the dispute was not all about rules or other legalisms; it had a subjective side and egos were involved. The padre wrote, "I find you lacking the proper spirit not because of your defense of royal interests, but for failing to give proper credit to the California Fathers, especially those of the South."[124]

The Jesuits Settle a Score

There was an epilogue to the years during which the Jesuits had to contend with Vizarrón, Bernal de Huidobro, and Alvarez de Acevedo. Once the Society of Jesus had set its machinery in motion, it was not easily denied — as these three opponents discovered.[125] As early as 1738, Jesuit complaints to the king produced official inquiries into the viceroy's actions during the early part of the California rebellion. During the investigation, the viceroy partially repudiated Bernal de Huidobro, claiming that the governor had misinformed him in several matters. By July 1740, Vizarrón produced a ringing endorsement of the Jesuit position in California and withdrew his support for the independent presidio at the cape.[126]

Gobernador Bernal de Huidobro had problems unrelated to California. When he returned to the mainland in mid-1738, he ignored Jesuit warnings of unrest at Sonoran missions and continued to feud with the missionaries. In 1740, a widespread rebellion of Yaqui caught him ill-prepared and incapable of quieting the rebels or protecting the missions and the Hispanic settlers.[127] When his principal sponsor, Virrey Vizarrón, lost his office, Bernal de Huidobro found himself in court facing numerous charges of malfeasance. In 1741, Capitán Alvarez de Acevedo was demoted to the rank of lieutenant and made subordinate to the captain at Loreto.[128] At the end of 1742, he was recalled from California and put on trial. The principal charges against Bernal de Huidobro and Alvarez de Acevedo were brought by Padre Provincial Mateo Anzaldo of the Society of Jesus. They consisted of a dossier of complaints gleaned from missionaries in California and Sonora.[129] Among the various accusations, one was reported to have been confirmed: both men were found guilty of illicit commerce with the Manila galleon.[130] Bernal de Huidobro's property was seized, and litigation dragged on for years.[131] Alvarez de Acevedo was formally forbidden to set foot on California soil.[132]

These extended proceedings demonstrated that the organized, cohesive Society of Jesus could outlast individual critics or opponents and eventually ruin them if it desired, but the Jesuits may have sensed that they had overplayed their hand in this case. Gobernador Bernal de Huidobro may not have been an admirable man, but he represented the Hispanic settlers on a frontier that was generating interest for its economic promise. The Audiencia of Guadalajara was in the midst of lengthy hearings that led to elaborate plans for the development of mining and agriculture in Sonora, pearling in the gulf, and the long-awaited civil colony in California. These were old dreams, but the new stirrings had vitality and the interest of Madrid.[133] Whatever the merits of the Jesuit case versus the ex-governor, its charges and counter-charges cast the missionary order in an unfavorably obstructionist and reactionary role.

By the end of Bernal de Huidobro's trials, a strangely conciliatory attitude toward him had appeared in Jesuit writings. After the invective of earlier times, it is surprising to find an official Jesuit history, written in the early 1750s, which contains such lines as, ". . . by the zeal and courage of the governor of Sinaloa were the Pericú, the Guaycura and Cora reduced, and the new garrison of [Cabo de] San Lucas established. . . ." In the same work, a royal cédula is cited which comments on peaceful conditions among the Pericú and Guaycura created "by the good conduct of the governor of Sinaloa. . . ."[134] Padre Miguel del Barco became a chronicler precisely to correct what he perceived to be errors in that book, but he was satisfied to quote the above line verbatim.[135] For whatever reasons, Manuel Bernal de Huidobro was rehabilitated in works by substantial representatives of the order that had been his bitterest adversary.

The deposed governor himself may have recouped more rapidly than his literary image. The final papers in the archives of the Audiencia of Mexico suggest a shattered career and a personal fortune claimed by courts and creditors, but another branch of the huge documentation of Spain in the New World contains a tantalizing footnote, a suggestion of the cashiered governor's resiliency. On 10 November 1748, the Audiencia of Santa Fé de Bogotá in the Viceroyalty of Peru recorded the appointment of Manuel Bernal de Huidobro as governor of the Province of Popayán.[136]

Jesuit Control of California Weakens

Between 1743 and 1746, various events created the illusion that California missionaries might regain lost ground with royal authorities, recover lost privileges, and renew the impetus of their dream. A new viceroy, Pedro Cebrián y Agustín, the Conde de Fuenclara, seemed to favor them in word and deed.[137] In 1744, a cédula came from the Council of the Indies which indicated that Jesuit missionaries would have the religious responsibilities in a proposed occupation of Alta California. At the same time, a cédula called for the payment of money long promised to California by previous decrees.[138] This evidence of royal interest and favor was interpreted as the best of omens. In 1746, however, the illness and death of Felipe V caused new alignments in the power structure. The old threat of Bourbon reforms was becoming more real and more imminent. Cédulas flew, and some were sharply critical of California practices, particularly the Jesuit resistance to a civil colony and economic development. There was also increasing dissatisfaction with California's static frontier. It had been twenty years since a new mission was established in the north, and royal officials were impatient to be off to San Diego and Monterey.

In response, the Society of Jesus in New Spain, from the provincial down to the missionaries of California and Sonora, began to deploy new plans and actions. Jesuit Provincial Cristóbal de Escobar y Llamas sent explicit directions to his men in the field; they were ordered to settle — yet again — the old controversy about the peninsularity of California and to seek supply routes across the Sonoran desert that could serve the new northern missions that were being planned for California.

In 1746, the task of exploring the gulf fell to Fernando Consag, who for over ten years had been Sebastián de Sistiaga's co-worker at Misión de San Ignacio.

This forty-three-year-old Croatian padre had explored extensively on land while evangelizing the gentiles, but reconnoitering the gulf at that time was quite another matter. One of Loreto's intermittent marine disasters once more had left California without a ship. The only available craft were the open canoes that were sailed or paddled from Loreto up and down the coast carrying supplies to mission landings. Nevertheless, the determined missionary organized and carried out an epic exploration. "On the ninth of June, 1746, we departed in four canoes from San Carlos," began Fernando Consag's diary, a work which was to be read by the King of Spain, quoted all over Europe, and printed in several languages.[139] His flotilla of four canoes was manned by six soldiers, a small force of his San Ignacio neophytes, and a group of Yaqui. The little fleet worked its way north for over a month. Each night it landed to cook, eat, and sleep. They had adventures with previously uncontacted Cochimí and ultimately with people speaking a Yuman dialect. They saw the first dog reported in California. Finally they came to the mouth of the Río Colorado and entered it. After bucking its great tidal bore and a storm, Consag found himself in the delta of a great river. Mountains rose to the west at his left, and a vast expanse of marshes stretched off to his right. The water had become entirely sweet, and no evidence of an arm of the sea lay ahead.

When Consag had sailed and then towed his canoes as far as seemed possible, he turned south with no doubts about what he had seen. Like Ulloa, Alarcón, and Ugarte before him, Consag was convinced that he had arrived at the head of a gulf; California was a peninsula. But the modest padre was disinclined to make overly positive assertions. His report of his discoveries was cautious in its conclusions. Once again, geographers who had no firsthand knowledge or tangible evidence sought to refute an actual explorer of the Mar de Cortés. Two Spanish naval officers who on occasion advised or informed the king, produced a joint publication: "The opinion of Jorge Juan and Antonio de Ulloa concerning the diary of Fr. Consag written in order to make clear the reasons which can be offered in contradiction of his assurance that the sea of California does not have an outlet to the north. . . ."[140] Even a highly placed Austrian Jesuit scholar was unconvinced after reading the printed version of Consag's report—and noted that there were many other doubters. The "Island of California," fantasized for more than two centuries, remained deeply entrenched as a figure of speech and popular belief in the outside world. For another generation, California Jesuits would have to read such frustrating views and dream of yet another opportunity to demonstrate what for them was an obvious truth.[141]

As a corollary to Consag's effort, the Jesuits attempted to determine the feasibility of a land route from Sonora to California, a development considered essential to the push to occupy lands along the Pacific shore that were claimed by Spain. Missionaries and soldiers in the Pimería Alta participated in the burst of activity following the royal decrees of 1744, but they were delayed by disturbances among the Pimas. Padre Jacobo Sedelmayr led three explorations down the Gila River to the Colorado, and in his final effort during November and December of 1750, he reached a point near the mouth of the Colorado.[142]

No immediate use was made of the knowledge gained during these expeditions, but a quarter of a century later it served Juan Bautista de Anza as he took colonists from Sonora to Alta California.

This great flurry of Jesuit activity during the late 1740s resulted in no economic or political advantages for the missionary order. Although the favorable cédula of 1744 was eventually upheld and reissued by the council of the new king, Fernando VI, its benefits proved illusory. No money was forthcoming, no powers were conferred. During the decade, the economic development of the northwest grew from being a local concern to one that excited regional planning and engaged the attention of the central government.[143] As enthusiasm and cupidity grew, the Jesuits were painted in ever-blacker terms as obstructionists with a stranglehold on the economic potential of the region.[144]

In this spotlight of attention and growing disapproval, California missionaries gave up a right they had cherished since the days of Salvatierra's original license to open California. In the last years of his life, Padre Procurador Jaime Bravo had become convinced that the presidio had to be more independent if he and his fellows expected Bourbon cooperation. He must have had the ear of his provincial, Cristóbal de Escobar y Llamas. Despite shocked and concerned reactions from other California Jesuits, the long-held right was renounced. When Bernardo Rodríguez was appointed to succeed his aged and blind father in 1744, he was nominated by Padre Visitador Sebastián de Sistiaga, but he was appointed by the viceroy.[145] Within a year or two, California Jesuits also renounced the right to specify the soldiers to be hired for service in their region. The captain thereafter made his own choices.[146]

The South in Transition

By the mid-1740s, events set in motion by the persistent Marqués de Valero thirty years before had nearly run their course. Before Valero's time, Salvatierra had managed to avoid royal requests and even royal orders for missionary activities in California's cape area. After Salvatierra's death, his successors reluctantly undertook the conversion of the peoples of the South. Their system, which worked well enough with the Cochimí, could not pacify or reconcile the warring factions of the southern cape. Rebellion, once unleashed, was beyond the control of the peninsular Jesuits and their modest forces. Appeals to other powers resulted in the loss of California's isolation. Strangers with civil and military powers came and ranged over the land. They brought the cloistered little Loreto colony ideas about individual rights and privileges that were scarcely imagined before. As these and other controversial issues were aired, California's people — gente de razón, converts, and heathen alike — were shown the spectacle of men who argued with the Jesuits and acted independently of them. The protracted rebellion also ended the ultra-provincialism of the cape peoples. Their isolation was lost as all resisted the common enemy, became refugees, and shared the same retreats. When the rebellion was over, only the

Uchití maintained their independence and carried on an active, armed resistance. However, all the native groups of the South retained their desire to escape the limitations of mission life and to flee the plagues that killed them faster than any armed conflict.[147]

As a by-product of the rebellion, the South was opened up and proved attractive to the peninsular Hispanic population. Land and water were there for the taking; economic opportunity beckoned to soldiers and their families. A few had the temerity to take steps that would have been suppressed before; now the padres failed to react. By 1746, the California pioneers were dead. In the turmoil of changing kings, councilors, and viceroys — and in a political climate of increasing criticism of the Society of Jesus — the later missionaries tried to avoid controversy. Salvatierra and Kino's dream of a theocracy was fading. Gente de razón, those weeds in their mission garden, were about to become a significant factor in changing California.

II

The Organization and Operation
of Jesuit California

The California Jesuits governed and supplied their mission as a unified venture, but it had distinct elements. The missionaries themselves formed a miniature bureaucracy with its own goals and esprit de corps even as they formed a part of the international Jesuit body. Their mission to native Californians was the end and the all of their effort. However, the California mission of their dreams could never have been established or maintained without a presidio under their control. That presidio, in turn, required soldiers and seamen who were also artisans and agriculturalists. They and their families formed a third entity, an incipient Hispanic pueblo. Within a few years of its founding, the colony was organized and operating much as it would throughout the seventy years of Jesuit control. Thanks to Juan María de Salvatierra's foresight, skills, and good fortune, that organization had a rare degree of autonomy, not only from many aspects of civil government, but also from the rest of the Jesuit hierarchy of New Spain. Padre Salvatierra and successive directors of the Jesuit mission were the effective governors of all Spanish affairs in California.

FIVE

The Jesuit Organization in California

The Visitador *of the Californias*

The superior of the California Jesuits, their *padre visitador*, got his title from one of his principal duties: to visit each mission at regular intervals, to evaluate its progress, and to work with its missionary to solve problems. The Jesuit order empowered California's padre visitador to order any of the missionaries under him back to the mainland for poor health, "loss of heart," or any other reason that he deemed important. He could send subordinate Jesuits to any place on or off the peninsula to further the interests of the California mission. He was the ultimate authority for all California purchases, and he could go to Mexico City at three-year intervals to inspect account books kept by his subordinate, the *padre procurador de Californias*. He might appoint one of his missionaries as his agent and send him to the capital in his stead. While there, the father visitor's deputy outranked the procurador de Californias and could order changes in the prosecution of California's affairs.[1]

The crown granted the father visitor control of the California presidio by giving him the right to hire and fire the captain, and, through that power over him, to influence the choice of all his personnel. This authority made California's Jesuit leader a quasimilitary figure; he was empowered to muster troops and hoist colors to signal the start of a campaign. He was also the highest civil authority on the peninsula since he had the power to appoint and depose those who administered justice.[2]

For all practical purposes, Juan María de Salvatierra served as padre visitador from the inception of the colony in 1697 until his death in 1717. Although he was appointed provincial of the Jesuits of New Spain in late 1704 and served until late 1706, he retained close ties with California and even managed a three-month visit in 1705. During his absences, his duties as father visitor were performed by Juan de Ugarte, who fully succeeded to the position at Sal-

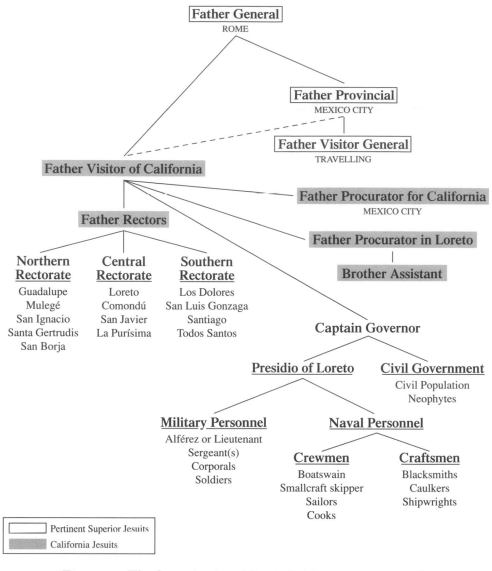

Figure 5.1 The Organization of Jesuit California c. 1730–1767

vatierra's death. By Ugarte's time, the burden of the leader's duties in the expanding mission chain led to the appointment of a new superior every three years.[3] To lighten the father visitor's load, the dozen or more missions were divided into three *rectorados* (rectorates): northern, central, and southern. The four or five padres in each rectorado were presided over by one of their number, a *padre rector*, appointed on a rotating basis to serve for three years. Each father rector worked with the missionaries of his group to find local solutions to as many problems as possible.[4]

Padres Visitadores *of Jesuit California*

Juan María de Salvatierra	1697–1717
Juan de Ugarte	1718–1722
Francisco María Piccolo	1723–1725[5]
Clemente Guillén	1726–1728[6]
Sebastián de Sistiaga	1729–1731[7]
Clemente Guillén	1732–1735[8]
Sebastián de Sistiaga	1736–1740[9]
Clemente Guillén	1741–1743[10]
Sebastián de Sistiaga	1743–1747[11]
Fernando Consag	1747–1750[12]
Miguel del Barco	1751–1754[13]
Lamberto Hostell	1755–1757[14]
Fernando Consag	1758–1759[15]
Miguel del Barco	1761–1763[16]
Lamberto Hostell	1764–1766[17]
Benno Ducrue	1767–1768[18]

The Visitador General *for Jesuit Missions in New Spain*

The California mission received its charter directly from the Jesuit general in Rome and had the right to keep its finances separate from those of the Jesuit Province of New Spain, but it was not autonomous in all things. California's padre visitador reported to and consulted with the *padre provincial* in Mexico City, chief administrator of Jesuit affairs in New Spain.

In 1725, Padre Provincial José de Arjó created a formal office for a *visitador general* who would represent the provincial and travel to all the missions of the northwest: Nayarit, Tepehuana, Tarahumara, Sinaloa, Sonora, and California. This visitor general was given the authority to make many ad hoc decisions, a necessary delegation of power since problems were often local and the provincial was far away and unfamiliar with the circumstances. A visitor general could appoint or transfer missionaries. He could order changes in mission practices.[19] He outranked any regional father visitor, including that of California. However, because of California's special status, these representatives of the provincial of New Spain acted more as advisors than directors in peninsular affairs.[20]

Jesuits selected for duty as visitors general were prominent men, usually men considered to have potential for higher office; five subsequently became provincials themselves, and two represented the province at court in Madrid.[21] During their rounds, visitors general kept records of their observations, collected extensive data, and submitted written reports to the provincial. The few of their reports that survive provide the frankest, most explicit, and most comprehensive available pictures of Jesuit missions and missionaries.[22] In addition, three visitors general required each California missionary to submit a written report on the state of his mission. The padres' responses included descriptions of daily activities, achievements, and special problems, as well as reviews of events at their missions since the previous visitation. These documents supply unique firsthand information.[23]

The visitor general rendered an important service to the missions by carrying news and gossip from one Jesuit region to another and then to the remotest missions of each. This internal communication was particularly welcome and important for California where few mainland missionaries otherwise went. In return, the visitors general carried home vivid pictures of the accomplishments and hardships of the new conversion. They were catalysts in the mainland network that provided contributions of food and animals that helped carry the California colony through its periods of greatest need.

In theory, visitors general were appointed triennially, the same term served by California's padre visitador. However, California records show that their visits were not that frequent or regular.[24]

Visitadores Generales *in Jesuit California*

Juan de Guenduláin	1726[25]
José de Echeverría	1729–1730[26]
Andrés Javier García	1737[27]
Lucas Luis Alvarez	1742[28]
Juan Antonio Baltasar	1744[29]
Agustín Carta	1752[30]
José de Utrera	1755[31]
Ignacio de Lizasoáin	1762[32]
Carlos Rojas	1766[33]

The Procurador de Californias

The Jesuit mission to California was Spain's most isolated outpost in North America and therefore had to cope with the longest supply lines. Salvatierra had foreseen the need for a supply officer in Mexico City — a subordinate who could handle finances, procurement, and shipments—but Padre Juan María began by assuming that he could handle the California end of the supply system himself. But California's needs, and the problems of meeting them, soon demanded more men and a more complex organization.

California's financing was uniquely independent of the sources and controls that pertained to other Jesuit mission areas. Kino, Salvatierra, Ugarte, and others had solicited contributions to open and sustain a Jesuit California. The resulting gifts from benefactors, whether monies or real property, were pooled to create an endowment, *el Fondo Piadoso* (the Pious Fund), earmarked for California use only. The padre visitador of the Californias had sole discretion in investing or spending Pious Fund revenue. When the crown began to pay soldiers' salaries, the money was put into a California account. The financial officer of the Society of Jesus in Mexico City controlled funds for other Jesuit missions in New Spain, but not those of California—indeed, he was not privy to the California books. Both the Pious Fund and royal payments for California soldiers were controlled by California's own business administrator, the *padre procurador de Californias*.[34] The latter was stationed at the Colegio de San Andrés in Mexico City but answered directly to California's padre visitador. The California procurador in Mexico City supervised every aspect of the Pious Fund, the investment of its assets, and the operation of its properties. He and his assistants kept account books for all incomes and expenses, including all disbursements for California's annual supplies.[35]

Every year, each California missionary submitted to Loreto a list of his own and his mission's needs as complete as his budget would allow. Each Jesuit employee did likewise. No one in California was allowed to send directly to any merchant or dealer to purchase anything.[36] Part of the Jesuit discipline and efficiency arose from channeling all purchases through the procurador de Californias. All the lists of mission and individual needs were consolidated into an itemized supply order called a *memoria*. Memorias were so important that a California soldier accompanied them all the way to Mexico City rather than trust them to disinterested hands.[37]

The procurador de Californias became a political figure. He was the highest California authority who could be readily contacted by the viceroy, so he was often called in for consultation or to explain decisions or developments in the distant colony. The procurador knew the system and did his part to promote cooperation; the account books of the Pious Fund show annual *regalías*, "gifts" of hundreds of pesos to the viceroy and his two principal secretaries.[38]

Padre Jacobo Baegert, a California missionary, offered a succinct description of the offices of the procurador de Californias:

> Once a year, the royal officials in Mexico delivered the full sum for the payment of the sailors and soldiers to the Father-Administrator [the procurador de Californias] who managed all the foundation estates of the missions. Of course a few thousand pesos were always deducted. They remained glued to the fingers of the officials as a "present." The administrator did not

send this money to California, and neither soldier nor sailor ever received any silver. It would be of no use to him, since there were no bakers, butchers, innkeepers, or merchants in California from whom he could have bought any necessities. The Father-Administrator, therefore, purchased with this pay everything, excluding food, which approximately eighty men and a number of wives and their children might need in the course of a year. He sent these commodities, together with the articles requested by each missionary, to Loreto.[39]

Such accounts of the work of the procurador de Californias imply a single dedicated Jesuit laboring in monastic isolation at several demanding jobs. In fact, as early as 1708, the procurador in Mexico City had an *hermano coadjutor* (a brother helper) as an assistant. In later years, he often had two such helpers in the viceregal capital and another at the Hacienda de Arroyo Zarco, headquarters of the Pious Fund's estates.[40]

Padres Procuradores de Californias

Padre Juan de Ugarte	1697–1700[41]
Padre Alejandro Romano	1701–1719[42]
Padre José de Echeverría	1719–1729[43]
Hermano Juan Francisco de Tompes	1729–1750[44]
Padre Juan de Armesto	1752–1767[45]

In addition, a Jesuit in Guadalajara acted as a deputy procurador to deal, as necessity arose, with the Audiencia of Guadalajara, and to make arrangements for supplies that could be purchased more advantageously in that city or in nearby Tepic. He could also help to expedite the annual passage of the supply train. During the first years of the California mission, the procurador in Guadalajara was Padre Matías Goñi, one of Padre Kino's Jesuit companions in California during the Atondo expedition. Later, Padre Feliciano Pimentel filled this post, to be followed around 1730 by Padre José Carrillo.[46]

The Procurador *in Loreto*

During his first years at Loreto, Juan María de Salvatierra acted not only as padre visitador, but also kept books, paid his hired help, and sent out annual lists of needed supplies to Mexico City, and, on occasion, to sister missions in Sonora.[47] However, by 1705, increased paperwork, additional duties occasioned by the creation of a more formal presidio, and Salvatierra's extended absence dictated that he get help. Hermano Jaime Bravo, a young Jesuit not yet qualified as a padre, was brought to Loreto to serve as hermano coadjutor, Salvatierra's administrative assistant. He collected orders from the missions and the presidio, sent requisitions to the procurador de Californias, received shipments, then inventoried and stored them for local distribution or shipment by mule or launch to other missions.[48]

Juan de Ugarte, Salvatierra's successor, served as both padre visitador and overseer of the presidio while continuing as missionary at San Javier. That arrangement further hindered already difficult communications since the procurador de Californias was in distant Mexico City and the hermano coadjutor had to remain at Loreto.[49] At Ugarte's suggestion, Padre Provincial Andrés Nieto agreed in 1728 to a new position: *procurador en Loreto*. Because no new men or monies were available, the title and the duties were given to Loreto's missionary. His burden was somewhat offset by the fact that his missionary duties were relatively light — Loreto, by then, was more a base and a port than a mission. Whereas a typical mission had five hundred or more isolated converts, Loreto had fewer than three hundred, and they were far more acculturated. Many worked and lived more as laborers for the presidio and the greater mission system than as mission neophytes.

As padre visitador general, José de Echeverría had the power to institute the new post of procurador in Loreto when he came to California in 1729, but he waited until he had visited the missions and talked to the missionaries before he acted. In 1730, he called a meeting of the most experienced missionaries — at San Javier, since Ugarte was too ill to travel. Padres Julián de Mayorga and Clemente Guillén joined Ugarte and Echeverría to discuss the new position. They were particularly concerned that the procurador's relationship with the presidio not be allowed to dilute the traditional powers of California's padre visitador.[50] Their deliberations produced a list of points that defined and delimited the post of procurador in Loreto:

1 The padre visitador of California shall continue to be superior of the presidio of Loreto. All of its soldiers, workmen, and sailors shall continue to be subject to his orders.

2 The padre at Loreto, in both his roles, missionary and procurador, shall be subject as before to the visitador. His immediate superior is the rector of Loreto's district.

3 The procurador shall give the proper governing of the presidio whatever attention is required. He shall have the power to enlist or dismiss such soldiers, sailors, or servants as he deems necessary. He will not need to advise the visitador of such actions if he is inconveniently distant; otherwise he should be notified as a matter of courtesy.

4 The selection of capitán, alférez, and cabo remains the sole province of the visitador. However, the latter should fill these posts only after consultation with the procurador and other missionaries.

5 The procurador at all times shall provide the provisions necessary to maintain the presidio and its sailing craft. Boats must always be in readiness to

transport goods needed for presidio and missions. However, these craft should not be required to sail during the dangerous storm season in August and September except in cases of extraordinary necessity.

6   The procurador shall keep accounts for all of the personnel of the presidio, paying them in the established fashion. He shall not accept into service more persons than are needed, give salaries to worthless people, or incur any avoidable expense.

7   The procurador shall not authorize any major expense, such as dismantling a ship, building another, or putting a new bottom on a vessel, without consulting the visitador. He should seek competent advice beyond that of mere boatswains and sailors before ordering work on a ship. He must be zealous to keep them in service, for ships are difficult to obtain and indispensable to the conversion of the Californias.

8   When a vessel is lost, the procurador must make an accurate report, have it approved by the visitador, and send it with any request to the viceroy for a new ship. If such a loss were due to criminal negligence by a boatswain or sailors, the captain of the presidio should institute judicial proceedings. Neither the procurador nor others, even with the excuse of charity, should hinder the pursuit of justice.

9   In cases where there might be no easy recourse to the padre visitador, the padre procurador shall have authority to issue certificates of service to persons being dismissed from mission employ.[51]

Years later, Padre Jacobo Baegert set down a concise description of the padre procurador's activities.

He received all the goods sent from Mexico. During the year, the soldiers and sailors were given on account whatever they requested within the limit of the amount of their salary. The administrator of Loreto was also obliged to report annually, under oath, to the Viceroy, stating that the number of soldiers was complete and that they had been duly paid. If one of them received his discharge and left, he was given linen or other goods for the amount of pay still due him.[52]

Padres Procuradores *in Loreto*[53]

Jaime Bravo	1730–1744
Gaspar de Trujillo	1744–1748
Juan de Armesto	1748–1752
Juan Javier Bischoff	1753–1757
Lucas Ventura	1757–1767

The Hermano Coadjutor at Loreto

The hermano coadjutor was not mentioned in the job definition for the procurador in Loreto that is cited above. No doubt the latter took the primary responsibility and made the major decisions, but contemporary documents show that the procurador's assistant did the bookkeeping and storekeeping for which his superior was responsible.[54]

Jaime Bravo held the post of hermano coadjutor until he became a full-fledged padre and missionary in 1720. By that time, Hermano Juan Bautista Mugazábal, recently converted from soldier to Jesuit,[55] had been made hermano coadjutor. He held the position for forty-one of the forty-seven remaining years of Jesuit tenure. Juan de Ugarte had sponsored Hermano Mugazábal in his novitiate as a Jesuit, and he was responsible for much of his training. Mugazábal's placement as coadjutor made shrewd use of the ex-soldier's fifteen years of experience in California. He had served as alférez of the presidio and knew its workings intimately. The year before he became a Jesuit, he commanded a boat that took shipwrecked pearlers back to the mainland and, while on that coast, he acted as Loreto's purchasing agent for wheat. In all, he was well prepared to judge personnel and to cope with all the practices and mal-practices of soldiering.[56] Hermano Mugazábal served as sole coadjutor for over thirty years; about 1751, he was given an assistant.

The hermano coadjutor at Loreto kept ledgers that encompassed the accounts of every mission and every employed individual in California. He was a go-between in every transaction. For example, a missionary would requisition whatever was needed at his establishment. If the requested items were in stock at the Loreto warehouse, the coadjutor had them collected, packaged, and sent by lancha or pack mule and soldier escort to their mission destination. Then he did the necessary bookkeeping to charge the mission's account. If items were not available in California, the coadjutor added them to that year's memoria to be obtained through the procurador de Californias.[57]

Hermanos coadjutor worked long hours on a year-round basis; from 1705 to 1767, they were the only California Jesuits not assigned to missions in addition to their other duties.[58]

Hermanos Coadjutores at Loreto

Jaime Bravo	1705–1718[59]
Juan Bautista Mugazábal	1719–1761[60]
Francisco López	1752–1759[61]
Joaquín López y Cía	1759–1764[62]
Juan Villavieja	1764–1767[63]

The Annual Drama of California Logistics

The procurador in Mexico City and his assistants had demanding jobs. They did all the bookkeeping for California procurement; they arranged and supervised the purchasing, collection, storage, and shipping of most of the supplies needed by a colony of over a hundred gente de razón and several thousand neophytes. Most buying was done in Mexico City. Where large amounts of goods or large sums were involved, the procurador de Californias solicited bids from merchants that the Jesuits trusted. Chosen vendors delivered merchandise to the Colegio de San Andrés, headquarters for California procurement and shipping. Some specialty items were ordered directly from their makers or importers; all commodities were carefully bought.

Durable goods were purchased at any time during the year that the procurador deemed advantageous. They were accumulated in the colegio's sizeable storehouse. Food was purchased for delivery close to the time when a shipment was put on the road. Particularly heavy or perishable items like sugar, flour, and wholegrain maize were purchased from dealers or agents who lived closer to Matanchel, the principal port of embarkation for California. Such supplies could be held in readiness for the pack train as it passed in transit.

By 1731, Pious Fund money had been used to buy an hacienda named Arroyo Zarco, about thirty-five miles north of the city of Querétaro. Arroyo Zarco functioned primarily as a sheep ranch, but it may have been purchased because it lay near the road from Mexico City to Guadalajara and offered storage facilities that could accommodate not only the accumulated purchases for all the Pious Fund's haciendas, but also the goods to fill California's annual supply orders. After 1734, most, if not all, Jesuit pack trains that headed for Matanchel were loaded at Arroyo Zarco.[64]

Fortunately, most of the memorias survive for all but the first ten years of the Jesuit colony in California. Each annual memoria runs from five to ten pages and lists the numbers, weight, or other measure of each commodity, as well as its cost.[65] The memoria for 1725 attracts attention because it is long, unusually self-explanatory, and written in the fine hand of Procurador de Californias José de Echeverría.[66] Moreover, 1725 was a typical year for its decade: no new mission was to be founded and no serious losses had been experienced during the previous year's supply delivery. Few items on the memoria were unique or unusual when compared to those of previous or later years. The nine-page invoice contains 220 entries that record thousands of separate items. No single article or loaded container could weigh more than about two hundred pounds, the practical limit to a mule's load for a long trip. The biggest and heaviest objects were a bell and clapper weighing 172 pounds and a pipe organ of unspecified weight that was disassembled sufficiently to be packed in three boxes. Most religious objects were listed together under the heading "Sacramentos," but otherwise the memoria indicated none of the specific recipients of any commodities. Nevertheless, most of those fall into a few major categories whose uses or users can be deduced:

Clothing   Most items were ordered in two or three grades of quality, reflected in their cost. For men, there were 66 linen shirts, 66 pairs of cotton hose, 168 pairs of silk hose, and 196 hats. For women, the invoice specified 52 under-petticoats, 41 pairs of long silk stockings, 20 pairs of short silk stockings, 36 pairs of short cotton stockings, and 132 rebozos, most of fine quality and costing from two to eight pesos each.* Included were 315 pairs of shoes, but they were not specified as men's, women's, or children's.

Fabrics and Notions   Thirty-three different woven materials were specified. Their prices spread from a quarter of a peso to nearly two pesos per yard, and their weights ranged from that of sackcloth to nankeen and fine silk. They included 2,600 yards of cotton cloths, 1,400 of linens, and nearly 1,200 of woolens. In addition, there were 270 yards of Flanders lace, 30 rolls of unspecified lengths of assorted costly fabrics, and 8 yards of expensive Chinese brocade. There were 90 rolls of ribbon or fancy banding material, much of it woven in figured patterns. Also included were 50 pounds of threads, cotton and silk; and finally, there were three hundred pesos' worth of silk yarn in skeins, material needed for the knitting and crocheting done by women of both the gente de razón and mission communities.[67]

Riding and Pack Equipment   Twelve saddle trees and various saddle parts on the memoria show that a small amount of saddle building was taking place in California. Included also were 53 pairs of stirrups in three categories, one for roping or round-up, and 55 pairs of spurs, about half of them with showy openwork or engraving at double the price of the plain vaquero type. There were 12 sets of high-quality reins with bells, and 7 dozen plain. Also included were 84 bits and 60 cruppers, the broad straps attached to either side of a saddle or pack saddle that passes beneath an animal's tail to prevent the saddle from sliding forward. Finally, there were 72 pairs of saddlebags fitted with small bells — apparently a popular small luxury.

Tools and Materials   There were 64 short planting hoes (*coas*), 26 long hoes, 38 woodcutter's axes, 14 brush-clearing machetes, and 24 knives specified for neophytes' use. For woodworking, there were 17 carpenter's adzes, 4 adzes of finer quality, 3 handsaws, and 45 drill bits. For metal work, there were 3 ball peen hammers, 6 pincers, and 3 large Spanish files. For general use were 84 belt knives of fine steel with sheaths, and 96 very inexpensive "English" knives. Hardware items included 6 large latches — perhaps for storeroom doors — 7 ordinary door latches, 16 chest latches, 12 Spanish padlocks "of a good make," 12 padlocks of lesser quality, and 6 tiny padlocks — possibly for use on personal storage chests. Materials for artisans' use included 45 pounds of steel, 6 pounds of wire, and 4,000 nails in different sizes, over half of them specified as shingle nails, a type with an unusually large head.

---

*For reference, a California soldier was paid about one peso per day.

CHAPTER 5

Domestic Items   The 1725 shipment included 12 *tercios* of soap, about 1,000 pounds. There were 50 wool blankets in two price categories and 180 others of unspecified materials and much lower cost. There were 144 combs, 20 pairs of gold earrings with gold wire loops, a box of unstrung pearl beads, and 2 bundles of coral, expensive, and probably destined to be cut, polished, and strung into adornments. Six tercios of tobacco were shipped, two tercios of a better grade, and four of regular quality. This luxury was used not only by padres and gente de razón; missionaries gave it to neophytes as a reward for special achievements.[68]

Food and Condiments   The following food items were included: 18 hams weighing a total of 160 pounds; 875 pounds of chocolate: 250 of fine quality and 625 regular; 150 pounds of fruit preserved in syrup; 140 pounds of *cajetas*, boxes of fruit preserves boiled down to make a stiff, moist confection; 25 pounds of peppercorns; 25 pounds of anise seed; 12 pounds of cinnamon; 6 pounds of rosemary; 6 pounds of cloves; 2 bags of unspecified sizes, one of bay leaves, the other of mustard seed.

Kitchen Utensils   Three 3 large griddles, one of iron and 2 of copper; 25 large pots for the preparation of chocolate; 30 large sets of pottery jugs and 10 sets of pottery jars; 32 dozen white glazed pottery vessels; 31 dozen fine Puebla dishes.

Military Equipment and Supplies   Two hundred pounds of gunpowder, 150 of high quality, and 50 of regular grade; 100 pounds of musket balls and 50 pounds of buckshot; 22 musket sheaths, 18 of high quality and 4 of common make; 13 long swords with scabbards and 12 additional scabbards; 13 embroidered sword belts, one of them used.

Mission Equipment and Supplies   Many items that were not intended to adorn churches or missionaries nevertheless appear to have been destined for mission use. These included oversized kitchen gear: a 42-pound copper kettle, 14 atole kettles, 72 atole sieves, 60 pozole ladles, 11 large frying pans, and 5 large and 14 medium copper jars. A few unusual clothing items must have been intended for neophytes or the unconverted; for example, there were 148 good-quality loincloths and 150 cheaper ones were specified "for barter."[69] There were also 130 dozen skyrockets and 48 dozen packets of firecrackers that were used during certain fiestas.[70]

Church Furnishings and Vestments   On the 1725 memoria, items in this category cost nearly three thousand pesos, one-sixth of the value of the annual shipment. Four padre's capes, in red brocade or white silk, cost one hundred and fifty and two hundred pesos respectively. Five cassocks ranged from forty pesos for plain black to over one hundred pesos for red or white. There were altar hangings, altar cloths, and chalice covers in rich cloths. There was a painted tabernacle and a painted retablo; the latter cost three hundred and eighty pesos. The organ that was broken down for transport cost three hundred and fifty pesos, and its builder was rewarded with a gift of thirty pesos more. Candles were a major expense; 325 of them, each weighing a half-pound, came to a total of one hundred and eighty pesos. Other items included candlesticks, rugs, and silver cruets for sacramental wine.

The contents of the 1725 memoria cost over nineteen thousand pesos. The shipment weighed over ten tons. Miguel Rodríguez Vaca owned and managed the *recua* (pack train) that took the supplies to the port of Matanchel. He was paid a total of 1,113 pesos, five and a half pesos for each hundredweight. His recua consisted of about 130 mules; at any given time, ten to twenty of these traveled without loads to rest or recuperate from worn hooves or other disabilities. Their journey covered five hundred miles and required two hundred and fifty hours of trail time, more than five weeks of elapsed time.[71]

The pack train that carried California's annual supplies followed the old, much-used camino real that ran through settled regions between Mexico City — or Arroyo Zarco — and Guadalajara. At Guadalajara, the road joined and overlaid an ancient trade route that led northwest across the Sierra Madre Occidental and continued on the same bearing across foothills and floodplains until it reached central Sonora and turned northeast to arrive amongst the pueblos of New Mexico.[72] By 1697, when they opened California, the Jesuits had been extending their use of this route for a hundred years while packing supplies to their missions in Nayarit, Sinaloa, and Sonora. Expert *arrieros*, muleteers, guided pack trains out of Guadalajara to arrive successively at the increasingly remote population centers of Tepic, Rosario, Culiacán, Mocorito, Villa de Sinaloa, El Fuerte, and Alamos. At any of these towns, the laden animals might be met by arrieros from individual missions who then transported their share of the goods up or down rivercourses to their destinations.

In times of Indian unrest, caravans worth many thousands of pesos were dangerously exposed along the camino real. To provide a safer alternative, landing places for cargo were established near river mouths so that necessities could be brought by sea.[73] At all times, ships could bring large, heavy, or particularly fragile merchandise.

Perils and Drawbacks of Supply by Sea

In principle, after 1718, Jesuit California was to have the use of two ships with crews, paid for by the crown. One would be large enough to bring the annual memoria or a dozen or more head of livestock from any port on the west coast of New Spain. The other, usually described as a lancha, had to be large enough to navigate the gulf safely in normal weather and to bring supplies from the Jesuit missions of the immediate mainland.[74] In fact, one (or both) of these craft was often out of service. Jesuit records are strewn with piecemeal references to maritime difficulties and disasters. Shipwrecks, captains charged with criminal negligence, and appeals to the viceroy for funds for new ships were recurrent

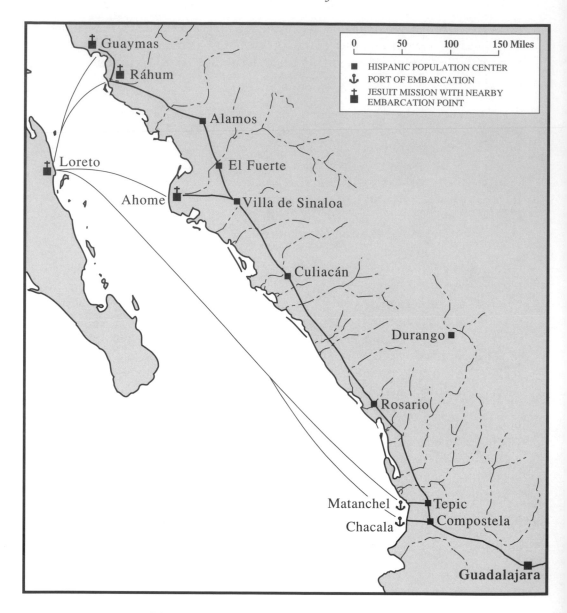

Map 5.1 Delivery Routes for California Supplies

themes reflected in the stated duties of the procurador in Loreto and the correspondence of the procurador de Californias.[75]

Winds and currents generally run contrary to ships sailing northwest along the west coast of New Spain. In almost any year, from July to October, some part of the Mar de Cortés and the adjacent land is devastated by a southern storm. From November to February, frequent strong north winds are dangerous to any small craft.

There are few natural harbors on the mainland coast between Matanchel and

Guaymas. The California peninsula lying offshore acts as a mammoth barrier reef blocking ocean swells and alongshore currents, altering tidal effects, and reducing the effects of onshore winds. Such sheltered coastal conditions are not seen elsewhere on the Pacific shores of the Americas. The lowlands are made up of the finest alluvium, and most coastal terrain is poorly suited to landing, loading, or unloading. Marshes or mud flats extend for several miles back of the beaches. These conditions hampered land access to bays or inlets near most of the towns and missions of the eighteenth century. Roads or causeways laboriously raised above the floodplains were often endangered or engulfed by torrential rains. Padre Jaime Bravo, long-time procurador in Loreto, described the Sinaloan and Sonoran landing places:

> . . . they can be entered only by launches or small ships, for they are not really harbors at all, but estuaries, and such boats take shelter in them. They have long, dangerous bars, and in order to enter them or sail out of them, the boats, when loaded, have to wait for the spring tides, that is when the moon is in conjunction or opposition. . . .[76]

Many maritime catastrophes involved unsheltered harbors with shallow waters and shifting sand bars onto which craft were swept.

The costs and uncertainties of shipping to Loreto motivated California missionaries to seek a land route around the head of the gulf. Major efforts were made as early as 1701 and continued in a series of land and sea ventures throughout Jesuit times, but the dream of driving cattle and packing supplies to California by land eluded Spaniards to the end of their hegemony in 1821. As bad as it was, shipping remained the best solution. The pack trains sent annually by the procurador de Californias terminated in the early years at Acapulco and in the later years at Matanchel, but even the latter port, so tantalizingly close to California on a map, often proved to be two weeks' sailing time from Loreto.[77]

The Poor Quality of West Coast Ships and Ship Repairs

Weather and terrain made up only part of California's maritime difficulties. During the seventy-year Jesuit presence in California, the colony built, bought, or was given twenty-two major ships. Twenty of these were lost, reduced to salvage, or retired as incapable of service. During a quarter of that time, the colony had no major vessel on which it could depend for vital supplies.[78] Boats and ships in use in the area were generally a poor lot. Most were built in Pacific ports, since the perilous rounding of the Horn was rarely undertaken by boats as small as those used in coastal trade. Local ship design and construction lagged behind those of Europe or the Caribbean. Iron was needed for many kinds of fastenings and fittings, but iron produced in the New World was very poor. As much as possible was imported from Spain, but again that was more difficult and costly for shipbuilders on the west coast. Poor or archaic designs resulted in craft with bluff hull contours and cumbersome rigging patterns that forced extremely long tacking legs when they were sailed upwind — the predominant condition as they plied northwest to Sonora or California.[79]

The soundest ships involved in west coast trade were built at Realejo,[80] a Pacific port in what is today Nicaragua, and at Guayaquil, today in Ecuador.[81] These vessels carried most of the growing coastal trade between the northern and southern hemispheres. North of Colima there was little economic activity, and hence little profit to be made in cargo. Most ships that visited northerly ports were built at Acapulco, Colima, and later at Chacala, Matanchel, and San Blas. According to various accounts, most of these craft were poorly joined from insufficiently aged timbers; planks were often so short that hulls lacked rigidity and structural integrity.

Operators along the coasts of Colima, Jalisco, and Sinaloa imported a few better vessels from Realejo and Guayaquil, but records suggest that these ships were often old by the time their prices suited the pockets of the marginal operators on the west-coast.[82] Most were purchased and brought north without being careened for adequate inspection. Damage from worm and rot frequently put them on the bottom within months of purchase. Even if detected in time, such damage required extensive renovations, and the same west coast shipyards that launched poorly built hulls offered deplorable repairs. Of the ships that served Jesuit California, few underwent major repairs and subsequently gave good or long service.[83]

Pirates

Pirates, or rather the fear of pirates, stunted the growth of west-coast ports and the development of commerce, transportation, and population during the seventeenth and eighteenth centuries. Francis Drake in 1579, and Thomas Cavendish in 1587, raided several coastal towns and villages. Cavendish, in particular, created an uproar by taking a Manila ship off Cabo de San Lucas. Pacific ports suffered periodic raids by English, Dutch and French buccaneers, and attempts to pursue the pirates uniformly failed. Fortifying ports proved costly and ineffective. Since the raiders had to land for food, water, and supplies, a passive form of defense was implemented. The rulers of New Spain urged the people to destroy crops, drive off livestock, and remove stores whenever the sea raiders appeared. Coastal settlements that might attract or sustain the corsairs were discouraged.[84] Ports that had been active stagnated. For many years, only fortified Acapulco engaged in regular trade, most notably the annual comings and goings of Manila galleons.

From its inception, the Jesuit colony in California was dependent on ships — sometimes pearling craft — to bring vital supplies, personnel, or messages. Padre Salvatierra was fortunate that he launched his venture at a time when there was no active piracy along the coasts of Nueva Galicia, Sinaloa, or the peninsula itself. The atmosphere was still charged with apprehension, but the lure of pearls had begun to tempt private enterprise back into the area.[85] In 1729, a principal argument for the maintenance of the presidio at Villa de Sinaloa, forty miles from the sea, was the necessity for its garrison in case pirates should invade the area in search of supplies.[86] As late as 1740, reports of privateers lurking off the coast of Nueva Galicia kept Loreto's supply ship in the port of Matanchel for days despite the fact that it was on an urgent mission to fetch grain for starving California.[87]

Soldiers' Pay and the Company Store

Whereas the crown's financial support for other presidios was placed in the hands of their captains, monies for the California presidio were delivered to the procurador de Californias. This difference troubled the Jesuits who knew that their detractors would use it to emphasize the degree and kind of control over the military enjoyed by the California missionaries. In 1718, the year that royal support for soldier salaries began, a charade was instituted at Loreto. Instead of receiving the royal funds like another presidial commander, Capitán Rodríguez wrote a letter in which he disclaimed any responsibility for the royal funds and deferred that obligation to the padre procurador in Mexico City. This request was signed by all soldiers at Loreto.[88] That procurador, who of course had always handled all royal and private funds, proceeded as he had from the first days of the conquest, receiving annual supply orders and putting them on the road to California.

When the annual memoria finally arrived at Loreto, it set off a flurry of activity. Supplies were usually overdue, so pressing needs had to be met. Trains of pack mules were prepared and, as rapidly as the goods could be sorted and invoiced, they were sent out to the missions and to the troops stationed in *el Sur*. The people at Loreto went directly to the warehouse, received their ordered supplies and signed, or made their marks, on the ledger sheets of their accounts. They had no alternative source for anything, other than a few trinkets brought in sub rosa by sailors.

The procurador in Loreto presided over a warehouse very much like the company stores operated by frontier mineowners of those and later times. The Jesuits equated cash with gambling, which they forbade, and incidental commerce, which they discouraged.[89] Thus, each soldier, sailor, or servant had an account with the procurador and received his salary as a credit on that account. Employees gave or sent the hermano coadjutor lists of their needs, drew items when they became available, and paid by reductions from their credit sheets. Each mission had a similar credit, an annual sum of five hundred pesos drawn from the Pious Fund. Occasionally, a mission had a surplus of harvests or animals; the excess was sent to the warehouse, and the mission was credited with its value.[90] None of these practices was limited to mission systems or to the frontier in general. In the absence of bank notes and with inadequate coinage, virtually the entire economy of New Spain operated on systems of credits and debits.[91]

Prices of all items, including the allowances for surpluses turned in to the warehouse, were determined by prices current in Mexico City. Some of these responded to fluctuations in supply and demand, but others were fixed by audiencias or viceroys.[92] The prices that the procurador de Californias paid for supplies were doubled when the goods were exchanged for the soldiers' pay credits. The mark-up was said to cover transportation costs, spoilage, and losses.[93]

In some ways, the operation of the Jesuit "company store" at Loreto worked in favor of soldiers and their families. They ordered supplies through the padre procurador who delivered them at prices that reflected careful buying. Even with the Jesuits' high transportation charges, most goods were less costly than at mainland presidios.[94] In 1718, Hermano Coadjutor Jaime Bravo reported that people at Loreto were charged from ten to fifty percent less than prices current at "other presidios" for a long list of items that included many popular forms of yard goods, most kinds of ready-made men's and women's clothing, horses, mules, writing paper, knives, tobacco, sugar, and more.[95] In 1729, viceroys began to regulate the prices charged to soldiers at northern presidios,[96] but California's maverick presidio was ignored in the process. Even so, as nearly as can be told from fragmentary and indirect records, the California supply system continued to deliver food and goods at lower prices.[97]

An incident in 1741 showed that California soldiers had learned how their pay scale and costs contrasted with those of their mainland brethren. The independent presidio at San José del Cabo had recently been suppressed and its command returned to the captain of the presidio of Loreto. The troops in this unit, now called the *escuadra del Sur* (the squadron of the South), were fresh from experiences with pay and supplies channeled through an independent captain, and the lessons were not lost on their fellows at Loreto. In concert, the men of the two divisions of the presidio signed a document requesting that the procurador de Californias in Mexico City continue to pay them in effects, as had always been the practice at Loreto.[98]

The Dependence of Jesuit California on Jesuit Sonora

Before their campaign to open California began, Salvatierra and Kino foresaw that money alone might not be able to sustain their California venture. Both padres recognized that Mexico City and Guadalajara were far away and emergencies were inevitable. Their prospective settlement would need a nearby, reliable source of food.[99] Therefore, Padre Kino pioneered missions that had the potential to create surpluses of livestock, missions located in the Sonoran territories near the part of California that he hoped to evangelize.[100] Coincidentally, Kino's own mission field, the Pimería Alta, lay just north of the most populous and prosperous of all the Jesuit missions, those along the broad, fertile banks of the Río Yaqui.

Kino and Salvatierra were men of stature who had regular dealings with important figures in society, finance, politics, and the church. They met little opposition when they decided to use Sonoran missions as their springboard and larder. No other Sonoran Jesuits had wide influence; none would have been likely to oppose contributions to so popular a venture as that of brother Jesuits opening California. Thus, as soon as Salvatierra's cross was planted on the opposite shore, Sonoran missions began to feel the pressure of his needs. One of his ships returned for provisions immediately after depositing the first shore party, and at least five more crossings for supplies were made during the first year of the settlement.[101] In October 1700, Kino collected and shipped seven hundred cattle donated by Jesuit missionaries in the Pimería and Sonora.[102]

In 1701, Salvatierra joined Kino on one of his many explorations northwest in the Pimería Alta, this time to look for a usable land route to California.[103] That objective was not achieved, but on his return to Guaymas, Salvatierra seized the opportunity to establish San José, a "California" mission that could serve as a supply depot near the great harbor.[104] Meanwhile, Salvatierra and Kino continued their letter-writing campaign to people in high places. In response, Padre Provincial Francisco de Arteaga congratulated Kino on the discovery of potential mission sites in the northwest, "because those missions, once established, will become the support of California."[105] Padre Juan María informed Tirso González, the Jesuit general in Rome, that Arteaga had instructed his missionaries in Sinaloa and Sonora to provide assistance to California. Salvatierra asked González to thank the helpful provincial and the missionaries who had responded with contributions.[106] The padres' active correspondence reflected not only California's long-term dependence on outside help, but also the acute food shortages at Loreto in 1701 and 1702. Shipments from the Pimería and Yaqui missions enabled the colony to survive.[107]

Padre General González conferred several powers on Salvatierra to facilitate his leadership, one of which was the right to transfer any unneeded or undesired missionary from California to Sonora or Sinaloa.[108] In 1703, Salvatierra used that power to send Padre Gerónimo Minutili to Sonora. There, he was trained by Kino and placed at Tubutama, a mission that raised cattle and served as a way station between Kino's headquarters at Misión de los Dolores and San José, the new California mission at Guaymas.[109] A year later, Kino sent the Jesuit general a glowing description of progress in California — and reminded him of the importance of the Sonora-California relationship by enumerating the contributions he was able to make through San José de Guaymas.[110] From 1702 to 1704, food shipments from the Pimería Alta and Yaqui missions continued to be crucial to Loreto's survival.[111]

In 1704, Salvatierra sent Padre Piccolo, his right hand, to Guaymas to further develop Misión de San José and to thank the missionaries of the Yaqui and encourage their continued support. Piccolo received many cattle from

Kino, most of which he shipped to needy California. Piccolo also received the news that he had been appointed padre visitador of the Sonoran missions.[112] Letters he wrote during his four years as visitador show that he kept close contact with Padres Kino and Minutili and channeled needed supplies to California.[113]

In 1706, Eusebio Kino still had his mind on what he called "the little sister across the gulf."[114] His plans were as ambitious as ever, encompassing nothing less than a ring of missions around the head of the gulf to serve and lead to the peninsular missions.[115] Padre Piccolo, then his superior, wrote to thank him for his continuing assistance to "the poor padres of California."[116] In 1709, while California suffered serious epidemics and food shortages, Kino rallied support. He heard from Salvatierra that, by disposition of the Jesuit general, Kino's principal obligation was to help California.[117] He had been the first driving force behind the Jesuits' return to California. During the twenty-six years after his own mission to the peninsula was suspended, he was probably the most vital benefactor of the new mission that took its place. Kino died in 1711 at age sixty-six. He has been recognized for his vision, but his efforts toward, and material contributions to, the development of the peninsular mission have been under-appreciated in California annals.

In 1709, Piccolo's term as visitador in Sonora ended, but not before another California missionary was strategically placed in Sonora. Padre Juan Manuel de Basaldúa, founder of Misión de Santa Rosalía de Mulegé, had been plagued by an unspecified chronic illness. It was decided that Piccolo, when he left Sonora, would take the post at Mulegé. Basaldúa, in turn, was sent to be missionary at Belén, the mission nearest the mouth of the Río Yaqui. Padre Miguel Venegas described the advantages of the transfer: "With this placement, Padre Basaldúa was able to provide much assistance to California; Guaymas has a spacious and protected port close to California and therefore is its most immediate recourse in case of urgent necessity. From here, Padre Basaldúa was able to provision the ships that shuttled across [the gulf]."[118]

Basaldúa's illness and transfer presaged a pattern in California affairs not likely to have been coincidental. Between 1709 and 1727, just five Jesuits were retired from California service. Each was represented as too ill to carry on such strenuous work; each was transferred to a missionary post in Sonora, and four of them ultimately were placed at prosperous missions on the Yaqui.[119] Padre Pedro de Ugarte's transfer elicited revealing words from Venegas: "Padre Juan María de Salvatierra ordered him [Ugarte] to the mission of Tórim on the Yaqui River because there he would be of the greatest use and advantage to California; he would be like a procurador for them, acting to gather up contributions, buy corn and cattle, and expedite shipping."[120] By the 1730s, California's demands on Sonora were so institutionalized that Padre Venegas was able to write:

> In addition to their annual supplies sent from Mexico City to the port of Matanchel . . . , the [California] padres solicit provisions and other necessities

from the missions of the other coast, sending now to the port of Yaqui, now to that of Ahome, and again to that of Guaymas. From these places they obtain what they need in exchange for California products: wine, panocha, native incense, and similar things.[121]

Padre Ignacio María Nápoli was transferred from California to Sonora or Sinaloa in 1726.[122] By 1735 — and probably before — he was shipping seed grains from Ráhum to Loreto in response to requests from Padre Jaime Bravo, the procurador in Loreto.[123] During his service in Sonora, Nápoli became known to Don Manuel Bernal de Huidobro, civil governor of the territory. When Bernal de Huidobro went to California to quell the rebellion in the South, he sent for Nápoli, hoping that the founder of Misión de Santiago might be able to help pacify the mission's rebellious neophytes. At the end of 1736, after several months of inconclusive efforts on the peninsula, Padre Nápoli was returned to Sonora to direct three adjacent missions on the Yaqui: Ráhum, Huírivis, and Pótam.[124] Meanwhile, California was beginning one of its worst famines, which Nápoli may have witnessed before he left. His response can be judged from eleven letters that California Jesuits wrote to him between 1737 and 1739.[125] First, it should be noted that all the California writers addressed Nápoli as "Padre Procurador," whereas no mainland writer used that title in any of thirty extant letters sent to him during that period. Jaime Bravo, then the padre procurador in Loreto, prefaced a request with the phrase, "since you are our procurador in those missions. . . ."[126] California's leader, Padre Visitador Sebastián de Sistiaga, wrote:

> Our procurador, you are doing good works. Thanks to God and His Blessed Mother . . . may they repay Your Reverence for the solicitude, care, zeal, and love with which you oversee the good of these poor missions and missionaries, helping meet their needs alike with whatever you have in your mission, or by begging aid and alms from the others. To show my affection, I had desired to send you a cask of wine, but none has come down to Loreto and what we have on hand is no good. Patience until another sailing.[127]

But Padre Nápoli, and California, faced an unusual problem: by 1739, Sonora itself was experiencing a famine of major proportions caused by an extended drought that ended in torrential, unseasonable rains. In the past, stores of grain and large herds of cattle had provided relief from such hardships. Nápoli, and his neighboring missionaries, had to make a choice between providing help to distressed California, or doling out their stores to alleviate Sonora's woes. The resident fathers broke with their local tradition; in 1739, they announced that they were reserving the bulk of their surplus provisions for the California missions. A small detachment of soldiers from the presidio of Loreto was sent to help Padre Nápoli in obtaining food from the Yaqui missions and to guard it while it was transported to a waiting California ship.[128] When neophytes in the flood-damaged region approached the prosperous

Yaqui missions for relief, they were turned away empty-handed. Allegedly, when Nápoli finally relented and released a niggardly amount of maize for sale, he demanded an exorbitant price.[129] At about the same time, Jaime Bravo, from Loreto, reproached Nápoli for denying help to Sonora's gente de razón, saying that a Jesuit had written that miners in Baroyeca complained that Nápoli had sold several hundred bushels of grain for silver and at very high prices.[130]

Whatever the details may have been, Padre Ignacio María Nápoli and his allegiance to California became key issues in the greatest uprising by native peoples against the Spaniards in the history of northwest New Spain.[131] The Yaqui revolt lasted fitfully for over two years; a thousand gente de razón and perhaps five thousand Yaqui and Mayo were killed. When it was over, civil authorities began to investigate its causes and take steps to prevent a recurrence. The neophytes had several reasons to complain but bitterly resented being required to work without pay to grow food for California and to haul it to ports and load it on boats. Such aired grievances struck at the heart of the Jesuit mission system. The padres had taught their neophytes to believe that they formed mission communities and that all their labor served communal purposes, that they truly worked for themselves. The argument that their labors were communal when their fruits were expended to further Jesuit goals over the horizon was far too abstract for the Yaqui to accept.[132]

The Yaqui revolt permanently changed life in the Jesuit missions of Sonora. Their people won greater freedom. They came and went almost as they wished, and fewer labored in mission fields or with mission herds. The missions thus produced less and never again had the great surpluses they had once enjoyed. Sonora's problems underscored the fragile, economically impractical nature of the mission to California. After forty years, it still depended on imported food. When the Yaqui revolt was over, California still begged food from Sonora, though the demands were lighter and less frequent.[133] The procurador in Loreto turned to Sinaloa to purchase needed food rather than to ask for contributions.[134]

Many of the world's isolated frontier settlements survived because they achieved a degree of self-sufficiency. Peninsular California never achieved that status in Spanish times. The Jesuit mission would survive for seventy years through an efficient, dedicated supply system, an integrated network linked to Guadalajara, Mexico City, and sister missions on the mainland. Procuradores, coadjutores, arrieros, and marineros were the unsung facilitators of a difficult operation.

SIX

The Presidio of Loreto

 Spanish presidios along the northern frontier of New Spain loom large in the legends of the region. Like most legends, these reflect romanticized and distorted perceptions. Presidios were not fortresses, they were not commanded or manned by trained military personnel. Their men seldom looked or acted in a manner to match a contemporary European's idea of a professional soldiery. The presidios in question were frontier garrisons manned by people more akin to militiamen than traditional soldiers. Captains of presidios were often Spaniards with military experience, but many were merchants, miners, or cattlemen who aspired to the power and perquisites of the post. Most presidial soldiers were recruited in the general areas of the presidios, lived there with their families, and retired there as well. Viceroys appointed presidial captains and gave them the responsibility to protect missions, settlers, mines, and the trade routes that made all the other activities possible. Presidial soldiers were the instruments of this protection, but their quasi-military chores seldom filled even a majority of days in a year. During times when demands on presidios were low, these men engaged in most of the same activities that occupied the rest of the frontiersmen.[1]

The Control and Financing of the California Presidio

During its first few years, Loreto's presidio was less a fact than a report. Padre Juan María de Salvatierra, the leader of the California Jesuits, was also the de facto governor or captain who controlled the activities of the presidio and made the arrangements for supplies and personnel — as he did for every other aspect of the conquest. Manpower at the presidio varied from a dozen soldiers to thirty or more and the numbers and the men changed frequently. Some "volunteers" were serving at the pleasure of benefactors who wished to provide enough manpower to see the Jesuit mission safely launched. Most of those enlistees stayed only long enough to satisfy their patrons at home. Two events attracted unwelcome attention to the state of affairs in California. In 1700, Salvatierra had to renege on his promise to finance his mission privately, and, in 1701, complaints against the missionaries by their own captain began to be heard in Mexico City.[2] Thereafter, the California Jesuits began to make changes that might create the form and perception of a more orthodox presidio. During Salvatierra's six years of contention with Virrey Alburquerque (1705–1711), less ambitious men were recruited as soldiers to give the presidio greater stability. Separate books were prepared in which to record the presidio's finances. Military affairs were reported to the viceroy in terms that implied a somewhat autonomous royal presidio, an entity separate from the mission, but there was no alteration in the presidio's agenda. Its operations were directed primarily toward the evangelical conquest.[3]

The Duque de Albuquerque and his superiors in the new Bourbon regime questioned the wisdom of allowing Jesuits to control any part of the king's military arm. Their position was strengthened by Salvatierra's requests that the royal treasury help to finance his mission undertaking. Albuquerque and other officials saw no reason why the padre should continue to enjoy all the concessions made to him when he promised to establish the desired presence in California at no cost to the crown. In 1706, the viceroy announced his intent to relieve the Jesuits of their special powers and to open California to colonists and normal economic development.[4] Salvatierra, his Jesuit cohorts, and their supporters bombarded governmental figures with counter-arguments, not the least of which was the relative success of the California mission—a success which to that time had been financed largely through Jesuit efforts.

Finally Albuquerque overplayed his hand. Salvatierra consulted elder statesmen of his order and, with their support, offered to relinquish the California mission so that the crown could award it to another order. The viceroy made his own consultations and concluded that he had no workable alternative to the Jesuits. He conceded by paying out a small part of the royal funds already owed to California by decree and by dropping, for the time, all threats to revoke the Jesuits' control of their military support.[5]

When Albuquerque changed his stand on Jesuit control of soldiers from outright opposition to de facto recognition, he established a precedent that would help to preserve California's unique presidio, but the specter of Bourbon intervention and the threat of change stimulated the California missionaries to justify the precious concessions they had received. When negotiations in 1717 resulted in putting twenty-five of their soldiers on the royal payroll, the Jesuits decided to reveal and explain their California modus operandi. They wrote precise rules to codify the positions, responsibilities, rights, and limitations of every person in the colony. Very few situations were not anticipated by some explicit rule.[6]

Elaborate legal codes and legislation proposing to regulate every aspect of social and economic life were typical of the Spanish presence in the New

World. Convoluted laws arose from governing complex societies with influential civil, religious, and military sectors. Pressure from these different factions often resulted in controls or concessions that were incompatible with each other or with the limits of the royal budget. Councils, courts, and viceroys were forced to compromise. Viceroys' archives bulged with complex proclamations and regulations from Spain that, because of slow communications and lack of information about New World conditions, were outdated or unworkable in the colonies. Laws of the period should not be read today with the assumption that they reflected legal, economic, or social realities. Superiors tacitly accepted the fact that a viceroy could acknowledge, or "obey" orders without acting upon them.[7]

Recruiting for the California Presidio

California Jesuits regularly discharged employees who did not meet their standards, but replacements were usually at hand. Times were hard in New Spain, and jobs were scarce. The Jesuits recruited by offering the rare inducement of fair wages paid regularly.

Spain, Iberian and colonial, was controlled by a pervasive bureaucracy, an awesome structure that towered high above its common citizens. Lost in the clouds were a legendary king, bishops, ministers, and councils, but at the level of frontier communities, power lay in the hands of priests, petty civil authorities, and presidial captains. Of these, only the military regularly found jobs for significant numbers of local men with no fortunes or connections. For a common man, enlistment at the presidio offered access to the power structure, even if it was but a toehold at a low level. A soldier had security, a degree of credit, and the possibility of a modest grant of land, a valuable asset that many captains had the power to bestow or arrange. These things tended to offset the fact that a soldier's pay was low and, outside California, often in arrears. Younger or illegitimate sons with little inheritance or education could gain prestige and perhaps property through honorable military service. Criminals and exiles enlisted at the presidios as a step toward social rehabilitation. The military was virtually the only government service, and therefore source of royal salaries, available to two major blocks of New Spain's population: *castas*, people of mixed blood, and Hispanicized Indians.[8] Both offered willing recruits, although some employers, including California Jesuits, discriminated against them.[9]

All over New Spain, when practical qualifications were similar, a Spaniard was preferred over other men for employment or advancement. Second in desirability was a *criollo*, a person of primarily European descent born in the New World. In the eyes of the law, a native American stood next, but this dictum had little or no social reality. In practice, below any white man, the order of descending prestige was: mestizo, mulatto, black, and finally Indian.[10]

During New Spain's first century, Indians and castas were usually excluded from royal military service, but in the course of the next century, the frontier and the presidios in the north and northwest became more remote from cities and supplies. The furious battles of the Chichimeca Wars dwindled to minor skirmishes in areas that bordered hostile Indian territory. Spaniards and even creoles became increasingly difficult to lure into service in these isolated, poor regions. People with criminal records or mixed blood gravitated to the frontier precisely because their skills were needed and prejudice yielded somewhat to that need.[11] Presidial captains were allowed considerable discretion in dividing up their budgeted payrolls, and some preferred to hire castas at low pay rather than to use higher wages to lure whites. This temptation was particularly strong in Sinaloa and Sonora where the poorer, landless part of the Hispanic population was strongly casta. That group formed the likeliest pool for militia duty or presidial service. By 1700, California drew the majority of its recruits from the same pool.[12]

Jesuit authorities in California readily employed castas and neophytes from the mainland as artisans, sailors, and servants; in the greater society of New Spain, such people regularly provided these services.[13] The Jesuits were less inclined to hire castas as soldiers; a study of Loreto's muster rolls and other pertinent documents indicates that the Jesuits hired a greater percentage of Europeans and creoles than were found at other presidios of northwest New Spain.[14] A soldier's role in California was quite different from that of his mainland counterparts. The missionaries were grudgingly aware that a soldier would serve to some extent as a role model for new converts and would be responsible for their discipline. Therefore, the padres excluded all men with records as criminals or exiles and tried to hire whites in the belief that they would maintain a greater distance from the native people and better represent European ideals.[15] Moreover, in California, missionaries and soldiers were thrown together for company. At each isolated mission, this meant one padre and one soldier. For weeks or months on end, a soldier would be the only person with whom a padre could have any real conversation.[16] Jesuit missionaries were urban sophisticates, products of polite society, and bearers of its manners and prejudices. They preferred to associate with Europeans rather than with frontiersmen from New Spain. However, Europeans were not to be a major factor in California's growing Hispanic population. Most men from the Old World served briefly at Loreto and moved on. Most did not bring wives or families. The majority of men who served at length, raised families, and retired in peninsular California were bred near the northwest frontier of New Spain.

In part, the recruitment of frontiersmen reflected necessity; they were near at hand when urgent needs arose for infusions of manpower. The rebellion of 1734 in *el Sur de California*, as detailed earlier, inspired a call for help that was answered by at least thirty gente de razón from across the gulf. Similar needs developed on the mainland and California reciprocated. The Yaqui revolt in Sonora in 1740 necessitated the formation of protective militia companies in adjacent areas. At least eight recruits in these hastily formed squads had recently served in California, and several others can be identified as men who later served on the peninsula. The pool of manpower in the greater area numbered only a few hundred men capable of fighting; some at least were prepared to go where they were most needed.[17]

In quieter times, the Jesuits chose carefully from this population. Their selections reflected both research and connections. During the first few years, men hired as soldiers came largely from substantial families in the environs of Compostela (see Map 5.1) where the Jesuits had interests of their own and an important benefactor who could suggest candidates and influence them to serve. A decade or two later, the presidio at Loreto began to attract some legacies from those early contacts in Compostela, sons and other relatives and connections of pioneers. California missionaries also depended on brother Jesuits who ran an administrative center and school at Villa de Sinaloa, an old presidio on the Sinaloa River (see Map 1.1).[18] Sinaloan Jesuits knew most of the dozens of young men growing up in their area and could provide candid opinions to guide those who hired for California. Most of the men from Compostela and perhaps half of those from Villa de Sinaloa were literate, reflecting the family background of the former and the educational opportunities of the latter.[19] Few presidios of the time appear to have hired so many literate men.

In drawing on these manpower pools, the California missionaries unwittingly followed a century-old pattern in which leaders in the northern expansion of New Spain hired the sons and grandsons of people who had carved out the previous frontier to help them to establish the next. The logic was inescapable; not only were they near at hand, they also were acclimated to many of the conditions and problems that would have to be faced. They embodied a working frontier culture which they would literally transfer to a new land by their presence. They practiced most of the crafts and other skills needed by a small, new colony.

Despite the advantages of their backgrounds and the advice that led the missionaries to hire them, the men available often did not conform to the requirements and preferences of their California employers. Jesuit historian Miguel Venegas's description of hiring practices betrays the common upperclass perspective of his day—as well as the absurd impracticality of yet another royal decree.

When there is a shortage of men at the presidio, they accept only those who come in response to summons or who volunteer of their own free will. By royal decree it is forbidden for any man not an español to be enrolled at any presidio, or to be accepted as a soldier. But because such men are scarce in regions so remote, and because it is not feasible to bring them from New Spain, it is impossible to observe this law in every particular. Although the Fathers would like to select as soldiers only the best that could be found, nevertheless, in those regions beyond the sea they are compelled by necessity to accept such soldiers as are available—mulattoes, mestizos, lobos, coyotes, and others of similar sort. Some of these, in their varying shades of color and

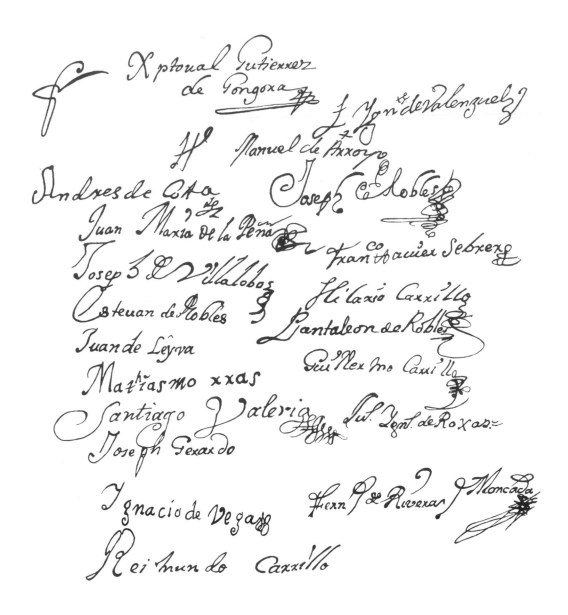

Figure 6.1 Signatures of Soldiers at the Presidio of Loreto, 1751

in the evil composition of their mixed blood, presently reveal the baseness of their character.[20]

> When it is necessary to accept as soldiers . . . persons of mixed blood, it is right that some distinction should be made between them and true españoles. They are told, when accepted, that they will receive only half-pay. This applies merely to the first two years. If they conduct themselves well and it is felt that they are necessary and useful after this lapse of time, they are given full pay as by special favor. In this way the fathers gain another advantage: they can increase the number of enlisted men in the presidio by giving some half-pay. Consequently, as a rule, there are more soldiers in the presidio than those for whom the King pays.[21]

By 1733, the frugal Jesuits started everyone they could, white or casta, as a *media plaza*, a man on half-pay. He remained in this lower position until he proved his worth or was discharged.[22]

Loreto's muster rolls for the years 1700–1767 are too scarce to be used to trace each soldier's career, but they and other occasional records provide insights into the racial composition of the presidio. Few *pardos*, or dark-skinned men, were ever hired, and even the lighter castas, such as mestizos, were hired less often than at other western presidios.[23] However, many men and women who passed as white and were called españoles at Loreto probably had some Indian or African blood. Along the frontier, any person with one parent a Spaniard or an apparently white creole and the other a white or light casta could be accorded español status.[24] Rules and practices in these matters were far apart. Popular, wealthy, or indispensable individuals were often perceived and publicly recognized as one or two shades lighter than less favored folk of similar heritage. Human nature, as well as law and custom, was always at work.

Despite their continuous efforts to choose well-recommended recruits and to weed out those who failed to perform to their satisfaction, the missionaries never ceased to deplore the quality and behavior of the men they hired. The Jesuit historian Miguel Venegas, writing in the 1730s, called California's soldiers "the greatest cross the missionaries had to bear."[25] However, this and other diatribes formed parts of arguments intended to impress viceroys and audiencias and to foster the perception that California soldiers could be kept in line only if the padre visitador in California had complete power over them. Venegas's description of the same Jesuits' dismissal of unsatisfactory soldiers suggests the degree to which they were accustomed to managing public perception:

> In the case of soldiers who leave because they are dismissed, the fathers charitably endeavor in every way to have regard for their credit and good name, and so they conceal everything that might be a blemish upon their reputation . . . and they refrain from saying that the men have been dismissed. Sometimes the fathers arrange that soldiers, dismissed for secret faults, publicly offer their resignations.[26]

Despite the rhetoric, California Jesuits found cooperative and reliable men, as evidenced by many soldiers' good performances and long service.

Regulations for Soldiers in California

Venegas explained how the indoctrination of California recruits was handled:

> ... when they first arrive for service at the presidio, there is read to them the grant of authority to the superior of the missions. Thereby they can understand the deference they must show to the superior, the obedience they must render to their captain, and, finally, the privileges they will enjoy because of military service in California."[27]

No document spells out the privileges promised during the years before 1719. A list from that year reflects the agreements reached by Hermano Jaime Bravo and Virrey Valero. Here, the Jesuits were concerned with emphasizing that soldiers at the California presidio were the equals of those maintained by the king elsewhere in northwest New Spain.

> 1   They shall enjoy all the rights and privileges that His Majesty grants to all the other officers and soldiers in his royal armies.
>
> 2   Their services shall be counted as performed in active warfare in the same way that this privilege has been granted to the soldiers of El Parral and certain other presidios.
>
> 3   Since His Majesty now pays the wages of the California soldiers, they are to be fixed, not in accordance with those of Veracruz, but on a scale with those of Sonora, Sinaloa and Nueva Vizcaya, the soldiers of which are paid more because they live in more remote places.[28] Similarly, the sailors will be paid as in Acapulco and not as in the Caribbean Fleet.
>
> 4   Their certifications of military service signed by the [Jesuit] superior of the presidio shall be accepted without question as if all the authority were actually subject to the Royal Audiencia of Guadalajara and the central government.[29]

These formalities aside, the Jesuits set down the specific regulations to which their soldiers would be subject, thereby codifying the rules they had tried to enforce since the beginning of their mission in California.

> After this [recitation of their privileges] they are informed of the rules which the father visitors have established to ensure their proper conduct. The most important of these are the following.[30]
> They are not to devote themselves to pearl fishing, although they are not forbidden to buy pearls from the Indians.[31]

They are not to subject the Indians to annoyance or set them a bad example.

Those who are married on the other coast shall not leave their wives there, but shall bring them along unless they are legally divorced.

Those who have children shall send them to school at Loreto to learn to read and write, and they shall pay the teacher his just fee.[32]

In addition to his weapons, each soldier shall keep two horses of his own,[33] and soldiers who leave the country shall sell their horses to someone else. They shall take turns, one after another, in taking care of the horses belonging to all of them according as they are assigned to this duty by the captain.

They shall be ready to take part in all military expeditions that may be made according as they are chosen for them.

Those who serve as guards at the missions shall be obedient to the fathers, and shall employ themselves in any task they are commanded to perform, in accordance with the practice and the needs of each mission.

Those who are stationed at the presidio shall be prompt to conform with the military practices there maintained.

Finally, they shall live as Christians should, and shall be a united body, preserving peace and harmony among themselves.

There are other injunctions, similar to the foregoing, by which the fathers seek to instruct the new recruits, so that they may comply with their obligations both as soldiers and as Christians. For this purpose they give talks in Spanish on spiritual topics to the soldiers at the presidio in addition to instructions to the Indians in their own tongue. The fathers see to it that the soldiers observe a Christian mode of life, that they hear Mass every day with proper attention and reverence, and that they repeat in chorus and with devotion the Rosary of María Santísima, and finally her Litanies. On Saturdays when this is over the fathers relate to them some instance of devotion to the Virgin Mary and exhort them to live as Christians and to receive the sacraments at some of the festivals during the year.

All evidence suggests that soldiers of the presidio of Loreto were substantially held to these rules throughout the Jesuit years. Nevertheless, men were attracted by the stability of the Jesuit organization coupled with the guarantee that California soldiers "shall enjoy all the rights and privileges which His Majesty grants to other officers and soldiers in his royal armies." In reality, that grand-sounding "privilege" was largely a mirage. All royal soldiers enjoyed the corporate prestige of royal service. Only a few fundamental rights and privileges were spelled out: limited benefits involved with retirement, legal protection, and reduction of certain taxes and fees. Because of merit or connections, some of the soldiers in other parts of the Spanish colonial domain were granted rewards like land titles, access to native labor, grazing rights, or ownership of domestic animals other than their mounts. These privileges might be bestowed by captains, governors, or viceroys. In New Spain's presidios, such concessions were especially prevalent and important. They attracted men to the military and contributed to local economic development.[34]

In California, relatively high wages and the Jesuits' prompt payments and fair dealings had to substitute for most of the fringe benefits enjoyed by mainland soldiers. California soldiers, from captain to recruit, signed a contract that made them servants of the missionaries. They were forbidden to employ California natives to do any labor. They were forbidden to fish for pearls, although in one significant concession they were allowed to deal with the natives in buying or trading for pearls.[35] Soldiers were not allowed to import commodities to sell or trade. The Jesuits who employed them set the low rates they could charge for private service as shoemakers, tailors, barbers, carpenters, and so forth. They were prevented from owning land or running their own herds because the missionaries argued that usable land, water, and pasture were so scarce that the missions needed it all. In fact, private grazing at some distance from missions could have been allowed and would have added significantly to food supplies, but the padres feared that this, like pearling, would lead to absenteeism and to misemployment of the natives. Such restrictions were justified and accepted in the early days of the colony when conditions were uncertain and manpower was at a premium, but in a few years career soldiers with growing families felt thwarted. Children meant added costs, but family men had no way to augment their incomes or gainfully employ their many children, usually a source of wealth in a frontier community.

In some ways, the peculiarities of the presidio at Loreto worked in favor of soldiers and their families. Around 1720, during his term as padre visitador, Juan de Ugarte initiated a policy of bestowing incentive pay on individuals with outstanding credentials or those who had displayed unusual zeal or productivity.[36] Moreover, though their pay — like that of all presidial soldiers — emanated originally from royal coffers, it did not pass through the hands of an unscrupulous captain. Pay was delivered regularly, and the captain had no opportunity to make deductions for any purpose or to make demands that his underlings serve his personal interests.[37] Supplies were generally less costly than those sold at mainland presidios.[38] There were no wine shops to extend credit, no money lenders were tolerated, no gambling was allowed. Soldiers were exposed to less temptation and were able to keep more of their earnings or to use them for relatively constructive purposes. These circumstances were made possible by the power placed in Jesuit hands and by the peninsula's isolation. They were unique to the presidio of Loreto and contrasted markedly with conditions in other presidios of New Spain.

California Jesuits were strict taskmasters; their soldiers probably worked harder at legitimate duties and chores than did their counterparts elsewhere. However, California soldiers were less likely to be asked to serve the private ends of their captain or his subalterns; officers at Loreto could have had little private business under those watchful religious eyes. Another important attraction for California service was its relative safety. In no other part of the heathen frontier were the bands of natives so small, their arms so primitive, or their warlike traditions so little developed—facts that became known in northwest New Spain as California's soldier pioneers returned to their mainland homes.[39]

Thus, California was a place of mixed blessings for its handful of incidental colonists. It was not designed for them, and it presented little opportunity for individual initiative. However, they were fairly treated in other ways. Their community atmosphere was unusually upright with a minimum of injustice, vice, or excess. It was a climate that attracted some and palled on many; the traffic of outgoing and incoming soldiers was brisk. Most left because they were discharged, but others must have done so out of frustration with such a paternalistic system.

California's rules were remarkable because they were formulated and administered by just one segment of Spanish authority: the religious. The Jesuits oversaw employee deportment at all times and made few compromises. Elsewhere, soldiers and servants had time at their jobs and time to call their own; employers were less involved in supervising the latter. Loreto and California were governed quite literally to the letter of their strict homegrown law. Rules codified for the operation of the religious colony provide a sketch of the directions and limitations that controlled the lives of California's people. The Jesuits' unusual requirements led to, or at least were linked with, the relatively disciplined behavior that became characteristic of the regional society. Most of these rules were peculiar to California, an important historical point. Assumptions about peninsular life under the Jesuits—civil, religious, military, or economic—should not be based on studies of corresponding mainland institutions. Distinctions arose early and were fundamental, none more so than the relationship between the father visitor and the captain of the California presidio.

The Capitán of the Presidio

The padre visitador of the Californias alone had the power to appoint a *capitán* for the presidio; his choice was then confirmed by the viceroy of New Spain. In guidelines laid out for the captain, the Jesuits called for an active and responsive surrogate who would appear to be the source of all commands. They hoped to blunt complaints from discharged soldiers who reported that they had taken their orders from missionaries, not officers. Venegas emphasized the captain's powers and duties—with no concurrent reference to the source of his orders:

> The government of the soldiers in both civil and military matters rests with the captain of the presidio by virtue of his office. He it is who commands them, who controls them, who gives them their orders as to what they shall do within the presidio and outside it. He it is who sends them on military campaigns, to make explorations, or to put down rebellions and uprisings. Finally, it is he who names the soldiers that are to reside at each mission. If some prove unsatisfactory to the fathers because of failure to comply with

their obligations, the captain sends others to take their place and recalls those first sent by transferring them to the presidio.[40]

The Jesuits were concerned about criticisms from government officials, military men, and influential citizens. They sought to present their captain as an equal to other royally approved presidial commanders. Venegas provided the imposing list of the California captain's powers and prerogatives that was proclaimed in New Spain.

1   He shall be chief justice of all California.

2   He shall be judge over the soldiers in military matters and also in matters political, civil, and criminal.

3   He shall likewise be governor and judge of all the other inhabitants such as sailors, the servants of the presidios and missions, and all the Indians.

4   He shall be the captain general not only of the land but also of the sea and coasts of California. Therefore, the chief ship of the presidio shall be called the *capitana*, and be entitled to enter all ports flying the flags proper to her rank. She shall omit to fly these flags only if she enters Acapulco when the Manila galleon is in port.

5   He shall be royal superintendent of all those who go to California to take pearls.[41]

Despite the duties, pomp, and trappings described in this and other documents, the California captain had no independent authority. The father visitor delegated power to the captain so that he could deal with the presidio's day-to-day affairs. In the Jesuit dictum, "the entire presidio, including captain and soldiers, should be subject to the authority of and at the disposal of the Padre Visitador . . . de Californias."[42] Viceroys had grudgingly acquiesced. The captain, therefore, was hired and retained at the discretion of the leader of the peninsular Jesuits. He was obliged to consult with the father visitor and carry out his orders and policies. In 1730, long after Salvatierra's death, this status quo was reiterated by a Jesuit visitor general during a tour of inspection: ". . . the Padre Visitador de Californias, since the beginning of the conquest, has been, and shall continue to be, the superior of the presidio; . . . its captain, workmen, soldiers, boatswains, boatswain's mates, and sailors take their orders from him."[43]

All presidial captains in New Spain, including the captain at Loreto, were subject to the ultimate authority of the viceroy, but mainland captains had no intermediate superior, particularly not one who lived in close proximity and oversaw every act. Manuel Bernal de Huidobro, governor of Sinaloa and Sonora and a presidial captain himself, scorned Loreto's military commander for his subservience.[44] This disrespect must have hurt the California captain in the eyes of his troops, most of whom were born and raised in Sinaloa or Sonora and were accustomed to their different pattern of authority.

However, California Jesuits were well served by the captains they chose. Esteban Rodríguez and his successors accepted the limitations placed on the captaincy and cooperated militarily with the primarily religious spirit of the undertaking they served. The California Jesuits' judgment and good fortune were emphasized in 1744 when, in an internally controversial decision, they renounced their power to appoint captains directly, yet continued to receive loyal support from the men given the post. Both Bernardo Rodríguez and Fernando de Rivera were recommended by a father visitor but were officially chosen and appointed by viceroys.[45]

Captains in Jesuit California[46]

Luis de Tortolero y Torres	1697–1699
Antonio García de Mendoza	1699–1701
Isidro Grumeque de Figueroa*	1701
Esteban Rodríguez Lorenzo	1701–1704
Juan Bautista de Escalante*	1704–1705
Esteban Rodríguez Lorenzo	1705–1744
Bernardo Rodríguez Larrea	1744–1750
Fernando de Rivera y Moncada	1751–1767

*Served too briefly to receive a viceregal appointment or royal confirmation.

The Alférez *and the* Teniente

The muster of soldiers at Loreto was short; twenty-five men garrisoned the presidio during most of its first forty years.[47] Some mainland presidios supported a captain, various lieutenants, sergeants, and corporals, but, for many years, the frugal Jesuits kept only a captain, an alférez, and one or two corporals.

The alférez was second-in-command. In the captain's absence, he assumed his superior's responsibilities, but in practice junior officers rarely had a hand in administration. California's correspondence and military affairs were simple and seldom pressing; most matters could be held in abeyance until the captain's return.

After 1741 when the second presidio, located in *el Sur*, was made dependent on Loreto and renamed the escuadra del Sur, it was commanded by a *teniente* (lieutenant). Thereafter, men of this rank also served as seconds-in-command at Loreto during all but two or three years when the post was vacant.

Alféreces

Isidro Grumeque de Figueroa	1698–1704[48]
Nicolás Márquez	1709–1710[49]

Juan Bautista Mugazábal	1714–1718[50]
José de Larrea	1718[51]
Francisco Cortés de Monroy	1719–1735[52]
Juan [Bernal] de Huidobro	1725–1727[53]
Juan del Valle	1725–1731[54]
José Antonio de Robles	1736–1737[55]
Juan Carrillo	174?–1748[56]
José Gerardo	1748[57]

Tenientes

Bernardo Rodríguez Larrea	1738–1744[58]
Pedro de la Riva [*Sur*]	1741–1751[59]
Cristóbal Gutiérrez de Góngora	1753–1755[60]
Blas Fernández de Somera	1758–1768[61]
Eugenio de Olachea [*Sur*]	1766[62]

Noncommissioned Officers

Loreto had no sergeants during the first three decades of the conquest. The post was introduced before 1733 and the presidio thereafter listed one or more *sargentos*. No document specified the exact nature of these men's work, but the job description in the royal regulations for presidios of northwest New Spain promulgated in 1772 probably gives a fair picture of the formal duties of the post:

> The sergeant should know from memory all the duties of the soldiers and corporals, and the penal laws, in order to instruct the company and to see to their compliance. He is not to overlook disorders, prohibited conversations, or incidents that might be contrary to obedience; he personally is to restrain and correct such things as quickly as possible, and to give a report afterward to his immediate superior, winning the respect of the soldiers by his good conduct and by the respect and obedience he gives to the officers.[63]

The same regulations urged that, whenever possible, literate men be chosen as sergeants. Each man known to have served as sergeant during California's Jesuit years was literate. After 1750, if not earlier, a sergeant at Loreto acted at times as company clerk.[64]

By 1715, California records show a soldier who held the rank of *cabo de esquadra* (corporal of the squad or detachment). He probably acted as a surrogate in the absence of a sergeant or a commissioned officer, conducted training and ceremonial drills, and received and relayed orders from officers to the appropriate soldiers.[65] An early and formal use of this title appears in a 1730 statement of the rights and responsibilities of the padre visitador; one was the power to choose "Capitán, Alférez y Cabo de Esquadra," as the three top positions at the presidio of Loreto.[66] The status of this rank is revealed in a 1751 muster of the presidio wherein Andrés de Cota and Fernando de la Peña appear on lines headed "cabo de esquadra" that fall below "sargento" and above "soldado."[67]

The simple term *cabo* (head or foreman) indicated a man other than a *cabo de esquadra* chosen to lead a detachment temporarily assigned to a specific task. Padre Clemente Guillén was escorted overland to La Paz in 1720 by a squad that included *el señor cabo* Ignacio de Rojas; Rojas was the soldier picked to lead that particular venture.[68] In another instance, the procurador de Californias in Mexico City sent a thousand pesos to the port captain in Acapulco to be given to "Alférez Don Juan del Valle, *Cabo del Barco de Californias*" so that he could pay his crew's expenses.[69] Serving as a cabo apparently brought no extra pay,[70] although it did confer a form of prestige evidenced in many non-military documents. In records of baptisms and marriages, for example, the name of Andrés de Cota usually appears, even after his death, preceded by the title "Cabo de Escuadra." To a lesser extent, this practice applied to Andrés López and Fernando de la Peña.

Sargentos

José Antonio de Robles	1730–1735[71]
Pedro de la Riva	1735–1741[72]
Cristóbal Gutiérrez de Góngora	1749–1753[73]
Manuel de la Torre Villavicencio	1751[74]
Francisco María José de Castro	1754[75]
Hilario Carrillo	c. 1752–1757[76]
José Francisco de Ortega	1757–1768[77]

Cabos de Esquadra

Juan Antonio Hinojosa	1715–1716[78]
Andrés López	1723–1724[79]
José Antonio de Robles	1727[80]
Andrés de Cota	1751[81]
Fernando de la Peña	1751[82]
Manuel de la Torre Villavicencio	1754[83]
José Francisco de Ortega	1756[84]

(Many officers and noncommissioned officers must have held their posts longer than the range of dates found in the scanty documentation.)

Common Soldados *in California*

During the seventy-year Jesuit stewardship of California affairs, the number of soldiers in their command varied from as few as eighteen to as many as sixty.[85] The fluctuations reflected the needs and economics of three distinct time periods. In the first, from 1697 to 1718, the California Jesuits themselves paid most of the cost of their presidio. When they feared attacks by the natives and planned extended explorations, they maintained as many as thirty-three soldiers. By 1701, it was apparent that the Californians presented less of a threat than had been feared. Many soldiers had come in the hope of finding opportunities to make fortunes and by that time were disillusioned and ready to leave. From 1701 to 1718, the number of soldiers at Loreto ranged from eighteen to twenty-six.[86]

In 1717, the deal was struck by which the crown agreed to support twenty-five soldiers in California, an arrangement that was not implemented for more than a year.[87] From 1718 to 1738, the Jesuits hired their allotted twenty-five men with royal funds and added as many others as they needed or could afford. Prior to the rebellion in *el Sur* in 1734, they kept around thirty men, but, because some were on half-pay, the requisition for royal funds typically reflected two or three men less than were carried on the payroll. Because of the rebellion, the number of troops at Loreto was raised to about sixty in 1735.[88] In 1738, the crown agreed to pay sixty soldiers, and divided them between Loreto and the newly formed Presidio del Sur de California at San José del Cabo. That distribution persisted until 1768 when the Jesuits were expelled.[89]

In 1729, following an inspection of the northern presidios of New Spain, Virrey Casafuerte issued a set of regulations for their future government. Specific provisions showed that the crown intended to protect the soldiers whose salaries they paid from private exploitation by their captains and from institutional exploitation by missionaries. In short, if they were paid to be soldiers of the crown, they were not to be worked for the benefit of others.[90] The presidio of Loreto was never visited by a royal inspector, nor was it specifically covered by Casafuerte's regulations. However, those regulations represented the views of most of the interested royal officials, and they implicitly condemned practices that had been commonplace in California since 1697. These rules and the related attitudes of high government figures probably emboldened Gobernador Bernal de Huidobro, during and after his 1736–1738 campaign in California, to voice his opposition to the way that the Jesuits employed and dominated their soldiers.[91] However, the frugal California Jesuits had reasoned from the start that strictly military duties would not fill the normal working hours of a force the size they needed to cope with probable challenges and emergencies. Their plans called for men who could perform a wide variety of services, few of which were strictly military. In the early years of the conquest, the need for skill and ingenuity was so intense that it dictated the choice of soldiers. Jesuit letters and reports from California depicted soldiers at work as masons, carpenters, leatherworkers, skippers, arrieros, vaqueros, farmers, scouts for trails and water holes, hunters of game, and collectors of native food plants. Most had skills in more than one trade. Individual missionaries, as well as the father visitor, came to realize the importance of having soldier-escorts with broad skills. Capable individuals were sought after and traded around.[92]

In spite of its small garrison, Loreto was the workshop for the entire conquest. This tiny body of men incorporated virtually the entire range of basic European technologies needed to sustain Hispanic life on the frontier. Survival depended on constant maintenance or replacement of every article that distinguished the newcomers' culture from that of the natives. Manufactured articles were not only slow, uncertain, and expensive to replace, but parts and even raw materials were lacking for long periods. As a result, there was a continual process of planing, carving, chipping, cutting, forging, riveting, grinding, punching, and stitching as the people of Loreto repaired their vital gear or manufactured replacements. Arms were overhauled, boats were scraped and caulked, pots and pans were soldered, tools mended, clothing darned and patched, and riding and pack gear restitched and gradually replaced.

Soldiers' uniforms were not, in fact, uniform. Different presidios adopted different cuts and colors.[93] Contemporary reports suggest that men at Loreto had no formal uniforms.[94] The Jesuits were practical, and they had virtually no visitors and little need to hold dress ceremonies. Only the captain and the alférez had uniforms appropriate to their rank, and they were outfitted at their own cost. For the other soldiers, local tailors and seamstresses, the latter often the soldiers' own wives, created coats and pantaloons in what they perceived to be the military style. To those outfits were added as purchased items boots and hats, but they apparently were not specifically military. The soldiers wore these hybrid "uniforms" to special events, like fiestas or ceremonies to greet a visitor general, and, in general, as their "Sunday best" attire.[95]

Soldiers in the field carried a heavy, knee-length coat, a garment made of several layers of buckskin bound together at the edges with a strong seam. This *cuera* was the presidial soldier's distinguishing feature and gave him the name by which he was known for over two centuries: *soldado de cuera*. A cuera was said to be able to resist penetration by arrows, but was also heavy (about seventeen pounds) and hot except during California's brief cool season. Soldiers did not wear cueras except in times of cold or danger; but when they slept, the many-layered garments gave welcome protection from the cold, dampness, and hard ground.[96]

The frontiersmen had firsthand experience with leatherwork. One or more soldiers at each presidio had enough skill to act as a *talabartero* (a proficient leatherworker). Such men were essential for the never-ending manufacture and repair of saddle and pack gear needed for a force that moved on horses, mules, and burros. They, or others with adequate skills, served as cobblers for the soldiers and other people of Loreto. The common footgear was the *tegua*, a rude replica of a conventional shoe, with supple leather uppers nailed to soles made of two or three thicknesses of hide. Teguas covered the entire foot and offered greater protection against California's omnipresent thorns than did open sandals.

Rawhide was prepared locally, although, at first, cured leather was obtained from Sonoran missions. However, leatherworkers in California quickly recognized local trees—most notably *palo blanco*—that yield tanbarks. Lime was already in demand as a constituent of mortar for masonry and *masa*, the dough for corn tortillas. Before long, simple kilns were built and limestone burned to make lime. With lime and a selection of local tanbarks, the hides of slaughtered cattle and of deer brought in by hunters were made into leather. The same curing processes were in use by peninsular ranchers in the late twentieth century.[97]

Descriptions of California soldiers' mounts and gear are rare and brief; Padre Jacobo Baegert provided one of the best.

> Their weapons are a sword, a musket, a shield, and an armor of four layers of tanned, white deerskin, which cover the entire body like a sleeveless coat. Otherwise they wear whatever they like; they have no uniforms. They serve on horseback or on mule, and because of the rugged trails, each man is obliged to keep five mounts. The soldiers have to buy these animals as well as their weapons, clothing, ammunition, and all their food.[98]

In addition to his animals, a soldier owned all the saddles, bridles, blankets, pads, and pack gear to fully equip his beasts for military, exploratory, or supply duty. One thread carries through all reports about the men of Loreto's presidio: they were exceptional riders and their mounts were superbly broken and conditioned. Experienced observers said they equaled or surpassed any of Spain's mounted troops in matters of hardiness and skill in the saddle.[99]

Over the years, European observers reported mixed opinions of the attainments of California soldiers in other military disciplines. However, all reports were tailored to the different needs of the writers. In 1730, Padre Visitador General José de Echeverría, in a letter to a benefactor, reported neat dress, orderly drills, and ready arms.[100] A few years later, Manuel Bernal de Huidobro, the anti-Jesuit governor of Sinaloa, belittled the men of California's presidio in every way.[101] Padre Baegert, always the most critical of the Jesuits, complained that they cared for little but riding, or running and rounding up cattle. In his eyes, they were not careful in their dress, did not care properly for their arms, and were ignorant of most military drills and courtesies.[102]

From the European viewpoint, some criticisms were justified. Most of California's early soldiers were Sinaloan or Sonoran cattle ranchers by birth and training. Their sons were later employed as soldiers, and their cultural pattern became even more attuned to California realities. In all the Jesuit years, these men had little need for the niceties of orthodox military training or behavior. During rare instances when fighting was necessary, great distances had to be traversed in intense heat, and an elusive enemy sought out in vast areas of broken, nearly waterless land. Soldiering under these conditions favored men who traveled light, who bore few arms and less armor, and who could break up into very small groups and move quickly whether advancing or retreating and

THE PRESIDIO OF LORETO

live off the land when necessary. Moreover, the technological skills of local frontiersmen were specifically appropriate to local needs; few European soldiers could have made similar contributions. California's jack-of-all-trades soldiers were eventually appreciated, whether or not they looked military to their European or mainland critics. Gaspar de Portolá, the last competent critic of the men of the "Jesuit presidio" and the first officer to bring Spanish troops to California, required only a month to conclude that many of his soldiers should be returned to the mainland and be replaced by men from the presidio of Loreto.[103] When Alta California was opened and supplies brought up the peninsula, *Californios*, men raised or born and raised in California, were compared to Catalans and recruits from nearby Sonora and Sinaloa. In spite of Spanish officers' initial prejudices, they soon reported that the Californios performed best.[104]

The Marinería at Loreto

Loreto was unique among the presidios of New Spain's northwest in its dependence on ships and in having a maritime branch, its *marinería*. The Jesuits needed a crew of sailors to man their craft, and another of craftsmen to keep them seaworthy.[105]

The colony's principal ship, the *Capitana*, provided and funded by the crown,[106] made the annual run to Acapulco or Matanchel and occasionally brought livestock from Sonora. This vessel required a captain and up to twenty men. Captains of Loreto's first ships were volunteers, usually sponsored by benefactors. Most were from Compostela, the home of most mariners and pearlers who worked out of the old port of Chacala (see Map 5.1). At times during the ensuing two decades, Salvatierra contracted with the same men, or others from Compostela, to take the ship on its annual supply run. At other times, particularly when the ship needed a major overhaul, one of California's padres was relieved of his mission duties and sent to Matanchel to supervise the work.[107] Over the years, the Jesuits had at least eight employees at Loreto, four of them Compostelans, who were competent to command the larger ships. Oddly, most were carried on the presidial books as soldiers or officers, never as ship captains.

Commanders of Loreto's Principal Ship

Capitán Esteban Rodríguez	1707[108]
Alférez Juan Bautista Mugazábal	1717[109]
Alférez Juan del Valle	1726–1732[110]
Soldado Juan Antonio Romero	1734[111]
Contramaestre Juan Agustín Sánchez	1738[112]
Sargento Cristóbal Gutiérrez de Góngora	1740, 1746–1750[113]

Soldado Nicolás de Peraza   1751[114]
Soldado Francisco Miguel de Aguiar   176?[115]

Two others, Compostelans Ignacio Pérez de Arce (1741–1746)[116] and Basilio de Rivera y Valle (1753–1756),[117] were specifically called ship captains and had formal command of the ships that carried annual supplies. They performed no other recorded service in California. Perhaps they contracted with the thrifty Jesuits to make supply runs only as needed. A full-time captain would demand a high salary, but would be under-employed for much of the year.

California's principal supply ship and its crew were based at the relatively snug, deep-water ports of Matanchel or Chacala (see Map 5.1). Loreto's open and shallow roadstead afforded no shelter from a storm and no adequate place to careen a sizeable vessel.[118] California lacked the planks, iron, and cordage needed for repairs. Further, the peninsular missionaries must have thought it unwise to have large groups of idle sailors on their hands during the intervals between voyages.

California Marineros

During the first forty years of the conquest, a group of sailors did live at Loreto: two crews to man the presidial sailing launches. Each was headed by an *arráez* (skipper), his assistant, and six or seven *marineros* (sailors).[119] Each man received about half a soldier's pay and more than earned it with his needed skills and fortitude. The colony depended on its larger craft as a lifeline to the mainland, but those ships were frequently out of service for extended periods. In the first fifteen years of the conquest, half a dozen were sunk or destroyed by storms.[120] Each loss placed a heavy burden on California's one or two launches. These tiny craft had to sail north and south along the coast to supply the peninsula's missions and frequently were needed to cross the gulf for emergency aid from Sonoran missions. Most of their sailing was tranquil enough, but since they were active throughout the year, they were exposed to severe seasonal dangers. The violent chubascos of summer and fall were notorious and could wreck any craft; the more common, cold "northers" of winter and spring could swamp a launch or drive it onto the peninsula's rocky, unsheltered eastern shore. Loreto's sailors, like most of their worldwide peers in those days, had considerable ability to recover from a mishap by effecting repairs and jury rigging their craft, but damage was occasionally irreparable. Some of the colony's darkest hours followed the loss of a launch. The hungry people of Loreto could then trust only to providence and scan the waters of the gulf hoping to spy a sail.

From time to time, accidents or lengthy overhauls changed the number of craft and crews at Loreto. In 1733, a total of thirty-nine seafarers manned two ships. By 1751, Loreto's muster listed eighteen men to crew the principal craft provided by the crown. Neither the launch usually maintained for trips to the other shore nor its crew were mentioned in the marinería muster for that year. Possibly the Jesuits laid off the crews of boats that were out of service.[121]

Around 1740, the number of seamen at Loreto was permanently reduced when a faster, less labor-intense method of carrying supplies to the most distant missions was adopted. Stores were sent by water rather than by mule trains. Two gulf-coast missions, one in the cape region and one near the northern mission frontier, were designated to receive the supplies and distribute them to neighbors. Each of the two missions provided its own launch, chose sailors from among its own neophytes, and employed a skilled arráez to command and navigate its cargo craft. Misión de Santiago performed this service for the missions in *el Sur*, while San Ignacio, Santa Gertrudis, and San Borja successively did the job in the north.[122]

During the Jesuit era, the majority of sailors on the northwest coast who were willing to work and live at Loreto were Filipinos, castas from the west coast of New Spain, or neophytes from Sonoran missions.[123] The Filipinos and castas were so important, in fact, that Padre Jaime Bravo petitioned the Audiencia of Guadalajara to excuse those with five years of California service from paying the tribute required by the law. In context, the purpose of his request was not so much philanthropic as intended to facilitate recruiting and holding these vital servants.[124] In time, California natives became good sailors and were regularly employed, but throughout the eighteenth century, Yaqui from Sonora made up a substantial percentage of Loreto's sailors.[125]

A few marineros who had important duties or long service appear repeatedly in Loreto's bookkeeping and anecdotal records. *Contramaestres* (boatswains) were prominent because they commanded Loreto's launches and became involved with handling sums of money and important messages. One contramaestre crossed the peninsula in the company of two or three sailors to take soundings for a chart of Puerto de Año Nuevo (now Bahía de San Juanico).[126] Another was given the unusual task of transporting potted plants across the gulf and tending them as he went.[127] Alas, the boatswains' misfortunes were more often recorded than their achievements. They were blamed for any damage or loss that occurred while they were in command.[128]

Contramaestres

Antonio Justo	1697–1701[129]
Sebastián Romero	1700[130]
Juan de Santo	1728–1733[131]
Guillermo Strafford	1721, 1741[132]
Juan Agustín Sánchez	1733–1758[133]
Pasqual Martín	1740[134]
Juan de Santiago	1751–1752[135]
Pedro Regalado de Soto	1733–1768[136]

Manuel de los Reyes   1756–176?[137]
José Joaquín de Robles   176?–1768[138]

Oficiales de Rivera

The Jesuit "naval base" at Loreto retained a crew of craftsmen, *oficiales de rivera*, as a beach gang in permanent residence. The group was headed by a *maestro herrero* (master blacksmith), a *maestro carpintero de rivera* (master shipwright), and a *maestro calafate* (master caulker and, usually, a rigging expert). Each of the maestros had two or three assistants, according to need. These artisans worked on the beach or very near it. Open structures called *tinglados* were built to provide shelter for men and materials. Tinglados were simply thatched roofs supported by forked tree trunks buried in the earth.[139] Each probably had a small, lockable room to store articles that might tempt theft. One tinglado served as a smithy with forge, anvils, and assorted tools, tanks, and troughs. Another housed the carpentry with its benches, vises, and clamps.[140] Nearest the beach, the caulkers stored their tools, hemp, and pitch. These workmen kept the necessities for careening launches or other small craft near at hand. Their gear included rollers and blocks-and-tackle to draw the boats high onto the beach, and tree trunks to prop them up. Rough planks and sawhorses were used as scaffolds for those who mended, scraped, caulked, and painted hulls.[141]

The oficiales de rivera who served at Loreto, with one exception, were castas.[142] They, like most of the sailors, were recruited in nearby mainland provinces, and they, too, were enlisted because of merit rather than for reasons of class or race. The California craftsmen must have been well chosen. They typically had long careers despite living and working under the noses of demanding employers. They were responsible for the upkeep of Loreto's smaller craft, the launches that plied back and forth to *la otra banda* for crucial food when the major ship was away or out of service. In 1755 and 1756, they were called on to do major overhauls on two ships, including replacing the exterior planking, and were praised by Loreto's padre procurador.[143] By and large, the boats on which they worked gave better service than did the larger craft that had to go to Acapulco or Matanchel to be careened. Moreover, when Loreto's craftsmen were called on to build larger ships themselves, their products performed admirably and served long and well.[144]

Calafates

Salvador Márquez (I)   1708–c.1740[145]
Salvador Márquez (II)   c.1740–1755[146]
Pedro Navarrete   1755?–1756[147]
José Joaquín de Robles   1756–176?[148]

Herreros

Juan Botiller	c.1730–c.1740[149]
Cristóbal Ascencio	c.1730–c.1755[150]
Juan Murillo	c.1760–c.1774[151]

Carpinteros

Manuel Murillo	c.1728–c.1760[152]
Francisco María Murillo	c.1756–c.1780[153]

The lives of Loreto's mestizo and mulatto craftsmen demonstrate that the frontier could be a haven for ambitious people of mixed blood. The majority founded families that made important contributions to the later population. Several were succeeded in their jobs by their own sons. Many of their descendants became landowners.

The Presidio of Loreto exemplifies the problem of studying California institutions through mainland counterparts. Loreto's unique religious direction gave it a different agenda and created different patterns of reports and records. The downfall of its Jesuit directors resulted in the loss or destruction of many of those records, during and after the expulsion. Moreover, neither of the major inspections of New Spain's presidios, that by Brigadier Pedro de Rivera (1725–1728) or that by the Marqués de Rubí (1766–1767), included Loreto. The peninsular presidio was thus ignored; all the data that was taken at other presidios during those inspections — and put into enduring records — had no California counterpart. Major studies of presidios have routinely avoided Loreto because of its atypical nature and the paucity of data on which to base a description and comparisons with other presidios.[154]

SEVEN

The Making of the Missions

Missions were the crux of the conquest.[1] During the first four decades of the Jesuit settlement, all Hispanic residents were missionaries or their paid assistants. Despite some rhetoric about the parallel royal agenda, soldiers, civilians, and converts alike took their orders from missionaries and toiled for the welfare of a miniature theocracy whose fundamental unit was a frontier mission.[2] In the Jesuit dream, missionaries would push out an ever-widening frontier, contact heathen, and add missions that would finally incorporate all of California's human geography. Their preliminary travail — tedious fund raising, procuring and transporting supplies, learning new languages, disciplining soldiers and servants — were borne as temporal costs of holy endeavors.

Both church and state expected missions to do more than effect religious conversions. The most idealistic Europeans came to the New World with the idea of transforming its people to look, act, and think like themselves. A half-century after the conquest of Mexico, mission practices were firmly directed toward the abolition of any pre-Christian practices, religious or secular, that were considered impediments to conversion or to integration with the greater Spanish economy.[3] As the Jesuits expanded their system of missions in northwest New Spain, they clung to the ideal of Europeanizing their converts in external matters such as dress, diet, and daily activities. They believed that people who looked and acted more like Europeans would also think and believe like Europeans.[4]

Before any instruction or conversion was undertaken, indigenous people had to be coaxed into congregating at mission centers, a tremendous change in their lives. At missions, people who had been members of autonomous bands had to be persuaded to accept a new concept: direct, tangible supervision by a judgmental higher power.[5] A mission's material offerings — stores of food, clothing, and a few simple manufactured items — may seem insufficient reason

TABLE 7.1 JESUIT MISSIONS IN CALIFORNIA (*Common names italicized*)

Mission Title + Indian Placename	Year	Founding Missionary
Nuestra Señora de *Loreto* Conchó	1697	Juan María de Salvatierra
San Francisco Javier de Biaundó [*San Javier*][a]	1699	Francisco María Piccolo
San Juan Bautista de Ligüí (or Malibat)[b]	1705	Pedro de Ugarte
Santa Rosalía de Mulegé	1705	Juan Manuel de Basaldúa
San José de Comondú[a]	1708	Julián de Mayorga
La Purísima Concepción de Cadegomó[c]	1720	Nicolás Tamaral
Nuestra Señora del Pilar de *la Paz* Airapí[d]	1720	Jaime Bravo
Nuestra Señora de *Guadalupe* de Huasinapí	1720	Everardo Helen
Nuestra Señora de *los Dolores* Apaté[e]	1721	Clemente Guillén
Santiago el Apóstol Aiñiní	1724	Ignacio María Nápoli
Nuestro Señor *San Ignacio* Kadakaamán	1728	Juan Bautista de Luyando
San José del Cabo Añuití	1730	Nicolás Tamaral
Todos Santos[f]	1733	Sigismundo Taraval
San Luis Gonzaga Chiriyaqui	1737	Lamberto Hostell
Santa Gertrudis de Cadacamán	1751	Jorge Retz
San Francisco de Borja Adac [*San Borja*]	1762	Wenceslao Linck
Santa María Cabujakaamung[g]	1767	Victoriano Arnés, Juan Díez

[a]moved after founding, but retained original placename
[b]mission abandoned in 1721; endowment used to found Los Dolores (q.v.)
[c]moved after founding and took on the placename of its new site
[d]moved to Todos Santos in 1748
[e]moved after founding, took new placename Tañuetía; moved again to a visita site, took name and
   placename of visita: La Pasión de Chillá
[f]site of two successive missions: Santa Rosa de las Palmas (1733), Nuestra Señora del Pilar de la
   Paz (1749)—the latter gradually came to be called Todos Santos; no Indian placename is known.
[g]originally located (1766) at Calamajué; moved 1767 and took new placename

for a people to have accepted so austere a regime as mission life, or to explain why they continued to tolerate it when they came to know its day-to-day reality. Part of the explanation must be sought in their old way of life, its rewards and successes balanced against its threats, trials, deprivations, and monotony.

The Californians who Attracted the Jesuit Mission

Very little can be known about some fundamental aspects of the peninsular Californian societies.[6] Only Jesuit missionaries had extended contact with them, and the former were bent on changing or obliterating the native cultures. The Jesuits recorded copious descriptions of Californians, but not as impartial observers. They omitted whatever was inconvenient and dramatized exotic details and what they perceived as general cultural backwardness. They sought to attract support for the Jesuit effort and convince their audience of the pressing need for Christian ministrations. They did not wish to portray functioning cultures, intact, and serving their people's needs, so Jesuits either did not describe social institutions and interpersonal relationships at all or did so in disparaging and belittling ways. As a result, little can be known about the peninsular people's religion, government, family life, or cultural traditions — and that little often has to be read between the lines, deduced or inferred from oblique or incidental references.

All California people believed in some form of deity. All had creation myths and various hero figures or personifications of forces of nature or of animals.[7] All had shamans who acted as intermediaries between the people and the supernatural. They interceded on the peoples' behalf to ward off illnesses, divert storms, ensure good harvests of pitahaya, etc. Beside the prestige of their positions, shamans exacted tribute in the form of food and offerings of hair that people cut from their own heads. If they were not satisfied with the attention and remuneration they got, they threatened to invoke the same scourges against which they purported to protect. Shamans equipped themselves with various symbolic devices — talismans carefully crafted of wood, intricately painted, carved, and inlaid with shell, mother-of-pearl, or pearls themselves. They made ceremonial cloaks from their people's offerings of hair. When engaged to treat the injured, shamans would wash and lick wounds. They blew upon or sucked at the bodies of ill patients through pipes or hollow reeds, or they manipulated the afflicted and, apparently by sleight of hand, appeared to remove mysterious intrusive stones or thorns they claimed had caused the sickness or pain. The Jesuits called all shamans *hechiceros*, or wizards. In the early years of the California mission, they made a sincere distinction between *hechiceros verdaderos*, true wizards, that actually had powers derived from pacts with *El Demonio*, the Devil himself, and *hechiceros falsos o embusteros*, liars or false prophets, charlatans who hoodwinked the people into believing they had any sort of supernatural power.[8] Later Jesuits discreetly dropped this issue. They referred to shamans either as quacks or, in the frontier context, as the misguided practitioners of heathen religion.[9]

Jesuits regularly noted the presence of the chiefs or headmen of bands that they encountered. This was particularly true during explorations when the cooperation of a headman could facilitate contact and lead to obtaining information and guides.[10] However, they recorded nothing about the way in which leaders were chosen, the degree of their power, the length of their tenure, or the nature of their duties.[11] The missionaries did give tacit evidence that these headmen were popular and successful when they appointed the same individuals to leadership roles in their mission organizations. The chroniclers made only occasional and incidental references to councils among Indians, presumably the familiar councils of elders. Their roles were never elaborated, though chiefs and elders were probably involved in preparations for the battles or skirmishes in which their bands were involved. All seventeenth- and eighteenth-century accounts of California that were based on extended Spanish contacts reported constant warfare or at least skirmishes between bands. These apparently had some bases in territorial disputes, but they often were of a more ritual character involving tests of manhood and solidarity of band members in carrying out what might best be called feuds, so small were the groups involved.[12]

Jesuits made numerous references to "marriages" arranged by Californians before they were converted and brought under mission influence.[13] Those of the Cochimí were the most stable and conventional to European eyes.[14] Those of the Guaycura and Pericú were described as more casual and shallow, with neither partner accepting much responsibility and the men, especially, not providing the support that the missionary chroniclers thought basic to such a relationship. Jesuits were scandalized by behavior that they called open adultery, by the apparent lack of adequate care for children, and by constant reports of abortion and infanticide.[15] They had no sympathy for rituals that had no recognizable European counterparts; one padre wrote:

> With boys and girls who have arrived at the age of puberty, with pregnant women, newborn children, and women in childbed, they . . . observe all kinds of absurd and superstitious rites, which for reasons of decency, cannot be described. . . .[16]

The Jesuits were shocked by the practice of killing the terminally ill and burying them forthwith.[17] Apparently, it did not occur to the missionaries that such isolated people, whose economy and problems in general so little resembled those of Europeans, might evolve relationships that did not correspond to European norms. In this, and in most judgments of alien cultures, the Jesuits displayed their most inflexible side and the least of their enlightenment.

It is easy to surmise that the long-range survival of the peninsular peoples had both evolved and depended on their cultural adaptations. Their bands were very small. The trading of sexual partners widely reported to take place between bands during occasional festivals would have enlarged the gene pools of both groups.[18] They often endured periods of drought or other phenomena that restricted their food supplies. Under such circumstances, abortion and infanticide were matters of survival. These people had no choice but to move constantly; at times they must have lacked the strength or the means to transport the very old or the very ill. Ending their lives must have seemed more humane than abandoning them.

Hispanic culture burst upon the Californians like a bombshell. Ships brought the strangers from across the water and who could know how many more might come? Spanish soldiers, armed and mounted as they were, quickly proved to be invincible foes with incredible powers. Missionaries strode boldly among them, backed by the soldiers, and proved to be super-shamans proclaiming entirely new ritual practices. Their own shamans and the people themselves were intimidated. Nothing they had in any way matched its Spanish counterpart. They must have felt powerless, especially when the strangers proved capable of following them even as they fled into their safest havens. In some ways, even the Jesuits often found them brave and determined, but they were cowed by firearms.[19] Feelings of inferiority developed but also feelings of hope and expectation. Missionaries gave them food. Missionaries promised them much. Life had been very hard and very uncertain. The strangers might indeed be able to make it easier.

Mission life offered change, and everything Spanish piqued the Californians' curiosity. Their traditional life was one of bare subsistence, so marginal and competitive that many were attracted and enthralled, initially at least, by the material advantages of the new system: food cost less in time and labor; soldiers appeared capable of protecting them from traditional enemies; there would be much more opportunity to settle down and see each other more regularly. This last aspect of mission life may have seemed like an extended version of the natives' own pitahaya festival, the one time of year when they could feed themselves easily enough to bivouac in one spot for two or three weeks and devote their time to social interaction.[20] The personalities and charisma of individual missionaries also must have been important factors in unconverted peoples' decision to accept new ways; with skill and conviction, the pioneer padres helped to make their faith attractive. Soldiers soon did more than provide protection; they were present to discourage neophytes from changing their minds, even to prevent them from running off and abandoning mission life.

California was not Christianized nor Europeanized quickly or easily. It was a long contest between a few missionaries, many scattered peoples, and a difficult environment. Chronicles of the struggle form the major part of the written history of Jesuit California, the first seventy years of the Spanish colonial presence.

Mission Endowments

Missions cost a great deal of money. Salvatierra figured that an endowment of ten thousand pesos would provide the annual income of five hundred pesos needed to support one establishment.[21] (In northwest New Spain, five hundred pesos would buy fifty head of cattle, or pay a little more than a soldier's annual salary with rations included, or purchase five hundred pairs of well-made shoes.) In the Pious Fund's early days, endowments from private donors sometimes carried less than desirable provisos. For example, in 1702, Juan Bautista López donated the income from a property located in central New Spain, and California's third mission, San Juan Bautista de Ligüí, was established on that income. However, López did not cede the property itself to the Pious Fund, only its income. His later bankruptcy ended the donation.[22] Heavily encumbered rural estates and associated bankruptcies were common in eighteenth-century New Spain as the fortunes of individual families rose and fell.[23] By 1705, Salvatierra had decided to found missions only on donations whose principal had been bequeathed and transferred directly to the Pious Fund, the private trust of his California mission. The Fund then invested the gift and earmarked its income for a designated mission.[24]

Missionaries for New Missions

Founding a mission required effort and organization before a site was chosen or prospective converts were approached. The missionary order had to inspire not only a donor, but also a padre. Jesuits recruited and prepared their novices so as to promote their zeal and exalt the work of the missionary. The fervor of this message is palpable in an exhortation for novices by seventeenth-century Jesuit missionary, Antonio Vieira (who took his theme from Jeremiah 1:7, ". . . for thou shalt go to all [*ad omnia*] that I shall send thee. . . .")

> This *ad omnia* is and must be the enterprise and the insignia of every true Missionary . . . not only to catechize the heathen, baptize the catechumens, and instruct the Christians, but also to nourish them when they are hungry, to clothe them when they are naked, to heal them when they are sick, to bury them when they die: as Teachers, as Fathers, as Pastors, as Tutors, as Doctors, as nurses, as servants, as their slaves in all things, in order to live with them always and in order to die with them, and for them, and also at their hands. . . . All this is signified by that *ad omnia*.[25]

Missionaries were not, however, created by inspiration and dedication alone. Each Jesuit underwent long training before being sent into the field. The Society's educational requirements were remarkable, even for probationers in religious orders. A typical candidate began in his early teenage years and served two years as a novice at a Jesuit house while he began a three- to five-year study of Greek and Latin classical literature. He then studied formal philosophy for three more years. Next, the candidate taught for two to three years in a Jesuit preparatory school or worked at local missions for the poor or sick. During or after all this, he studied theology for four years.[26] Then experienced missionaries tried to prepare the candidates to deal with problems in human relations and equip them with the practical skills they would need in very demanding circumstances. The prospective missionary and his order invested a great deal of time, money, and effort to bring him to the threshold of a missionary career.

Even then, the uncertainties of life might intervene. Padre Benito Guisi came within sight of his goal in California but was drowned by a storm in the gulf.[27] Padre Pedro de Ugarte, a brother of Padre Juan, arrived in California, learned a local language and founded Misión de San Juan Bautista at Ligüí but in a few years was returned to the mainland because of ill health.[28] Furthermore, a man prepared, selected, and put to work might prove unsuitable for local conditions. Padre Gerónimo Minutili, a native of Sardinia, arrived at Loreto late in 1702 while the colony was at a low ebb in people and supplies. Brimming with zeal, he roamed the land, preached to any heathen he could find, and chafed at restrictions that prevented him from building his own flock. After a year, Minutili was transferred to Sonora and assigned to the mission at Tubutama. In California annals, there is implicit relief at his departure. The Jesuit colony did not need a caged lion to add to its trials.[29]

Once in the mission field, a candidate served an apprenticeship under experienced eyes. No matter what capabilities or experiences he might have, each newcomer had to learn to cope with the unique problems of his new location and its people. He learned to direct the planting, care, and harvest of crops that were thought suitable for local conditions. Most important, he had to master a language, often with two or more dialects, of the people to whom he would minister.

Since 1550, the government of Spain had ordered that its New World citizens be taught Spanish as quickly as possible, as the vital first step toward integrating them into the economy of the empire, but from the start, the religious orders gave that accomplishment a low priority; they had a different agenda.[30] They would not wait to deliver their religious message in a tongue that the average adult convert might never master. Jesuits, in particular, were activists; their leaders directed them to devote whatever time was needed to learn to communicate directly with unconverted people.[31] By doing so, they became independent of interpreters. They delivered their own messages, and they could judge the natives' receptiveness or their expressions of doubt and resistance. It was a plain case of "knowledge is power," and, as a corollary desirable to missionaries, converts who were not fluent in Spanish were better insulated from casual contact with most secular Hispanic people.

The leaders of Jesuit mission provinces sought to make efficient use of their missionaries' language studies. After a padre had toiled among new and linguistically distinct people, he was ordered to create a grammar and a glossary; such works could reduce the time needed to add new missionaries to the field.[32] However, for a newly arrived missionary-in-training, New World language studies were in no way equivalent to learning an additional European language in which every word or construction would have an approximate equivalent in his native speech.[33] The semantic difficulties encountered in California presented a particularly severe test. Mainland missionaries evangelized people whose languages belonged to major family groups with related structures and logic — and often with recognizable root words. In California, the three linguistic groups spoke languages that were not only unrelated to each other but had no apparent affinities with mainland languages.[34] Padre Jacobo Baegert, who served for seventeen years among Guaycuran speakers at Misión de San Luis Gonzaga (1751–1768), commented on the challenge of indoctrinating his people:

> They have no words to express whatever is not material and not perceptible to the senses and can neither be seen nor touched, no words to express virtues and vices or qualities of feeling. There are no terms which relate to social, human, or rational and civil life. . . . It would be futile to look in a Guaycura dictionary, for instance, for the following words: Life, death, weather, time, cold, heat, world, rain, reason, memory, knowledge, honor, decency, peace . . . , feeling, friend, friendship, truth, shame, faith, love, hope, desire, hate, anger, gratitude, patience, meekness, industry, virtue, vice, beauty, happiness. . . .[35]

Any of these absent concepts that was essential in teaching Christian doctrine had to be laboriously synthesized in awkward phrases made up of known word/idea relationships. Not only had these native Californians no means with which to express abstract qualities, they had no way of signifying the abstract form of a tangible object. For example, *bed are, ed are, ti are,* and *keped are* translated readily as "my father," "your father," "his father," and "our father." Yet Baegert added: "There is not a single Californian who could understand and answer if I asked the meaning of *are.* . . . They could never dream, think, or speak of the obligation of 'a father'. . . ." [that is, "father" as a generalized concept].[36] Bridging fundamental semantic gaps required immense patience, a quality that was already being tested by many aspects of a missionary's demanding vocation.

Despite the difficulties, California Jesuits achieved a high level of competence in peninsular languages. The most explicit report on their linguistic prowess was made by an unusually conscientious and observant visitor general, Padre Juan Antonio Baltasar, who came to the peninsula in 1744. He referred to several of the local missionaries as eminent linguists and, among the remainder, found only one to criticize for inadequate familiarity with the language of his neophytes. Baltasar was, however, surprised and disappointed to find that another Jesuit goal, the subject of a directive to all missionaries, had not been achieved. No California missionary had produced a study of a major language or a regional dialect, "not even a grammar." A previous visitor general had ordered one veteran padre to produce a Cochimí grammar, but "in his spirit of perfection, he never finished it. . . ."[37] Three brief Jesuit studies of California languages have been uncovered, but none was ever available to a California missionary.[38]

Much the same story describes Jesuit accomplishments in a related arena. From the beginning of missionary work in the New World, some of the religious argued that ethnographic studies would give succeeding missionaries insight into native cultures and the thought processes that arose from them. Bernardino de Sahagún, a great Franciscan pioneer in New Spain, likened such studies to those of a physician: one had to know the nature of a disease in order to counteract it. Confessors, he urged, would be better able to respond to penitents if they were able in some measure to understand their perception of good and evil.[39] Although the zeal for such formal studies diminished with the advent of the Counter Reformation, most California Jesuits became informal students of their neophytes' cultural past. Unfortunately, few put their findings on paper.[40] Weariness and a simple lack of free time must have inhibited scholarly pursuits. Only Padres Miguel del Barco and Jacobo Baegert are known to have created organized bodies of ethnographic data.[41]

Candidates for the Society of Jesus were carefully chosen, trained, and evaluated before becoming full-fledged members, and many small bits of evidence create a particularly flattering collective portrait of the men who represented the order in California. As far as official evaluations go, they fared much better than their mainland counterparts in the detailed report made in

1744 by Visitor General Baltasar.[42] They also shone in other appreciable ways. They were unusually supportive of each other and evinced very high esprit de corps. Their brothers in Sonora and the Tarahumara, by contrast, lodged many formal, written protests against fellow missionaries, brother helpers, and even their own father rectors.[43] Moreover, from an intellectual standpoint, no California Jesuit evidenced the degrees of superstition or naive religiosity displayed by some Jesuits at mainland missions.[44]

From his earliest days as a recruiter of California missionaries, the practical Padre Salvatierra insisted on candidates who enjoyed robust health.[45] However, that health did not always endure, and California padres also suffered from the human frailties of loneliness and homesickness. Salvatierra recognized the symptoms and made it a rule that each padre come to Loreto annually to perform the spiritual exercises mandated by the founder of their order, Ignacio de Loyola.[46] When they were there, he would invite them in for chocolate and jolly them along with such phrases as "Come on, old man, and cheer up. . . ." He insisted that they perform the dances of their regions; he played the guitar and sang with them.[47] Later, as the expansion of the mission system made distances greater, neighboring missionaries were encouraged to visit each other to combat the depression that arose from their isolated condition. Nevertheless, during the seventy years of Jesuit tenure in California, half a dozen padres were plagued by combinations of just such mental difficulties and serious illnesses. Their indispositions must have slowed progress and had a depressing effect on the psychological climate at their missions.[48]

Soldiers at Missions

The founders of Jesuit California had practical experience in other mission fields. They understood that soldier employees would be essential threads in their mission fabric. The missionary's job, at best, was lonely and dangerous. At times, he had to leave the mission and go to the aid of a sick or dying member of his flock. If his mission could not accommodate all its people, he needed to go forth to take confessions. Every early report and memoir that touches on these matters echoes this refrain: the padre's life would be swiftly forfeited if he did not enjoy a soldier's protection.[49] Moreover, at home in the *cabecera*, the headquarters of his mission, he needed help with the discipline of his neophytes, and the presence of a single soldier usually prevented open unrest or rebellion.[50] Padre Miguel del Barco summed up the argument for a soldier's full-time presence:

A single soldier serves an important purpose at a mission because the Indians regard him with much respect, knowing that he is there as the captain's representative. He is able to punish for disorders and chastise for impudence. If a matter is more serious, or might have far-reaching consequences, the soldier can inform the captain so that they be averted. The

Indians know all this, and because of that, and their fear of firearms, they are held in check more by the presence of one soldier than by many other mission servants.[51]

Soldiers played conspicuous roles in a mission's religious life. They attended all services and, in the first months at a new mission, they filled all the ceremonial roles beneath that of the padre. They functioned as choir, acolytes, and congregation while neophytes watched and learned. The apparent fervor and seriousness of the soldiers provided an important example for neophytes. In 1697, Salvatierra observed that the piety of his fighting force was a positive influence on natives recently vanquished in battles around Loreto.[52]

Early in the development of each mission, efforts were made to impress the potential converts with the existence of the Spanish king and with his temporal power. Soldiers were introduced as that king's representatives, fiercely dedicated to protecting his possessions and subjects, fiercely determined to punish anyone who flouted his authority. To make the maximum impression, skirmishes or mock battles were fought by mounted soldiers using sword and shield, lances, or even firearms charged with powder alone. The first such display was held at Loreto in 1698. Governor Andrés de Rezábal of Sinaloa had just sent a gift of two sets of leather armor for horses. Salvatierra ordered a pair outfitted and saddled, then had his soldiers stage a rousing tourney. The Californians had recently been in a battle with the Spaniards and had lost men to their muskets. This spectacle was intended to deter further resistance by showing off, for the first time, the speed and mobility of horses.[53]

When neophytes committed serious crimes, the soldiers were expected to run them down and bring them back for discipline.[54] As with mock battles, the theatrical possibilities of public punishment were exploited. Venegas explained how it was done:

> Before any sentence is carried out, whether at the criminal's mission or at the presidio of Loreto to which he has been brought, measures are taken to make certain that the Indians of his pueblo or such of them as are in Loreto shall be present at the execution of the sentence. In this way news of his punishment may be spread abroad among his people and may serve as a warning to the rest. To this end, through an interpreter, the reason for his arrest is made public along with the crime or crimes which have been proved against him, and the punishment to which he is condemned in consequence. In this way the offender is chastised for his crime, and the other Indians are warned by his chastisement. This justice is executed by the captain, or, at his orders, by the soldiers. Thus, the whole country is held in subjection, and all the Indians are submissive and obedient to the man whom they recognize as His Majesty's officer.[55]

Early in the period of contact with a new band of gentiles, a variant of this justice was used as a none-too-subtle lesson; opportunity was provided by the first case of serious misbehavior among the prospective converts. In a well-rehearsed charade, the captain of the presidio made a pretense of meting out a dire punishment, even a death sentence. At the moment this harsh justice was to be carried out, the padre would intercede, rescue the wrongdoer, and exact a public promise of exemplary behavior. This system was effective because, on rare occasions of serious or oft-repeated crimes, there was no staying hand; soldiers laid on the lash or executed the offenders. At Misión de los Dolores as late as 1747, nine men accused of repeated rustling from the mission's herds were rounded up and shot.[56] That sort of news spread swiftly and surely and added to every soldier's aura of power and implicit threat. California natives were made to fear the civil-military sector of Spanish life and to regard the padre as their stern but friendly protector and intermediary.[57]

Despite their paternalistic, almost adversarial role, the soldiers were not viewed with disfavor by most converts. During the years when the first ten missions were opened, the presidio usually had twenty-five soldiers. They were assigned singly or in small groups — called an *escolta*, or escort — to the individual missions. Such a force could scarcely have controlled one to two thousand converts had they been determined to defect or resist. A majority of neophytes felt threatened by unconverted bands and by troublemakers in their midst. They had little charity or trust for their old enemies and considered soldiers their chief and best defense. Some natives probably admired the men of the presidio simply because they were symbols of power. Some neophytes, usually older boys or young men, were "adopted" by soldiers as assistants and companions. A degree of mutual loyalty and affection developed.[58]

Conditions of employment for California soldiers and servants varied widely from mission to mission. Some missions, usually those on frontiers frequented by unconverted Indians, were considered too dangerous for the families of their servitors. In such places, the padre and a soldier often shared quarters and even the necessary housekeeping chores.[59] Some missions were especially poor in land or water; providing food was a problem, and that limited the number of Hispanic families that could be accommodated. Native Californians differed in their attitudes and degree of cooperation in different mission settings; the rebellion in the South underscored that point. Finally, and not least important, the character and personality of the missionary influenced the ambience within his compound. At one mission, records show that soldiers served in the escolta for several consecutive years.[60] At another, a padre reported that, within a four-year span, he sent more than a dozen men back to the presidio because of "evil habits."[61] Typically, a soldier or servant stayed at a mission two or three years before being reassigned.

While the terms of the Jesuits' California license gave their missionaries a degree of control over soldiers not found elsewhere on mission frontiers, this did not make them ideal companions for the padres. Jesuit missionaries were educated, sophisticated people, mostly European and from elite backgrounds, but their order could afford to put only one of them at each mission. Their daily companions were the much humbler people hired to serve them. Most soldiers and servants were born on the uncouth frontier of New Spain and raised with little formal education. Indeed, their rustic origin with its associated folkways and beliefs made them objects of scorn in private communications among Jesuits — who at times gave them the pejorative title of "the Sinaloas," clearly linking churlish behavior with the culture found on that frontier.[62] In their letters, missionaries emphasized that they and the soldiers had no meeting of minds but rather a marriage of necessity. Padre Juan de Ugarte summed up the missionary attitude, and the irony, by quoting an ancient aphorism: "We cannot live with them, and we cannot live without them."[63]

However, some of the Jesuits' reports had political aims and their allegations do not correlate with other contemporary evidence. In private letters, Piccolo and Ugarte himself betrayed real regard for some of their soldiers.[64] Most telling is a statement volunteered by Padre Miguel del Barco, a thoughtful, perceptive veteran of the human relationships that worked and did not work in Jesuit California. After the expulsion, after political and diplomatic restraints on his pen had been largely removed, Barco wrote:

> . . . the captains always took care to select, for the missions in which padres had to stay alone, those soldiers who showed the best judgment and conducted themselves in the most honorable and Christian fashion. Had they not had these qualities, they would have caused the gravest concern for the missionary, and when they were alone in charge of a mission, their misbehavior would have upset and misled the Indians.
>
> But the captains made such careful choices that, for the most part, the soldiers at the missions performed well and honorably and gave much relief and comfort to the padres. . . .

Barco added an even stronger statement. He said that the soldier, in theory, had no need to do more than act as a military guard. He could refuse to assist further as a foreman, although, said Barco, no soldiers really took that attitude. They contributed what they could to mission welfare, partly to please the padre, partly to be diverted by doing something active and useful.[65]

Mission Mayordomos

California soldiers took on a second, non-military role when they were stationed at missions. Their function as guards was usually accomplished by their presence and continued vigilance; it did not keep them busy, yet there was much to do. In short order, soldier guards became the padres' right-hand men, *mayordomos*, or foremen of the missions. In this role, they usually had custody of the mission's food supplies and tools, both kept under lock and key. They also trained and supervised neophytes in the activities of agriculture and herding.[66] Once a mission was well established, the padre might be sent a man hired specifically for his usefulness as a mayordomo. Whoever filled this position

Figure 7.1 California Mayordomo with Bull
(Drawing by Padre Ignacio Tirsch, S. J.)

acted as a supervisor and inspector, making sure that neophytes followed approved procedures and avoided or rectified mistakes.

The most descriptive Jesuit statements about their California mayordomos were penned as they defended themselves against criticisms solicited from California veterans by Virrey Vizarrón as he feuded with the Jesuits in the aftermath of the 1734 rebellion. Soldiers publicly aired complaints about the missionaries' control over them and requirements that they perform tasks more appropriate for servants than for soldiers. The Jesuits were stung to respond. Miguel Venegas was just completing his history, and he detailed specific duties and activities of mayordomos in his defense of Jesuit practices.[67] Venegas gave a prominent place to the mayordomo's responsibility for rounding up and branding cattle or cutting out those needed for food and bringing them to the mission for slaughter. When Venegas reported that the soldier serving as mayordomo always had neophyte assistants, he intended to belittle soldiers' complaints of overwork. This report also underscores the role of soldiers, and California's gente de razón in general, in educating and training neophytes. Venegas's remarks about a mayordomo grabbing yearling calves by the tail and throwing them to the ground for branding are also useful because they coincide perfectly with a drawing made in the 1760s by a California Jesuit.[68]

Venegas detailed a mayordomo's custodial responsibilities: he doled out staple foods to the cooks for each meal, inspected the cooking to be sure that everything was used properly, then supervised or personally ladled out the servings. He distributed tools for use either in the compound or in the fields; he later called them in and locked them safely away. When it was time to hand out craft materials, the mayordomo arranged that they reached the right hands in the right quantities. He distributed clothing when so instructed. In case of a padre's extended illness or absence, his soldier companion directed every vital mission activity until the missionary's return or replacement.[69]

The position of mission mayordomo had a direct relationship to the California presidio. Some soldiers were recruited and put on Loreto's presidial payroll as *medias plazas*, apprentice soldiers on half-pay. Records of several medias plazas show that they were first assigned to serve as mayordomos, vaqueros, or in some other mission servant capacity; only later did they appear on lists of regular soldiers on full pay.[70] Further evidence of this practice is provided by the two principal California Jesuit memoirs in which duties carried out by men who were called "mission servants" were later described as activities of "soldiers."[71] From the Jesuit viewpoint, the practice of using men on half-pay served useful purposes beyond the obvious economy. Missions needed servants; recruits who had some skills to offer could be usefully employed during a probationary period. Furthermore, by serving first as mission servants, they could be trained and evaluated under a missionary's constant supervision. A soldier, by contrast, had duties that took him away from the mission and away from any effective control other than his loyalty and discipline.

The entrada

Expanding the mission system was a goal always in the air, even as existing missions were developed. Lengthy and costly explorations were carried out, not only to find and evaluate potential mission sites, but also to satisfy royal councils that the Jesuits were making an effort to chart and pacify their parcel of the lands claimed by Spain. Explorations were planned when missionaries had received repeated reports of significant bands of accessible gentiles. Other explorations were made for primarily geographic purposes, like those in search for ports for the Manila ships or to determine the insularity or peninsularity of California.[72] However, missionaries accompanied all expeditions, and attempted to assess the mission potential of all areas visited.

When the missionaries found an area frequented by several receptive bands of heathen, they began planning to introduce Christianity and the concept of a missionary's ministrations. The first overt step was an *entrada*, at which the missionary handed out food and gifts — such as blankets and steel knives — to attract and hold the gentiles' attention. Useful Spanish trade goods had a long history as enticements in the mission fields of New Spain and were powerful lures for people who spent nearly all their time searching for and preparing food, and who had no weaving or metalworking technologies. The padre also depended on his accompanying neophytes to influence the heathen.

Four or five soldiers were a vital part of an entrada. They acted as the padre's bodyguards. They handled, or at least oversaw, the many chores and details of an extended pack trip. Their presence gave heart to their neophyte companions, who were often going into what had once been enemy territory. Soldiers represented Hispanic tradition and culture when they took part in demonstrations of religious services; they provided the lead for neophyte voices in chants, responses, and choruses staged to impress the unconverted.[73] Entradas were not expected to have an immediate effect and were in no sense military conquests. On the contrary, the missionary hoped that good reports from his mission had spread into the hinterland and aroused favorable interest. By making personal entradas, he gave the natives a chance to meet the storied strangers, sample their hospitality, and listen to their exhortations and promises.

Some early California entradas were not planned or carried out as skillfully as those of the mature conquest. One entrada, to Ligüí, twenty miles south of Loreto, was more fortunate than wise. In July 1704, Salvatierra and the recently arrived Pedro de Ugarte ventured south along the beach accompanied by a soldier and two interpreters. The small size of the party was due to the current shortage of soldiers and the apparent friendliness of the people previously encountered on the Loreto plain. As the visitors approached Ligüí, they were startled by a group of Monquí men who leaped out of ambush and showered them with arrows. The situation seemed desperate, or so Salvatierra's subsequent description implies, but the soldier, far from being panicked or routed, charged the Monquí, firing his musket and then brandishing his sword as he came. This wild apparition, reinforced by rumors of Spanish prowess, unnerved the local warriors; they threw down their arms and lay prostrate. The wondering padres gave thanks to their patron saints, but Salvatierra did not forget his debt to the soldier. His report of the incident gave the man's full name, Francisco Javier Valenzuela, and that rare personal touch was dutifully copied by Jesuit historians. Thanks to Valenzuela, the padres were able to speak to their recent attackers, forgive them, make gifts, and ultimately to retire with a successful entrada.[74]

Each new mission aroused the curiosity of nearby unconverted people. Small delegations soon came to observe mission life. The Jesuits reported that these bands often departed leaving requests that a padre visit them in their distant encampments, each typically consisting of a unit that the Spaniards called a *ranchería*, usually less than a hundred people who belonged to an extended family or to a group of interrelated families.[75] Padre Piccolo responded to many such requests and made extended entradas from Misión de Santa Rosalía de Mulegé to visit groups of Cochimí at sites or, at least, in areas that were soon served by the missions of La Purísima, Guadalupe, and San Ignacio (see Map 3.2). Piccolo was the first California missionary to use an entrada to capitalize on the mission visitors' curiosity about agriculture. During visits to their lands,

TABLE 7.2 EXPLORATIONS THAT LOCATED EVENTUAL MISSION SITES

Year	Padre	Base	Resulting mission
1699	Piccolo	Loreto	San Javier[a]
1701	Salvatierra	Loreto	San José de Comondú[b]
1703	Piccolo Basaldúa	Loreto	Santa Rosalía de Mulegé[c]
1709	Piccolo	Mulegé	La Purísima
1716	Piccolo	Mulegé	San Ignacio
1719	Ugarte	Mulegé	Guadalupe
1720	Guillén	Malibat	Los Dolores[d]
c.1747	Consag	San Ignacio	Santa Gertrudis
1766	Linck	San Borja	Santa María, San Fernando[e]

[a]The 1699 exploration is discussed in chap. 2, pp. oo–oo.
[b]P. Salvatierra's 1701 exploration in the Sierra de la Giganta is described in chap. 8, pp. oo–oo.
[c]The complex 1703 exploration is discussed in chap. 3, pp.oo–oo.
[d]The context of the 1720 exploration into *el Sur* is discussed in chap. 4, pp. oo–oo.
[e]P. Linck's 1766 exploration is discussed in chap. 11, pp. oo–oo. Misión de San Fernando de Velicatá was founded by the Franciscan, Fray Junipero Serra, in 1769 on a site discovered — and noted for its mission potential — by Wenceslao Linck in 1766.

Piccolo planted garden patches in suitable places.[76] Later, when Padre Nicolás Tamaral was opening Misión de la Purísima, he planted a field of watermelons. The crop was a success, and his converts loved the fruit. Tamaral pressed his advantage by presenting melons to an unconverted ranchería during an entrada. That band was so impressed that they joined the fold on the spot.[77] Even if the recipients of these demonstrations did not learn enough to produce crops, sprouting seeds and growing plants reinforced the concept of agriculture that had been carried home and reported by mission visitors — and furthered the process of acculturation.

If an unconverted ranchería were close enough to a mission, it might be invited to visit and participate in the community's activities. Usually, however, this was impractical or undesirable; gentiles might find old enemies among the mission neophytes, and chronic food shortages made it risky to assemble large populations at the missions.[78] A more common practice was to wait until several related bands made repeated requests for missionary attention. Then a padre was sent to live among them and begin their instruction, and he and his escort would intensify the search for a suitable mission site.

Sites for Missions

To retain its hold on converts, each mission had to be a reliable source of food. Grains were imported whenever possible, but no mission could depend on such costly fare with such uncertain delivery. Therefore, the cabecera of each mission required a certain amount of arable land and reliable water. As many neophytes as necessary were engaged in agricultural activities. They had to feed their own group, help to feed the bands that made monthly visits, and if possible create a surplus to be offered when all the mission's people congregated seasonally for church festivals. Nevertheless, the Jesuits' choice of mission sites proved to be the weakest link in their chain of preparations. Despite their recognition of food as a crucial element, the Jesuits repeatedly selected locations that could not sustain the necessary agriculture. Often, this realization came to them only after much time, money, and energy had been expended in building roads, erecting structures, and clearing land.

Inexperience with peninsular people contributed to unwise site selections. The fundamentals of aboriginal life in California were quite alien to the padres. Experience among more sedentary groups in other mission fields predisposed the Jesuits to expect the Californians to have strong emotional ties to certain locations. They attached too much significance to the places where natives were first encountered or where they seemed to congregate. The missionaries did not fully appreciate, until later, the immense area over which a band ranged during its annual rounds of foraging; they failed to realize that supporting a mission's people on irrigated agriculture required many times the volume of water that the same group used while practicing its ancestral hunting and gathering regime. Such early misconceptions led to mission sites with woefully little water, chosen simply because they were the best within the known stamping grounds of a given people. Padre Ignacio María Nápoli, writing in 1721 about his selection of what proved to be the first of three sites for Misión de Santiago, voiced the temptation that led to many mistakes.

> To be sure, it might have been better to found it at [either of two other sites], but those are uninhabited places distant from the Indians. It was necessary for me to direct my feet to where the people live; to attain our chief objective of converting them, I have to be among them.[79]

The Jesuits also were misled by their ignorance of the peninsula's natural environment. Salvatierra and most of his cohorts had cut their missionary teeth in arid or semi-arid land. They supposed that knowledge gained during their mainland experiences could be applied directly in California. In fact, the character of water resources in Chihuahua and Sonora is significantly different from that on the peninsula. However dry the mainland climate, areas in which missions were successful are watered by large rivers that originate in high mountains with annual rains (see Map 1.1). Even if these rivers run only part of each year, dependable water supplies can be had from shallow wells. Crops were planted on floodplains or on terraces along rivercourses, places which are rather easily irrigated and where soil tends to remain moist.

However, there are no rivers on the peninsula. Although watercourses begin in moderately high mountains, the peninsula lacks a consistent annual pattern of rainfall. When rains do fall on the narrow ribbon of the peninsula, runoff waters quickly traverse the short distances down steep slopes to porous, sandy plains and the ocean. Even with much runoff, little water is retained in natural

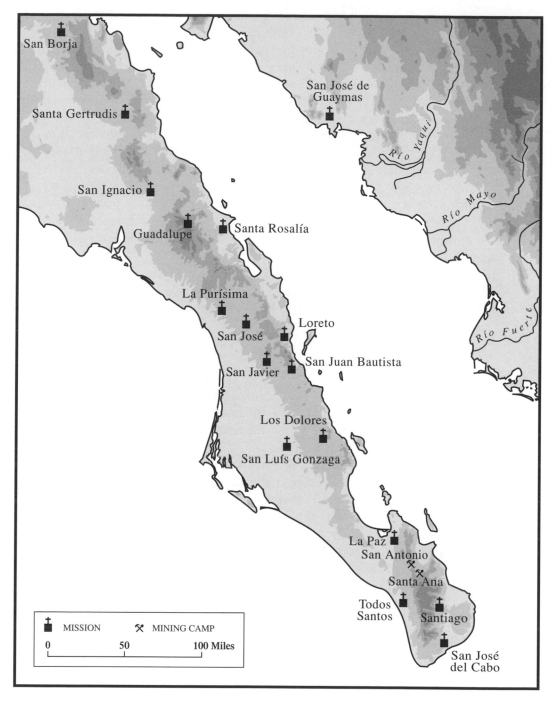

San Borja

San José de
Guaymas

Santa Gertrudis

Río Yaqui

San Ignacio

Río Mayo

Guadalupe

Santa Rosalía

La Purísima

Río Fuerte

Loreto

San José

San Javier

San Juan Bautista

Los Dolores

San Luís Gonzaga

La Paz
San Antonio

Santa Ana

Todos
Santos

Santiago

✝ MISSION   ✗ MINING CAMP

0   50   100 Miles

San José
del Cabo

Map 7.1 Missions Founded by California Jesuits, 1697–1762

storage either on the surface or below ground at depths reached by shallow wells. These conditions pertain to both the central peninsula, composed of ocean-bottom sediments overtopped by volcanic flows, and the south, where a ridge of intrusive granite is partially overlaid by skirts of sedimentary origin. As a result of this unusual hydrology, sources of water are scarce, and each yields only a small quantity. In their pre-mission adaptation, the natives had depended on an intimate knowledge of *tinajas* (bedrock catchments), places known to contain water for predictable periods after heavy rainfall. Early in their California experiences, the missionaries might have observed that a large band spent weeks in an area, but not have realized that such a stay was possible only during a rare year when a large tinaja had filled.[80] On at least one occasion, the Jesuits were misled when they found an apparently promising location for a mission, only to learn later that their discovery had followed several unusually wet years. Thus, another partially developed site had to be abandoned and the project moved to a point many miles distant.[81]

The Jesuits gradually learned to select better locations, but their education was expensive. Of nine missions founded in the first twenty-four years of the conquest, one was abandoned and five had to be moved to better sites.[82]

Road Building

The Jesuits struggled to cope with California's broken, rocky terrain as soon as they began to expand their enclave beyond Loreto. They endured a painfully slow pace as their mounts moved over it. Plans to build and maintain a camino real were made early and followed faithfully throughout their tenure on the land. Once a mission site was chosen, a trail was cleared to connect it with the nearest older establishment. Missions were located at water sources, so Indian footpaths usually indicated the best routes between them. Often the camino real was created simply by widening and smoothing an old trail.

The Jesuits, or particularly skilled soldiers or masons, laid out the camino real using stakes to indicate the sightlines of its course. Then soldiers and neophyte men took over a formidable task. They cleared the larger, loose stones out of the pathway and laid them in neat borders along the sides. They leveled the path as much as possible, chipping away protrusions from buried rocks, and filling holes with small debris. They moved rocks weighing hundreds of pounds by using iron bars and hardwood tree trunks as levers. They constructed switchback trails on hillsides by clearing paths in the tumbled rocks. On particularly steep slopes, or where there was bedrock, they built up carefully chinked walls of dry-laid rock, then backfilled them with rubble to form suitably wide turns or stretches of trail.

When the camino real was complete in a mission's area, similar if narrower trails were built to each of the mission's subsidiary pueblos. All of these many miles of trails were maintained, and after major storms, substantially restored.

The trails permitted pack animals and men to cover as much as twenty-five or thirty miles a day in country where, without such roads, they would have labored harder to make a ten-mile advance.[83]

The cabecera *and its* visitas

The cabecera, or headquarters, was each mission's ceremonial, administrative, and economic center. Here the church was built and the principal services held. Here lived the padre and his soldiers and servants. Here was the storehouse for the mission's food and other supplies. The goal of bringing all converts to live permanently at the cabecera was a cherished one, but a typical new mission was called on to encompass twelve to fifteen rancherías — about a thousand people. No missions consistently produced enough food to support such a concentration. Earlier in the evangelization of hunting-and-foraging people, a plan was worked out whereby a cabecera was settled by a few bands that had lived nearby. Others were grouped into new units that could be brought in monthly for indoctrination at the cabecera, or visited monthly by a circuit-riding padre. Each of these new groups usually consisted of two or more pre-contact bands, now collectively called a *pueblo de visita*. The principal encampment for such a group became a visiting station of the mother mission, called a *visita*.[84] Visitas were located at watered sites that from time to time had supported encampments of one or more rancherías. Occasionally a visita gave its mission access to more arable land and water, but usually it provided only an area where traditional hunting and gathering could sustain its people. Through these satellite pueblos, the missionaries began religious instruction, introduced the concept of a broader community, and began the process of breaking down old rivalries and fears.

When the missionary was acquainted with the people of a visita, he appointed a leader, usually called a *capitán*, to help in coordinating the headmen of the still somewhat autonomous rancherías that formed the new aggregate group.[85] One of this capitán's main duties was to make sure that the ranchería leaders (who, confusingly enough, were also called captains) assembled all bands of a pueblo de visita at the cabecera on schedule. Each pueblo de visita was to report at a specific phase of the moon — the Californians' only calendar — for a three- to seven-day exposure to the full range of mission life.[86]

When a pueblo arrived at the cabecera for its monthly mission experience, each of its people went through the steps of a personal ritual. Before any other activity or greeting, each visitor went directly to the church, knelt, crossed himself, recited an *Ave Maria*, sang the *Alabado*, a favorite hymn of praise, and went to greet the padre. The neophyte was then ready for whatever the day might hold. While permanent residents of the mission went to work, the padre performed the ceremonies that prepared the newly arrived ranchería for confession. In this he was assisted by the *temastián*, an apt neophyte trained as a catechist who traveled with the visiting group.[87] During the following days, the transient group attended church, received some schooling and some training in practical arts, and had a chance to watch the mission community in action. When the pueblo departed, each person repeated his personal visit to the church and, upon saying his farewells to the padre, received gifts of food and clothing.[88]

Occasionally, the cabecera had no food to spare and could not host extra mouths, or a visita was too occupied with seasonal food gathering to break off for a long trek to the mission. In such cases, the missionary left his headquarters and took the church to the people. While there, he would conduct Mass, then remain a day or two to perform baptisms or marriages, catechize neophytes, and confer with those chosen to be leaders and teachers. A missionary might be called to a visita at any time to attend an ill or dying neophyte.[89] In the early days, these excursions were great trials. The missionary and his escort had to pack along all the food they would need. The terrain was usually rough, and the distances could be so great that the padre was in the saddle for two days in each direction. He had no house or bed, so he slept under a tree or a pile of hastily cut branches. Gradually, as conditions permitted, roads were cleared and each visita was outfitted with a chapel, a one-room house, and a strong, lockable storeroom in which church trappings and some food could be left in safety.[90]

From the missionary point of view, visitas were an unwelcome necessity. A recurrent lament runs through the first fifty years of California Jesuit writings, a regret that all neophytes could not be permanently accommodated at mission headquarters. The mission center made powerful new impressions with its buildings and its organized and imposed activities. A sedentary way of life in itself was new, and when a ranchería had to subsist away from the cabecera three weeks out of four, some missionaries agonized that the people's old ways would be reinforced. They would move without restraint or supervision from one familiar haunt to another and be exposed to constant associations with their past, its natural and supernatural elements. No wonder that padres were anguished when droughts or other disasters caused food shortages and regular mission inhabitants had to be released to forage for ancestral foods. Some missionaries believed that an atavism took place as soon as neophytes were out of their sight. Especially, they conjured up visions of widespread unchaste sexual behavior, the ultimate anathema to the celibate padres.[91] In describing aboriginal customs, Padre Salvatierra had provided the explicit details on which such fears could be based:

> It has to be understood that the three month harvest season for pitahaya is like the Mardi Gras in some parts of Europe in which a good part of the men submit to an ecstasy; the natives here are so enraptured, giving themselves over to fiestas and dances at gatherings of the usually distant rancherías. They make offerings of food and buffoonery in the enjoyment of which they pass entire nights of merrymaking, the foremost comics being the best mimics.

Also, these gatherings serve as times for excessive lovemaking, trading of women, and practices that maintain the customs of the tribe.[92]

The padres worried that neophytes away from the mission might die without religious rites, and they suffered pangs of guilt during any group's enforced absence. This was not diminished by their observation that many, even most, of those who died in their presence did not seem repentant about their pasts or fearful of the future.[93] One padre preserved the refrain from a song intoned at appropriate moments by soldiers. Californians, it ran, "eat without disgust, live without shame, and die without fear."[94]

However, seasoned missionaries knew the problems and pitfalls that visitas allowed them to circumvent; they understood the necessity for half-way measures. At times, it was necessary that one of them step in to temper the zeal of superiors who wished to end the compromise that visitas represented. In 1730, the enthusiastic and activist visitor general, Padre José de Echeverría, ended his inspection of California missions with a list of suggestions that, owing to the powers of his office, could be considered as orders. Echeverría indicated that the padres should call in rancherías to live at the cabeceras. He urged firmness in the enforcement of his order; each padre was to achieve the desired goal "with gentle pressure, or, if that were insufficient, with harsh means." Head of the California Jesuits at that time was Padre Sebastián de Sistiaga who drew on twelve years of experience at the mission system's northern frontier, the very area in which the operation of visitas was most necessary. The California veteran was undoubtedly sympathetic to the basic idea; every missionary wished to have the advantages conveyed by a united flock under his direct, daily supervision. Sistiaga wrote a generally conciliatory response to the visitor general, but he expressed unflinching resistance to Echeverría's dictum on visitas. He pointed out that rancherías around old missions could be ordered in with little difficulty; other missions lay beyond them, and they effectively had no place to hide. Rancherías attached to new missions on the frontier were less familiar with mission life and less certain to comply with such an order. They had the option of retreating into the world of heathen that lay beyond. Not only that, but the spectacle created by the harsh measures that would be needed to bring them in against their will would turn the unconverted against the missions and their message. Sistiaga reminded Echeverría that the newly converted were still attached to their ancestral lands; it would take time to wean them away.

Padre Sistiaga had to differ with another of the visitor general's directives, a plan to give land to neophyte men, teach them how to cultivate it, and make them responsible for their own subsistence. Sistiaga explained that there was limited land, water, and seed grain; all had to be used under supervision to achieve the greatest advantage. Furthermore, when newly converted men were asked to work, they complained a great deal, were slow and uncertain in reporting, contributed little labor, and were inclined to dawdle or even to sneak off and hide. If they came at all, they expected to be fed morning, noon, and night, and even to be given clothing. Finally Sistiaga voiced the concern that probably most deterred the missionaries from encouraging anything but group activities at their visitas. Any sort of individual project would give a neophyte too much freedom and expose him to too much temptation. The padres could not be present, and native officials, even if they could be trusted, could not supervise projects carried out by people scattered about the area occupied by the visita's band. Padre Sistiaga painted a graphic picture of the consequences for his visitador general, one that no Jesuit could condone:

> Planting and working the fields [at visitas] makes them hotbeds of other problems, giving the men of those places the means to solicit favors of women and create wantonness with the greatest of ease. My Father Visitor General, the women of these lands are not wooed with money, yard-goods, linens, etc. He who has food — which is so often lacking — can obtain whatever he fancies. The women do not hold back, they are easily influenced. If the plantings are so used, they result in a disgusting harvest.
>
> This is not overcautious speculation that I report, I have learned by experience. The captain of a ranchería, now dead from dysentery, planted a little field. Hidden in his garden plot, [the captain] had a young girl from up north, his reason for maintaining the planting."[95]

There is no indication that Visitador General Echeverría offered further suggestions for dealing with the visiting stations of the California missions.

Evidence suggests that neophytes at visitas were healthier than those who lived at missions — and that the latter made psychological and physical gains when they got time away from the monotony of mission life. This was noted by at least a few Jesuits. Padre Jacobo Baegert wrote, "some missionaries here are of [the] opinion — and some experiences cause me to agree — that in California one meets respectively better Christian people among those who wander around in the brush and who come to the mission every month or six weeks than those who are always living in the mission."[96] Neophytes who lived away from the cabecera encountered the stimuli of their former life and engaged in more spontaneous activity. Groups of men and boys flushed out deer and drove them near hunters, armed with spears or bows-and-arrows, who waited in blinds made from piled rock. Others went to the Pacific shore, made *balsas* (rafts) by binding bundles of reeds, launched them into lagoons that lay behind sand bars. There, in marshes, on spits, and in open waters, they collected eggs of waterfowl and turtles, took shellfish, and killed fish and turtles with wooden spears.[97] When available, freshly gathered fruit, seeds, roots, and hearts of agaves eaten in the field made up a more nutritious vegetable diet than dried wheat and corn at the mission. Along with the bounty of the seashore, newly caught grubs, lizards, snakes, deer, rabbits, and bats were more beneficial than beef, especially since they made up a larger proportion of the total diet than did meat at the mission.[98]

Conversion

Acceptance of the Catholic religion by the heathen should be free and spontaneous, since faith,
as Saint Ambrose notes, is a voluntary act of understanding, wrought by the free exercise of
will, and is incompatible with necessity or coercion.

PADRE MIGUEL VENEGAS, CITING A COMMENTARY ON II CORINTHIANS
AS A CORNERSTONE OF JESUIT CALIFORNIA.[99]

Spanish missionaries in the New World succeeded in attracting native Americans to join them in creating hundreds of mission centers. Missionaries regularly reported to their superiors, government officials, and benefactors that their message so moved the converts that they became agents in further evangelization. This was widely interpreted as a sign that the tidings of the Catholic faith were spreading and attracting converts, but evidence suggests that religion was but one of several inducements that drew Indians to mission compounds.

Many of New Spain's ethnic groups seemed to lack the abstract concepts necessary for an understanding of Christian theology. Word-of-mouth reports from new converts to the unconverted probably stressed material conditions at the missions — food, activities, and the novelties of European technology — rather than the missionaries' teachings. Initially, most natives had little idea of what was expected from them in return for the material benefits they received. It is likely that most joined missions for new experiences or to escape ancient problems and not with the intent to adopt new beliefs.[100]

In California, more than in most areas of the New World, the lives of indigenous people centered on an imperative, unending search for food. To these people, the mission appeared to be an inexhaustible larder with easy access.[101] For societies with such precarious existences, religious conversion — or the little part of that concept they understood — may have seemed like a small price to pay for security and relative leisure. As the Californians settled into mission life, temporal aspects of acculturation, such as the form and content of their new surroundings and daily lives, had more impact than abstract spiritual principles.[102] They probably viewed the mission in simple socio-economic terms — although the padres demanded that a great deal of everybody's time be spent in religious activities.

When the few available missionaries began to evangelize large populations in the New World, they necessarily performed mass baptisms; reports of these created a public perception in Europe of a sort of wholesale religious activity. However, soon after those beginnings, the missionary orders began to demand that prospective converts take instruction and learn certain basic ideas and brief texts before they were baptized.[103] Only newborn babies and small children were baptized at first contact, an acknowledgment of the high rate of infant mortality. In their early years in new areas, including California, the Jesuits withheld baptism from adults because of the uncertainty of the conquest and their horror of having to withdraw and leave behind Christians with no pastor.

Later, in recognition of the shallow nature of most conversions, the Jesuits demanded years of study and some demonstrable learning before they bestowed the privilege of baptism.[104] These prerequisites, however, cost every Jesuit missionary time, effort, and discomfort. Because few adults were fully admitted to the faith, the padres were absolutely committed to visit and, if necessary, baptize all neophytes who were reported to be dangerously ill. Every missionary made many excursions to minister to rancherías as much as forty miles from the mission. Sometimes the padre arrived too late and was upset by his failure.[105] Native officials saw how emotional a missionary could become when one of his flock died without baptism or final rites. Some may have become overcautious; others may have used the situation to express a subtle form of resistance. Many of the illnesses that they reported were not severe and the victims had recovered, or nearly so, by the time the hurrying padre arrived.[106]

During the successive epidemics caused by the introduction of European diseases, the padres offered food, some primitive nursing, the solace of their presence, and the message of the church. They were genuinely puzzled by the devastating progress of the diseases and seem not to have recognized the mission's role in their spread.[107] They combated their own feelings of helplessness with consolations provided by their faith. They believed that children they had baptized were blessed by being taken before they had sinned; their salvation was assured. The missionaries took a degree of perverse pleasure in noting that Californians who had rejected them and the mission, especially those who blamed the padres for the epidemics, were cut down by disease just as surely as those who had come to the Christian fold. That fact was pointed out to converts.[108]

From the early days of New World evangelism, missionaries found that they could facilitate conversion by conferring official status on native leaders. Appointments of this type began with the conquest of Mexico and were introduced in Sinaloa by the Jesuits a century before their California venture began.[109] This practice promoted a smoother transition by preserving some of the discipline and authority of the aboriginal social order. A ranchería chief, renamed *capitán* (captain of a converted band) by the padre, retained prestige and a semblance of power as he became an honored and recognized functionary in a new mission's social order. Ironically, another aspect of the ranchería's old order was lost even as the headman was allowed to hold on to some of his authority. In Indian groups, the headman's role was not hereditary or bestowed for life; he was usually a temporarily elevated member of an informal council of elders who helped to guide the band in religious and procedural matters.[110] But it did not suit the California missionaries to deal with deliberative bodies; they were looking for administrative assistants to occupy the lower rungs of their authoritarian ladder. The missionary himself would dictate in the sorts of cases that once had concerned the councils of elders.

California missionaries were particularly dependent on their appointed captains because they were needed to carry out approved routines far from missions and the padres' watchful eyes. When the missionaries chose leaders for the rancherías, they usually selected the men who had been leaders before conversion, perhaps in part to reward their willingness to bring their people to the mission. Thereafter, incumbent leaders seem to have been retained as long as they were able and remained cooperative and pious. Some duties of the capitán of a roving ranchería were simple: he was responsible for the erection and maintenance of a large cross wherever his band camped, and he was responsible for bringing the ranchería into the cabecera at the appointed day of the lunar month.[111] Other aspects of the captain's role were difficult. The new alliance preserved some aspects of his power and prestige, but forced him to acknowledge a higher authority, and, in the name of that authority, assert more control over his people than he had exercised in pre-mission days. He had to prevent his people from having any recourse to deposed shamans or pagan rites. He had to demand previously unknown forms of labor and deny practices that had been traditional and popular.

When the captain of a ranchería was not capable of taking religious responsibility for his group, a temastián attended his band when it left the mission; he was supposed to continue the people's instruction and influence them to maintain Christian practices.

Missionaries consolidated their control over ranchería captains by choosing a *gobernador* (governor of converts) to rule over them.[112] This individual lived at the cabecera and worked regularly with the padre. A California Jesuit, Jacobo Baegert, described a governor's duties:

> . . . to bring those present at the mission into the church at a given signal and, at the proper time, to round up those who had been roaming the fields for three weeks and to lead them to the mission. They were supposed to prevent all disorders and public misconduct, to review the catechism in the morning before the natives left the mission and in the evening after they had returned, to persuade them to recite the rosary in the fields, to punish culprits for minor offenses, to report serious crimes to the proper authority, to see that the natives preserved silence and were reverent during religious services, to attend the sick in the field, and bring them to the mission, and similar duties. As insignia of their office and the power vested in them, each carried a staff, sometimes one with a silver knob. Most of them were proud of their positions. . . . [113]

The gobernador at a mission was responsible for pursuing and arresting a neophyte who had fled. Every mission had a jail and one or more sets of leg irons. Cases of minor crimes were handled at the mission; major or repeated crimes were referred to the captain of the presidio.[114] As the missions matured, the California padres felt that the governors of their converts should be given greater trust and responsibility. After about 1740, Indian gobernadores were allowed to distribute food to the neophytes, previously a chore reserved for soldier-mayordomos or the padres themselves.[115]

The padre of each mission picked a male convert living at the cabecera to fill the post of *alcalde* or *fiscal*, the padre's lay helper in church activities. This functionary saw to it that people attended the appropriate ceremonies and helped to supervise behavior during their course. Each missionary picked an older boy or young man whom he perceived as capable, and trained him to serve as his *paje* (page). A page was usually at the padre's side, learned excellent Spanish, and interpreted in cases where the padre's command of an idiom was inadequate.[116] Some of these men spoke or understood several different languages or dialects and were called *intérpretes*. Pajes accompanied missionaries when they traveled and often carried messages from mission to mission; thus, they tended to become the best known and most sophisticated of the neophytes.[117] One who became especially well acculturated, who understood and could convincingly assume Spanish ways, was called a *paje ladino*.[118]

In picking officials for convert groups, Sonoran missionaries often favored acculturated neophytes from older missions or even men of mixed blood, either more loyal to the padres than to the people they helped to control.[119] But from the first days of their California mission, the Jesuits made their appointments from within the local groups, thus avoiding one of the tensions experienced by their mainland brethren.

The captain of the presidio of Loreto, in his role as governor of California, appointed such convert officials. In theory, they then acted as his agents in extending his civil authority. Because the tranquility and efficiency of a mission depended in part on the character and intentions of neophyte appointees, the missionaries wanted the captain to select convert leaders in whom they had confidence, i.e., those chosen at their suggestion. California Jesuits considered this matter so important that they based part of their argument for their continued control of the presidial captain on the significance of his powers of appointment.[120] As long as the captain remained a Jesuit employee, appointments of neophyte officials were made, de facto, by the missionary and merely confirmed by the captain.[121]

The early steps in evangelizing a new group tested any missionary's ingenuity. He not only had to introduce wholly new religious concepts, but he also sought to bring about immediate changes in behavior. If old forms of song, dance, or games seemed lewd or irreverent, they were forbidden — as soon as sufficient control was established. In their place, the padres promoted European equivalents, familiar to the missionaries and therefore considered safer and more decorous.[122] Neophytes, particularly women, were clothed, both to help them develop the approved sense of modesty and to spare the sensibilities of Jesuits.[123] As they began to teach Christianity, the Jesuits attempted to eradicate manifestations of what they called "the old, false religion."[124] Younger people responded readily, but the old were slower to accept change; many must have come to missions only as an alternative to being left alone.[125] Whatever reservations the new congregations may have harbored, they accepted the padres' demands that they abandon the material trappings associated with their old beliefs. Converts stood by without reported protest as the

newcomers burned cultural artifacts that the missionaries believed had religious significance.[126] Converts also gave up other material symbols of their
past, such as the age-old practices of tattooing and nose and ear piercing.[127]

In training their converts, the padres made good use of the Californians'
attraction to European music. Salvatierra was said to have played the flute and
sung simple songs to beguile children. Later, he taught religious texts by setting
them to music that the children could sing themselves.[128] Loreto and San Javier
were equipped with small organs,[129] and neophytes learned to play viols of
several sizes, but the biggest emphasis was on choral music. Most missionaries
made some effort to train groups of singers to perform for church services.[130]
By common consent, the most skillful choirmaster in California was Padre
Pedro María Nascimbén, born in Venice in 1703. Nascimbén spent almost
twenty years at Mulegé (1735–1754) where he trained singers and choruses
that invited admiring compliments from fellow missionaries and visitors general as well.[131] Nascimbén's successor offered an anecdote that illustrates the
Venetian's devotion to music — and inadvertently exposes some unusual facets
of mission life.

> Padre Fernando Consag, then padre visitador, was to come to Santa Rosalía
> with soldiers to punish certain Mulegeños for some extraordinary mis-
> behavior. Padre Pedro knew of this some days ahead of their arrival and sat
> down to compose a song that would serve as an act of contrition; it began:
> 'Que viva Jesus . . .' and was as tender as his kind heart could desire. And he
> taught his delinquent sons to sing it. Using the skills of a teacher of musical
> arts that he had been, he trained them for the day when the Father Visitor
> would arrive. Then Father Pedro with a rope around his neck and in the habit
> of a penitent, accompanied by his sons, began to sing as Father Fernando
> approached. He, hearing the tender new song and admiring Father Pedro's
> imitation of his chaplain Jesus, could not but pardon the offenders. . . .
>
> Further, touching on the point of music, I cannot do less than tell the great
> benefits and advantages created by Father Pedro, not only in this mission but
> rather in all those of this province, in that every day on rising, on retiring,
> after the morning rosary and the evening, even at times of work, there would
> be sung now litanies of Our Lady, now acts of contrition, now verses of Our
> Lord Jesus Christ and His Holy Mother, and of many saints, spreading light
> and being admired in whatever place encountered. A boatload of those who
> came to dive for pearls arrived at these missions and were captivated by the
> range of songs, most of them composed and taught by Father Pedro. Then
> Father Pedro arranged that these people learn some of the music and sing it.
> Otherwise, the songs heard among the pearlers were not very holy.[132]

The missionaries placed special emphasis on winning over and indoctrinating the children of converts.[133] They were required to go to school, which the
Jesuits used as a major tool in their efforts to replace ancestral folkways with
their own idealized and attenuated version of Hispanic culture.[134] Their curric-

ulum was based on church activities—to familiarize mission youth with the Mass and train them to respond appropriately in church. Classes were also aimed at preparing the young to raise Christian families. In time, this training allowed the missionary to conduct religious services with the same group participation found in congregations of "old Christians," or people born to the faith. Classes were segregated by sex, met several days a week, and continued until the students reached marriageable ages—about twelve or thirteen for a girl, a little older for a boy.[135]

Religious training was begun with group repetitions of musical or chanted ritual passages. The neophytes were innocent of Spanish or Latin, so at first they were taught to parrot the responses in the Mass. Soon, they participated in other ceremonies. Couples who had paired off before converting were urged to take formal Christian vows. Soldiers served as godparents and witnesses at the first baptisms and weddings, but before long neophytes enjoyed taking part in these rituals.[136] They served enthusiastically as godparents and witnesses, in part because the padres had little gifts or favors for participants in baptism and wedding services; crosses, rosaries, and bits of cloth were mentioned by Salvatierra.[137] As they became more accustomed to mission life, converts were offered material and psychological incentives to learn basic religious practices and to repeat certain prayers and anticipate responses.

The padres also taught crafts, moral lessons, Spanish, and, to boys at least, reading and writing.[138] Two centuries of experience confirmed that mission youth so instructed would have less interest in or devotion to the ideas and practices of their parents. Too, the padre, as teacher, was creating a personal bond with his students and training future helpers to assist him in the indoctrination of their elders.[139] However, the education of the young continued to hold out a promise that frustrated missionaries. They were the only available teachers, and they were already overworked. They knew and believed in the advantages of regular schooling, but most could provide it only intermittently.

In a few months or years of mission life, most neophytes achieved at least a superficial patina of Christian practices and Hispanic life style. They dressed and were housed in acceptably Hispanic ways. Their overt activities—social, economic, and religious—were imitative of European models. There were, however, signs that changes were only skin deep. After years of missionary experience with adult converts, some California Jesuits, in moments of candor, wrote of their profound doubts about the sincerity or conviction of most conversions.[140] At least one padre, Jacobo Baegert, admitted doubt that neophytes had any comprehension of even the most basic Christian principles or dogma. In a letter to his brother, also a religious, he spoke of the California natives' generally passive attitude and their disinclination for disputes, particularly verbal. He surmised that they had been attracted to the missionaries' message by curiosity and handouts of food. After that, rather than undergoing a religious conversion, they had been awed into staying at missions by soldiers' demonstrations of might and by missionaries' floods of rhetoric.[141]

Indian Resistance

From the missionary point of view, the conversion of California natives proved to be a slow, unsteady process marked by setbacks. Some gentiles rejected all the padres' proposals for years and continued to forage for survival in lands beyond mission control. The most profound rejection of the whole mission effort was expressed by the great rebellion in *el Sur* in 1734 when neophytes at two missions conspired to overthrow the padres, destroy the missions, and take back their independence. Several smaller revolts followed but with less disruption or loss of life.[142]

Although the majority of converts at most missions seem to have stayed with the Jesuit program and made some effort to contribute to viable communities, a smaller percentage of people resisted in various ways ranging from total rejection to simple non-cooperation.[143] Some Californians submitted themselves for conversion but lost their enthusiasm and held back from full participation in mission affairs. Some neophytes feigned cooperation with mission arrangements but took every opportunity to steal tools, crops, or livestock.[144] From time to time, here and there, a few mission dwellers simply took to their heels and abandoned their missions entirely.[145] Even among apparently contented neophytes, there were regressions. Out of sight of the missionaries, men doffed their new clothes. People turned to traditional healers for relief from ills.[146]

Neophytes who displayed no overt resistance were often not as cooperative or willing as the padre wished. They were inclined to promise their pastor anything he desired and then forget to perform. When they did work, it was often inefficiently, without enthusiasm, and with little apparent regard for the outcome. Neophytes exasperated some padres by their failure to confess, or worse, their failure to recognize sin—as defined by missionaries—and to identify themselves with it.[147]

Not surprisingly, the missionaries found it difficult to accept responsibility for the shortcomings they perceived in their "converts." Several charged that Californians were larcenous, lazy, perverse, dull-witted, wanton, and so forth, although some were perceptive enough to see a relationship between their program and the untoward responses. Padre Miguel Venegas, writing from reports by unspecified missionaries, summed up an unusually frank report of resistance to conversion and mission life:

> [Our] enemy is self-indulgence, armed with all the lawless passions. Accustomed to the freedom of the licentious heathen life they formerly enjoyed, Indians find it very hard and burdensome to give up ancient vices and submit to the purity of Christian ways . . . although at the beginning the heathen may be docile and peaceable — as long as the missionaries give them presents and bestow benefits on them — nevertheless, when the padres at length suggest change in their habits and mode of life, necessary if they are to be accepted for baptism, they become recalcitrant, and are incensed against the missionary

preaching to them — especially when they learn that they must live under his authority and submit to punishment for their crimes. . . . Fear of such punishment then leads them to plot vengeance and to form conspiracies against the padre's life. . . .[148]

The Jesuits had only themselves to thank for problems that appeared in the wake of their gifts — which were frankly designed to entice converts.[149] People who had never before received gifts quickly came to regard them as entitlements; they were bound to be disappointed when the gifts slowed or ceased after they had joined a mission group. Nor should the Jesuits have expected that their mission discipline would be easily understood or accepted. They knew that no form of corporal punishment had been commonly practiced by the native Californians,[150] yet they presided over a system in which a "culprit is either given a number of lashes with a leather whip on his bare skin, or his feet are put into irons for some days, weeks, or months."[151] No doubt many of the mission-imposed castigations were doubly resented because they punished behavior that had been commonplace and acceptable prior to the advent of the Jesuits. A transgression in point would be adultery, apparently a wholly introduced concept, that was punished with twenty-five lashes. A boy of twelve was whipped "for a shameful vice," probably masturbation.[152]

The Jesuits blamed many of their problems during the conversion process on the machinations of the men that they called hechiceros, the shamans that they lost no opportunity to discredit. As missions were formed, authority, honors, or privileges were rarely given to the men who had been shamans. Native healers and spiritual leaders always were charged — and sometimes with reason — with resisting conversion and fomenting opposition to the new faith.[153] Unrest might have been reduced if the Jesuits had found a way to place those once-important men in significant mission posts, but missionaries were skeptical about their sincerity and jealous of their past influence.[154] When rancherías left the padre's watchful eye, they were accompanied by his delegates who could counteract the influence of shamans, or at least report their activities.

California missionaries did not want to give authority to the very leaders who had exercised religious influence in pre-mission days and who might in any way be prepared to debate missionary precepts.[155] If a shaman wished to accompany his former subjects into a mission community, he had to bring in all the paraphernalia of his profession, "instruments of his diabolical arts," which the converts then publicly "trampled, mocked, ridiculed, and stoned," before throwing them into a bonfire. The Jesuits reported these as edifying ceremonial events.[156] At a ranchería attached to Misión de la Purísima in the 1720s, one shaman renounced his previous practices in such a public ceremony but later backslid and dared to perform rituals of the past. He misjudged the degree to which the missionary had influenced his converts. When reporting the outcome of this episode, Padre Tamaral was able to exult: "Men of the hechicero's ranchería seized him to take him before Capitán Rodríguez for justice, but on the way they kicked and beat him so that he died. They buried him under a mountain of spiny *nopal* [prickly pear] to do to him in death what he had done to others in life."[157]

On the whole, Jesuits did not overreact to the threat of former shamans living among their neophytes. No mission policy dictated their ostracism or punishment, as long as they were discreet and did not openly question a missionary's authority.[158] Decades after a mission was formed, shamans might live as neophytes within the walls, be recognized as hechiceros, and continue to attract neophytes who looked to traditional healers for relief from ills.[159] However, they were discredited whenever possible, and neophytes were discouraged from turning to them.[160]

Mission Agriculture

Most New World missions were founded with agricultural self-sufficiency as one of their goals,[161] but few missionaries encountered the need to train their converts in the mysteries of the new technology as completely as did those of the California peninsula. The natives had no concepts or words relating to agriculture or livestock. No one had planted a seed, tried to domesticate an animal — or imagined what could result.[162] The padres and their employees introduced every associated practice. Years after these introductions, they still had to supervise agrarian practices closely to prevent neophytes from eating seeds and slaughtering breeding stock.[163]

California lacked water, in comparison with most other mission fields, and some of its watered places had no arable land nearby. In the few locations that had both springs and soil, every sort of crop was tried — fruits, vegetables, and cereals — some well adapted to the conditions and others not. Jesuit prejudices and priorities resulted in a great deal of effort, land, and water expended impractically. Like other Europeans in the New World, they clung to the familiar foods of their homelands as symbols or even causative elements of a civilized way of life. Wheat was an inefficient crop, poorly suited to conditions in the central or southern parts of the California peninsula.[164] The missionaries insisted that it be planted for years both to satisfy their desire for bread and to demonstrate the triumph of Old World agriculture over the collection of native foods. An eyewitness described the practices used to grow wheat, beginning with the tillage:

> The plow of California consists of a piece of iron shaped like a hollow tile, with a long point or beak on one end. On the other end a wooden stick is inserted into the hollow iron which permits the plowman to guide the plow. It has no wheels, and the oxen drag rather than pull it.[165]

The next step after turning over the soil was to cut irrigation canals with a plow, contour fashion, at intervals of about ten feet. Then laborers released water into these trenches, allowed the field to stand until it was not unduly muddy, and sowed it in the following manner:

> A man with a digging stick in hand places himself at the head of a furrow. On the slope of one side of the furrow at the highest point reached by the water, he makes a hole that is long but not deep. Farther along, by two or three handbreadths, he makes another hole like the first and continues forward. Simultaneously, he makes similar holes on the other side of the furrow, so that he makes one to his right and then one to his left, taking care that they are not opposite each other.
>
> The wheat that is to be sown in the morning is put into water the previous night in order that it carry this moisture along with it and so sprout sooner. Immediately behind the man making the holes goes another man, carrying the wheat in a small container in one hand and with the other he tosses the wheat into the holes. When the soil is good and has rested, or when it has been well manured, four to six grains are sufficient. When it is not of such good quality, one uses ten to twelve grains; if the soil is meager, a few more. . . . When the wheat has been thrown into the hole, the same man tosses on it the soil that the digging stick just displaced. Alternatively, a boy follows the sower and covers up the wheat with said soil.
>
> After the wheat sprouts it is watered and if there are some bare spots they are reseeded. And one continues to irrigate so that the whole field is watered each week.[166]

A mission mayordomo taught neophytes to use appropriate tools and domestic animals. Some of his crew were set to drive off crows or other birds that dug up seeds or shoots. Unfortunately, they had no means to combat rodents that worked at night. If they or birds, locusts, or a parasitic smut did not destroy the crop, mission wheat fields yielded harvest-to-seed ratios ranging from sixty-to-one, for the poorest, to three hundred-to-one, for the best.[167]

California missionaries tried to breed and raise the common domestic animals at their missions. Cattle adapted well to the forage and water available around several of the missions. By the 1730s, their numbers had increased enough to yield substantial supplies of meat and useful by-products.[168] As their numbers increased, so did the area over which they had to range. Increasing effort and expense went into managing and protecting them. Those chores required herders and saddle animals trained to work in the pursuit and round-up of cattle. Mission mayordomos could not cope with such tasks in addition to their other duties, so professional vaqueros, usually mainland mulattoes, were hired onto mission staffs to undertake the herding and train the mounts.[169] Mountain lions limited the increase of herds; one small mission lost fifty calves and colts in a year. Missionaries sought the help of neophytes to combat this menace. In the early days of the California missions they introduced an incentive: any man who killed a mountain lion was rewarded with the gift of a bull. This practice continued throughout Jesuit times.[170]

Horses and mules, particularly the latter, were indispensable for the transport of men and materials; the missions could not have been established or maintained without them. However, horses and mules did not adapt to browsing off the native shrubs as well as did cattle. They suffered just as severely from depredations by renegade or unconverted Indians and the numerous and rapacious mountain lions. Mules, in particular, were difficult to breed. Throughout the eighteenth century, peninsular people were never able to raise enough to meet the demand. They counted on Jesuit missions in Sonora to make up the shortfall. Burros, on the other hand, adapted easily and came to be used as poor substitutes for mules, both for pack and saddle.[171] Dogs were rarely mentioned in Jesuit records although they accompanied the pioneers and were to be found at Loreto and apparently at all the missions. Some must have provided the typical service of watchdogs and the same or others were used in herding sheep and goats.[172]

Another inefficient use of scarce mission resources resulted from the missionaries' anxiety over the nakedness of the Californians. At a mission, a convert woman was expected to wrap herself in a blanket if she approached a padre, even though the Jesuits apparently propagated a myth to spread the belief that they literally did not see women.[173] California Jesuits regularly devoted the majority of their own five-hundred-peso annual stipends to buying and transporting yardage to clothe their naked neophytes.[174] In addition, they mandated that one to two thousand bushes of a perennial variety of cotton be grown at most missions. A significant share of available land, water, and labor must have been devoted to its culture — with a proportionate reduction in the missions' ability to produce or collect food. Equally wasteful, in practical terms, was the raising of sheep with an eye to using their wool for clothing and blankets. Sheep lost much wool to the omnipresent thorns and did not tolerate the heat well. Goats gave little meat or milk, yet were raised at great cost in labor to provide skins that could be used to clothe women. Mountain lions severely limited the herds of both these *ganado menor* (small livestock); despite great efforts to create herds, sheep and goats never became an important part of the mission economy during the Jesuit years.[175]

However, even if all mission agricultural efforts had been directed efficiently, they might not have succeeded, not while congregations were closely tied to mission centers. California natives had supported themselves before conversion — and in greater numbers — but to do so they had had to roam the land, year in, year out. Missionary plans called on converts to settle down to village life, both to achieve religious ends, and to create pueblos, the Hispanic social units desired by royal authorities. Despite the problems caused by unrecognized weaknesses and deficiencies in their methods, the padres labored mightily; most never despaired of producing the food that was the keystone of their plan. Some padres worked the greater part of their adult lives in directing neophytes to develop plots of land that could never have supported more than a few dozen people. Others worked at sites with the potential for copious production. There were periods of success, but no peninsular mission was destined to achieve long-term self-sufficiency.

The perverseness of peninsular life convinced some of the more ascetic Jesuits that it was the most glorious place on earth, a foretaste of the worst trials the spirit might encounter. Sigismundo Taraval wrote of fellow California Jesuit, Julián de Mayorga, founder of Misión de San José de Comondú, ". . . he asked specifically to be sent to a mission of the Californias, for these he believed were the most abandoned, desolate, and remote of all the missions, as they undoubtedly were, are, and always will be."[176] But even the most self-mortifying padre must have suffered anew when faced with the responsibility for feeding his mission children.

The tenacious Jesuits dreamed and planned and labored over the farms and ranches designed to support their missions. If application alone had assured results, they would have brought their desert arroyos into bountiful production, but when the most intelligent and energetic efforts were expended, when elaborate irrigation systems were devised and constructed, when plots of land were finally in full production, and when large groups of people were becoming dependent on them, the worst catastrophes occurred. At intervals of a few years, most regions were visited by rampaging chubascos. Deluges struck the hard rock uplands and ran off, channelled into steep gorges. In minutes, waters roared down onto mission sites and obliterated entire agricultural installations, carrying off crops, embankments, soil, and irrigation works.[177] There were extended droughts.[178] Plagues of locusts, sometimes year after year, ate every leaf in the land.[179] At times, everyone was hungry — padre, soldiers, neophytes, and domestic herds — and a mission's life came to a virtual halt while its people went out to forage from mountains to beaches.

Indigenous Food Resources

The colony at Loreto was nearly starved out several times in its first decade, primarily because it was forced to obtain food supplies from such far places and then transport them across the water. During each crisis, neophytes were sent out to forage in their ancestral fashion, and they were soon accompanied by the presidio's gente de razón who learned to appreciate, if not to savor, such items as heart of mezcal (*Agave* species), stems, seeds, and root of the *saya* (*Amoreuxia palmatifida*), seeds of *Yucca* and *Cercidium* species, and leaves, flowers, and fruit of many cacti, most notably *nopal* and *pitahaya*. At all times, but particularly before the agriculture at San Javier, Comondú, and San Ignacio began to produce, missionaries reported periodic dependence on indigenous food sources. *Vinorama* [*Acacia brandegeana*] produces edible seeds earlier in the spring than any other mid-peninsular plant. Since the native Californians often had difficulty finding adequate food in the winter, they feasted on these seeds despite the fact that they have a strong, medicinal flavor and caused the people who ate them to give off a disagreeable odor in their breath and through their skin. Padre Miguel del Barco reported that it was a hardship for a padre to be closed up in church with a congregation who had been eating vinorama.[180] Monotonous mission food probably caused the converts to crave other items from their traditional diet. As late as 1755, a missionary at Comondú wrote:

> For want of garden and farm produce, most of the Californians live on what nature affords them, albeit scarcely, in their countryside: wild tree-fruits, plants, roots, seeds. And inasmuch as there is little rabbit or deer meat, they devour that of squirrels, lizards, field-mice, cats, worms, snakes, and bats. This year the country was overrun by a locust plague. The natives built fires in the early morning while the locusts still clung to the trees, and then picked up the insects, which had fallen to the ground roasted or half-raw, to eat as tasty morsels.
>
> [Even] when we missionaries give them more decent nourishment, they long to retire occasionally to the brush in order to gather wild fruit, worms, and bats, all of which they regard as the tastiest delicacies. Recently I allowed the smaller Indian boys of my mission to make such an excursion into the woods. They soon returned with a rich booty of 125 bats; they roasted them to medium-rare and devoured them right before me without the least hesitation or reluctance![181]

Nevertheless, the Jesuits opposed the regular use of native foods. When neophytes roamed in search of food, the missionaries agonized over their concomitant loss of control. Padre Sigismundo Taraval illustrated the extent of their desire to supervise their converts at all times, when, in the midst of a food shortage, he wrote:

> In the immediate vicinity of our camp were many of the tart pitahaya,[182] the only thing that, throughout the Californias, might be termed a luxury. These were coveted by the Indians; no matter what orders were issued by the captains, and, despite all I could say, they would not restrain themselves. Whenever they went out, hatchet in hand, after wood, or sought water or anything else, they invariably strayed away. So irremediable was this evil that it was a strong temptation to wish that the Californians had never acquired this habit.[183]

A mission community was far larger, perhaps by a factor of ten, than the population that had occupied its area in pre-mission days. Native foods available within a day or two's walk could not have supported even a modest-sized mission's inhabitants on a regular basis. For example, mezcales, the agaves that were roasted and eaten as an emergency winter ration all during the mission period, were so reduced around some mission centers that a hundred and fifty years later they are still scarce or absent.[184]

Women at Missions

The male-dominated Jesuit world was prepared to avoid the normal interactions of domestic life. The vocabulary of the Jesuits was rich in concepts of father, son, and brother, but lacking in concepts of mother, daughter, and sister, and in the dynamics that produced and reproduced both sets of concepts as part of a whole.[185]

Jesuits came to California with a plan based on their European, upper-class concept of an ideal human society—an ideal also affected by their order's ascetic outlook and vows of celibacy. The missionaries were shocked by the native Californians' open embrace of sensuality. One reported that the Californians had no thoughts for anything but food and women.[186] As a result, the Jesuits made strenuous efforts to instill a European sense of morality and shame. During times when mission women had to be sent out into the countryside to forage, they went only in supervised groups.[187] Unmarried women were confined at night in locked dormitories.

Jesuits agonized a great deal over what they took to be rampant adultery among Indians, but that judgment was based on their preconceptions, because they did not understand California customs.[188] They had not studied the Californians' traditional society, the responsibilities associated with membership in a band or family, or in relationships like marriage or parenthood. By observation, missionaries gradually learned a bit about these important social interactions, but that knowledge played little part in mission proceedings. The Jesuits had not come to adapt to local customs, they had come to impose their own simplified version of European behavior. As it happened, the relationships and dynamics of the old ways differed drastically from those proposed to take their place.

In the European scheme, men had the prime responsibilities as breadwinners, they went forth to do the work that garnered family income. Women were assigned domestic roles that tended to be confined to houses and perhaps adjacent gardens. Little is known about women's status in California's pre-contact societies—about their rights, their influence, their ceremonial responsibilities—but every observer agreed that California women worked as hard as men, probably harder, at all food-gathering activities. They did the heavy preparation, wielding ponderous stone manos while grinding seeds and other plant materials on metates.[189] Unless times were desperate, men spent most of their time in groups—hunting, playing games, and exchanging stories. Therefore, women in California bands had always made crucially important economic contributions, and that conferred a vital sense of worth and involvement, not only from the women's perspective but from that of all members of their miniature societies.

At missions, women's labor potential was scarcely tapped, in part because of the missionaries' preoccupation with "appropriate" women's roles and perhaps in larger part because the padres viewed women as the more controllable element in adultery. The padres conceived an exaggerated determination to keep all women, married and single, under their watchful eyes. About a third of the neophyte women had a child or two to tend, but most worked only at other domestic chores; they did some food preparation but no cooking, that was communal and done by men. Thus, women were shifted from vital activities at the center of life to less useful and less valued sedentary chores at its periphery. In the missions, a majority were underemployed and underexercised. Women's status, health, and morale must have been eroded in the process.[190] Ironically, women had been the first and most willing recipients of the mission message. During most entradas, the padres reached out to women with special gifts and attention because they wished to baptize babies and small children. Women were receptive because they perceived the promised mission life as less threatening and arduous than that which ancestral customs had thrust upon their gender.

Fiestas

The Jesuits placed a heavy emphasis on a continuous calendar of activities for neophytes; they knew that it was essential to fill the long days and keep everyone busy. Routine labors and the weekly rounds of church ceremonies occupied most available time, but they also led to monotony. To provide anticipation and enlist enthusiasm, the padres held out the promise of livelier and more popular activities in the offing—fiestas. These events were part of church tradition and entrenched in Hispanic society, but they were also tailored for local appeal. The Jesuits emulated their missionary counterparts all over the world by incorporating recognizable elements of local culture into fiesta activities. Peninsular societies had been accustomed to an extended autumn festival when fruit ripened on the pitahaya and when, for a brief interlude, living was easy.[191] These native celebrations included feasting, singing, dancing, the relaxation of marital arrangements, and enjoyment of contests, pantomimes, and exaggerated buffoonery.[192] The more decorous of these activities were retained in mission fiestas but redirected toward Christian themes.[193] On the day of a mission's titular saint and on Christmas, Corpus Christi, Easter, and some feasts of the Most Blessed Virgin, mission servants slaughtered bulls, roasted them, and divided the meat among the neophytes. Padres distributed mission produce—melons, pomegranates, and fresh or dried figs—more generously than usual. The padres offered prizes of clothing or food that encouraged neophytes to compete in footraces and archery or to enter contests of dancing. The place became, in effect, a rural carnival.

All the rancherías came in together for Holy Week, the only such congregation of the year. At the overflowing church, padre and chorus made special efforts to perform the religious ceremonies with great pomp and solemnity. Processions of penitents were organized, and everyone was involved as much as possible in the fervor of the moment.[194] The actual celebrations and the preparations for them stimulated the mission's people and gave them a sense of community and involvement with their new religion.

Most of a missionary's energy and resources, however, were not devoted to such periodic activities. His church building and its furnishings had a daily influence on the converts, and he worked constantly to preserve and improve its mystique. Most mission churches were plain, adobe structures, plastered inside and out, but all accounts agree that they were decorated and furnished with as much splendor as the Pious Fund could afford. Neophytes were treated to the sight of high, gold-leafed altars and linen altar cloths richly adorned with lace; carpets led to the altar, and different colors were brought out for special occasions. The dim interiors shone with crucifixes, candlesticks, chalices, and other altar vessels, all of solid silver. Candles and incense were lavishly used. Grand-scale paintings adorned the walls, and the padre wore elaborate brocaded, silk-lined vestments. Choirs wore colored robes and sang from stalls raised above the congregation. No California mission tolled fewer than three bells, and trained neophytes sounded them to good effect. Every effort was spent to make the house of God a place of wonder for the converts and a glorious retreat when they were called in from the hard work and routine of their daily lives.[195]

All this splendor had a cost, and neither mainland Jesuits nor benefactors were asked to bear all of it. California padres, as a group and as individuals, made continuing efforts to enhance their own churches by motivating their neophytes to produce saleable surpluses of crops and other products. These they sold to local soldiers, or sold or traded either to nearby missions or to those across the Gulf of California. Thus, by helping to adorn the church, neophytes contributed in a tangible way and one that created a sense of teamwork and participation. Of course, church finery was by no means the only reason to introduce market economy to the missions. Food and clothing would always require the lion's share of any return from sales of produce, but it is evident that elegance, too, had its priority.[196]

The Mission and the Market

Missions could have used any surplus crops or products to advantage. In most years, a Manila galleon put in at San José del Cabo in need of food and stores; a mission could send anything that was needed or desired by the ship's company and obtain exotic goods in exchange.[197] A mission could also send its products to the padre procurador's warehouse in Loreto to receive a credit on its account for the value received.

Soldiers and their families influenced economic planning at missions. Soldiers received no pay in cash, but rather a credit with the warehouse at Loreto and a food ration distributed to them where they served. The padres had personal as well as mission use for credit at Loreto's warehouse, so they planned to produce commodities that would be in demand among their paid helpers.

The soldiers' rations included only a few staples and had to be augmented with fresh foodstuffs from mission gardens. A soldier could also afford a few luxuries, such as *panocha*, sugar cakes made by boiling down juice pressed from sugar cane. Soldiers had no land of their own on which to raise crops or keep livestock, yet they were required to keep five riding animals fit for duty at all times and at their own expense. They bought horses or mules from the missions whenever they were available.[198] Soldiers were dependent on arrangements with missions to provide their mounts with feed and care.

In these and other ways, the men and their families stationed at missions became captive customers for mission products. But in this interchange, the missionary was not always the seller. Soldiers often had skills or possessions that a padre wanted. One account tells of a soldier being paid to erect a house. In another, a man-at-arms sold his own dooryard chickens to fill the missionary's pot.[199]

California's wine was considered excellent, similar to a Madeira or sweet sherry. The peninsular Jesuits were always beholden to some of their counterparts in Sonora for gifts of food and domestic animals, principally oxen and riding mules. Wine was one of the few valued commodities with which they could return the favors.[200] California missionaries admitted to sending jugs of wine to Jesuit higher-ups and to some royal officials whose favor they sought, notably the port captain at Acapulco, in hopes of directing his attention to their needs while one of their ships was being careened, or when they needed to procure marine gear.[201] The wine's reputation outran the missions' ability to produce it, and it became something of an embarrassment as well. California had a good product in a region where wine was in demand as a luxury and as a part of the sacrament. Jesuit chronicler Miguel Venegas was so proud of the accomplishment — and so indiscreet — that he crowed about sales of the wine in the regions of Mexico City and Guadalajara at a time when the production of wine for other than sacramental purposes was illegal.[202] A rumor soon circulated that California Jesuits were reaping great and untaxed profits from extensive vineyards.

One contemporary account indicated the actual volume of wine produced in a year in California. Early in 1755, in his confidential report to his superior, Visitador General José de Utrera noted that four missions — San Javier, San José de Comondú, La Purísima, and San Ignacio — together produced nearly four thousand gallons of wine. He reported that, in addition, San Javier, La Purísima, and San Ignacio collectively produced fourteen hundred gallons of *aguardiente* (brandy).[203] Utrera did not visit in a year of exceptional yields; San Ignacio was the biggest producer of both wine and brandy, but due to a flash flood, the harvest of 1754 was only a third of what it had been in each of the preceding two years. The magnitude of Utrera's figures seems to belie the Jesuits' usual claim that peninsular missions produced only enough wine for sacramental needs, or, in good years, a small surplus they could sell or trade to help them to embellish their churches or stock their storehouses.[204]

Neophytes provided the labor that made all this mission production possible, but they received no pay or extra benefits as recompense for either routine work or extraordinary labors, like road building, performed beyond the immediate areas of their missions. Unpaid neophytes served as sailors, rowers of supply canoes, assistants in pack trains, and as militiamen during the rebellion.[205] No wonder missionaries were often portrayed as directors of slave-labor camps. In the Jesuit definition of mission life, each convert was a shareholder in a communal system; he was not paid in cash or credit because he was considered to be working for himself as part of the unit. He was directed to work for everyone's good and therefore his own. That philosophy—or rationale—served as a defense against those who charged the Jesuits with exploiting their charges. However, there was nothing communal about the processes of defining goals and assigning work; missionaries directed every governable aspect of their converts' lives.

There were other inconsistencies in the Jesuits' communal argument. Indians in some Sonoran missions were made to work to produce food for needy California. Converts at California missions that had better agricultural production were asked to share their harvests with the neophytes of poorer missions. It is doubtful that those who were ordered to be donors really understood and supported the larger communal benefits from their enforced charity. In California, another deviation from purely communal behavior grew within individual mission communities. Some time around the 1740s, missionaries began to allow some neophytes to develop small industries of their own. Many who seized this opportunity were women, otherwise little utilized in daily mission labor. This concession must have grown out of missionary attempts to appease neophyte discontent by accommodating popular activities that offset the monotony and drudgery of the converts' daily chores. Jesuit writings of the time did not chronicle their gradual acceptance of private economic activity in their missions. The existence and the details of this development first appeared in memoirs written after the Jesuits were expelled. To those accounts can be added indirect evidence that would otherwise have remained obscure, and a surprising picture of diverse small industry and commerce emerges.

Neophyte men hunted down many hundreds of deer each year and preserved their skins.[206] Although these people had not cured leather before the coming of the Jesuits, as converts at the missions they became proficient at tanning deerskins, using lime and tanbarks stripped from native shrubs; *torote* [Bursera microphylla] produces a dark red-brown leather, *mezquitillo* [probably *Krameria grayi*] creates a soft, ivory-colored leather. These cured deerhides, called *gamuzas*, were a popular trade item, eventually as far away as Spain itself.[207] Neophytes also cultivated private garden patches to produce vegetables and, after some years, fruit from their own trees. They raised chickens, goats, cattle, and especially horses, the animals they most admired.[208]

When mission people slaughtered cattle, most of the meat was converted to jerky; bones and meat scraps went directly into mission soup pots. Any fat they could separate, they rendered and stored in skin bags or bladders for use later in cooking beans or frying the ultra-lean meat. Before the Spaniards came, the people of California made a sort of moccasin and useful containers from the rawhides of deer. At the missions, they learned to transform the more durable cattle rawhide into containers for the backs of pack animals, covers for saddle trees, ropes, cords, or thongs — the latter vital for tying things up and forming packs. They learned to tan cowhide using palo blanco as the tanbark. With the resulting leather, they made shoes and saddle coverings and other riding and pack equipment. They made many — in time, probably thousands — of the bags in which they carried produce or gear back and forth to the fields or from mission to mission. All of these utilitarian items were in constant demand. When California began to develop a local economy, neophytes must have produced such goods on their own time as trade items. One padre described mission people plaiting the hair from cattle tails into halters to convert even that snippet into trade goods.[209] Neophytes from missions near the coasts collected the shells of the turtles they took at sea and profited by sending them through the supply network to faraway Guadalajara where they were in demand.[210]

Padre Juan de Ugarte at Misión de San Javier hired Antonio Morán, a skilled weaver from Tepic, to make cloth from mission-raised fibers and to train neophytes in his craft. Morán came to San Javier in 1709, spent several years at this post, and drew a salary similar to that of a soldier.[211] The weaver's students were primarily women, because they were the underemployed element in the potential workforce. In time, the more successful of the California weavers taught their skills to women from other missions.[212] In the later Jesuit years, neophyte women wove creditable blankets on their own time, using mission-grown cotton and wool bought with shares of the product.[213] Other women learned to knit fine, well-made cotton stockings that were more durable than silk. Even officers of the garrison found these hose sufficiently elegant for their use. Neophytes of one mission learned how to weave cuttings from palm fronds to make light, serviceable hats that missionaries and no doubt others used while traveling or working in the sun.[214] Using Sonoran baskets as examples, women learned to split slim canes of young *carrizo* and create rude but useful baskets of their own.[215] By heating and mashing the flexible branches of the bush *matacora* (*Jatropha cuneata*), women made little bundles of fiber that they could twist, weave, and sew together to form trays and even crock-shaped containers that had many uses.[216] Mission women also made a sweet preserve by roasting hearts of mezcales. This aboriginal food remained popular well into mission times.[217]

The Californians' traditional hunting-and-gathering society evolved on the move; they spent only a few weeks each year at any one location. After being detained in a mission compound, many tried to get away. Sometimes they used pretexts that were acceptable to the Jesuits, such as visiting relatives or friends at other missions, but often they simply ran away. As neophytes became more Hispanicized and made more contributions to the economy, they had more and more legitimate reasons to travel: they hoped to buy or sell products at other places, to collect on debts owed to them, and the like. Missionaries knew that these were often excuses, that the real goal was diversion, but they could use the converts' strong motivation to advantage. Padres gave the required written permits as rewards for good citizenship or for the quality or amount of work—in short, they traded them for subservience to the system.[218] The system was also changing to accommodate the development and needs of its population. Individuals applied their newly learned crafts and economic understanding to private commerce. They were allowed, to some extent, to travel for their own purposes. They acquired credits and contracted debts. Their handcrafts became articles of trade. Missions were acquiring more of the attributes of Hispanic pueblos.

At Loreto, the neophytes' produce and handcrafts might be sold or traded to the families of soldiers or sailors, or even to other local neophytes who had become part of the workforce.[219] Those same Loretans, when they held jobs as arrieros or drovers, traveled out to other missions in the line of duty. They probably did a little clandestine trading and certainly carried news and messages, thereby becoming part of the interchange and intercommunication between the sequestered inmates of the several missions. Many of Loreto's people appear in the record books of other missions; for example, in different months of 1753, Carlos de la Cueva and Féliz Gándara, identified as inhabitants of the pueblo of Loreto, served as godfathers at San José de Comondú.

Loreto was the heart of the colony, the mother church, the government, the presidio, the seaport, the general store, and the only place where all elements of California society could meet. Loreto was the magnet that drew gente de razón, neophytes, even missionaries when opportunities arose. The influx of transient neophytes eventually became so great that they outnumbered the residents. Theft became a problem. Discipline was threatened. The padre visitador finally had to curtail the number of travel permits issued, and the presidial captain restored order by chasing off unauthorized visitors. However, this extended episode reveals the neophytes' longing for personal freedom and the stimulation of the larger and more varied society outside the walls of their own missions.[220]

EIGHT

Misión de San José de Comondú

The cycles of life at California missions — daily, seasonal, annual, and generational — were the common experiences of most California people, missionary, Indian, or gente de razón. Pictures of their lives depend on knowledge of the mission context, but the stories of individual missions, their neophytes, or the gente de razón in their employ are difficult to document. Only the padres made a practice of writing, and few of them were inclined to chronicle the particulars of their mission operations. Nonetheless, each padre did keep up his mission's *libros de misión*, books of baptisms, marriages, and burials. Those registers could have been prime sources for vital statistics and data on social organization. Unfortunately, time, neglect, and a turbulent history left the Jesuit libros de misión in great disarray, the majority lost or in scattered pieces.[1]

However, there are survivals. The registers from Misión de San José de Comondú contain the majority of entries made between 1736 and 1768, the longest span of time covered by known books from Jesuit California.[2] With a few other documents that describe earlier events at Comondú or provide data contemporary with the libros de misión, a connected history can be sketched. Fortunately, San José was an early, representative, and important mission.

Background for a New Mission

In 1699, Padre Juan María de Salvatierra made his first entradas among the people of Londó.[3] During the following year, he established a formal visiting station called San Juan at Londó in honor of Juan de Caballero y Ocio, the donor who provided for its support.[4] Salvatierra found the people receptive, and he knew where to look for more of their kind. Padre Kino and Almirante Atondo had explored to the west and there met Cochimí who were related to

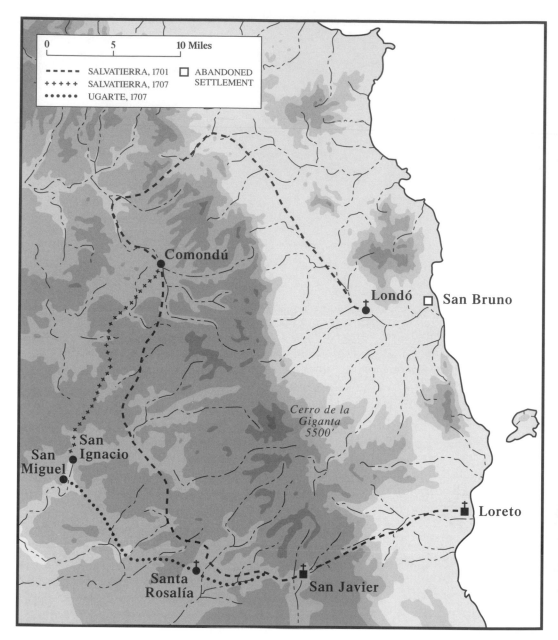

Map 8.1 Explorations of the Comondú Region

the people of Londó by both blood and language. Padre Juan María was anxious to visit them and begin their conversion, but the founding of Misión de San Javier then occupied the available soldiers and resources.

In 1701, while Salvatierra was at San Juan Londó to hold services, local neophytes described the route by which they crossed the forbidding Sierra de la Giganta, immediately to the west. Salvatierra had time, men, and animals, so he decided to explore the reported trail with his informants as guides. The padre was delighted when they showed him an easy way into mountains that, as Padre Juan María told it, Almirante Atondo had been able to climb only with the aid of ropes and elaborate trail-clearing efforts.[5] Once the uplands were attained, the missionary marched to the south and stumbled onto what he took to be fertile green basins. He decided to go through them to reach San Javier from the north, a feat never before attempted. From there, his party could return to Loreto on the newly constructed camino real, thereby "circumnavigating" the nearly six-thousand-foot peak of La Giganta. Salvatierra gleefully anticipated surprising Francisco María Piccolo by descending from the supposedly impassable north.

Salvatierra later wrote a clear description of the trail that took his party through "fertile plains," which the astute padre correctly identified as *playas*, drainage basins with no outlets. However, his opinion that rain would make them into useful agricultural fields proved invalid. Playas dry up quickly, leaving first quagmires, then expanses of fine dust.[6]

For the enthusiastic Salvatierra, the high country's agricultural promise was more than matched by the warm welcome extended by its many inhabitants. Local Cochimí presented forty-three of their children for baptism, and many conversions seemed possible. A recent event suggested a sacred name for this auspicious place. Benefactor Caballero y Ocio had shipped to Loreto a large statue of Saint Joseph with the infant Jesus on one outstretched hand. The craft bearing the statue was hit by a furious squall while crossing the gulf. The sailors invoked San José with fortunate results. Pursuant to this omen, Salvatierra named the highlands San José de la Giganta.

A third of the way through his circle tour, Salvatierra visited a valley that his guides called Comondú. It was a center frequented by the Cochimí who roamed northwest of Loreto and San Javier, and whose children he had just baptized. The spot had an elevation of 1,200 feet and lay near the headwaters of a modest watercourse. Its permanent water supply was a modest spring, really an active seepage choked with rushes, but the padre carried away memories of many receptive Cochimí and the baptisms he had performed. In his mind, Comondú was a prospective mission site.[7]

The following year, 1702, Padre Francisco María Piccolo went to Mexico City and Guadalajara on a crucial fund-raising campaign. In answer to Piccolo's appeal, Jesuit California's foremost financial benefactor, José de la Puente Peña Castejón y Salcines, the Marqués de Villapuente, promised and later delivered thirty thousand pesos to provide endowments for the missions of San José de Comondú, La Purísima, and Guadalupe.[8]

Founding Misión de San José de Comondú

San José de Comondú apparently was founded after no more entradas than Salvatierra's exploratory visit in 1701. Comondú lay fairly near Loreto, and its

Cochimí were closely related to bands at Londó that Kino had evangelized and Salvatierra had converted and then regularly visited from his base in Loreto. Comondú people were accustomed to visiting their relatives under conversion at Londó.[9] Out of curiosity, some probably went to Loreto and were among the visitors mentioned during the early contact period. These unconverted Cochimí witnessed firsthand how their Monquí neighbors were treated, especially how they were fed and clothed. In time, they began to clamor for a padre and a mission of their own.[10]

By 1707, the people of Comondú were deemed prepared to form a mission, primarily by their exposure to religious life at Londó and Loreto. A building site was chosen: a level shelf of sandy soil and rocks along the east side of the seasonally active watercourse and a safe distance above it. (Such a shelf is the remainder of an earlier, broader floodplain, and is called an *ancón* by peninsular people.) The site was enhanced by an adjacent hill that was a handy source of fragmented volcanic rock, a valued building material, but construction was delayed for a year by the illness of the designated missionary, Julián de Mayorga. The newly arrived Spaniard reacted badly to Loreto's hot climate and to the pervasive diet of atole and dried beef, perhaps the earliest indication of the notorious California dependence on beef jerky.[11]

Mayorga's former life contrasted dramatically with the conditions he now faced. He was born in 1670 to a patrician family in the town of Villarejo de Salvanés, twenty-six miles southeast of Madrid. He was educated at the court of Madrid where he studied grammar and humanities at the Imperial College. At the tender age of twelve, he was admitted as a novice to the Society of Jesus. After a brilliant career as a student at the important Jesuit college in Alcalá de Henares, Mayorga devoted himself to working through the stages required to become a full-fledged Jesuit. That done, he turned his back on the prestige and comforts of beckoning European opportunities and asked to be sent as a missionary to California. He taught philosophy at the Imperial College during a waiting period and then was appointed to his chosen field by the general of his order. Just before he boarded a ship in Cádiz in 1705, a clerk jotted down his description: "a good physique, coarse features, and a swarthy complexion."[12] By 1707, he was at Loreto, but was so ill that his personal mission was threatened with an early end.[13]

Padre Salvatierra was impressed with Julián de Mayorga's determination and allowed him time to recover. Mayorga gained strength and was finally considered fit to found the mission at Comondú. In 1708, an impressive expeditionary force set out to install him in his new post. His companions included Padres Juan María de Salvatierra and Juan de Ugarte, Capitán Esteban Rodríguez, several soldiers, some arrieros, and neophyte helpers. Their long pack train bore trappings for a church and equipment for a mission.

At Comondú, Mayorga was introduced, extolled, and offered as pastor. The gentiles were asked to bring in their unbaptized children, and many did. Padre Mayorga performed the baptisms in a ceremony made as grand as possible for the encircling crowd. Meanwhile, Padre Ugarte directed soldiers and neophytes in building a thatch-roofed, open-sided structure from the trunks and branches of local trees. Then Padre Visitador Salvatierra consecrated the new mission as San José de Comondú, a contraction of Salvatierra's former name for the area, San José de la Giganta, and Comondú, the Cochimí name for the immediate area in which the mission had been placed.[14]

After the labors and rites of the founding, Mayorga was left with one soldier for protection and help.[15] However, Ugarte, his neighbor missionary at San Javier, soon returned with enough soldiers and neophytes to build a house and a small but serviceable church of adobe blocks. Ugarte brought a dozen cows, two bulls, and a few goats to initiate the mission's herds and to supply milk. The experienced and energetic Ugarte supervised the preparation of a garden patch, although the spring was so choked with roots that Padre Mayorga had to clear it extensively before he could get enough water to irrigate even the smallest planting.[16]

Mission Organization and Routine

Julián de Mayorga hoped to begin work immediately on a full-scale church for San José, but 1709 brought an epidemic of smallpox that lasted over a year and killed half the converts at Loreto, San Javier, and Comondú. Many who lived needed nursing for weeks before they could care for themselves. Matters were made worse by a year-long shortage of food and supplies from the mainland. A pall of gloom cloaked the missions. The padres trekked back and forth trying to arrange and direct the feeding and nursing of their charges both at the cabeceras and out in the countryside. Concurrently, they tried to be everywhere to perform last rites and arrange burials. The few people who remained fit enough to help during this plague were compelled to dig five or six graves a day at each mission. Padre Mayorga was called from Comondú to Mulegé to administer the sacraments to a desperately ill Francisco María Piccolo. Piccolo finally rallied and recovered, but the plague and surrounding events distracted and weakened Mayorga for a long time. When the epidemic passed, the population at Comondú was so reduced in numbers and debilitated that constructions were carried out in slow, intermittent steps.[17]

Meanwhile, Mayorga was studying the Cochimí language with an interpreter from Mulegé, one of many neophytes from that mission who provided linguistic services and made their group noteworthy for such skills.[18] As he gained the power of speech, the new missionary introduced his flock to the basic practices of the Catholic faith and to the social and political infrastructure of a mission. Then he began to delegate some authority and responsibilities to chosen neophytes.

In addition to routine daily religious services at Comondú, special solemnities were practiced for baptisms and marriages. The newly baptized were given little crosses that they wore proudly around their necks—symbols that subsequently helped the padre to remember those that he had christened.[19]

They were also given Christian names to use with phonetic approximations of their native names, e.g., Pedro *Panayí*, Juan *Molocué*, and Isabel *Chiyigán*. Others were identified with their rancherías, as in Micaela de Kasalkyñí, Catalina de Calopú, or Basilio de San Miguel. Gertrudis *de casa* belonged to the group located permanently at the cabecera; the words "de casa" indicated a member of the "household." A generation later, Spanish surnames were bestowed. The diplomatic Jesuits did not have to look far for choices. In short order, unwitting neophytes were given the names of all Pious Fund benefactors, all recent viceroys of New Spain, some of the Jesuit hierarchy, most California missionaries, and many local soldiers.[20]

Padre Mayorga organized neophyte boys and girls into separate classes and began to inculcate basic practices to be observed in church services as well as to introduce concepts of Christianity and Hispanic social behavior. However, this schooling was impeded by the padre's chronic illness and interruptions caused by his frequent several-day absences as he traveled to serve the visitas of Misión de San José.[21]

Visitas of Misión de San José

The site for one of San José de Comondú's eventual visitas was discovered during the aging Padre Salvatierra's last significant exploration. Around 1707, before the founding of Misión de San José de Comondú, Salvatierra had come from Loreto to hold services at Londó. At the same time, Padre Ugarte was visiting Santa Rosalía, home ground for a ranchería attached to his mission of San Javier. By chance, the two padres independently received news—perhaps from some soldiers who were traveling in the line of duty—of a large arroyo cut into the great mesa that slopes to the west from the highest peaks of La Giganta. An abundance of water was assured by reports that the canyon was choked by a dense growth of *carrizo* (*Phragmites communis*), a false cane that grows only around permanent springs or streams.[22]

Each padre was outfitted for travel at the time, and each decided to go and assess the new find. The watercourse proved to merit its enthusiastic reports and to bear the formidable Cochimí name *Cadandugounó*. By coincidence, the two parties met face-to-face in the impressive arroyo, despite their different approaches. Water was everywhere; the arroyo receives subterranean waters from the series of nearby playas that lie above its 1,000-foot elevation. When the padres met, Ugarte had already chosen a promising location for agriculture which he named San Miguel and later developed into an important visita for Misión de San Javier.[23] Salvatierra selected a farming site two miles to the north to support agriculturally poor Loreto; he named it San Ignacio in honor of the founder of his order (see Map 8.1).

At Padre Salvatierra's death in 1717, Padre Visitador Juan de Ugarte took a logical step by transferring Misión de Loreto's two visitas to the jurisdiction of San José de Comondú. Ugarte knew from experience that the padre at Loreto had many administrative duties that served the whole system and had little opportunity to ride out to minister to visitas. Moreover, the people of San Juan Londó and San Ignacio spoke the Cochimí dialect of Comondú, not the Monquí of Loreto. This change enlarged and extended Padre Mayorga's responsibilities. San Juan Londó was located to the east, thirty miles away by a circuitous trail. San Ignacio lay two arroyos to the south of the cabecera, twenty miles distant by trail.[24]

San Ignacio was a godsend for the mission at Comondú, despite its irksome distance from the cabecera. Padre Mayorga faced a classic California predicament; he had to develop a mission site chosen more for its supposed ability to attract converts than for its potential to support them after conversion. Having little water or arable land at his disposal, he was forced far afield to garden at his visita of San Ignacio. The padre and his mayordomo would have to spend a great deal of time traveling to supervise distant workers. Nevertheless, Mayorga made this development a priority and oversaw the creation of irrigation ditches, garden plots, a chapel, and a storeroom.[25] Later, San Ignacio was one of the peninsula's most productive sources of fruits, vegetables, and cereals. In 1726, Padre Visitador General Juan de Guenduláin[26] reported that San Ignacio was producing figs, wine, and, most notably, enough sugar cane to yield thirty or forty packloads of panocha annually. Rice was less successful. Although over two hundred bushels had been harvested, rice required back-breaking labor and consumed more precious water than did other crops. Guenduláin found that the culture of rice was a hardship for neophytes and ordered it abandoned.[27]

Mayorga Builds his Church

When the health of Padre Mayorga and his converts permitted, the missionary and his soldier escorts staked out foundations on a roughly north-south axis for a larger and more permanent church at Comondú. They planned a simple adobe structure because no nearby source of lime had been found and no masons were available to build with stone. The width of the building was limited to twenty-one feet by the maximum length of timbers available to support the roof. With deductions for three-foot thick walls, the interior was only fifteen feet wide, but it was made sixty-two feet long to accommodate the neophytes at the cabecera. Padre Mayorga combined a sacristy and storehouse under the same roof by extending the already hall-like plan an additional twenty-five feet.

Neophyte laborers dug trenches and collected rocks of appropriate shapes and sizes for the foundation. Foundation walls of fitted and chinked stone were laid up to a height of two and a half feet, that is, from the bottom of the trench to about a foot or more above ground. When food was available to support labor, adobe blocks were manufactured, and the side walls were gradually laid up to a height of about ten feet. The end and intermediate walls were built even

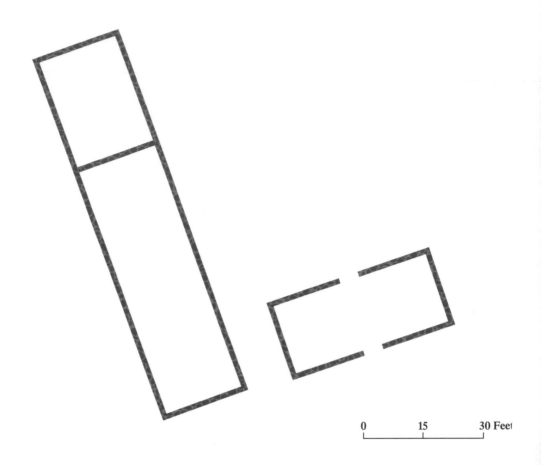

Figure 8.1 Padre Mayorga's Church and House at Comondú

The adobe church is represented today by its still-complete stone foundations. The walls of the chinked-stone house stand to a height of over six feet and show two doorways.

higher into gable points to match the rafter angle and to bear the ridgepole. Eight years after the founding of Misión de San José, the roof members were put up and the church was thatched.[28]

In early October 1716, the little colony in California staged a joyous celebration to dedicate the new church. The thanksgiving mass, sermon, and concourse of peoples was the most splendid event recorded in the annals of Comondú. Salvatierra came from Loreto to preside and was joined by Padre Piccolo from Mulegé and Padre Ugarte from San Javier. Delegations of neophytes marched over from these neighboring missions and filed into the south-facing door of the new church.[29] No doubt a grand fiesta followed the formalities; it was the last over which Juan María de Salvatierra would preside. The founder of California's permanent Hispanic settlement died during the following year.

The System and the Circumstances Test the Padre

Each mission created or exposed its own problems, and each missionary encountered unique challenges. Comondú's Julián de Mayorga had to try to reconcile several rancherías that proved poorly compatible and resented being asked to work and live in close proximity. Mayorga was fortunate that he faced no open mutiny or violent rebellion; but he also failed to win his people over to an enthusiastic view of mission life. His simplicity, his lack of ulterior motives, and his dedication — proven by years of effort — apparently earned him and his mission a degree of acceptance, but his message fell on partially deaf ears; his people resisted change and subjected him to many signs of displeasure.[30]

In 1720, Juan de Ugarte, then the padre visitador, called on each missionary to send a progress report to Padre Alejandro Romano, the long-time procurador de Californias recently appointed to be the Jesuit provincial of New Spain. Mayorga's report survives as a poignant sketch of early California.[31] On the material side, Mayorga noted, buildings at Comondú consisted of the church, a residence for the missionary, and a storehouse, all built with walls of double rows of adobe blocks "as strong as the character of this earth permits." Cattle were not mentioned, mules were few, but he had horses in sufficient numbers, and they were multiplying, thanks to fertile brood mares. The lesser herds, mostly goats, satisfied local needs, as they did at the neighboring missions, but that year, they had suffered a worrisome die-off. The drought that reduced their forage had also stunted the mission's crops.

The distant visita of San Juan Londó had only a few religious ornaments and a couple of shacks to house the padre and his escort. Construction of a proper chapel had been started earlier, but was not active at the time. San Juan had a few goats, but no other livestock, and no agriculture. A meager water supply was obtained from a batequi dug in the bed of the arroyo and had to be allowed to stand to clear sufficiently for drinking or kitchen use.

San Ignacio, with its abundance of water, presented a brighter picture. Two irrigated garden plots collectively produced ten to fifteen bushels of corn. Earlier, the missionary had found two small locations for grapes. Now he was making good wine. However, problems had arisen that threatened San Ignacio's agricultural promise. Mayorga noted the encroachment of sterile, alkali-crusted patches wherever his people had cultivated and irrigated—a problem for those farming the arroyo to this day. He remarked wearily on the *avenidas* (flash floods) that so damaged the visita's installations each year that much time was lost on repairs. He feared these rampages would scour the soil from the arroyo bottom, leaving only a pile of stones or pure bedrock, and his plantings were beset by worms and locusts.[32] Despite these problems, San Ignacio produced all of Misión de San José's crops.

Mayorga was hesitant to raise the topic of religion in his report. "As for spiritual matters, I do not know what to tell your reverence. Nearly all [my people] are baptized, but very few are preparing for communion. . . ." Mayorga's time was so divided by the necessity to travel to the visitas that he had very little to spend with any one group. The tired and ailing missionary noted the persistence of pre-Christian beliefs, gloomily observing that "most of the adults here now were reared with barbarous customs, false beliefs, and witchcraft which, in my judgment, are abroad in the land more than one might like to believe."[33]

Julián de Mayorga finished his report with a touching statement of his desire to help his poor charges, his frustration at his illnesses—"hypochondria," he called them—and a profound melancholy that was always with him, lowered his spirits, and at times left him barely able to lift his hand.

In fact, although the Jesuit system had evolved for over a century and had achieved comparative success, it remained an almost impossibly demanding test of its missionaries. They were sent out singly, largely as an economy. They were trained and expected to build and run centers for a new civilization among hundreds of people totally alien to it, under orders to delegate as little authority as possible to servants or neophytes. The Jesuits' role as superhumans enhanced their image with their benefactors and made each the indispensable hub of his mission, as one long-time California missionary suggested:

> [The] missionary was the only refuge of young or old, the sick or the healthy. Upon him alone lay the responsibility for everything which had to be done. From him the natives solicited food and medicine, clothing and shoes. . . . He alone had to mediate quarrels, look after small children who had lost their parents, care for the sick, and find someone to watch over a dying person. . . . [Missionaries] did tailoring and carpentering, or practiced the professions of masonry, cabinet-, harness-, brick-, and tile-making, or were physicians and surgeons, choirmasters and teachers, managers, guardians, hospital attendants, or constable.[34]

Missionaries paid the terrible price exacted by all those responsibilities and the endless workload. Intense loneliness and despair must have overtaken others beside Mayorga, isolated as they were and beset by hordes of essentially unsolvable problems.

A Distant Rebellion Affects Comondú

A decade passed between Padre Julián de Mayorga's pessimistic report of 1720 and his next known activities. Entries in the record books from San Miguel show him performing baptisms there between March 1731 and August 1734, despite the fact that San Miguel was a visita of Misión de San Javier. Padre Juan de Ugarte, San Javier's veteran missionary, had died in late December 1730. When Mayorga came to minister to his own visita at San Ignacio, he could spare San Javier's new padre, Agustín María de Luyando, a hard two-day trip by riding for twenty minutes to perform needed rites at San Miguel.[35] San Miguel's libros de misión show the presence of others who became part of the Comondú story. By 1730, a veteran soldier, Peruvian Juan Miguel Montaño, was at San Miguel to direct neophyte labor and to protect the mission people from unconverted Guaycura who ranged up from the south along the Pacific shore in search of food.[36] Between 1732 and 1735, Juan Antonio de Aguilar, Montaño's successor and later his son-in-law, served as a godfather at San Miguel on several occasions.[37]

In 1734, the rebellion in the South sent shockwaves throughout the peninsular missions.[38] Many southern converts had run away from their missions and joined rebellious gentiles. Similar defections were feared in other areas. By the beginning of 1735, Capitán Rodríguez had informed his Jesuit superiors that the rebellion could not be contained by the twenty-five men of the presidio and the handful of sailors, mainland volunteers, and local neophytes available to him. A call was sent out for warrior volunteers from the ranks of converts of the more northerly California missions. Two months later, fifty-six men from the congregations of San Javier and San José de Comondú were prepared to march. The recruits were armed only with bows and arrows, knives, and spears since the missionaries did not permit firearms in the hands of converts.[39] A few soldiers were needed to guide and oversee the recruits because they knew only the territory of their missions, regions that coincided roughly with the areas once roamed by their aboriginal bands. It is probable that a veteran soldier was selected from the escolta of each mission; in this way the neophytes had leaders with whom they were acquainted and in whom they had confidence. The visita of San Miguel sent recruits and its soldier, Juan de Aguilar.[40]

On 12 March 1735, the combined forces from the two missions left San Javier and trudged down its arroyo and across the northern extremities of the Magdalena Plain. They turned southeast and hugged the lowest slopes of the diminishing Giganta range. After traversing a hundred miles, they went up an arroyo into the heart of the range to arrive at Misión de Nuestra Señora de los Dolores, headquarters of the Jesuit effort to repacify the rebellious South (see Map 7.1). Los Dolores hummed with a babel of tongues and cultures. The heretofore sheltered Cochimí from San Javier and Comondú rubbed shoulders with Pericú from the region of Cabo de San Lucas, Guaycura from the areas of La Paz and the Magdalena plain, and Yaqui and Mayo from Jesuit missions across the gulf in Sonora. The march to the warring South and subsequent experiences forcibly changed the point of view of the parochial neophytes. In the ensuing months, they were exposed to new ideas and thought-provoking experiences, like the spectacle of Spaniards — missionary and soldier alike — frustrated in efforts to control peninsular natives.

One hundred California neophyte warriors "from the various missions" accompanied Gobernador Bernal de Huidobro and his troops when they went to La Paz in February of 1736. Padre Taraval, the principal chronicler of the rebellion, made few references to their contributions or casualties, but, in general, he described very low losses among the anti-rebel forces.[41] Most deaths were caused by the epidemics that were ravaging all the natives of the southern peninsula. Surviving veterans from the northern missions presumably returned to their homes after the governor of Sinaloa left California in mid-1737.

Misión de San José Is Moved from Comondú to San Ignacio

Epidemics and fear had created bad conditions at the southern missions, even before the rebellion. Those conditions, by chance, brought some assistance to the overworked Padre Mayorga. A few months before the fighting began, most neophytes of the mission at La Paz were transferred to the care of the mission at Todos Santos. Guillermo Gordon, the Scottish Jesuit who had been serving at La Paz, was reassigned to San Miguel, which gave the visita a padre of its own for the first time since Nicolás Tamaral served his apprenticeship there in 1718 and 1719;[42] once again, San Miguel had almost the status of a mission.[43]

The rebellion in the South also created the circumstances for an unusual visit to San Miguel by the ex-California missionary, Padre Ignacio María Nápoli. In December 1735, Gobernador Bernal de Huidobro brought Nápoli with him as an advisor when he came to California to quell the uprising. While the governor made arrangements to travel to the scene of the fighting, Nápoli visited missions near Loreto, bringing news of the insurrection and of the outside world; on 15 January 1736, he performed a baptism at San Miguel.[44]

A resident missionary was assigned to San Miguel for reasons other than Padre Gordon's availability. San Miguel was not a typical visita. Juan de Ugarte had foreseen the value of its unusually good land and water resources and expended time and labor for years to develop its gardens. Since it could sustain fifty or more families, its economic significance was greater than that of some peninsular missions.[45] Furthermore, though the visitas of San Miguel and San Ignacio were under two miles apart, each lay a long, troublesome ride from its mother mission. By tending to both, Gordon provided much-needed relief to the missionaries at San Javier and San José. Padre Agustín María de Luyando,

Ugarte's successor at San Javier, was busy learning to handle the affairs of a populous, important mission, and Padre Mayorga's health was deteriorating; he faced increasing difficulty in riding to his distant visita, or even in performing his daily tasks at home.[46]

Padre Mayorga was now in his mid-sixties and had been infirm for years. It is difficult to explain why he was not relieved of his heavy responsibilities. Less than ten years later, a padre visitador general was recommending that the frail Padre Clemente Guillén be retired to a Jesuit college on the mainland or, if that proved difficult, he be sent to live at Loreto where he could be comfortably housed and cared for.[47] Mayorga, however, simply struggled on. As he felt his life nearing its end, he directed the construction of a stone-and-mortar house, larger and finer than his adobe, so that his successor would be properly housed.[48] In 1736, when Padre Mayorga was sixty-five, he was so ill that he was taken, probably on a litter, to San Javier where Padre Luyando could see to his physical and spiritual needs. Julián de Mayorga had been the hub of the new way of life in the Comondú region for twenty-eight years. That continuity ended with his death on 10 November 1736.[49]

Probably due to his age and devotion to his original works, Mayorga had never relocated his headquarters from Comondú to the more advantageous San Ignacio.[50] Padre Visitador Sebastián de Sistiaga must have decided to make this move even before Mayorga's death, judging by its logic and the speed with which it was carried out. By December 1736, Comondú's people and possessions were moved—another disturbing event in their lives.

This transfer initiated an unusual round of changes in placenames. Misión de San José de Comondú was known by its full title to distinguish it from Misión de San José del Cabo which had been founded at the tip of the peninsula in 1730. Now the Comondú mission's full title was uprooted along with its people and replanted in the new location. Thus, the name San Ignacio was eliminated from the vicinity.[51] The mission's original site became a visita known as Comondú Viejo, "Old Comondú." The arroyo that now held San José and San Miguel soon came to be called Comondú—as it is to this day.

The move made such close neighbors of San José and San Miguel that logic dictated that they be under the same administration. In 1737, Padre Gordon, already serving at San Miguel, was named as interim administrator of both the arroyo's religious communities. San Miguel was removed from the jurisdiction of Misión de San Javier and made a pueblo and visita of San José de Comondú.[52]

Transition and Trouble

More changes and disturbances came to San José de Comondú in its new location. In July 1737, Padre Francisco Javier Wagner, a young, newly arrived German, became Julián de Mayorga's official successor. Padre Guillermo Gordon, who had filled in for nine months, signed the last entry in the separate records of San Miguel on 15 September 1737 — then disappeared from California's known documentation.[53]

Wagner was born in 1707 at Eichstatt, a town located midway between Nuremberg and Munich in Germany's Catholic south. After the usual education for a Jesuit recruit, he volunteered for missionary service around 1733. The necessary travels and further training in Spain and New Spain occupied four additional years. From Mexico City, Wagner wrote letters to his family that betray considerable smugness about German culture and material attainments, but his records also show that he received high marks in his studies of the Spanish language.[54]

The neophytes of Misión de San José were confused and shaken by the sudden introduction of unfamiliar elements into their once ordered lives. Padre Mayorga had converted or baptized nearly all of them; he was the only missionary who had lived in their community. On the heels of their padre's death, they were disturbed by recurrent rumors from the north of neophyte unrest at Misión de San Ignacio.[55] Troops from Loreto rode north to investigate, creating more rumors and tension as they hurried through the chain of missions along the camino real. Then, most of Comondú's people had to leave their old mission home to rebuild at a new site under an unfamiliar leader. Neophyte veterans of the campaign against the Southern rebellion began to return after months or years of exposure to influences very different from those they had known at their isolated mission. All these things contributed to uncertainty and division in the community.

Mayorga knew that his neophytes had undergone imperfect conversions. His report to a superior, "barbarous customs, false beliefs, and witchcraft . . . are abroad in the land more than one might like to believe" may be recalled.[56] Little is known about the pioneer padre's compromises with his converts, particularly his accommodation of former shamans — presumably, he tolerated and controlled them in a balance that produced a workable mission environment and met the expectations of his superiors — but as soon as Wagner took the reins, trouble began. He was young and inexperienced. He was only a few months into his first experiences as a missionary — his first attempt to direct and interact in a complex form of human relations — and his first exposure to the isolation and responsibilities inherent to the post. By May 1738, it was alleged that deposed shamans were conspiring against him. A serious attempt was made on his life: an arrow was shot at him from an ambush in the night. Most of Wagner's flock remained loyal and sheltered him, but he remained fearful. He lacked the security of a soldier's presence because an edict by Gobernador Bernal de Huidobro, in the aftermath of the rebellion in *el Sur*, had taken the military away from the missions to be concentrated at the presidio and two other supposedly strategic locations.[57] At daybreak after the arrow shot, Padre Wagner rode away to seek protection in the house of Miguel del Barco, his missionary neighbor at San Javier.[58]

Before long, Teniente Bernardo Rodríguez and a few soldiers from Loreto were sent to San José to investigate the attack. The arrow that had been loosed at Wagner provided key evidence: experienced soldiers knew that a missile and its maker could be positively linked, an interesting ethnographic sidelight. On that basis, the assailant was identified. Though he had fled, he was pursued, captured, and hanged. Several others were found guilty of plotting against the padre and were heavily flogged. Within three weeks, it was reported that those who had been beaten were conspiring again. The lieutenant and his men returned and rounded up the rebels. They were marched to Loreto from whence they were banished to the mainland, a virtual death sentence in cultural terms.[59]

A New Soldier for Comondú

The unrest among San José's neophytes ended by July 1738, and there was no further rebellious behavior in the environs of Wagner's mission, but the attack on Wagner had reinforced the long-held Jesuit conviction that each mission needed at least one armed, experienced soldier to protect the padre.[60] In 1742, a routine reassignment put soldier Juan Antonio de Aguilar and his wife and infant son on the camino real from Loreto to San Javier to take up a post at Misión de San José de Comondú. Between 1732 and 1735, while still a probationer on half-pay, Aguilar had served as a guard at San Miguel. His superiors probably returned him to the vicinity because they sought a seasoned man with local experience.[61]

The way to San Javier was familiar to Aguilar from his previous service, but he also may have ridden over it while courting his wife, María Dolores Montaño. Her Peruvian father was an old associate of San Javier's long-time missionary, Padre Juan de Ugarte. Indeed, Juan Miguel Montaño merited two of the few commendations that Jesuits bestowed on their soldiers in any official reports.[62]

As the Aguilars approached Comondú from the southeast, they saw before them a panorama of red-brown cinder cones and mesas that has changed little to this day. To the east, no more than twenty miles away, rises Cerro de la Giganta, but that highest summit in the sierra is scarcely visible due to intermediate peaks. Every geographic feature — cones, mesas, eroded slopes, and wide basins — is dotted with cacti great and small and leguminous trees. However, the typical panorama seen from the camino real does not tell a traveler the whole story. Through millions of years, waters from violent storms did not merely cut the gullies and basins that scar the sweeping mesas, they carved a few deep, narrow canyons below the line of sight, arroyos not even suspected until they open up at a wayfarer's feet. In the broadest and deepest of these are San Miguel and San José de Comondú, places packed with native palms, and — ever since mission times — dates, figs, vineyards, and kitchen gardens. This was the view beheld by Juan de Aguilar in 1742, this and the sight of a mission village, still under construction, that had replaced the thatched huts that he remembered from his visits to bygone San Ignacio.

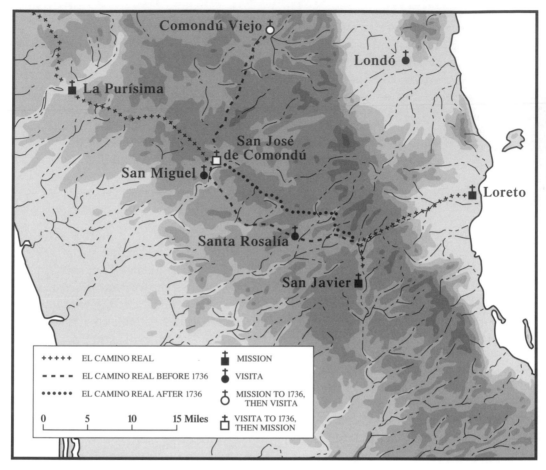

Map 8.2 San José de Comondú, Neighboring Missions, and El Camino Real

The padre was a stranger, as were most of the neophytes who had moved with the mission. Yet, in this familiar terrain, the soldier was also greeted by old acquaintances. He would have recognized San José's Hispanic mayordomo, Miguel Caravajal. In 1734 and 1735, during the last year and a half that Aguilar spent as a soldier guard at nearby San Miguel, Caravajal had been the *sirviente* (missionary's aide). During Aguilar's previous service in the area, he had stood as godfather to four newborn children of neophytes, doubtless because he had some connection to the parents. Now, on his return, he was greeted by five of those parents: Damián, whose wife Manuela had just died; Basilio and María; and Antonio Boyi and Isabel. Antonio was particularly conspicuous; he had become Padre Wagner's page, his principal interpreter, messenger, and informant for the minutiae of neophyte affairs.[63]

Aguilar's first duty at his new post was to approach the padre deferentially, present himself and his family, and offer to relieve the missionary of those responsibilities that a soldier could appropriately assume.[64] The broad outlines of his major duties can be sketched with some confidence, but a detailed daily routine for a soldier at a Jesuit California mission is difficult to reconstruct. In Comondú's record books, the soldier stationed at the mission was most frequently called *el compañero* (the padre's companion, which indeed he was), but neither he nor his job were commonly mentioned in formal reports. That is small wonder; acting as mayordomo, he supervised what might, in other contexts, be called labor gangs and sweat shops. As a soldier, he had to protect the missionary himself, guard food and supplies, pursue runaways, and punish wrongdoers. Even an outline of a soldier's role would tend to remind readers that a mission was not the cherished ideal community of teacher and converts, but rather a frontier institution with stern regulations, practical compromises, harsh conditions, and, at times, grim necessities.

The libros de misión and detailed reports by Jesuit visitors general provide specific information about the population encountered by Aguilar at San José in the early 1740s. The total headcount was a little over five hundred, and they comprised about one hundred and fifty families.[65] This accounting included San José itself and the mission's three pueblos de visita: San Miguel, Comondú Viejo, and San Juan Londó. However, the mission's people represented far more than four rancherías. The libros de misión mention neophytes from Blandá, Cadejundé, Cadenchó, Calagá, Calopú, Ibogomó, Juliagá, Nebocool, and Pindojol, bands designated by use of the different Cochimí names for the areas with which they were identified before converting.[66] Four other bands were distinguished by Hispanic names: La Bahía, La Cueva, San Juanico, and San Pedro.

A Day at the Mission

The Jesuit program placed a great deal of emphasis on formal organization of life at mission centers; the Jesuit plan resulted both from European mindset and from experiences with New World people. Missionaries were imbued with the idea that neophytes could be "civilized" by being led to imitate European life. Experiences in other mission fields had taught the Jesuits that radical changes in a society required the imposition of a regimen that left few idle hands or empty moments.[67] Converts were given organized activities and the padre, his soldier, and his servants provided daily supervision. Existing documents from Comondú and other missions nearby make possible a reconstruction of an ordinary day at Misión de San José de Comondú *c.*1740.[68]

When dawn began to break, Andrés, the neophyte sexton, tolled the Ave Marias on the bells of the church. Hispanic soldiers, servants, and their families rose promptly because it was their duty to arrive early, take prominent places at the front of the congregation, and lead in prayers and responses. In the early days of a mission, they were expected to provide the padre with a chorus, or at least a strong base to sustain the uncertain vocal efforts of the recent converts.[69] However, Comondú was a mature mission, and the entire congregation knew the *Alabado* and a few other pieces used regularly in the various services. As the neophytes entered, they broke up and sat in four separate groups: men, women, boys, and girls. They joined in prayer and proclaimed the Blessed Virgin. The *Alabado* was sung, first by men, then by women, then by both. Singing was led by two neophyte women, Inés and Chepa, designated as *cantoras* (singers) and picked for strong voices and musical ability. At other times, the cantoras probably helped in teaching the young to sing.

Worshippers whose work was needed to start the mission day rose from devotions and began their chores. Some served as the kitchen staff and prepared breakfast. One of the two soldiers would have gone at this time to unlock the storeroom and dole out foodstuffs to neophyte cooks[70] named Cheype and Francisco. One cook headed a group that prepared atole for most of the mission's people, and the other was in charge of preparing a more nourishing *pozole*, a thick soup of cornmeal, beans, bones, and perhaps a few scraps of meat. This was reserved for fieldworkers, the sick, and old people.

People who had no immediate duties stayed in church and took part in the daily Mass. That finished, they said prayers, sang the *Alabado* again, and went to take breakfast. The padre blessed the food and ladled it out to all who had attended the service. Miguel Caravajal, the mayordomo, supervised the feeding of those who did heavy, physical work.

After breakfast, some men took tools and went to work in the fields. Their accompanying soldier or mayordomo supervised their efforts and taught techniques for preparing the soil, planting, irrigating, and weeding. He put groups to work on the routine chores of the day, each directed by a man who had shown some ability to take responsibility. Other men were led off to work on special problems; for example, a good deal of time had to be spent in replenishing earth washed away by irrigation water or an occasional flood. Men were sent out with leather bags to collect laboriously the only earth available, sandy soil from thin deposits along the banks of the arroyo. When they had a load, it was shouldered and returned to be spread over any gullied areas in the plantings.[71]

Women, if willing and apt, were trained and supervised in crafts by the mayordomo's wife, the wife of a soldier, or even an artisan imported for the purpose.[72] Some were taught to spin cotton and wool, others to weave, others to knit stockings and caps. These activities, and the making of pottery as well, were unknown in pre-mission days. Although the mission had been in operation for over a generation, such crafts had not yet become fully a part of the local culture.[73] In these and other pursuits, gente de razón and native Californians associated daily and spent long hours side by side in mission workplaces. As years passed, these contacts were a vital if unrecognized part of the deliberate and incidental transfer of European culture and technology that characterized the missions of the New World.

At ten in the morning, the sexton again tolled the bells, and the boys and girls who were being prepared for catechism went to church. Segregated by sex, they chanted the catechism in unison, then sang the *Alabado*, which they were bade

Misión de San Javier de Biaundó, Located in a Deep Canyon in the Mountain Area Called Viggé by Its Cochimí Inhabitants.

A Limekiln, Dry-Laid from Volcanic Rock Fragments, Stands Midway between the Missions of San Javier and San José de Comondú.

The Llano de San Casimiro, Typical of the Natural Water Catchments above San José de Comondú.

Rangelands for Rancho Santa Gertrudis Where Capitán Esteban Rodríguez Ran California's First Privately Owned Cattle.

The Site of Santa Ana, California's First Mining Camp and Secular Village; Cerro de la Balleña Looms to the Southeast.

*Ruins of an Eighteenth-Century Silver Refining Installation at
the Real de Santa Ana.*

Adobe Ruins on the Site of the Real de Santa Ana

El Camino Real Crosses the Llano del Gentil As It Approaches Misión de San Borja from the South.

to perform "with proper feeling."[74] Much emphasis was placed on efforts to keep unmarried men separate from women and boys apart from girls. The Jesuits attached extreme importance to the ideal of chastity — and they desired to reassure superiors and benefactors of their zeal in promoting that ideal. A report, written specifically about Comondú in 1744, tells more about the process: " . . . in the main mission or town, boys and girls are brought up separately with the proper reserve, especially the girls, who are placed in charge of an upright woman of prudent judgment, although an Indian, to take care of them."[75] Thanks to the invaluable libros de misión, this rustic governess can be identified as Felipa Priora — in a mission context, *priora* can only have referred to a keeper or supervisor of women.

At midday, the bell was sounded anew, and all knelt, prayed to the Virgin, and sang the *Alabado* one time through. Then a noon meal was dished out. Those doing heavy work got pozole again. Old men, women, and children were allotted atole mixed with a bit of pozole. After the meal, everyone took a siesta until the hour of two, then work was resumed. At five, the bell was tolled, and boys and girls again went to church to recite the *Angelus* and the catechism. At the end, they took turns singing the *Alabado*.

The end of a mission's busy and regimented day was described by Padre Nicolás Tamaral of nearby Misión de la Purísima:

At nightfall, the Ave Marias are tolled and all kneel to acknowledge the Most Blessed Virgin, then a supper is served similar to the noonday meal. After eating, all go to the church and, with the padre, recite the invocation and responses of the Rosary and Litany. This is done then and not before, because everyone is free of duties and able to pay full attention to his most important devotions. After chanting the Rosary and singing the *Alabado* in the church, all leave; the men with their temastián and the women with their temastiana, to totally separate places where they practice the catechism and then retire. The older boys and bachelors have a room apart where they sleep; married couples have their own little houses because it is customary, when any of the mission flocks marry, to build them a house where they can live and sleep in decency.

Tamaral's unique picture of life at a California mission is idealized and rather abstract. Indoctrination and ritual are emphasized in a presentation tailored carefully for an audience of Jesuit superiors, wealthy patrons, and important civil servants sympathetic to the Jesuit mission cause. For these readers, a remarkably repetitive, regimented schedule was made to sound joyous and serene; neophytes were portrayed as docile, eager for enlightenment, fervent, and faceless.

A fuller, more realistic picture of mission life emerges when Tamaral's account is fleshed out with other material which reveals vital elements that he omitted. He largely ignored the community's incidental social life and the presence and activities of soldiers' and servants' families. Tamaral and the other padres probably viewed these dependents as having minor influences on mission affairs, so routine and unremarkable that they were not worthy of note. In fact, in their family life, in their pursuit of daily chores, in their socializing—either with each other or with the neophytes—gente de razón embodied Hispanic customs and practices.[76] Their active, visible participation in church services, their appearances as witnesses at neophyte weddings, and their sharing in neophyte godparent rites influenced the spiritual, or at least the ritual, development of the community. They were a major influence in making a mission—quite apart from its planned routine and stated objectives—into an incipient Hispanic village.

A Mission Construction Crew

Most of the Hispanic people whose names appear on the pages of mission registers from San Miguel and San José de Comondú can be identified from other sources as well. Soldiers, for example, appeared annually on muster and payroll documents. Most of these have been lost, but examples from the years 1718, 1733, and 1751 are available.[77] The padres occasionally recorded their servants' exceptional performances or interesting adventures, and some soldiers placed personal orders for goods that were entered in California's annual master supply lists, most of which survive.[78] Other gente de razón are known primarily from the extant libros de misión. The Comondú books provide the only known information about a group of temporary employees, a construction crew that began work at San José shortly after the mission was moved.

The need to import skilled labor arose early in the conquest of California and persisted for many years. In 1699, Padre Salvatierra wrote to the Audiencia de Guadalajara to request that a certain mason be sent to supervise the construction of Loreto's first masonry church.[79] In 1762, Padre Miguel del Barco reported that the construction of his stone church at San Javier (1744–1758) ". . . had various interruptions because of the difficulty of finding a satisfactory master builder who would go to so remote a land."[80] The builders at San José had no chronicler other than the padre who recorded their participation in the ceremonies of baptisms and marriages, yet a story emerges. Beginning in 1737, over a period of eight years, this crew built the structures necessary for the new mission center.

Jacobo Baegert, a California Jesuit who designed a mission church and oversaw its construction, left a concise account of the process.

> Building material, like workable stone, limestone (and the necessary wood for burning it), is difficult to find at most missions. It takes much effort to transport these and many other materials to the proper places. However, . . . time, industry, hard work, patience, and a large number of donkeys and mules will overcome all difficulties. Many California natives learned stone masonry and brick laying. A missionary, a carpenter, or a competent soldier supervises

the construction, or a master builder from another place is engaged for pay. The common labor is performed by Indians who, while the building is under construction, do not have to roam the fields in search of food. For scaffolding, any kind of rough lumber and poles will do. Should some pieces be too short, then two or more of them are tied together with strips of fresh leather [rawhide]; also the trunks of palm trees are used for scaffolding. When none are available nearby, they are sometimes brought from a distance as much as eighty or more hours away. Except for the three missions in the south, the land is full of common building stones. It is therefore possible to construct within a few years and with little expense such a respectable California church as would do credit to any European city.[81]

Juan Clemente Padilla, *el albañil* (the mason), was the foreman of the builders gathered at the new Comondú.[82] Masons served as *maestros* (master craftsmen or foremen) on most construction jobs in New Spain. In an area chronically short of timber, stone-and-mortar was the common medium for serious building, and masons rather than carpenters were called on to lay out proposed structures by using the levels, chains, rods, and other tools of their trade. Padilla's name first appeared in Comondú's records in early 1739 and was entered repeatedly until 1747. The names of Felipe *el Carpintero* (the carpenter) and Manuel el Carpintero also appear regularly between late 1738 and 1744. Their lack of Hispanic surnames suggests that they were neophytes from mainland missions,[83] a source of skilled labor and other support personnel for California from the first days of Salvatierra's conquest. Since they were born and raised in missions established generations earlier, they spoke Spanish and were otherwise much acculturated. When placed in a community of relatively new converts whose language they did not speak, they acquired the status of lowly gente de razón.

Juan Clemente Padilla probably came from a town in Sinaloa, or he may have come from as far away as Guadalajara. Such artisans, with their mixed blood and humble social status, were people of suspect virtue to the Jesuits or, for that matter, to "polite" society in general. Following Jesuit practices, before such a man was employed, he, his work, and his family would have to be known to one of the order whose opinion was trusted. On that basis, the builder would be given a contract to gather a crew and report for duty in California. Such crews were very small, a handful of artisans who could train the available neophytes to be their assistants.

When San José was transferred to its former visita, the existing buildings, irrigation system, and earthworks were inadequate for the suddenly greater numbers of people and the resulting need for greater production. Juan Clemente Padilla and his crew were brought in to build a new physical plant. A nearly contemporary description indicates the scope of the construction that the mason undertook.[84] The first priority was a temporary adobe chapel that would serve until time, materials, labor, and money would make possible a permanent and handsomely built stone-and-mortar church. An equally temporary structure was thrown up to serve as the padre's quarters. The mason's crew also built a storehouse in which supplies and harvests could be locked securely, and from which they could be dispensed as needed. They erected dormitories: one for unmarried women and another for older boys and bachelors. Padilla and his crew used one basic construction method: stone foundations, raised and tamped earth floors, walls laid up with adobe brick, and the whole timbered over with rafters of palo blanco or palm trunks and thatched with palm fronds or bundled carrizo.[85] In addition to these larger, communal structures, the crew built houses for soldiers and servants and their families and for married neophytes. Miguel del Barco described in minute detail the process of building these houses using forked tree trunks, mud and wattle, rafters, and thatch. His account is doubly valuable because it provides evidence that construction methods used in the eighteenth century were virtually identical to those in common use in the central and southern peninsula to this day. Since very similar structures are traditional in Sinaloa, it is probable that this regional style of building was brought across the gulf from the homeland of most of the early colonists.[86]

Juan Clemente Padilla and his helpers did more than erect buildings. Though San José was blessed with a large spring and a flowing stream, it was necessary to build and maintain *acequias* (open ditches either unlined or lined with stone and mortar) to conduct water to plots of arable land.[87] This work required a mason's skills and experience because the inclination of each acequia had to be carefully engineered. Padilla also must have overseen the construction of *pilas*, small reservoirs used to accumulate spring water to be used for irrigation. Finally, the mason may have supervised the construction of retaining walls that were back-filled with earth to create level gardens at elevations convenient for irrigation. Such constructions were pioneered at San Miguel by Padre Juan de Ugarte soon after he envisioned the arroyo's agricultural potential.[88] Similar terraces and stone-lined irrigation ditches are still in daily use at Comondú in the late twentieth century.

In most years, the new Comondú could be made to produce agricultural surpluses that became crucial not only to its own people, but to the survival of the system. The presidio often had short-term food shortages and several of the other missions were never able to supply their own basic food needs. They depended at times on transfers from more productive sisters.[89] The development and maintenance of San José's agricultural capability — and expenditures for salaries to do so — continued to be vital all through the Jesuit years.

Agriculture at Misión de San José

Misión de San José's basic crops were wheat and corn. In 1753, the only year in which harvests were reported in precise figures, the yield of wheat was seventy-two tons and that of corn was thirty-three tons. That harvest probably represented the mission's needs for the year with a ten to twenty percent surplus.[90]

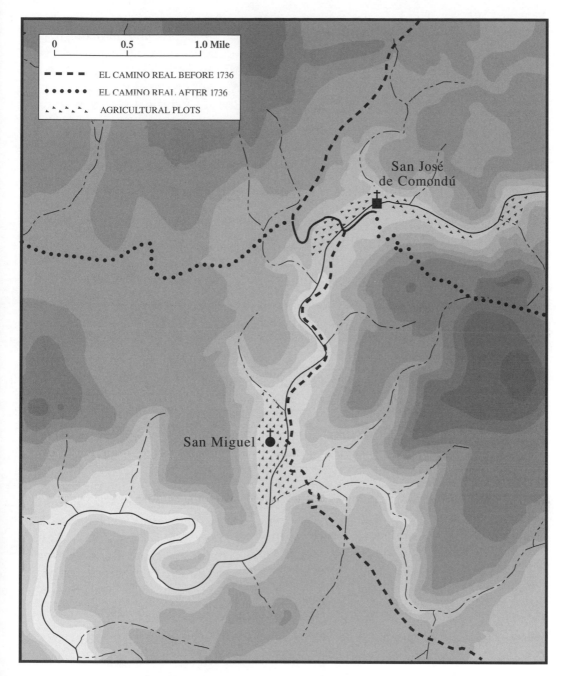

Map 8.3 Misión de San José de Comondú and the Visita of San Miguel

The climate, soil, and water resources of Arroyo de Comondú were even better suited to orchards and vineyards. Padre Juan de Ugarte initiated the first plantings at San Miguel as early as 1714 and experimented intelligently with every feasible sort of fruit tree.[91] By the time Misión de San José was relocated to the same vicinity, certain trees had prospered and provided the cuttings or seed required to plant the mission's new orchards.[92] Principal successes were oranges, pomegranates, olives, lemons, bananas, and especially figs and grapes. The last two were the basis of real trade because they yielded dried fruit and wine, products that could be stored or transported to become valuable trade items.

In 1744, Comondú's grape plantings were described as "four small vineyards," which undoubtedly included those at San Miguel.[93] In 1767, the mission possessed two wine presses, one large and one small, and an assortment of large containers used in the preparation, fermentation, and storage of wine. These included tubs and vats as well as seventeen barrels and 140 *tinajas* (casks of about eleven-gallon capacity). In addition, San José had two stills for the preparation of brandy.[94] Stoppers or seals for the wine and brandy containers were made from peninsular materials. Large openings were stopped with plugs carved from the pithy wood of the tree called *corcho* or *colorín* (*Erythrina flabelliformis*); smaller-necked vessels were sealed with the wax that exudes from the trunks and branches of *palo brea* [*Cercidium praecox*].[95]

A curious tale relates to the fermenting and storing of wine at San Miguel. During his early years at San Javier, Juan de Ugarte made a call at his visita of Santa Rosalía. Heathen from the north also came in, curious to see Spaniards and their novel possessions. When they noticed the great copper pots used in making pozole, the guests remarked that they had others of a similar nature in their land. Ugarte sent his soldier escort, Alférez Juan Bautista Mugazábal, to investigate. When the soldier and his guides arrived at their goal in the mouth of Cadegomó arroyo, the alférez found his informants fearful and far from eager to produce the copper vessels. After much coaxing, some young men took Mugazábal to the beach and showed him where they were buried in sand. The party soon unearthed seven large copper water jars, each with a capacity of over nine gallons ["70 *cuartillos*"]. Local Cochimí had found them on the beach many years before. Because they were so foreign to the Cochimí's experience, they were taken to a cave and lined up with their mouths facing out — these mouths being the aspect that most fascinated their finders. Everyone in the area came to see and wonder, but soon there was a local epidemic, and the council of shamans and headmen decided that it was due to evil exhalations from the alien "mouths." Young men were recruited to charge up to the jars and plug their offending mouths with mud and weeds. Thus stifled, they were returned to the beach and buried.

The jars were plainly of European make, but Ugarte knew that they had not been part of the baggage hauled across the peninsula in 1684 by Admiral Isidro de Atondo's party, the only foreigners known to have visited the area. Padre Miguel del Barco reasoned that they were not from a shipwreck because no other flotsam or artifacts had turned up in the greater area. He concluded that men from some ship, perhaps a Manila galleon, had put ashore with the jars to look for water. Perhaps they were surprised by Cochimí and took to their longboats, leaving the heavy vessels behind. Ugarte had them taken to San Javier, leaving one off at San Miguel as he passed. Barco reported that the jars served throughout the Jesuit period as admirable containers in which to prepare wine.[96]

Sugar, another of San Ignacio's successful crops, was the basis of a small but profitable industry in panocha, cakes of crude brown sugar. The construction and equipment needed for their manufacture were collectively called a *trapiche*, which included a sugar-cane press, a very large copper cauldron, and molds in which the *piloncillos* (cone-shaped cakes of panocha) were cast. The presses were made in Sinaloa—and later in California itself—from the hardwood of mesquite.[97] A mule or burro was harnessed to a long lever attached to the core of the press. The animal walked in endless circles to turn the rollers of the press as cane was fed in. The resulting juice was sluiced away from the press to catchments, from which it was scooped up in buckets to fill the cauldron. That great pot was heated by hardwood and dried cane stalks fed into a furnace chamber below. When the pressings were boiled down to the proper consistency, the viscous liquid was ladled into the molds and allowed to cool and harden. San Ignacio's reported annual production of forty loads (about seven thousand pounds) of panocha, allowed some sweets for the people of Comondú and a nice surplus to exchange for credit at the warehouse in Loreto.[98]

Other harvests in the arroyo of Comondú—beans, watermelon and other melons, squash, and garbanzos—were too scarce or perishable to become items of commerce and were consumed locally.[99]

Individual Neophytes

Libros de misión for San José offer many small clues to the organization of the mission's society, particularly the contributions made by certain individuals.[100] Most prominent are the records of the neophyte officials appointed to assist the padres' administration of mission rules.[101] The first mention of a governor in San José's record books is dated March 1739 when "Joaquín el gobernador" and his wife acted as godparents to a newborn child of neophytes from Londó. This Joaquín appeared as a godfather the previous December, but simply as "Joaquín de Comondú," which indicates that he was one of the group of neophytes who had inhabited the original site of the mission and moved with it to the new location. The baptismal record provides evidence of the governor's status. Between 1739 and 1743, he served six times as a godfather and his wife four times as a godmother. No other neophyte man or couple appear as often in this role. Moreover, the governor and his wife had two sons, born in 1739 and 1743, and on each occasion gente de razón acted as godparents.

Surprisingly few captains of rancherías appear in the records of San José, although they should have been prestigious choices for godfathers or witnesses at weddings. Between 1738 and 1740, an exception appears that may help to solve the mystery. In those years, Francisco, "capitán de San Miguel," and his wife Ignacia appeared five times, always in the role of godparents. Their headquarters lay a half-hour's stroll from San José. San Miguel had always been operated much as if it were a mission; it had established agriculture and people in fixed dwellings. Francisco and Ignacia could have spent a good deal of time at San José as well as at their nominal post in San Miguel. No doubt the padre influenced the choice of godparents and witnesses, and he suggested neophyte officials or other individuals he knew well and of whom he approved. In this respect, Francisco had a huge advantage over any capitán who spent three-fourths of his time away from the mission.

Records show that certain neophytes were identified with their occupations, usually over long periods of time. They provided necessary services and probably were some of the mission's more loyal and hard-working subjects. At Comondú, in addition to the already mentioned page, sexton, cooks, singers, and governess, several neophytes are named whose jobs lay outside the mission compound: Bernardino Vaquero, Julián Vaquero, and Vicente Vaquero (cowherds), Blas Pastor (shepherd), Felipe Arriero and Mateo Arriero (mule and burro drivers). Missionary letters describe these as jobs difficult to trust to neophytes. Outside the immediate purview of missionary or soldier, unconverted Californians or runaway neophytes often connived with their fellows who had jobs as herders or drivers. Even mature missions suffered heavy losses when they were betrayed in this fashion and their livestock killed and eaten. At San José, however, although Padre Wagner was ill and absent from his mission more than most of his fellows, there are no reports of excessive losses.

Since every male performed some sort of labor, Miguel Gañán (laborer or teamster), whose name appears often, may have worked as a plowman or teamster rather than a simple laborer. Ignacio Pescador (fisherman) must have had notable skills and returned significant catches to acquire his epithet. An odd nickname, "Quelites," was given to one neophyte as a Christian name since he appears to have had no other. *Quelites* meant edible herbs; the name suggests that the man was known for skills in finding wild plants for food or perhaps for acting as an herbalist and making folk remedies.

In addition to indicating specific occupations, libros de misión from San José provide an assortment of neophyte nicknames. The missionary, reflecting the practices of the day throughout New Spain, used all sorts of descriptive terms to distinguish individuals among his hundreds of charges. He listed Clemente Tuerto (the one-eyed), Ignacio el Manco (the one-handed), Juan Bautista el Chato (the moon-faced), and Pablo Gordo (the fat) [Gordo was not simply a family name; in one entry the padre wrote *"Pablo de la Paz vulgo el Gordo"* ("Pablo from La Paz, commonly called the Fat")]. Salvador el Sordo (the deaf) died at Casalquiñí in 1738, while Juan el Ciego (the blind) and his wife lived for many years at the mission. Baptismal entries for two children born to Manuela

Ciega (the blind) form melancholy vignettes; each contains the phrase "by a father unknown."

Dramatic stories are suggested by entries in the vital records of Comondú. One concerns another handicapped neophyte, Andrea la Coxa (the lame), a woman from San Miguel, and, tangentially, soldier Juan de Aguilar. Aguilar's name first appeared in the local records on 19 July 1732, when he acted as a godfather at San Miguel to an infant son of Hermenegildo and his wife Andrea. In 1736, her husband deceased or long departed, Andrea gave birth to a daughter—no father listed. This child's baptism also shows an oblique tie to Aguilar; Antonio Boyi stood as the baby's godfather just as Juan de Aguilar had served as godfather for Antonio's child three years earlier. In a society of several hundred people, instances of interrelated godparenthood are usually more than coincidences. They reflect circles of friendships or occupational ties.

In 1739, Padre Francisco Javier Wagner noted in the Book of Burials that María Antonia, mother of Andrea la Coxa, had died without last rites because at the time of her death she was out wandering in the arroyo of Cadegomó, a watercourse downstream from the old site of Comondú. On 24 September 1740, Wagner wrote in the same book of burials, ". . . at this time, Andrea la Coxa drowned in San Miguel" [or "choked to death"; *se ahogó* could mean either. However, September is the high season for chubascos, the area's wettest and most violent storms.]

The books of births and burials also sketch out a dismal pattern for Julián the Vaquero and his wife, Jacinta (written *Hyacintha* in the records). Between 1737 and 1743, five children were born to them, and four perished in infancy. In that period, an older daughter and Julián's mother died as well. The case was more extreme than most, but sickness and death made up a relentless part of daily mission routine. In those years, thirty-three percent of the children died before the age of two, and Comondú had a net gain of only fourteen people. In seven subsequent years, matters worsened and there was a net loss of seventy-five. In 1744, San José's neophyte population was counted at 513, yet since 1708 1,563 people, mostly infants, had been baptized.[102] These people, who "died without fear," lived with death as a beckoning neighbor.[103]

Social Interaction

While building roads, fetching supplies, delivering produce, and performing many other mission chores, soldiers and neophytes traveled and worked together away from the mission. It is likely that friendships formed, which may in part account for the ritualized relationships between specific soldiers and particular neophytes that appear in mission baptismal records. Although neophytes usually served as godparents to other neophytes, soldiers were often asked to act as godfathers to children of neophytes. This suggests that respect and friendship existed, not merely fear. Even in his policeman's role, the soldier was often protecting the interests of the majority, the neophytes who lived by mission rules.

Traces of soldiers' relations with converts, or of their own careers, or the careers of gente de razón in general, are more in evidence at Comondú than at any other mission — or, indeed, in the system as a whole — thanks to the survival of the invaluable libros de misión from San Miguel and San José. Those records are criss-crossed with the comings, goings, and doings of gente de razón who lived or served in their area.

The first soldier-guard to appear on those pages was Juan Miguel Montaño, who served at San Miguel in 1730 and 1731. His wife was Magdalena Miajuan, apparently a native Californian and perhaps a local neophyte. Juan Antonio de Aguilar, later Montaño's son-in-law, was posted at San Miguel from 1732 until 1735 when he left to fight the rebellion in the South. By the first days of 1737, if not before, the soldier at San José de Comondú was Juan Carrillo, an español and founder of the Carrillo family so prominent in later California affairs.[104] San Miguel's book of baptisms shows that, in the few months after his arrival, Carrillo performed the emergency baptism of a neophyte child, and that his daughters María Ignacia and Micaela acted as *madrinas* (godmothers) to other neophyte children. Juan Carrillo's status is firmly established by a February 1738 entry in San José's baptismal record. The occasion was the baptism of Felipa, newborn daughter of Miguel Caravajal, the mayordomo, and his wife, Prudencia. The godmother is shown to have been "Ifigenia, wife of Carrillo who is stationed as a soldier at San Miguel." San Miguel ceased to have separate books in 1737, but, in those of San José, there are additional entries showing that Carrillo, his wife, Ifigenia Millán, and daughters Micaela, María Ignacia, and Josefa, continued to act as godparents from time to time until the summer of 1742, when Carrillo was reassigned and his place taken by the returning Juan de Aguilar.[105]

These three Carrillo daughters were born during the mid- to late 1720s and would have been adolescent or preadolescent during the time in which Padre Guillermo Gordon allowed or encouraged them, on six occasions, to serve as madrinas to newborn children of converts. This is the earliest instance of a practice that recurred throughout California's mission history. Certain padres apparently considered the immature daughters of gente de razón as desirable godparents — and seldom employed their brothers in the same role. Young girls may have appeared to these isolated celibate males as ideal models of purity not yet tarnished by the realities of adulthood. Some such consideration must have overcome an obvious disadvantage: the girls' relatively brief tenure at any one mission would prevent them from carrying out all but the most preliminary of a godmother's traditional responsibilities.[106]

Hispanic women were mentioned in few mission-related writings other than their unavoidable inclusion in the libros de misión. Jesuits were discouraged in the strongest terms from associating with any women, but most specifically with español women who were seen as a greater temptation; presumably their cultural background would make them more attractive companions. Missionaries were specifically forbidden to have women as cooks or to have women, even blood relatives, in their houses for any reason whatever. Rules of their order prohibited Jesuits from entering a house occupied only by a woman.[107] To mention a woman in writing would have conveyed the undesirable message that she had occupied a Jesuit's thoughts. These conventions created a real gap in the documentation, a failure to record and report the roles of women in early California.

In 1742, there were five gente de razón families in residence at Comondú, those of the mayordomo, the soldier, the mason, and the married carpenter. Unfortunately, one of Padre Wagner's idiosyncrasies was to ignore the family names of Hispanic women.[108] He made an exception of Aguilar's wife, María Dolores Montaño, for no apparent reason, unless it was the fact that her father was a well-known man who had served in the immediate area.

Miguel Caravajal's wife was named Prudencia. She and Caravajal apparently were married in 1737; she appeared as a godmother at San José in late 1736 simply as "Prudencia," but thereafter was regularly listed as the wife of Caravajal. Juan Clemente Padilla's wife was identified only as María Antonia. She bore no children during the couple's eight years at Comondú, but they brought at least two children with them, daughters Manuela and Petra, who were about five to nine years of age at the time of their arrival in 1738. The carpenter named Felipe was married to Isabel. The other carpenter, Manuel, was the only single man among San José's gente de razón. By 1747, he too had taken a wife. Jesuit policy, based on long experience, encouraged the employment of married men for work at missions. Unmarried men were more inclined to have sexual designs and influence on neophyte women, and Indian men had always been suspicious and resentful of men who came among them with no women of their own.

Baptismal records provide clues to relationships between the Jesuits' Hispanic servants and neophytes at San José. Gente de razón acted as godparents to many of the neophytes' children. Some cases undoubtedly resulted from friendships or social politics at the mission. For example, two sons of Joaquín, governor of the neophytes at the cabecera of Misión de San José, were baptized in 1739 and 1743; godparents to the first were Juan Clemente Padilla and his wife; godmother to the second was Prudencia, wife of mayordomo Miguel Caravajal.

In some cases of *compadrazgo* (godparental ties), there are no clues as to the relationship of parents to godparents. Perhaps María Antonia, wife of Padilla and many times a godmother, was simply a favorite of the missionary, a trusted person deemed suitable and usually available. In other cases, real bonds of friendship no doubt were involved. In 1739, María Antonia acted as godmother to a daughter of a neophyte couple, Juan Bautista Sombra and Ana — and their child was named María Antonia. In 1743, María Antonia de Padilla served as godmother to a son of the same couple, certainly not a chance occurrence. Similarly, Juan de Aguilar stood as godfather to a son of neophytes Basilio Sánchez and María at San Miguel in 1733; at San José ten years later, Aguilar's wife was godmother to the same couple's daughter. All these events, recorded in a short span of years, give strong if not very explicit evidence of the impact of gente de razón on a mission community.

Although gente de razón were often involved in neophytes' ritual ceremonies, they depended almost entirely on each other for their own. When the Caravajals' son, Nazario José, was baptized in 1740, his godparents were Juan Padilla and his wife Antonia. The previous year, when a short-lived daughter was born to Felipe the carpenter and his wife, the Padillas were also the godparents. A month or so after Juan de Aguilar and his wife arrived at San José, she served as godmother to the Caravajals' third child, daughter Francisca Luisa. This pattern of gente de razón acting as godparents to each other's children remained constant throughout California mission times. When a child was born at an isolated mission, friends or family members traveled long distances to help during the confinement and to participate in the baptismal ritual. This demonstrated the efforts made by the Hispanic population to maintain all aspects of its traditional society even in difficult circumstances.

Rarely did an Hispanic child have neophyte godparents. However, on the tenth Sunday of 1743, Padre Francisco Javier Wagner opened "The Book of Baptisms, Marriages, & Burials performed at this Mission of San José de Comondú since the year 1736," and penned the 535th numbered entry in the baptismal section: "On the 10th of March, I solemnly baptized Francisco Javier, infant son of Señor Juan de Aguilar and María Dolores Montaño. The godparents were Clemente de la Cruz and Bernarda," both neophytes. In Jesuit baptismal entries, surnames were usually included for children born to gente de razón, but customarily omitted for the offspring of neophytes — another reminder of status differences. Previously, Wagner had ignored this convention, but now, inexplicably, he changed his ways. On the outer margin of the page, in a column reserved for the child's name and entry number, Wagner carefully wrote out "Francisco Javier de Aguilar." The date — 10 March — is not a day identified with the Jesuit Saint Francis Xavier. Most probably, the child was named for the padre who baptized him, a fairly common practice in those times. However, Wagner had not urged the use of his name by his servants or neophytes; among the hundred boys that he baptized, only this one was named "Francisco Javier," and none was named "Francisco."

The End of a Padre and a Period

By early 1742, Wagner was suffering from an unspecified chronic illness. Over a period of at least two years, his disability prevented him from keeping adequate records of his mission's financial transactions.[109] Comondú's libros de misión graphically portray Wagner's declining health in the progressive deterioration of his handwriting and his attention to form and details. Increasingly, his entries show that gente de razón and even neophytes visited the sick or performed emergency baptisms in his stead.

Since the Jesuit leadership was aware of Wagner's precarious health, and because he was held in high esteem — Padre Visitador General Baltasar described Wagner as "beloved by all"[110] — assumptions can be made about the quality of the men assigned to him. Miguel Caravajal had served under Padre Gordon and stayed on when Wagner arrived in 1737. A mayordomo's ability, vigor, and general cooperativeness were essential to a smoothly run mission. Given Wagner's condition, Caravajal's contribution was doubly important, and the missionary must have been satisfied with his work. Subsequent events also show that Caravajal was a valued employee: after he left Comondú in 1744, he was placed on the roster of the presidio of Loreto as a soldier on full pay, a real promotion from his role as a mission servant. Caravajal continued to serve as a soldier until at least 1752.[111] The endorsement of Juan de Aguilar by the Jesuit leadership can also be inferred. Wagner's illness was apparent by the time Aguilar was assigned to San José in mid-1742. The soldier's appointment must have represented a form of recognition for his previous performance at the post. Such a selection had old precedents; the Jesuits' management strategy involved shuffling padres, soldiers, servants, and even neophytes to obtain the best combinations at all their missions.

In August 1743, Padre Jacobo Druet, the Italian missionary stationed at Misión de la Purísima, came to San José to make his solemn profession in Wagner's presence; these vows ended a Jesuit's final probationary period.[112] By September, Padre Wagner's entries in the vital records at San José traced the accelerating decline of his health. During that month, Padre Miguel del Barco from Misión de San Javier visited Comondú and recorded an emergency baptism that he had performed. Plainly, he was helping Wagner with duties the sick man could not complete.[113] In November, Wagner baptized the child of a convert woman by a heathen father. By the time he tried to place the entry in the book, he noted that he could not remember the mother's name, a disability that had not appeared before.

On 23 January 1744, Padre Visitador General Juan Antonio Baltasar and Padre Miguel del Barco rode over from Misión de San Javier. Barco performed an emergency baptism to spare Wagner the effort. The next day, Baltasar inspected the mission facilities and discovered the progressive deficiencies in Wagner's bookkeeping. No balance of the mission's credits and debits with the procurador in Loreto was found. Baltasar ordered Wagner to return to San Javier with Barco to rest and be nursed back to health.[114] During February and early March, Barco traveled repeatedly to Comondú to perform needed services. By 14 March Wagner was back at work, but it was a brief, gallant effort. In the first six months of that year, Barco, Juan de Aguilar, and even a neophyte performed emergency baptisms, six in all. On 27 March 1744, Wagner preceded a baptismal entry with the simple statement, "Gravely ill as I am . . ." Wording and handwriting became progressively more confused. By summer, he had to be relieved of his duties and sent to San Javier, where Barco could be his doctor and nurse. Wagner last wrote in the books of his mission on 27 July 1744. He did not complete or sign the entry; the task was carried out by Padre Druet who, like Barco, had been coming to help at San José as time permitted.

It was a devastating season for everyone in the south-central peninsula. From August to October 1744, the Sierra de la Giganta was lashed from end to end by storms and torrential rains, an especially severe season of tropical hurricanes. First, plantings were washed away, then the earth and retaining walls that had contained them.[115] In the midst of that gloom, Padre Francisco Javier Wagner died; the day was 12 October 1744. San José's book of burials is complete for the period, but there is no entry for the fallen padre. Death overtook him at San Javier, and he was buried by his neighbor and host, Miguel del Barco.[116] Less than a month passed before a greater blow fell on the region. During a Sunday Mass, the church at Misión de Guadalupe collapsed, its footings weakened by the tremendous rains. The walls and roof crushed scores of worshippers; a hundred eventually died, one-seventh of the mission's population.[117]

Life at Comondú must have been difficult during its padre's last agonizing year. The mission servants had extra duties; everyone felt the lack of direction and security when their accustomed leader was incapacitated and then taken away. When Padre Wagner died, more and greater changes added to the confusion. Out of necessity, San José was run like a visita of La Purísima for more than a year; Padre Jacobo Druet shuttled back and forth, making the long day's ride between missions. Comondú's people not only had to adjust to a new padre with different ways, but also to one who barely understood or spoke their language. Druet was characterized by his superiors and his peers as a driven worker, ascetic, stubborn, and lacking in diplomacy.[118]

Familiar faces disappeared; names of members of the Caravajal and Aguilar families vanish from the records, never to reappear. By the fall of 1745 a new, young missionary, Padre José Rondero, had arrived to take over San José. New soldiers came, as did a new mayordomo; only Juan Clemente Padilla and his family stayed on another year, the last reminders of Padre Wagner's brief administration. Padilla then left to work at Manuel de Ocio's mining operation in *el Sur*, the story of which is told in Chapters 10 and 11.[119]

Times of Loss and Shrinkage

Padre José Rondero assumed the duties of missionary at San José de Comondú in September 1745. He was about twenty-seven years of age, born in the city of Puebla de los Angeles in Nueva España in 1717 or 1718. No record indicates that he had previous missionary experience, and his relative youth also suggests that this was his first fieldwork. His indoctrination was harsh and somber.

The mission had suffered a steady demographic decline since its founding — as did all California missions.[120] Few census figures are available, but two of them illustrate the trend at San José. In 1744, the greater mission population consisted of 513 individuals in 150 family groups. (Apparently a family was defined as a married couple and their children; widowers and widows were listed as additions.) Ten years later, in 1754, the mission had only 387 people in 109 families.[121] The mission's books of baptisms and burials do not give a direct measure of population totals, but they do show that the rate of loss due to infant mortality accelerated sharply during the seven years of Rondero's stay. On average, during Wagner's time, nine infants under the age of two and seventeen other people died each year. During Rondero's years, the figures jumped to nineteen infants and eighteen others, despite the fact that the same average number of children (twenty-eight) was born each year. The padre, like most of his California fellows, not only spent a large proportion of his time acting as a nurse, but he also had to appoint and train many of the able-bodied to help him. Much of their labor was expended in the procurement and distribution of food so that those laid low by disease did not also starve.[122] Additional labor was required to bury the dead.

All told, the population of the greater mission, as measured by baptisms and burials, gained fifteen people in Wagner's time and lost over a hundred in Rondero's. A decision was made before 1750 to consolidate the populations of the pueblos de visita at the cabecera. Apart from the desire to supervise neophytes as closely as possible, a major motivation for these moves may have been to put all available hands to work in the orchards and fields of San José and San Miguel; their agricultural production was important to the whole system.[123] Over the next few years, the bands that had occupied the regions of Comondú Viejo and San Juan Londó were withdrawn from their ancestral areas to become permanent residents of San José.[124] This shrinkage of the area occupied by the mission's people — and their concentration at the cabecera — worsened the average diet and exposed them to even more deficiencies and diseases.

Gente de Razón Visit Comondú

Three months after his arrival, and four days before Christmas of 1745, Padre Rondero made an entry in San José's baptismal record. Gertrudis Acevedo, wife of the mission's guard, Manuel Villavicencio, had delivered a child, Gertrudis María de la Expectación. Rondero performed the baptism and noted the infant as an *española*, thereby fulfilling an unwritten obligation to record the caste of gente de razón. The baby girl's godmother was Doña Loreta Rodríguez, daughter of the now aged and retired Capitán Don Esteban Rodríguez, and widow of Don José Antonio de Robles, once alférez at Loreto. At his death, Robles apparently left little estate to support his family. His widow was financially dependent on her father.[125] Perhaps she came to Comondú because her oldest boy had been assigned there as a soldier. Loreta's presence may account for the other Rodríguez relations who soon began to appear in the mission's record books.

A year and a half later, in August of 1747, Loreta's youngest sister, Doña Josefa Rodríguez, gave birth at San José to daughter Francisca Javiera. Padre Rondero this time served as godfather and Padre Francisco Domínguez, a Jesuit missionary from Sonora unaccountably spending the summer at Comondú, performed the ceremonies.[126] Josefa's husband was Sargento Don Cris-

tóbal Gutiérrez de Góngora, and, in their child's baptismal entry, Padre Domínguez listed the parents as residents of Loreto, which creates a puzzle. A man
as important as Gutiérrez de Góngora would never have been assigned as a
mission guard, nor would he have been accompanied by his pregnant wife when
traveling on presidial business. The likeliest explanation is that Gutiérrez de
Góngora did not come to Comondú; the father was always listed in a baptismal
entry whether he was present or not. His wife probably had come to take
advantage of her sister Loreta's help and Comondú's cooler climate. Loreto is
exceedingly hot in summer and fall; temperatures of 115°F are common.[127]

Other family members came to assist, or simply to be present, during Josefa's
confinement, delivery, the succeeding ceremonies, and the subsequent domestic arrangements. In September 1747, Padre Rondero recorded the burial of a
child, Mariano de Ocio, son of Rosalía Rodríguez, another of Loreta's sisters.
Rosalía's husband, Manuel de Ocio, was far away in the South, opening his first
mines. A few days after Mariano's burial, the name of Doña María de Larrea
appeared, and soon reappeared, listed among godmothers to newborn children
of neophytes. María de Larrea had been widowed by Esteban Rodríguez's death
in 1746, and now she was free to travel whenever she could help her family.
Perhaps the young Mexican missionary acted in deference to the Rodríguez
family. He may have been glad to invite such relatively genteel company to his
new and lonely post.

In 1748, Hilario Carrillo, Juan Carrillo's eldest son, was assigned as San José's
soldier; only eight years had passed since his father held the same post. Hilario's
wife was Josefa de Pazos, a native of Compostela. During this couple's stay at
the mission, and during Rondero's administration, they received a visit from
Antonio Patrón and his wife, Catarina de Pazos, who was Josefa's sister.[128]
Antonio and Catarina acted as godparents and were entered in the record book
as residents of Tepic. A few months later, Alférez Don José Gerardo[129] and Don
Nicolás de Peraza served as godfathers in baptisms performed by Rondero. In
1750, yet another visitor appeared on the baptismal pages: Doña Rosalía Heras,
wife of soldier José Marcelino de Estrada, stationed at San José del Cabo as a
member of the Escuadra del Sur.[130]

By April 1751, Padre Francisco Inama, Rondero's successor, had arrived at
the mission. There followed an unusually long transition period of six months
with both padres in attendance. Rondero then went to Loreto and took ship for
Sonora, where he continued to serve as a missionary until 1767, the end of
Jesuit tenure.[131] After Rondero left Comondú, the libros de misión reveal that
the number of visits by gente de razón decreased markedly. In comparison with
the padres who served before and after him, Rondero either attracted a greater
number of visitors, or was more likely to involve them in the mission's ceremonial life. In any case, this vignette reveals California's gente de razón engaged in many of the traditional but little-reported activities that maintained
and renewed their emerging society. They are seen traveling for days to assist
family members and to take part in rituals or even going as far for social visits.

To a degree, these exercises were recreational, as certainly were the impulses to escape Loreto's heat and enjoy the oasis-like setting of Comondú, a thousand feet above the sea and freshened by Pacific air.

The Last Jesuit at Comondú

Padre Francisco Inama, a native of Vienna, was just thirty-two when he signed his first entries — burial notices for two Guaycura women — in a Comondú mission register on 28 April 1751.[132] Padre Rondero must have been weary and depressed by all the deaths he had attended in his more than six years at the mission. Between April and October, Inama conducted all the burials while Rondero performed all the baptisms.[133]

Inama was not an imposing physical presence. The scribe who entered him in the records of those leaving Cádiz for assignments in the Indies described him as fair, of poor physique, and with a face pitted by the pox.[134] Nevertheless, the new man had an inquiring mind, energy, and good health. When he arrived in Mexico City, the Jesuit padre provincial of New Spain was Juan Antonio Baltasar who knew California well from his 1744 visit. Baltasar judged Inama to be a good candidate for California service and had him on the road by December 1750 in the company of fellow German speakers Jorge Retz and Jacobo Baegert.[135]

Inama had taught humanities in the Jesuit colleges of Passau, Linz, and Sopron — all near his native Vienna. He had studied natural science as well and had an avocational interest in zoology. He brought a kit of instruments to Comondú that included magnifying glasses, a microscope, and dissection tools. Inama was particularly interested in the anatomy of rattlesnakes. Another California missionary with whom he was corresponding (probably Ignacio Tirsch[136]) held to ideas, old-fashioned even in those days, of plant and animal fluids as "humours" (blood, phlegm, black bile, and yellow bile), and of the sympathetic or antithetical "textures" of different substances, such as snakes' teeth and a man's flesh. Inama made an extended and careful study of the rattlesnake. He learned about the articulation of the teeth; about their successive development, and about the venom sacs and the delivery of the liquid through the hollow teeth. When he had obtained answers to most of his questions, he wrote an argument based on his studies to refute his colleague's naive assertions. Inama's report is precisely and clearly written. His procedures, results, and interpretations seem to qualify as outstanding early work in this field.[137] In the person of Francisco Inama, European enlightenment had come to Comondú. A generation earlier, California Jesuits had sent for barbers to bleed them; now Padre Inama corresponded or conversed about natural science with Padre Barco, his sophisticated neighbor, in terms quite compatible with modern scientific practices.

By February 1754, the time had come for Francisco Inama to take the final solemn vows of the Jesuit order. He rode for two or three days to reach Loreto and made his profession to Padre Juan Javier Bischoff, a fellow German speaker.[138]

On 19 January 1755, San José de Comondú welcomed a rare guest, Padre Visitador General José de Utrera, who was completing an inspection tour of most of the Jesuit missions of northwest New Spain. In just one day, Utrera examined the mission facilities, observed its activities, inspected its books, asked questions of its padre, and took notes. Later, those notes became part of the visitor general's report to the Jesuit provincial in Mexico City.[139] This document contains itemized data on crops, livestock, and the state of conversion at each mission that he visited. It is the best single source for economic information about the Jesuit missions of northwest New Spain in the mid-eighteenth century.

On 21 January Utrera rode off to inspect missions to the north. At the newest, Santa Gertrudis, founded in 1751, Utrera had the opportunity to baptize a California infant.[140] Subsequently, he returned to visit the southern missions, and his route took him through Comondú. While there, Utrera baptized a second neophyte child. In both cases, the local padre wrote out the entry in the baptismal record, but Utrera signed, attesting that it was he who had performed the rites.[141]

Official Jesuit inspectors, like Utrera, were among the very few visitors to California in Jesuit times — and their visits were infrequent and brief. However, the missionaries' isolation was reduced by one of their organization's thoughtful services. Through their procurador in Mexico City, they could order and eventually receive publications that kept them abreast of much European writing, including that relating to the peninsula. California's seven German-speaking Jesuits were particularly indebted to Padre Procurador General Juan de Armesto's assistant, Hermano José Goebel. In 1759, Juan Javier Bischoff, then missionary at La Purísima, wrote to thank Goebel not only for sending the best medicines he had received since coming to the peninsula, but also for "*gacetas, papeletes, y mercurios*" (periodicals of politics, science, and literature) that contained news and contemporary thought.[142] The printed materials must have been seized upon hungrily by each missionary and circulated all around the mission chain.[143] Of particular interest were geographies and purported ethnographies that dealt with California.[144] However, the California missionaries also had complaints about their procurador. Some found Padre Juan de Armesto, Procurador de Californias from 1752 to 1767, arbitrary and dictatorial in his responses to some of their requests, refusing some and supplying inferior or dilapidated substitutes for others. The padres understood that they were prohibited from buying directly from any merchants, but they resented Armesto's resistance to allowing them to spend their own credits to obtain items that could be had from brother Jesuits on the mainland. They felt that the opinions of two provincials supported their right to such transactions.[145]

Francisco Inama's education and experience more than qualified him to teach at San José de Comondú's separate schools for boys and girls. Neither the number of classes held each week nor the curricula were mentioned, but

Visitador General Utrera's description of the schools as *"como seminarios,"* implies that the mission's children were given some elements of a general education with, no doubt, a heavy emphasis on religion and church ritual. Young people attended these classes for several years; Utrera reported that they were expected to participate until they were married. Padre Inama not only taught all the classes, but also paid from his stipend for books and materials, as did the padres of other missions.[146]

Considering Padre Francisco Inama's skills as a scholar, researcher, and teacher, it is surprising to find that Utrera reprimanded him for failure to keep proper accounts of his mission's credits and debits with the warehouse at Loreto. When Utrera ordered Inama to overhaul his bookkeeping, he also may have suggested that he make a fresh copy of old baptismal records from the visita of San Miguel. In any event, this important visita's records survive only in a verbatim copy in Inama's beautiful, legible hand.[147]

Guaycura Bolster a Declining Labor Force

By the mid-1750s, the agricultural potential of Misión de San José and nearby San Miguel could no longer be fully exploited. The death rate at San José was not as high as it had been in the 1740s, but the mission's economy—as well as its psychological climate—suffered from the continuing high mortality. Padre Inama performed 108 marriages between 1753 and 1768. In forty percent of those, both partners had been widowed; in another twenty percent, one partner had already lost a mate.[148] At the beginning of 1755, the greater mission of San José de Comondú had 387 people in 109 families; by 1762 those numbers were reduced to 350 people in 95 families.[149] At the same time, Comondú counted twenty-five hundred cattle, but only about five hundred were truly being herded, and fewer than that had been branded. The remainder roamed nearby areas as nearly wild strays called *ganado alzado* (runaway cattle).[150] Other animals had increased in numbers. By 1761, the mission had over a hundred saddle or work horses, one hundred and thirty brood mares, fifty mules, and over two thousand sheep and goats.[151] However, the decrease in men of working age caused a decline in the care and utilization of these herds. When that problem was compounded by a several-year drought in the mid-1760s, all the mission's cattle became essentially wild, and the number of sheep and goats was halved.[152] Labor-intensive agriculture probably suffered similar losses. By 1755, most of San José's crops were raised at San Miguel, using terraces and irrigation works created forty years earlier by Padre Juan de Ugarte. Thanks to Ugarte's foresight and engineering, San Miguel was easier to work and less subject to flash flood damage than were the fields of San José, which lay nearer the bed of the arroyo.[153]

No formal Jesuit policy addressed the problem of decreasing manpower, but the libros de misión show the demographic response to the local shortage of people. During Rondero's time, a few Guaycura were baptized. After 1752, they appeared regularly and in increasing numbers in records of births, marriages, and burials. The source of these people is indicated by the baptism at Comondú in 1752 of the son of Rosalía, a Guaycura, widow of a Guaycura who had run away from Misión de San Luis Gonzaga. San Luis was founded fifteen years earlier, in 1737, but it had lacked a full-time missionary for several of those years, had little agriculture, and only a small village at its cabecera. The people for whom it was established were scattered, and for many it was the first Christian contact. They still supported themselves primarily by hunting and gathering over a vast area of the Pacific slope between San Luis and Comondú.[154] Those from the more northerly parts of that range typically found themselves closer to San José than to San Luis.[155]

Meanwhile, two generations of mission life had diminished the Cochimí's old animosity for the Guaycura, so needy Guaycura felt safer in coming to the predominantly Cochimí mission. In 1753, the baptism of an infant daughter of Miguel Carrillo, "Capitan de los Waicuros," and his wife, Antonia, at San José suggests that a band of some size had come to the mission. By 1755, the influx of new groups was just one of Padre Inama's added burdens. Padres José Gasteiger of Misión de Guadalupe and Pedro Nascimbén of Misión de Santa Rosalía had died a year earlier. Benno Ducrue had had to leave his mission at La Purísima in Inama's care during an interim while he filled both the dead men's shoes. Francisco Inama wrote to his sister, a Carmelite nun, explaining the difficulties of dividing his time between two missions and coping with two languages, Cochimí and Guaycura:

> The latter tribe, recently converted, came to us here from the coastal lands along the Pacific Ocean. They keep me busy because of their ways, which are still rather savage. They are accustomed to sleep on the sand under the open sky, and it has cost me no little effort to get them to live in a hut. In order to protect their sick from sun and wind, I had them brought under a roof; but this proved a source of greater suffering than the illness itself.
>
> If a horse or mule, overburdened by its load, died, they would enthusiastically plunge in and devour the carrion, utterly disregarding all my sermons against such a disgusting habit. They are now, however, approaching a better way of life.[156]

No doubt the need for workers contributed to the padres' tacit acceptance of the informal transfers of Guaycura to Misión de San José de Comondú. Judging by the discrepancy between the mission's birth and death records on the one hand, and its population figures on the other, San José must have acquired about two hundred Guaycura recruits between 1744 and 1762.[157] Padre Inama must have had some success in marshaling his reduced workforce for agriculture. Cochimí men and boys, in their second and third generations of acculturation, had the basic skills required for most of the activities that contributed to the mission's economy. The more recently arrived Guaycura stepped in at the level of unskilled labor and began the learning process.

Neophytes were not formally paid for their work, but the missionary had ways to reward people who performed well or volunteered for extra services. He could award small portions of tobacco to neophytes to smoke or snuff.[158] He might apportion extra clothing, or showy yardage, or bits of ribbon. He could allow a man a small, private garden plot. He sometimes lent tools to a man who wished to do work for himself.[159] He might give a family a sheep or goat or chicken to raise as its own. As indicated earlier, he might also give passes that allowed a man or a family to travel on personal business or to see relatives. At times, Padre Inama allowed neophytes who had been moved to the cabecera from the abandoned visitas at Londó and Comondú Viejo to make nostalgic returns to their old homes and to forage for their traditional foods.[160] Inducements like these that stimulated productivity were particularly significant at Comondú. By the 1760s, the populations of California's most fertile missions, Santiago and Todos Santos, had declined so drastically that San José de Comondú, even in its reduced state, was producing the peninsula's most dependable crops.[161]

A Stone Church and an Itinerant Carpenter

Beginning in 1744, Padre Miguel del Barco had a crew working at San Javier on a magnificent church of cut stone, California's first to be capped by a vaulted roof. This building was not dedicated until 1758, in part because it took several years to obtain a maestro capable of supervising the delicate craft of cutting porous stone, *tezontle*, a vesicular basalt, and erecting vaults with crossing arches.[162]

Once those church walls were completed, the experienced masons and stoneworkers were free for other work. Francisco Inama may have borrowed some of these artisans to work at San José. In fact, on 10 March 1754, "Señor Sebastián Manríquez and his wife Francisca Antonia Estrada, residents of Loreto," appeared as godparents in Comondú's book of baptisms. During the next four months, the couple, or sometimes she alone, repeated this service. In each entry, Manríquez was identified as master carpenter, or simply carpenter. These laconic entries indicate one of Antigua California's most ubiquitous and colorful characters.

On the payroll of the presidio of Loreto in the year 1733, the master shipwright's first assistant was Sebastián Manríquez, and the third was Antonio Manríquez. The highest pay drawn by a married sailor, fifty percent more than any of the others—and more than double that of the carpenter's apprentices— belonged to one Francisco Manríquez. The sailor came from the area of the village of Jalisco, six miles south of Tepic. Francisco's wife was Augusta Regina; the lack of last name in Jalisco's parish church records suggest that she was a casta or an Indian. In all probability, Sebastián and Antonio were children of this couple. Sebastián was born at Compostela, fourteen miles from Jalisco, and the employment of closely related men was common at all levels in Loreto.

Sebastián Manríquez appears in several books of mission records and in various documents, identified by name, and usually as "el carpintero."[163] If all such books were extant, he would probably be found in most, so much in demand were his skills. It was almost certainly he to whom Jacobo Baegert referred, in his typically depreciating fashion:

> In Loreto . . . were two so-called carpenters, two so-called cabinetmakers, and as many blacksmiths. At times another cabinetmaker of this type, carrying all his iron tools in his trouser pocket, roamed the country trying to earn a little at the missions if there was no lack of wood.

Manríquez's presence as a carpenter at Comondú in 1754 probably indicates that church building had begun. Unfortunately, Padre Inama did not make a plain statement like that of a fellow Jesuit. At Misión de San Ignacio, on 23 April 1764, Padre José Mariano Rotea baptized a daughter of Sebastián Manríquez and described him as "the craftsman stationed here to work on the building of the church. . . ." (This great church graces the plaza of San Ignacio to this day.[164])

Manríquez was employed at Comondú from 1754 to at least 1760, a good indication of the time needed to build the church, and a modest amount of time compared to other California church constructions. An inventory of San José's possessions, made in 1767, lists tools probably used in the work: ten picks, seven masonry trowels, a plumb bob and line, calipers, wood planes, mallets, chisels, an auger, gouges, saws, axes, "and other pieces" presumably of less interest or value. The mission had a reasonably well-equipped smithy with a forge, anvil, forceps, hammers, and files.[165] Construction materials, necessarily, were of local origin. The sources of tezontle and lime probably were the same as those used in building the great church at San Javier. A large lime kiln still stands beside a trail between the two missions.[166]

When Padre Visitador General Utrera came to Comondú in early 1755, he found a stone-and-mortar church "with three vaulted naves," no doubt meaning a principal nave and two side aisles. The middle aisle was already nicely paved, and the others awaited the same treatment. Utrera found the church well appointed and commented in particular on a fine alabaster baptismal font from Puebla. In 1762, Visitador General Lizasoáin's typically brief description of the church suggested that it was completed: "a well-vaulted church, with good decoration." A retrospective Jesuit account identified Inama as the builder, and also noted that "[the church] had three naves," a floorplan unique in California.[167]

In 1773, the edifice was described in more detail in an inventory made before it passed from Franciscan into Dominican hands:

> A church with three vaulted naves and three entries; near to them on the inside are three holy water basins. [The church] is paved with cut stone, and also has wooden grillwork, a vaulted choir-loft in which there is an old hand-

organ and a bassoon. There are three altars; the principal altar surround is new and gold leafed, has a sculptured image of San José with the Child, his halo in silver, and the blossom on his staff in silver as well.[168] There is also a sculptured image of San Miguel, and seven panels depicting various saints.

This inventory goes on to describe in detail both side altars, two confessionals, a baptistry with the noted alabaster font, and, on the main walls, many painted panels. Outside, two graveyards were walled about with stone, but one was unfinished. There was no belfry, but six small- to medium-sized bells were suspended from a wooden framework set up outside near the entrance. Separate but adjacent were a stone-vaulted sacristy with many church furnishings and a stone-vaulted house for the padre, a structure that Lizasoáin also praised in his terse report.[169]

Sebastián Manríquez's wife, Francisca Antonia Estrada, died during the carpenter's second year at Comondú. In May 1757, the widower married Juliana Bustamante, daughter of neophytes Salvador Bustamante and Teresa. Her parents were prominent in the mission's ceremonial life, as attested by many entries in the baptismal and marriage records over a twenty-five year period. Juliana herself made a dramatic appearance in the book of baptisms. It was she for whom Padre Miguel del Barco performed an emergency baptism in September of 1743 when Padre Wagner was too ill to handle the mission's affairs.[170] At the time of his second marriage, Manríquez was on the payroll of the presidio of Loreto so, like any other of its soldiers, sailors, or artisans, he had to obtain a marriage permit from the father visitor. Padre Inama did not fail to indicate that he had the permit in hand when he performed the ceremony.[171] Official witnesses at the service included Juan Molocué, San José's gobernador, and Clemente Ferrer, the long-time fiscal.

Juliana Bustamante bore a son, Ignacio Javier, the following year when she was still fourteen years of age. She had four other children for whom baptismal records exist, and there were doubtless others for whom records are lost. Two daughters bore the same name, María Josefa. When the first died, her name was passed on to the next born daughter. At least three of Sebastián and Juliana's children matured, married, and had a long-term impact on California's population.[172]

Comondú and Alta California

Sebastián Manríquez's adventures, and those of several other gente de razón who figure in the story of San José de Comondú, continued into California's next period of major expansion, the opening of Alta California. Veteran carpenter Manríquez was in his mid-fifties when the first expedition went north in 1769. Nevertheless, the old artisan went along as an arriero and spent at least six years in the new establishments or in the frontier region between the once-Jesuit missions and San Diego. His active career ended about 1775, but he apparently lived on for several years—into the 1780s—at San Diego. Luis Gonzaga Manríquez, who was born at Comondú in 1773, the son of Juliana Bustamante and Sebastián Manríquez, served as a soldier at the presidio of San Diego in 1790, long after the opening of Alta California.[173]

Two other men born at Comondú had earlier and greater impacts on the Spanish expansion and the development of the new area. One was Francisco Javier Aguilar, born on 10 March 1743, the son of Soldier Juan de Aguilar and María Dolores Montaño. The young Aguilar followed in his father's footsteps and enlisted in 1768 to take part in the land expedition that founded San Diego and Monterey. He served as a soldier in the frontier region for twenty-five years, rose to the position of sergeant, served another decade, acquired lands and honors, and lived to the ripe age of seventy-eight.[174] The second Comondú-born pioneer of Alta California was Francisco María Ruiz, baptized on 3 September 1754 by Padre Inama. At eighteen, Ruiz became a soldier, thereafter an officer, and finally captain of the presidio of San Diego. Upon retirement, he built what was perhaps the first home outside the presidial compound and became a founder of San Diego's Old Town.[175] Francisco María Ruiz was the son of Juan María Ruiz and Isabel Carrillo. Juan María Ruiz had come to Comondú early in 1754 to serve as Inama's soldier-mayordomo just as the local church building was begun. Ruiz was from El Fuerte, the old presidial town on the Río Fuerte in Sinaloa. His Ruiz forefather settled there in the early seventeenth century, and the family had grown large. A few years before coming to Comondú, Juan María Ruiz enlisted at Loreto. There also, he married Isabel Carrillo, daughter of Juan Carrillo, described earlier as a soldier-guard at San José de Comondú.

In 1748, Juan Carrillo died and while his older children were self-sufficient, his wife and two youngest offspring needed support.[176] His son-in-law Juan María Ruiz stepped forward. Ruiz's household at Comondú in 1754, and for some years thereafter, included his mother-in-law, Ifigenia Millán, and Mariano and Antonia Victoria, the younger Carrillo children, as well as Ruiz's wife and their succession of six children. For the next three years, the record books of the mission show these people and other members of the extended Carrillo family participating in a tightly knit, family-only version of the rituals of compadrazgo.

Both of the Carrillo children that Juan María Ruiz helped to raise played important roles in Alta California. Mariano became a sergeant of the presidio of Loreto, rode in the first land expedition to San Diego, and served in the new establishments of the north — finally as alférez at Monterey — until his death in 1782. He was buried by Fray Junípero Serra. Antonia Victoria Carrillo married José Francisco Ortega, also a 1769 pioneer to San Diego and San Francisco. He was a sergeant and later lieutenant at San Diego and Loreto. Ortega and his wife settled in the Santa Barbara area, and their children became important citizens and progenitors of many people who are still residents of the area.[177]

In 1755, the Carrillos at Comondú welcomed their sister Micaela when her husband Martín de Olivera was assigned to join Juan María Ruiz as a soldier-escort at Misión de San José. Sons of this couple also became important *pobladores* (settlers) of Alta California.[178]

The handful of gente de razón associated with Misión de San José de Comondú thus continued a trend two centuries old in which the families of frontiersmen provided manpower for opening and settling the next frontier of northwest New Spain. Moreover, San José's invaluable libros de misión reveal the patterns of marriage and mutual assistance that created the extended families that were needed to perpetuate Hispanic society in such a harsh and remote environment.

The Declining Jesuit Years

By the time Francisco Inama took over San José de Comondú, the initial problems of mission establishment were past. There were no further insurrections and no reported conspiracies. There were no heathen left to convert, and no large groups of people to indoctrinate or train in mission skills. The padre and soldiers no longer were needed to provide all the discipline and know-how. Young people could learn from well-trained elders who had experienced the regimes of every padre in the mission's history. Antonio Boyi, once a page for Padre Wagner, and his wife Isabel still appeared in the record books over thirty years after their names were first set down. Others long-identified as vaqueros and fishermen were available to impart their skills.

Men were no longer identified as captains of separate bands. Little time was spent roaming the countryside to collect wild food; when it was done, the impulse sprang more from tradition than necessity. Most available men were employed in agriculture and stock-raising. San José had become a tightly knit society, communal in the sense that everyone worked for the common good, but not because it was governed by committee. Only small matters were handled by its native officials: Juan Moloque, the governor, and Clemente Ferrer, the fiscal. All major responsibilities and decisions were still assigned to the missionary. A characterization written by Inama shows that both he and the neophytes had attitudes conditioned by this severely paternalistic system:

> . . . the natives are a meek, kind, joyous people, desirous to know our holy religion. . . . After they have been christened, they are perfectly obedient to the orders of their missionaries or to those of the *caciques*, the town officials who govern in their name, and avoid all which might offend either group.[179] They entertain for us a deferential affection, a blind obedience, a child-like confidence, and are most concerned for our well-being. It is precisely these characteristics that cause us missionaries so much concern, work, poverty, and numerous privations in our vocation—and at the same time render it light and joyful. Here we must be, day and night, 'all things to all,' as well for their body as for their soul, and sacrifice ourselves all the more because they receive no other help, counsel, guidance, or care.[180]

By the mid-1750s, the Bishop of Guadalajara, realizing that he would never visit California, decided to empower a California missionary to act as his substitute and bring the rite of confirmation to the peninsular neophytes. He chose Padre Lamberto Hostell, who made the long and strenuous round of all the California missions and confirmed over six thousand neophytes. At Comondú, as at the other missions, this was a grand event, solemn and festive.[181]

In the early 1750s, Padre Inama had acted for extended periods as a substitute for ailing or deceased padres within his rectorado. Now, such duties were infrequent; the local missionaries were young men, except Miguel del Barco who was blessed with exceptional health. At the end of the decade, Inama was appointed padre rector of the central mission group. This was a duty, doled out on a rotating basis, rather than an honor or form of recognition. The rectorship cost Padre Inama long rides on the camino real as he made the required visits to the Jesuits in his district, but he must have welcomed the opportunities to socialize.[182]

By the 1760s, activity was decreasing in the area that included San José and its neighbors, San Javier and La Purísima. Populations were declining, and no major constructions were under way. Inama decided to consolidate even the people of his visita at San Miguel, a scant two miles away, into the cabecera at San José.[183] The heathen frontier was so far to the north that, when a new mission, San Borja, was being planned for Adac—a site near Bahía de los Angeles—only the missions of San Ignacio and Santa Gertrudis were asked to contribute mission produce and livestock. The camino real was quiet; supplies and men from Loreto traveled to the new establishment by boat. Padre Inama was able to have an occasional visit with his nearest neighbor missionary, Juan Javier Bischoff at La Purísima, and he exchanged notes on naturalism and common concerns with Miguel del Barco at San Javier. Perhaps he engaged in other, unrecorded avocations. Several of his contemporaries cultivated gardens of exotic flowers and herbs. At least one may have been a hunter; Padre Carlos Neumayer, received a shipment of two muskets and a shotgun ordered on his own account.[184]

In January 1762, Comondú had a three-day visit from Padre Visitador General Ignacio de Lizasoáin. He would have taken meals and slept in Padre Inama's house; the setting can be visualized with the aid of a nearly contemporary inventory.[185] There were five beds of hides stretched over wooden frames, each apparently with a bedside table.[186] A trunk listed was probably used by the missionary to protect clothing and personal objects from omnipresent dust. Inama had a writing desk of Honduras mahogany and a bookcase holding over a hundred volumes. He could offer meals on a dining table with tablecloth, napkins, and six chairs. The table could be laid from a large set of Chinese porcelain dishes with thirty-six plates of various sizes, cups and saucers, and saltcellars.[187] The visit gave Francisco Inama a rare opportunity to use some of these things and to share evenings of conversation and to offer the chocolate, brandy, and pipes of tobacco that the padres were said to enjoy.[188]

As always, the missionary at San José was thrown together with at least one soldier and his family. By 1762, this compañero was Matías de Morras who had been on the rolls of the presidio of Loreto since 1751 or before.[189] Morras was married to María Loreta de Cota, a daughter of Loreto's long-time cabo de escuadra, Andrés de Cota, deceased by 1762. María Loreta's younger sister, María Josefa, also lived at Comondú, chaperoned by her sister and brother-in-law. The next few years brought local events typical of the intertwined lives of gente de razón in Jesuit California. At a ceremony in the church on 19 March 1762, Padre Inama married María Josefa de Cota to Juan Miguel Camacho, mayordomo of Misión de la Purísima.[190] Witnesses were Matías de Morras and his wife. When the Morras couple had a son in 1764, and again when they had a daughter in 1766, the godfather was José Cristóbal Ramírez, Padre Barco's soldier-companion at San Javier.

Several years of relative comfort and stability ended in 1764 with the return in force of two old nemeses: locusts and drought. Comondú was less affected than most missions of the central and southern peninsula, but the scourges persisted for years; Padre Inama felt pressure to keep up his agricultural output to assist in what became a peninsula-wide food crisis.[191] The work was increasingly difficult because his neophytes continued to be victims of epidemics and the slower attrition of syphilis.[192] Misión de San José de Comondú no longer offered heady prospects for evangelization, conversion, and new worlds to conquer. Nearly all the formerly scattered Cochimí and Guaycura of the northwestern Giganta now lived in the mission village. They spoke at least some Spanish, practiced Roman Catholicism to a degree, and dressed and worked much like other poor citizens of the Spanish colonial world.

The missions of *el Sur* were moribund; San José and its mid-peninsular neighbors were declining rapidly; only the north with its potential for new establishments held out the prospects that had attracted the religious to the California mission field. Padre Inama betrayed that thought as early as 1755: "I shall gladly hand over my well-cultivated apostolic field and penetrate deeper into the interior of the country in order to till the land still covered with thistles and thus render it fit to receive the seed of the gospel."[193] However, experienced missionaries were rarely released to work on the frontier; their hard-won missions in Antigua California represented a base of resources with which the ambitious order could work toward its long-held goal. The established padres held that thought to justify their labor, now almost that of curates in dwindling, isolated parishes far from other rewards.

NINE

The Pueblo of Loreto

An Ebb and Flow of People

 At the end of 1698, one year after landing in California, Padre Juan María de Salvatierra reported that he was celebrating Christmas at Nuestra Señora de Loreto with more than one hundred convert families, all well instructed in Christianity.[1] His mission's total population must have been around four hundred, the largest number of native Californians that would occupy the Loreto area during its Jesuit years.[2] That total included most members of the rancherías of Tuidú, Yeltí, Niodí, Bonú, Notrí, Chuenquí, Nopoló, and Ligüí that occupied the coastal lowlands stretching from about ten miles north of Loreto to Ligüí, thirty miles to the south. These groups made up an entire Guaycuran sub-culture, called Monquí. The mountains that virtually surrounded Monquí lands were inhabited by bands of Cochimí with whom the Monquí coexisted under circumstances ranging from extended truces to constant skirmishes. The Monquí absorbed the first impact of the Spanish intruders. When they embraced the newcomers, they received protection, a new religion, an altered way of life — and new diseases. Their numbers plummeted.[3] A measure of their decline can be taken from Padre Jaime Bravo's report of 1730: thirty-three years after its founding, Loreto's mission counted only 134 neophytes, and that included every member of the above-named Monquí rancherías, all of whom by then were living at Loreto.[4]

The Jesuits had compelling reasons to locate all the Monquí at the mission. Loreto, as headquarters, port, and supply center of their system, needed a flexible pool of local manpower. By 1744, the number of resident neophytes was up to 150, implicit evidence that families were imported from other missions to maintain the capital's population.[5] Subsequent counts of Loreto's neophytes — 100 in 1755, 109 in 1762, and 120 in 1767 — give few clues to local population dynamics.[6] However, the Loreto missionary submitted a report in

1762 that sheds more light on the matter: "since 1744, 38 have been baptized, 88 married, and 309 have died."[7] The wide disparity between births and deaths shows that people were continually relocated to the mother mission.

Gente de razón employed at Loreto were also enumerated from time to time. Soldiers numbered between twenty-five and thirty from 1698 to 1738. After the establishment of the presidio in *el Sur* in 1738, thirty positions were invariably assigned to Loreto and a like number in the South.[8] However, as few as eight soldiers, and never more than fifteen, were actually stationed at Loreto; the balance were posted at other missions or away on expeditions or delivery chores.[9] The number of sailors varied more widely, ranging from as few as eighteen to as many as thirty-nine.[10] The count of craftsmen attached to the presidio fluctuated between three and a dozen.[11] Numbers of seamen and shipwrights were largest in the mid-Jesuit years and sharply reduced by the end of the era.

The households of Loreto's soldiers and sailors were seldom counted and reported. Jaime Bravo's *informe* of 1730 comes close to a direct count; after stating that the presidio totaled 175 people, he gave the individual numbers of soldiers, sailors, artisans, mule drivers, and vaqueros. Then he added, "the rest of the souls, which are 99 of the complement of 175, are wives of the married soldiers and [married] men of the marinería, their children, and some servants that they keep in their houses at their own expense."[12] In 1762, Padre Visitador Lizasoáin reported a firm figure for the entire presidial community, exclusive of neophytes; under the heading "R. Presidio," he wrote "Individuals, in all, 274."[13] This figure, compared to Bravo's, shows an increase of one hundred gente de razón at Loreto during the intervening thirty-two years. Finally, at the time of the Jesuit expulsion in 1768, Loreto's inhabitants, including neophytes, soldiers, sailors, and their families, numbered a few above four hundred.[14] Gente de razón gains had balanced neophyte losses during the seventy-year Spanish occupation of the Loreto area.

The Physical Development of Loreto, 1697–1698

When Salvatierra's party landed in 1697, it found a primitive Monquí settlement at Conchó "about half an harquebus shot from the sea," perhaps ninety or a hundred yards.[15] To locate their own enterprise, the newcomers looked first at the water holes that lay south of the Monquí encampment. These were marshy pools near the mouth of an otherwise dry watercourse that cut across a mile-wide alluvial fan after emanating from the sierra to the west. Sixty or seventy yards to the southwest at an elevation about ten feet above the water holes, the newcomers found level ground about twice as far from the beach as was the Indian camp. They walked this low mesa until they found a level spot at the head of the slope that ran down to the pools where they could water animals. The marshy, reed-filled area to the north would keep unfriendly Californians outside the effective range of their bows and arrows but within reach of Spanish muskets. Padre Salvatierra estimated this site to be two harquebus shots from the sea. Further searching produced no better alternative and on 19 October 1697, the second day at Conchó, the mesa site was chosen.[16] A few days after the decisive battle that allowed the Spanish party to keep its foothold, Salvatierra and the nine other pioneers were joined by Padre Francisco María Piccolo and the crew of the supply launch. With this work force of over a dozen men, and with the help of an unspecified number of Monquí volunteers, the founder of the new California mission began to direct the construction of a chapel, three smaller buildings, and defensive walls for a presidio.

In those days, the mesa was covered with large mesquites, low, spreading hardwood trees with trunks ranging to two feet or more in diameter and up to ten feet in height. Some of these were left standing to support a stockade and to shade and uphold sacks of food and items of gear that frontiersmen suspended by ropes for protection from animals and runoff water. Other mesquites were cut to provide logs for a palisade that was embellished with thorny branches. These defenses formed at least two concentric squares that enclosed the visitors and their possessions in a fortified corral.[17]

Within the stockade, the workers laid up rock fragments with adobe mortar to build the walls of a chapel and three adjacent rooms.[18] These they covered with shed roofs thatched with grasses.[19] Some idea of the simplicity of these pioneer structures can be gained from the time devoted to their construction. The chapel was begun on 30 November and dedicated on 8 December. It housed the party's few religious articles, including a portable altar. One of the adjacent rooms served as the padre's quarters, another as a mess hall and captain's quarters, and the third as a small warehouse for supplies, arms, tools, and saddle gear.[20] In the following days, the pioneers erected simple structures called *ramadas*, houses of branches, to serve as soldiers' dormitories.[21] Their roofs were also thatched and their sides probably infilled with woven branches and rushes daubed with adobe to stop winter winds. This mud-and-wattle technique was in common use on the mainland.

The following year and a half were filled with evangelical labors, hardships, and pressing demands on everyone's time; only a few simple, utilitarian structures were added: large ramadas to provide shade for carpenters and smiths at work, corrals for cattle and beasts of burden, and pens for goats. Work parties dug batequis, or shallow wells, with their rims at elevations a foot or two above the standing pools. These were fenced to prevent fouling by livestock. People took pails down to the batequis to bail out water filtered through the sands of the arroyo.[22] Loreto looked more like a busy encampment than a village or fort.

The Mission Removed from the Presidio, 1699–1700

In each community that Spaniards occupied or created in the Americas, great attention, effort, and expense were devoted to erecting an impressive church.

This symbolized not only the power of the new regime but also the importance of the community. Neophytes were involved in church constructions both for their invaluable labor and to give those who participated a greater attachment to the mission itself: " . . . one has an especial fondness for the work of one's hands."[23]

By the summer of 1699, the California missionaries were determined to replace their crude chapel with a more impressive place of worship. As with other aspects of his California cause, Juan María de Salvatierra had planned ahead to obtain men who could help him in its construction. An example of his foresight appears in a list of requests to the Audiencia of Guadalajara, dated 14 March 1699:

> He asks that there be sent to him an officially appointed mason, competent to build the Holy House of Loreto. Joaquín, the foreman of the work on the cathedral, knows that I have already spoken to one man. He can be summoned by the Señor President [of the audiencia], and an agreement can be reached as to the proper wage which he shall earn in California.[24]

However, this inquiry bore no fruit. Loreto's first masonry church was not built by craftsmen from Guadalajara but by soldiers and neophytes under the direction of Padre Piccolo and Capitán García de Mendoza.[25]

Construction of the church was slow and difficult. Food was short and little could be used to lure neophytes into becoming laborers. Desirable building materials, such as workable stone and proper roof beams, remained out of reach for the undermanned and financially strapped colony. Nevertheless, the padres undertook to fulfill their vows to Nuestra Señora de Loreto. Each Sunday they exhorted their men to help them meet the challenge. After such a sermon on 27 June 1699, the soldiers promised to devote themselves at once to building the church. They left the chapel and began to clear a chosen site about four or five hundred feet west of their fortified compound.[26] Two hours into their labors, an overdue supply ship was sighted. The promise of food soon drew converts into the workforce. In five days, the ship was unloaded and the area for the new place of worship was clear and level. On 2 July Piccolo and García de Mendoza stretched and pegged cords to outline a modest church, about fifty-five feet long by seventeen feet wide, inside measure.[27] The plan called for the facade and portal to face south, as does the later church that now occupies approximately the same location.

Workers dug trenches and created foundations by setting in large fragments of basaltic rock, omnipresent in the mid-peninsula. Shortages of money and skilled labor dictated that they build the walls of adobe blocks rather than cut stone. Neophytes had to be trained to make forms, mix adobe, and proceed through the steps required to produce usable sun-dried blocks.[28] Prior to laying up the walls, the workers were directed to fell mesquite trees and adze their trunks into timbers for lintels and door- and window-frames.[29] These they would key into the adobe masonry as it was raised.

The construction project at Loreto required building materials that would take time to acquire or prepare. The many long, straight *vigas* (roof beams) had to be imported. The hard local woods had to be brought from greater and greater distances and laboriously worked to shape. When Salvatierra realized how much time the completion of his church would require, he ordered the construction of an interim chapel on the west side of the new church. A year passed before his building crew got to the point of thatching this smaller, simpler structure with bundles of carrizo.[30] The missionaries used its dedication as an opportunity to display the pageantry of church ceremonies and to show off their vestments and church ornaments. These not only attracted and impressed the Monquí, but lifted the spirits of padres and soldiers as well. Salvatierra told how, on 8 September 1700 — not by chance the Nativity of the Blessed Virgin — Our Lady of Loreto's image was "transferred to the new adobe house, all white-washed and adorned with paintings, statues, an altarpiece, and a canopy. It resembles a veritable paradise. . . ." The padres and their retinue of soldiers, sailors, and neophytes joined in a dedicatory march and ceremonies.[31]

At about the time the builders started the permanent church and the chapel, they also put up three rooms of adobe, white-washed and roofed like the chapel, to serve as the padre's house. On 21 and 22 September, a furious rain-and-wind storm caused a flood that undercut the walls of the house and caused them to topple. Fortunately, the building had been standing empty to allow its adobe to dry. It was soon rebuilt, its three rooms in line from east to west and attached to the northeast corner of the church to form a right angle.[32]

Loreto's First Church and Mission Compound, 1700–1707

Work continued on the larger church that had been laid out and begun in 1699. The size and cost of the building slowed the project, and it was delayed further whenever manpower had to be diverted to other efforts. The church was finally dedicated on 8 September 1704, with five missionaries present. The image of the Virgin was moved with great pomp and ceremony from the chapel into the new church whose high ceiling was still an open gable with a thatched roof. The long vigas that would eventually be topped by fired tile and adobe to make a proper flat roof were not yet available.[33] Even so, the California neophytes could now see a mission church whose scale and trappings were comparable to those built elsewhere on the Hispanic frontier.

At this time, Salvatierra was called away to Mexico City to meet with Virrey Alburquerque; soon thereafter he was made provincial of New Spain's Jesuits and was able to visit California only once in more than two years. In his absence, Padre Juan de Ugarte directed local affairs and, with characteristic skill and energy, furthered the building program. He oversaw the erection of a larger dwelling for the padre and a smaller structure to house visiting missionaries. With these additions, the mission complex formed three sides of an open square, fifty-five feet on a side.

Ugarte's additions were of stone and mortar. It had been learned that cement could be prepared from a limestone deposit found on nearby Isla de Coronados. Ugarte sent a crew to crack out fragments of the mineral. These were brought to Loreto, dumped into kilns built for the purpose, fired, then fine-ground on stone mills to make the cement. Ugarte had adobe tiles fired to serve as pavers and roofing units. He imported the vital roof beams from the environs of a Jesuit mission in Sinaloa. He also caused a surprise to be prepared for his superior: a garden orchard, probably walled in, with its own well. When Salvatierra returned to Loreto in early 1707, his encampment had become a settled, permanent village.[34]

During the next year or two, Padre Pedro de Ugarte, Juan's younger brother, directed a few more additions to the mission. He closed in the final side of the compound, presumably that on the south, by building a small house to use when he was in Loreto between stints as missionary at Ligüí or supervisor of ship repairs at Matanchel.[35] The church complex now looked a bit like a fortress, but in fact was so little threatened that its new form served only to provide privacy for the padres and prevent petty theft.

After a few years, enough long, strong roof beams of cedar were obtained from Sinaloa to span the seventeen-foot interior width of the church nave. At last, the typical flat roof could be put on the church. This was composed of beams, a layer of fired tile, several inches of adobe, and a final exterior field of tile sealed with *alquitrán*, a mixture of pitch, tar, grease, and oils.[36]

West of the church compound and outside its walls, two long rows of adobe huts faced each other, homes for Loreto's neophytes.[37] The location probably was selected to put the new converts at the door of the chapel built in 1699 — and on the side away from the presidio. At about the same time, a house for unmarried women was built inside the compound. A well about nine feet deep was dug in the center of the neophytes' enclosure. Its lining formed a circular stairway with twenty-three steps that wound down to the water level.[38]

A clearing was made near the permanent neophyte homes as a campsite for the converts who streamed in from other missions. This camping place was particularly busy and populous during Loreto's fiestas when neophytes from near and far tried to get away from other responsibilities in order to attend.[39]

Coral (or some other sea animal) produced *piedra múcara*, a lightweight, calcareous "rock," that washed up in chunks on the beaches around Loreto. The padres directed workers to gather these up, fire them in a kiln to form lime, grind them to a powder, and mix them with sand and water to make a white stucco. That material was plastered on all the masonry buildings in the village, a treatment that improved their appearance and protected the underlying adobe bricks.[40] Now, with her little groups of well-roofed, white-stuccoed buildings standing out on the low mesa, rustic Loreto at last had a Spanish colonial look. Loreto was changed but little for three decades after the church was finished. September chubascos ripped through the village in 1717 and again in 1728. Ensuing flash floods roared out of Arroyo de las Parras and cut swaths through low-lying parts of the village, but repairs were made, and life went on.[41]

Jaime Bravo Builds the Great Church at Loreto — and a House

The next significant physical changes to Loreto were made around 1740 when Padre Jaime Bravo began to erect a larger church. His simple but massive stone-and-mortar construction endures to this day, albeit much modified. Bravo's edifice astonished even Padre Visitador General Juan Antonio de Baltasar, a sophisticated Swiss. In 1744, Baltasar wrote that "Father Rector Jaime Bravo . . . has just finished building a structure that resembles a school. It surpasses anything we have in our missions this side of Guadalajara. Neither Chihuahua nor Parras can boast so fine a building, whether church, residence, barn, or warehouse. It is so sturdy, firm, and solid that all are amazed."[42]

Baltasar's comparison of Bravo's building to a school, barn, or warehouse resulted from its plainness and awkward dimensions. Another Jesuit made a similar observation: "The church of Loreto is very large, yet consists of only four artless walls and a flat roof made of well-joined beams of cedar wood."[43] Padre Jaime desired a grand structure, so he made it over a hundred and fifty feet long. His church is a bit less than twenty feet wide inside; the width was limited by the length of timbers available for ceiling beams. However, in keeping with his desire for a grand scale, the walls were raised some twenty-eight feet before the cross-beams were placed. The church's generous length and height consort oddly with its narrowness and give it the feeling of a grand hallway.[44]

The physical relationship between the old church and the new was not described. According to local tradition, the great stone church was built in the same spot as the original.[45] That would have preserved the integrity of Padre Piccolo's burial site in front of the altar of the church in which he last served. It is likely that Bravo's new church began as an extension of the old, perhaps by building the northern end of the new one behind the older church. That way, the north end, with the altar, could have been completed before the old church was dismantled, and services could have continued uninterrupted.

At Bravo's death in 1744, the new church was in use, though incomplete in some details. Bravo's successor, Padre Gaspar de Trujillo, installed the high altar, described by a near contemporary as "gold-leafed, and very splendid and showy." The same report continued: "Trujillo also fulfilled the long-standing dream to have an organ and other instruments to alternate with or accompany parts of the sacred services of the church, making them thereby more harmonious and solemn."[46] Some important adjunct, perhaps the bell tower with the baptistry in its base, remained under construction until Trujillo's successor, Padre Juan de Armesto, celebrated a formal dedication of the building during his tenure as padre procurador in Loreto (1748–1752).[47]

While he had masons and materials at hand, Jaime Bravo seized the opportunity to build a large residence for himself as padre misionero and procurador, and for those who came after him.[48] His massive stone-and-mortar edifice, sixty-seven feet long and thirty-one feet wide, with walls three feet thick and ten feet high, is located on the southwest corner of the public square that faced the church. The size and quality of this house struck Visitor General Baltasar as an embarrassment to the missionaries. In his report to the provincial, he pointed out that the money came from profits on supplies and food sold to soldiers at double the purchase price. Even with the high shipping costs and spoilage factors figured in, Baltasar felt that the procurador's profits were too great.

> . . . the doubt arises whether the presidio and houses for the captain and soldiers (of which there is almost nothing) should not have been built from these profits. If the profits belonged to the soldiers, then they are justified in protesting on seeing how comfortably the Padres are housed while they are so neglected. This matter must be satisfactorily corrected.[49]

Baltasar's point of view produced no change in the status quo. Bravo submitted a defense of the project, then died the same year. The provincial must have thought that punishment enough; he did not offer the redress asked by the visitor general.[50]

Bravo's "mansion" endured. When Gaspar de Portolá came to Loreto nearly thirty years later, it was the house he commandeered for his own use. In all likelihood, it is the house that padres and then governors used until the end of Loreto's reign as regional capital in 1829. It is occupied as a residence to this day.

Loreto's mission compound had acquired its final Jesuit form. Padre Baegert described what lay alongside the new church.

> The other three wings contain six small rooms each, approximately six yards wide and as many yards long, with a light hole toward the sand or the sea. The vestry and the kitchen are found here, also a small general store, where the soldiers, sailors, their wives and children buy buckles, belts, ribbons, combs, tobacco, sugar, linen, shoes, stockings, hats, and similar things, for no Italian or any other trader ever thought of making a fortune in California.
>
> Next to this quadrangle are four other walls, within which dried steer and beef meat, tallow, fat, soap, unrefined sugar, chocolate, cloth, leather, wheat, Indian corn, several millions of small black bugs which thrive on the grain, lumber, and other things are stored.[51]

Juan Javier Bischoff, padre procurador in Loreto from 1752 to 1757, initiated the raising of a *muralla* (a dike of large boulders) to divert floodwaters from the church complex. The possible scope of such a project can be appreciated today by inspecting the remains of the muralla built at about the same time at Misión de San Ignacio. In its heyday, the dike at San Ignacio was three miles long, forty feet wide and twelve or more feet high. Loreto was a more important place with more vital structures to protect, but its dike was not as large. Loreto had less than one tenth of San Ignacio's labor force and a much smaller supply of nearby boulders.[52]

Presidial Constructions

The development of the presidio roughly paralleled that of the mission since it was subject to the same financial restrictions and availability of labor and materials, but the Jesuits never gave a high priority to improvements for the military compound. Presidial structures were usually added, enlarged, or renewed with markedly less expensive and less substantial methods and materials than those devoted to the mission. Esteban Rodríguez accepted this subordination as a natural part of his contract as captain. He came to California as a Jesuit servant and ally. During his forty-three years as captain, he did not attempt to promote the temporal aspects of his command at the expense of mission objectives. By about 1740, when Jaime Bravo had the funds to make major improvements at Loreto, Rodríguez was nearly blind and at the end of his tenure. He made no complaint when the presidio was overlooked during Bravo's building program.

The presidio remained in the immediacy of its original location, less than a quarter of a mile from the beach.[53] That first hastily built fortification formed a square surrounded by two or three rows of palisades and heaps of thorny branches. Ramadas were built to shelter the soldiers and the supplies. Gradually, adobe rooms replaced these temporary shelters. By 1702, Padre Piccolo could report, ". . . the fortification consists of an entrenchment laid out in the form of a square large enough for a military plaza and soldiers' quarters. The building material of . . . the soldiers' quarters is good adobe with tile roofs."[54] From 1704 to 1706, Juan de Ugarte directed a building phase in which the presidio's perimeter wall was reinforced, a capacious stone-and-mortar storehouse was added, and the soldiers' quarters were expanded to house thirty men.[55]

The presidio's square plan served several purposes. Each room made use of the perimeter wall as one of its own, and each shared two interior walls with neighboring rooms. This arrangement saved materials and labor and formed the enclosed space needed for a parade and drill area, as well as a place to saddle and load animals. The presidio got tiled roofs much earlier than did the church. This was partly because the rooms were smaller and more readily framed over, but more importantly because the roofs were just inside the defensive wall and, had they been thatched, would have been vulnerable to attack by fire. After 1707, no mention was made of changes or additions to the presidio for about forty years. Reports do suggest nearby storerooms and workshops used by soldiers and craftsmen. It is likely that some were modest structures of adobes, but more would have been inexpensive, quickly erected ramadas.

To build a ramada, a construction crew cut four *palo blanco* trees so that their first forks were about eight feet from the butt end.[56] They implanted these vertically to form the corners of the building. They then set two taller forked trunks in the middle of each end to support a ridgepole. The workers buried all these posts to a depth of about two feet, enough to withstand some lateral force. Palm logs were split or palo blanco trunks were trimmed to serve as ridgepoles and eave supports. The builders set these horizontal members into the forked tops of the standing posts; then they used smaller branches of palo blanco as rafters. They bound each joint of this house of poles with broad thongs of wet rawhide, which shrank as they dried to form tight bindings. Finally, they thatched the roof with palm leaves or carrizo stalks.[57] In Loreto's climate, this was a useful structure. It gave excellent protection from the fierce sun and occasional rains. The sides were open to any air movement and allowed the people easy entry or access to stored objects.

Large, open-sided ramadas were called *tinglados*. Some were built as workshops for carpenters, blacksmiths, and other artisans. Some were used as tackrooms for the diverse gear needed for riding and pack animals. Others served as shelters for goods being unloaded from ships, or as staging areas for supplies to be loaded onto pack trains bound for other missions.[58]

Padre Procurador Juan de Armesto was responsible for the last major building erected at Loreto in Jesuit times. In 1751, the captain of the presidio wrote a formal receipt for a new *cuerpo de guardia* (guardhouse) completed that April. The old building, he noted, had been destroyed by a furious storm. The new one was solidly built of stone and mortar and could withstand any tempest. He was careful to note that the building's cost, fourteen hundred pesos, was very moderate for such work. This document reflected Visitador General Baltasar's disapproval of some of Jaime Bravo's earlier building expenditures and Juan de Armesto's determination to justify his own.[59] The guardhouse no doubt was part of the presidial compound's perimeter. It served as both barracks for unmarried soldiers and as a guardroom for men in the watch rotation.[60]

Hispanic Society Recreated in Frontier California

From the earliest daylight, Loreto was astir. Bells were tolled to call neophytes in for religious services and instruction. Simple meals were cooked and served. Domestic animals were taken from corrals and driven out to spend the day in the upper flats browsing on the sparse herbs, brush, and leguminous trees that grew from the sandy soil. A smith and his helper fired a forge, caulkers prepared oakum and worked on small craft careened at the top of the beach. Small parties went out to hunt and fish, often to return empty-handed. A few neophytes tended a garden patch under the direction of a soldier. A string of mules was loaded with supplies, then picked its way along a rocky road toward an outlying mission. Later in the day, the *leñeros* (firewood gatherers) returned to the village. These men and boys drove burros loaded with faggots of dead branches wrenched from mesquite trees, or wood cut from palo blanco trees downed and tossed in tumbled confusion by a recent chubasco. Other crews returned with fresh-cut branches of green mesquite or *dipúa* [*Cercidium microphyllum*] which were needed to feed any riding or pack animals penned up for use in the following days.[61]

Juan María de Salvatierra had intended a spiritual conquest and the creation

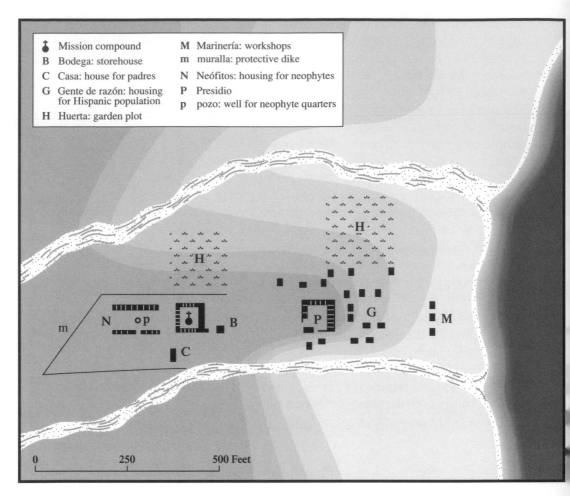

Key:
- ⚓ Mission compound
- **B** Bodega: storehouse
- **C** Casa: house for padres
- **G** Gente de razón: housing for Hispanic population
- **H** Huerta: garden plot
- **M** Marinería: workshops
- **m** muralla: protective dike
- **N** Neófitos: housing for neophytes
- **P** Presidio
- **p** pozo: well for neophyte quarters

0   250   500 Feet

Figure 9.1 Conjectural Plan of Loreto c. 1760[62]

of an ideal mission, but an Hispanic village also took root in California's rocky soil. Most of the mission's employees were products of pueblos on New Spain's northwest frontiers. When they brought in their families, built dwellings, and began to socialize, they unconsciously formed a pueblo. This unintended by-product of the mission effort was inevitable; even the missionaries unconsciously thought of the pueblo as a pattern for the way people should live and imposed the form on their neophytes.

Many Hispanic communities in New Spain included a high percentage of Indians, or had them living nearby and interacting in the same economy with gente de razón, but nowhere other than Loreto were indigenous people the principal focus of such a community's directors. Nowhere else were they so protected and cultivated while living in close proximity to Hispanic soldiers and their families. In California, gente de razón were instructed to mobilize and guide neophyte manpower to achieve mission goals. They were expected to act as role models, teachers, and supervisors of neophytes under mission tutelage.

At the same time, soldiers and servants were barred from hiring converts to work for them or from imposing on their charges in other economic or personal ways.

This teacher-and-student, master-and-apprentice relationship was not limited to men. As the soldiers brought in their families and their women began to take part in Loreto's affairs, neophyte girls were assigned to them as helpers and students. The association of the two groups of women must have started awkwardly. They had no common language and shared few cultural experiences.[63] The women from New Spain were old hands at household chores; they swept floors, washed clothes, sewed and mended. They made tortillas and prepared the other staple dishes of their regional Mexican cuisine. The converts saw that all of this was approved by padres and soldiers, and there was a great deal of social pressure on them to learn these new skills. Before long, neophyte women copied the newcomers in dress and action.[64] They learned Spanish from their unofficial mentors and then began to take verbal direction, which speeded their acculturation.[65] Thus, a rather small number of Hispanic women at Loreto, and even more limited numbers of their sisters living at missions, were able to establish Hispanic families and transplant the whole range of their family practices and domestic arts and crafts to this frontier location.

The education of children was not overlooked. Soldiers and sailors were charged for their children's tuition, and their sons, at least, were given elementary educations in reading, writing, number concepts needed to keep simple accounts, and certainly in singing and in religious doctrine. Selected neophyte children were included in the same classes. Some of the young Californians excelled in their studies; the padres referred to them as *ladinos*, individuals apt at acquiring the Spanish language and Hispanic ways.[66] Most of the young gente de razón who matured to be soldiers and sailors did learn to read and write. In the 1750s, Padre Juan Javier Bischoff, then procurador in Loreto, arranged to place a small library in the presidio's guardhouse and to put books aboard all Loreto's boats. The expense and effort was said to have been justified because it provided a wholesome diversion.[67]

Loreto differed from other pueblos of New Spain in its unusual balance of Hispanic men, women, and children. A census taken in 1730 indicated that gente de razón of all ages and sexes numbered 175. Twenty-nine of these were soldiers, forty-one were men of the marinería, and six were arrieros and vaqueros. Most of the remaining ninety-nine were wives and children of the seventy-six men enumerated, but the ninety-nine dependents also included an unspecified number of servants who were paid by the soldiers and lived in their houses.[68] Thus, if each man were taken as the head of a household and the servant total was as few as five, each household would consist of only two and a quarter people. Several factors contributed to this unusually small number of women and children. The Jesuits would seldom allow an unmarried woman to come to California.[69] Most soldiers were young; some were unmarried, and those who had wives as yet had few children.[70] A number of sailors and artisans were either unmarried or kept their wives and families at their mainland homes.[71] Some older children were probably sent back to family centers on the mainland, places with better opportunities for apprenticeship, employment, and marriage.

California was truly an island for its Hispanic people. Most mainland pueblos had neighboring hamlets, usually within a day's ride, but from Loreto excursions to see relatives were long, difficult undertakings and required formal permission from the missionaries. Loreto's isolation and its function as a mission base gave the place an unusually sober mien, part of which was due to the method by which its Hispanic people were selected. Each man signed a contract and was expected to live up to its terms. If he failed to perform satisfactorily, he was returned to the mainland and another took his place and was tested in turn. Some gave good service but tired of the restrictive atmosphere; many left California voluntarily.[72] Long-time employees were, therefore, an exceptionally capable, disciplined, and upright group. There were no flippant or rowdy elements, no frivolous entertainments, and no unseemly displays of drunkenness or affection. Compared to their mainland counterparts, California's gente de razón must have appeared remarkably upright in their behavior and submissive to religious authority.[73]

Church attendance was a condition of employment. Padre Salvatierra boasted that soldiers were expected to "hear mass every day with proper attention and reverence, and repeat in chorus and with devotion, the Rosary of Most Holy Mary, and, finally, her litanies." He concluded by saying that on Saturdays there was a compulsory sermon and that soldiers were urged to take sacraments often. Hispanic women and children attended as regularly as men. Such measures provided good examples for neophytes.[74] An account written in 1730 shows that after three decades the formalities were undiminished:

> Every Sunday afternoon the *español* children [children of the gente de razón] file out of the church after their Sunday School lessons singing the opening of the catechism. They go down to the pueblo and from there to the presidio from where they proceed, accompanied by the soldiers and the remainder of the people, back to the church where they are received by the padres. All enter the church in procession and singing. After the preaching of the gospel in Spanish, they are given a sermon which is received also by most of the Indians, almost all of whom now understand the Castilian tongue.
>
> On Wednesdays, Fridays and Saturdays, at the pealing of the bells, all the military and other folk assemble for the Rosary. They recite as a chorus before the main altar and sing the litanies to Our Lady of Loreto.[75]

Not only was church attendance expected, but deportment in the temple was monitored and regulated. For forty years (1720–1761), Hermano Juan Bautista Mugazábal performed as a self-appointed overseer of the house of God. He watched over those attending services or visiting the church, ready to reprove any who talked or failed to pay proper respect.[76]

Jesuit hiring practices produced an unusually homogeneous frontier community in Loreto. The missionaries excluded workers from the lowest levels of mainland society because native Californians performed most menial chores. Very few people who took jobs in California were from the mainland frontier's upper strata; those who had status or wealth in more typical Hispanic centers did not care to submit to the limitations imposed by the Jesuits. Men from the upper echelons of New Spain's society who did volunteer to serve in California's military during its early years were dependents of Jesuit benefactors, or younger sons hoping to have a role in a successful conquest — an involvement that, in the Spanish world, would bring prestige and advantage later in life. Few brought families or remained many years.

Despite the absence of Hispanic grandees or laborers, nascent Loreto was by no means a classless society. The new community was dominated by an aristocracy: the educated, upper-class European and creole Jesuits. They paid everyone's wages, and they controlled community life. The church was the principal social center, and a padre presided at any of its functions. From the pulpit, missionaries directed the colony on moral and spiritual affairs. From the lectern, they taught the sons of the presidials and even some promising neophyte youths to read, to write, and to sing.[77] They funded, orchestrated, and presided over the great fiestas that were the high points of public social life, and they officiated at weddings, baptisms, and funerals, the central events of family life.

Like the padres, officers and even petty officers of the presidio were Europeans or creoles. Though they stood well below their employers in power and prestige, their social group dominated everyday affairs. Despite his subservience to the Jesuits, the captain received at least some of the respect traditionally shown to a frontier military leader. He also commanded attention as the civil authority who presided over gente de razón and neophytes. The visitador had the power to override the captain's authority but in practice seldom did — it was considered expedient to have the people respect and at times fear their highest-ranking officer.

For such a small group, California's gente de razón were remarkably diverse in racial and national origin. During its seventy years, the colony's padres originated in Spain, Italy, Sicily, Scotland, Alsace, Lower Rhineland, Bavaria, Austria, Bohemia, Croatia, Honduras, and New Spain. Its soldiers hailed from Spain, Portugal, Malta, Sicily, England, Peru, and New Spain. Besides Indians and castas from the lands around the gulf, Loreto's sailors usually included *chinos*, Filipinos who had come on Manila ships and stayed in New Spain rather than risk another harrowing Pacific crossing.[78] Vaqueros, arrieros, and craftsmen included, perhaps predominantly, mulattoes. Mission servants were either mestizos or neophytes trained in the long-established Sinaloan or Sonoran missions. No doubt other men with diverse origins worked in California without having their birthplaces recorded.

The traditional Hispanic social order was innate in gente de razón, whatever their origin. They adopted appropriate roles dictated by unspoken rules known to all. Many clues show how the colony's people regarded each other. Some status relationships are obvious; the white and the educated were accorded higher standing. Gradations of pay and the relative prestige of occupations had their effects. The levels of esteem in which Loreto's people were held by their padre-employers and by each other were indicated in other ways. In their private letters, as well as in entries in church records, California Jesuits accorded the honorary title of *don* to any man in their employ who was born in Spain. An español of good family, particularly if he were literate or had some distinction like previous meritorious service or important relatives, might be called *don*, especially in his later years. The Jesuits never used this title in referring to any man considered a casta.

A great deal of the social interaction in any Hispanic society can be inferred from baptismal records. A key is found in the relationships between the principals in those ceremonies and the people they chose to act as godparents. Compadrazgo, the ties between people through godparenthood, was a social custom with certain informal rules in addition to religious obligations. In most cases, a man or woman served as a godparent to a child of his or her social equal: a family member, friend, or colleague. As an honor to the parents, a person might act as godparent to offspring of social inferiors. Rarely did anyone appear in the records as godparent to a child of his or her social superiors. When this did occur, another more important godparent was usually listed first. Where fairly complete baptismal and, therefore, godparental records are available, diagrams can be made to show the relative prestige of a community's members.[79] Unfortunately, most of Loreto's vital records have been lost; there is not enough evidence to reconstruct all the individual and family relationships that made up even that small society.

A second and more obvious relationship emerges from marriage records. In such a caste-conscious society, marriages were usually contracted between people of similar status — if that were possible. But socially equal partners were often unavailable at tiny Loreto. Choices then devolved to partners who might be seen as suitable, if not equal. Such situations stimulated individuals or families to arrange marriages in which their status was improved by unions with their betters. The social acceptance of individuals and the social distance between families can be gauged by a study of who married whom, and by studying those who were asked to be witnesses. Although the marriage registers from Loreto are missing — and with them, all records of witnesses — other sources reveal the names of partners for about a third to half of gente de razón marriages in Jesuit times.[80]

The elements in Loreto's population ranked by assessing the chain of command and factors such as pay, forms of address, race, marriage, and compadrazgo were[81]

Missionaries
Captain
Alférez/teniente
Soldiers from Spain

Non-commissioned officers
Español soldiers

Master craftsmen[82]
Mestizo soldiers
Boatswain/arráez
Craft apprentices or assistants
Neophyte servants from mainland missions
Sailors

Neophyte officials: governor, captain, fiscal, etc.
Neophytes with jobs: page/interpreter, vaquero, etc.
Other neophytes

Analysis of Loreto's society reveals predictable prejudices. The greatest separation between any of its levels was the gap between españoles and all of the castas below them. A second conspicuous separation lay between neophytes, bound as they were to missions, and all those who were brought to work in California. Neophytes were both protected and discriminated against by the rules that restricted their activities.

Officers and Spanish and español soldiers tended to marry within each other's families or into those of their mainland counterparts. Marriages between soldiers and neophytes were rare; only a half dozen can be documented, all in the first half of the Jesuit years. Social mobility and intermarriage were more frequent among the lower ranked groups.

The Jesuits themselves were a continuing force in molding the community. Men who could not live up to their expectations and those who did not care to do so were winnowed out. Some who chose to remain were destined to do more than serve a stint on the California peninsula; they had come to stay. They founded the pioneer families that gave continuity to Spain's foothold in California.[83]

The Jesuit influence created differences between California's gente de razón and their more casually assembled mainland counterparts. Most can only be inferred or surmised, but at least one is measurable. The men and women hired and brought to work in California bore a distribution of Christian names derived from many areas, although primarily that of northwest New Spain where the Jesuits had considerable influence. Despite that, names in California show a markedly greater degree of Jesuit cultural persuasion. Jesuit icons like Ignacio of Loyola [Ignacio, Ignacia], Francisco Javier [Francisco, Francisca], and Luis Gonzaga [Luis]; middle-European saints like San Juan Nepomuceno [Juan, Juana] and Santa Gertrudis [Gertrudis]; and California's designated patroness, Nuestra Señora de Loreto [Loreta], were reflected among the commonest names bestowed by gente de razón.[84] José María and Mariano were so common as to be prototypically Californian. Otherwise notable were the names Manuel and Pedro, frequently found among men hired to come but virtually never bestowed on those born on the peninsula.

TABLE 9.1 GIVEN NAMES OF HISPANIC PEOPLE IN CALIFORNIA, C.1720–1767 (*in order of frequency*)

Men born elsewhere	Men born in California	Women born elsewhere	Women born in California
Juan	José	María	María
Francisco	Ignacio	Juana	Josefa
José	Francisco	Gertrudis	Gertrudis
Manuel	José María	Antonia	Francisca
Pedro	Juan	Teresa	Loreta
Antonio	Luis	Ana	Ignacia
Ignacio	Mariano	Rosa	Teresa
Miguel	Joaquín		
Diego	Salvador		

Homes for gente de razón

About two to three and a half dozen mud huts are scattered over the sand, without order, looking more like cowsheds of the poorest little village than homes, and usually containing but one single room. These are occupied by the married soldiers, the few sailors, the one and a half carpenters and equally numerous blacksmiths, and their wives and children, and serve as lodging, living room, storeroom, and bedroom. . . .[85]

Thus did the dour German, Padre Baegert, describe the housing for presidial families in 1768. In all likelihood, their homes were distributed on the mesa west of the presidio. Each had a primary room of adobe, but despite Baegert's belittling description, many may have had lean-to additions or outbuildings of ramada construction — as was the custom all over northwest New Spain. These useful adjuncts, fabricated almost without cost, could be modified to serve several purposes. The sides could filled in with vertical palings taken from skeletons of the numerous cardón, the giant cactus of the region. In places like Loreto with long hot seasons, this version was widely used as a cookhouse until late in the twentieth century. The openwork siding allows ventilation to dissipate heat and smoke, yet acts as an effective windbreak. In a more elaborate variation, all four sides, aside from doors or windows, were filled in with panels of woven sticks. If desired, these could be plastered with adobe to make a local version of mud and wattle. This technique gave protection against the wind, rain, and dust that swept across the mesa.[86] Floors in all these simple structures, and in some of the more substantial buildings as well, were of packed earth, easy to prepare and maintain, and more comfortable underfoot than other available materials.

With no convenient water and only poor, rocky soil near the houses, kitchen gardening was minimal. Hispanic families probably cultivated flowering plants and herbs in containers, but it is unlikely that they had many trees or shrubs. They did raise a few dooryard chickens.[87] Finches, cardinals, doves, and possibly parrots were caged as pets, as were tiny ground squirrels and kangaroo rats.[88] Dogs were brought to Loreto early in its settlement, primarily to aid in the herding of goats, an industry that soon moved to the mountain missions.[89] A Jesuit commented on the dogs kept by gente de razón, incidentally revealing something about the way dogs were raised, a bit of folklore, and another side effect of decades of intermittent food shortages.

> The Sinaloans . . . say that dogs bred in California have no loyalty. This follows from their silly belief that here a perfidious star influences dogs to have bad natures. Let them take more care in raising their dogs and they will see that they are no different from dogs in other lands. Let their masters give them proper food from birth and they will not go about robbing jerky from ranches, kitchens, etc. Let them make sure that there is no lack of food in the house, because, if dogs have to get it some other way, they have little regard for their master; indeed they have as many masters as will give them mouthfuls to eat.[90]

Homes of the gente de razón were loosely dispersed on Loreto's mesa for a reason. Separation gave neighbors privacy and allowed houses and privies to be farther apart than would have been possible in a compact grouping. Water pollution from privies presumably was negligible. Serious health hazards from this source would have been minimized by the distance from the water source, the height of the mesa, a very dry climate, and a small population.

Furniture and Implements

Each household was outfitted with simple but durable wooden furniture: a table and chairs, a chest or two, a cupboard of some sort, and bedframes. These last were rectangular, heavy, wooden frames with a leg at each corner. Frequent holes were drilled on all sides so the frame could be strung like a tennis racquet with strips of rawhide that dried to form a taut lattice. A skin was thrown on this gridwork to prevent it from biting into the sleeper; for further comfort, a pad of mezcal fibers was placed over the hide. Imported blankets completed the sleeping gear. Chests were probably of the round-topped type, called *arcones*, that were popular at that time and later on the adjacent mainland. These were used to protect finer items of clothing or other delicate objects from otherwise inescapable dust.

Although most soldiers may have been capable of simple woodwork, the hardness of local woods inhibited casual carpentry.[91] The softer, more readily split woods required to build most furniture had to be imported—at some cost.

Although the presidial shipwrights could not have been employed full-time on the often absent vessels, the missions had first call on their time and skills. Eventually, however, at least one carpenter offered his services to Loreto's inhabitants.[92]

Items handcrafted in California showed little innovation in form or use. Recently arrived Europeans may have introduced some new ideas, but most implements and furnishings, like the dwellings, were patterned after models found elsewhere in northwest New Spain.[93] The adobe stove is an example. Adobe bricks were used to build a structure about five feet long, three to four feet wide, and two and a half feet tall. This boxy shell was then filled with earth tamped until the whole formed a flat-topped solid. More adobe bricks were added on top to create three or four open fireboxes, each a foot wide by two feet deep. A line of large bricks at the back served as a place to set pots and pans off the flames. Fires were built in the boxes and fed with dry mesquite twigs which produce a hot, nearly smokeless flame. The cook placed iron rods across the top of one or more fireboxes to support pots and pans, or topped a fire with a *comal* (a flat sheet of earthenware or metal) on which to bake tortillas.

A few of the crafts widely practiced in New Spain were conspicuously absent at Loreto. Little pottery was made on the peninsula, partly because of the scarcity of suitable clay. Pottery vessels of all sorts were imported from Sonoran missions.[94] Little weaving was done at Loreto and that with imported fibers; the area could not support sheep or cotton. Little soap was made — slaughtered animals were very lean because of the sparse browsing, and most of the fat they did yield was needed to prepare beans and tortillas.[95]

To an urban observer, Loreto would have seemed rude and makeshift. Its great distance from urban centers discouraged the importation of niceties other than trappings for the church and personal adornments for occasional use. Most objects, aside from weapons, tools, and a few kitchen utensils, were crudely manufactured from local materials.

Housekeeping, Food, and Food Preparation

Housekeeping at Loreto was simple, but it involved much drudgery. In addition to assigned duties that supported the greater mission system, everyone devoted much time to maintaining the traditional way of life. Houses were built on a mesa high enough above watercourses to offer protection from most flash floods, but the elevation and the distance from the village spring made fetching water a continuous chore. It was impractical to do laundry at home when water had to be brought so far; clothing was carried down and washed on rocks near a batequi or in the dry watercourse near the springs. Collecting firewood was another never-ending labor, and, as nearby sources were depleted, wood gatherers had to go farther and farther afield.

Poor soil and a meager water supply made agriculture at Loreto difficult and unproductive. As the population of native Californians fell and more hands were required to carry out Loreto's larger responsibilities, it became expedient to obtain agricultural products — largely dry staples — from other missions, or from Sonora, rather than to produce them locally. Subsequently, Loreto's people had little access to fresh fruits or vegetables. Minor exceptions were sweet mesquite, deliberately planted for its edible young foliage and pods[96], and coconuts that eventually flourished in the damp soil where the watercourses north and south of the presidio intersected the beach.[97]

Loreto did pursue cattle raising. The mission maintained vaqueros who tended herds that roamed the coastal plain. Around 1750, Loreto reclaimed the site of its one-time visita of San Juan Londó when it was abandoned by Misión de San José de Comondú. Loreto soon had herds totaling over a thousand cattle, a resource that increased the people's dependence on meat and utilization of animal products.[98] Many experienced ranch hands were available for a *matanza* (slaughter), and they wasted nothing from the felled steers. Padre Baegert described the uses of some of the products:

> Cattle, sheep, and goats had to supply the meat for the healthy and the sick, but they were also needed for their tallow, used to make candles and soap, and in caulking ships and boats. They also furnished the fat used to prepare beans. In California, as well as elsewhere in America, the beans are not prepared with butter churned from milk, but with the rendered fat and marrow of the bones. For this purpose, every time a well-fed cow or ox was killed, a rare occurrence, every bit of fat was carefully cut from the meat, rendered and conserved in skin bags and bladders. This fat was used for the preparation of food and for frying the very lean or dried meat. Some of the hides were tanned for shoes and saddles and for bags in which everything was carried from the field to the mission or anywhere else.[99] Other skins were used raw to make sandals for the natives, or were cut into strips for ropes, cords, or thongs, which were used for tying, packing, and similar tasks. The natives used the horns to scoop up water or to fetch food from the mission.[100]

The butchers also salted some hides to preserve them for future uses. The people hauled hoofs and bones back to the *real* to make soup stock. They roasted livers and kidneys and ate them on the spot. One of their principal interests was to produce *tasajo* (jerky) which they prepared by cutting the meat into thin strips, salting it, and hanging it over ropes to dry in the sun. Lightweight, long-lasting, and nutritious, tasajo was the arid peninsula's all-purpose trail food, a vital component of every traveler's stores. Men of the gente de razón were the most mobile members of the population, and their taste for tasajo became proverbial, a trait that would be remarked upon by most observers for the next century and a half. An old saying of gente de razón — reported in Jesuit times and still remembered in the area — captures the spirit of this taste: "*Que un tasajo bien salado, no hay cosa mayor. Se bebe tinas de agua, que es tanto mejor.*" [There is no better thing than a well-salted piece of jerky, after which you drink tubs of water—which is so much the better!][101]

Tasajo was the basis of a popular ingredient in the folk cuisine of northwest New Spain. Dried, cured tasajo was placed on a large *metate* (the aboriginal grind stone) and beaten with a hammer stone until it separated into string-like fibers, called *machaca*. These were then soaked in water and used as part of various sautéed or simmered dishes, along with rice, vegetables, chiles, etc.

Food preparation differed widely between the neighboring but distinct communities of neophytes and gente de razón. Neophyte crews prepared and cooked their group's simple, communal meals of gruels, soups, and stews. Among the gente de razón, food preparation and consumption was on a family basis, and their food required more labor to prepare. Wheat flour was often available, but cornmeal had to be hand ground on metates in each home. Chiles and rock salt were also ground as needed. Soup stock was made by boiling bones, offal, or dried meat. Dried meat and fish, pounded into machaca, were mixed with vegetables—particularly onions, garlic, and chiles—to make sautéed dishes. Garbanzos and dried beans were popular but required long cooking on fires that had to be stoked and tended.

Salt was needed to prepare jerky and to preserve hides, as well as for other purposes. A bountiful source lay near at hand; Isla del Carmen has a natural *salina*, or salt pan, less than thirty miles sailing distance from Loreto. There sea water evaporated and left several inches of pure salt that could be broken up with bars and hauled to the beach. This resource had commercial promise, so Padre Salvatierra attempted to get a monopoly on the salt harvest to help finance his mission.[102]

The land and the adjacent gulf provided a few table items. Sea turtles were an old source of food for the Indians, but—strangely in the light of its later popularity—the meat was disdained by gente de razón because of its fishy flavor.[103] Use of turtle eggs was never mentioned. Some fish were caught, but the gente de razón, through inexperience or lack of gear, were poor fishermen. No records indicate fish as an important dietary adjunct.[104] Hunting was only sporadically successful. Men were adept enough at this art, but deer and mountain sheep, the principal game animals, were scarce and wary due to continual hunting. Gente de razón gathered a few herbs, fruits, and edible roots or stems from the mesas and mountains. Some were identical to those that they knew and used on the opposite coast. Others were introduced to them by local Californians. They brewed a variety of teas from local herbs to supplement their limited supplies of popular but costly chocolate. Neither coffee nor Asian teas were as yet imported for use along the frontier.

Clothing

Imported, readymade clothing was limited to headgear, cloaks, coats, fine shirts, stockings, and a few shoes and boots. Most of these items were saved for ceremonial wear rather than daily use.[105] The great majority of clothing had to be cut and sewn by hand. Apart from child care, cooking, and maintenance chores, sewing was a woman's most time-consuming activity. Dozens of different kinds and colors of yard goods were delivered on each annual supply order. Loreto's previously cited supply order for 1725, as well as those for most other years, abounded in materials for would-be elegant wardrobes: costly, showy fabrics of varied types and colors, brocaded banding tapes, ribbons, and the like.[106] Patterns were either imported or worked out by local seamstresses.

Little is known about the style of clothing worn in early Loreto. A few documents mention odds and ends of clothing, but there are few specific clues to indicate their appearance.[107] Few descriptions referred to daily garb. Workaday clothes were patched and rustic; garments deteriorated quickly in contact with California's unrelenting rocks and thorns. However, on Sundays or during fiestas, the people of the frontier village worked a great transformation. They dressed up and cut surprisingly stylish figures as they went to and from the church or socialized during their day of rest. In later years, the Jesuits provided some verbal and visual pictures. Padre Baegert, on his way to California in 1751, was moved to write, "I could not wonder enough about the show-off of the womenfolk, especially when we came to Culiacán at the time of Lent and saw the women going to confession. We hardly saw such a show-off in Mexico City, not to mention in Alsace, for I noticed them dressed in velvet or in a gold material."[108] Since Sinaloa was the cradle of so many of California's early gente de razón, it is logical to suppose that Loretans imitated their peers on the mainland. The Sinaloans, in turn, had copied what was in vogue in Guadalajara and Mexico City. It is difficult to guess at the accuracy with which styles were imitated and revised as copies of copies moved outward to the frontiers. Baegert observed that some of these creations were quite extravagant. In the 1760s, Padre Ignacio Tirsch made color sketches showing several examples of elaborately dressed Hispanic women in California. His corresponding pictures of neophytes show similar but simpler clothing, probably their best as well.[109]

Women's everyday garments included dresses or skirts and blouses, petticoats and stockings. For warmth, they wore shawls or *mangas*, a poncho-shaped overgarment, rather than coats. During the day, in all but the coldest weather, it is likely that men and women wore shirts and undershirts rather than any sort of wrap. Teguas, homemade by local leatherworkers, were the working footwear of both sexes.[110] Women wore scarfs over their heads when they went to church or out into the sun. Both men and women wore hats of felted material or woven of straw or palm fiber. These were smaller and had flatter brims than their Mexican counterparts of today. Soldiers also had cocked hats for dress occasions and felt hats with low, flat tops and wide, flat brims. Most headgear was imported from the mainland.[111]

Hair styles are as difficult to trace as styles of dress. The scant evidence suggests that in the first decades of the colony men had rather long hair and caught it back with a thong. Moustaches were popular.[112] At least some soldiers and some missionary fathers wore beards; they reported that the Californians, who had none, were intrigued and tugged at those of the Spaniards to see if they were some sort of disguise or mask.[113] Español men, in particular, may have grown beards or moustaches to emphasize their European blood. In the last years of Jesuit California, Padre Tirsch's drawings depict clean-shaven men and gente de razón who dressed like their counterparts in the settled interior of New Spain.[114]

Tirsch's neophyte women all appear with a single braid to the middle of their backs. Hispanic women apparently wore their hair long and tied back, braided, or up in one or two buns.[115] Ribbon was mentioned frequently in lists of stores. It could have served to tie or adorn women's hair, but may have been used primarily in sewing. There were no descriptions of combs as hair ornaments, though they may have been so used. Jesuits, virtually the only sources of information on California matters, were disinclined to think or write about women.[116] Fortunately, Padre Tirsch did not apply this ideal to his drawings.

Health, Medical Treatment, and Medicine

Gente de razón enjoyed better health in California than did their counterparts in most mainland locations.[117] Very little was reported about the native Californians' health, except their susceptibility to imported contagious diseases and the tragically high mortality that ensued. Single epidemics of smallpox or some of the so-called childhood diseases carried away a quarter or more of the native population.[118] Gente de razón had much greater immunity to these diseases. This inequity, apparently an act of providence, reinforced the Hispanic sense of superiority and detracted from the neophytes' morale and already low self-esteem.

Accidents must have been commonplace and received treatment according to the skills and experience of those available to offer care. For serious injuries, people turned to a soldier who had been trained as a barber-surgeon.[119] He could stitch and cauterize wounds, apply tourniquets, and set bones using splints.[120] As late as 1734, such a man was sent from Loreto all the way to San José del Cabo to bleed Padre Tamaral who believed that he needed that treatment.[121] In 1720, a soldier, possibly the same man, was called on to bleed all the horses in Padre Guillén's caballada to more quickly "expel their fatigue" after they had borne the first land expedition from Ligüí to La Paz.[122] California documentation does not mention bleeding of humans or animals after the 1734 account.

Midwives were probably the most crucial medical practitioners in the colony—and they were excluded from Jesuit reports. This omission was due to the padres' studied delicacy in matters pertaining to women and to the fact that the midwife's work was considered routine, unlike treatment performed during emergencies or epidemics, and was offered by a relatively large number of women.

The padre at Loreto, like those at the more remote missions, set up a room with a few beds to act as an infirmary. Here, he (or neophytes trained by him) administered medicines, proffered food and drink, and generally tended the ill. In times of epidemics, larger shelters — such as tinglados — were thrown up, and the sufferers, often with only mats on which to lie, were cared for as well as the healthy could manage.[123]

Home remedies had to suffice for the majority of ailments. The padres had sources of prepared medicines, but the amounts they received suggest that these filled only their personal needs.[124] California's supply lists show little more in the way of bulk remedies than a few sorts of leaves fancied as medicinal teas, and some tars and unguents used as liniments, perhaps as much on pack and saddle beasts as on people. A few widely known medicinal plants — such as castor bean, the prototypical laxative — were introduced.[125] Folklore and practical experience also indicated a wide variety of reportedly efficacious teas, ointments, and poultices made from local herbs. Padre Ignacio Tirsch made a painting of the red-flowered shrub, *tabardillo* (*Calliandra californica*), and captioned it "very good against a high fever."[126] Padre Miguel del Barco, an astute and critical observer, agreed in that assessment and went on to describe the preparation of the medicine. Among his many descriptions of medicinal plants, Barco particularly extolled the virtue of the dried, powdered bark of *palo blanco* (*Lysiloma candida*) as a treatment for infected wounds, recounted the many medicinal uses of jojoba (*Simmondsia chinensis*), and described the preparation of a balsam, valuable in treating sores and wounds, made by boiling down the liquid obtained from the pulp of the *cardón* (*Pachycereus pringlei*).[127] Many such medicines are still used by isolated or poor Baja Californians.

Fiestas

Despite their serious purpose, missionaries did not suppress all gaiety, nor was it their wish to do so. Some California Jesuits had well-developed senses of humor and even a love of fun.[128] Their tight control of village decorum was based on their ideas of appropriate behavior in a mission setting. They allowed or encouraged dancing, singing, the playing of musical instruments, and certain games and contests that they perceived as attractive but harmless elements in the celebration of fiestas.[129] Fiestas were held on days of special significance for all Catholics, for Jesuits, or for the people of Loreto. Fiestas served several purposes: to remind everyone of important religious events; to allow times for merrymaking with special foods, music, dancing, and acts of mimicry and pantomime, and to attract any unconverted Californians who might attend. A report by Salvatierra shows that even in little Loreto, a fiesta could be a beautiful, awe-inspiring event.

> The month of December now began. During this month we celebrated with great solemnity the Feast of the Immaculate Conception and the feast of our patron, San Francisco Javier. Since the launch *San Francisco Javier* was in

the bay, within sight of the real, we sent powder down to it and two small guns, and in this way the salutes fired on land were answered from the sea. The whole launch was hung with lanterns and was made beautiful with lights. Rockets were sent up, both on sea and on land. The water was very calm, and the lights were reflected in it.

In the same letter, the father visitor described Loreto's first major Christmas feast.

> Hundreds of neophytes came to the festivities and more than a hundred of these New Christians performed native dances. These dances are very different from those of the tribes on the mainland coast. These Indians have more than thirty dances, all of them different. They are performed in costume, and they are designed to give instruction in various pursuits and occupations, such as making war, fishing, traveling, carrying babies, packing loads, and other things of this sort. The boy of three of four years of age prides himself on properly playing his part in the dances. These children act as if they were already mature, skilled performers vying with one another. It amused all of us very much to watch them.[130]

Dance, music, and festivals were among the few activities in which Spanish and native American cultures coincided. All were incorporated into the mission's religious practices and formed rare examples of pre-Christian influences that were tolerated by missionaries. Dancing, in particular, was an activity shared by converts and gente de razón. The Californians had many dances portraying men, animals, and situations, often humorous and appreciated by the padres and their helpers. The people from Europe and New Spain had their own regional folk dance repertories. Both groups performed dances in a spirited and good-natured form of competitive entertainment. Piccolo encouraged his soldiers to teach their dances to the converts. Salvatierra reported with relish that he took part in these events himself. His performances, of course, were roundly applauded.[131]

Many letters and reports from Loreto in its first years radiate a sort of communal joy, a camaraderie in which missionaries, gente de razón, and neophytes were joined. Doubtless some of this was due to the first Jesuits' enthusiasm for their venture. Some can be attributed to the innocence of the Californians and their delight in new experiences, and some to the whole group's isolation and everyone's need for companionship and shared experiences.

Fiestas created an annual round of colorful events that broke the spell of dull routine and brought all elements of the community to a single focus. Padre Jaime Bravo's 1730 description of Loreto's celebrations gives a remarkable view of the extent to which presidial forces were utilized in the mission's ceremonial activities:

All the church functions are carried out with all possible propriety and solemnity. Those of Holy Week are celebrated with whatever pomp is permitted by the poverty of the land. Foodstuffs are guarded by armed soldiers from the moment they are put in the warehouse. Likewise the chancel, inside and out, is watched over by Indians armed in the fashion of this land.

The ceremony of washing the feet of those that represent the twelve apostles is very solemn as performed with the assistance of all the men of the presidio, the marinería, and others who perform it in church and there make their offerings. The apostles' banquet is presented as grandly as possible. The cooks are the captain's wife and the wives of the other principal men of the presidio. They take the food in servings to the tables where it is distributed by the padres, the captain, the alférez, and the more responsible men of the presidio and marinería. The ceremony is greatly edifying.

At all the processions of Holy Week, Corpus Christi, the Immaculate Conception, the major supplications [San Marcos], or whatever others are to be celebrated, the military presidio also assists, outfitted in their uniforms and arms — as they do also when they attend church. During the processions of Corpus Christi and Immaculate Conception, the soldiers march all around the presidio compound in close order drill, firing off continuous salutes until the flag of the presidio is brought out and they return to their quarters.

When the sacrament is taken to one who is ill or when a burial is performed, some of the soldiers provide a ceremonial escort.[132]

Occasionally, special events allowed additions to the regular fiesta schedule. A ceremony was organized to greet Padre Visitador General José de Echeverría when he landed at California's capital in 1729. Echeverría's letter to the Marqués de Villapuente preserves his view of Loreto in action.

. . . at five o'clock in the afternoon . . . the garrison came down to the beach to receive me; the alférez, who carried an old-fashioned banner of Spain, and who, after the ceremony, did not fail to perform a salute with his lance; the sergeant with his halberd; the soldiers dressed in long coats, with hats in the Spanish fashion, shoes without ornament, broad-swords, and shields hanging freely from their shoulders. Some of them had moustaches, and all of them bore themselves like valiant men. They gave their salute, and then, keeping excellent order, preceded me to the gate of the church yard, which is enclosed with a wall of rough stone and mortar. . . .

Though the church is small, not large enough to contain the throngs of people who attend, it is very handsome, and its decorations excellent. . . . If your Lordship could see [the Indians] officiate at a sung Mass, you would go mad with joy, for they achieve a great harmony, and employ many bagpipes. All those who live in the pueblo go to Mass, which is celebrated every day. The men sit on the right side of the church; the women, by themselves, on the left. When the Mass is finished, they praise the Lord in song; the men sing first, and the women follow. The boys remain for instruction in Christian doctrine, and likewise, in a separate section, the girls. In the afternoon they gather for the Rosary, which they repeat in chorus. This whole place has become a Heaven. . . . The men come to church in their trousers and shirts of sack-cloth; the women wear their flannel petticoats and cotton chemises. . . .[133]

Padre Echeverría summed up his sense of Loreto with the phrase, "this new, happy, miniature Christian kingdom. . . ." He was painting a very rosy picture for California's most generous benefactor — but the images offer rare hints of life in Antigua California.

Storytelling, Loreto's Principal Pastime

Most entertainment was spontaneous, created and enjoyed whenever company and time were available. In all likelihood, the most fundamental and enduring was the recounting of anecdotal history, still the popular choice at remote peninsular ranches in the late twentieth century.[134] Individuals were proud of their native places and enjoyed describing their sights, activities, and people. In this way, they gave themselves identity and preserved vestiges of their origins. Exchanges of this sort went on without end. Each teller was versed in the oral history of his family and other notables of his region. A conversation might begin on almost any topic: strong men, fortunate occurrences, great storms, heroism, or disgrace. Each person would have a contribution, and the total rounds far exceeded *The Thousand and One Nights*. Most places in those days perpetuated oral traditions, but on isolated frontiers the practice was especially valuable as an entertainment and pastime.

Travelers, whether sailors, messengers, or muleskinners, carried news and had rapt audiences; they practiced their storyteller's skills with fresh material, always eagerly awaited in isolated places.[135] Loreto's position as headquarters and supply center for all California missions made it the prime recipient of all tidings and rumors generated in its own hinterland, and put it in the path of reports from the gulf, the opposite shore, and the mainland in general.

Sailors made constant round trips to ports on the west coast of New Spain. There they met other sailors, townspeople, and the arrieros who transported cargoes between ports and inland towns and missions. On each return, they brought news and gossip to enliven Loreto's inbred conversational fare. Another class of mariner made longer voyages. In at least ten different years, scattered between the 1720s and the 1750s, Loreto's principal ship was sailed to Acapulco under the command of an officer of the presidio, or an español soldier with appropriate skills.[136] These men carried important mail, delivered or picked up sums of money in the form of drafts, made significant purchases, transported padres, and otherwise carried out the business of the colony. Their viewpoints were more like those of California's leaders than those of simple sailors. They returned with different observations, news, and rumors tuned more to the interests of California's small elite.

All too often, Loreto's ships and sailors created news — frequently colorful, occasionally tragic. In 1700, California's best ship was lost on a sand bar near Ahome. In 1709, a launch loaded with badly needed supplies was blown far north of Puerto Yaqui by a furious storm and wrecked on a beach. In 1713, a new ship was hit by successive storms as it tried to reach Loreto. Eight people were drowned, including two children and Padre Benito Guisi, on his way to a mission post. In 1715, Loreto's supply craft was hit by a storm and all her precious cargo had to be jettisoned to prevent her from being swamped. Other ships important to the colony were lost in 1740, 1741, 1742, 1746, 1749, 1754, 1756, and 1759. An entry in California's account book preserves a vignette of the 1740 loss. It records "100 pesos sent by Padre Jaime [Bravo] for masses to be said for the soul of the drowned mate of the sloop. . . ."[137] In many more instances, boats were disabled and blown far north or south of their usual routes. Crews were overdue for weeks or even months, and their families suffered cruelly during their long vigils.

On at least two occasions, the people of Loreto were eyewitnesses to marine disasters. In September 1717, a three-day chubasco ripped through the Loreto area, flooded the arroyos, washed out the crops of two missions, and carried Mateo, the young son of a boatswain, out to sea where he drowned. When two pearling craft foundered just to the south in the same storm, four men were drowned and the survivors came to Loreto. In September 1728, another chubasco caught the supply ship *San José* in the midst of being unloaded onto lighters off Loreto's beach. One anchor chain broke and the storm-driven craft dragged the other anchor along the sandy bottom. All hands were threatened; a boatswain was swept overboard and driven, half-drowned, into the haven of a mangrove thicket. A woman and her child, lashed to a crate, were tumbled by wind and wave before being washed, unhurt, onto the shore. Finally, the ship was beached to keep it from sinking.[138]

Prior to the opening of the second presidio in *el Sur* in 1738, presidial employees, other than soldiers and servants stationed at missions, had their families at Loreto. When soldiers were away on any sort of campaign, those families watched the trails as they waited for reports. California was a fairly safe frontier. Conflicts with natives were usually brief, and very few soldiers or servants were killed or severely injured during the entire eighteenth century, although on occasion, dramatic and sad stories had to be told.

In 1701, after Capitán García de Mendoza and other soldier-adventurers were discharged from the presidio, one of their replacements was José Pérez, a youngster from Puebla, hardly more than a boy. By the summer of 1702, all the people of Loreto were suffering from a dire shortage of food and were making every effort to obtain edible native plants, fish, and game. Padre Salvatierra described an incident of the time:

Just as we were half used up by hunger, we were overtaken by the prospect of a battle that could have finished us. A young soldier, José Pérez, had married an Indian girl from the mountains. At the time of the *pitahaya* harvest, the other natives enticed her to take part in their evil practices for that occasion. The soldier set out secretly, against the orders of the captain, in search of his wife. On his arrival in a mountain ranchería, he killed an old Indian because the man opposed the girl's return. The natives then slew the soldier and called for a concerted attack against all of us. Many agreed to such an action, but others refused to take part, and thus we were spared. Otherwise, how would it have gone with us, loaded down with arms, but with empty stomachs?[139]

In the early part of 1706, Padre Juan de Ugarte wished to explore south of the new mission at Ligüí, hoping to find a site and people for an additional mission. Since Padre Salvatierra had left three months before to begin what was to become a two-year stint as the Jesuit provincial of New Spain, Ugarte was shorthanded and sent Hermano Jaime Bravo to explore in his stead. Bravo, Capitán Rodríguez, seven soldiers, and a few neophytes arrived at Ligüí at the end of their first day and rested the next. Then they set out southward along bluffs above the steep, rocky coastline. After most of a day's scrambling over difficult trails and steep passes, the Jesuit and three of the soldiers were well ahead of the others who were slowed by burdened pack animals. Bravo's group stopped to wait and explored a bit on foot around its *paraje* (a waiting or stopping place).

As the men with the pack train were about to catch up, they came across the coals of a fire left by local Guaycura fishermen. One of the soldado-arrieros bent over the coals to light a cigar and found the remains of broiled fish, including several livers. He called out to his fellows to share his find. A neophyte companion warned the soldier that the liver, from a fish called *botete*, was poisonous. The soldier refused the advice contemptuously, gave each of his fellows a piece, and began to eat. A second man ate a bite, and a third tried a taste; the latter two took no more because they did not like the odor of the liver. The fourth wanted nothing to do with it but avoided comment by dropping his chunk in his saddlebag. Then the men mounted and went to join Bravo's group, waiting within their sight. All those who had tried the fish liver were sick by the time they caught up. The instigator had eaten the most and became violently ill and thirsty. He took water and died in half an hour. The second man lived longer and was able to say his farewells. The third was miserably sick for a day. Even the soldier who had only handled and smelled the deadly liver was dazed and ill for hours. The party retraced its steps and endured grisly and difficult labors to return their caravan and the two bodies over the great rock pile that blocks the coastline south of Ligüí.[140]

Forty years later, in July 1747, a group of Pericú paddlers aboard the supply canoa from Misión de Santiago murdered their Filipino arráez, stole a shipment of supplies intended for the soldiers of *el Sur*, and attempted to wreck their craft on the beach.[141] The commander of the Southern troop sent three men with experience to salvage the canoa: two soldiers and a civilian, the last identified only as *un andaluz* (an Andalucian). The little team began its work at the seashore, but at nightfall took refuge from a possible attack in a nest built from crates and boxes that had filled the canoa. The andaluz found the sleeping quarters too hot and confining. He went outside, found a slope with air movement, stripped himself bare, and lay down with his musket and sword at his side. In the night, he awoke amidst a shower of arrows. Terrified, he leaped up and ran for the boxed-in refuge of his mates. At dawn, the Indians were gone, but so were all the naked man's arms and clothing, including his shoes.[142]

In the summer of 1765, a party of three soldiers were ordered by their captain to go to a mining camp in *el Sur* and take charge of prisoners who were to be returned to Loreto. They saw the tracks of a large mountain lion as they neared the paraje where they planned to spend the night. Despite the heat of the season, Juan María Ruiz wrapped himself for the night in a mantle of strong fabric because he feared these animals that were known to have attacked the native Californians. Nevertheless, he was attacked. While still partially wrapped, he grabbed the beast by a leg and called out to his companions for help. By the time they were able to distinguish the animal in the dark and kill it with their knives, Ruiz was terribly mauled. He recovered for a time, but finally died of his wounds, probably because they became infected. The death of Juan María Ruiz was keenly felt in Loreto because he was a good man who had served in California for years, married into the prominent Carrillo family, and left a wife and six children.[143]

These dire tales are culled from a long list; others offer humor, adventure, or instruction. Lurid accounts attracted the most attention, demanded the most repetition, and had the longest lives.

Other Diversions

Tobacco was available at Loreto's warehouse, and many Hispanic men, even the padres, made cigars. They also smoked pipes.[144] Some undoubtedly knew how to create *pulque*, an alcoholic drink made by fermenting a watery slurry of roasted mezcal hearts, and they knew how to distill pulque to make a beverage which they called *mezcal*, the generic name for the liquor more familiarly known outside Mexico as "tequila." However, these would have been difficult activities to conceal in California. The padres kept their own wine and brandy production under lock and key and forbade the making or distribution of alcohol by others. Sailors may have sneaked liquor in from time to time, but no doubt did most of their drinking away from Loreto. The reverend fathers allowed a little wine to be sold, but it was very expensive and could not have constituted a serious problem.[145]

The Californians had been inveterate gamblers in their pre-Christian days. The padres were anxious to put an end to it, so they frowned on wagers and games of chance. Presidial soldiers were also legendary for their betting and gaming. It is safe to assume that these habits were not easily given up or soon forgotten. Such pastimes were probably practiced surreptitiously or disguised against missionary disapproval. In 1731, Padre Visitador Sebastián de Sistiaga wrote to Capitán Rodríguez, thanked him for his letter, and told him how relieved he was to hear that the game of bowling indulged in by the soldiers was simply honest recreation that involved no betting.[146] Cards were sold at the company store, presumably for purely social games, and, surprisingly, chess is mentioned now and then, as a pastime of soldiers.

Profanity was anathema to the Jesuits, especially in the mission setting. Salvatierra reported that one of his soldiers had heard of a German army tradition by which any man who blasphemed or used foul language paid the fine of a pound of chocolate or its price. The padres reported that the garrison at Loreto adopted the practice, dedicating the proceeds to decorating the newly built chapel.[147]

Little was reported about music-making outside of church, but such a universal diversion was too commonplace to have invited descriptions in serious chronicles. During his stay in California, Padre Kino wrote that soldiers in his escort had guitars and harps, and that they took them along on explorations and sang and played in the evenings.[148] These "harps" were probably the small, many-stringed instruments, traditional in the Galician province of Spain, that were strummed to accompany songs. Since singing and playing instruments were popular activities at fiestas and on the trail, they must have been practiced regularly at Loreto as well — there were few other recreations in that straight-laced environment. It is likely that people gathered during the warm evenings to enjoy performing and listening.

Travel played a minimal role in the lives of presidial folk, with the exception of sailors and the soldier sent annually to Mexico City to deliver the order for supplies. Other men were occasionally given permission to visit the mainland in order to marry, to settle estates, or to assist in mission or presidial affairs such as cattle drives to shipping points.[149] Women were seldom reported as traveling back and forth across the Vermillion Sea, though existing baptismal records for Loreto in the years 1701–1715 show the birth of very few children to gente de razón. Wives may have left the uncertain conditions in primitive Loreto and returned to give birth at the homes of their mainland families. If so, they stayed long enough to get their babies through the first critical months. The help of women relatives and the availability of ample fresh food were powerful attractions after life in Spartan Loreto.[150]

California had few visitors. Its Jesuit government answered directly to the viceroy. Since he and his advisors had neither the time nor inclination to travel to far provinces, California received no inspections from royal authorities. A few boatloads of pearlers were the only outsiders who visited the colony during its first decade. After 1704, pearlers were required to put into Loreto to show their licenses before they began operations. A law of that year not only made the captain at Loreto responsible for inspecting their permits, but also ordered him to determine the amount of their subsequent take in pearls and to collect the royal fifth.[151]

Pearlers generally were considered nuisances by the missionaries. Their dealings with natives created problems and, when shipwrecked as they often were, they had to be fed and accommodated until they could be returned to *la otra banda*.[152] At times, however, pearlers could and did aid the colony. The Loretans also lost ships and, on a number of occasions, depended on pearlers to carry news or men to the mainland for help; pearlers even made round trips, returning with much-needed supplies for the mission and pueblo.[153] Loreto's gente de razón did not share the padres' yearning for isolation and were less concerned about exploitation of the Californians. They must have considered contact with pearlers as rare diversions.

Loreto Evolves

Despite the Jesuits' resolve to isolate California, Loreto was not destined to remain the "new, happy, and miniature Christian Kingdom" that Visitador General José de Echeverría imagined he had seen in 1729.[154] From its inception, the place was a divided camp: on the one hand, it was a port, fortress, and supply center; on the other, it was the mother mission of the new Utopia.

As years passed, Loreto became more a presidio and village and less a religious center. New missions and missionaries required more supplies and services. Neophytes at Loreto were necessarily exposed to increasing economic activity. They learned to speak Spanish, and to speak it well.[155] As needs arose, they were trained and asked to help with nearly every chore performed by gente de razón.[156] They gradually became assistants to sailors, smiths, carpenters, masons, farmers, arrieros, vaqueros, and soldiers. Some who were especially adept were regularly employed. As neophytes worked alongside gente de razón, attitudes changed. Some of them enjoyed their new responsibilities and began to regard their work and its rewards as the focus of their lives. Gente de razón found them less alien and the social gap began to close. Neophytes' lives were changing but not as the missionaries had intended.

As ruler and overseer of Loreto, Salvatierra must have been aware of its degeneration as a mission, but he was also a pragmatist, more inclined to work for the future than to agonize over the past or present. He realized that the hybrid capital of his colony could never be an ideal holy mission. He saw that its people were often needed to perform tasks for the greater conquest. In the end, he accepted the compromise of a relatively secular Loreto. Rather than make an heroic and probably futile effort to keep gente de razón and neophytes truly separate, he allowed expedient interaction to progress. His successors followed suit. Loreto's house of worship became, in effect, a parish church. The community became home to the personnel that administered, protected, and supplied the expanding mission system.

Even if the missionaries were disappointed by Loreto's low estate as a mission, they were sustained by their chosen work and its inborn rewards; they could look beyond to broader horizons. Gente de razón got less satisfaction from their efforts, and their prospects were limited. Their lives were circumscribed not only by the dictates of their superiors but also by their extreme isolation. When all contemporary accounts have been sifted, when all reasonable inferences have been made, and when allowances for human optimism and resilience are factored in, the sober conclusion remains: for ordinary people, life at Loreto was serious, subdued, and Spartan. They had been brought to California as servants and were expected to carry out orders well and willingly. They were supposed to remain inconspicuous and to create no problems or distractions for padres or neophytes. These were the padres' requirements and expectations during all the Jesuit years. Such demands were unusual, and many could not satisfy them.

Survival at Loreto demanded people who could obtain gratification from very simple or very abstract sources. Life became a test of inner resources. No wonder men constantly entered and left California employment. No wonder families who stayed formed a closely knit community of serious, upright people.

III

The Decline and Fall
of Jesuit California

The California Jesuits had rivals in the secular church, in government, and in the ranks of entrepreneurs who sought to reduce Jesuit authority and to profit from or gain access to the sequestered peninsula. The Jesuits constantly called upon their connections, wealth, and diplomatic skills to maintain their monopoly. At one point, they nearly lost control of their own presidio, but averted that threat by adroitness and good fortune. Paradoxically, the most effective challenge to their hold on California came from the very people they brought to help them in its conquest. When the missionaries put oppressive restrictions on opportunities for their own soldiers and servants, and their families, they invited competition and disobedience.

One soldier seized an opportunity and demonstrated to other California gente de razón the possibility of independent wealth — or at least independent subsistence. California's little Hispanic community began to divide into those willing to remain subservient and those seeking self-sufficiency. Social and economic life became more active — and more chaotic — as the Jesuits grudgingly yielded part of their authority and holdings to some of their former hired helpers.

Finally, suddenly, ironically, the seventy-year Jesuit adventure in California was ended — not by internal problems, but by a decision made half a world away.

TEN

A Challenge from Within

In the 1740s, California missionaries finally began to feel that the neophyte rebellion, with all its human and economic costs and upheavals, was behind them. They raised new money to restart the delayed expansion of their missions to the north. They extended themselves to please and placate their critics in high places. Since the crown and its councils still wondered aloud whether California was an island or a peninsula, Jesuit leaders hurried to provide a conclusive answer. A new exploration to the head of the gulf and the mouth of the Colorado River was planned and carried out by Padre Fernando Consag in 1746.[1]

In 1740, every person in California—with one colorful exception—was a California native, a missionary, an employee of the mission system, or a member of an employee's family. The exception was an ambitious man who was determined to challenge the status quo. Within a decade, he would unleash a new force in the land: private enterprise involving entrepreneurs and paid laborers.

Throughout the 1740s, the attention of California's rank-and-file Hispanic people was not directed toward evangelization or geography. Their attention was riveted on new developments that benefited friends and relatives. In the South, a few ex-soldiers had begun to work little ranches or garden plots; a former servant was now a tanner selling his own produce; private individuals slaughtered wild cattle and sold the products. Overriding such small matters was the great and continuing news: *one ex-soldier had made a fortune—in California*. He was not only hiring local men but was bringing dozens of others from across the water to work for him.

Such opportunities had no precedent in Jesuit California, but by the mid-1750s gente de razón could participate in an emerging secular economy. In their own land, rudimentary forms of mining, pearling, ranching, and trade were materializing. A civilian village grew as a consequence, and its social life contrasted strongly with that in Jesuit centers. The abruptness with which all this occurred must have astonished everyone on the peninsula. For half a century, the Jesuits had used their special powers to avoid all these things; suddenly, a faction had arisen that challenged their authority and acted independently. In a classic irony, the missionaries found themselves pitted against the growing clan of their oldest, most valued, and most trusted employee.

Esteban Rodríguez, The Good and Faithful Servant

Esteban Rodríguez Lorenzo was born about 1665 at Tavira, twenty miles northeast of the port of Faro in the Portuguese province of Algarve.[2] Rodríguez emigrated to New Spain in 1688 and worked his way up to a position as mayordomo at a Jesuit hacienda near Tepotzotlán.[3] Padre Juan María de Salvatierra met him there and recruited him to help open California. Rodríguez was one of Salvatierra's brave party of ten that landed on the beach at Loreto in 1697. Four years later, Rodríguez was chosen to be captain of the Jesuits' presidio, and, except for a brief hiatus during 1704–1705, occupied that post until 1744. During this remarkably long tenure, the Portuguese served his religious superiors admirably, performing the military services they required and accepting the limitations of the California captaincy. Indeed, he went beyond the purely military by volunteering his services as a mason and supervisor of constructions at most new missions.[4]

As a captain on the frontier, Esteban Rodríguez also held the civil posts of governor and *justicia mayor* (chief justice). Nominally, the powers inherent in these offices were not directed by the Jesuits. As the ostensible representative of the crown, the captain dealt with visiting pearlers, inspected their licenses and collected the royal fifth of their harvest. If charges or allegations were leveled against members of the small civil community, he presided over hearings, settled disputes, and carried out the laws.[5] He used his own judgment when sentencing neophyte wrongdoers, on occasion imposing the death sentence in the face of some opposition from the missionaries.[6] Nevertheless, in most situations, Rodríguez was notably faithful in his adherence to the principles of his employers and punctilious in carrying out their wishes. The various fathers visitor during Rodríguez's long tenure respected his opinion and valued his support, but they deferred to him primarily because they were anxious to maintain the impression that the king's representative had some autonomy in operating the "Royal Presidio." However, Rodríguez was unable to get well-deserved recognition from the crown, his nominal employer. A succession of viceroys and other bureaucrats who disapproved of the Jesuits' "private" military force, displayed their resentment by withholding final confirmation of Rodríguez's appointment.[7]

By the late 1720s, Esteban Rodríguez had become a major figure in the California legend. Dozens of missionary reports and letters extolled his accomplishments and his devotion. As he neared sixty and suffered the advancing disabilities of age and hard service, discreet inquiries were made about retirement and a royal pension. At a time when an unusually large number of the higher royal officials were less than friendly to the Jesuits, the matter of the captain's unconfirmed appointment was used to deny a routine stipend or the honors that would seem to have been deserved.[8]

Meanwhile, Rodríguez and many others in California knew how an earlier captain had been favored by the crown and its councils in New Spain. Luis de Tortolero y Torres, like Rodríguez, had been one of Padre Juan María de Salvatierra's heroic pioneers. Although Salvatierra virtually forced Tortolero's resignation, he was anxious to show his gratitude for his captain's invaluable early contributions — and to make service in California attractive to prospective applicants.[9] As the recent conqueror of California, the missionary was playing with a strong hand. In response to his requests, the Audiencia de Guadalajara, the region's royal high court, appointed California's first retiree to be *alcalde mayor* (district magistrate) of Santa María del Oro de Tequepexpa, a gold-mining town near both Compostela and Tepic. In the act of this appointment, the audiencia promised a better position when a vacancy might occur.[10] By 1702, Tortolero occupied the much more lucrative and prestigious position of alcalde mayor of Compostela.[11] There, the ex-captain of California governed a jurisdiction with some hundreds of Spanish or creole inhabitants, several with real wealth and influence. Tortolero subsequently married well and acquired land and slaves in the neighborhood of Tepic. He lived until 1730, a well-known California veteran located virtually on the road of those who traveled back and forth between the peninsula and the interior of New Spain.[12]

The missionary order was embarrassed by its failure to achieve some commensurate reward and recognition for the far longer service of the vastly deserving Rodríguez. To make amends and show gratitude, California Jesuits broke one of their otherwise inviolate rules. Before 1730, they granted Rodríguez's wish to run private cattle and use a parcel of browsing land in an area north of Todos Santos. The captain's request already had a history; he had been eyeing the area since he assisted Padre Bravo during the opening of a visita at Todos Santos in 1724.[13]

During the establishment of missions in the South, soldiers and other gente de razón found themselves faced with temptations they had not known elsewhere in California. A detachment of troops, varying from as few as four to as many as twelve, was located at the La Paz mission. An escort of two to five soldiers served at Misión de Santiago. Periodic disturbances at all the area's missions led to calls for small squads of soldiers to pursue rebels or other wrongdoers into the farthest corners of the cape region. Even in times of peace, soldiers' duties led them to explore their environs. The missions kept cattle, horses, sheep, and goats, but had little grazing land in their immediate vicinities. New converts could not be trusted to tend domestic animals, so soldiers served as herdsmen for both mission and presidial animals. The soldiers took them far afield to a succession of places since pasturage was soon exhausted at any one spot.

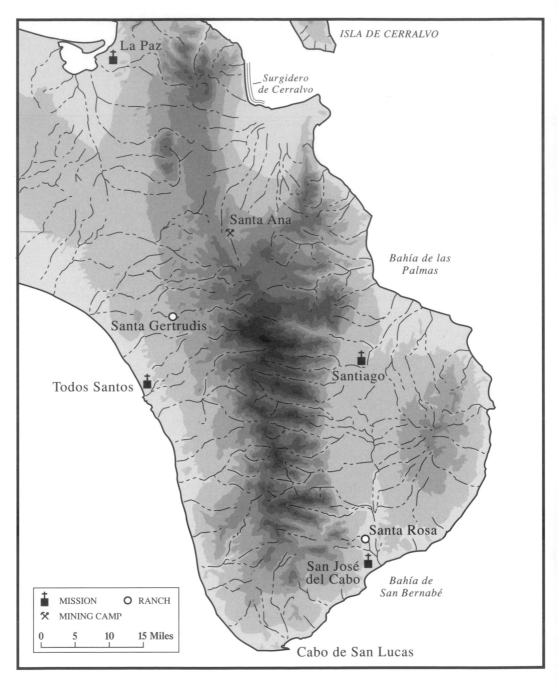

Map 10.1 Settings for Activities of the Extended Rodríguez Family

Water and pasture were more abundant in the cape region than in any place the soldiers had seen to the north. When Capitán Rodríguez was emboldened to ask for permission to own cattle and have the run of some land near Todos Santos, Padre Visitador Ugarte agreed to the plan. The arrangements were informal and verbal; they did not address the potential conflict created by this permission to use land understood to belong to whatever mission controlled Todos Santos. From the late 1720s until 1734, two soldiers were assigned specifically to tend the captain's cattle at or around Rancho Santa Gertrudis, thirteen miles northeast of Misión de Todos Santos.[14]

Suddenly, in 1734, Rodríguez's ranching was disrupted, as were all other Spanish activities in the cape region. The neophyte insurrection created a period of five or more years in which cattle were either killed and eaten by rebels, or, as happened with a majority, escaped all human attention and became truly wild.[15] These multiplied rapidly and, despite constant round-ups and no little hunting, were destined to be a feature of the region for over a century.[16]

When the rebellion was finally quelled, Esteban Rodríguez was past seventy and nearly blind. He retained his job only as a source of support for his family and because he could lean on his eldest son and second-in-command, Bernardo Rodríguez.[17] By 1743, his condition demanded retirement and the Conde de Fuenclara, viceroy at the time, was petitioned for a proper pension. No direct response was ever obtained. The aged captain could hope for support only through the generosity of his long-time Jesuit employers.

The Jesuits must have had intimations of difficulties with Rodríguez's heirs over the rights to personal property and land use granted to the captain. To forestall such problems, they made a bid to buy back these privileges. The blind, aged Rodríguez was in no position to refuse. Not only had he lost his salary, but one of his daughters recently had been widowed and now depended on him to support her and several children.[18] In 1745, the needy ex-captain accepted a Jesuit offer of one thousand pesos to renounce his claims to ownership of cattle.[19]

Padre Miguel del Barco, serving a term as visitador in those days, frequently found himself in Loreto. Writing thirty years later and well into his own old age, he recorded poignant memories of the aged captain's last years. In his conduct and his emotions, Esteban Rodríguez was the frankest of men; he avoided euphemisms or courtesies that obscured the truth. He had always been an active participant in church services and never abandoned the practices of the early conquest during which he led prayers and singing for the education of neophytes. Barco tells us that in his last years, the blind captain still raised his voice, cracked and quavering, and that, although it fell harshly on everyone's ears, he was sure that God found it most gratifying, and that mortal listeners were moved rather than annoyed.[20]

In Loreto's book of burials, Miguel del Barco wrote and signed this entry: "On the fourth of November of 1746 died Don Esteban Rodríguez, captain commander and one of the first conquerors of California. He received the Holy

Sacraments and was buried in the church at the place where the captains are accustomed to sit."[21] This was a touching tribute. Rodríguez, the last survivor of the California colony's ten pioneers, became the only secular figure known to have received the honor of burial within the church.

The life that began in a seaside town in southern Portugal ended in a seaside village in Antigua California, a pueblo which Rodríguez had helped to build with his own hands. There he lies within steps of Francisco María Piccolo and Jaime Bravo. It is the resting place that would have been preferred by Juan María de Salvatierra, Rodríguez's employer and friend.

The First Family

In 1704, Esteban Rodríguez resigned his captaincy and returned to the mainland where he traveled as far as the Mexico City. In a few months, his replacement at Loreto had proved unsatisfactory and Padre Salvatierra personally sought out the Portuguese and persuaded him to resume his California service. Rodríguez was back at his post by August 1705, nothing of consequence having occurred on the peninsula in his absence.[22] However, Rodríguez's brief return to the mainland had one portentous outcome. In that time, he met María de Larrea, a woman from Magdalena, an hacienda near Tequila on the road from Matanchel to Guadalajara.[23] A Jesuit described her as coming from one of the most honorable families of Nueva Galicia.[24] During the following year, the two were formally engaged and began to make wedding plans. In the spring of 1707, Esteban Rodríguez was allowed to take the ship going to Matanchel to await the supply train from Mexico City that carried California's annual order. During the interim, the captain married María de Larrea, then brought her back to rustic Loreto.[25]

It is evident from every report that Rodríguez chose well and that his employers approved. One Jesuit wrote, "a woman of exemplary character and of great charity; she has devoted herself to teaching the Indian women how to perform the tasks incumbent on civilized women".[26] Another echoed and amplified those thoughts: "Ever since setting foot in this land, she has been serving as nurse for the Indians, both men and women, and caring for them in their rancherías. Her house is a hospital where the ailing from our missions gather, receive very kind treatment, and are much edified. She is teaching the Indian women not only to sew and to embroider, but even to read."[27] More significantly for later history, María de Larrea bore seven children who survived into mature adulthood. She and her husband thereby created California's preeminent pioneer family. In addition, they fashioned the household around which California's small social life centered.

The living room or, in hot Loreto, the *corredor* (open-air porch) of Capitán Don Esteban Rodríguez's home must have been the premier salon of secular influence. The coterie that centered on the Casa Rodríguez undoubtedly began as a social group. The captain's shaded corredor would have been the natural gathering place for people who had any sort of education, who craved polite society, or who cared to keep alive the amenities of Spanish culture. Even in remote Loreto, the captain could afford to make modest offerings of such appreciated luxuries as chocolate, brandy, and pipes of tobacco, but other, more significant attractions drew company.[28] Apart from the padres—who were much more difficult to approach and cultivate—Rodríguez was the one man who had substantial ties to both church and civil government. His favor could make a difference in a man's life. Jobs were scarce in New Spain, and Esteban Rodríguez must have found himself petitioned to use his influence to obtain posts for various relatives, friends, and acquaintances. It is likely that most, if not all, the officers employed during Rodríguez's captaincy were selected by him from lists of applicants or promoted by him from the ranks of troops that, in large part, had originally been hired on his recommendation. By 1718, and probably earlier, Rodríguez's alférez, his second officer, was Don José de Larrea, almost certainly an immediate relative of the captain's wife.[29] The alférez who served at Loreto in 1737 was Don José Antonio de Robles, a son-in-law of Esteban Rodríguez and María de Larrea.[30] Such nepotism was the rule during the years of Rodríguez's service and repeated a pattern of favoritism based on blood or marriage ties that was common in most presidios—and to employment throughout the Hispanic world.

For his part, the captain profited from the friendship and understanding of the subalterns on whom he depended; their good and willing service could make his job easier. Furthermore, when they were men with attainments or family distinction, credit was reflected on his command. As time went on, Rodríguez had another reason to cultivate young men with promise; he and his wife had four daughters maturing in tiny, remote Loreto. It was imperative that suitable marital prospects be available.

All but a few fragments of Loreto's libros de misión have disappeared, making it impossible to determine the exact years in which the children of Esteban Rodríguez and María de Larrea were born or to be sure of the order in which they came. The following reconstruction of their birth years fits the available facts.[31]

| Loreta | 1708 | Manuel | 1712 | Simón | 1716 | Josefa | 1720 |
| Bernardo | 1710 | María | 1714 | Rosalía | 1717 | | |

José Antonio de Robles, Husband of Loreta Rodríguez

At Loreto, in September 1724, Loreta Rodríguez was married to Don José Antonio de Robles, a gentleman from Valladolid—now Morelia, Michoacán—an important colonial city one hundred and fifty miles west of Mexico City.[32] No record is available to show the dates of Robles's arrival or departure but he did make out a long document, apparently as paymaster at Loreto, in 1733. Robles was still at Loreto in December 1735 and witnessed the first document signed in California by the governor of Sinaloa, who had just arrived to lead the campaign against the rebellious natives of the South.[33] Military men were in short supply during this struggle and Robles probably stayed in California until 1738 or later. Then he returned to Valladolid with his wife and a family of four sons. Perhaps other children were born in Valladolid. Then Robles died. In common with many men of good family who have gone to find work on frontiers, José Antonio de Robles apparently had little in the way of inheritance or personal fortune. By 1745, the widowed Loreta Rodríguez brought her children back to California. Reports that Esteban Rodríguez had the responsibility for supporting a large family even in his old age undoubtedly referred to Loreta and her children; his other daughters were married to men with good incomes and his sons were self-supporting.[34] All four of the known Robles sons eventually served in California as soldiers; their adventures extended into the Alta California of later times.[35]

Cristóbal Gutiérrez de Góngora, Husband of Josefa Rodríguez

Near the town of Compostela in Nueva Galicia was an estate of Alonso Dávalos y Bracamonte, the Conde de Miravalle, a man of great wealth who had been the first to respond to the Jesuit drive for funds when California was opened. Several of Miravalle's relatives, retainers, and employees appeared on Loreto's payrolls in those early years, a time when competent assistance was vital to the survival and progress of the mission. One of the men so involved was Cristóbal Gutiérrez de Góngora, who served in California as a soldier between 1699 and 1701 and was close enough to Miravalle to have a daughter baptized in the count's private chapel, with the count's younger son as godfather.[36]

By the end of 1702, Cristóbal Gutiérrez de Góngora was back in Compostela with the prestigious post of alcalde mayor, awarded by the Audiencia of Guadalajara. Not only did the proceedings of his appointment refer prominently to his California service, but in taking the position, he succeeded none other than Luis de Tortolero y Torres, his commanding officer in California.[37] By 1706, Gutiérrez de Góngora was married to Rosa de la Torre y Redondo, daughter of a prominent and prosperous family, and younger sister of Tortolero's wife, Isabel. On 23 September 1708, their son Cristóbal María was baptized in the parish church. Shortly after, Gutiérrez de Góngora and his wife moved to Tepic where three more sons were born.[38] Luis de Tortolero and his wife lived nearby. Records of godparenthood show that these couples continued to associate with the petty nobility and gentility of both Tepic and Compostela for another twenty years.[39]

In 1735, Gutiérrez de Góngora's son and namesake enlisted as one of the mainlanders who answered the Jesuit's first call for help in combating the

insurrection in *el Sur*.[40] Like many men from Compostela, the younger Cristóbal Gutiérrez de Góngora had experience as a sailor; for several years he was
paid as a soldier at the presidio of Loreto, though he actually served as skipper
of Loreto's supply ship. Between 1739 and 1747, his name appears frequently in
the California *procurador's* account books as he sailed to places as distant as
Acapulco and traveled inland to Guadalajara and Compostela to buy grain or
arrange for shipment of his cargoes.[41]

In the early 1740s, the younger Cristóbal Gutiérrez de Góngora married
Josefa Rodríguez, the captain's youngest daughter. A son, José María, was born
to this couple around 1745.[42] A daughter, Francisca Javiera, was born in 1747 at
San José de Comondú.[43] Josefa Rodríguez died soon after, as apparently did
Francisca Javiera, of whom there is no further record. Cristóbal was remarried,
by about 1749, to María Serafina Quintero. Gutiérrez de Góngora probably
met his second wife during one of his several mainland visits and made the
match through his important family connections in the neighboring communities of Compostela, Tepic, and Jalisco. After this marriage, the couple returned to Loreto; their son, Francisco Javier, was later described as an "orig-
inario de Californias."[44]

Cristóbal Gutiérrez de Góngora rose to be sergeant and finally lieutenant at
Loreto. He was a man of some education; the several surviving documents from
his hand display erratic spelling even for those highly individualistic times, but
they look elegant in his florid and graceful script.[45]

Manuel Rodríguez and Simón Rodríguez

None of Esteban Rodríguez's three sons married. Manuel left California to
pursue an education and a career in Mexico City. Simón enlisted as a soldier at
Loreto at about the age of seventeen. He apparently served in his father's force
during 1734–1735 as he attempted to quell the rebellion in *el Sur*. Simón
remained a soldier for a total of thirteen years, leaving the presidial service
about 1745.[46] The few known details of his later life appear in the next chapter
of this work.

Manuel Rodríguez finished his education for the priesthood in Mexico City
about 1730. In that year, Padre Jaime Bravo in Loreto, most likely at Manuel's
request, wrote to a California benefactor, the Marqués de Villapuente, asking
him to arrange a chaplaincy for the young Rodríguez.[47] The following year,
Bravo and Esteban Rodríguez submitted affidavits on behalf of Manuel to the
Santo Oficio (the Holy Office of the Inquisition) which had the responsibility for
certifying the fitness of a candidate for the priesthood on the basis of family and
blood.[48] Further references show that Manuel Rodríguez stayed in the area of
the capital city, but do not reveal his employment.[49] Manuel apparently never
revisited California, but he retained an interest in his family and a possible
inheritance.[50]

Bernardo Rodríguez

Bernardo had the most distinguished career of the three Rodríguez sons. He and brother Manuel were destined originally for careers in the church; one California missionary wrote an urgent request to the Jesuit provincial requesting a scholarship for them at San Ildefonso, the order's *colegio* (preparatory school) in Mexico City.[51] Bernardo graduated not only from San Ildefonso but also with some distinction from the University of Mexico as a Bachelor of Arts. He then studied theology for a year, but by early 1731, when he was about twenty-one years of age, he was back at Loreto.

Information on Bernardo Rodríguez's education is taken from a letter of recommendation written on his behalf in 1731 by Padre Julián de Mayorga, founder of Misión de San José de Comondú. Mayorga addressed the Holy Office of the Inquisition in Mexico City, acting as that body's duly appointed California representative. His petition noted the recent death of Don José de Larrea, who had held the largely honorary Inquisition post of *notario y alguacil mayor*. This officeholder theoretically could act as a notary legitimizing representations to the Inquisition, and would be expected to seek out or report cases of heresy in his area. It is likely that such an official was designated for California because of its potential for contact with foreign ships with Protestant crews. Mayorga's testimonial reveals what he perceived to be the Holy Office's priorities. He described Bernardo as "a very white person, of honorable birth, and literate to a degree rarely encountered around here" [i.e., in California]. A related document shows that the candidate was appointed to the post later in 1731.[52]

In 1733, Bernardo Rodríguez signed as a witness on a payroll made out by his brother-in-law, José Antonio de Robles.[53] Bernardo's relationship to the presidio at that time was not indicated. Perhaps he held some non-military job in the warehouse, an institution that always needed a literate man who could keep books. Subsequent events indicate that Bernardo Rodríguez was active as a soldier between 1734 and 1737, probably in pursuit of the rebellious neophytes in the South. In late 1735, the Governor of Sinaloa, Manuel Bernal de Huidobro, was dispatched by the viceroy to take additional troops and lead the campaign to quell that rebellion. Reports from the governor convinced the viceroy that a new presidio should be located at San José del Cabo. The new troop was created by viceregal orders issued in 1736. The first captain appointed was Don Bernardo Rodríguez, and he probably received this empowerment in 1737, given the usual pace of royal funding and the slow communications between the capital and California. In any event, Rodríguez held the position only a few months, after which he was replaced by one of Bernal de Huidobro's favorites. According to Jesuit chronicles — the only available reports on the case — the governor found Rodríguez too deferential to Jesuit desires.[54]

This setback cost Bernardo Rodríguez none of the Jesuits' support. After he was removed from the captaincy of the cape presidio, he returned to Loreto and, because of his father's disabilities, became the de facto commanding officer of the presidio. The California Jesuits formally nominated him to be its lieutenant, but Virrey Vizarrón ignored their request; the officer therefore served, like his father, without proper portfolio. Nevertheless, he continued to act as his father's lieutenant and presumably his surrogate in most matters, considering the captain's age and infirmities. It was Bernardo who responded to Padre Francisco Javier Wagner's call for help in May 1738, and it was he who headed the small force that hunted down Wagner's attacker, hanged him, and exiled a few of his supporters.[55]

By 1743, Bernardo's father was blind and could no longer pretend to perform the presidial captain's duties. The Jesuits were relieved when the viceroy honored their request and appointed the son to take the father's place.[56] A telling proof of their confidence in Bernardo emerges from the simple statement — in Padre Barco's great memoir — that the Jesuits then renounced their absolute right to choose California's captain governor, and left the whole business of selecting and hiring soldiers to the younger Rodríguez, a privilege that even his revered father never enjoyed.[57] Plainly, the primary motive for this change was to blunt the impact of repeated complaints about the lack of autonomy for California's presidial commander; but it is equally plain that the missionaries would not have chosen that time for the change unless they trusted their captain.

Bernardo also followed in his father's footsteps in his public devotion to the church and in his private piety.[58] Jesuit reports and chronicles, both contemporary and retrospective, convey approval and appreciation of Bernardo's efforts and achievements. Padre Fernando Consag's report to the viceroy of his momentous 1746 exploration of the upper Gulf of California and mouth of the Río Colorado includes an example. The missionary gratefully reported that Rodríguez had come all the way from Loreto to the mission at San Ignacio to deliver men and supplies, the latter his own contribution. Although Rodríguez was unable to accompany the expedition, Consag reported that he selected capable soldiers, made the loan of a canoe, and personally escorted the party from San Ignacio to the gulf at San Carlos, forty miles to the north. There he stayed, assisting with preparations, until the party sailed. Thereafter, when a report filtered back that the padre and his men had been ambushed and slain, he sped to San Carlos to take immediate action — finding, as it happened, that the rumor was false and that all was well.[59]

Rodríguez was born, raised, and educated under the Jesuits' aegis. He had studied theology, never married, and seems to have enjoyed a warm and comfortable relationship with the religious. For the Jesuits, however, there was a troubling aspect to Bernardo Rodríguez's years as captain. His health was poor, though his specific ailments were never named. In 1747, he had a breakdown and had to be sent to Guadalajara for treatment ("curazion"). His condition was serious enough that soldier José de Gerardo was sent along as his aide and escort.[60] The first indication of Rodríguez's return to the peninsula comes in a letter, written on 1 October 1748 to Francisco de Güemes y

Horcasitas, Conde de Revillagigedo, then viceroy of New Spain. In this document, he joined with Padre Visitador Barco and the Jesuit Procurador in Mexico City in requesting permission to move the soldiery in the South from San José del Cabo to Todos Santos. The stated purpose was to shorten supply lines and to have a more centrally located force in the greater cape region.[61]

Successive epidemics in 1742, 1744, and 1748 had almost depopulated the San José del Cabo area.[62] As a result, the missionaries planned to close two missions, Nuestra Señora del Pilar de la Paz and San José del Cabo, and consolidate their neophytes respectively at Todos Santos and Santiago. Moving the southern military force to Todos Santos would position it nearer to the remaining missions and keep its personnel under closer missionary scrutiny. But there was a negative aspect to the proposed change. The idea of moving the subpresidio of the South had been initiated by the lieutenant in charge, Pedro de la Riva. He had already proven to be an independent officer, at times even defiant; his employers could have suspected him of ulterior motives in any of his acts. Worse, in light of Bernardo Rodríguez's failing health, Riva was the only other commissioned officer on the peninsula. Within the military system of New Spain, he could have been considered the prime candidate for California's captaincy.

Pedro de la Riva, Husband of María Rodríguez

Pedro de la Riva is at once one of the most interesting and least known of the gente de razón who lived and worked in Jesuit California. He was born in 1700, most probably a son of Don Juan de la Riva Salazar, the latter a native of El Parral in Nueva Vizcaya, a military captain, assistant *alcalde mayor*, and landowner in Sonora.[63] Juan de la Riva was well known to California and Sonoran Jesuits; as early as 1706, he signed as a witness to a document attesting to Padre Kino's good work in converting Pimas as far away as the Río Colorado.[64] Juan de la Riva gave significant assistance to Padre Juan de Ugarte during his 1721 gulf explorations,[65] and earlier he had testified on behalf of the Sonoran missionary, Padre Agustín de Campos, who had been accused in a paternity suit.[66]

On New Year's Day 1731, Padre Nicolás Tamaral reported that "Ribas" was at Misión de los Dolores as one of the soldado-vaqueros on a cattle drive to bring a herd from Tamaral's old mission of La Purísima to his newly founded mission at San José del Cabo. This terse entry was Pedro de la Riva's first documentary appearance in California.[67] In 1733, he was listed on Loreto's payroll simply as "Pedro de Ribas," a married man.[68] Years later, two of his sons gave Loreto as their birthplace, in the years 1732 and 1738, and their parents as Pedro de la Riva and María Rodríguez.[69] A Jesuit letter confirms that this María was the captain's daughter.[70]

By March 1735, Riva had been promoted to sergeant and was at the head of a detachment of soldiers stationed at Misión de los Dolores to resist an anticipated attack by rebellious neophytes and unconverted Californians during the great uprising that had begun in the South a few months before. Padre Taraval, the principal chronicler of the rebellion, described Riva as the military man most involved in the difficult problems of intelligence and disinformation that plagued the force attempting to restore the missionaries' concept of order to the region.[71]

In 1739, when all of California was suffering from a total drought and an accompanying shortage of food, the need for foodstuffs from Sonora became so intense that Padre Jaime Bravo, the procurador in Loreto, had Capitán Rodríguez assign Sargento Pedro de la Riva and an unspecified number of soldiers to cross the gulf to help in collecting and transporting grain.[72] Since Sonora was also experiencing a drought and food shortages, supplies taken for California became controversial. California's soldiers may have been needed to get grain away from the Yaqui—who shortly would be in full revolt themselves against both missions and presidios.[73]

In 1740, Arzobispo Virrey Vizarrón withdrew his support for the independent presidio in California's cape region, in part, no doubt, because of three years of Jesuit pressure in high places. On the advice of his attorney general and his auditor, the viceroy decreed three significant changes on the same day, 13 July 1740.[74] He removed Capitán Pedro Antonio Alvarez de Acevedo from command of the presidio of the South and returned him to the mainland.[75] He reduced the southern presidio to the escuadra del Sur, a dependency of the presidio of Loreto, commanded by a mere lieutenant.[76] Finally, the viceroy appointed Pedro de la Riva, then a sergeant at Loreto, to the new lieutenant's post, making pointed references to the subordinate nature of his position.[77] Since the Jesuits retained most of their traditional control of the presidio, the viceroy's order would seem to have returned all the peninsula's military to their fold.

It might be supposed that Pedro de la Riva was promoted as a result of recommendations by his immediate superiors and relatives-in-law, Esteban and Bernardo Rodríguez. Later revelations suggest that this was far from the case. In his appointment, the viceroy said he was "taking heed of the ability, loyalty, and experience of Don Pedro de la Riva Salazar, and the services he has rendered while in the Presidio de Nuestra Señora de Loreto."[78] To earn these accolades, the appointee must have been involved in the continuous fighting that had so occupied both the Californian and Sinaloan troops between 1735 and 1738. If so, it was under the eye of Gobernador Bernal de Huidobro, who supervised this activity and demonstrably had the ear of the archbishop-viceroy. When Capitán Alvarez de Acevedo's clashes with the missionaries made him a political liability, the governor of Sinaloa may well have suggested Riva as his replacement, knowing his turn of mind and its potential. This supposition is reinforced by Virrey Vizarrón's related actions and by later missionary reports.

Vizarrón fully confirmed Pedro de la Riva to be the lieutenant in command of the escuadra del Sur even as he turned a deaf ear to Jesuit pleas for the confirmation of Bernardo Rodríguez to the lieutenancy at Loreto. By 1743, Riva had not only shown that he was aware of these circumstances, but he was involved in a dispute with at least one local missionary. In that year, Padre Visitador Sebastián de Sistiaga, a veteran of a quarter-century on the peninsula, wrote to his superior in Mexico City:

> . . . [Bernardo Rodríguez] has only the empty title of lieutenant. The lieutenant of the southern presidio has brighter prospects since he knows that Don Bernardo lacks both the title and the confirmation in office. The man has stated that he recognizes no superiority in Don Bernardo, saying, 'if he possess it, let him give proof of it.'
>
> In fact, the southern lieutenant could even handcuff Don Bernardo! Hence, Don Bernardo can do nothing in the south, where he should have gone to investigate what was stated by Don Pedro de Ribas (that is the southern lieutenant's name) against the reputation and good name of one of the Jesuit missionaries. . . . Don Bernardo has not gone south, nor does he dare to go, in order not to run into a disagreement with him.[79]

No other document tells so eloquently the low estate of Don Esteban Rodríguez's health and influence, not to mention the division in his family. He was still the titular head of the Presidio of Loreto; his position took precedence over that of his son-in-law, Riva, not only by rank, but by terms of a specific clause in the latter's commission. At any earlier time, these circumstances would not have arisen, or would have been summarily handled, but now the lion was old, blind, toothless, and unable to defend those who had depended on him for over forty years. This situation pressured the Jesuits into retiring the old man and making a strong plea that his son be appointed in his place. The prospect of Pedro de la Riva obtaining the captaincy loomed over them, as Sistiaga's observations show. Their subsequent haste accounts for the fact that the changeover was pushed through in 1744, despite the lack of a pension for the retiring captain.[80]

Meanwhile, Pedro de la Riva seems to have been audacious in taking advantage of his royal military appointment to leave the peninsula and further his own affairs. His wife, María Rodríguez, had died within two or three years after the birth of their third son in 1738.[81] By about 1743, Riva had gone to the mainland to marry Doña María Isabel Carrera del Valle, a member of the petty gentility in the mining and cattle grazing hinterlands southeast of Tepic. By early 1747, she too had died and Pedro de la Riva was in the Real de Santa Bárbara de las Mojarras seeking permission to marry his late wife's second cousin. In his petition, he was described as "teniente de capitán del Presidio de San Joseph del Cabo," and as a resident of the mining village of Chimaltitlán, near Santa Bárbara. The claim of residence simply meant that he owned land at Chimaltitlán since he patently had been serving in California and would continue to do so, at least on a part-time basis, for four more years. His request for a matrimonial dispensation was granted, and he soon married Doña María

Teresa de Liñan y Mejía, the youngest daughter of impoverished but well-connected parents.[82] There is no apparent evidence to show whether either the second or third wife came to California, but it can be inferred that the third, at least, may have been involved in rearing Riva's young sons.[83]

Pedro de la Riva's next reported acts occurred during the fall and winter of 1747–1748 while Bernardo Rodriguez was in Guadalajara for medical treatment. The Filipino mayordomo of Misión de Santiago was murdered by the neophyte paddlers of the mission canoe he was piloting from Bahía de las Palmas to Bahía de San Bernabé, the landing place for Misión de San José del Cabo. The culprits took to the hills, but Riva and his men hunted them down. After an investigation, the lieutenant held a trial; the two men judged most guilty were given the customary interval to "prepare themselves to die like Christians," then they were executed.[84]

In a more perilous action, Riva and his forces fought at length with a band of the Uchití, a people nominally assigned to Misión de Nuestra Señora del Pilar at La Paz, but then in revolt and occupying hilly country to the southeast (see Map 4.3). Riva represented this group as so dangerous that he had to make open war on it. In the course of his punitive campaign, he captured twenty children, aged four to ten years. The lieutenant could not spare men to act as full-time captors, nor did he have provisions for so large a contingent. Rather than let them run away and rejoin their rebellious parents, he hustled them off to La Paz, put them in a canoe, and sent them to Loreto. Following his directions, the Uchití children were parceled out among the missions of Loreto, San Javier, San José de Comondú, and Guadalupe.[85]

Perhaps further enraged by this loss, the Uchití attacked the soldiers at La Paz. In one action, Riva's force took fifteen or sixteen captives. Before long, the lieutenant ordered that they all be shot, and it was done. Riva explained that another force of the Uchití was approaching to give battle. He had no suitable prison structure and no leg irons. He could not spare men to act as guards to keep the prisoners from attacking when the soldiers turned their backs. He could not release them for fear that their numbers, coupled with their knowledge of his camp, would result in a disastrous return attack. Padre Miguel del Barco, whose account preserves this story, seems to have been shaken at the decision and its consequence. He speaks of the soldiers' thoughts, "seeing their miserable prisoners killed, almost in cold blood by their own hands, as if they were brute beasts of the woods." No attack followed. Barco is generous enough to suggest that Riva's "attackers" might have been driven off by the sounds of all the executioners' musket fire. Considering that the Uchití were already a group much reduced by epidemic disease and fighting during the long years of the earlier rebellion, these two incidents amounted to acts of genocide. Barco tells us that, just twenty years later, one youth at Todos Santos was the last Uchití survivor.[86] In an ironic footnote, Capitán Bernardo Rodríguez, who had suffered at Riva's hands, and Padre Visitador Miguel del Barco, who had been his critic, had to swallow their pride and appear to endorse one of his military actions: On 3 November 1749, they co-signed a letter to Virrey Revillagigedo asking him to authorize the royal treasury to pay 1,924 pesos to cover the cost of Pedro de la Riva's 1747–1748 campaign against the Uchití.[87]

Teniente Riva also asserted his independence by taking and using a ranch-sized parcel of watered land near Santa Rosa[88] in the great arroyo that leads down to the site of Misión de San José del Cabo. Here, he probably used soldiers or soldier's sons—and perhaps a few of the Pericú—to raise food and run cattle that could be sold to his troop. In this, he was achieving, in miniature, one of the economic advantages that the commanders of military posts usually enjoyed along the Hispanic frontier. Earlier, Capitán Alvarez de Acevedo had run into intense Jesuit opposition when he tried to occupy a more secluded tract on which to run his presidio's herds, but Riva's position was now so secure and isolated that the Jesuits apparently chose to ignore his defiance of the sweeping mission claims.[89]

In fact, during the 1740s, missions of the South were virtually unworkable. For fourteen years, native peninsular groups that had never become reconciled to settled life had been pursued and coerced. Many of the most adamantly resistant were killed in battle or executed for "crimes" like persistent cattle theft. Moreover, the number of Californians resigned to mission life was drastically reduced by waves of epidemic diseases like smallpox and measles, and by the slower killer, syphilis. The survivors represented many different small, linguistically distinct groups, most of whom had once been at least wary rivals and often bitter enemies. By 1748, the decision had been made to redistribute the people of the southern missions in an attempt to create more homogeneous and practical-sized units.

In 1748, Misión de Nuestra Señora del Pilar de la Paz was moved sixty miles south to the arroyo of Todos Santos where it obliterated short-lived Misión de Santa Rosa.[90] Pericú neophytes who had been uneasily accommodated at Santa Rosa, cheek-by-jowl with its Guaycura contingent, were trooped off to Misión de Santiago, always a purely Pericú community. Misión de San José del Cabo—also Pericú—was reduced to a visita of Santiago. Some families were left to work the cane fields of San José; the others were consolidated at Santiago. On paper, this was a tidy solution. Four missions were reduced to two. All Guaycuran people south of Misión de los Dolores were concentrated at Todos Santos, and all Pericú were ministered to from Santiago. However efficient this scheme was, there were terrible costs in human terms. These battered people—who had undergone war, epidemics, and abrupt separation from ancient cultures—now had to leave their ancestral areas, the lands and beaches of their hunting-and-gathering past. Moreover, they were tied to their newly assigned locations by the drastic measure of detaining their children at the missions; a missionary at Santiago noted that "parents and relatives, for love of the children, remained pacified. . . ."[91] By all accounts, the people of the South thereafter suffered either desperate outbursts of rebellion, or sank into profound melancholy. Their end was near.

In the course of these many moves in 1748, an unusual personal history came to light, one that involved Pedro de la Riva and illustrates another kind of impact on Californians of the cape region. At Todos Santos lived a teen-aged boy named Ignacio Arriz, a ward of the mission and a servant in the missionary's house. He was born in the area just before the great upheaval of 1734. His father was Don Joseph de Arriz (also spelled in various documents: Harris, Arris, and Ariz), an Englishman[92] who had served as a soldier at Todos Santos. Ignacio Arriz's mother was a Pericú woman to whom the Englishman was not wedded, though, by 1742, Harris was legitimately married to Rosa Ugueti, a Pericú by whom he had a daughter.[93] Harris apparently died or departed at about this time, but his son was kept on at the Todos Santos mission and educated by Padre Bernardo Zumziel.[94]

Capitán Bernardo Rodríguez journeyed south in 1748 to transfer the presidio from San José del Cabo to Todos Santos and to oversee the movement of mission people and goods. At Todos Santos, he met Ignacio Arriz and became aware of his situation. The youth, in effect, was indentured to the mission, or attached to it as a neophyte was understood to be, but he had the appearance of a European as well as an elementary education. Rodríguez must have felt that Ignacio belonged among gente de razón. He used his authority to "put him at liberty" — the chronicler's words — or, in practical terms, to raise him to the status of gente de razón. At this same time, Pedro de la Riva, as lieutenant of the Escuadra del Sur, moved to Todos Santos. Finding young Arriz apt and perfectly acquainted with the area, Riva took him on as his personal servant, or orderly. In this way, Ignacio Arriz moved from one world to another, the first step of what was to be a long journey that would include the conquest of Alta California.[95]

Pedro de la Riva tends to emerge from the few known documents as a harsh, threatening presence. In part, this reflects the Jesuit view that he was a turncoat, a threat to their traditional control of California affairs. Their opinions create a tangible bias because they composed most of the records by which the man may be known. Riva left some personal touches that support, but, at the same time, flesh out and humanize his detractors' portrait.

The man was probably well above average height; his sons, Jacobo and Mariano, were described as "tall" when they joined a militia company.[96] Riva was vain and concerned with image; he ordered various lavish pieces of personal adornment to be sent from the capital, and was apparently the first California soldier to so indulge himself. He was the only Jesuit employee known to have asked that a bundle of unspecified personal possessions, addressed to him, be sent from Mexico to California.[97] He had spirit and a degree of audacity — unless Padre Sistiaga's report of his challenge to Bernardo Rodríguez was a total fabrication. He was an active and decisive military man, too brutal, perhaps, for his religious employers — but they had damaged their credibility on this score by constantly decrying Gobernador Bernal de Huidobro's supposed coddling of arrogant rebels.

Pedro de la Riva contracted three prestigious marriages. María Rodríguez held the highest social status available in California, and his other wives belonged to the rural elite of Nueva Galicia. Riva was concerned with his family's image as well as his own. He ordered various bits of finery—"a fashionable rebozo," "some bracelets"—in all likelihood for his second wife.[98] He tried to give his family advantages beyond outward appearances. The Jesuits' own account books show that Riva sent one son, unnamed, to the Jesuit school of San Ildefonso and paid for it with the better part of a year's salary. A letter written by Jacobo de la Riva shows that he studied at the Colegio de San Juan in Mexico City during the 1750s.[99] Pedro de la Riva's employment of Ignacio Arriz appears to have had no ugly motivation but to have been a useful experience for the boy, as Arriz's later military record suggests.

All things considered, Pedro de la Riva was probably a fairly typical military officer on the Hispanic frontier, but in California the Jesuits had enjoyed decades of unquestioning, devoted service from the Rodríguezes—father and son. They were understandably reluctant to accept less, and, in their view, Riva's bad relations with these two Rodríguez men were less troublesome than his close relations with his brother-in-law, Manuel de Ocio.

Manuel de Ocio, Husband of Rosalía Rodríguez

In the fall of 1734, a missionary and three soldiers made a dramatic escape in the hectic first days of the southern insurrection.[100] During that summer, converts of the four southern missions began to defect. Those who fled soon influenced others to join them. Dire rumors circulated among faithful neo-phytes, soldiers, and even missionaries. Before long, armed bands of rebels blocked roads and prevented inter-mission travel and messages. The over-worked presidio—only twenty-five men in those days—could not provide adequate protection for all the missions.

Padre Sigismundo Taraval, founder and padre of Misión de Santa Rosa at Todos Santos, did have a soldier-guard. In addition, two other soldiers were in the area of Todos Santos; Taraval ascribes their presence to Divine Providence. In fact, pairs of soldiers were assigned to this area to tend mission cattle and those belonging to Capitán Rodríguez.[101] Taraval named the three soldiers with him: Manuel de Ocio, Nicolás López, and Pedro Pertiguero. It is easy to surmise that Ocio and López were the erstwhile cowboys. Ocio, in later years, was devoted to cattle round-ups and cattle raising; moreover, just two years later, he would become a son-in-law to Rodríguez. López was from Guadala-jara, prime cattle country. Pertiguero, a Genoese, no doubt was the experienced sailor that Taraval would later give thanks to God for providing.

Small groups of frightened neophytes from the more southerly missions brought reports to Todos Santos that collectively suggested that most of the southern converts had rebelled. One of the soldiers at Todos Santos—un-named in Taraval's account—was ill and had received permission to return to Loreto. He and a mission youth left for La Paz where they planned to get a canoe from the mission guard and sail to the north. In two days they returned, bringing the grisly news that they had found the young soldier, Don Manuel Andrés Romero, butchered and the buildings of Misión de la Paz despoiled.[102] All three soldiers openly advised Padre Taraval to return with them to La Paz and escape to the north. Taraval was furious at the suggestion that he abandon his post and more so at what he called the soldiers' insubordination which he supposed would dishearten his neophytes.

Less than three weeks later, several Pericú from San José and Santiago straggled into Todos Santos, exhausted from their efforts to make haste and avoid discovery. They reported that Padres Tamaral and Carranco had been killed by rebels, assisted by some of the missions' supposedly faithful neophytes. The soldiers held a hasty meeting. Two of them approached the padre and asked what he proposed to do. Taraval later described the encounter:

> I told them the hour was now late, that I would think it over during the night. . . . "No, no, father", they replied, "we are in danger here; the Indians are uniting; we are powerless to resist so many barbarians! Does your reverence wish us all to die? Surely not! We have mounts ready and perhaps, by this special dispensation of the Almighty, we may have a chance to escape." Having made these remarks, one went to saddle the horses without waiting for a reply. The other began to collect belongings for the journey.[103]

Taraval was in an agony of indecision. He deeply resented the soldiers' independent decision. He feared every step of the trail to La Paz and the real or imagined perils of taking to the sea, but if he was immobilized, Manuel de Ocio and his companions were not. The missionary remembered what ensued:

> The time I spent turning all these obstacles over in my mind, the soldiers used in saddling, giving instructions to the Indians, and collecting what was necessary. Whatever the soldiers did, everyone else followed. In less than a quarter of an hour, they were prepared to depart. I saw that the desire to go was general, so I too was forced to leave.[104]

Padre Taraval went on with an eloquent account of the night flight to La Paz through rebel-held territory, anguish on the beach when no canoe was found, joy when a faithful neophyte provided another, and the group's eventual escape to Espíritu Santo Island. At every turn, the padre's fears were a worse torture than reality. Taraval's memoir also reveals the reason that he survived while his brother missionaries perished. Though no admirer of soldiers, he grudgingly made clear the debt he owed to them. At each critical step, it was they who made the decisions and initiated the actions that led the little party from danger. It is easy to imagine Sigismundo Taraval, had he been as isolated as his fallen brothers, likewise forfeiting his life. He was saved almost incidentally, swept along by the soldiers with the few faithful neophytes in their wake;

". . . whatever the soldiers did, everyone else followed. . . ." Perhaps the padre had a flash of insight when he ascribed the soldiers' presence to Divine Providence. Manuel de Ocio, throughout his long life, displayed very little in the way of godly behavior, but at every juncture, he acted with just the toughness and resourcefulness that got everyone out of Todos Santos alive.

Ocio's Background and Personal Affairs

Manuel de Ocio first appears in California's records as a soldier with full pay on Loreto's payroll for 1733. His position, two-thirds of the way down the list suggests that he had not been on the peninsula for long, since these musters were usually made out in order of seniority. He was paid as a single man and given the title of *don*, as were only four others among thirty soldiers.[105] This honor probably signified little more than that he was a native of mother Spain.[106]

Ocio himself indicated that he was born in the year 1700,[107] but other details of his background and early life are singularly lacking, especially for a man of his eventual prominence. The largely antagonistic chroniclers of his time and place were little accustomed to recording the affairs of their employees and offer only a few tantalizing scraps of information. Padre Baegert said that Ocio was born in Andalucía; Padre Taraval said he hailed from Old Castile. Unfortunately, both informants were non-Spaniards; either could have been insensitive to regional accents typical of those distinct provinces of Spain. However, Baegert is the better source; he took an interest in Ocio and his affairs, and referred to him repeatedly in the course of his memoirs. Moreover, it was he who bothered to mention that Ocio had been trained in his youth as a black-smith—although it is clear, in context, that Baegert produced that fact to suggest the relatively humble beginnings of California's only pretender to wealth. Taraval mentions Ocio by name only once, despite admitting that the soldier was instrumental in saving his life.[108]

After the flight from Todos Santos, there is no record of Ocio's whereabouts for several years. In 1736, he married Rosalía Rodríguez, one of the captain's younger daughters,[109] and the couple had two sons, Antonio and Mariano. No evidence suggests that there were other children, and, remarkably—considering the prominence of the Rodríguez family and the number of documents generated by its activities—there seem to be no records of these sons' birth dates or even birth years. Other evidence suggests that the boys were born between 1738 and 1742.[110] No direct report of Rosalía Rodríguez's death is known. Ocio, in a deposition made in 1754, calls attention to rights that he inherited from her at her death on some unspecified earlier date.[111]

Ocio must have continued to serve as a soldier, attached for a year or two at a mission, then stationed for a time at Loreto. In 1741, a second fateful event found Manuel de Ocio stationed at Misión de San Ignacio. Again, the resourceful Spaniard rose to the challenge.

Pearls Launch Ocio the Entrepreneur

An extraordinary event supplied Manuel de Ocio with the opportunity for a new career and the basis for a fortune. Miguel del Barco, already a missionary in California at the time, described the occurrence:

> Because of an unusual storm, or some other reason unknown, the sea cast up a great multitude of pearl oysters, mounding them on certain beaches from the 28th parallel on to the north.[112] This area, to that time, had not been worked by pearl hunters. The Indians of that coast, recent Christians, knowing that soldiers desired and bought pearls, began to bring them in abundance to the men of the escort at Misión de San Ignacio, then the heathen frontier.[113]

Manuel de Ocio was one of those soldiers with a chance to profit, but he alone had the determination, skills, and connections to make the most of it. The Cochimí who found the pearls wanted goods in trade. Ocio, as a son-in-law of the captain, had the best opportunity to make arrangements with the warehouse in Loreto and apparently got the lion's share of the windfall. He was able to resign his position as a soldier, take ship with his treasure, and proceed to Matanchel and Guadalajara. In short order, he exchanged his newfound wealth for pearling canoes, crews, and merchandise to trade with Cochimí who were still collecting the pearls cast up by the sea. Ocio thus became the first California-based entrepreneur.

> [Ocio] returned the following year with two well-stocked canoes and set sail for the new oyster beds of the north from which he took great gains. He carried his pearls back to Guadalajara, and with the proceeds of their sale, made major preparations for the following year's pearl diving. That was 1743, in which he did so well that he took as much as five arrobas [or about 125 pounds] of pearls to Guadalajara, an event that caused great wonder in that city. But they ceased to wonder even at these riches when, in the following year, on returning from pearl fishing, he brought back eleven arrobas of this precious commodity.[114]

Ocio's success caused a sensation, and he could not hope to keep the new pearl area to himself. After the first year, other pearlers, principally from Sonora, flocked to the scene of the bonanza.

> But this [competition] did not hinder Ocio from making profits; on the contrary, it augmented them. Finding himself with more capital [than the other pearlers], he took a mother ship and three canoes with many people for diving and many bales of clothing, knives, and other things of various sorts that would tempt the taste of divers and any others about. All of these goods were displayed in the pearling camps, bringing to their owner the greater part

of all the pearls in which his divers had an interest, and also those of the divers brought by the other entrepreneurs.[115]

Beds of pearl oysters were found in several places along the coast of northwest New Spain, but those off the gulf shores of the California peninsula, particularly the adjacent islands, were the most prolific. From Bahía de las Palmas, a few miles north of the Tropic of Cancer, 23°30' N. Lat., to Bahía de San Carlos, 27°30' N. Lat., pearl oysters were located at depths up to eighty or a hundred feet on rocky bottoms in almost any place protected from the violent actions of waves and currents created by storms. Along the coast that continues to the northwest, a species of pearl-bearing clam grew in similar but sandy locations.[116] Pearling camps had been set up seasonally along that coast for more than a century before 1740 and had always offered untapped possibilities for profit. *Armadores de buceo* (diving outfitters) provided small sailing craft, or mother ships, and these carried several canoes. They found crews for both sorts of craft in various west-coast ports and other principal towns by offering shares of the pearls to be taken.[117] In Ocio's time, most armadores and their crews came from Compostela, the home base of many of the gulf's pearlers for two centuries.[118] Divers were usually Yaqui, the Sonoran ethnic group that regularly produced hard and willing workers in such diverse fields as cattle herding, sailing, diving, and mining.[119] Ocio was uniquely situated to employ native Californians, some of whom not only knew how to dive, but may also have known the best places to find oysters.

The mother craft would sail to a *placer* (oyster bed) and debark its dugout canoes. The crew set up a camp on the beach as temporary living quarters, and canoes, each with a crew and two to four divers, went to selected points over the placer. Divers swam to depths perhaps as great as forty feet to bring up oysters and a man in the canoe kept track of the take. At the end of the day, the oysters were distributed according to a contracted formula. Out of each ten, for example, the armador might take five since he provided the food, drink, boats, tackle and transportation. Two would be reserved for the crown — the royal fifth — and three would go to the diver himself.

After the division, the shells were opened and the occurrence of pearls was a matter of luck. Of course, over a season, each sharer got approximately his proportionate share of pearls, though there were stories of individuals said to have been amazingly fortunate in this game of chance. The oysters were eaten and the shells hauled away from camp to a distance where the rotting stench was tolerable. The beautiful mother-of-pearl was wasted; there was, as yet, no demand for this material in New Spain and, hence, no profit for the entrepreneurs who had access to it by the ton.[120]

Most armadores were able to finance only shoestring operations, or chose to risk the smallest possible amount of capital in each of these uncertain ventures. They often rented their craft from others and got together no more than the minimum supplies that would keep their crews at work. Pearling camps, places where two or more private flotillas might assemble, were potentially lively places for commerce, but their development was severely limited by lack of capital and imagination among those who ran the operations.

Manuel de Ocio, with his shrewd instincts for profit making, recognized the wasted opportunities. He saw that divers began to acquire pearls as soon as the season started, yet could not convert them to any advantage or diversion until they got back to the mainland. Most divers, in fact, did not return to any real supply center even when the season ended; they ended up selling their pearls at poor prices to the armador for whom they labored.

Ocio, with the advantage of capital derived from his windfall, brought in the sorts of wares that divers wanted, took them directly into the camps, and traded daily for pearls throughout the season. The result, as revealed by Padre Barco, was predictable: "By taking advantage of this opportunity, Manuel de Ocio was able to amass in three months a quantity of pearls which perhaps no individual in all the world will ever be able to equal in so short a time. . . ."[121] Ocio had taken a first step in diversifying his entrepreneurial activities.

Barco added that Ocio would have possessed a fortune of inestimable value had these pearls been of first quality, but they were not.[122] California pearls had always yielded a high percentage of discolored and irregularly shaped specimens. Nevertheless, enough were of desirable quality to enable Don Manuel to bank sums in Guadalajara that were the basis for all his subsequent ventures, profitable and unprofitable.[123]

Ocio in Guadalajara

The pearl-rich Manuel de Ocio burst upon the Guadalajara stage in 1743 — and made an even more dazzling return in 1744. His timing was exquisite. For several years, the Audiencia of Guadalajara had been vigorously investigating ideas and proposals for the promotion of economic development in its territory. Guadalajara merchants, bankers, investors, and ranchers — and the civic leaders that arose from those same groups — sought to throw off the yoke of Mexico City, whose favored position as the capital had led to laws and practices that allowed its merchants to dominate all of New Spain's regional economies. The president of the Audiencia de Guadalajara, Francisco de Aysa, Marqués del Castillo de Aysa, initiated a series of hearings in 1740. The audiencia called in men who had been engaged in any sort of activity — commercial, exploitive, military, or religious — on the coasts and on the underdeveloped northwest frontier. It inquired into all aspects of shipping, pearling, mining, and colonization. California was much on the audiencia's mind; any secular development there would fall under Guadalajara's control.[124] Gobernador Manuel Bernal de Huidobro was called for testimony. The audiencia listened with interest to the first civil authority to evaluate the peninsula's economic potential since the return of Almirante Atondo in 1685. Not surprisingly, considering his opposition to the Jesuit monopoly, the governor was optimistic about California's resources and about plans for civil development and colonization.[125]

In 1742, local lawyer Matías de la Mota y Padilla produced an influential book, *Historia de la conquista de Nueva Galicia*,[126] that argued eloquently against Mexico City's economic monopoly over all of New Spain and the inefficiency of a system designed to benefit only one geographic area and one clique of businessmen. In 1743, Castillo de Aysa and the audiencia brought out an ambitious plan to promote economic growth, colonization of the frontier, increased coastal trade and shipping, and military protection for all the foregoing. Most of the specific steps proposed, especially those that required large outlays of public monies, were never realized. However, in 1743 and 1744, the issue and the opportunities had the attention of Guadalajara's elite, and it was into their circle that Ocio came with his hundreds of pounds of pearls.[127]

The shrewd Ocio must have realized early in his pearling career that he had become a merchant, and that much of his success would depend on the costs of his supplies and trade goods. In Guadalajara, he cultivated the people who had wholesale dealings in the commodities he needed. The ex-soldier soon joined forces with members of two prominent and wealthy merchant families.

Since the late seventeenth century, men of the Sánchez Leñero family had been emigrating to New Spain from the little Spanish town of Tembleque, near Toledo. By Ocio's time, they had built up wholesale businesses in Mexico City and Guadalajara. Already prosperous, they eventually commanded great wealth and owned large haciendas and trading posts in more provincial places, like Tepic, that lay on the road to Matanchel and California.[128] The sale or lease of tax collecting and other administrative activities was common in the Spanish empire and, by 1745, Manuel de Ocio had joined with Don Juan Manuel Sánchez Leñero to take a five-year lease on the right to collect — and keep — the royal share of all pearls taken in California and on the Pacific coast in general. For this concession, the entrepreneurs agreed to pay fourteen hundred pesos each year to the crown.[129] For Ocio, this was informed speculation. He would not have to make further payments to the crown, and he had some basis for estimating the probable savings. In addition, he could cruise the pearling areas in his boats and collect the quinto from the other armadores then at work. The government leased out this right to get cash in advance and to avoid the difficulties and temptations involved when sending its own employees.

Ocio's second and more important Guadalajara alliance was with Antonio Ignacio de Mena, a member of an old creole family with excellent connections. Mena was also a merchant and, as such, ready to invest in new locations and potentially profitable enterprises. A man in his position usually was called upon to lend money and extend credit to a would-be miner or provincial merchant, but Manuel de Ocio presented a most unusual case; here was a potential frontier associate who had capital but needed access to the less tangible advantages of social position and economic and political influence.[130] Shortly after arriving in Guadalajara, Ocio joined Mena in what became a legal partnership and a linking of families.[131]

Early in 1743, probably on Mena's advice, Manuel de Ocio began a remarkable campaign of real estate acquisitions in Guadalajara. On 6 March, he concluded an agreement to purchase an estate from the executors of Doña Ana de Mena. For two thousand pesos paid down and another thousand due in October, Ocio received a complex of five dwellings adjacent to the Convent of Santa Mónica. The principal house consisted of eight rooms, a patio sixty feet square, and a corral forty feet square. The second house had four rooms and a patio and corral described as "capacious." The other houses ranged downward in size.[132]

Some of Ocio's purchases consisted of strategically placed land with a single structure. In the last days of 1743, he paid Alexandro Contreras twelve hundred pesos in gold reales for a property located on the corner of "the street that goes to the Convent of San Agustín, where it is crossed by that called Las Animas." This acquisition consisted of a store that formed the corner, an entrance vestibule, a salon, a bedroom wing, a principal patio, a second patio, a kitchen with its own patio and various fruit trees, and a corral.[133]

A few months later, in May 1744, Manuel de Ocio paid twenty-five hundred pesos in cash for a two-floor house and a separate structure. In March 1745, he bought an unspecified number of houses from an estate that had been willed to a women's religious house; the price was thirty-six hundred pesos. Ocio continued to make such purchases until he had at least fourteen houses in the Guadalajara area.[134] These investments may have been motivated by the ratio between selling prices and rental income. Typical interest rates of the time were five percent or less. Ocio must have been looking for a better return on his money, as well as cash or credit generated in Guadalajara where he most needed it. Through his new connections, he could have rents collected and applied to the costs of supplies that were sent on to him in California where his other enterprises continued.

Ocio Brings Mining to California

During Manuel de Ocio's several protracted visits to Guadalajara, he and Antonio de Mena must have had long discussions about the specifics of deriving wealth from California. Pearling alone was a risky basis. After the first year or two of bonanzas, the great oyster beds around the 28th parallel yielded drastically less each season.[135] Those of the South provided a steadier take but showed no promise of higher yields.[136] However, the ex-soldier had another ace in the hole: samples of ore that had been collected on the peninsula. Mining was a subject familiar to any alert Spanish entrepreneur. Silver, in particular, had created great fortunes in northwestern New Spain. If California had any serious mining potential, Ocio, with his firsthand knowledge and his newly acquired wealth, was the man best positioned to make a strike.

From Mena's point of view, the prospect of a mining bonanza in California was doubly promising. Not only was he associated with the man most likely to succeed in exploiting California, but also, as a merchant already supplying entrepreneurial ventures on the gulf, he would have the position, the capital, and the organization to take advantage of any large or sudden demand.[137] All Guadalajara businessmen knew the history of Zacatecas, Hidalgo del Parral, and other great silver strikes to the north; fortunes could be made by people with money to invest or supplies to sell. Moreover, Mena was a man with social and political ambitions beyond mere profit. Aysa's commission had focused attention on Guadalajara's stake in the frontier. In late 1744, a royal decree, prompted in part by the Aysa report, called for the founding of a Spanish civil settlement in California, a place that would serve as a refuge in any future rebellion, provide help to the Manila galleon, and work crown lands to the advantage of the treasury.[138] Opening a mining operation in California's South would be a timely and prestigious move. With all these incentives, Mena and Ocio formed a company with the intent of establishing settlers in California and "bringing gain to the Crown" — that is, making profits and paying taxes.[139]

For nearly half a century, the lower half of the peninsula had been informally prospected by soldiers, some of whom had previous mining experience. Even the Jesuits had once had ore samples collected and sent to a viceroy at a moment when they badly needed to emphasize the value of California and the continued funding of their conquest.[140] A 1740 description of the peninsula, now attributed to Esteban Rodríguez, mentioned the presence of silver at a site he called Santa Ana.[141] (Santa Ana had replaced the indigenous name, Marinó, in 1723 when Padre Ignacio María Nápoli chose to locate a new mission on the spot.)[142]

Manuel de Ocio knew the Santa Ana region well. As a soldier, he picked up supplies at the *surgidero* (landing place) on the gulf shore opposite the prominent island of Cerralvo and escorted them to his assigned base at Todos Santos, sixty miles away. The trail he followed passed within a few hundred yards of Santa Ana, elevation 1500 feet, on its way to the peninsular divide, 2500 feet at the pass. Moreover, the surgidero of Cerralvo was a place much frequented by pearlers because of its freshwater spring and the nearby oyster beds that yielded some of the best pearls in California's waters. During his years as a pearler, Ocio went there annually, either to take pearls or to collect the quinto from other armadores.

Ocio knew the opportunities and the obstacles involved in occupying Santa Ana. The site was not near a mission, nor was the area in use as mission pasturage. These assets suggested that the Jesuits would not seriously oppose its appropriation as they had opposed Capitán Alvarez de Acevedo's attempt in 1740 to annex a watered place claimed by Padre Tempis for Misión de Santiago.[143]

However, even if the missionaries did not oppose the taking of Santa Ana, another group could be expected to contest any intrusion. An antagonistic band of Uchití still roamed their ancestral land, the hills and mountains that lie ten to fifty miles south-southeast of La Paz. The Uchití were unrepentant over their prominent part in the rebellion in the South ten years earlier. They had never returned to their nominal mission "homes," and, by the mid 1740s, they were the principal group that harassed the missions that remained in the South. Santa Ana was located in the heart of their range.

Ocio once again was in a position to take advantage of the circumstances. Pedro de la Riva, his aggressive and independent brother-in-law, was the commanding officer of the troops stationed in the South. Ocio and Riva were close, at least in business matters; to his business partners in Guadalajara, the entrepreneur could have reported his military kinsman as a potentially useful ally.[144] When Manuel de Ocio returned to California, he explained his plans and ambitions to Riva and probably offered whatever inducements were necessary to enlist his invaluable support in making Santa Ana safe from the Uchití.

In times past, the Jesuits had been able to argue against a civil colony on the grounds that it could not be self-supporting and that such an installation would diminish the resources needed by the missions and corrupt their neophytes. No serious challenge to this position had arisen during their half-century tenure, largely because the crown did not care to venture the large costs, and no private capitalists had had the desire to reach so far out for a risky venture with uncertain rewards. Manuel de Ocio was different. He possessed insider's knowledge, adequate financial backing, military support, and took advantage of a political climate in which his efforts would be widely applauded. It is likely that Pedro de la Riva welcomed Ocio's propositions. He, too, was ambitious, and his recent skirmishes with Jesuit authority prove that he was willing to take risks and press for advantage.

Teniente Riva could contribute an important service in the founding of a mining camp at Santa Ana; he and his troops could scatter or destroy any Uchití who occupied the area.[145] The escuadra del Sur was headquartered at San José del Cabo, over sixty miles from Santa Ana by trail, but by 1748, the southern troops had been relocated to Todos Santos, a move likely to have been made because of Riva's persuasions and petitions. From that nearby base, Riva and his troops soon killed a significant number of Uchití men and exiled a score of their children.[146] The stage was set for the next phase of Ocio and Mena's grand plan.

While conditions in California were thus being stage-managed for his benefit, Ocio continued his annual pearling during the July to October season. He and Mena arranged for needed supplies and the construction of a sailing craft suitable for transporting men and goods back and forth across the Gulf of California. Ironically, in 1748, just after Ocio's new ship went into service, California's regular supply ship, *Nuestra Señora del Carmen*, was wrecked by a storm at Ahome. In April 1749, the Jesuits were forced to ask Ocio to transport badly needed supplies, then, and thereafter, as needed. He was paid by the presidio of Loreto.[147]

By 1748, Ocio had laid claim to Santa Ana and begun to develop the place with a newly hired crew. Initially, Ocio had brought in several dozen men, some already living in California—ex-soldiers, soldiers' sons, and ex-mission servants—and others were mineworkers from New Spain.[148] As a rule, married men were hired. They were less inclined to approach mission women, and thereby would create less resentment of the whole mining venture among the missionaries.[149] In addition, Ocio and Mena envisioned Santa Ana becoming first a *real de minas* (the officially chartered seat of a miner who paid taxes) then a *villa*, a formally organized town complete with families, domestic animals, and other aspects of Spanish civilization.[150] In the first days of Santa Ana's development, families must have been left at home, but before long they were brought to live in or near the mining camp — and to suffer from its many problems.

Santa Ana began to produce silver, but that was not a commodity that could be eaten or worn. No doubt Ocio started his mining operation with certain stores on hand. No doubt, as well, his employees brought clothes, tools, and perhaps a few other possessions with them; but all these things were short-lived under California's harsh conditions, and all were difficult to replace. Then, too, when Don Manuel laid in food and other stores, he may have underestimated the sizes of families and the numbers of job-seekers or hangers-on. California was experiencing yet another frontier economic phenomenon. Despite the difficulties in crossing the gulf, a crowd was gathering in response to rumors of a possible silver bonanza.

Before long, the already poor, dwindling missions of the South were involved in Santa Ana's relief. The sixty or seventy souls at Santa Ana had no priest and no place to go for even minimum religious observances. The missionaries felt compelled, on occasion, to make the long day's ride and hold services, but problems soon came knocking at the missions' own doors. Hungry people with silver came there trying to trade for food and clothing; hungry people with nothing came there to beg.[151] California Jesuits had always treasured control over their own interests and isolation from those of others. In the South, by 1750, both were being undermined.

The Rodríguez Era Ends

From the beginning of his captaincy in 1744, California's Jesuit community must have been troubled by Bernardo Rodríguez's delicate health. They chose him for the post, despite this serious handicap, because he was the only qualified, available man who could be depended on to support their program wholeheartedly. As his condition worsened, another threatening development became known. In Mexico City and in Rome, higher Jesuit authorities were becoming increasingly sensitive to criticism directed at the order's temporal power — the growth of its wealth and influence — particularly when this power was represented as frustrating the ambitions of others in matters that might benefit the crown. To some Jesuits, the image of a captive presidio, particularly one funded in part from the royal treasury, provided critics and enemies with too inviting a target. Even one veteran California Jesuit, Padre Jaime Bravo, came to hold this belief, and, to the consternation of his fellows, lobbied for the renunciation of much control over California's military.[152] Bravo's death in 1744 ended his influence, but not the controversy.

By 1747, Rodríguez's worsening health and the specter of Pedro de la Riva were almost palpable in Jesuit communications. In a letter to the padre in Madrid who represented New Spain's Jesuits at the royal court, Padre Visitador Sistiaga pleaded for the continued power to select captains and junior officers as well. The old missionary sketched the alternative in dark tones:

> . . . a commanding officer has many temptations . . . he has familiar friends in attendance upon him; in the presidio, he usually has supporters and kinsmen. The captain will seek to promote their profit and advantage . . . and these men act in their own interests and ignore their duty to God and to His ministers.[153]

Three years later, in December 1750, Capitán Don Bernardo Rodríguez Larrea died at age forty. The acting commandant of the Presidio of Loreto was Teniente Pedro de la Riva.[154] The Jesuits had more reason than ever to fear their fallen captain's kinsmen acting in their own interests and ignoring God's ministers. Riva chose that moment to order a silver-inlaid musket, gold-plated spurs, and a beaverskin hat.[155]

Changing the Guard in Loreto

In the last days of 1750, Miguel del Barco was taking his turn serving as California's padre visitador. He and his council must have welcomed the overdue opportunity to propose a new captain since the years of Esteban Rodríguez's dotage and his son's illness had seen some Jesuit interests neglected and left in disarray, and the Jesuits would need all the allies and power they could muster. Even as Bernardo Rodríguez died, Manuel de Ocio was attempting to have the official status of his mining camp raised to that of a villa, a town with the right to an *alcalde*, or judge. Such a post would be filled by Don Manuel or one of his people. Loreto's own military detachment in the South, adjacent to Ocio's camp, was under the command of Pedro de la Riva. In these trying times, the missionaries must have wished that they still had the power to select their own man.[156] As it was, they faced the reality of circumstances like those they had endured in Sinaloa and Sonora for more than a century, the galling necessity to share power and territory with antagonistic economic and military interests.

The imminent threat posed by Manuel de Ocio made it imperative that the Jesuits use all their powers and influence to obtain a captain sympathetic to their ambitions and methods, one who would be energetically supportive and place their desires ahead of his personal interests. On the other hand, exactly that sort of appointment had provoked anti-Jesuit grumblings in high places and provided ammunition for the diverse factions that lobbied against the order. It was true that during his four years in office, Virrey Revillagigedo had generally supported Jesuit positions, and his predecessor, Virrey Fuenclara, had accepted their nomination of Bernardo Rodríguez. Still, the winds of favor might be shifting. Fernando VI, king for only four years, had appointed ministers and instituted policies friendly to economic development and designed to give the crown greater control over all institutions involved in the economy, including the religious orders. Jesuits were also mindful of the Marqués del Castillo de Aysa's recent proposals for deriving more royal income from California.[157] Given the tenor of the times, a strong case could be made for a new capitán and justicia mayor who would be more responsive to royal interests and less bound to those of the missionary order.

Moreover, in order to maintain credibility within New Spain's military community, the Jesuits had to nominate a man whose appointment could be justified to the viceroy on the grounds of his military knowledge and experience. Such a nominee, by necessity, would have to be a man already serving in California. Jesuit relations with presidial officers in other parts of New Spain were strained or broken, and the California Jesuits' own plans called for immediate expansion toward the north. It was no time to consider a chief officer who did not know the country or its people, but, ironically, it was also a time when the two ranking officers on Loreto's roster loomed more as liabilities than as assets.

The difficult and defiant Teniente Pedro de la Riva must have known that the Jesuits disapproved of some of his previous actions, but he may still have harbored hopes for promotion. He held the second-highest rank and a proper royal commission to his post. He was the interim commander of the presidio — at Bernardo Rodríguez's request. He had served longer than any potential claimant. During the long years of the rebellion in the South, he had seen more action than any other man who remained in the Loreto company.

The competent Sargento Cristóbal Gutiérrez de Góngora also may have felt that he had some claim to California's top military position. In 1750, prior to Bernardo Rodríguez's death, Gutiérrez de Góngora was sergeant, second-in-command at Loreto, and the third-ranking officer on the peninsula. He had appeared on Loreto's muster rolls for seventeen years. His family was honorable and had old California and Jesuit connections. He was literate. Unlike his various brothers-in-law, Gutiérrez de Góngora is not known to have engaged in any private activities of which the Jesuits disapproved, but the sergeant does not seem to have demonstrated command potential. His known career consisted of desk work and piloting supply craft. Beyond their personal shortcomings, both these men were brothers-in-law of Manuel de Ocio. It was unthinkable to the Jesuits that they employ one of Ocio's relatives or familiars in a post that carried with it the concurrent duties and powers of justicia mayor, chief justice of the entire peninsula. Despite the seeming lack of suitable candidates, Padre Visitador Miguel del Barco, no doubt after consultation with his fellow missionaries, lost no time in nominating a replacement. Bernardo Rodríguez died at Loreto on 1 December 1750. By the end of the month, both Padre Barco and Padre Juan de Armesto, the procurador in Loreto, had submitted letters informing the viceroy, the Conde de Revillagigedo, of the choice made by their group.

By June 1751, Revillagigedo's response had arrived in Loreto, bringing welcome news to missionary eyes. Privately, to Procurador Armesto, he acknowledged receiving the news of Rodríguez's death and the appointment of Pedro de la Riva as interim commander.[158] Then the viceroy proceeded to the real business at hand:

> The command and administration of the presidial company require firmness, courage, prudence and other endowments for their best fulfillment conducted in the interests of both majesties. The father visitor, the rectors, and all the missionaries agree in proposing to me that Don Fernando de Rivera y Moncada be appointed to the vacancy. He is qualified in all the desired ways, principally for Christian conduct, temperance, knowledge of the land and of the habits of the Indians. He has traveled every part, from the south to the latest conquest in the north, attending to his duties as sergeant. He took part in the subjugation of the Uchití nation which had rebelled and in that expedition confirmed and added to the many proofs of his good conduct.
>
> As your reverence wishes, and in consideration of his merits, I agree to name him as captain, believing that this will best serve their majesties and the advancement of Christianity in these Islands of California.[159]

Thus, as the darkest of dark horses, Fernando de Rivera broke into California's documentation. He appears as if he were a convenient invention created to solve the Jesuit dilemma; in some ways, perhaps he was. His fellow soldiers, who had rubbed shoulders with him for years, must have been astonished by his elevation to the captaincy; there is no indication that his nomination had been made public before the viceregal appointment reached California. That spring in Loreto, on 5 April, Sargento Gutiérrez de Góngora made out an extensive payroll document, noting that he was acting as second-in-command to the absent Riva, who was presumably carrying out his usual duties in *el Sur.* All the men on the muster were listed, including Fernando de Rivera, but this is the earliest known California document on which his name appears.[160] Of his previous activities, even his previous presence on the peninsula, not the least mention survives, and here, in early 1751, Rivera had no other rating than soldier. It is probable that when the Jesuits represented Rivera to the viceroy as having been a sergeant, they were stretching a point and referring, without explanation, to a temporary duty and title.[161]

After nominating Rivera, in fact, the Jesuits arranged an assignment that would assure their candidate of favorable notice at the level of audiencias and the viceroy. They chose him to lead an expeditionary force to accompany Padre Fernando Consag on an exploration of lands to the northwest of the site he had chosen for the new mission of Santa Gertrudis (see Map 11.1). Consag's account of his 1746 voyage to the mouth of the Río Colorado had received much attention; a new push into unknown and heathen lands would be sure to attract interest among royal authorities who could share credit for any noteworthy discoveries, enlargements of the realm, or conversions to the faith. The expedition was carried out in May and June of 1751 and, predictably, Rivera y Moncada was singled out for praise when the missionary made his official report.[162]

Such maneuvers may have produced the desired reactions in Mexico City, but, in Loreto, Rivera must have seemed to lack not only rank, but also age, seniority, and experience. He was just twenty-six years old and had served in California for eight years, far fewer than several of the men who outranked him before his appointment. When word of Rivera's elevation became public, it surely caused surprise, chagrin, and disappointment, particularly within the Rodríguez family circle. Ironically, that circle included Manuel de Ocio. He, more than anyone, challenged the Jesuits' control of the peninsular economy both through acts and legal representations. As captain, Rivera would be called upon to adjudicate disputes between Ocio and the Jesuits, and to enforce his judgments. Despite the apparent deficiencies of his training and the awkward circumstances of his appointment, Fernando de Rivera proved to be an inspired selection. During the next sixteen years, he would deliver the service for which his employers must have prayed.

ELEVEN

The Mission Yields
a Share of California

During the 1740s, the control of events and developments in California began to shift from missionaries to secular individuals. One of the latter was Manuel de Ocio, the self-made entrepreneur and rival to the missionaries for the peninsula's useful land. Another was Fernando de Rivera, captain of the presidio as well as supporter and virtual employee of the Jesuits. Each of these determined men commanded a sizeable following, employees in Ocio's case, and presidial subordinates in Rivera's. Both had agendas. Ocio's was the simpler. He sought all possible avenues toward wealth and prestige. Most were blocked or impeded by the Jesuits as they defended their original claims.

Rivera's professional goals and duties constituted an apparent conflict of interest. As captain at Loreto, his de facto role was to implement Jesuit plans to expand their mission system, as well as to maintain the status quo at older establishments. With the captaincy, however, Rivera also acquired the traditional auxiliary roles of governor and judge over the civilian population. In the latter capacities, Rivera acted as the crown's representative and should have been independent of Jesuit influence. The history of California's isolated and unique presidio, Jesuit-founded and Jesuit-dominated, made the legitimacy of Rivera's double role questionable, particularly in the eyes of Manuel de Ocio.

Between 1750 and the Jesuit expulsion in 1768, California affairs were dominated by the actions and rivalry of these contrasting frontier figures.

Fernando de Rivera y Moncada

In July 1751, a few months before his twenty-seventh birthday, Fernando Javier de Rivera y Moncada was installed as captain of the presidio of Loreto.[1] During the ceremony, Rivera was presented with a symbol of office, a *bastón*, or staff with a silver handle.[2] From that moment, the young man exercised the captain's traditional powers. However, bureaucrats in Mexico City and Madrid had only begun the labyrinthine process by which a frontier official obtained royal confirmation and appointment. Rivera had accepted a demanding job at a particularly difficult time. As capitán, he needed to reunite a splintered presidio by asserting his authority over his former superior officer, Pedro de la Riva, lieutenant of the troops in *el Sur*. As gobernador and justicia mayor, Rivera would have to govern and judge the new and growing secular population within his jurisdiction.

Capitán Esteban Rodríguez's civil duties had been carried out in a California under strict Jesuit control and rarely extended beyond governing the converts. His responsibilities with gente de razón were limited to dealing with a few transient pearlers or the crew and passengers of the annual Manila galleon.[3] During Bernardo Rodríguez's brief captaincy, California acquired a secular presence outside Jesuit control. Manuel de Ocio obtained ships and hired crews that occupied camps along the peninsula's southern gulf coast; he opened mines, hired miners, and created a village at Santa Ana. All were far from Loreto and in an area dominated by his brother-in-law, Pedro de la Riva, the least subservient of California's soldiers. Some of Ocio's enterprises challenged Jesuit claims and encroached on established Jesuit rights; all were activities that Loreto's captain was supposed to oversee or regulate. However, Bernardo Rodríguez's poor health — and perhaps his family ties — prevented him, or the Jesuits through him, from actively responding to Ocio's challenges. The viceroy's ready support for Fernando de Rivera's captaincy brought these covert strains and conflicts into the open. Pedro de la Riva now had to defer to Rivera as his commanding officer, and Manuel de Ocio had to contend with him as justicia mayor. In contrast to his predecessor, Rivera would prove to be tenacious and effective in defending Jesuit interests and the dignity of his command.

The first years of Rivera's captaincy were neither a time of watching and waiting, nor of standoffs and inactivity. Ocio and the Jesuits were on the move, defending their positions, advancing their interests, testing the limits of each new situation, and planning for the days ahead. The missionaries, aided by their energetic young captain, expanded their mission chain for the first time in over twenty years. In July 1751, baptisms began for Misión de Santa Gertrudis, located in a rocky valley near the intersection of the gulf coast and the 28th parallel.[4] The Jesuits also made changes in personnel and procedures. Padre Juan Javier Bischoff was chosen to administer the mother mission at Loreto and its busy community. According to the chronicles, he instituted a broad campaign to reduce the incidence of undesirable conduct, such as excessive drinking, loitering, and gossiping. He ended an unnamed scandal among the soldiers and sailors of the presidio by picking out the least wholesome men and banishing them. Descriptions of these actions, and their timing, suggest that reforms to reassert Jesuit standards of decorum and piety were overdue. This new broom swept away discipline problems that had arisen during Bernardo Rodríguez's illnesses.[5]

During the following year, Capitán Rivera filled the places on the presidial muster left vacant by Bischoff's zealous firings. Several long and notable careers thus began, including those of Francisco Javier de Ochoa from El Fuerte in Sinaloa,[6] José Velázquez, a frontiersman born in San Ildefonso de Ostimuri,[7] and Francisco de Aguiar from Guadalajara.[8] Velázquez may have originally come to California to be a miner; his previous residence was the mining camp of La Cienega (Cieneguita), Sonora.[9] Before his enlistment, Aguiar had had experience as skipper of his own oceangoing craft, and he may have come to the peninsula originally as a pearler or trader. He was to follow in the tradition of Teniente Cristóbal Gutiérrez de Góngora by commanding Loreto's ships to ports as far off as Acapulco to obtain California's allotted supplies.[10]

At the same time, Manuel de Ocio was expanding his holdings and trying to fill Santa Ana's needs—and make profits in the process. He sent men out to hunt and slaughter wild cattle to supply the mining community with meat and hides. He put more men and money into the development of his own herds, ranging them over any convenient, unused pasturage; he started a long series of petitions to the crown for powers or concessions that would add prestige and legitimacy to his activities. Meanwhile, other men in California's small civil community were plotting their own independence. Ex-soldiers, soldiers' sons, and miners were looking for opportunities to obtain land and cattle, or to find and exploit new sources of minerals.

Fernando de Rivera and the men of the presidio were involved, directly or obliquely, in all these activities. Each new mission establishment required a large contingent of soldier-guards during its early days, then a smaller, permanent escolta to serve the missionary. The captain organized the soldiers and arrieros needed for major explorations and usually elected to take their lead. As the crown's judicial representative, he investigated crime, apprehended criminals, held court, and carried out sentences. He also adjudicated all civil disputes, whether they were small claims or contests over the ownership of large tracts of land or thousands of cattle.

Rivera's Origins in Compostela

The new captain of the presidio of Loreto began his California service in 1742 when he was but seventeen.[11] Like so many of Loreto's recruits for nearly a half-century, Fernando de Rivera came from Compostela, had direct connections with that center's political and economic leadership, and was born into its criollo gentry. Early in the century, his father, Don Cristóbal de Rivera y Mendoza,[12] held office in Compostela, first as public and royal notary and then as *alcalde ordinario*, or municipal magistrate. By 1711, the elder Rivera had acquired the prestigious post of *alférez real*, member of the municipal council and bearer of the royal standard in civil and religious ceremonies. He held that office until 1724, or perhaps a year or two later.[13] Although the regional office of alférez real was openly sold to a high bidder, it represented the crown and was awarded by an astute viceroy to people who would reflect credit on him and be acceptable to the wealthier and more aristocratic citizen taxpayers.[14] Rivera y Mendoza's tenure demonstrates that he had some wealth and was esteemed by the more important of his neighbors. Available documents record his official and ceremonial status without suggesting the sources of his income or the nature of his daily affairs. Those sources do show that he owned a few slaves, a common situation for a man at his level of Nueva Galician society.[15]

By marrying Inés del Valle y Guzmán, Rivera y Mendoza allied himself with other well-to-do and prominent families. Late in 1718, after bearing three sons and four daughters, Rivera's wife died. In less than a year, he married Josefa Ramón de Moncada y de la Peña, a woman with family connections in both Compostela and Guadalajara.[16] They had two daughters, then two sons. Fernando Javier, the elder of the boys, was baptized on 14 November 1724. His godfather was Bachiller Don Basilio Ramos, a prominent cleric in the region and a family friend. Fernando could have been named for his mother's brother, Fernando Ramón de Moncada.[17]

When he was about nine years of age, Fernando de Rivera's childhood was marred by the death of his father and the resulting changes in the family's financial status.[18] In accordance with Spanish law, the estate was divided among the lawful issue, in this case, eleven children. Later, when Fernando was grown and drawing pay, he regularly sent money to help support his mother.[19] Her need probably influenced his military enlistment at an unusually early age. His birth in Compostela virtually predestined him for service in California.

Rivera's Years as a Common Soldier

Beginning in 1742 when he was eighteen, Rivera served for six years under Teniente Pedro de la Riva in the escuadra del Sur, the southern detachment of the presidio of Loreto.[20] He was assigned as a soldier-escort at Todos Santos on an off-and-on basis, though one stint lasted for more than three years. During this service, Rivera witnessed successive epidemics that decimated all native groups in the region.[21] At Todos Santos, he came to know Joseph Harris, an Englishman and fellow soldier, and his young son, Ignacio.[22] Rivera's friendship with the son continued for nearly forty years. During Rivera's early service, the South was a quiet place for a soldier whose only non-routine duty was the pursuit of neophytes accused of crimes. California's isolation from the outside world was profound, and the cape region, lacking even Loreto's mail and supply ships, offered few distractions. In earlier years, Manila galleons made annual visits to the strand below Misión de San José del Cabo which, for a week or two, took on the atmosphere of a carnival. However, after rebelling neophytes surprised and killed a landing party in 1734, galleon visits were interrupted for several years.[23]

In 1742, the year Rivera began his service, George Anson, an English commodore, was known to be lurking off Acapulco, so the Manila ship was held in port. Undaunted, Anson sailed for the Orient and, in June 1743, took the eastbound galleon *Covadonga* in a pitched battle off the Philippines. After that, no trans-Pacific traders left Manila for three years.[24] This interruption of the usual Manila-Acapulco trade had a bizarre consequence that did enliven California's South for a time. In Java, Dutch traders learned of Anson's exploit and the chaos it had caused. They imagined that the interruption in the Manila trade might incline New Spain to trade with others. Two Dutch ships were outfitted, loaded with desirable cargoes, and put to sea. They were separated by a storm in mid-Pacific. At the end of 1746, one of them, the *Hervating*, put into San Bernabé with the same urgent needs as a typical Manila galleon.[25]

Spanish colonials were forbidden to trade with, or even to offer assistance to, foreign vessels. Such orders emanated from the always xenophobic councils in Madrid — and their views were repeatedly impressed on viceroys in the New World.[26] California Jesuits, located as they were on a vulnerable frontier, had received repeated reminders of this national policy, but the visit by a Dutch trader found the missionaries unusually vulnerable to temptation. Mainstay crops had repeatedly fallen prey to massive attacks by locusts; the Dutch had a large cargo of rice and were ready to trade for water and any meat and vegetables that the missions could accumulate. They soon succeeded in overcoming their hosts' prejudices — and their good judgment as well. Padre Carlos Neumayer, who spoke Dutch, moved down from Santiago to San José del Cabo, and the missions and the merchants began to trade necessities.

The Hollanders arranged to stay a month while they recuperated. The largely Protestant ship's company impressed everyone with its seriousness and good behavior, especially in its deference and respect for the padres and the church. Surprisingly, they were able to cajole Padres Neumayer and Sigismundo Taraval, the rector of the missions of the South, into penning letters on their behalf to the Jesuit procurador in Mexico City, letters that, in effect, endorsed the idea of Dutch trade with New Spain. Perhaps uneasy about their collaboration, the California Jesuits decided to explain matters to their own superiors and to civil authorities in the capital. After consultation, they wrote various letters and reports and gave them to a volunteer letter carrier, Juan Nicolás de Estrada, a soldier in *el Sur*, who would go on the *Hervating*. They persuaded Pedro de la Riva, Estrada's superior officer, to give him a formal pass to the mainland for official business.

However, when the Dutch arrived at Matanchel, they were prevented even from landing. When Juan Nicolás de Estrada was put ashore to explain his mission, he was clapped in irons and taken before the president of the Audiencia de Guadalajara, who ordered him sent to Mexico City. Virrey Revillagigedo was read the Jesuits' letters and became so incensed over the whole affair that he had Estrada tortured to procure the "true" story of all that had taken place. In April 1747, after two months of imprisonment, the unfortunate Estrada was released. The Jesuit procurador saw to it that he was given fifty pesos and allowed to return to California.[27] The Dutch traders never gained the slightest acceptance, lost several landing parties trying to procure necessities, and finally, in desperation, put to sea bound for Java. No word of their fate appears in Spanish records, but California's Jesuits soon felt the viceroy's outrage. A strong letter of rebuke was sent to Padre Neumayer and a most pointed warning to the Jesuit provincial of New Spain. Jesuits, in brief, were not even to speak to foreigners. However, that limitation remained academic in California. By all accounts, no other foreign ship landed on the peninsula during the remaining quarter-century of Jesuit tenure.[28]

The monotony of life in the South was interrupted again in the years 1747 and 1748 by Pedro de la Riva's campaign against the ever-resistant Uchití and by Manuel de Ocio's occupation of Santa Ana, which brought his men into conflict with remnants of the same band.[29] Fernando de Rivera served under Riva during this action, but his personal efforts are known only from an abbreviated reference in Virrey Revillagigedo's letter confirming Rivera's nomination to the captaincy: "He took part in the subjugation of the Uchití nation . . . and in that expedition confirmed and added to the many proofs of his good conduct. . . ." These words reflected what His Excellency had been told by the Jesuits as they pressed for Rivera's appointment.[30]

Fernando de Rivera's most conspicuous acts of leadership would be played out on California's northern frontiers, at first in furthering Jesuit plans, later in pursuit of the far-flung ambitions of the crown. However, his apprenticeship in the South had exposed him to the awakening of secular life on the peninsula. Far from Loreto and Jesuit supervision, he rubbed shoulders with men who were pressing for private enterprise, private landholdings, and more independence. Later events would make plain that Rivera remained concerned for the welfare of these former companions and for their families, even as he served the very different interests of missionaries and royal officials.

Rivera Confirmed and Outfitted as Captain

In March 1753, Fernando de Rivera received the coveted royal confirmation of his appointment. A royal decree had been issued on 9 September 1752 and sent to Mexico City. On 25 January 1753, Virrey Revillagigedo added his note of compliance and transmittal and sent the decree on to California.[31]

With his final confirmation in hand, the always-cautious Rivera felt justified in ordering the finery that the California captain would be expected to display, not only in the event of a higher official's visit, but weekly while leading his men to church, or while attending any fiesta. When Rivera assumed the captaincy, Padre Juan de Armesto had been the missionary and procurador in Loreto, the Jesuit most responsible for helping the inexperienced officer to adjust to his duties, perquisites, and ceremonial responsibilities. In 1752, Armesto was promoted to be procurador de Californias and sent to Mexico City, and in 1753, Rivera found himself asking a friend to supply the accouterments of his post. His order begins formally enough:

Memorandum of that which I ask your reverence to send me from Mexico City — and the money which I hope can be charged to my account and sent to my mother in Guadalajara.

However, he soon displays an unusual ease and familiarity in one of the most revealing documents known to have come from his hand. Fernando de Rivera's emotions can be imagined; his thoughts probably went back to the Compostela of his early youth, its official pomp and ceremony, and his sense of his father's role in festive events. He certainly remembered the financial need in his childhood home when, before anything else, he asked the procurador to send his mother fifty pesos in silver.

The youthful captain then asked Armesto to secure him an outfit of practical and ceremonial arms:

A well-made musket with a good quality sheath
A pair of flared-barrel pistols
A dress rapier, not too broad, with the handguard and other usual parts inlaid with silver
A cutlass decorated in silver. . . .

Then he turned to clothing and adornments:

A riding coat of crimson velvet well provided with eyelets
Two and a half yards of blue velvet
A pleated coat in the military style
Four widths of fine Brittany linen
Six dozen heavy silver buttons. . . .

Finally, he asked the favor of Armesto's assistance in obtaining certain items. "Take 200 pesos or whatever Your Reverence deems necessary to have made two heavy cloaks of Bayonne serge, closed with one or two tie-strings," and "as to the pleated coat, let's put it that if you can find a person of my stature in Mexico City, you can take his measurements." Juan de Armesto replied, "Ask for whatever you personally need, and for anything more, if we have it among our stores. . . ."[32]

More than a dozen documents survive that Rivera wrote during his first two or three years as captain. They reveal a man with a reasonably good education, particularly as compared to others raised near the frontier. His penmanship was firm and distinguished, his ideas expressed economically and with conviction. In fact, it is his persistently terse and businesslike style — even judged by today's standards — that betrays the fact that he lacked the education of an urban gentleman of the times. His writings display none of the elaborate circumlocutions used, or at least attempted, by most men with pretensions to elegance. True, Rivera dutifully wrote out the flowery forms expected in salutations and complimentary closings, but between these he addressed himself to matters at hand with economy and directness. His letters to audiencias, or even such a personage as the viceroy, were not as self-effacing or subservient as those written by his university-educated predecessor, Bernardo Rodríguez.[33]

Rodríguez Versus Rivera

During his first years as captain, Rivera's relations with the extended Rodríguez family degenerated. His sudden promotion had leap-frogged him over the backs of Rodríguez family members. Then he had a hand in curtailing some of Manuel de Ocio's plans. Worst of all, he was placed in a position of open legal conflict with the entire clan — including the revered *mamá*, María de Larrea — over Bernardo Rodríguez's estate. All these problems were less personal than official; they grew out of Rivera's duties as justicia mayor.

Bernardo Rodríguez died leaving a small orchard, doubtless some horses and mules with their trappings, and various unspecified personal effects. Among his last acts, Bernardo named Pedro de la Riva as his interim successor. When Riva took over the temporary command, he thereby became the judge responsible for the execution of Rodríguez's will. He began by ordering an inventory and appraisal of the estate. A total value of over thirteen thousand pesos was determined,[34] a small fortune in those days — and one that suggests that Rodríguez had found some unrecorded way to profit from his years as an officer. The appraised amount was about double the total of all the salaries he drew in his nearly twenty years of service. The heirs had every reason to expect a favorable outcome to any legal proceedings and an early distribution of the assets because the authority in charge was a family member. However, the case was complicated by the claims of creditors and Riva could not close it before he was replaced. Fernando de Rivera thereby inherited what became a most contentious duty.[35]

Bernardo Rodríguez left sizeable debts. One appears plainly on the Jesuit books in early 1751: "... charge 2,033 pesos against the account of the defunct Capitán Don Bernardo. . . ."[36] As California's magistrate, Rivera had to reconcile Jesuit claims — and perhaps the claims of others — with the relatively non-liquid assets of the deceased and the probably unrealistic expectations of the heirs-in-waiting.

In California, little currency circulated, so there was virtually no cash economy. A forced sale created a buyers' market, one limited not only to those who needed or valued the property being sold, but also to those who had significant credit at the warehouse or on the payroll books. Rivera followed law and tradition in ordering that Bernardo Rodríguez's estate be auctioned. A list was circulated proclaiming the event and the property involved. The auction was held, but the proceeds amounted to only fifteen hundred pesos — a sum that was consumed in paying debts. The heirs were incensed. They expressed shock at what they took to be scandalously low selling prices. They claimed to have asked for inventories and the corresponding sales information, and to have been refused by the justicia mayor. At some point in 1752, Simón Rodríguez abused Rivera in writing and to his face. The captain held that his honor and the dignity of his office had been denigrated. He had Simón placed in leg irons and incarcerated for an extended period of time — the first recorded occurrence among California's gente de razón of such an aggressive offense and such stern justice.[37] Another part of New Spain's everyday life had finally come to the sheltered peninsula.

Months passed, during which Fernando de Rivera celebrated his formal appointment and led a difficult journey of exploration to the north.[38] Meanwhile, his detractors were at work. Simón Rodríguez remained in prison, and his family continued to be outraged. Manuel de Ocio — who had much experience petitioning those in high places, and in contesting Rivera's authority — probably arranged the action that followed. Simón's brother, Manuel Rodríguez, resident in Mexico City,[39] was contacted and informed of the family situation in California. Manuel obtained a lawyer and, through him, in May of 1753, made a representation to the viceroy. The principal plaintiff was stated to be María de Larrea, Bernardo's mother and presumably the chief beneficiary deprived of property by Rivera's allegedly illegal acts. In what amounted to a suit against the California captain, the viceroy was requested to order that Rivera release Simón Rodríguez and give an accounting of the disposition of Bernardo's estate to Pedro de la Riva, or, in case of his death or absence, to Manuel de Ocio. The viceroy was also asked to fine the captain one thousand pesos if he should fail to follow these orders, and to put Riva or Ocio in charge of supervising Rivera's compliance.

Virrey Revillagigedo's first reaction was favorable to the plaintiffs. He ordered Simón's immediate release — but only if his offense was as represented by the plaintiff petition. He ordered the fine, as requested, but declined to appoint Riva or Ocio as watchdog. In this, Revillagigedo showed both wisdom and caution. California was far away, and he had heard only one side of the case. He was not ready to completely override the authority of the justicia mayor, nor to demand an act that could only be undone after months of waiting on the mails.[40]

When Rivera received the viceroy's letter, he doubtless responded as promptly as Loreto's intermittent sailings permitted, but his letter cannot be found today. Fortunately, Rivera's parallel letter to inform Padre Armesto of these matters does survive. Rivera told Armesto that he had released the jailed Rodríguez, as ordered, but he had not turned over the inventory or auction proceedings to Ocio. He guessed that the viceroy did not realize the extent of Don Manuel's personal interest in the case. Furthermore, Rivera wanted the higher authorities to know that the individuals who had bought the auctioned items had enjoyed their use for two years and considered them as their own property. He had submitted the full particulars of the sale, but wanted legal advice from his superiors before he reopened that matter. Rivera also sent the viceroy his own report of Simón Rodríguez's behavior and the mountain of claims and complaints he had received from that person. The young captain reveals his exasperation and his rusticity in describing these experiences. In vernacular phrases seldom seen in correspondence between officials, he speaks of Simón's efforts to wear him down with paperwork— "*moliendome con papeles . . . ; la marimaña de papeles . . . .*"—and to make a commotion out of proportion to the facts— "*tales cosas se buigan de recio.*" When Ocio tried to get him to sign an apparently innocent document, Rivera did not do so because he knew that he would only hurt himself: "*conoci que me espinaba*". To close his report, Rivera expressed doubt that he deserved to be fined a thousand pesos, but awaited the viceroy's pleasure in that regard.[41]

When Revillagigedo received the requested documents, he referred the whole matter to his legal counsel for military matters, the *auditor de guerra*.[42] The auditor's decision is the last word known in this case. He found that María de Larrea had been wronged. The inheritance she had the right to expect had been dissipated in unfortunate auction proceedings. However, the auditor did not find Rivera entirely at fault. His inexperience was noted as well as the fact that he had conducted all proceedings in a legal fashion. To attempt to redress the wrongs, the auditor ordered that a man experienced in such matters, Don José Bon of Culiacán, be summoned to California. There, he and Rivera would jointly take depositions from all parties to the auction and submit a full report to Mexico City from whence further actions might be ordered.[43]

Simón Rodríguez' and his co-plaintiffs did not fare well in the auditor's report. The petitioners were judged to be severely at fault for failing to identify Riva and Ocio as their brothers-in-law, even as they sought to involve them as authorities in the case. Simón Rodríguez's behavior was judged as an affront to an officer of the crown, an offense that required the captain to take action. However, Rivera was reprimanded for the severity of his response. He should have remembered the honor due to the Rodríguez family. He was reminded that Simón was not, after all, a common criminal and should not have been humiliated to such a degree. Rivera was admonished to ponder all this and make future punishments of California folk better fit their offenses.

The auditor de guerra concluded that the justicia mayor of California was young, his intentions had been good, but he had not had legal training or experience. He recommended that no fine be imposed. Virrey Revillagigedo read his auditor's report, added his endorsement, and ordered that it serve, in toto, as his official reply.[44]

Trials of the Justicia Mayor

The controversies that swirled around Fernando de Rivera during the first years of his captaincy were exacerbated by his youth, his inexperience, and the suddenness of his elevation. His challengers intended to test his resolve; Rivera was the new watchdog set to guard Jesuit interests after a period of laxness that had benefited some. The captaincy carried with it the duties of governor and provincial justice. Rivera was called on to investigate and arbitrate any case in which written charges were proffered. He became an intermediate target for bolts aimed at the Jesuits, or for the resentment of anyone impeded by California's rules or practices. Most often, the resentful person was Manuel de Ocio, whose interests often conflicted with those of the missions.

Don Manuel and the missionaries were quick to make complaints when they felt that their rights were threatened. Each time the entrepreneur made a claim or was charged with usurping land, water, or cattle, the justicia mayor had to conduct hearings, take depositions from witnesses, hear the accusers and plaintiffs, and hand down a decision. Rivera drew on the laws, decrees, and other precedents that seemed pertinent to him. He usually supported Jesuit claims and found against Ocio. The latter was outraged, or feigned to be so, each time his claims were denied and his ambitions thwarted. He appealed several decisions to the Audiencia of Guadalajara, or to the viceroy, usually including broad charges against Rivera for connivance with the missionaries, as well as the usual allegations that the Jesuits opposed all development of California resources.[45]

It is difficult to fault Rivera's logic or sense of justice as reflected in the records of his few surviving decisions. He was bound by California's unique legalities, which were Spanish colonial law modified by the pro-Jesuit concessions that had been proclaimed and upheld in various decrees during more than half a century. Rivera was responsible for none of the rules, but they had to form the basis for his findings. Legal counselors to viceroys and audiencias understood these things, but most others did not. Ocio could have influenced some to see Rivera as a biased judge, one who put the interests of the Jesuits before all else.

Exploring to the North

Jesuit efforts to convert the natives of the cape region, from their outset in 1720, seemed to go wrong. Within fifteen years, a rebellion against the missions left the place depopulated and a target for exploitation. After that tragic experience, the missionaries were fortunate to have a larger and more promising evangelical objective. Their efforts in the South had been largely forced upon them by bureaucrats anxious to establish a port to facilitate the Manila trade. The missionaries' primary dream had always impelled them northward to complete the conversion of the peninsular natives, join forces with their Sonoran brothers, and push a Christian frontier up the Pacific Coast toward the coveted goal of Monterey. Peninsular missions at Comondú (1708), La Purísima (1719), Guadalupe (1720), and San Ignacio (1728) had been steps toward that goal. The rebellion in the South drained away energy, supplies, and money for a decade, but even when that flow was stanched, the situation within the Loreto presidio impeded northward expansion. Unity, morale, and military effectiveness had deteriorated during the dotage of Esteban Rodríguez and the illness of his son and successor.

Despite these problems, Padre Fernando Consag had devoted years to preparing for a new northern mission. He had trained a German padre, Jorge Retz, to serve as its missionary. Consag had accumulated animals and supplies, and, particularly, had labored to indoctrinate the bands of neophytes who would form the new mission. The informal confirmation of Fernando de Rivera as captain in 1751 gave California Jesuits the confidence they needed to take their first step northward in over twenty years. In July of that year, Retz opened Misión de Santa Gertrudis.[46] Additional missions were planned, and, in 1753, the indefatigable Consag readied another exploration to seek a suitable location. A sense of renewed purpose infused the long-stalled California missionaries.

Consag's 1746 canoe exploration of the upper gulf turned up no promising sites along the gulf coast. The exploration he and Rivera headed in 1751 fared in a generally north-northwesterly direction, and it too revealed no desirable locations. Now the persistent Croatian was determined to explore the cordillera that lay between his previous routes. In preparation, he had assembled supplies and recruited neophytes to guide and assist the venture. Soldiers were needed to guard against hostilities from unconverted Cochimí and to maintain order and discipline among expedition members. When Rivera was told of the venture, he insisted on bringing soldiers from Loreto and again taking the lead.

In the spring of 1753, the expedition left San Ignacio and went north-northwest to Bahía de los Angeles, a place known to Consag from his 1746 visit by water. Unsatisfied, the explorers pushed on, this time to the northwest to skirt the west flank of a peculiarly rugged and arid sierra, one that later would be known as Calamajué or La Asamblea. Eventually the party arrived at a huge arroyo with much water and stands of tules and carrizo, but the water was so salt-laden that the place was deemed unusable as a mission site. The explorers, and particularly their animals, were tired, bruised, and thirsty. All returned to San Ignacio with no more solace than the knowledge that the Cochimí they had encountered had not resisted their incursion and had proved tractable and receptive.[47]

Rivera's Marriage and Family

On 19 January 1755, a unique bit of California history was played out in the parochial church of Compostela, Nueva Galicia. A congregation of the area's most prominent families was witness to the wedding of Don Fernando Javier de Rivera y Moncada, Capitán del Real de Loreto de California, to Doña María Teresa Dávalos y Patrón. The event must have seemed extraordinary and romantic even at the time; Fernando de Rivera was far away in California, and his elder half-brother, Basilio de Rivera y Valle, stood in his place as a proxy bridegroom. Records of hundreds of weddings at dozens of churches in northwest New Spain during the mid-eighteenth century reveal no other that was solemnized in the absence of a principal.[48]

Capitán Rivera needed the viceroy's approval to leave the area under his jurisdiction.[49] His duties must have prevented him from seeking, or perhaps from receiving, a leave of absence. The practical and ecclesiastical arrangements for the wedding were carried out through the good offices of the same Basilio de Rivera. He was then captain of the bark *San José*, which was owned by the crown, but lent to and operated by the Jesuits to supply Loreto from Acapulco and Matanchel. Basilio and his brother, Cristóbal de Rivera y Valle, were in Loreto on 8 November 1754, when Fernando de Rivera dated the power of attorney that made Basilio his proxy.[50]

Rivera's bride came from a family whose connections with California were already old. Her father, Don Diego Dávalos, was the son of a Compostela merchant of the same name who had sold grain to Salvatierra during the first years of the California colony. The bride's mother, Doña Antonia Patrón y Romero, was a niece of Don Juan Antonio Romero Gil de la Sierpe, who captained the ship that first brought Salvatierra and his party to California.[51]

No records suggest how the match was arranged. Rivera is not known to have left the peninsula in the years between 1742 and 1755. He may have done so, though it is more likely that the principals had known each other as youngsters in Compostela and that the marriage was contracted by their prominent families.[52] Basilio de Rivera, shuttling between Loreto and Compostela, added a human touch to these unusually impersonal arrangements. After the wedding, Teresa probably came to California on her brother-in-law's ship, escorted by a member of her family.

Despite Loreto's isolation from mainland society, Teresa had the same entrée with local people that her husband had enjoyed all through his California years. Several of the presidial families were Compostelans. A cousin of the captain, Cabo Fernando de la Peña, lived at Loreto with his wife and several children. Moreover, Teresa Dávalos's hometown was on the supply route between California and Guadalajara. Through her merchant father, she could have met, in her own home, most of the soldiers who facilitated the purchase and transfer of supplies.

During the next twelve years, the couple produced four children. Juan Bautista Francisco María was born at Loreto and baptized by Padre Juan Javier Bischoff on 5 October 1756. Doña Teresa was apparently attended by her parents at the time of the birth, and for some weeks thereafter.[53] Another son, José Nicolás María, was born at Loreto and baptized by Padre Lucas Ventura on 8 May 1758. A third son, Luis Gonzaga Francisco Javier María, and a daughter, Isabel, were born before 1767.[54]

A Few Activities in Quiet Times

Fernando de Rivera's captaincy coincided with a period in California that was described a little over a century later by historian H. H. Bancroft as a virtual blank: "It is not possible to form a connected and complete narrative . . . for the remainder of the Jesuit period. Only a few events are preserved in the records; but they are the most important, and from them . . . the reader may picture the monotony of peninsula happenings and progress in these years. Even the Jesuit chroniclers found nothing of interest in the dry record."[55] Perhaps it would be closer to the truth to say that the Jesuits were relieved to have little to report. Most evidence of secular affairs in California during their regime derives from controversies that produced revealing paperwork: reports, charges, denials, pleas, and defenses. Rivera's years were marked by little more dissent than Manuel de Ocio's perennial nipping at Jesuit heels. Viceroys and other officials asked few questions, little information was volunteered, and today the archives are correspondingly bare. Nevertheless, there are records of a few events that had later significance or further illustrate the quiet character of the times.

In early 1752, Pedro de la Riva left California service and moved to the Tepic region of Nueva Galicia.[56] Three years later, Cristóbal Gutiérrez de Góngora, then in his mid-forties, retired from California service and took up residence in the vicinity of Tepic.[57] Thus, at about the time of his marriage, Fernando de Rivera had no commissioned officers. Since the captain might become ill, or be called upon to lead an exploration or travel the length of a very long peninsula, there was a clear need for an officer qualified to act in his place. Finally, in 1758, Don Blas Fernández de Somera was hired as lieutenant at Loreto through an unusual form of nepotism. His brother, Miguel Fernández de Somera was a Jesuit missionary at Ocoroni, Sonora, a post he had held for twenty-five years.[58]

In the spring of 1759, Rivera made pointed reference to Fernández de Somera's presence and competence when he applied for the viceroy's permission to take a two-month leave of absence to visit his mother in Compostela. His request for leave was granted, and he was reminded to leave the lieutenant clear instructions for any contingency. In the fall of 1761, the captain once again asked to visit his mother, but she died before he could have reached her.[59]

In 1759, California's new supply ship, *El Aguila*, was wrecked on the gulf coast southeast of Misión de Santiago on her maiden voyage; Rivera went to investigate both the responsibility for the loss and the possibility of saving the hull or salvaging parts of the wreckage. News and doings were at such a low ebb in California that this matter occupied most of the known correspondence for over a year.[60] *El Aguila* had been built at royal expense in Realejo, Nicaragua, specifically for California service. The loss was devastating. The peninsular missions were left with no supply ship larger than lanchas, the open sailing craft that plied between Loreto and the ports of sister missions in Sonora. Now the California visitador had to reopen the business of getting approval and funding for yet another new craft. The royal treasury was always in arrears; its guardians had demonstrated their anger and dismay at the loss of *El Aguila* and their disinclination to reinvest at such risk. Padre Miguel del Barco once again was visitador in California; he showed the same decisive hand that had elevated Rivera y Moncada during his first visitorship.

Shipbuilding at Loreto

Forty years earlier, Padre Juan de Ugarte had a ship built on the beach at Mulegé under the direction of his English pilot and shipwright, Guillermo Strafford.[61] Miguel del Barco knew a Filipino, Gaspar Molina—a sailor in California as early as 1733—who had shown ability at boatbuilding, albeit only of small craft. Barco and Padre Lucas Ventura, the procurador in Loreto, called Molina out of retirement in Sinaloa and gave him an audacious commission: build a full-scale, oceangoing supply ship, and do it at Loreto. The Jesuits must have calculated that they could fund Molina's efforts themselves, hoping eventually to convince the viceroy and his advisors that they should be reimbursed.[62]

The presidio of Loreto imported wood from Matanchel and provided the full-time services of its own marinería—a crew of artisans that may have been augmented for the project.[63] In August 1761, Molina launched *Nuestra Señora de la Concepción*, a vessel of his own design, forty-eight feet long at the keel. All her curved members had been adzed out of appropriately shaped trunks selected from the great mesquite thicket that flourished at Londó, twenty miles north of Loreto.[64] All possible salvage from *El Aguila* was reused, but Padre Barco could not resist describing the parts of the original craft as inferior in size and strength to those fabricated by Molina. As soon as *La Concepción*—as she was soon called—had been shaken down, Barco and Ventura wrote to the viceroy to explain what had been done, the great success that had been achieved, and the incredibly small cost—ten thousand pesos, or about half of the cost of *El Aguila*.

Actually, the Jesuits had undervalued their work by nearly half, and planned to make up the difference themselves. Barco, writing with no restraints after the expulsion, explained that they asked for less than the cost so that no one would be tempted to accuse them of profiting from their self-imposed task. The claims made for the quality of *La Concepción*'s construction and seaworthiness were not exaggerated. She served long and well, but, ironically, she would be also be the ship that was used to carry California's Jesuits away into exile. As for Gaspar Molina, his success led to another commission; before 1768, he had launched the slightly smaller *Nuestra Señora de Loreto*—popularly called *La Lauretana*—which served even longer than her sister-ship as a fixture on the Sea of Cortés.[65]

Opening a New Mission—San Francisco de Borja

Shortly after Capitán Rivera completed his investigations and reported on the wreck of *El Aguila*, he again became involved in the Jesuit push to the north, this time to add the new mission that had been planned by Padre Fernando Consag since 1746. Consag had conceived the idea during his gulf voyage when he found a large and receptive ranchería at Bahía de los Angeles. Consag and Rivera's expeditions of 1751 and 1753 were unsuccessful searches for adequate

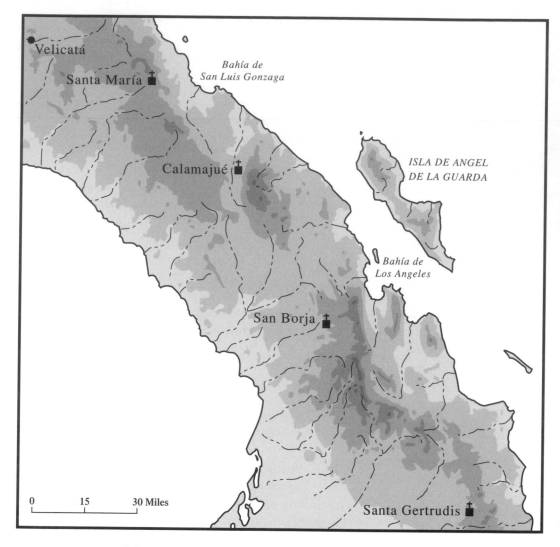

Map 11.1 California's Northern Missions, 1751–1767

land and water to support this mission; both ventures had bypassed Adac, a site in the mountains some twenty miles southwest of the great bay. Several years later, Padre Jorge Retz, missionary at Santa Gertrudis, got word of Adac; it was soon reconnoitered and then chosen to be the cabecera of the mission that would be named for San Francisco de Borja, and popularly called San Borja.

Consag and Retz were the two men most qualified to work on the northern frontier; both knew the land and the people, but Padre Consag was in frail health, and Retz was considered too involved in consolidating and developing Santa Gertrudis. Instead, in 1759, a young Mexican Jesuit, José Mariano Rotea, was sent to San Ignacio to train under Consag. Unfortunately, Padre Fernando's remaining days were few; he died on 10 December of that year. Rotea by then knew San Ignacio well and was the obvious choice to succeed the deceased padre. San Borja would have to wait.

In 1761, a new man was at hand—a young Bohemian, Wenceslao Linck. He was sent to train with Retz and, by 1762, was ready to move northward. Linck had several advantages over most of his mission-founding predecessors. Donors had made generous gifts. The useful harbor at Bahía de los Angeles facilitated the shipment of supplies from Loreto, and the large, cooperative ranchería at the bay could supply labor for the overland leg of the journey, as well as for mission construction.[66]

Adac proved to be less than an ideal cabecera. The spring and fields alike were meager, yet there were many neophytes to accommodate. Early in the establishment period, it became apparent that the site was seriously short of the pasture land and water needed to support the necessary livestock. Fernando de Rivera took charge at this crucial juncture.[67] The captain had moved his headquarters temporarily to San Borja so he could supervise the soldiers and provide an example for the attendant workers—the arrieros, vaqueros, carpenters, masons, and their assistants—who might be faint-hearted when sent to a remote heathen frontier. When Rivera realized that grazing land and water would be crucial to the mission's survival, he took two soldiers with ranching experience and rode out to canvass the area.

They spent days eliminating adjacent lands. To the north was useless desert and to the east an escarpment, an impassable drop-off onto a more arid plain. To the south, a succession of deep arroyos offered water but little land. Rivera decided to explore some heights about twenty miles southeast of Adac, a somewhat forlorn hope since water was seldom found on high mesas. Nevertheless, after much searching and many difficult climbs, the little party came upon a broad mesa, today called Las Cabras, that had not only pasturage but a running spring that scattered pools of water down the course of a rivulet. Rivera thought the mesa could support up to eight hundred cattle as well as the necessary horses, mules, and burros.

By the end of 1763, Rivera's assessment had proved accurate. Over six hundred head of cattle were brought to the area, as well as eighty mares for breeding much-needed mules. The herders who brought the animals from the more southern missions had an unforgettable experience as they neared their goal; on the high mesa, they experienced a heavy snowfall, the first that any of them had seen.[68]

In 1764, a new missionary, Padre Victoriano Arnés, arrived in California and went to work on the northern frontier. He was sent to train under Linck and to learn the native dialects used around San Borja. Early in the following year, a second recruit, Padre Juan José Diez, joined Linck and Arnés. The newcomers were anxious to found a mission. Men, money, and materials were available, but no suitable site had been discovered within a desirable distance. Practical experience had convinced the padres that new establishments should not be more than forty or fifty miles from a neighbor. Having extra missionaries at San Borja meant that Linck could leave for a thorough exploration.[69]

Wenceslao Linck's diary of his journey has been lost. However, as the venture neared its end, he wrote a brief letter to Padre Procurador Juan de Armesto that discloses only a hint of the itinerary, but suggests several interesting things:

> On August 1st I set out . . . in company with the Captain, two Spanish soldiers, and two Germans. The Germans came on the Manila Galleon after escaping from the English. Because of their vigorous strength and unflagging diligence in working, they have given me much assistance on all occasions.[70]

The captain was Rivera y Moncada, the soldiers remain nameless, and no more is known about the intriguing Germans. Sixteen friendly Cochimí completed Linck's force, and their travels extended for an incredible five months. The party penetrated northward as far as the southern peaks of the Sierra de San Pedro Mártir; they encountered snow and bitter cold, and finally returned to San Borja by way of the Pacific plains.

Such a lengthy trek suggests a diligent search. Linck made another trip north just a few weeks later, and his surviving diary reveals the thoroughness of the earlier reconnaissance. In his journal of the second trip, the padre displays an intimate knowledge of the geography and population of a place called Velicatá. He probably recognized its potential during his first visit and stopped to evangelize the people as well as to explore the surroundings.[71] Within a year, a number of thatched utility structures were erected at Velicatá as it was developed into a visita of Santa María, the final and most northerly Jesuit mission in California.[72]

Before long, Fernando de Rivera's knowledge of the northern peninsula was put to use. Four years after his long trip with Padre Linck, he led the first overland march to San Diego. He chose the proven and developed site at Velicatá as his base and staging area. His experiences in 1765 influenced the choice of a route, the selection of supplies and animals, and the daily travel routine of the important later expedition.

Trials and Labors of Manuel de Ocio

Most references to Manuel de Ocio paint him as a man of totally mundane, grasping interests whose activities invariably impeded the selfless labors of his one-time employers, the California missionaries. However, most references to Ocio were written by those same missionaries, and they represent a narrow viewpoint. Using the broader standards of eighteenth-century colonial life, Ocio emerges simply as a hardheaded, practical opportunist—a typical character on a developing frontier. Like most successful New World entrepreneurs, Don Manuel was an immigrant from Spain. None of his varied activities was unique. California had seen pearlers long before his time, and northwest New Spain had had its share of prospectors, miners, merchants, shipowners, traders, and ranchers. Ocio was notable in that he was all of these things in California, and several with considerable success. In the process, he coped with some of the longest supply lines, smallest labor pools, and most isolated areas that had faced entrepreneurs in New Spain, and most of the time, he had to contend with Jesuit opposition, not only in California, but also in Mexico City where his petitions for permits, licenses, and property rights were heard and debated.

Opening Santa Ana was a major accomplishment for one man, even one with Ocio's pearl-engendered wealth. In 1747, he had already put in years of planning and months of work just to assemble the needed men and supplies in Sinaloa, get them aboard ships, and deliver them to el surgidero de Cerralvo, the beach nearest Santa Ana. Even then, his crew was not free to start work. The would-be mineworkers were harassed by remnants of the Uchití who remained at large in the rugged foothills north of the six-thousand-foot cape sierra.[73] Their threat was staved off by force of arms, but there remained Santa Ana's heat, the labor and drudgery of transporting supplies from the distant beach, and the building of structures and mining devices from sparse trees and granite earth.

While Manuel de Ocio struggled to create a mining town in a wilderness, his wife, Rosalía Rodríguez, and his two young sons, Antonio and Mariano, were situated with her mother, the recently widowed María de Larrea, in the more secure environment of Loreto. In August 1747, Josefa Rodríguez, Rosalía's sister, was expecting a child. She had moved to Comondú to be with her sister Loreta and to enjoy a better climate during her confinement and delivery. María de Larrea and her daughter Rosalía, with her two little boys, left the stifling heat of Loreto and went to Comondú to be present at the birth and baptism and to offer Josefa the assistance she would need. When her child, Francisca Javiera, was born on 22 August the visitors stayed on to help and to enjoy the cool Pacific air that moderates the climate of Comondú. For over thirty years, María de Larrea had impressed the Jesuits with her kindness and diligence in the service of their cause. Now, in her later years, the mission records show that she acted as a helper to Comondú's Padre Francisco Domínguez, a missionary visiting from Sonora who had only a few weeks' experience in California.[74]

That summer in Comondú, Mariano de Ocio became ill. He was no more than five or six, not old enough to understand the honor of his grandparents or to enjoy the wealth of his father. All of that gained him only the small distinction noted in the Book of Burials for Misión de San José de Comondú, "On the thirteenth of September, there died and was buried in this holy church, the child Mariano Ocio, son of Don Manuel de Ocio and of Doña Rosalía Rodríguez. . . ." It is the only entry among hundreds that specifies interment in the sanctuary.[75] Within four or five years at most, Rosalía Rodríguez also died.[76] Manuel de Ocio, the worldly success, was a widower, alone with his son Antonio who was still a young child.

CHAPTER II

Raw Ore and Refined Silver

By late 1748, Ocio and his hirelings at Santa Ana were ready to try their hands at mining and refining silver.[77] Work was begun by digging pits on the flanks of a nearby mountain called Cerro de San Pedro in pursuit of a vein of dark minerals clearly visible in a generally gray-brown granitic matrix. Digging was done with hammers, chisels, and iron bars — and may have been facilitated by blasting powder.[78] Miners shovelled ore fragments into leather hampers, slung them over mules, and took them to a simple mill that consisted of a great stationary millstone, several feet in diameter, and another of equal size that lay on it and was turned around a central shaft by mulepower. Small chunks of ore were fed through openings near the center of the upper stone. The ore worked outward as the mill turned and was emitted at the edges as a powder and sand mixture. The pulverized ore was then subjected to one or the other of two relatively simple thermochemical refining procedures that could be carried out in primitive circumstances.

Smelting was the favored method for refining rich ore. This required simple stone furnaces or ovens with large leathern bellows to provide blasts of air. First, the ground ore was burned in small furnaces to eliminate its sulfur content. Then, it was mixed with litharge, lead, and charcoal, and smelted in a large, pyramid-shaped Castilian furnace. The resulting compound was burned again in the small furnaces to separate lead from silver.

The actual smelting took about twenty-four hours, so it offered the miner an immediate evaluation of the take from his mine. However, the process was primitive and inefficient; it failed to refine perhaps a third of the silver. Moreover, the furnaces consumed great quantities of charcoal and wood, and the litharge and lead, though inexpensive, were heavy and had to be shipped across the gulf and then hauled by muleback from Ocio's landing at the surgidero de Cerralvo.

The second refinement process had the advantage of working on poorer grades of ore at about the same efficiency as smelting. It was a rapid, heat-induced amalgamation called the *cazo* method. The ore was placed in a *cazo*, or copper cauldron, mixed with salt, copper pyrites, and mercury, then smelted. The disadvantage was that the copper of the cazo tended to alloy with the silver. Moreover, the whole process depended on mercury, an expensive ingredient that was particularly heavy and troublesome to transport.[79]

When Manuel de Ocio reviewed the early results of his mining in a petition to the viceroy, he reported half of his first thousand pounds of silver as *plata de fuego* and half as *plata de azogue* — which meant that half had been produced by smelting and half by amalgamation.[80] However, since smelting was well known as a procedure applied to relatively rich ores, Ocio may have exaggerated the proportion of plata de fuego to enhance his own status by creating a more favorable perception of the Real de Santa Ana among high officials. A report made only fifteen years later, by an expert in silver refining, shows that the cazo method was then the most successful and most widely used in California.[81]

Santa Ana's People and Problems

Manuel de Ocio founded the Real de Santa Ana as a step in his drive to be honored and rewarded as the man who finally opened up the wealth of fabled California. Quite incidentally, his mining camp brought a very different novelty to the peninsula: a class of people that, up until then, had been carefully excluded from its sheltered society. Previous immigrants, whether white or of mixed blood, had been handpicked by the Jesuits. The missionaries held their employees to high standards, not only for competence, but also for obedience, temperance, and moral integrity. If a man failed to meet their standards, the Jesuits were not slow to end his contract and return him to the less demanding mainland.[82]

Manuel de Ocio hired his sailors, arrieros, vaqueros, and mineworkers less fastidiously. Although he knew the concerns of the Jesuits about the kind of people brought to California, his interests were in economy and efficiency. When his men and their families were assembled at Santa Ana, they were not only common frontier folk, they were also strangers to each other. Their new community had no infrastructure, no upper class but Ocio and his assistants, and, perhaps more significantly, no priest and no church. Jesuit descriptions of the place are brief and circumspect but leave no doubt that the living conditions of its inhabitants were miserable.[83] More candid reports about contemporary mining camps on the mainland describe drunkenness, whoring, and general dissolution.[84] In any event, illegitimate children born to Santa Ana women soon appeared in the baptismal records of Misión de Santiago.[85] No doubt more were recorded at Todos Santos, the nearest mission, but its libros de misión are lost. Most distressing to the Jesuits was the fact that neophytes were curious about the new activities and began to gather at the mining camp. When they found that they could exchange their labor for trade goods, neophytes found more excuses to absent themselves from missions. The missionaries sternly forbade this — with indifferent results.[86]

There were other problems as well. Although Santa Ana was producing encouraging amounts of ore and even a fair share of refined silver within a year or two of its founding, it also suffered from an acute lack of basic things, from clothing and equipment to food. Manuel de Ocio encountered the same problems that had plagued the Jesuits. In fact, California's great distances, adverse weather, and shortages of water, manpower, shipping, money, supplies, and provisions afflicted everyone who attempted a major California enterprise during the century that followed.

When it became apparent not only that there was an overwhelming need for stores, but that there would be some silver to pay for them, Ocio embarked on an additional career as sole owner and proprietor of a commissary. He knew the territory well; he reprised the system by which he had brought trade goods to corner the market in California pearls. From Antonio Ignacio de Mena in Guadalajara, Ocio bought food, clothing, tools, utensils, and other supplies, had them packed over the mountains to Matanchel, and then used his boats to bring them across the gulf.

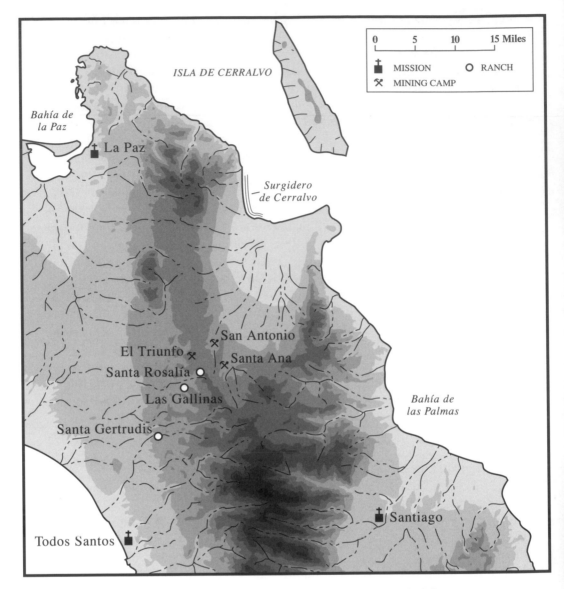

Map 11.2 El Sur, *Cradle of Private Enterprise in California*

Even these stores did not solve all of Santa Ana's problems; goods brought at so much cost and effort were not doled out to just anyone. Ocio operated a company store and advanced food and goods, at very high prices, against the wages of those who were gainfully employed. Soldiers stationed in the South were lured by Ocio's imports, some of which were very tempting when compared to the meager offerings at the presidial warehouse in Loreto. When their credit ran out at Ocio's store, some soldiers went so far as to trade in their precious mounts and firearms.[87]

Mining folk without income or credit were forced to forage or to beg abjectly at missions. Men, women, and children were reduced to rags and asked for some of the fabric the Jesuits imported to clothe their neophytes, but the missionaries were hard pressed to feed and clothe their own. At first they refused to part with food or supplies, and did so reluctantly even when the mineworkers became desperate.

Soon the mining camp placed more burdens on the missionaries. Ocio had not provided a priest for the seat of his mining venture. Since the workers' families had no means by which to travel the many miles to mission church services — and since the missionaries hoped to keep them from mingling with neophytes — the padres went without recompense to Santa Ana to celebrate the Mass and shepherd the leaderless flock. By the time the mining camp had struggled through three or four years, the local missionaries, Francisco María Badillo at Santiago and Carlos Neumayer at Todos Santos, were heartily sick of the relationship. The father visitor, in turn, put all possible pressure on Ocio, personally and through high civil and ecclesiastical leaders, to get a pastor for Santa Ana. The tiny secular community — only about seventy souls living outside Jesuit jurisdiction — threatened to realize the missionaries' worst fears about unsupervised gente de razón.[88] California was finally becoming integrated with the rest of the frontier of northwest New Spain; her small sources of wealth had attracted a diverse civilian population.

Ocio's Push for Power and Favor

By 1751, two of Manuel de Ocio's mines had produced enough silver that they qualified to be registered with the crown — the process that would guarantee his claims. In June of that year, he appeared before Teniente Pedro de la Riva and his witness, Sargento Manuel de la Torre Villavicencio, provided the needed geographic descriptions, and displayed two lots of silver bars, one said to have been produced by amalgamation and the other by smelting. Riva made out the required documents to register the mines as El Triunfo de la Santa Cruz, the first discovered, and San Pedro y San Pablo. Each was located about ten miles from Santa Ana.[89]

The registration of these mines improved Ocio's status and prospects. He now had protected claims to certain lands and mineral rights. His simple camp now qualified as a *real de minas*, a source of mineral wealth that paid a share to the crown, and its owner was given status accordingly. In fact, this esteem may have been somewhat exaggerated because of California's long history of profitless ventures. Ocio was aware of his reputation as the peninsula's first entrepreneur and was determined to push for any advantages that his new status could confer. His needs and desires coincided, and he made his first serious bid to control herds of cattle, grazing land, and permanent water sources.

Santa Ana's lack of a dependable local source of food was a crucial stumbling block. The canny Spaniard was aware that if he owned or controlled land and cattle, he could facilitate the entire operation and make good profits by running a meat market as part of his company store. To that end, Ocio sent hirelings to occupy Santa Rosa, a *sitio* (a place with water and grazing land) in an area the Jesuits had claimed for the use of the recently closed Misión de San José del Cabo. Once the missionaries knew of this attempted takeover, they asserted their claim by protesting to the justicia mayor, Fernando de Rivera. The whole case was a repeat of Capitán Alvarez de Acevedo's attempt to use El Salto a decade earlier.[90] Ocio argued that the mission was defunct and, in any case, that the mission system as a whole was making no use of the sitio. He alluded to the great need of his workers and made pointed references to their present and potential contributions to royal coffers. The missionaries, as usual, claimed that all mission lands were held in trust for their neophytes and that Santa Rosa would be needed for future herds of Misión de Santiago.

Rivera probably recommended in the Jesuits' favor, and in any event the matter was referred to the viceroy for a final decision. In 1753, Virrey Revillagigedo found for the missionaries and forbade Ocio to occupy Santa Rosa, but Don Manuel was undaunted. This was only one of the many confrontations that he would provoke, and the first skirmish in what was to become persistent if bloodless guerrilla warfare over cattle, land, and water.[91] The competition for resources between missionaries and entrepreneurs that was typical in other parts of the northern frontier of New Spain now had arrived in California.

Ocio had planned to press the viceroy on another front even before the unfavorable decision was delivered. By the first days of 1753, he and Antonio Ignacio de Mena were prepared to make a major push to create a profitable monopoly in the development of California resources. One key to increasing their power and their degree of control lay in convincing royal authorities, notably the Audiencia of Guadalajara and the viceroy of New Spain, that California had real potential, and that Ocio had made large and successful efforts at development—at his own expense. In return for their exertions and expenditures, Ocio—and, more covertly, Mena—sought certain concessions that the authorities had the power to bestow.

Ocio's first step was to remind governmental bodies that he was producing silver and paying taxes in California, the perennial quiet rebuke to the Jesuits who had long inferred that California would become an economic asset to the crown, but who had never delivered a peso. Ocio reported the registry of three mines in 1751 and 1752; he also offered proof of having produced over a thousand pounds of silver. More importantly, he showed that on 11 April 1753 he had paid the royal fifth to the treasurer of Guadalajara.[92]

Before making formal overtures to audiencia or viceroy, Ocio orchestrated a prelude designed to call attention to the plight of the honest working men who were trying to eke out a living—and pay taxes—in difficult California. Certain citizens of California "found themselves in Guadalajara" for the Holy Week of 1753. While there, five of them asked to appear before the Licenciado Don Francisco López Portillo, member of the Audiencia of Guadalajara. The visitors petitioned for help in developing the mining industry in California. They asked that the captain of the presidio be required to guard and defend them against "invasions and hostilities of barbarous Indians." The witnesses reported that the Uchití nation had done great harm to the works of their neighbor, Don Manuel de Ocio, killing one of his employees and wounding his mayordomo. They reported that the California captain had ignored repeated requests, even written requests, for assistance. A petition was produced as evidence of the captain's callous inattention.

The message of the pilgrims from California was plain. If the presidio would suppress the Uchití, the miners could proceed with prospecting and producing silver—and thus contribute to the greater good. The petitioners assured the official that the mines would have no harmful effect on the California missions or their converts. All Indian mineworkers would be imported from the main-land, not recruited locally.[93]

Manuel de Ocio was also in Guadalajara, no doubt by design. He used the occasion to petition the bishop to appoint a secular priest to minister to the inhabitants of Santa Ana. The need was reported to be great. There were two hundred souls to be served, and the nearest priest was a missionary over thirty miles away. The Padre Visitador of California had been asked to provide the needed ministrations, but he claimed that he could not spare a padre. Ocio proposed an ordained priest for the post, one Bachiller Don Mateo Adolfo Falembock, German by birth, but a resident of the bishopric of Guadalajara. The bishop agreed to the proposal, specifying that Ocio be responsible for the priest's pay of six hundred pesos a year. To that end, the bishop asked for surety in the form of a note on Ocio's "fourteen houses located in this city and worth more than 11,000 pesos." Don Manuel signed his agreement, and Antonio Ignacio de Mena witnessed his signature.[94]

Ocio, as might be imagined, was not primarily concerned with the spiritual welfare of his employees and their dependents. His and Mena's first major goal was the elevation of Santa Ana, Ocio's seat of power, from the status of *real de minas* to that of *villa* (a royally chartered frontier settlement). Villa status would offer more rights and privileges, such as a degree of self-government and a permanent justicia mayor. Ocio, as the virtual owner and operator of Santa Ana, would thus be in a position to have greater powers conferred on him and to exercise other rights de facto. A villa was required to have a priest in residence and a suitable building dedicated and decorated as a church, hence Ocio's interplay with the bishop.

The Bishopric of Guadalajara had a little self-interest in the matter as well. Technically, California and Sonora fell into its allotted area of religious juris-diction. In fact, those areas had always been administered by Jesuits, and the missionary order did not report to or derive its powers from any regional bishop. If a secular priest were installed in the area, however, he would fall under Guadalajara's control. To extend his influence as much as possible, the bishop appointed Falembock not only as curate to Santa Ana, but also as *capellán de canales adentro*, chaplain of the entire Gulf of California.[95] This would give substance to Guadalajara's claim to spiritual sovereignty over the waters, the islands, and any ports or enclaves that the missions could not legitimately include in their territories.

Having laid the groundwork as best he could, Manuel de Ocio then had petitions placed before the viceroy. He asked to have Santa Ana made a villa. He claimed that the place had more than two hundred families, a grossly exaggerated figure. He represented it as having good soil, a benign climate, fodder for cattle, brush and trees for firewood, materials for construction, good water to drink and with which to irrigate crops, good access by sea and land, and now, by order of the bishop, a priest. Anyone familiar with Santa Ana's subsequent history, or the place as it is today, would be hard pressed to recognize it from that description. The wily promoter did not fail to note one important missing element in his utopia: "a person to exercise civil and criminal jurisdiction. . . ." Don Manuel did not name himself as a candidate, but the suggestion lingers over his petition.

By some unrecorded means, probably Jesuit friends in high places, Fernando de Rivera was apprised of Ocio's doings. On 9 July 1753, the captain penned a report to the viceroy on the status of California affairs. The natives were at peace, he wrote, due to the effects of their conversions, baptism, and benign mission life. However, his own service to the crown and that of his men was threatened by an insidious and disruptive influence. Manuel de Ocio had placed his own desires ahead of the welfare of the king's representatives. Ocio had many soldiers in his power because he imported goods on his boats and sold them on credit at excessive interest rates. Ocio was exploiting this advantage. Since he required horses and mules for work in the mines and reduction mills, he was inducing soldiers to sell mounts that were essential to their military duties. The captain had to prohibit these sales and punish offenders. In general, the purchasing power of Ocio and his workers had left the troops and missionaries with many shortages, but particularly of riding and pack animals. That problem was more than usually difficult to overcome since the ship in the missions' service, that of His Majesty, lacked the capacity to transport livestock.

Manuel de Ocio had the wits to turn some of this criticism to his advantage. For five years, he had been asking for viceregal permission to build and operate a "covered ship", that is, a ship large enough to make long voyages and carry large cargoes. Now he asked the viceroy for the right to buy horses, mules, and supplies freely in California. The welfare of his mines and mineworkers would depend on it *while he, Manuel de Ocio, awaited his license for the larger ship.* Parenthetically, Ocio noted that such a ship would be a valuable addition to the support and defense of the peninsula "against enemy invasions."[96]

Virrey Revillagigedo considered all the requests, claims, and counter-claims. On October 26, 1753, he issued a decree that further illustrated his celebrated wisdom and diplomacy. Capitán Rivera was ordered to sell to, assist, and protect Ocio—in short, to further the development of his ventures in all the ways asked by the miner. At the same time, however, the captain governor was to order all things in such a way that the interests of the missions and the presidio came first and were not compromised. It was indeed a Solomonic decision.

Meanwhile, Ocio was not turned away. He was empowered to build his large ship and small ones as well, but he was ordered to trade with recognized merchants of the area ruled by the Audiencia of Guadalajara; he was specifically forbidden to traffic with Acapulco. Revillagigedo underscored this warning to Ocio in a way that transparently demonstrated his understanding of Ocio and his breed. The viceroy appended a directive to the governor and other officials of the Port of Acapulco. The king's employees were ordered to keep a sharp lookout for any sign or appearance of the aforesaid Don Manuel de Ocio in Acapulco. If Ocio were to appear, they were to take the strongest measures to curb his activities and to notify the viceroy immediately.[97]

Opportunities and Limitations for Manuel de Ocio

By his carefully considered responses to all the various California petitions of the early 1750s, Virrey Revillagigedo defined and delimited the rights of those who contested for power and opportunity. He declared no clear-cut winners or losers, nor did he banish any parties or interests. Rather, he maintained order while giving official recognition to an uneasy coexistence that persisted during California's remaining Jesuit years. The viceroy reiterated the crown's long-standing, traditional support for the missions as its prime force and first consideration. He gave his blessing to the practice, if not the concept, of a presidial force selected and guided by missionaries. At the same time, Revillagigedo represented his monarch's keen interest in stimulating commerce and tax revenues. The viceroy was careful to regulate but not to discourage or eliminate private enterprise in California. He recognized Manuel de Ocio's mining claims and his roles as miner, merchant, pearler, and collector of the real quinto on pearls.

The Jesuits must have been pleased when the viceroy saw through Ocio's misrepresentations during the premature attempt to have tiny, poor Santa Ana raised to the status of a villa; with his rejection, the viceroy ended Ocio's dream of wielding legal power in his miniature bailiwick. However, Revillagigedo's rejection was notably restrained. He did not upbraid Ocio for his attempts to mislead; he merely restated the stringent—and unmet—requirements for villa status, and let the matter rest. Moreover, the viceroy encouraged Ocio, and entrepreneurial interest in general, by allowing private, California-based ships to ply gulf waters, and private, California-based people to trade both with the local missions and with duly licensed mainland merchants.

Despite his continued support for the California mission cause, and his endorsement of some of the Jesuits' traditional perquisites, the viceroy had significantly narrowed their authority. Salvatierra and Kino's plan to isolate the peninsula from commerce had resisted attack for half a century. Now private enterprise was openly recognized and made part of the official scheme for California.

Ocio's Tactics for Ranging his Cattle

Manuel de Ocio was energetic and tenacious. Although each new phase of his private career was opposed in some way by the entrenched missionaries, Ocio initiated and maintained an astonishing array of endeavors. Padre Jacobo Baegert, who had an eye for temporal affairs, paid grudging tribute to the man's industry. He wrote of Ocio:

> . . . his wealth is derived more from pearl fishing, his butcher shop, his general store, and his unbelievable thrift than from his mine. He alone sells all the meat to his fellow miners and their helpers, and also all the cloth, linen, tobacco, rags, and so on, which they and their families wear and which they use to pay their workers. He is the only man who is in a position to buy merchandise and bring it from Guadalajara over land and sea; also he was the first to take possession of the land over which his cows were grazing.[98]

Baegert's last remark indicates the direction that Ocio's ambitions had taken by the start of the 1760s. Pearling was seasonal, and, by then, mining prospects had dwindled.[99] Ocio adapted. Without abandoning his other ventures, he strove to augment his wealth and status by building great herds—a tangible, growing form of wealth. Ranching equated with traditional Iberian conceptions of success, so it should have been no surprise that a Spaniard reached out for land and cattle. In Spain, possession of land was synonymous with petty gentility; range animals were regarded as a particularly estimable form of property.[100] Cattle ranching was also a logical extension of Ocio's other activities. Miners and their families needed meat, fat, and leather, and—a most important point—they produced silver with which to pay for their needs. The miner-rancher had long been a fixture in mineral-rich parts of northwest New Spain.[101]

Ocio began to buy cattle around the time he established Santa Ana. Depositions made years later reveal that he purchased Rancho Santa Rosalía and its herds from the owners, his brothers-in-law Simón Rodríguez and Pedro de la Riva, and Riva's sons.[102] Reports of this acquisition, made by several parties, prove that, in addition to Esteban Rodríguez, other active and retired soldiers did own cattle and private ranches in the South—a fact never mentioned in Jesuit reports.[103] In the early days of his mining career, Ocio also sent his cowhands out to pursue wild cattle, descendants of strays from mission herds and, as he always contended, from the herds of his father-in-law.[104]

However, there was little California land that money could buy. When Pedro de la Riva received royal confirmation of his lieutenancy and was put in charge of the escuadra del Sur, the Jesuits apparently did not contest his right to award small grants of land to a few soldiers. However, the basic Jesuit position stated that all California land belonged to the neophytes and that the missionary order guarded and conserved it in trust for their converts' futures. Ocio could counter these claims only by invoking old Spanish laws that provided inducements and rights to colonists. These were the grounds on which he had attempted to justify the seizure of Rancho Santa Rosa in 1751, the petition that was rejected by the viceroy.[105]

Ocio was too persistent to be dissuaded by one adverse decision. The council chambers of Mexico City may have been familiar ground to the Jesuits and their supporters, but Ocio had an advantage when the arena became unoccupied land in California. He devised a hit-and-run campaign based on the concept of squatters' rights; he simply occupied any desirable land that was not grazed, cultivated, or patrolled by mission personnel.

Ocio sent his vaqueros, with cattle, into the greater area bounded by La Paz, Todos Santos, and Santiago. They would make a base camp at a *paraje* and, before long, the nearest missionary would hear of the occupation and protest. Ocio would press his arguments: the land was not in use, and his miners needed food. The padres could not go to war; they could only appeal to California's justicia mayor, Fernando de Rivera. Rivera would conduct hearings and make decisions, usually in favor of the missionaries. By the time a particular case had been argued, Ocio's men and cattle might have occupied one or more other sites, and the wrangling would continue.[106]

Land and water were but the means to an end. Ocio sought great herds of cattle; an obvious step in that direction was to round up the numerous maverick descendants of the animals dispersed and lost during the rebellion years. In Santa Ana's early days, Ocio occasionally sent his employees out to slaughter a few wild cattle, but during 1753 and 1754, he ordered many of these round-ups on the deserted hills and plains west and southwest of Santa Ana.[107] Padre Carlos Neumayer protested Ocio's activities, claiming that the wild herds were the property of Misión de Todos Santos. Ocio, as usual, responded that he and others had rights to parcels of land in that area and that the cattle in question were fair game since they were unbranded and running wild on land not worked by the mission.

Lengthy hearings over this argument dragged on for months and appear to have ended inconclusively. The Jesuits produced records to show that they owned the rights to all wild cattle. Rivera upheld that claim, but did not find that the missions held rights to all unused grazing land. Padre Neumayer proposed a negotiated settlement that would have allowed Ocio to slaughter wild cattle profitably and still make payments to the mission. Ocio demurred, and his own uncompromising counterproposals were not acceptable to Neumayer.[108]

There the hearings ended, but part of the aftermath is revealed by later documents. In the following decade, active and retired soldiers received a total of about ten grants of land located either in the area just north of ex-mission San José del Cabo, or to the north and east of Misión de Todos Santos.[109] Later depositions show that a compromise was worked out regarding wild cattle. Sworn statements show that Ocio's vaqueros went out with their counterparts from the mission, took unbranded cattle, and paid the mission a fee in silver. Two of Ocio's former employees incidentally related that their master had never slaughtered from his own herds when it was possible to take wild cattle and pay the mission.[110] Common sense and many Jesuit complaints suggest that when Ocio's men found wild cattle on lands far from missions and unpatrolled by mission vaqueros, they were taken without permission or payment.

Missionaries in *el Sur* inferred that Ocio was little concerned with the plight of the people he had brought and virtually stranded in California and that he was content to let neighboring missions provide for them in times of need. Hungry mineworkers and their families certainly did go to missions for relief, but their final resort seems to have been Ocio's cattle, or the wild cattle that his round-ups brought to camp. No one tells us how, or if, Ocio was compensated, but several accounts of Santa Ana's second decade report that beef was the staple diet and that some had no other sustenance, not a scrap of bread nor fruit nor vegetable. As mentioned previously, the predominance of meat in the peninsular diet persisted for a long time and elicited comments from many visitors.[111]

Ocio's Plans for his Son and Heir

By the 1760s, Antonio de Ocio, Don Manuel's only surviving child, was an adolescent, old enough to take an interest in his father's affairs and to show signs of becoming a working heir. His potential probably contributed to his father's continued enthusiasm for new activities, honors, and recognition. Too, there was a marriage to be arranged. Don Manuel's long-time associate, Antonio Ignacio de Mena, had an eligible daughter, but the Mena family was well connected and prosperous. Young Antonio would need wealth and prospects to be welcome among the elite of Guadalajara.

Manuel de Ocio, no doubt prompted by Mena, endeavored to enhance his family prestige and coffers. Each bishopric collected its *diezmos* or tithes, a levy of ten percent on all "fruits of the earth," the products of agricultural and animal husbandry, in its own district. Direct collection was impractical, however, when dealing with distant, lightly populated areas. As the crown, in similar conditions, auctioned the rights to the real quinto, so the bishop could offer the collection of tithes to the highest bidder. In 1762, Ocio purchased California's tithes from the Bishop of Guadalajara.[112] Ocio did not envision another fortune made by collecting the church's rights from California's humble gente de razón. Only the missions had significant crops or killed substantial numbers of cattle, and at that moment, missions were exempt from tithes. However, secular church groups in New Spain were pressing law suits to force the Jesuits to pay at least something on their produce. Ocio had reason to believe that if the Jesuits lost these suits, he would be ideally situated to profit from the change. In any case, his purchase of the California tithes, even as a largely symbolic gesture, established him as a personage of some importance in the powerful bishopric and assured him of a stake in the peninsula's future civil development. In the meantime, these arrangements made him known to more important people in Guadalajara, some of whom were opponents of the Jesuits and possible allies in his ongoing efforts to open California to further economic development.

Antonio de Ocio and the business of his marriage raised Padre Baegert's sardonic pen. Antonio, he wrote, "was born and raised in California and received his cavalier-like training and education among his father's cowherds until his marriage to a highly respected person. . . ." Baegert demeaned the alliance with short strokes, saying that Manuel de Ocio "bought a wife in Guadalajara for his only son and heir for twenty thousand guilders."[113] Quite apart from Baegert's intention to deprecate all that was California, it is likely that he failed to appreciate the connection between the right kinship and social and financial success in New Spain. Ocio was not simply showing off wealth, he was opening an important door for his son.

By 5 June 1767, Antonio was wedded to Doña Manuela de Mena, daughter of Teniente Coronel of the Militia Don Antonio Ignacio de Mena and his wife, Doña Josefa Sánchez Calderón. As part of the marriage agreement, Antonio went before a notary and made out a paper acknowledging his obligation to pay a dowry amounting to the tenth part of the family fortune to which he was the sole heir. Providentially, this document lists the Ocio family assets and appraises their total worth.[114] Since the young man was yet a minor, his father guaranteed the dowry payment. To make this binding, Manuel de Ocio had given the elder Mena letters acknowledging the obligation and deeds to some of his Guadalajara property as well. The dowry sum was fixed at six thousand pesos, which placed the Ocio estate at sixty thousand. Don Manuel had succeeded in securing a prestigious union, but he had paid a substantial price. This becomes especially apparent when comparisons are made with other marriages among Guadalajara's elite; most dowries were paid to the grooms.[115]

The list of Ocio's assets contains few details and no surprises; nevertheless, it does come from a time when the aging entrepreneur's holdings were near their peak. Most interesting is the figure given for cattle holdings: sixteen thousand head, including horses and mules. Beyond that, there was an hacienda for extracting silver by both methods, and with it a general merchandise store and outbuildings for workers. These structures formed the heart of the Real de Santa Ana. Also listed were no fewer than seven boats and ships: Ocio's supply craft and pearling canoas. Finally, there was an unspecified number of houses in Guadalajara, one of which was occupied by Antonio and his bride.[116] If all this really was worth sixty thousand pesos, Don Manuel had amassed an estate ranked among Guadalajara's two or three hundred largest fortunes, though nearer to the middle of that group than to the top.[117]

Other Soldiers Turn to Business

In the 1750s, the population of Loreto included about two hundred and fifty gente de razón, all direct or indirect dependents of the mission system. Sons of long-time presidial employees had preference when openings appeared on the payroll. Naturally, priorities began at the top. Eight of Esteban Rodríguez's grandsons remained in California and took employment as soldiers despite the fact that their fathers had died or retired to the mainland.[118] Loreto needed the services of more than soldiers, sailors, and the artisans of the marinería. Gradually, retirees from the presidio and men from presidial families found informal employment as tailors, barbers, or cobblers, or in exercising other necessary skills. The missionaries controlled these occupations by vigilantly supervising the prices that were charged. There is no evidence that they allowed their employees or their families to occupy private land, even as squatters, or to engage in such forbidden commerce as moonshining or dealing directly with pearlers.

Things were different in the South. Manuel de Ocio had showed the way to step out of the Jesuit camp and into private enterprise. Increasingly, men who ended mission service either joined Ocio or struck out on their own. Many had sons, and the mission system could find places for few. The remainder had to leave the land of their birth to compete abroad or find something to do in California outside mission walls. With increasing opportunity, more retirees and young people stayed in California — some to work for others, some to occupy unused land and become de facto ranchers.

These newly independent folk were quick to capitalize on any useful product of the land. Hunting the peninsular mule deer had been a pre-historic occupation, and one continued in mission times. Padre Baegert estimated that his neophytes at Misión de San Luis Gonzaga killed over five hundred deer a year.[119] The same pursuit became a preoccupation of soldiers shortly after the conquest. Now, private individuals began to hunt assiduously, not just for the valued meat, but for the hides. These were expertly tanned, using solutions derived from native trees and shrubs, to create gamuza, the light, pliant garment leather that had become a prized item of commerce. Gamuzas could be traded profitably — if illegally — to men on the Manila galleon or exported to the mainland.[120] No doubt, such endeavors by people who had struck out on their own, were closely watched and provided much grist for the popular gossip mills in all corners of the land. Only a few, however, created businesses that generated paperwork and thus left records.

Gaspar Pisón y Guzmán

The first man who came near to emulating Manuel de Ocio was Gaspar Pisón y Guzmán, a young Spaniard from Andalucía — by chance, Ocio's home province as well. Pisón was born about 1724 in Alcalá de Guadaira, a small town ten miles east of Sevilla.[121] By 1745, he was in Tepic and married to Rosa Francisca de Acevedo, a native of that region. There, in January 1746, she bore a daughter. By then Don Gaspar was in California, serving as a soldier.[122]

In 1747, Pisón was released from the presidio of Loreto. According to his later testimony, he became a resident of Santa Ana in the very year that it was founded, so he must have been one of Ocio's pioneer assistants in opening the mines and mills.[123] The young *andaluz* had some education; he wrote a good hand and expressed himself easily in writing. His duties at Santa Ana are easy to imagine. Plainly, Don Manuel needed to carry on some correspondence and to keep account books, yet, although he could sign his name with a flourish, no documents in his hand are known to exist. Furthermore, Pisón, or someone like him, must have supervised the California operations while Ocio was off pearling or making his months-long trips to Guadalajara. Another possible assistant was Ocio's brother-in-law, Simón Rodríguez, who also resigned from the presidio around 1747.[124]

In 1756, Pisón opened a new mine, called Santa Gertrudis, some ten miles north of Santa Ana.[125] Since the mine's environs were scarcely habitable, a camp was set up on a nearby hillside at an elevation of 1,300 feet and next to a permanent spring called San Antonio. The camp's founder was Simón Rodríguez, who may also have had an interest in the mine.[126] The *real de minas de San Antonio* thus became the peninsula's second non-mission pueblo and, since Santa Ana was abandoned in a few decades, San Antonio stands today as the oldest continuously occupied civil community in all the Californias.

In 1764, Manuel de Ocio apparently chose not to reapply as collector of the quinto on pearls. By then, Pisón also was in the business and obtained the license. Pearling returns had diminished drastically, but Pisón is reported to have made a profit and pursued the business as long as he was able.[127]

Gaspar Pisón's private life in California was something of a scandal. He kept his wife, a son, and a daughter in Tepic and saw them only when he went to the mainland for supplies or to sell pearls or silver. Meanwhile, by common report, he kept company with mineworkers' wives and drank a great deal, some of his bouts lasting for a week or more. Worse, Pisón lost control of his tongue when in his cups. Then, by all accounts, he would blaspheme all the holies from God downward, and defame or vilify anyone who raised his ire. On one occasion, he had the bad judgment to get intoxicated in staid Loreto. His performance so outraged the people that he was brought before Fernando de Rivera, and the justicia mayor sentenced him to several days of hard labor. When he was released, two soldiers escorted him to his boat and waited until his crew set sail and scudded off. When he was sober, Pisón seems to have been a good-natured, kind-hearted man, and, in the main, his neighbors forgave his weaknesses.[128]

Simón Rodríguez and the Real de San Antonio

From all evidence, Simón Rodríguez was a frustrated, ineffectual man. Despite the advantage of his family's good name and three hard-working and successful brothers-in-law, bachelor Simón produced little to mark the passage of his life. He joined with one brother-in-law, Pedro de la Riva, and his sons in the ownership and perhaps the operation of the cattle ranch, Santa Rosalía, which they eventually sold to Ocio.[129] Perhaps this sale provided Don Simón with the funds to develop San Antonio. Rodríguez's first anecdotal entry in California letters was occasioned by his intemperate attack on Capitán Fernando de Rivera over an inheritance.[130] Elsewhere, Padre Jacobo Baegert disparaged him as a failed but grandiose buffoon:

> [Simón Rodríguez] became so rich digging for silver that he begged for money to pay his passage to Spain, so he could, as was rumored, apply at the Court of Madrid for a pension, because he was an offspring of the first Spanish-California captain. It is certain that he brought to Madrid neither six pennies nor a Spanish real from his California silver mine.[131]

Simón's new mining community at San Antonio added another burden on the overworked padres at Santiago and Todos Santos, who now had to minister to yet another distant flock. Only a few months before, they had been forced to resume the heavy burden of riding more than twenty miles to conduct services at Santa Ana. In late 1753, Ocio installed his chosen curate, Don Mateo Adolfo Falembock, at the mining camp. Falembock served there for over two years. By 1755, he had become involved in difficulties over runaways from Misión de Todos Santos, but he had returned them to the mission and was on good terms with Padre Carlos Neumayer, the missionary. He had also registered some alleged complaints of neophytes against "the captain and soldiers who led detachments," charges that sound suspiciously like echoes from the curate's employer, Manuel de Ocio.[132] However, neither Ocio nor Falembock was happy with the religious arrangements at Santa Ana; by 1756, the discontented curate fled from the lonely camp, and Santa Ana's spiritual chores reverted to the unwilling missionaries.[133]

The missionaries did, however, find one small solace in the Santa Ana situation. Despite all his rancorous differences with the Jesuits, Ocio opened his house with bed and board whenever a padre came to offer religious services. Padre Miguel del Barco was fair-minded enough to recall this hospitality and added that Ocio spread a good table. At San Antonio, however, there was no such recompense. In addition to the long ride and the unpaid service, the padre had to bring his own food and anything else that he and a helper or two might need during their stay.[134] Padre Francisco María Badillo at Misión de Santiago made a great issue of these and other difficulties. In 1759, he was transferred to the Jesuit mission at Carichí in the Tarahumara. A Jesuit chronicler says that he left the peninsula after bitter disputes with mineowners.[135]

Juan Nicolás and José María de Estrada

Juan Nicolás de Estrada was the soldier who was imprisoned and coerced to give testimony during the 1747 attempt by Dutch traders to deal with Spanish officials. Estrada first appeared on the presidio's rolls in 1733 as an unmarried soldier drawing full pay.[136] Within a few years, he had married Juana Morillo, and their eldest child, José María, was born at San José del Cabo in 1743.[137] A daughter, María Teresa, followed, and then a son, José Bonifacio, who was born in 1750 at the cape mission.[138]

Juan Nicolás de Estrada indicated his literacy by witnessing several legal documents.[139] His sons were well educated, although there is no clue as to how this was arranged. Records show that Estrada served in the South at least until late 1754.[140] Estrada's next documentary appearance sheds some light on his activities after retirement from the presidio. In June 1761, he stood before a notary in Guadalajara and signed a paper that read, in part: "Juan Nicolás de Estrada, miner on the California peninsula in the Real de San Antonio, agrees to pay Don Antonio Ignacio de Mena 560 pesos for trade goods. . . ." Payment was specified to be in plata de azogue at seven pesos for each *marco* (half-pound), and paid by May of the following year.[141] Estrada met his commitment. In May 1762, he and his elder son, José María, aged nineteen, were back in Guadalajara. This time, Juan Nicolás obtained 840 pesos worth of merchandise from Mena, loaded up, and then headed toward Matanchel for the return voyage.[142] At the Hacienda de San Leonel, a way station on the road, the senior Estrada died from an unspecified malady.

José María de Estrada demonstrated his character and his sense of responsibility. He turned around and went back to Guadalajara. He convinced Mena that he could carry out his father's contract. A new agreement was drawn up and signed. There, for the first time, appears the elegant signature from a hand destined to generate hundreds of documents and keep Loreto's account books for two decades.[143] The next notarial entry involving the young Estrada suggests that he was succeeding in business and perhaps that he was shrewd enough to shop around for his needs. In 1764, he was back in Guadalajara and purchased 963 pesos worth of trade goods, this time from Don Marcos Mendoza.[144] In 1765, he sold a sailing launch to the presidio of Loreto for one thousand pesos.[145] A noteworthy career was under way.

The Bitter End of an Old Feud

In June 1766, Fernando de Rivera and Manuel de Ocio were engaged in a familiar proceeding. Ocio was suing the mission community of Todos Santos over the usual matters: the rights to take wild cattle and to use certain lands. He charged that vaqueros from Todos Santos, in running the mission's herds, encroached on ranch sites that he was using and to which he had just claims. He also charged that servants of the mission had driven off or slaughtered some of his cattle. In his opening petition, Ocio made pointed reference to the years of adverse decisions that he had suffered from the justicia mayor. He detailed his great labors and the costs he had incurred for "the public good." He issued almost a challenge to Rivera to bring forth another pro-missionary finding, saying that if justice could not be had in Jesuit California, his just cause would be placed before the king!

The hearings went on for days, and a parade of witnesses was called. The questions and answers make plain that Ocio had no new claims and no new proofs of injury. His real audience or court of appeal was far away in New Spain. The veteran entrepreneur's rhetoric seems less designed to convince the immediate justicia mayor than to catch the ears of a royal tax collector, a bishop's treasurer, or any official interested in colonial expansion. In any event, Rivera ignored the larger issues over which he had no jurisdiction. He found little merit in Don Manuel's claims and handed down a decision which, among other things, denied the plaintiff exclusive rights to certain lands or to the unbranded cattle roaming on them.

Several aspects of this judicial process portend subsequent events. Ocio accused Rivera of malice, saying that when Todos Santos had a mayordomo named Estanislao Sotelo, Ocio's cattle were left alone and his lands were not invaded. He complained that Rivera had hired Sotelo away to be a soldier and, under subsequent mayordomos, Ocio's cattle and rights were abused. During the hearings, Don Manuel also delivered a great broadside in which he called Rivera a tool of the missionaries. The rancher bluntly proclaimed that he loved his king—and created tax money for him—whereas Rivera loved only the reverend fathers. Surely this accusation was meant for distant ears. Rivera responded by instructing Ocio to moderate his rhetoric and not address the king's representative as he would one of his laborers. When Ocio was absent from one hearing, José Francisco de Ortega appeared before Rivera armed with Ocio's power of attorney. Ortega proceeded to plead Ocio's case as forcefully as if he were the old soldier himself.[146] The encounter foreshadowed a time when Rivera and Ortega would be associates but not always allies in the dramatic opening of Alta California.

Shortly after Ocio's disappointment with the results of this suit, a series of cruelly conceived charges against California Jesuits was presented to the court at Madrid and then forwarded to the viceroy in Mexico City. As soon as the Jesuits were able to make a copy, it was sent to the peninsula to inform the accused missionaries. The charges, as received by Padre Visitador Lamberto Hostell, were these:

First: that the soldiers are paid only in merchandise and that at excessive prices ordered by the padres.

Second: that the Señor Capitán does not actually command the troops and that the padres fill all vacancies, hiring and firing at their arbitrary wish—on which account the soldiers do only the fathers' bidding.

Third: that the padres hinder work at the mines, that they obtain the silver which is taken out because the miners have to buy corn and other supplies necessary for their existence from the missions at excessive prices, etc.

Fourth: that the padres secretly work mines on their own account.

Fifth: that with the silver thus obtained, the padres engage in commerce with Manila galleons and with Dutch ships which are accustomed to arrive on these coasts.[147]

Sixth: that the Indians work hard for the padres' benefit and are paid only with cooked corn.

Seventh: that the padres prevent the entrance of españoles to the missions because they wish to keep the Indians in ignorance of the fact that they have a king and so that they will continue to believe that they have no superiors other than the missionaries themselves.[148]

It is difficult to imagine that these charges did not originate with Manuel de Ocio. Some of his banking or business associates in Guadalajara may have passed a list of the miner-rancher's fuming complaints to a highly placed Jesuit enemy, perhaps the Bishop of Puebla. The accusations certainly betray a knowledge of California's circumstances, even when represented in such a distorted fashion, but they also suggest a familiarity with old slanders against the Jesuits that had long circulated and gained some acceptance in the outside world. In this, the missionaries paid a price for their treasured isolation. In all of California's colonial years, no official of the central government had ever visited;[149] no impartial observer could now be called to testify for the defense. Anyone who knew California would have seen through most of these charges at once, but those few were Jesuits or Jesuit employees — suspect witnesses — or a handful of miners or pearlers inclined to side with Ocio. The irony of this situation must have come home forcefully to the frustrated Jesuits.

At about the same time that these charges first circulated, Padre Procurador Armesto was having more than the usual difficulty in getting the royal funds nominally assigned to support the presidio at Loreto. Soldiers' salaries were draining his California accounts.[150] Jesuit leaders in New Spain decided to take an extreme position in order to discredit their detractors' claims. California missionaries had long been discouraged by the prospects for the remaining southerly missions, Santiago and Todos Santos, with their declining populations. These same missions were considered to have the best agricultural futures and were most coveted by their near neighbors, Manuel de Ocio and California's other entrepreneurs and landholders. Therefore, the Jesuits sent the viceroy a letter in which they offered to renounce their claim to these two missions. To make the offer more impressive, they made the further sweeping suggestion that they would renounce all their California missions if called upon to do so by the king's representatives.[151] The Jesuits also renewed old offers to undertake the opening of new missions north of their latest, Misión de Santa María.

In California, Padre Visitador Lamberto Hostell asked some old-timers on the presidial rolls to reply directly to the charges made against him and his brother Jesuits. Beside Capitán Rivera, Teniente Don Blas Fernández de Somera and five soldiers were asked to comment on the allegations while under oath. Four of the five soldiers — Miguel Cordero, Raymundo Carrillo, Juan Luis de Osuna, and Felipe Romero — were noncommittal in their testimony, as if they somehow knew that a great controversy was at hand and wished to avoid taking a strong stand. Only Don José de Robles spoke out boldly and denied all the charges. Teniente Fernández de Somera penned an explicit and forceful rebuttal to each allegation, using such ringing phrases as, "[such-and-such a charge] is as false as the soul of Judas," but it remained for Rivera to sum up for the defense. His painstaking and lengthy, point-by-point refutation went far beyond mere testimony and became a testimonial. The charges were turned around and made into bouquets (if neophytes are asked to work, it is only just, for the padre works and sacrifices many times as much for them). In peroration, Rivera announced himself indignant at all the charges, called them insults to religion, and engaged in a final tribute to the entire Jesuit effort.[152] These depositions were collected and sent to Mexico City and Spain along with the offers to renounce all or part of the California missions.

The entire episode had an ironic twist, and no one was to suffer from it more than Fernando de Rivera y Moncada. By the time the rebuttal was received in Mexico City and Madrid, the expulsion of the Jesuits had been decided upon. The opinions of Rivera and his mates could scarcely have been welcome. Moreover, Lamberto Hostell's choice of witnesses would have proved unconvincing even had the Jesuits received a fair hearing. Rivera was an interested party in that he owed his post to Jesuit influence and was one of those belittled by the accusations. Blas Fernández's testimony could easily have been called biased since his older brother, Miguel Fernández de Somera, was a Jesuit missionary in Sonora — one of the many, as it happened, who would die as a result of abuses during the expulsion. Furthermore, a simple inquiry would have showed that Don José de Robles, the soldier who denied all the charges, was a grandson of Esteban Rodríguez, the original pro-Jesuit captain.

The only significant result of this ill-timed defense was to arm high officials, including those who would soon come to California to expel the Jesuits, with documentary proof of Fernando de Rivera's loyalty to the very cause that was now anathema. He deserved a better introduction to his new superiors.

TWELVE

The Expulsion

The Work of José de Gálvez

In 1759, Carlos, king of Naples and Sicily and a son of Felipe V's second marriage, inherited the crown of Spain as Carlos III. He was forty-three years old, ambitious, and experienced. He knew that power required money, and he planned to reshape the government of his new domain to increase its efficiency and stimulate its commerce. Don Carlos busily asserted the ideas and administrative talents that were to make him the most effective of Spain's Bourbon rulers. Within four years, he had initiated a significant reorganization and was actively planning to extend his governmental reforms and economic policies to the colonies. In short order, waves of the royal will crossed oceans and began to be felt in all colonial areas. Eventually, California was affected more than most.

The king planned to install a visitor-general as his instrument in each major overseas region. Each of these appointees would represent the crown and temporarily outrank the local viceroy and audiencia. Service in the New World, however, was distasteful to many able and highborn Spanish officials. The first man chosen to serve as the king's visitor to New Spain managed to sidestep the appointment; the second had to be threatened with imprisonment and fines before he grudgingly put to sea. This man, Francisco Anselmo de Armona, managed to avoid the unwelcome chore by dying before making landfall in America.[1] In haste, a third choice was made: José de Gálvez, an Andalucian petty nobleman of modest means who recently had been appointed to a municipal judgeship in Madrid. Gálvez seized the opportunity provided by the visitorship and parlayed it into an active and controversial career.

José de Gálvez arrived in New Spain in mid-1765. Because of his hurried appointment, he was asked to employ as many as possible of the assistants who had sailed with his predecessor. These included Matías de Armona, brother of the deceased visitor.[2] Armona was involved in many of Gálvez's operations in New Spain, including those in California.

Visitador General Gálvez had a remarkable penchant for creating grand-scale plans, working them out in minute detail, and using his great authority to get them launched. His activities in New Spain were legion. Gálvez planned to introduce new taxes and new governmental bodies to collect them. He instituted royal monopolies on tobacco, salt, gunpowder, and playing cards. Gálvez also intended to revitalize flagging efforts to collect the *tributo*, an annual payment of money or goods theoretically owed to the crown by all free men.[3] New Spain, like Spain's other New World colonies, had a large, restive lower class of Indian or mixed blood. These people were wretchedly poor; many were unemployed, and most had little opportunity in the Spanish system. Rulers and privileged citizens saw them as a perpetual threat, a barely restrained mob with the potential for armed revolt. It was they who would bear the heaviest burden of José de Gálvez's fund raising, and he anticipated enforcement problems. In addition to his own reforms, the visitor had been instructed to assist the viceroy in strengthening the imperial defenses. To prepare for an uprising, Gálvez ordered the conscription of local militias and arranged that they be supported by local levies.[4] He must have realized, however, that this created yet another economic burden that would incite resistance.

For a year, Gálvez studied the society and economy of New Spain and made plans. The Marqués de Cruillas, viceroy at the time, resented the intrusion of the king's visitor and questioned various aspects of his power. He stalled most matters while awaiting answers to inquiries he had sent to Spain. Cruillas received one direct imperial reply. He was relieved of his post and replaced by Carlos Francisco de Croix, the Marqués de Croix.[5] This changeover reflected the confidence that king and council had in Gálvez; Croix was a trusted Bourbon retainer appointed specifically to work with the visitor and to give him free rein to institute his reforms. As the summer of 1767 approached, the visitor prepared to install his new governing bodies, taxes, and conscription. Just then, the viceroy received a secret royal command that added a formidable task to the list of reforms. Carlos III ordered the governors of all areas claimed by Spain to arrest all Jesuits and send them to the mother country. Their lands and other properties were to be confiscated and held for the crown.

This coup promised to be profoundly unpopular. Jesuits still wielded great influence as confessors and as teachers and were held in the highest esteem by most of the upper class, Spanish and creole. Moreover, through their charities and their missions, Jesuits had the support of the same humble folk who would bear the brunt of the impositions soon to be instituted in the name of the crown. Virrey Croix was faced with the task of tearing apart the society he governed—and of doing so suddenly, under terms that precluded diplomacy.

The stark demands of the royal order must have been shocking, though no high Spanish official could have been completely surprised by the decision. The prospect of a Jesuit expulsion must have been discussed privately in government circles for several years. In 1759, the year Carlos III ascended the throne, an anti-Jesuit chief minister of Portugal had successfully uprooted the entire Jesuit organization in that country and confiscated the order's wealth for the crown. France was involved in a long court procedure that was leading toward an end to Jesuit influence in that country. In many ways, the Society of Jesus was the victim of its own success. Its positive public image and popular respect were offset by a growing legion of detractors. The Society exceeded other Catholic orders in wealth and influence. Hence it wielded the greatest power and was best able to create or seize opportunity. Jesuit landholdings, agriculture, and industry paid less tax and little or no tithes compared to private competitors. The Jesuits had many opponents among businessmen and the secular clergy — who in the Spanish world were members of the same upper class and came from the same influential families. On various frontiers — Sonora has been cited as an example — Jesuit missionaries dominated most of the available labor force and protected it from private exploitation.[6] Jesuits won battles with local civil authorities by going over their heads to more central seats of power where Jesuit influence was strongest. There was a further galling element in these contests. Hispanic society was strongly xenophobic; when foreign missionaries out-dueled local civil or military leaders, they left smoldering chauvinistic resentments.[7]

Finally, when the Jesuits were perceived to be vulnerable, they were charged with undermining the authority of kings and popes and their downfall began. When Carlos III decided to make a complete break with the order, he was no innovator but rather the latest and most prominent head of state to elect an option that promised wealth and an end to an oft-resented domestic rival. If the expulsion was not their idea, the Spanish king and the Spanish bureaucracy made a memorable business of carrying out its complex execution. The royal command traveled to the far reaches of the vast empire with noteworthy speed and secrecy, and was implemented with unusual efficiency. In nearly all parts of New Spain, the surprise arrests of the Jesuits took place on the same day, 25 June 1767.

In some localities, notably a few mining areas, there was public resistance to both José de Gálvez's "reforms" and the uprooting of Jesuits. Stones were thrown, and government officeholders were threatened. Although no large or serious revolts took place, the incidents fitted into the visitor's plans. By representing these ad hoc uprisings as major threats to authority, he could assert the absolute power of the crown. Gálvez personally took six hundred Spanish troops into troubled areas of Guanajuato, San Luis Potosí, and Michoacán. He rounded up hordes of the disaffected, set up criminal courts, and meted out the harshest punishments seen there in generations. Eighty-five men were hanged and their bodies mutilated; seventy more received enough lashes to maim or cripple; over six hundred were sent to prison; a hundred others were banished. All were Indians or castas. The visitor accompanied these affairs with a harangue: "Vassals of the throne of Spain were born to be silent and obey — not to debate or discuss the affairs of Government."[8]

California was too remote to be included in the basic timetable for the Jesuit expulsion; it became a sequel to the main event. While authorities in New Spain were preparing to seize the Jesuits in their regions, a body of Catalán officers and enlisted men was traveling to Sonora to take part in a campaign to pacify rebellious Seris, Pimas, and their allies. At Tepic, it was overtaken by an order from Virrey Croix. Fifty-year-old Capitán Gaspar de Portolá, was thereby appointed governor of California and deputized to carry out the removal of its Jesuits.[9] He and a body of troops were ordered to the port of San Blas to await the ships that would carry them to Loreto. Meanwhile, all other ships, whether serving pearlers or carrying routine supplies, were banned from California's shores. At about the same time, Franciscan missionaries from the College of San Fernando near Mexico City were directed to replace the Jesuits in California's missions. They too were put on the road toward San Blas and a major role in California history.[10]

The Year of Changes

In September 1767, a mysterious encounter sent waves of rumor and speculation up and down California. A group of travelers making its way along the narrow coastal strip south of Loreto spied one of Manuel de Ocio's sailing launches inside Puerto Escondido, a snug harbor favored by all comers during the summer-to-fall chubasco season. Their curiosity aroused, the Californians went down to the beach. Pearlers regularly visited this coast each summer, but this year, though their season was well along, none had yet appeared. Perhaps the launch's crew could provide some explanation. As they approached, the people on shore saw some sailors they knew, but, in addition, five men in unfamiliar military uniforms. The strangers declined to land and refused to answer questions about their purpose or their destination. They did, however, reveal that a new governor had been appointed to direct California affairs and that he would arrive with Franciscan friars for California's missions. The sloop sailed south and was later reported to have landed at La Paz, where it waited for several days. An authority on the launch sent a local man south to the mining villages with a royal permit to requisition food. The messenger repeated the news that the visitors were forbidden under penalty of death to reveal their mission. Once provisioned, the launch sailed out of the bay and disappeared.[11]

This peculiar visitation gave the Jesuits much cause for speculation. Most widely believed was the explanation that the viceroy of New Spain had accepted the Jesuits' offer to renounce all or part of the present California missions. The Franciscans, they thought, were to replace at least some of the Jesuits, and a new governor had been appointed because the Franciscans would not be given command of the presidio.[12] After seventy years of jealously and assiduously laboring and politicking to protect their rights in California, the Jesuits finally viewed the prospect of change with some resignation. A series of misfortunes in the last few years had worn down their resources and their spirits.

For four successive years, devastating clouds of locusts had decimated crops at all but the northernmost missions. Herds were reduced to half by the shortage of forage. The rural estates in New Spain on which the Pious Fund depended for its income suffered poor years at about the same time. To compound that loss of income, for at least two years royal bureaucrats had failed to release the usual payments to support the presidio of Loreto, and they turned deaf ears on Jesuit pleas for relief. When no credits were left at the Loreto warehouse, missions used up their small reserves of stored food, tools, and yard goods. Only a quarter of the neophytes could be properly clothed. Loreto reduced the scale of its annual supply orders, but even these exceeded the reserves in California accounts. Juan de Armesto, the procurador de Californias in Mexico City, reported his mounting shortages of cash and credit not only to the padre visitador in California, but also to the provincial. At the beginning of 1767, Padre Salvador Gándara, provincial at the time, sent a directive to Padre Benno Ducrue, California's visitador, telling him to discharge the crew of one ship, lay off some of the shipwrights, and reduce the number of soldiers retained by the presidio. These measures seemed so draconian that, in March, Padre Ducrue convened a meeting of most of his missionaries. They agreed to the reductions in the marinería but could not accept cuts in the soldiery. To tide them over after that decision, they suggested using Loreto's small surplus of funds to pay the men to the end of the year, and then to offer some of them the choice of resigning or accepting the old entry-level position of media plaza — in other words working for half-pay. Fernando de Rivera was informed of the problems and the plans. He declined flatly to reduce the number of his men, saying that only orders from the viceroy would give him that power. The Jesuits sensed that Rivera felt threatened, and they feared that he might hand in his resignation — to be replaced by a man chosen in Mexico City who would be neither sympathetic to their cause nor energetic in carrying out his duties.[13]

No group of California Jesuits had ever been so vulnerable to the temptation to give up the struggle. None of their predecessors could have heard rumors of change with such mixed feelings. Some of the older missionaries probably considered the possibility of returning to their homelands or retiring to a Jesuit college or home. Younger missionaries must have contemplated their roles in their order's offer to expand the chain of missions northward. Perhaps they imagined pioneering, as Padres Linck and Arnés had recently done. Some may have thought about transfers to other Jesuit mission fields. But no one suggested or even imagined the fate that would be theirs.

At last, a king's envoy bearing a statement of royal intent arrived in California on 30 November 1767. Lookouts at San José del Cabo spotted masts, sails, and finally the hull of a familiar small schooner approaching from the east. *La Lauretana* anchored just offshore at San Bernabé, the open roadstead whose long beach served as a landing place for supply vessels and the Manila galleon.[14] No large throng could have witnessed this coming because, several years earlier, most of San José's diminishing flock was moved to Santiago, the adjacent mission to the north. However, because the Jesuits continued to provision the annual Manila galleon, and because San José provided the peninsula's best combination of land and water, a small settlement of gente de razón and neophytes remained to range livestock and tend the valuable gardens.[15]

Local workers would have watched the ocean horizon as a matter of course. They expected a Manila ship at any time, and they could profit by contacting its people and making trades before the missionary was notified and the formal visit began. Of course, local coast watchers would never have mistaken the little schooner that appeared in the east for the grand galleon that should have rounded the cape to the west; but simple curiosity must have attracted them to the beach. Their reward was to witness the arrival of the first Spanish civil authority to visit the California colony since the days of the neophyte rebellion thirty years earlier. Gaspar de Portolá and twenty-five armed and uniformed soldiers landed on the long arc of sand.[16]

The new governor and his men had been at sea for over forty days. Their orders were to sail directly into Loreto, surprise the Jesuits, and seize control of their presidio and administrative apparatus before they could resist or secrete their wealth.[17] Instead, the seafarers had been buffeted by storms and separated from the two other craft with which they had embarked at Matanchel. They knew nothing of the fate or whereabouts of the sloop that carried twenty-five Catalonian Volunteers, or of the sailing launch that carried a secular priest and fourteen Franciscan missionaries.[18] When Portolá's ship finally managed to approach the peninsula in the cape region, the new governor decided not to be bound by the viceroy's orders. He chose solid ground over putting prow to windward and trying to tack up the gulf in island-dotted waters off a dangerous coast.[19] Despite the numbers in his party and their ready arms, Portolá must have been relieved to find the Californios friendly and merely curious about the circumstances of his arrival.[20]

Portolá's party was led a few hundred yards to the tiny village. Don Gaspar asserted his right to command and instructed his hosts to notify the nearest missionary of his coming and to command the padre to meet him at San José. A local man immediately saddled up and rode off to Misión de Santiago, distant thirty miles — seven hours' ride for a motivated Californio. By then, the governor may have had a fair idea of the lay of the land and the distances he would have to cover to carry out his orders. During the forty wearying days out of Matanchel, while his craft tacked into winds or ran before them, Portolá had had ample time to learn that most of the schooner's crew were native Californians. He must have quizzed them about the locations of missions, the communications between them, and many other details that would be useful to the man who was to take over and run the peninsula.[21]

Padre Ignacio Tirsch, a thirty-four-year-old Bohemian, administered Santiago at that time and therefore became the first California missionary to hear of the governor's arrival and to wonder what it might portend. Tirsch knew that Capitán Rivera was in the area. As he hastened to comply with Portolá's summons, he sent a messenger to find the captain and ask him to join the conference in Santiago.[22]

Padre Tirsch knew about the mysterious visitors who had sailed into Puerto Escondido and La Paz two months earlier. When the messenger reached him with the latest news, he must have assumed, as did the Jesuits whose memoirs are known, that the reported new governor and Franciscan missionaries represented a group sent to realize the Jesuits' offer to give up all or part of California. As Tirsch made the day-long ride from Santiago to San José, he knew that an historic change was in the offing, but it is unlikely that any premonition prepared him for the magnitude of the shock he was about to receive.

If the padre and later the presidial captain rode toward the confrontation full of wonder and misgivings, Portolá himself must have speculated a bit about his own reception. Though his fears had been somewhat allayed, he could not have entirely discounted the warnings from his superiors and the stories he had heard on the mainland. Some idea of the nature of these rumors can be gained from versions carefully included in all the firsthand memoirs by California Jesuits who experienced Portolá's coming. Padre Miguel del Barco later wrote, "with the fabulous tidings that had made the rounds about the riches of California in padre hands, it was told also that such was their power and arrogance that they would dare much. Should the king wish to remove them from the land, they would resist, rebel, put the peninsula under arms, and its taking would be a difficult enterprise."[23] Padre Benno Ducrue wrote that "the governor had come with no little fear. He had heard that the California neophytes were equipped with ten thousand muskets and a vast amount of powder in order to resist any attempt which might be made to invade their country."[24] Even if these tales were exaggerated by disgruntled Jesuits, they probably reflected stories told by Portolá's men after the pressure was off and they were hobnobbing with the Californios. The voyage from Matanchel must have given Portolá some inkling of a peaceful outcome to his venture. The seamen on his schooner knew the peninsula and its people intimately; they would have painted a very different picture from that imagined by distant royal functionaries.

Gaspar de Portolá came to his new calling as a career army officer, a *militar*, not a bureaucrat. He was a native of Catalonia and had thirty years of service behind him, campaigns in Italy and Portugal, and both honors and wounds. He had come to New Spain as a captain in the Regiment of Dragoons of Spain in late 1764; his recently acquired governorship probably resulted from favorable reports by his superiors to Virrey Croix or Visitador General Gálvez.[25] As he waited at San José del Cabo, he must have sensed that the campaign ahead of him was to be a very different challenge, both in human relations and environment, than anything he had yet encountered.

Padre Tirsch rode into San José del Cabo and into the midst of the party of visitors. He welcomed them warmly and put himself at their disposal. The governor, plainly relieved to find the missionary with only a small and unarmed escort, was pleasant and deferential. After an exchange of greetings, he and the missionary retired to a private place where he could explain his written orders from the king. In a matter of moments the Jesuit was informed that, within Spanish domains, the Jesuit order had been outlawed and dispossessed of lands, buildings, and all other wealth. The Jesuits' royal assignments were cancelled; they were relieved of every responsibility, spiritual and temporal. Finally, all were to be arrested and sent under guard, first to New Spain, then to Spain itself, then exiled beyond the borders of all nations that had joined in their expulsion. It was reported that Padre Tirsch accepted this dictum with a profound calm.[26] If Portolá was amazed at such resignation, it was in part because he did not yet appreciate what it had meant to be a missionary in fabled California or the exceptional hardships then being experienced.

When Fernando de Rivera y Moncada joined the conference, the governor must have met him cautiously and with the liveliest interest. Rivera's position was unique among New Spain's presidial captains because his rank—indeed, his entire career—was owed to Jesuit favor. Furthermore, only months had passed since the viceroy had received spirited defenses of California Jesuits authored by Rivera and his lieutenant.[27] Ironically, this sincere testimony, under normal circumstances, would have been taken as a mildly self-serving, ritual exercise. In 1767, however, it received a very different reading. Arriving, as it did, immediately after the king's expulsion order, it focused attention on Rivera and the Presidio of Loreto as almost traitorously dedicated to Jesuit interests.

As Portolá and Rivera exchanged greetings at isolated San José del Cabo, the anti-Jesuit fervor in Mexico City must have seemed far away. Storms and adverse winds had delayed Portolá's arrival and induced him to land far from his objective. He had only half his men, little of his traveling gear, and no missionaries with which to replace the Jesuits. To carry out his unhappy assignment, he was dependent upon a force of soldiers whose loyalty was in question and on the very Jesuits he had come to depose. Rivera, for his part, also had mixed feelings. He had been demoted from his position as California's premier civil and military official, but his job had already been in jeopardy and Portolá brought news of activities in which he might well find a role.

Two accounts describe the meeting between the California captain and the newly arrived governor. Padres Baegert and Barco, though men of opposite temperaments and different opinions, felt the same regard for Fernando de Rivera and gave the same interpretation of his impact on Portolá. Baegert concentrated on material concerns: "The captain of the old California soldiery, Don Fernando de Rivera y Moncada, a man of great virtue, scrupulously conscientious and a faithful servant of the King of Spain, happened to be in this region when the governor arrived in San José. Portolá secretly conferred with him for several hours and was rudely shaken out of his dreams of California treasures, of the wealth of the missionaries, and of other such things."[28]

Barco was more concerned with honor and allegiance than with treasures: "After having talked to the Santiago missionary and much more with Capitán

Rivera — who knew the Jesuits to the core, their sentiments and their loyalty — [Gobernador Portolá] became entirely persuaded that he had nothing to fear from the padres, not the slightest thing, and that they would obey the king's orders to the letter even if no troops accompanied them; even a single communication from the Lord Viceroy declaring His Majesty's decision would have been sufficient. . . . Capitán Rivera was able to give those assurances with the security of knowing about the [Jesuits'] offer to renounce all their mission provinces and especially California. Furthermore, this same captain knew full well that, in case this universal renunciation was not accepted, the California missionaries had attempted shortly after to give up at least the two southernmost missions [i.e., San José del Cabo and Santiago], those with the best land and most fame for their riches."[29]

These accounts and subsequent events demonstrate that Portolá accepted Rivera, at least temporarily, as an ally and advisor. For the moment, he was the only subordinate who could effectively carry out any of the governor's orders. The Catalán probably planned to retain all the California troops until his new order was established at Loreto and he understood the local situation and had had a chance to make long-range plans. In this, the governor showed his experience and the generally good judgment that were factors in his subsequent success with most of his difficult California assignments.

The first problem that faced the strange junta at San José was to obtain mounts and saddles for the trip to Santiago, a sixteen-hour ride for such a large group. The far more demanding ten or twelve day trek to Loreto would come next. Probably at Rivera's suggestion, Portolá sent a letter by soldier-courier directly to the procurador in Loreto, Padre Lucas Ventura, asking him to obtain as many additional mounts and saddles as possible and to start them south on the camino real so as to meet the governor's party. Tirsch, meanwhile, headed back to Santiago where he had his own people round up mounts and equipment, load them up, and return to San José to bring the newcomers to his mission.[30]

When he reached Santiago, Gobernador Portolá was introduced to his first California mission. While others made ready for the long journey ahead, he surveyed what had been the core of California life for seventy years. He saw how poor the mission was in food and supplies and how dependent on the direction and authority of its missionary. Since the replacement Franciscans were delayed for an indefinite period, Portolá would have to delegate some authority to supervise the mission after he removed the Jesuits.

Among his original orders, Portolá apparently was given a plan to cope with this transition: a local soldier or mayordomo was to be put in charge until he was properly relieved. At Santiago, the governor appointed Padre Tirsch's soldier-escort. The soldier accepted responsibility for supervision of daily activities and for all mission property, other than the church and its religious furnishings. He was left to guard the storehouse, the gardens, and the herds against theft or waste and was to be subject to the governor's orders, not to any missionary's. If there were a time lag between Jesuit departure and Franciscan arrival, the soldier at each mission would be responsible for its entire day-to-day operation. Such a special appointment — one that carried unusual or additional duties — was known as a *comisión*. Soldiers so appointed came to be called *comisionados*. That part of mission property given to them to administer was known as the mission's *temporalidades*, its temporal or worldly holdings. As it happened, the comisionados faced extraordinary problems with the ongoing drought and the concommitant food shortages, and they took measures that angered the Franciscans who took over the missions six months later. For several years after, the words *comisionados* and *temporalidades* were employed and manipulated in many rancorous ways as great changes were made and remade in mission jurisdiction.[31]

The widely believed rumors of California's wealth were based on supposed bonanzas of pearls and silver. Since the expulsion of the Jesuits was carried out everywhere with simultaneous royal confiscation of their property, Spanish officials in New Spain looked forward to seizing some treasure — perhaps a great trove — in California. It is probable that the viceroy gave his emissary specific orders for its seizure and for making inquiry as to its sources. When Gaspar de Portolá had completed his arrangements at Misión de Santiago, he was ready to inspect the mines located at Santa Ana and San Antonio, a day and a half's ride from Santiago. Padre Baegert wrote the only description of this reconnaissance: "After having inspected the misery of San José and Santiago, [the governor] visited the poverty-stricken mines. . . . There, too, he was astonished to see the poor huts and apparent poverty of the miners."[32] That Portolá chose not to dwell on any of these visits in his first reports to the viceroy should surprise no one. Knowing the interests and expectations of his superiors, this seasoned veteran of the Spanish system concentrated on reporting his primary assignment, the expulsion itself, and after that, his own most pressing problems: lack of equipment, supplies, and suitable personnel. There was no need as yet to burst the bubble of expectations in Mexico City.

Padre Baegert provided a capsule description of Portolá's next move northward to his new capital: "With more than forty people in his company he hastened his departure for Loreto . . . [which] he saw with little comfort on December 17, after ten days of travel and forced marches. Only once on his journey did he find human beings and shelter at a mission [La Pasión]. The daily march was not just four or five hours, as is customary among soldiers, but ten and more. . . ."[33] Nothing in Portolá's own letters in any way contradicts Baegert, but that embittered Jesuit chronicler focused narrowly on Portolá's discomfort and disillusion and failed to perceive that this was a journey of discovery for all concerned. The "more than forty people" comprised two groups traveling together, but with very different backgrounds. The newcomers, Gobernador Portolá, Alférez José Lasso, Capellán Pedro Fernández, and twenty-five Catalán dragoons, were distracted and tormented by their first encounter with overland California travel. They probably had little personal interest in the Californios other than to learn a few of their skills — in the interests of survival — and to be grateful for their assistance and envious of their more appropriate clothing and gear.

The thirteen or more old California hands included Fernando de Rivera, two or three soldiers in his escort, and various arrieros selected by Tirsch or Rivera from gente de razón at San José, Santiago, and Santa Ana. The latter group would have found little to interest them in the familiar countryside or travel conditions, but they must have been fascinated by the novelty of so many new faces and foreign ways. Other than crews and passengers on the Manila ship, people living in California simply had not been exposed to outsiders. The present group was not only outlandish, but also represented the all-powerful mother country; and they had come to effect unprecedented changes — rumors of which were now flying to all corners of the land with the couriers dispatched to carry the governor's orders.

Thus, for everyone in the caravan, that trip was an elementary education. The most interested and motivated student must have been Gaspar de Portolá. The governor apparently had Fernando de Rivera much at his side during those tiring days; when he later wrote to the viceroy that Rivera had worked hard to make the journey a success, it is likely that he referred to the captain's direction of the many physical activities of the cavalcade.[34] However, Rivera's greatest contribution was his experience and point of view — the fruits of twenty-five years of peninsular duty — that could give his willing listener some realistic sense of the components and problems of his new command.

On 28 December 1767, eleven days after his arrival at Loreto, Gobernador Portolá sent his first communication, a detailed ten-page report, to Virrey Croix. Don Gaspar's time had been filled with business related to the expulsion, and his report devoted two pages to that topic. Uppermost in his mind was impressing the viceroy with his convictions about the extraordinary demands of his assignment in California. The hardships of his recent trip dominated his thoughts. The governor described the rugged land he was to administer: the heat, the rocks, the thorns, the lack of water and pasturage, the great distances between sources of help or supplies, and the astonishing amount of work required from all hands. All of Portolá's comments could have been clipped from reports by any overland traveler in California in the seventeenth, eighteenth, or nineteenth centuries; but since the Catalán was not a mere traveler — it was his task to govern and perhaps defend this inhospitable place — he was deeply concerned about doing his job while coping with such adverse conditions.

In his frank and personal letter to Croix, Portolá sketched out a plan. He reminded the viceroy that he had been ordered to review Loreto's troops as soon as the Jesuits had been expelled. Reading between the lines, it is apparent that Croix had suggested removing the presidio's commissioned officers and evaluating its enlisted men to find any that might profitably be added to the governor's command, but now that Portolá had seen the country and what it did to his own men, and had had the opportunity to watch Fernando de Rivera and some of his troop in action, he saw an imperative need to forestall changes in personnel at the presidio of Loreto.

After a scant month in California, Portolá found that half his Spanish dragoons should be returned to mainland duty: ". . . they are incapacitated from so much fatigue and work. . . . This is not the case, I assure your excellency, for the company of the Californias, for I found both its men and animals in very good condition." Presently he came to the point: "It is certain, Sir, that in order to carry out the service in this country, it is more necessary to have a cowboy than a soldier to care for so much livestock by day and to guard it by night. For this reason, I find it convenient and necessary to retain as many soldiers as possible from the said company and even, temporarily, the two officers who serve as captain and lieutenant. . . ." This last line indicates that Portolá's original instructions had anticipated the removal of these officers. It seems to be an assurance to the viceroy that this perhaps unwelcome turn of events should persist only until better arrangements could be made.[35]

Portolá explained the system by which Loreto's soldiers had been paid. He firmly supported the wisdom of its idiosyncrasies, particularly that of paying the men higher-than-usual wages but expecting them to buy and maintain uniforms, arms, and riding animals. "I well know, Sir, that this is a great expense to the king, but, although lowering their pay by giving them animals was discussed, it would not only be inconvenient but also more costly, for the time would come when the soldier would not be able to perform his service, for since the animals would not be on his bill, he would neglect them or abandon them, or perhaps deceitfully sell them and give the excuse that they had been lost—which happens often and easily because of the mazes of thickets whose thorns can scarcely be penetrated." The governor mentioned that his orders "discussed" changes in the method of paying California soldiers, but apparently Rivera y Moncada's opinions made sense to the receptive newcomer.[36]

The Expulsion Is Carried Out

On arrival at Loreto, Gobernador Portolá presented himself to the ranking Jesuit authority, Padre Procurador Lucas Ventura. Portolá reviewed the accommodations, and chose some rooms for himself in the padres' living quarters, the large stone building that Padre Jaime Bravo had built twenty-five years earlier. The following day he sent a letter to the superior of all peninsular missionaries, Padre Visitador Benno Ducrue, at his post at Misión de Guadalupe. He invited the father visitor to come to Loreto, because he, the governor, was too exhausted to travel farther. Portolá's message, no doubt carried by one of the usual soldier-couriers, arrived at Guadalupe on 20 December; it had traveled an impressive sixty leagues—about one hundred and fifty miles—in two and a half days. When Ducrue had read and digested the contents, he wrote hurried notes to the remaining missionaries. The next day, he set out for Loreto and arrived on Christmas Eve.[37]

As soon as he had written to Ducrue, Portolá set more of his plan in motion. He was acutely aware of his superiors' interest in Jesuit possessions, but he had already seen enough to guess that they were going to be keenly disappointed in California. To protect himself, he decided to obtain a signed inventory from each mission before its padre was relieved of his responsibilities. To this end, he sent Capitán Rivera with an escort to tally the contents of the northern missions, and dispatched Teniente Blas Fernández de Somera and a few men to handle the missions south of Loreto.[38] When these teams of inventory takers completed their work at the northern and southern extremes of the mission system, they were to send the resident missionary to the first neighboring mission on the road back to Loreto. There the first padre would pick up the second, the two would go to the third mission, and so on, so that all the padres from the north and the south would arrive at the capital in just two parties. Until that time, each missionary was instructed to continue with his work as before.[39]

In deference to the holy festival of Christmas, Portolá greeted Padre Ducrue at Loreto without reference to the decree of expulsion, presenting only a letter of introduction from the viceroy informing the visitador about the coming of the new governor and asking that he be welcomed by missionaries and neophytes alike.[40] These contradictory acts, the ordering of inventories on the one hand and withholding the formal presentation of bad news on the other, illustrate both the ceremonial and practical aspects of Spanish life. The governor was a gentleman, religious and humane. He had no desire to bully or humiliate those he had come to depose; every subsequent Jesuit account extolled his kindness, courtesy, and compassion. Avoiding the Christmas feast as a time to deliver the decree of expulsion illustrates Portolá's ritual sensitivity.

By that time, all the missionaries knew their fate; Tirsch had sent letters from Santiago and, in addition, every courier on whatever errand must have carried some version of Portolá's orders. Portolá knew that the word was out. Before Ducrue presented himself at Loreto, the governor wrote to the viceroy that he had already received letters from most of the missionaries "in which they show themselves subordinate to the royal will . . . proof that they have known for some days everything that is happening".[41] He was prepared to bow to protocol, but did not feel justified in wasting time while he waited for the visitador to arrive in response to his summons. That was why he sent Rivera and Fernández de Somera out to inventory the missions and give practical ultimatums to their padres before their superior had officially received the royal decree. Everyone involved understood compromises between protocol and necessity.

On Saturday, 26 December 1767, the governor finally carried out the long-delayed formal presentation of the king's decree of expulsion. Six months had passed since its promulgation in Mexico City, a fact that speaks volumes about the reality of California's isolation. The Jesuits present at Loreto—Padre Visitador Benno Ducrue, Padre Rector Lucas Ventura, Capellán of the Presidio Francisco Javier Franco, and Hermano Juan Villavieja—were met by

Gobernador Portolá, who was accompanied by his alférez, his secretary, and a sergeant of the dragoons. The royal decree containing the order of expulsion was read and immediately signed by those present.[42] Again, Portolá observed the symmetry of ancient protocols: the king's enemies — a leader and three subordinates — were ritually vanquished by the king's retainers — a captain and three subalterns.

This disclosure of the actual expulsion document revealed orders that the governor had kept to himself for nearly a month; his forbearance bespeaks both his humanity and his practicality. In the official proclamation, the Jesuits were forbidden from celebrating Mass or participating in any other ecclesiastical functions. By postponing the formal delivery, the governor was able to maintain a semblance of normal daily life during an upheaval that would have been far more wrenching — and difficult to administer — without the missionaries' participation. Furthermore, the decree ordered that the Jesuits be locked in their rooms and guarded by soldiers until they could set out on their voyage. Portolá assumed the responsibility for ignoring this command; Ducrue says the governor told him that this was due to the absence of the successor Franciscans and the governor's desire to prevent unrest among the people. These doubtless were considerations, but it is easy to believe that this was also an extension of the kindness and courtesy that characterized Portolá's handling of the whole difficult affair.

The next step was the formal transfer of mission property to the crown. The governor took the keys to the presidio and the warehouse along with Padre Lucas Ventura's accounting. The great treasure of the California Jesuits amounted to about seven thousand pesos in cash and another sixty or seventy thousand pesos worth of stores, much of it yardage destined to be traded for soldiers' pay credits or mission produce.[43] Portolá's report of this transfer betrays no overt sign of disappointment, but that and every subsequent communication showed that he had fully recognized the woeful lack of everyday necessities, especially food. He emphasized that disaster could be averted for only a month or two unless new provisions arrived.[44]

After the fateful decree was proclaimed and signed, it took five more weeks to complete the details. Rivera and Fernández de Somera proceeded with their inventories at the successive missions, and the padres began wending their way toward Loreto. An epidemic was ravaging the neophytes at San Borja, so Padre Wenceslao Linck was allowed an extra week to nurse and comfort the stricken. Jorge Retz, padre at Misión de Santa Gertrudis, was a corpulent and somewhat infirm man who, at best, had difficulty with travel. The expulsion order found Retz with a severely injured foot. He was carried by teams of his neophytes the more than two hundred miles from Santa Gertrudis to Loreto. This devotion to Retz is especially notable because the Jesuits had lost the power to command.[45]

By 2 February 1768, all members of the Society of Jesus were gathered at Loreto, and the following day they prepared to depart. Gobernador Portolá closed his eyes once again to the royal order and allowed a final mass at which

Padre Visitador Benno Ducrue preached to all of Loreto's assembled people and nearly all received communion. A further service was held later in the day. The governor ordered that the Jesuits embark well after dark so that no large crowd would gather, but he misjudged the people. Ducrue, writing several years later in Germany, recalled the scene: "As we walked down to the shore, behold we were surrounded on all sides by the people, the Spanish soldiers among them. Some knelt on the sand to kiss our hands and feet, others knelt with arms outstretched in the form of a cross, publicly pleading for pardon. Others tenderly embraced the missionaries, bidding them farewell and wishing them a happy voyage through loud weeping and sobbing. This sad spectacle moved the Governor to tears."[46] Finally, as midnight approached, the sixteen missionaries were carried on soldier and neophyte backs through shallow water to the skiff that would lighter them out to *Nuestra Señora de la Concepción*, anchored offshore. In a final considerate act, Portolá sent with them an escort composed of Alférez José Lasso and six dragoons to deliver them safely in Mexico City and give the viceroy a firsthand account of California affairs.[47]

Truly, neither Portolá nor any of the other newly arrived Spaniards could possibly have appreciated the impact of the changes they wrought or the emotional ties being broken as the leavetaking reached its poignant climax. For seventy years, people in California had known no other masters, religious or secular. Most of the native Californians present were born at peninsular missions; most gente de razón were either born and raised in Jesuit California or in Sinaloa or Sonora where Jesuits also managed most religious and social affairs. Moreover, the soldiers and servants had been hired by the Jesuits and most had served under them for years. Each soldier had put in time at a mission where he and a Jesuit were sole companions for months on end. Jesuits had performed their weddings, baptized their children, nursed and buried their family members. For seven decades there had been no constant in California life more central than the Jesuit presence. Now, unexpectedly and in a matter of weeks, all that was swept away. The loss was not ideological for the people on Loreto's beach. They were losing their familiar leaders, the missionaries who had always been the upper stratum of their society. Their replacements would be strangers whose arrival was still only a rumor. There is little reason to doubt that most California people shared a state of shock, uncertainty, and confusion.

The ordeal was prolonged through the next day; anchor was weighed but *La Concepción* stood becalmed just offshore, sails limp. On Thursday, 5 February a wind sprang up. The little two-masted bark sailed away from the very spot where, seventy years before, Juan María de Salvatierra had founded his mission and California's first permanent colony. When the sails of *La Concepción* disappeared among the islands to the southeast, an era truly ended.[48]

Thanks in part to their delayed arrest, and to the escort provided by Gaspar de Portolá, the California Jesuits avoided the brutal treatment accorded many of their mainland brothers, dozens of whom died from the hardships forced upon them. All California missionaries reached Spain. The northern Europeans then returned to their homes; those from Spain and New Spain eventually were exiled to the Papal States in Italy. With the worldwide suppression of their order, they became wards of the mother church—which had little for them to do. Most of those who had served in California ended their days quietly in Bologna.[49]

The people they left behind in California scarcely had time to mourn or to rejoice. The same hand that swept away the Society of Jesus now called on them all, in one way or another, to man or support a new adventure. Now they were to open a new California to the north. The course of the next half-century was in preparation.

Epilogue

The Aftermath

Gálvez in California

On 5 July 1768, five months after the Jesuits departed, Visitador General José de Gálvez disembarked at the surgidero de Cerralvo from a little ship that belonged to Gaspar Pisón. The most powerful man in New Spain had been at sea off-and-on for five weeks, trying to make the crossing from San Blas; now he was in California to assess royal interests and further royal aims. In a few days, he requisitioned Manuel de Ocio's buildings at Santa Ana as headquarters for himself and his retinue; Ocio moved off to his ranch in nearby Las Gallinas. Gálvez came with a four-part agenda for California: to install the Franciscans in the missions, to set up a civil government, to promote colonization and economic development, and, most important, to establish Spanish enclaves at San Diego and Monterey, presences that could forestall encroachment by other Europeans.[1]

Gálvez conferred with Franciscan Padre Junípero Serra, leader of the contingent of twelve Franciscan missionaries who had been sent to replace the Jesuits. The missionaries had been in their new posts three months and they had many problems to lay before the powerful leader. The visitor general was newly arrived, but full of plans. Gálvez had come to California convinced that the Jesuits had either mismanaged potentially rich missions, or that they had used them and their people as bases and tools for the secret development of great resources, perhaps pearls and silver or gold. Thus, he had come with unreasonable expectations. Because Gálvez had long since voiced his suppositions publicly, he had created conditions that made it doubly difficult for him to accept reality.[2] Within days of his arrival he saw missions that had no wealth and their few people sickly and dispirited. He found poor, tiny mining operations creating only marginal profits. The mining experts that he brought with him assured him that improvements could be made, but no one had the temerity to promise a secure industry, much less Gálvez's anticipated bonanzas.

The Fate of the Peninsular Missions

Secretly, José de Gálvez may have been startled and discouraged when he saw the poor potential of the fabled California peninsula, but he did not let his disappointment inhibit his natural bent for reorganizing people and institutions. When he realized that the missions of the South had relatively good agricultural prospects but were fast becoming depopulated, he decided to consolidate their Pericú people at Santiago and bring down the Guaycuran neophytes of Los Dolores and San Luis Gonzaga to occupy Todos Santos. He so ordered, and it was done at the end of 1768. According to all contemporary observers, the people thus displaced were alienated and uncooperative, the least Hispanicized of all peninsular groups. Forcing them to move nearly one hundred and fifty miles to the south, entirely out of their ancestral territory, made them no more cooperative. Moreover, they suffered the common lot of all California neophytes in that they had lost their accustomed padres and now were being asked to accept and learn new routines.

California mission herds were much reduced, and other food supplies had been nearly exhausted during the six months of drought and famine in which the missions were administered by the Portolá-appointed comisionados. Now they suffered additional losses; Gálvez and the Franciscans found it necessary to requisition and remove mission stores and trappings to facilitate their ambitious plan to open and occupy the vast new territory north of Jesuit California. By 1772, only four years after the shift from Jesuits to Franciscans, the old California missions once again changed hands, this time to the care of Dominican missionaries. By the time the Dominicans took possession, the oft-raided peninsular religious communities were in a sorry state. Their new caretakers complained to the viceroy about shortages of implements, staple foods, and particularly church trappings. They requested accountings for possessions, now missing, that were listed in the inventories Portolá ordered when he removed the Jesuits in 1768. Squabbles ensued. Franciscans blamed the comisionados, defended their acquisitions, referred to old orders that might justify their actions, and appealed to governors to verify their claims.[3]

All the peninsular missions that the Jesuits had left in operation continued to suffer demographic declines. Most began to acquire small populations of gente de razón, often the families of ex-servants, mayordomos, or soldiers. By 1782, the neophytes at Comondú numbered less than a score.[4] By the end of the century, Comondú had become an Hispanic village dominated by español and mestizo families that ran cattle and worked small plots of land. The few surviving neophytes huddled around the mission and worked as laborers.

The mission ideal, translated all over the Americas into fact by dedicated men with the best intentions, brought converts to the edge of Hispanic society, but never taught them to create a place for themselves within it. C. H. Haring, in commenting on the once-flourishing Jesuit mission in Paraguay, enunciated the problem: ". . . from a larger viewpoint the Jesuit regime was in many respects a failure. The Indians were never really taught to be much more than helpless, dependent children. They lived in a perpetual minority. Isolated from Spaniards and from their own kind, they were never trained to govern themselves or take their place in the civilized society about them."[5] Charles Polzer, a modern Jesuit historian, has observed, "As the passage of time has shown, the missions were preparing the indigenous populations for nonexistent places in [the larger] society. . . ."[6] After the Jesuits were forcibly removed from California, Franciscans and Dominicans attempted to bring the missionary work to a satisfactory conclusion. They too failed.

A few peninsular natives married into or cohabited with the society of gente de razón and added their genes to the growing Hispanic population, but most could not compete and were not accepted; disease took the outcasts. A century and a half after Salvatierra brought mission influence, all of California's people — all the Pericú, Guaycura, and Cochimí — were gone, their cultures forgotten, their eyes closed, and their faces shrouded.

Civil Government and Economic Development

Despite its poor prospects, José de Gálvez retained his grand vision of colonizing the sterile peninsula. Before he returned to the mainland in 1769, he designed a plan for Santa Ana down to the layout of streets, the location of houses, and the planting of shade trees. He began a program to distribute mission lands to deserving gente de razón and even to neophytes.[7] He decreed communal lands and water rights. He appointed his adjutant, Matías de Armona, to head the new civil government on the peninsula while Portolá was engaged in the expedition to Monterey. He installed an inspector of mines, a collector of taxes, and the tribute. He planned a school where youths from the missions could learn trades. He formed three militia companies to protect the old mission area while the men of the presidio were involved in opening the new California territory.[8] He arranged for a priest for the combined communities of Santa Ana and San Antonio. El Sur, as envisioned by Gálvez, would be transformed from a mission serving the narrow goals of the Jesuits into a promising civil community that would grow to be an asset to the crown and provide the resource base needed to assist Manila galleons. In April 1769, just before he left the peninsula, Gálvez went to Loreto and drew up plans to revitalize and improve it in much the same manner that he had ordered for Santa Ana.[9]

Just as Gálvez had deceived himself about sequestered Jesuit riches, he failed to perceive the truth about the peninsula's lack of resources. There were no readily exploitable assets, so there was no economic base for his ambitious community. To escape such unpromising conditions — and the inevitable failures that could blight their careers—the people that the visitor general left to administer the area managed within a year or two to arrange transfers for themselves. Many recently arrived colonists departed when they could get passage to the mainland. A few years later, the only vestiges of Gálvez's grand plans were the documents in which they were ordered.[10] Most of the humble people that he brought to work mines either had gone home or joined the local gente de razón in subsistence ranching, usually as squatters rather than legitimate landholders. A few entrepreneurs made their living as miners, pearlers, or merchants, but their activities were on a small scale; no one made a fraction of the profits enjoyed by Manuel de Ocio in his heyday.

Hopes were soon dashed for the California residents who hoped that civil government would open up opportunities stifled during the years of missionary rule. The new reality was harsher than the old. In 1769 and 1770, Antonio de Ocio, Gaspar Pisón, and perhaps a few other local men were lured into card games with the officials that Gálvez had installed. Ocio gambled away over five thousand pesos. Neither Manuel de Ocio, nor Antonio after him, was able to get the government of Spain to repay him for the ships, riding and pack animals, pack gear, and cattle that Portolá and Gálvez requisitioned to bring their parties to California, outfit them, and especially to supply the first land expeditions to San Diego and Monterey. Don Manuel was murdered by two of Gálvez's imported miners while they robbed his storehouse in 1771; it was a grimly ironic end. He had profited in safety while sparring with the Jesuits, but lost much of his wealth and met a violent death under the civil regime for which he had waited so long. Gaspar de Pisón's California career took a tragi-comic turn; during his many drinking bouts, he blasphemed publicly and denounced royal authorities. At last, both missionaries and civil officials tired of his bad example and had him banished permanently from the peninsula—although Pisón contended that the charges were amplified to justify the confiscation of his property. Don Gaspar spent the last ten years of his life in vain efforts to return to California to recover his mines and other holdings. José María de Estrada fared better. The young entrepreneur turned his back on private business to enlist at the presidio as an assistant to the *comisario*, the officer in charge of the royal warehouse at Loreto. After two of his superiors were fired for incompetence or dishonesty, Estrada was made comisario and filled the post with distinction; his were the neatest, most complete and accurate records that were kept during the last fifty years of the warehouse operation. He was elevated to the rank of alférez and would have gone higher but for his untimely death at the end of 1791. His son, José Mariano, served as an officer in the new California territory and founded the Estrada family in that region.

Gálvez's Plan for the New California

Spanish imperial policy—to some extent determined by Gálvez—had established the occupation of San Diego and Monterey as a high priority. The

Spanish crown knew that foreigners were exploring and planning to exploit areas on the northern fringes of New Spain; this prompted a flurry of activities in the late eighteenth century. In 1768, José de Gálvez feared that Russian and British incursions on the northwest coast might lead to permanent, threatening presences. These fears compelled the Spanish to move northward in California. Established areas were forced to provide the requisite men and materials. Peninsular California, because of its proximity, was hit especially hard — given its extreme poverty, small population, and the depletions already suffered under the new regime. Gálvez commandeered animals, equipment, supplies, and even the services of neophytes for his great push to open and occupy the northern lands that came to be known as Nueva California, and later as Alta California. He gave the Franciscans, under Padre Junípero Serra, the task of establishing missions in Nueva California, and they had little choice but to seek and get the government's permission to take some of the remaining possessions from the old Jesuit foundations.

As he planned the occupation of Nueva California from Santa Ana, Gálvez called Padre Serra to his side and conferred with him about a two-pronged expedition to the north. Gálvez planned to send the Catalán soldiers — who had accompanied him to the peninsula — by ship to San Diego. That was supposed to be an easy undertaking, and the seaborne troops would thus be well prepared to march on by land to Monterey. They set sail from La Paz in January 1769. A month later, more supplies were embarked for San Diego on a second ship.

Fernando de Rivera was appointed to command the party that would scout out a land route to San Diego. Rivera's troop of twenty-five, made up of his own soldiers from the presidio of Loreto and experienced California arrieros, was supported by over forty neophytes recruited — or ordered out — from the northerly missions of Santa María and San Borja. Rivera and his followers established a northern base at Velicatá, the site that the captain and Padre Linck had discovered three years before.[11] In late March 1769, Rivera's group headed northwest to break trail, establish camp sites, herd livestock, and generally prepare the way for Portolá's party, which was to follow in three weeks. Food was short, and the neophytes were expected to forage for most of what they needed. That plan failed; several neophytes died along the way, and more deserted.

Rivera's overland party found Gálvez's seaborne contingent in San Diego harbor, but they were in terrible straits from scurvy and other privations. Over a dozen Catalán soldiers died, and demands on the California soldiers increased. Most of them took part in the two subsequent expeditions led by Portolá to the region of San Francisco and Monterey. Most spent over two years in Nueva California before they were allowed to visit their homes. Many of these pioneers later returned to the new territories and served long stints.[12]

José de Gálvez and Virrey Croix in New Spain, as well as the king and many royal officials in Spain, expected to receive news of adventures and achievements on the promising new frontier. Officers and missionaries in the field wrote frequent reports of Spanish progress. Now that there were two Californias, one old and familiar, the other new and exotic, two names were needed. With the opening of Nueva California, the old, settled area of the peninsula began to be called Antigua California, partly in contrast to the new, partly in recognition of its two hundred years of Spanish explorations, labors, dreams, and disappointments.[13] For the men of Loreto who served far to the north, "Antigua California" summoned up visions of familiar homes and traditional lives.

However, in all the excitement and promise of the Nueva California venture, it was convenient for higher officials to forget Antigua California's indispensable contributions. José de Gálvez and Junipero Serra could take implicit credit for the availability of the men and means that powered the land expedition which proved so vital in the campaign to the north. The peninsular missions had provided essential supplies, but the Jesuits were gone and need not be acknowledged. The presidio of Loreto had provided most of the manpower, but its Jesuit past could be ignored and the roles of its men subordinated in the rounds of accolades accorded recently arrived Spanish officers. Manuel de Ocio's little empire provided the ship that made possible Portolá's coming; the further use of his ships, his mules, mule drivers, and stores made possible the prompt launching of the expedition to the north. Without that which was commandeered from Ocio, Gálvez's plans would have had long setbacks. But Ocio received no thanks and ultimately no reward nor even the recompense promised by royal officials.

New California gradually came to be called Alta California. While serving there, Fernando de Rivera y Moncada took on higher office with higher levels of responsibility, but reached emotional depths in concurrent disagreements and rejections. Twice he served as governor of the new region, but he was never able to please Padre Serra and his followers. In an acrimonious conflict over the precedence of authority, military versus religious, Rivera was excommunicated by a Franciscan missionary—a bitter blow for the sincerely devout captain. In 1781, after he had returned to Loreto as captain, Rivera led a party of settlers from Sinaloa and Sonora to Alta California over Kino's old trail through the Pimería. At the Yuma crossing of the Río Colorado, Rivera's scouts reported hundreds of hostile Yuma warriors in the area. Rivera sent the settlers and a small escort to the northwest into the desert; they eventually arrived safely in San Gabriel. The captain and his remaining soldiers fought the Yumas in a delaying action at the river's edge, where they were overwhelmed and slain. Rivera was fifty-seven and had been a California soldier for forty years. His widow was left destitute; she was never able to collect any part of Rivera's last five years of pay, held up as it was by disputes with missionaries and higher civil authorities. Like Manuel de Ocio, his old adversary, Fernando de Rivera's happiest times were those under the Jesuit regime.

For many years, most of the soldiers who were nominally assigned to the presidio of Loreto served in some capacity related to the new establishments in the north. In the beginning, they were simply detached to serve under the military command of Gaspar de Portolá. When the presidio of Monterey was founded in 1770, some were transferred to that command, but even as other presidios were established at San Diego and Santa Bárbara, half or more of Loreto's forces served in the northern part of the peninsula. Beside guarding Dominican missions, they had the important responsibility for packing and guarding deliveries of mail and supplies through the two hundred and fifty miles of terrain between Velicatá or Bahía de San Luis Gonzaga, in the south, and San Diego, in the north. At first, no mission or pueblo offered shelter or assistance in coping with the region's unpacified Indians, but gradually, a string of missions closed the gap and the men of Loreto were stationed as their guards and mayordomos.

Many soldiers who served at Loreto during Jesuit times, and some who were born during Jesuit control, had significant careers in Alta California. Several retired in the north to operate ranches on grants of land—and thus became pioneer settlers and, in several cases, founders of important Alta California families. Others received similar, though smaller, landholdings in Antigua California; these grants at first were in *el Sur*, later in the neighborhoods of peninsular missions and ex-missions in other areas. The process of privatization that the Jesuits had resisted for so long accelerated and became the norm.

Ironically, the most lasting Jesuit influence on both Californias was the community of handpicked gente de razón they had brought to the peninsula. The Jesuits had carefully chosen upright workers who could help to operate their mission endeavor and live harmoniously within its rigid confines. Those gente de razón carried on even as the missions faded away. They settled in Alta California early and received a large share of land grants. When the United States took over the area, descendants of peninsular colonists were in the upper class of California Mexicans; they met the invaders on a more equal social footing than their humbler neighbors. Over the years, their group tended to merge with the North Americans rather than being shunted aside by them.

The gente de razón who remained in Antigua California paid a price for the unworldliness caused by the strict controls and limitations they had accepted as Jesuit employees. When conventional government came, they were poorly prepared to compete for the political favor of officials, to cope with a cash economy, or to engage in any form of organized commerce; they had been denied all experience with such matters. In short order, newcomers dominated the business affairs of the small peninsular community and controlled most of the small supply of cash. Antigua California's people became further isolated after Spain lost control of Mexico and the missions faded away. They had no real representatives in Mexico City. They were largely overlooked by their church and by their new government. Despite this lack of services, supervision, and education, successive generations remained industrious, family-oriented, law-abiding, and tolerant of each other and of strangers. Two hundred years after the Jesuit expulsion, their descendants lived in ways that reflected credit on the traditions of their pioneer ancestors and on the judgment of those padres who long ago set the standards for their society and policed its formative years.

Abbreviations Used in Appendixes and Notes

N.B. Herein, "Padre" is abbreviated as "P." The names of most printed sources are given in abbreviated forms. See the bibliography for full information on each. In most cases, no citations are provided for particular baptisms, marriages, or burials. The reader may assume that these facts were derived from the record books of the appropriate missions. Information on these mission records will be found in the bibliography.

AGI	Archivo General de Indias, Sevilla.
AGNM	Archivo General de la Nación, México, D. F.
AHBCS	Archivo Histórico de Baja California Sur, La Paz.
AHH	Archivo Histórico de Hacienda, México, D. F.
AIPG	Archivo de Instrumentos Públicos de Guadalajara.
TBL	The Bancroft Library.
BNM	Biblioteca Nacional de México, México, D. F.
FHL	The Family History Library, The Church of Jesus Christ of Latter-day Saints.

Appendix A

Spanish Kings and Viceroys of New Spain

The following individuals were involved in California affairs from 1691 when Salvatierra and Kino began their campaign to obtain permission to place a mission on the peninsula, until 1768, when the Jesuits were expelled from California—as well as from the entire Spanish world.

Kings of Spain

Carlos II   (born in 1661) 1665–1700
Felipe V   (born in 1683) 1700–1746
Fernando VI   (born in 1713) 1746–1759
Carlos III   (born in 1716) 1759–1788

Viceroys of New Spain

Gaspar de Sandoval Silva y Mendoza, Conde de Galve
    20 November 1688 – 27 February 1696
Juan de Ortega y Montañez, Arzobispo de México
    27 February 1696 – 18 December 1696
José Sarmiento Valladares, Conde de Moctezuma
    18 December 1696 – 4 November 1701
Juan de Ortega y Montañez, Arzobispo de México
    4 November 1701 – 27 November 1702
Francisco Fernández de la Cueva, Duque de Alburquerque
    27 November 1702 – 15 January 1711

Fernando de Alencastre Noroña y Silva, Duque de Linares
    15 January 1711 – 15 August 1716
Baltasar de Zúñiga y Guzmán, Marqués de Valero Ayamonte
    15 August 1716 – 15 October 1722
Juan de Acuña, Marqués de Casafuerte
    15 October 1722 – 17 March 1734
Juan Antonio de Vizarrón y Eguiarreta, Arzobispo de México
    17 March 1734 – 17 August 1740
Pedro de Castro y Figueroa, Duque de la Conquista
    17 August 1740 – 23 August 1741
Pedro Cebrián y Agustín, Conde de Fuenclara
    3 November 1742 – 9 July 1746
Francisco de Güemes y Horcasitas, Conde de Revillagigedo
    9 July 1746 – 9 November 1755
Agustín de Ahumada y Villalón, Márques de Amarillas
    10 November 1755 – 5 February 1760
Francisco Cagigal de la Vega
    28 April 1760 – 5 October 1760
Joaquín de Montserrat, Marqués de Cruillas
    5 October 1760 – 24 August 1766
Carlos Francisco de Croix, Marqués de Croix
    24 August 1766 – 21 September 1771

Appendix B

Jesuit Personnel at California Missions, 1697–1767

 This distribution of padres and hermanos coadjutores is drawn from sources judged too numerous to cite individually. Principal among them are *libros de misión*, Venegas, "Empressas Apostolicas," Barco, *Historia natural y crónica*, and Burrus and Zubillaga, *El noroeste*. Contradictions have been resolved in favor of documentation generated by persons closest to the scene. No Jesuit is placed at a mission without specific documentation, but a few of the time spans are conjectural at one or the other end. Each mission was normally directed by one resident Jesuit. Any of several conditions might place two or more at the same mission in the same year: (1) one padre was reassigned or retired during a year and another took his place in the same year; (2) the assigned missionary was ill or absent and another was sent as a substitute; (3) a veteran missionary was assigned another as a trainee.

Each padre who is listed with no qualifying statement may be assumed to have been the principal missionary assigned to that mission during the indicated period of time.

Guadalupe (*Nuestra Señora de Guadalupe de Huasinapí*)

1720–1735	Everardo María Helen
1724	Ignacio María Nápoli — substituting for Helen during illness
1726	Francisco Osorio — substituting for Helen during illness
1736–1754	José Gasteiger
1755–1768	Benno Ducrue

La Paz (Nuestra Señora del Pilar de la Paz Airapí)

1720–1728   Jaime Bravo
1725   Lorenzo Carranco — training to take over Santiago
1728–1733   Guillermo Gordon
1734–1736   Vacant during rebellion
1737–1748   Visited by Bernardo Zumziel from Santa Rosa[1]
1746–1747   Visited by Juan Javier Bischoff from San Luis Gonzaga

La Purísima (La Purísima Concepción de Cadegomó)

1719–1730   Nicolás Tamaral
1725–1726   Francisco Osorio — substituting for Tamaral during absence
1730–1732   Sigismundo Taraval
1733–1753   Jacobo Druet
1753–1754   Benno Ducrue
1755–1757   Visited by Benno Ducrue from Guadalupe, Francisco Inama
             from San José de Comondú
1757–1766   Juan Javier Bischoff
1766–1768   Juan Diez

Loreto (Nuestra Señora de Loreto Conchó)

1697–1704   Juan María de Salvatierra
1697–1699   Francisco María Piccolo
1701   Juan de Ugarte
1702–1703   Geronimo Minutili
1704   Pedro de Ugarte — training to open San Juan Bautista
1705–1720   Jaime Bravo (brother assistant)
1707–1717   Juan María de Salvatierra
1719–1729   Francisco María Piccolo
1720–1761   Juan Bautista Mugazábal (brother assistant)
1728–1744   Jaime Bravo
1744–1748   Gaspar Trujillo
1747–1752   Juan de Armesto
1753–1757   Juan Javier Bischoff
1755–1762   Francisco López (brother assistant)
1757–1768   Lucas Ventura
1760–1764   Joaquín López y Cía (brother assistant)
1763–1765   Julián Salazar
1765–1768   Juan Villavieja (brother assistant)

Los Dolores *(Nuestra Señora de los Dolores Apaté)*

1721–1747	Clemente Guillén
1747–1768	Lamberto Hostell

San Borja *(San Francisco de Borja Adac)*

1762–1768	Wenceslao Linck
1764–1766	Victoriano Arnés — training to open Santa María
1765	Juan Diez — training to open Santa María

San Ignacio *(Nuestro Señor San Ignacio de Kadakaamán)*

1725–1728	Sebastián de Sistiaga — preparing people and site
1728–1733	Juan Bautista María de Luyando
1728–1747	Sebastián de Sistiaga
1732–1733	Sigismundo Taraval
1734–1759	Fernando Consag
1759–1768	José Mariano Rotea

San Javier *(San Francisco Javier de Biaundó)*

1699–1703	Francisco María Piccolo
1702	Juan de Ugarte
1703–1704	Juan Manuel de Basaldúa — training to open Santa Rosalía
1704–1730	Juan de Ugarte
1718–1719	Juan Bautista Mugazábal — novice under Ugarte
1718–1719	Nicolás Tamaral — training at visita of San Miguel to open La Purísima
1731–1738	Agustín María de Luyando
1734–1737	Guillermo Gordon — padre ministering to visita of San Miguel
1738–1768	Miguel del Barco

San José de Comondú

1708–1736	Julián de Mayorga
1737–1744	Francisco Javier Wagner
1745–1751	José Rondero
1751–1768	Francisco Inama

San José del Cabo Añuití

1730–1734	Nicolás Tamaral
1735	Vacant during rebellion
1736–1738	Sigismundo Taraval
1737	Miguel del Barco–substituting for absent Taraval
1738–1740	Lamberto Hostell
1741–1746	Sigismundo Taraval
1747–1751	Carlos Neumayer

San Juan Bautista de Ligüí (or Malibat)

1705–1708	Pedro de Ugarte
1709–1711	Francisco de Peralta[2]
1711–1714	Visited by padres available at Loreto
1714–1720	Clemente Guillén[3]

San Luis Gonzaga Chiriyaqui

1737–1738	Lamberto Hostell
1739–1740	Visited by Clemente Guillén from Los Dolores
1741–1745	Lamberto Hostell
1746–1750	Juan Javier Bischoff
1751–1768	Jacobo Baegert

Santa Gertrudis de Cadacamán

1751–1768	Jorge Retz

Santa María Cabujakaamung

1766–1768	Victoriano Arnés
1766	Juan Diez

Santa Rosa

1734	Sigismundo Taraval
1735–1736	Vacant during rebellion
1737–1750	Bernardo Zumziel
1751–1752	Juan Javier Bischoff

Santa Rosalía de Mulegé

1705–1709	Juan Manuel de Basaldúa
1709–1718	Francisco María Piccolo
1717	Nicolás Tamaral
1718–1726	Sebastián de Sistiaga
1725	Francisco Osorio — substituting for the absent Sistiaga
1727–1730	Juan Bautista María de Luyando[4]
1731–1732	Visited by Sebastían de Sistiaga from San Ignacio, Everardo Helen from Guadalupe
1733–1734	Guillermo Gordon
1735–1754	Pedro María Nascimbén
1755	Visited by Benno Ducrue from Guadalupe
1756–1757	Joaquín Trujillo
1757–1759	Francisco Escalante
1759–1760	Julián Salazar
1760–1768	Francisco Escalante

Santiago el Apóstol Aiñiní

1724–1726	Ignacio María Nápoli
1726–1734	Lorenzo Carranco
1735–1736	Vacant during rebellion
1736–1746	Antonio Tempis
1747–1750	Sigismundo Taraval
1750–1751	Bernardo Zumziel
1752–1753	Juan Javier Bischoff
1753–1759	Francisco María Badillo
1759	Francisco Escalante
1760–1763	Julián Salazar
1763–1768	Ignacio Tirsch

Todos Santos

1752–1764	Carlos Neumayer
1764–1766	Francisco Javier Franco
1767–1768	Juan Javier Bischoff

---

1. P. Zumziel divided his time between Todos Santos and La Paz. Since Todos Santos had a larger population and abundant agriculture, it was no doubt his seat, while La Paz became in effect a visita. In 1748, La Paz was abandoned as a mission and Todos Santos received its entire population.

2. P. Francisco de Peralta was absent much of the time — in Loreto, due to illness, and in Matanchel

supervising repairs on a California ship. From 1709 to 1713, Misión de San Juan Bautista was run like a visita of Loreto.

3. P. Clemente Guillén went to Loreto in April 1717 and ran that mission until November 1718. Meanwhile, San Juan Bautista was once again treated as a visita.

4. The libros de misión show that P. Luyando, despite being the nominal founder of Misión de San Ignacio in January 1728, actually spent most of 1728–1730 at Misión de Santa Rosalía while P. Sistiaga tended San Ignacio.

Appendix C

Jesuits Who Visited or Served in California, 1697–1768

 Jesuits appointed to serve on the peninsula, or men appointed to any religious or civil posts in the New World, are usually easy to identify through documents that name them to posts or otherwise track the selection process. It is often more difficult to verify that people appointed actually arrived and served. Months and even years passed between the time a candidate was nominated in New Spain, then appointed or confirmed in Spain, and finally received his orders. Meanwhile, a man might be assigned elsewhere, become ill, or die. Several Jesuits were selected for California service but demonstrably did not report and are found working in other mission fields or other enterprises of the order.

Members of the Society of Jesus for whom I have been able to find documented presences in California are listed alphabetically—with birth and death years, nationality, type and dates of service or activities. Dates preceded by "post-" are not those of deaths, but rather indicate the last year in which the individual can be documented as alive. Dates for events in California have been determined wherever possible from libros de misión. References to baptisms or marriages at California missions imply that the sources are the appropriate libros de misión, which may be found in the Bibliography but are not cited— following the practice employed elsewhere in this text. Major sources of biographical information, when available, are indicated. The quoted physical descriptions of some Jesuits are those written at Cádiz on exit documents when the men left for the New World. These are located in AGI, Contratación, legajo 5550.

Compiling lists of Jesuits with California service, or those who set foot on California soil, has served as a parlor game for scholars for over a century. Lists were produced by Bancroft (1884), Engelhardt (1929), Decorme (1941), Dunne (1952), and Burrus (1984). Each participant has tried to refine previous entries and add new names—as is the case here—but no end is in sight.

Documents continue to be located, additional priests or brothers of the order continue to be found.

Alvarez, Lucas Luis (1688–1760)   Born in Veracruz, New Spain. Missionary in the Tarahumara, 1726–1737, and Sinaloa, 1737–1758. Visitador general, inspected California in 1742. Burrus, *Jesuit Relations*, pp. 209–15, 235 n. 7.

Armesto, Juan de (1713–1795)   Born in Villa de Monforte de Lemos (also given as San Cristóbal de Cermela), Lugo, Spain. "Average physique, slim, fair-skinned, thin beard, scar below the hair on his right forehead, blue eyes." Procurador in Loreto from May 1747 until the end of 1752. Left to serve as *procurador de Californias* in Mexico City, 1753–1767. Expelled in 1767; exiled and died in Bologna. Ducrue, *Account of the Expulsion*, p. 26.

Arnés, Victoriano (1736–1788)   Born in Villa de Graus, Aragón, Spain. "Medium physique, pallid complexion, slim, thin beard, eyes and hair black." Missionary assistant at San Borja, 1764–1765; founder and missionary at Santa María, 1765–1768. Expelled 1768; died in Rome. Ducrue, *Account of the Expulsion*, p. 22.

Badillo, Francisco María (1719–1783)   Born in Palencia, Spain. Missionary at Santiago, 1753–1759. Transferred to the Tarahumara mission of Carichic. Expelled to Bologna where he died. Decorme, *Jesuitas Mexicanos*, vol. II, p. 543; Roca, *Jesuit Churches*, p. 238.

Baegert, Jacobo [Johann Jakob Baegert] (1717–1772)   Born in Schlettstadt, now Sélestat, Alsace, France. "Poor physique, fair skin, corpulent, thin beard, and thick lips." Missionary at San Luis Gonzaga, 1751–1768. Expelled 1768. Wrote useful letters from California, and, after the expulsion, an important description of Jesuit California. Died at Neustadt in the Rhenish Palatinate. Baegert, *Letters*, biographical data on pp. 19–28.

Baltasar, Juan Antonio (1697–1763)   Born in Lucerne, Switzerland. Missionary in the Sinaloan mountains, 173?–1736; rector of the Colegio de San Gregorio in Mexico City, 1736–1744. Visitador general, inspected California in 1744. Author of an important report on California, a result of his visit. Provincial of New Spain's Jesuits, 1750–1753. Burrus, *Jesuit Relations*, p. 203; Dunne, *Juan Antonio Baltasar*, pp. 33–43.

Barco, Miguel del (1706–1790)   Born in Casas de Millán, Estremadura, Spain. "Average physique, tan complexion, light-colored eyes, red-brown hair." Missionary at San José del Cabo, 1737, San Javier, 1737–1768. Expelled 1768. Wrote an extended manuscript that is the major source of historical information for the latter half of California's Jesuit years. Exiled and died in Bologna. Barco, *Historia natural y crónica*, biographical data on pp. xvii–xxxi; Burrus, *Jesuit Relations*, p. 38–39.

Basaldúa, Juan Manuel de (1675–post-1714)   Born in Michoacán, New Spain. Missionary assistant at San Javier, 1703–1704. Founder and missionary at Santa Rosalía de Mulegé, 1705–1709. Transferred to Sonoran missions for poor health, 1709. Burrus, *Jesuit Relations*, p. 67.

Bischoff, Juan Javier [Johann Xaver Bischoff] (1710–post-1769) Born in Glatz, Bohemia, now Klodzko, Poland. "Small stature, fair-skinned, blond, blue-eyed, thin beard." Missionary at San Luis Gonzaga, 1746–1750; Santa Rosa, 1751–1752; Loreto, 1753–1757; La Purísima, 1758–1766; Todos Santos, 1767–1768. Expelled 1768; returned to homeland, but no further data available. Ducrue, *Account of the Expulsion*, pp. 15–16.

Bravo, Jaime (1683–1744) Born in Aragón, Spain. Hermano coadjutor at Loreto, 1705–1718. Elevated to status of padre, 1718. Founder and missionary at La Paz, 1720–1728. Procurador in Loreto, 1728–1744. Wrote many useful letters and informes. Salvatierra, *Selected Letters*, p. 50.

Carranco, Lorenzo José (1695–1734) Born in Cholula, New Spain. Missionary briefly at Todos Santos, then at Santiago, 1726–1734. Killed by a rebellious group that included some of his own neophytes. Taraval, *Indian Uprising*, pp. 225–28; Burrus, *Jesuit Relations*, p. 34.

Carta, Agustín (1699–1767) Born in Cagliari, Sardinia. "Good physique, dark-skinned, slim, nose somewhat broad." After teaching at Jesuit colleges in Mexico City (1744) and Querétaro (1748), he became a missionary in the Pimería Alta in 1751. As visitor general, he came to California in 1752. He served as provincial of New Spain, 1755–1760. Nunn, *Foreign Immigrants*, pp. 45, 153; Decorme, *Jesuitas Mexicanos*, vol. I, pp. 431–32.

Consag, Fernando [Ferdinand Konscak] (1703–1759) Born in Varazdin, Croatia. "Good physique, fair-skinned, reddish-brown hair, large blue eyes, a scar on his chin." Missionary assistant at San Ignacio, 1733–1746, during which time he was usually working with peoples to the north preparatory to founding a new mission. Missionary at San Ignacio, 1747–1759. Burrus, *Jesuit Relations*, p. 36; Barco, *Historia natural y crónica*, pp. 289–92.

Diez, Juan José (1735–1809) Born in Mexico City. Trained during 1765 at San Borja to be a founder of Misión de Santa María but became ill. Assigned to La Purísima 1766–1768. Expelled in 1768. Died in Ferrara, Italy. Ducrue, *Account of the Expulsion*, p. 18.

Domínguez, Francisco (1707–post-1751) Missionary at Chínipas, 1737–1743, then Navojoa and Caamoa on the Río Mayo in Sonora. In 1747, his missions did not operate because they received no supplies. Somehow Domínguez was invited to San José de Comondú where he performed and recorded baptisms in April and September, 1747. In 1749, he was moved from the Sonoran missions to those of Nayarit. AGNM, Missiones 22, fold. 24–24v, 103, 105v, 107, 111, 120.

Druet, Jacobo (1698–1753) Born in Torino, Italy. "Good physique, reddish-brown hair, and a scar on the right side of his jaw." Missionary at La Purísima, 1733–1753. Burrus, *Jesuit Relations*, p. 68, 235 n. 10.

Ducrue, Benno (1721–1779) Born in Munich, Bavaria. "Tall, slim, fair-skinned, with two moles on the left side of his face." Missionary at La Purísima, 1753–1754; Guadalupe, 1755–1768. Expelled 1768. Wrote an important historical account of the expulsion of the California Jesuits.

Died in Munich. Ducrue, *Account of the Expulsion*, biographical data on pp. 7–9.

Echeverría, José Antonio (1688–1756)   Born in Spain. Procurador de Californias, 1719–1729. Visitador general, inspected California in 1729–1730. Wrote several useful letters related to his visit. Burrus, *Jesuit Relations*, p. 68.

Escalante, Francisco (1724–1806)   Born in Jaén, Andalucía, Spain. Missionary at Santa Rosalía de Mulegé, 1757–1759; Santiago, 1759; Mulegé, 1760–1768. Expelled 1768; exiled in Bologna — but said to have died in his place of birth. Ducrue, *Account of the Expulsion*, pp. 18–19.

Franco, Francisco Javier (1738–1807)   Born in Agreda, Castilla la Vieja, Spain. "Poor physique, thick-featured, dark-skinned, eyes and hair black." Missionary at Todos Santos, 1764–1766, Loreto, 1767. Expelled 1768; exiled and died in Bologna. Ducrue, *Account of the Expulsion*, p. 24.

García, Andrés Javier (1686–1764)   Born in Beturia, Estremadura, Spain. Visitador general, inspected California in 1737. Provincial, 1747–1750. Burrus, *Jesuit Relations*, p. 68; Decorme, *Jesuitas Mexicanos*, vol. I, p. 387; Roca, *Jesuit Churches*, p. 259.

Gasteiger, José [Joseph Gasteiger] (1702–1754)   Born in Leobli[?], Archbishopric of Salzburg. "Of small stature, fair-skinned, blonde hair and beard, large mouth." Missionary at Guadalupe, 1735–1754. Venegas, "Empressas Apostolicas," párrafo 1007; AGNM, Californias 60 bis; Nunn, *Foreign Immigrants*, p. 155.

Gilg, Adamo (1653–post-1711)   Born in Rymarov, Moravia. Missionary among the Seris of Sonora, 1688–1710?. Performed four neophyte baptisms at Loreto, 19 September 1705. Nunn, *Foreign Immigrants*, p. 156.

Gordon, Guillermo [William Gordon] (1698–post-1751)   Born at Aberdeen, Scotland. "Fair-skinned, medium blonde, slender of face." Took Loreto's supply ship to Acapulco in 1728. Missionary at La Paz, 1728–1733; Santa Rosalía de Mulegé, 1733–1734; San Miguel — a visita of San Javier, 1734–1737. Left California by 1738; next appears in records in 1744 at the Jesuit Colegio de Espíritu Santo at Puebla where he was resident until at least 1751. AGI, Contratación, leg. 5550 contains Gordon's "Declaration" on departure for the New World, Cádiz, 21 June 1723; Nunn, *Foreign Immigrants*, p. 156 n. 8, gives a brief, documented account of Gordon's activities in the conversion of English Protestants in Mexico City, 1724–1727. Gordon's family may have left Scotland during the devastating famine of 1696–1704. Bangert, *A History of the Society of Jesus*, pp. 322–23.

Guenduláin, Juan de (c. 1681–1748)   Born in Oaxaca. Taught and served as rector of several Jesuit colleges, 1708–1724. Visitador general, 1724–1726. Died while serving as rector of the Colegio de San Ildefonso, Mexico City. Roca, *Jesuit Churches*, pp. 263–64.

Guillén, Clemente (1677–1748)   Born in Zacatecas, New Spain. Missionary at San Juan Bautista Malibat, 1714–1717; Loreto, 1718; Malibat,

1719–1720; transferred mission south from Malibat to found Los Dolores, 1721; at Los Dolores, 1721–1747. Died in Loreto. Led significant expeditions of discovery; wrote several important diaries and letters. Guillén, *Overland Expeditions*, biographical data on pp. 19–26.

Helen, Everardo [Everard Maria Hellen] (1699–1757) Born in Xanten, North Rhine, Germany. Missionary at Guadalupe, 1720–1735. Suffered poor health during missionary years; retired for that reason to the Jesuit seminary at Tepotzotlán. Barco, *Historia natural y crónica*, pp. 260–61.

Hostell, Lamberto [Lambert Hostell] (1706–post-1773) Born in Bad Münstereifel, near Bonn, Duchy of Jülich, Lower Rhineland. "Average physique, fair-skinned, blue-eyed, blonde hair and beard." Missionary at San Luis Gonzaga, 1737–1738; San José del Cabo, 1738–1740; split time between San Luis Gonzaga and Los Dolores, 1741–1743; San Luis Gonzaga, 1744–1745; Los Dolores, 1746–1768. Expelled 1768; last reported living in Düsseldorf in 1773. Ducrue, *Account of the Expulsion*, pp. 9–12.

Inama, Francisco [Franz Inama von Sternegg] (1719–1782) Born in Vienna, Austria. "Poor physique, fair skin, pitted by smallpox." Missionary at San José de Comondú, 1751–1768. Expelled 1768; returned to Austria and served as a diocesan priest after the universal suppression of the Society of Jesus. Ducrue, *Account of the Expulsion*, p. 17.

Linck, Wenceslao [Wenceslaus Linck] (1736–post-1790) Born in Neudek [?], Bohemia. Missionary at San Borja, 1762–1768. Expelled 1768; returned to his native land and last reported in 1790 serving as a priest at Olmütz, now Olomouc in the Czech Republic. Linck, *Diary of 1766 Expedition*, biographical data on pp. 14–30.

Lizasoáin, Ignacio (1717–1789) Born in Pamplona, Países Vascos, Spain. "Tall, slim, fair skin, and dark brown hair." Missionary in Sonora, 1751–1766. Visitador general, inspected California in 1762–1763. Provincial of New Spain at the time of the expulsion, 1767. Lizasoáin, "Noticia de la visita general de P. Ignacio Lizasoain Visitador General de esta Prov. de Nueva España . . . ," pp. 1–47, document 47, García Mss., W.B. Stevens Collection, Library of the University of Texas; Decorme, *Jesuitas Mexicanos*, vol. I, p. 433; Burrus, *Jesuit Relations*, pp. 40–41.

López, Francisco (1699–1783) Born in Venezuela. Hermano coadjutor at Loreto, 1755–1762. Burrus, *Jesuit Relations*, p. 68; AGNM, Californias 60 bis; Barco, *Historia natural y crónica*, p. 334.

López y Cía, Joaquín (no biographical data) Hermano coadjutor at Loreto, 1760–1764. Ignacio Lizasoáin, "Noticia de la visita general de P. Ignacio Lizasoain Visitador General de esta Prov. de Nueva España . . . ," p. 3, document 47, García Mss., W.B. Stevens Collection, Library of the University of Texas; AGNM, Californias 60 bis, exp. 15 (in this chronological *expediente*, under years 1760, 1762, 1764).

Luyando, Agustín María de (1698–1752) Born in New Spain; brother of Juan Bautista (q.v.). Missionary assistant at San Javier, 1730; missionary at

San Javier, 1731–1738. Transferred to a post in the Mexican Province of the Society of Jesus. Burrus, *Jesuit Relations*, p. 68; AGNM, Californias 60 bis.

Luyando, Juan Bautista de (1700–1757) Born in Mexico City. Benefactor and founder of record of Mission San Ignacio, for which Sebastián de Sistiaga made the actual on-the-ground preparations. Missionary, dividing duties with Sistiaga at San Ignacio and Santa Rosalía, 1727–1733. Retired to New Spain for reasons of health. Burrus, *Jesuit Relations*, p. 35; Barco, *Historia natural y crónica*, p. 264.

Mayorga, Julián de (1670–1736) Born in Villarejo de Montalban, near Toledo, Spain. "Good physique, coarse features, swarthy complexion." Missionary assistant at Loreto, 1707. Founder and missionary at San José de Comondú, 1708–1736. Taraval, *Indian Uprising*, pp. 257–62.

Minutili, Geronimo (1669–post-1709) Born on Sardinia. Missionary assistant at Loreto, 1702–1703. Transferred to Sonoran mission at Tubutama, 1703. Venegas, "Empressas Apostolicas," párrafos 525, 527–29.

Mugazábal, Juan Bautista (1682–1761) Born in the Basque province of Alava, Spain. Served as soldier and alférez of the presidio of Loreto, 1704–1718; was admitted as a brother to the Society of Jesus, 1719; served as hermano coadjutor at Loreto from 1720 until his death. Barco, *Historia natural y crónica*, pp. 294–95.

Nápoli, Ignacio María (1693–1745) Born in Palermo, Sicily. Began efforts to found Santiago in 1721. Served at Guadalupe in 1724. Became founder and missionary at Santiago, 1724–1726. Transferred to Sonoran mission of Ráhum, 1726. Dismissed from the order for refusing to accept a transfer, 1727, but reinstated in 1730. Returned to California for a year (1736) during the neophyte rebellion of 1734–1736. Served until his death at Tecoripa, Sonora. Nápoli, *The Cora Indians*, pp. 13–29.

Nascimbén, Pedro María [Pietro Maria Nascimbene] (1703–1754) Born in Venice, Italy. "Good physique, hair and eyes dark, pock-marked, and with a large nose." Missionary at Santa Rosalía de Mulegé, 1735–1754. Musical; trained notable neophyte choirs. Barco, *Historia natural y crónica*, p. 262.

Neumayer, Carlos [Carl Neumayer] (1707–1764) Born in Wroclaw, Silesia, now Poland. "Tall, fair-skinned, hair dark red-brown, small eyes, a pockmark on his right cheek." Missionary at Baborigame among the Tepehuanes, 1740–1744; transferred to California, 1746; missionary at Santiago, 1746–1747; San José del Cabo, 1747; Guaymas, 1748–1749; San José del Cabo, 1750–1751; Todos Santos, 1752–1764. Died at Todos Santos. AGNM, Misiones 22, exp. 1 fol. 94; Burrus, *Jesuit Relations*, p. 255.

Osorio, Francisco (1696–1750) Born in Spain. "Tall, fair-skinned." Missionary at La Purísima, 1725–1726. Transferred to Sonoran mission at Mochicagui, 1727, later to the Tarahumara. Burrus, *Jesuit Relations*, p. 69; Venegas, "Empressas Apostolicas," párrafos 1096, 1100; AGNM, Californias 60 bis; AGNM, Misiones 22, fols. 93, 95, 104.

Peralta, Francisco (1682–1728) Born in Spain. "Medium complexion, reddish-brown hair." Missionary at San Juan Bautista de Ligüí, 1709–1711. Left California to supervise a ship's repair, became ill and was transferred to Ráhum, Sonora. Burrus, *Jesuit Relations*, p. 69; Piccolo, *Informe de 1702*, p. 178; Venegas, "Empressas Apostolicas," párrafos 773, 774, 874–75; AGNM, Cárceles y Presidios 5 fol. 102.

Piccolo, Francisco María [Francesco Maria Piccolo] (1654–1729) Born in Palermo, Sicily. "Fair complexion, blond, blue-eyed, tall." Missionary in the Tarahumara, 1684–1697. Missionary at Loreto, 1697–1699; founder and missionary at San Javier, 1699–1703. Temporarily assigned to Sonora as visitador, 1704–1709. Missionary at Santa Rosalía de Mulegé, 1709–1718; Loreto, 1718–1729. Piccolo, *Informe de 1702*, biographical data on pp. 2–13.

Retz, Jorge [Georg Retz] (1717–1773) Born in Düsseldorf, Germany. "Tall, fair-skinned, ruddy-faced, blue-eyed." Founder of Mission Santa Gertrudis and its only missionary, 1751–1768. Expelled 1768; died in Trier, Germany. Ducrue, *Account of the Expulsion*, p. 20.

Rojas, Carlos (1702–1773) Born in Mexico City. Missionary at Arizpe, Sonora, for thirty years. Was appointed visitador general in 1764, but his rounds were delayed by illness. Rojas inspected California in 1766. Expelled 1767; died in Spain. Pradeau, *Expulsión de los Jesuitas*, pp. 210–14; Nentvig, *Descripción geográfica . . . de Sonora*, pp. 148–49; Barco, *Historia natural y crónica*, p. 331.

Rondero, José (1717–1768) Born in Puebla, New Spain. Missionary at San José de Comondú, 1745–1751. Transferred to Sonoran missions. Expelled 1767; died during the expulsion "death march" at Ixtlán del Río. Pradeau, *Expulsión de los Jesuitas*, pp. 219–20.

Rotea, José Mariano (1732–1799) Born in Mexico City. Missionary at San Ignacio, 1759–1768. Expelled 1768; exiled and died in Bologna, Italy. Ducrue, *Account of the Expulsion*, p. 19.

Salazar, Julián (1728–1790) Born in Chiapas, New Spain. Arrived at Loreto in 1758; missionary at Santa Rosalía de Mulegé, 1759–1760; Santiago, 1760–1763; missionary assistant at Loreto, 1763–1765. Transferred to the mission at Bácum, Sonora; served there 1766–1767. Expelled 1768; became a secular priest in Spain; died in Zaca, Spain. Pradeau, *Expulsión de los Jesuitas*, p. 224.

Salvatierra, Juan María de [Giovanni Maria Salvatierra] (1648–1717) Born in Milano, Italy. Missionary in the Tarahumara, 1680–1693. Rector of the Jesuit college in Guadalajara, 1693–1695; rector and master of novices at Jesuit seminary of Tepotzotlán, 1696. Founder of the Jesuit mission to California, 1697. Missionary at Loreto, 1697–1704, 1707–1717. Provincial of the Jesuit Province of New Spain, 1704–1706. Salvatierra, *Selected Letters*, pp. 18–53.

Sistiaga, Sebastián de (1684–1756) Born in Oaxaca, New Spain. Missionary at Santa Rosalía de Mulegé, 1718–1730 — also spent part of most years

1725–1728 preparing Indians for the anticipated mission of San Ignacio; shared duties at both Santa Rosalía and San Ignacio with Padre Juan Bautista Luyando, 1728–1733; shared duties at San Ignacio with Padre Fernando Consag, 1735–1747. Wrote several reports on conditions in Jesuit California. Retired for poor health to Puebla, New Spain, 1747. Four of Sistiaga's reports and biographical data in Burrus, *Jesuit Relations*, pp. 111–48.

Sotelo, Juan María (no biographical data)   Performed both a marriage and a baptism at San Ignacio, 25 April 1762.

Tamaral, Nicolás (1686–1734)   Born in Sevilla, Spain. Missionary assistant to Piccolo at Mulegé, 1717; missionary assistant to Ugarte at San Javier—working primarily at the visita of San Miguel, 1718–1719. Founder and missionary at La Purísima, 1719–1730. Chosen by Visitador General Echeverría, founded and served as missionary at San José del Cabo, 1730–1734. Killed by rebellious neophytes during the general uprising of 1734. Taraval, *Indian Uprising*, pp. 228–32; Burrus, *Jesuit Relations*, pp. 149–50.

Taraval, Sigismundo (1700–1763)   Born in Lodi, Italy. "Medium complexion, dark eyes." Missionary at La Purísima, 1730–1732; San Ignacio, 1732–1733. Founder and missionary at Santa Rosa, 1733–1734. Displaced and preoccupied by the rebellion, 1735–1736. Missionary at San José del Cabo 1736–1738. Went to Mexico City to consult about the finances and controversies of the rebellion, 1739–1740. Missionary at San José del Cabo, 1741–1746; Santiago, 1747–1750, at the time that San José del Cabo was reduced to a visita of Santiago. Left California in 1750; stationed at the Jesuit colegio in Guadalajara until at least 1761. Taraval, *Indian Uprising*, pp. 9–18; Burrus, *Jesuit Relations*, p. 35–36; Nunn, *Foreign Immigrants*, p. 163.

Tempis, Antonio [Anton Tempis] (1703–1746)   Born in Olmütz, Bohemia, now Olomouc in the Czech Republic. "Tall, fair-skinned, blonde hair and beard." Missionary at Santiago, 1736–1746, where he died. Barco, *Historia natural y crónica*, pp. 236, 313–15.

Tirsch, Ignacio [Ignác Tirsch] (1733–post-1769)   Born in Komotau, Bohemia, now Chomutov in the Czech Republic. Missionary assistant to Padre Procurador Lucas Ventura at Loreto, 1762–1763; missionary at Santiago, 1763–1768. Tirsch had a keen interest in natural history and created a valuable series of drawings and watercolors of California plants, animals, Indians, and—rarest of all—gente de razón. Expelled 1768; returned to Prague, 1769—no further record. Tirsch, *The Drawings of Ignacio Tirsch*, biographical data on pp. 15–24.

Trujillo, Gaspar de (1704–post-1756)   Missionary at Belén, Sonora, 174?–1743. Transferred to California: Loreto, 1744–1748; San José de Comondú, 1748. Rector of the Jesuit Colegio del Parral by 1753. Bayle, *Misión*, pp. 228–29; Burrus, *Jesuit Relations*, p. 69; Burrus and Zubillaga, *Misiones Norteñas*, 92, 308.

Trujillo, Joaquín de(1726–1775)   Born in Fresnillo, Zacatecas, New Spain. Missionary at Santa Rosalía de Mulegé, 1756–1757. Missionary in the Tarahumara in 1764. Transferred to Puebla *c.*1765. Expelled to Italy; died at Faenza. Decorme, *Jesuitas Mexicanos,* vol. II, p. 544; Roca, *Jesuit Churches,* p. 300.

Ugarte, Juan de (1662–1730)   Born in Tegucigalpa, Honduras. Procurador de Californias in Mexico City, 1697–1700. Missionary at Loreto, 1701; at San Javier, 1702, 1704–1730. Barco, *Historia natural y crónica,* p. 255; Villavicencio, *Vida de Ugarte.*

Ugarte, Pedro de (1671–1745)   Born in New Spain, brother of Juan de Ugarte. Trained at Loreto, 1704. Founder and missionary at San Juan Bautista de Ligüí, 1705–1709. Transferred to Sonoran missions because of poor health. Venegas, "Empressas Apostolicas," párrafos 533–37, 715, 762–74, 786.

Utrera, José de (1707–1776)   Born in Vélez, near Málaga, Spain. "Tall, blonde, slim, high forehead, small nose, and large mouth." Served as rector of the colleges in Zacatecas and Tepotzotlán. Visitador general, inspected California in 1755. He was expelled to Bologna, Italy, where he was elected to the shadow post of provincial of New Spain in exile, and where he died. Utrera's visit to California is recorded in "Nuevo estado de las Missiones de esta Provincia de la Compañía de JHS . . ." [unsigned manuscript in Utrera's hand], pp. 101–219, Document 67, García Mss., W. B. Stephens Collection, Library of the University of Texas. Entry #881, "Libro de Bautismos, Casamientos, y Entierros . . . de Sn. Joseph Comondu" (under heading of "Año de 1755") reads: "En 11 de Febrero bautizo solemnemente. el Padre Visitador General Joseph de Utrera. . . ." Utrera also baptized an infant at Santa Gertrudis on 31 January 1755, the same date as his inspection of the mission's books. Nentvig, *Descripción geográfica . . . de Sonora,* Apéndice, p. 195; Decorme, *Jesuitas Mexicanos,* vol. II, p. 433.

Ventura, Lucas (1727–1793)   Born in Muel, Zaragoza, Spain. "Medium complexion, corpulent, fair-skinned, dark eyes and hair." Padre procurador in Loreto, 1757–1768. Expelled 1768; exiled and died in Bologna, Italy. Ducrue, *Account of the Expulsion,* p. 23.

Villavieja, Juan Antonio (1736–1816)   Born in Villa de Soto, La Rioja, Spain. Hermano coadjutor at Loreto, 1765–1768. Expelled 1768; exiled in Bologna, Italy; returned to Spain in 1816 and died in Cádiz. Ducrue, *Account of the Expulsion,* p. 25.

Wagner, Francisco Javier [Franz Xaver Wagner] (1707–1744)   Born in Eichstatt, Bavaria. Missionary at San José de Comondú, 1737–1744, where he died. Barco, *Historia natural y crónica,* p. 236; Dunne, *Black Robes,* pp. 303–11.

Zumziel, Bernardo [Bernard Zumpziel] (1707–post-1767)   Born in Westphalia, Germany. "Tall, fair-skinned, hair and beard blonde, eyes blue, ruddy-faced." Missionary at La Paz/Santa Rosa (combined), 1737–1748; Santiago, 1750–1751. Transferred to the Jesuit college at León, 1751; then to their Colegio at San Luis Potosí before 1755. Burrus, *Jesuit Relations*, pp. 207, 223; Ducrue, *Account of the Expulsion*, p. 182; Nunn, *Foreign Immigrants*, p. 162.

Appendix D

Founders of Peninsular California
Families, 1697–1767

These are the progenitors of families that would become important in the growing Hispanic populations of both peninsular and Alta California. Biographical data on most is scarce. The minimum criteria for inclusion here are a documented presence in California during the years 1697–1767 and evidence of the birth of one or more children who contributed to the permanent population. Names of spouses are given in parentheses. Most of these men and women were identified as *españoles*, people of predominantly caucasian extraction; only the exceptions are noted here. Estimated birthdates are preceded by "*c.*" Dates preceded by "post-" are not those of deaths, but rather indicate the last year in which the individual's presence in California can be documented. In most cases, these people's residence in California must have been longer than the scant documentation can confirm.

Citations are located in brackets. A few documents that are cited many times are represented by abbreviations:

1718   Loreto payroll document, 31 July 1718. AGNM, Californias, vol. 80, exp. 3.

1733   Loreto payroll, 31 July 1733. AGNM, Californias, vol. 80, exp. 3.

1751   Loreto muster roll, 13 October 1751. AGNM, Californias, vol. 80, exp. 53.

1768   Rolls of enlistees for militia service at the Real de Santa Ana, November 1768–February 1769, AGI, Guadalajara 416.

Ignacio de Acevedo   Born *c.*1690, died post-1728 (Juana María Macías). Probably raised in the region of Villa de Sinaloa. Soldier at the Presidio of Loreto, 1712 to post-1725 [San Javier Baptisms #844, 906, 912, 1072, 1073, 1076; *1718*; Burrus and Zubillaga, *Misiones Mexicanas*, p. 239]. Literate [*1718*]. See also Index.

Francisco Miguel de Aguiar   Born 1727 in Guadalajara, son of José Antonio de Aguiar and Maria Antonia Manzana, died 1805 at Loreto [AHBCS, Político, docs. 32, 456] (María Antonia Castro). Enlisted at Loreto in 1752, promoted to *cabo* in 1772. Elevated to sergeant in 1776 after re-enlisting in 1775. Cited for valor in two engagements with hostile Indians while leading the *escolta* of Misión de San Gabriel. Twice commanded the detachment of troops at the Real de Santa Ana. Retired by 1788 [AHBCS, Político, docs. 32, 138, 149, 158, 169; California Archive, vol. 5, p. 24]. Literate. See also Index.

Juan Antonio de Aguilar   Born c.1705, died pre-1775 [AHBCS, Político, doc. 33] (María Dolores Montaño). If, as is likely, Juan de Aguilar was the son of Cayetano de Aguilar [*1718*], then Cayetano is the founder of the California family. Juan served as a California soldier from at least 1733 [*1733*] to post-1744 [Comondú Baptism #583]. See also Index.

Miguel de Alvarado   Born c.1715, died post-1752 (Wife's name unknown). Soldier in California by 1742 [Comondú Baptism #516]; signed as a witness to a report [AGNM, Californias, vol. 80, exps. 53, 55] and appeared on the muster roll of the presidio of Loreto in 1751 [*1751*]. Miguel was the only adult male Alvarado with a documented presence in California between 1700 and 1760. Several Alvarados reported their births in Antigua California during the years of Miguel's service; it must be assumed that he was their father. Literate.

Pedro Antonio Amador   Born c.1735 at Cocula, Nueva Galicia, son of José Amador and María Josefa Carpio, died 1824 at Santa Clara, Alta California (María de la Luz Ruiz, María Ramona Noriega). Enlisted at the Presidio of Loreto in 1764 [Eldredge Papers]. Went to Alta California in 1769 but returned to Loreto by c.1771; served at the presidio until 1784 when he was transferred to Santa Barbara [AHBCS, Político, doc. 102]. Literate.

José Gabriel de Arce   Born c.1724 at Villa de Sinaloa, son of Francisco de Pereda y Arce and Rosa López [AHBCS, Político, docs. 30, 113], died 1800 at San Fernando de Velicatá [San Fernando Burials #1784] (Ana Gertrudis Velasco, María Josefa Aguilar). Enlisted in the Escuadra del Sur by Pedro de la Riva in 1749 [AHBCS, Político, docs. 29, 113]; served as a soldier at Santa Gertrudis (1752–1756) and mayordomo at Guadalupe (1757–1768). Member of the first land expedition to Alta California, 1769; returned to serve at Santa Gertrudis by 1771. Promoted to corporal in 1774, sergeant in 1780 [AHBCS, Político, doc. 113], retired 1785, then worked as mayordomo at missions of El Rosario, Santo Domingo, and San Fernando de Velicatá [see record books of said missions]. Full brother of Sebastián de Arce (q.v.). Literate.

Sebastián Constantino de Arce   Born c.1736 at Villa de Sinaloa [AHBCS, Político, doc. 30], died 1795 at La Purísima de Cadegomó [La Purísima Burials #666] (Josefa Rafaela Espinosa, Francisca Velázquez). Enlisted at the Presidio of Loreto in 1759. Went to Alta California in 1769 and on to Monterey in 1770. Assigned to the troop of frontier guards serving under

Alférez José Velázquez (who was also Arce's father-in-law) from about 1773 to 1781. Mayordomo at Mulegé and La Purísima until his death. Brother of José Gabriel de Arce (q.v.). Semi-literate.

Juan Botiller   Born *c.*1700, probably in area of Villa de Sinaloa, died post-1741 [The Bancroft Library M-M 1875, "Documentos Históricos Mexicanos sobre Indios Mayos y Yaquis"] (Inés Márquez). Master blacksmith at the Presidio of Loreto in 1733 [*1733*], leader of a militia troop in the vicinity of the Río Mayo resisting the Yaqui revolt of 1740–1741. See also Index.

Juan Miguel Camacho   Born *c.*1742, died before 1803 (María Josefa Cota). Enlisted at Presidio of Loreto before 1762 when he was the soldier-mayordomo assigned to Misión de la Purísima de Cadegomó [Comondú Marriages, 19 March 1762]. Later served as soldier and mayordomo at Santa Gertrudis and El Rosario [see record books of said missions]; retired with viceregal consent in 1796 [AHBCS, Político, document 276].

Juan Carrillo   Born *c.*1690, died 1748 [Loreto Burial cited in Bancroft, *North Mexican States*, vol. XV, p. 462 n.] (Ifigenia Millán). Enlisted in the Presidio of Loreto by 1715 [San Javier Baptism #59], served at Loreto and several missions (records survive from San Ignacio, 1731 [California Archive, vol. 5, pp. 33–34], and Comondú, 1736–1742]. Continued on active duty until death. See also Index.

Francisco María José de Castro   Born *c.*1725 at Villa de Sinaloa, died 1770 at Loreto [Loreto Burials, Harvard Univ. Library] (María Zeferina Limón). Enlisted in Presidio of Loreto, Escuadra del Sur, before 1751 [*1751*]. By 1754, Castro had been promoted to sergeant and entrusted to conduct a series of legal hearings [AGNM, Provincias Internas, vol. 213, exp. 3]. He remained in the south until 1768 [AHBCS, Político, docs. 152, 202], then was made mayordomo of Misión de la Purísima [Crosby, *Doomed to Fail*, pp. 16–17]. Literate.

Juan Crisóstomo de Castro   Born 1729 at Villa de Sinaloa, son of Ignacio de Castro and Regalada Castro [*1768*], died post-1786 at Todos Santos [Todos Santos Marriage #103] (María Sebastiana de la Higuera). Enlisted in Presidio of Loreto, Escuadra del Sur, by 1757, and served for ten years, largely as mayordomo of Misión de Todos Santos. In 1768, he received a land grant from José de Gálvez and was made sergeant of a militia company created at Gálvez's order at Santa Ana. Castro continued to be mayordomo at Todos Santos for several years and then stayed as a settler [Crosby, *Doomed to Fail*, pp. 11–13]. Literate. Castro's brother, Salvador de Castro (Gertrudis Carrillo), born in 1730, came to California at the end of the Jesuit period. He also got a land grant [AHBCS, Económico, doc. 13] and worked for years under his brother as the mayordomo of a ranch of Misión de Todos Santos [AGNM, Provincias Internas, vol. 166, exp. 1, fol. 92]. Semi-literate.

Juan José Ceseña   Born 1729 at Hostotipaquillo, Nueva Galicia, son of José Ceseña and María Ignacia [*1768*], died post-1773 (Loreta Márquez). Enlisted in Presidio of Loreto, Escuadra del Sur, before 1751 [*1751*]. He and his wife were described as *de color quebrado*, persons of mixed blood, probably white, Indian, and black. In 1768, he was made sergeant of a militia company at Santa Ana [*1768*]. Meanwhile, and until 1773, Ceseña was mayordomo of ex-mission San José del Cabo, at that time a major ranch and visiting station of Misión de Santiago [AGNM, Californias, vol. 2, exp. 2]. Literate.

Miguel Cordero   Born 1706, died post-1766 [AGNM, Provincias Internas, vol. 7, exp. 11] (Angela Núñez). Enlisted in the Presidio of Loreto before 1733 [*1733*], was stationed at Loreto until at least 1742 [AHBCS, Jurídico, doc. 47], but by 1751 was serving in the Escuadra del Sur [*1751*]. Retired by 1766 [AGNM, Provincias Internas, vol. 7, exp. 11]. Literate.

Andrés de Cota   Born 1708 at El Fuerte [AGNM, Provincias Internas, vol. 213, exp. 3], died before 1762 [Comondú marriage, 19 March 1762] (Angela de León). Cota probably enlisted at Loreto by c.1730; he appears on the 1733 payroll as a married soldier on full pay—at a time when most recruits served two or more years on half-pay. Literate. See also Index.

José Antonio Domínguez   Born c.1730, died post-1766 [AGNM, Provincias Internas, vol. 7, exp. 10] (María Robles). Enlisted in the Presidio of Loreto after 1751 but before 1754 [AGNM, Provincias Internas, vol. 213, exp. 3]. Served with the Loreto half of the presidio [above citations and AHBCS, Político, doc. 169]. Literate.

José Marcelino de Estrada   Born c.1715, probably at Tepic or Compostela [*1768*], died 1778 [AHBCS, Jurídico, doc. 4] (Rosalía Heras). José Marcelino and his brother Juan Nicolás (see below) may have been the sons of California soldier Diego de Estrada and his wife, Gertrudis de Chávez, natives of Compostela. (Diego was a married man on full salary at Loreto in 1733 [*1733*]. José Marcelino and his wife lived in Tepic in 1740 [*1768*]. He enlisted in the Presidio of Loreto by 1750 [Comondú Baptism #757]. By 1751, he was serving in the Escuadra del Sur [*1751*] and continued there through 1754 [Misión de Santiago Baptisms #234, 235]. Before 1762, José Marcelino and his brother, Juan Nicolás, had obtained title to a plot [*sitio*] of watered land [AGNM, Provincias Internas, vol. 7, exp. 10].

Juan Nicolás de Estrada   Born c.1712, died 1762 [AIPG, Protocolos de Antonio de Berroa, tomo V, fols. 258v–60] (Juana Morillo). Enlisted in the Presidio of Loreto before 1733 when he was an unmarried soldier on full pay [*1733*]. Attached to the Escuadra del Sur by 1751 [*1751*], resident in *el Sur* the rest of his life. Literate. See also Index.

Cristóbal Gutiérrez de Góngora   Born 1708 at Compostela [Compostela Baptisms, FHL microfilm #654341], died pre-1786 (Josefa Rodríguez, María Serafina Quintero). Literate. See also Index.

Gerónimo González   Born c.1720 in Zacatecas, died post-1768 [*1768*; AHBCS, Económico, doc. 9] (María Teresa Liñán). González was an *español* and his wife a *mulata*. Their many children were identified as mulattoes in church and military records. González was enlisted in the

Presidio of Loreto by 1743 [AHBCS, Económico, doc. 9]; attached to the Escuadra del Sur by 1751 [*1751*], and resident in *el Sur* through the remainder of his known life [Santiago Baptisms; AHBCS, Económico, doc. 9]. Literate.

Francisco Graciano   Born *c.*1705, died post-1732 (María Luna). Graciano is known only from a statement by his son Antonio in 1768 in which he gave his parentage, his age as thirty-six years, and his birthplace as Loreto. Francisco must have been a servant of the Jesuits and probably, like his son, a *casta*, a man of mixed blood [*1768*].

Francisco Javier Heras   Born *c.*1710, died post-1744 [*1768*] (Juana López). Enlisted at the Presidio of Loreto before 1733 when he was an unmarried soldier on full pay [*1733*]. Left California by 1740 when one son was born at San Leonel, Nueva Galicia; another was born there in 1744. Both sons were in California by 1768 [*1768*].

José Ignacio de la Higuera   Born *c.*1730, probably at Villa de Sinaloa, died post-1783 (María Gertrudis Armenta, Ana Rita Bojórquez). Probably a brother of José Joaquín (see below). Enlisted at the Presidio of Loreto by the mid-1750s; soldier at northernmost peninsular missions from 1766– 1782 [Baptismal records of Santa Gertrudis, San Borja, El Rosario]; formally retired in 1783 [AHBCS, Político, docs. 83, 95].

José Joaquín de la Higuera   Born *c.*1725 at Villa de Sinaloa, died post-1768 [Crosby, *Doomed to Fail*, pp. 20–21; San Borja Baptism #2090] (Juana Nepomucena Heredia). He was probably the brother-in-law of Juan Crisóstomo de Castro (q.v.). Higuera first appears in known California records in early 1763 as a soldier at the newly established frontier mission of San Borja [San Borja Marriges]. By 1767, he was mayordomo of that mission [San Borja Baptism #2039].

Luis de Iribe   Born *c.*1706, died post-1777 at Rancho el Salto near Todos Santos [AGNM, Provincias Internas, vol. 7, exp. 10; Todos Santos Marriage Investigation, 15 December 1777] (María Teodora Romero). Iribe was an *español*, his wife a *mulata*. Their children were identified as mulattoes in church and military records. Iribe enlisted in October 1734 in answer to Loreto's call for mainland volunteers to put down the neophyte rebellion in the cape region [AGNM, Californias, vol. 80, exp. 6]. In 1751, he was a member of the Loreto division of the presidio [*1751*]. By 1766 he had retired, held a land grant at El Salto near Las Gallinas, and was called illiterate [AGNM, Provincias Internas, vol. 7, exp. 10].

Andrés López   Born *c.*1695, probably at Villa de Sinaloa, died post-1728 [Son Ignacio born at Loreto, 1728, *1768*] (Rosa Sotomayor). Other than his son's report of parentage and birthplace, López's California career is known only from H. H. Bancroft's report that a "Captain Andrés López" acted as a godfather at Loreto in 1723–1724. Bancroft almost certainly was misreading the abbreviation for *Cabo* [corporal] as the abbreviation for *Capitán* [Bancroft, *North Mexican States*, vol. XV, p. 462 n. 26].

Francisco Ginez de Lugo   Born *c.*1725, probably at Villa de Sinaloa, died after 1758 [Northrup, *Spanish-Mexican Families*, pp. 215–16] (Gertrudis Armenta). Presence in California, 1753–1758, demonstrated by reported births of son Luis Gonzaga and daughter María Guadalupe at Loreto in those years. Lugo and his wife probably lived in California while these children matured.

Francisco Salvador de Lugo   Born *c.*1735 at Villa de Sinaloa, died 1805 at Santa Barbara [Northrup, *Spanish-Mexican Families*, pp. 210–11] (Juana María Martínez). Lugo and his wife served as mayordomos of Misión de San Ignacio in 1760 [San Ignacio Baptism #2349].

Sebastián Manríquez   Born *c.*1715, probably in the Tepic-Jalisco-Compostela area, died after 1775 [*1733*; San Fernando Baptism #968] (Francisca Antonia Estrada, Juliana Bustamante). For details of Manríquez's long and eventful California career. See also Index.

Salvador Márquez   Born *c.*1680, died post-1733 [Loreto Baptism, 9 July 1708; *1733*] (María de la Cruz). Márquez was a casta employed at Loreto at least by 1708 and probably a year or two earlier. He and his wife had a child at Loreto in that year, then served as godparents at San Javier three times in 1714, indicating employment at that mission [San Javier Baptisms #982, 1047, 1052]. By 1733, he was the master caulker at Loreto and still married [*1733*]; by 1751 he was succeeded in his job by his son and namesake. See also Index.

Pablo Regino Mayoral   Born *c.*1730 in the Philippine Islands, died post-1768 [Loreto Baptism, 7 May 1768, Harvard Univ. Library] (María Josefa de Castro). In the baptismal record of their daughter Gertrudis, Mayoral was called *chino marinero* [Filipino sailor] and his wife *india* [Indian]; both were said to be inhabitants of Loreto.

José Hilario Moreno   Born *c.*1730, died post-1764 [*1751*; AHBCS, Político, document 83] (María Loreta de la Peña). Enlisted in Presidio of Loreto, Escuadra del Sur, before 1751 [*1751*]. This couple continued to live in *el Sur* while he served at Misión de Santiago, at least until 1754, and then took up mining at San Antonio before 1764, as shown by the recorded births of four children [Santiago Baptisms, 1753, 1754; AHBCS, Político, document 83].

Manuel Murillo   Born *c.*1700, died post-1751 [*1751*] (Teresa de Acosta). Murillo and his wife were *castas*, probably mestizos, as indicated by racial epithets applied to various members of their family. Murillo was the master shipwright of Loreto's marinería in 1733 [*1733*] and still held the post in 1751 [*1751*]. By the late 1750s, Manuel's sons held both his old post and that of master blacksmith. See also Index.

José Ramón Noriega   Born 1733 at Cosalá, Sinaloa, died post-1790 [living at time of wife's burial, La Purísima de Cadegomó Burials, 1790] (Clara Aguirre). Noriega first appears in California records as a witness to a legal document at San Antonio in June of 1766. In December of that year he was identified as the mayordomo of Misión de Santiago. He received a Gálvez land grant, enlisted in the local militia, then served as a soldier in both Alta and Antigua California [Crosby, *Doomed to Fail*, pp. 10–11]. Literate.

José Gabriel de Ojeda   Born *c.*1725, died post-1774 [San Borja Baptism #2623] (María Ignacia Josefa de Rojas). Ojeda began his service as a soldier with the Esquadra del Sur before 1745 [AGNM, Provincias Internas, vol. 211, exp. 15]. In 1762, he performed an emergency baptism at a mining camp [name lost to page damage] near Misión de Santiago [Santiago Baptisms, 1 September 1762]. A sixth son was born to Ojeda and his wife while he was in command of a detachment stationed at San Borja in 1774. Four sons later served Loreto as soldiers. Literate.

Martín de Olivera   Born *c.*1724, reportedly at Loreto [San Gabriel Marriage #141] died post-1756 [Comondú Baptism #918] (María Micaela Carrillo). Olivera must have arrived in California by *c.*1745, about the time that he married Micaela Carrillo and they began to have sons who reported that they were born on the peninsula. Possibly, he enlisted at Loreto and was assigned as a mayordomo to a mission in *el Sur*, which would explain why he was not on the presidial muster roll of 1751 — a precedent is provided by the case of José Gabriel de Arce, known to have been enlisted in 1749, but missing from the same 1751 list. Or, Olivera may have come to California to work for Manuel de Ocio in the mid-1740s and only taken up soldiering *c.*1754 when his name does appear as a soldier-witness to legal hearings at Todos Santos. [AGNM, Provincias Internas, vol. 213, exp. 3]. In 1756 Olivera was stationed as soldier-escort at Comondú [Comondú Baptism #918]. Literate.

José Francisco de Ortega   Born 1734 in Celaya, Guanajuato, died 1798 in Santa Barbara [Hoja de Servicio, Archivo General de Simancas, leg. 7278, IX, 44] (María Antonia Victoria Carrillo). Enlisted at the presidio of Loreto in 1755, promoted to sergeant by 1757 — the most rapid advancement in the history of the presidio. May have taken time off from military duties to be involved in mining at Real de Santa Ana [Temple, "El Gran Capitán de Nueva California," p. 5]. Gálvez re-enlisted Ortega as sergeant in 1768, put him to work at the royal warehouse [Temple, p. 7]. In 1773, Ortega was promoted to lieutenant and spent years at this rank in Alta and Antigua California. Literate. See also Index.

Juan Luis de Osuna   Born 1715, probably at Villa de Sinaloa, died post-1774 [AGNM, Provincias Internas, vol. 7, exp. 11; AGNM, Californias, vol. 36, exp. 10] (Ana María Alvarado). Enlisted at Loreto by 1749 [Comondú Baptism #730], was assigned to the new mission of San Borja in 1762 [San Borja Baptisms #6–9]. In the first days of 1768, Governor Portolá appointed Osuna to be the comisionado who would run Misión de Santa Gertrudis until the awaited Franciscans were authorized to accept the responsibility [Crosby, *Doomed to Fail*, pp. 19–20]. Illiterate [AGNM, Provincias Internas, vol. 7, exp. 11].

Fernando de la Peña   Born 1714 at Compostela [Compostela Baptisms], died after 1754 [AGNM, Provincias Internas, vol. 213, exp. 3] (María de Arroyo). Peña was one of the Compostelan volunteers who came to California in 1734 to combat the neophyte rebellion and avenge the death of their fellow townsman Don Manuel Andrés Romero [AGNM, Californias, vol. 80, exp. 6]. In 1751, he was the *cabo de escuadra* of the Escuadra del Sur [*1751*]. Literate.

Diego Pérez   Born 1738 at Tepic, died post-1797 [AHBCS, Jurídico, document 47] (Rosalía Cota [sometimes given as Rosa María], Antonia Valenzuela). Pérez and his wives were mestizos. Pérez was probably the son of the Diego Pérez, an unmarried soldier at Loreto in 1733 [*1733*]. The younger Diego came to California in the mid-1760s [AHBCS, Jurídico, document 47], and by 1769 — probably earlier — was skipper of Misión de San Borja's supply launch as it plied regularly between Loreto and Bahía de Los Angeles. For over twenty years Diego Pérez was preeminent among the presidio's small craft personnel.

Felipe Romero   Born *c.*1721 at Río Chico, Sonora, the son of Manuel Romero and Agustina León, died post-1789 [*1768*; California Archive, vol. 5, p. 41; AGNM, Provincias Internas, vol. 7, exp. 11, fol. 109v.] (Juana Liñán). Romero was a mestizo [California Archive, vol. 5, p. 41 — Romero mistakenly called Luis in this copy of parts of the original document, but facts fit Felipe]. Enlisted at Loreto in 1740 [AHBCS, Económico, document 6], was part of Padre Consag's military escort during his 1746 exploration to the mouth of the Río Colorado [Barco, *Historia Natural*, p. 370]. Romero retired in the 1760s, but was made a sergeant of a militia company at Real de Santa Ana in 1768. He also received a Gálvez land grant in 1768, and the next year got title to the lands of Misión de San Luis Gonzaga when it was closed and the neophytes moved to Todos Santos [*1768*; AHBCS, Económico, document 6]. See also Index.

Juan María Ruiz   Born *c.*1725 at El Fuerte, died 1765 near La Paz [Barco, *Historia Natural*, p. 18; Bancroft, *History of California*, vol. II, p. 540 n.] (Ana Isabel Carrillo). Enlisted in Presidio of Loreto before 1751, served in the Loreto division until at least 1759 [*1751*; Comondú Baptism #2005]. See also Index.

Francisco Gabriel Salgado   Born *c.*1730, died pre-1787 [El Rosario Marriage #279] (María Lucía Alipaz). Enlisted in Presidio of Loreto by *c.*1765, served at northern missions the remainder of his career. Promoted to sergeant by 1778 [AGNM, Californias, vol. 36, f. 329; El Rosario Baptism #477; AHBCS, Jurídico, document 5].

Antonio Trasviña   Born *c.*1730 at El Fuerte, died after 1773 [Santa Gertrudis Baptism #1934; Bancroft, *Pioneer Register*, p. 18] (Mariana Verdugo). Enlisted in Presidio of Loreto by 1760, served at northern missions [Santa Gertrudis Baptism #1934], then went north to Alta California in the first years of the new establishments [Bancroft, *Pioneer Register*, p. 18].

Juan Diego Verdugo   Born *c.*1720 at El Fuerte, son of Blas Verdugo and María Micaela de los Rios, died 1780 at San Gabriel [Northrup, *Spanish-*

Mexican Families, vol. II, pp. 318–19; San Gabriel Burial #102] (María Ignacia de la Concepción Carrillo). Enlisted in Presidio of Loreto by *c.*1744, was stationed at Loreto or nearby missions at least until *c.*1762 [Birth dates and places of children, La Purísima Baptism, 16 September 1757; La Purísima Burial, 22 September 1757; Santa Gertrudis Baptism #1935]. Verdugo and his wife were in Alta California from *c.*1776 to 1780 [San Diego Baptisms, 1776; San Gabriel Confirmations, 1778; his death, 1780].

Anastasio Verduzco Born *c.*1740, died 1818 at Caduaño [AHBCS, Jurídico, document 109] (María Ignacia de los Santos Ruiz). Enlisted before 1765 by which time he was mayordomo of Misión de Todos Santos. By 1766, he held the same post at La Pasión (Misión de los Dolores) [AGNM, Provincias Internas, vol. 7, exp. 10]. Served among the first soldiers in Alta California, 1769–1773 [Bancroft, *Pioneer Register*, p. 19], then at Loreto, where he was a corporal by 1780 and retired in 1787 [AHBCS, Político, docs. 49, 169]. He then served as mayordomo at Misión de la Purísima de Cadegomó until after 1788 [La Purísima Baptisms copied in: Martínez, *Guía Familiar*, p. 130]. Verduzco founded Rancho Caduaño near Santiago in the 1790s [AHBCS, Político, document 404].

Manuel de la Torre Villavicencio Born 1706 in Guadalajara, died post-1759 [AGNM, Provincias Internas, vol. 213, exp. 3; AGNM, Californias, vol. 68, exp. 7] (Gertrudis Acevedo). Enlisted at Loreto *c.*1732; in 1733 was a probationary soldier on half-pay [*1733*]. In 1734, worked as a soldier-cowboy on the ranch of Capitán Esteban Rodríguez [AGNM, Provincias Internas, vol. 213, exp. 3]. He was promoted to sergeant by 1751 [*1751*]. In 1759 he was in Acapulco, apparently to meet and inspect the promised California ship, *El Aguila*, arriving from Realejo [AGNM, Californias, vol. 68, exp. 7]. Literate. See also Index.

Glossary

The meanings of some terms in this glossary varied from region to region in the greater Hispanic world. The definitions offered are those understood in Jesuit California, 1697–1767.

Acequia: An open ditch, either unlined or lined with stone and mortar, to conduct water to plots of arable land.

Aguardiente: A distilled liquor made from local alcoholic ferments; in Jesuit California, a grape brandy, a product of several missions.

Alabado (short for *Alabado sea el Santísimo Nombre de Jesús*): A favorite hymn of praise taught to neophytes at missions.

Albañil: A stone or brick mason.

Alcalde: A local magistrate, usually a member of the municipal council.

Alcalde (Indian alcalde): A neophyte given limited responsibilities in directing and supervising mission inmates, chosen by a padre and appointed by the captain of the presidio—a man performing the same duties might instead be called a *fiscal*.

Alcalde mayor: A chief magistrate in charge of a district; a regional governmental post combining judicial, administrative, and tax-collecting duties—subordinate to the *gobernador* of the region.

Alcalde ordinario: A municipal magistrate.

Alférez: The lowest ranked of military officers, approximately equal to a modern lieutenant.

Alférez real: A municipal official, often a member of the town council, in charge of other-than-religious public ceremonies; bearer of the royal standard in civil and religious ceremonies.

Alquitrán: A mixture of pitch, tar, grease, and oils used as a caulking material for hulls of ships.

Ancón: An alluvial shelf that runs along an arroyo just above the watercourse.

Andaluz: A native of Andalucía, southern province of Spain.

Aparejo: A pack saddle made from two thicknesses of leather sewed at their edges; draped over the back of pack animals and offered little padding at the spine but, on each side, provided a large pouch, stuffed with straw, to protect the beast's vulnerable ribs.

Arcón: A chest with a vaulted lid; the common container to protect good clothing from dust.

Armadores de buceo: Pearling entrepreneurs with ships, stores, tools, and crews and finances necessary for pearl diving expeditions.

Arráez: Skipper of a large dugout canoe or a sailing launch.

Arriero: A muleteer.

Arzobispo: An archbishop.

Atole: A cooked mixture of water and grains; a staple mission food.

Audiencia: A royally appointed regional appellate high court which had some legislative authority and acted as an advisory council to a viceroy; also, the region of such a body's jurisdiction.

Auditor de guerra: A judge-advocate to a military command.

Azogue: Mercury, a vital ingredient in refining silver by the amalgamation process.

Avenida: A flash flood channeled by an arroyo into an overwhelmingly destructive rush of water.

Balsa: A raft made by binding bundles of reeds or the pithy trunks of *corcho* (q.v.); used by California Indians for fishing platforms and transportation.

Banda: See *otra banda.*

Bastón: A baton with a silver head, a symbol of office given to a presidial captain.

Batequi: A temporary water hole in the sandy soil at or near the bottom of an arroyo or near an estuary.

Bestia de carga: Pack mules or burros.

Bestia de silla: Riding animals collectively; either riding mules or a mixed group of riding mules and horses (see *caballada*).

Botete: A fish with a poisonous liver.

Caballada: Properly, a group of horses; often a group of horses and mules.

Cabecera: The headquarters or seat of a mission.

Cabo: A man designated to head a detail of soldiers or workers; a foreman.

Cabo de esquadra: A corporal; the presidio's lowest non-commissioned officer.

Cacastle: A crate made from the straight wands of *guatamote* (*Baccharis glutinosa*), a common plant of arroyo beds.

Cajeta: Fruit (and sometimes milk) boiled down to a stiff, moist preserve.

Cal: Lime in powder form, prepared by grinding kiln-fired pieces of limestone.

Calafate: A caulker of ship and boat hulls — and usually a rigging expert; a regular position in the *marinería* of the presidio of Loreto.

Californio: A person raised or, later, born and raised in California.

Camino real: A principal road or trail for mounted travelers or pack trains.

Canoa: A dugout canoe large enough to carry men and supplies in the gulf.

Cantora: An Indian woman trained as a singer and a leader of singers in mission church services.

Capellán de canales adentro: A secular cleric appointed by the bishop of Guadalajara as chaplain of the entire region surrounding the Gulf of California.

Capitán: Captain of the California presidio.

Capitán (Indian capitán): A neophyte official with duties in directing mission inmates (see *gobernador*).

Capitana: The chief ship of the presidio — so called because a captain commanded the presidio.

Cardón (*Pachycereus pringlei*): The giant columnar cactus of the California peninsula; its skeleton has many uses as a building material and its sap and fruit have been regarded as medicinal.

Carpintero de rivera: A shipwright or ship's carpenter.

Carrizo (*Phragmites communis*): A false cane commonly found growing in permanent springs or streams and used as an indication of immediate subsurface water; the stems were used as a material for thatched roofs, woven infill walls, sleeping mats, coarse baskets, etc.

"de casa": A phrase descriptive of an inhabitant of the *cabecera* of a mission — to distinguish him or her from an inhabitant of a *Visita*: Literally, a member of the mission "household."

Casta: A person of mixed racial heritage; a generic term for any mixtures of African, Asian, American, or European blood.

Cazo: A copper cauldron used in refining silver from silver ore.

Cédula real: A royal decree issued by a council over the king's signature.

Chino: A Filipino, many of whom came to New Spain on returning Manila ships.

Chubasco: A violent summer storm common to the Sea of Cortés and surrounding lands.

Coa: A short planting hoe or digging stick.

Colegio: A school or seminary.

Comal: A flat sheet of earthenware or metal for cooking tortillas.

Comisario: The officer in charge of a royal warehouse.

Comisión: A special appointment — one that carried unusual or additional duties.

Comisionado: A soldier appointed to carry out a *comisión.*

Compadrazgo: Fictive ritual kinship through godparenthood.

Compañero: Literally "companion"; a missionary's usual term to indicate the soldier assigned as a guard/mayordomo to his mission.

Conquista: A conquest.

Contracosta: The term for the Pacific coast of the peninsula employed by people in California in the 18th century (see *otra banda*).

Contramaestre: A boatswain; sometimes a skipper of one of the presidio of Loreto's smaller sailing craft.

Corcho or *colorín* (*Erythrina flebelliformis*): A small tree with balsa-like wood; native Californians bound together five or more of the trimmed trunks to form rafts (*balsas*) to be used in lagoons or even on the open ocean.

Corredor: A covered, open-sided porch.

Coyote: A person of mixed African, American Indian, and European heritage.

Criollo: A person of primarily European descent born in the New World.

Cuera (from *cuero:* hide or leather): A heavy, knee-length, usually sleeveless coat made of several layers of buckskin bound at the edges with a strong seam; this distinctive garment gave the presidial soldier the name by which he was known for over two centuries: *Soldado de cuera.*

Cuerpo de guardia: A guardhouse and bunkhouse for men on duty at the presidio.

Cuesta herradura: A graded switchback trail for riding and pack animals.

El Demonio: The missionaries' usual term for the Devil.

Diezmo: The tithe or tenth part of agricultural produce collected by each bishopric.

Dipúa (*Cercidium microphyllum*): A leguminous tree whose cut branches are an important fodder for animals that have to be tied and fed, as during service in a pack train.

Don, doña: A title of honor, in California accorded to any Spaniard, officer, or person from an important, respected family.

Encomiendas: Patronage over a designated number of natives.

Entrada: An expedition in which a missionary, a few soldiers, and sometimes a few converts visited a new area to learn about, and make themselves known to, its people.

Escolta: The escort or squad of soldiers assigned to protect a missionary at a new mission.

Escuadra del Sur: The division of the presidio of Loreto created in 1742 when the previously independent Presidio of the South was transferred to the command of the captain at Loreto.

Español, española: A person of primarily European blood with the cultural characteristics of a Spaniard; a person regarded as worthy to be recognized as white, regardless of heritage from other racial stocks.

Fiscal: An attorney for the crown and legal advisor to the audiencia.

Fiscal (Indian fiscal): An mission Indian official appointed by the captain (see *alcalde*).

Gamuza: A deerhide tanned like a chamois.

Ganado alzado: Half-wild to wild stray cattle.

Ganado mayor: Cattle.

Ganado menor: Sheep, goats, or pigs; any mix of these.

Gente de razón: Literally "people with the capacity to reason," but in fact meaning people born into Christianity; in simple terms, any non-Indian people.

Gentil: A heathen Indian.

Gobernador: Governor of a region or province, subordinate to a *virrey.*

Gobernador (Indian gobernador): A neophyte official with duties and responsibilities in leading mission inmates, particularly in the padre's absence; chosen by a padre and appointed by the captain of the presidio—a man performing the same duties might instead be called a *capitán.*

Güéribo (*Populus brandegeei*): The giant poplar indigenous to the higher sierras of central and southern peninsular California; its wood was used for shipbuilding in Jesuit times.

Hacienda: A rural property typically devoted to raising sheep or cattle.

Hechicero: A wizard or sorcerer; the pejorative name given to Native American shamans by Jesuit missionaries.

Hermano coadjutor: A Jesuit brother helper; in California, an assistant to the *padre procurador.*
in Loreto.

Herrero: A blacksmith.

Indios auxiliares: Indian auxiliaries recruited from the ranks of reliable neophytes in older, established missions to assist in explorations or the establishment or defense of new missions.

Informe: A written report.

Intérprete: A neophyte who spoke good Spanish and assisted a padre as an interpreter.

Justicia mayor: A regional justice appointed by a governor; in California, the post was combined with the captaincy of the presidio.

Ladino: An Indian who proved unusually adept in learning and using Spanish and adopting Hispanic dress and ways.

Lancha: A sailing launch; the smallest boat used regularly to cross the Gulf of California.

Leñero: A gatherer of firewood.

Libros de misión: A mission's books of vital records, usually separate registers of baptisms, marriages, and burials.

Lobo: A person of mixed American Indian and African racial background.

Machaca: Dried meat or fish made more palatable by pounding into stringy fragments.

Madrina: A godmother.

Maestro: A master craftsman; a foreman of a crew of artisans.

Manga: A poncho-shaped overgarment worn by women instead of a coat.

Marco: Half a pound (used as a measure of refined silver).

Marinería: The marine facility of the presidio of Loreto; the sailors and ship's craftsmen of that facility.

Marinero: A sailor.

Masa: Corn treated with limewater, ground to coarse flour, and mixed with water to create the dough from which tortillas are made.

Matacora (Jatropha cuneata): A low growing shrub whose pliant branches yielded fibers used by native Californians in their basketry.

Matanza: A slaughter of herd animals.

Mayordomo: A foreman or supervisor of a mission under the padre, or of a ranch under the owner.

Media plaza: A soldier on half-pay during a probationary period.

Memoria: An annual shipment of supplies; the itemized list of orders that preceded an annual shipment.

Metate: A grind stone or mortar, used with a *mano* (handstone) as an all-purpose grinding or mashing tool by both mission Indians and gente de razón.

Mezcal (Agave species): A plant whose heart, when roasted, provided a staple of Indian diet both before conversion and an important emergency food for a half-century after.

Mezquitillo (probably *Krameria grayi*): A very small woody shrub whose bark is used in tanning so-called "white" leather, usually from deerskin.

Militar: A military man.

Monte: Unused land covered with chaparral; the herbs, shrubs, and trees covering such land (*en el monte* translates as "out in the bush").

Muralla: A dike of large boulders piled up to divert floodwaters of an arroyo from a mission or from its agricultural fields.

Nopal (Opuntia species): The prickly-pear cactus whose leaves and fruit are eaten by men and cattle.

Notario y alguacil mayor: An official of the Holy Office of the Inquisition who would be expected to seek out or report cases of heresy in his area.

Oficiales de rivera: The collective craftsmen of Loreto's *marinería*.

Oidor: A judge; a judge seated on an *audiencia*.

"Otra banda": "The opposite shore;" then — and now — the peninsular California term for the coastline of Sonora and Sinaloa.

Padre general: Jesuit ruler in Rome.

Padre provincial: Jesuit head of each geographic area in which the Society of Jesus was represented.

Padrino: A godfather.

Paje: A neophyte youth selected by a missionary to serve as his page or assistant.

Palo blanco (Lysiloma candida): Multi-trunked tree with white bark; different parts of the plant serve as building material, tanbark, and medicine.

Panocha: Cakes of crude brown sugar made by boiling down cane pressings; the staple sweet of New Spain's frontiersmen and poor.

Paraje: A stopping or camping place with water and pasturage sufficient to support the *caballada* of a party for the length of its stay.

Pardo: A dark-skinned casta, or person of mixed blood.

Patio process: A physical-chemical process of refining silver ore by grinding and amalgamating with mercury.

Pedrero: A large mortar designed to fire a charge of stones or balls.

Peso: The monetary unit of Spanish America; eight *Reales* added up to one peso.

Piedra múcara: A lightweight, calcareous coral skeleton that washed up in chunks on the beaches near Loreto, was gathered, fired in a kiln to form lime, ground to a powder, mixed with sand and water to form a white stucco, and used on all the masonry buildings of the village.

Pila: A small reservoir used to accumulate water during the night so that the volume needed for irrigating a planted area was available as needed.

Piloncillo: A pyramidal or cone-shaped cake of *panocha*.

Pitahaya: Any of several so-called organ-pipe cacti; *pitahaya dulce [Lemaireocereus thurberi]:* the commonest and tallest, whose summer and early fall maturing fruit formed the major part of the Indian diet — and was abundant enough to provide the year's only respite from hunting and gathering and allow an opportunity for rancherías to gather and socialize; *pitahaya agria [Machaerocereus gummosus]:* sour pitahaya, a large, semi-recumbent plant with apple-sized fruit — considered by many the finest of the peninsula's native fruits.

Placer: A bed of pearl oysters; offshore areas where oyster beds were abundant.

Plata de azogue: Silver produced by amalgamation.

Plata de fuego: Silver produced by smelting.

Playa: A sandy beach or, inland, a drainage basin with no outlet; a natural sump.

Poblador: A first settler — who often claimed credit for opening and developing an area.

Pozole: A thick soup of cornmeal, beans, marrow bones, and scraps of meat.

Presidio: A frontier military garrison; the fortified location and community of such a garrison.

Priora: An Indian woman at a mission trusted as a keeper or supervisor of girls or young women.

Procurador de Californias: Jesuit California's own business administrator, stationed at the Colegio de

San Andrés in Mexico City and subordinate to California's *Visitador.*

Procurador en Loreto: The padre in charge of California's supply orders, warehouse, stored goods, payroll, and bookkeeping — in all of which he was assisted by the *hermano coadjutor;* in practice, he was also Loreto's missionary.

Pueblo: The populace; a village or town occupied by the *Pueblo.*

Pueblo de visita: The inhabitants of a *Visita;* a *visita* site, if it had a chapel and/or dwellings.

Pulque: An alcoholic drink made by fermenting a watery slurry of roasted mezcal hearts.

Quelites: Edible herbs.

Quinto (quinto real or *real quinto):* Originally, one-fifth of the gross take of any natural resource claimed as a right by the crown; in practice, the percentage collected varied.

Ramada: Literally, a house of branches; a simple structure made by setting forked posts in the ground as corners and laying other posts across them as superstructure, the whole to be roofed with thatch.

Ranchería: An organized, autonomous band of hunting-and-gathering Indians occupying a well-defined territory; after mission contact, such a band was named for the principal geographical site in its territory.

Real de Loreto (often written by Jesuits simply as *real*): The greater compound of the royal presidio and mission at Loreto.

Real de minas: A mining camp; the seat of a miner who paid taxes.

Rectorado: A rectorate; a territorial division of a regional Jesuit mission system supervised by a padre rector.

Recua: A pack train; the pack, riding, and replacement animals that formed a pack train.

Regalías: "Gifts" to royal officials in appreciation for, and anticipation of, their interest and attention.

Religioso: A man bound by vows to a religious order.

Salina: A salt pan, a natural surface deposit of salt in an inlet from the sea.

Santo Oficio: The Holy Office of the Inquisition.

Saya (Amoreuxia palmatifida): A low plant found in the clays of basins on the high mesas of the central peninsula; it has edible roots, stems, and seeds and was an important winter food resource for Indians in times of drought.

Sargento: A sergeant.

Sirviente: A missionary's paid helper, usually a *Casta* from the area of a Jesuit mainland mission.

Sitio: A parcel of land with water and grazing potential.

Soldado de cuera: A presidial soldier on the northwest frontier of New Spain (see *Cuera*).

El Sur: The part of the California peninsula from the latitude of the north end of the bay of La Paz southward to Cabo San Lucas.

Surgidero: Roadstead or anchorage; a landing place on an open beach.

Tabardillo (Calliandra californica): A low shrub whose flowers and leaves are regarded as medicinal.

Talabartero: A skilled leatherworker.

Tasajo: Jerked meat, salted and dried.

Tegua: A rustic handmade shoe with supple leather uppers nailed to soles made of two or three thicknesses of hide.

Temastián: A neophyte trained as a catechist.

Temporalidades: A mission's lands and non-religious possessions.

Teniente: A lieutenant, or the officer second-in-command of a military unit.

Tercio: One-third of a normal pack-animal load; about sixty pounds.

Tezontle: A vesicular basalt, light in weight and so employed in the construction of vaults for masonry structures.

Tinaja: A water catchment in the bedrock of a watercourse; a cask of about eleven-gallon capacity.

Tinglado: A utility structure consisting of a thatched roof supported by forked tree trunks buried in the earth; a shed.

Torote (Bursera microphylla): A low, spreading tree whose multiple trunks are disproportionately enlarged; the bark is used in tanning *Gamuzas* (q.v.).

Trapiche: An arrangement of a press, a cauldron, and a fireplace that allowed sugar cane juice to be extracted and boiled down to produce *Panocha.*

Tributo: An annual payment of money or goods theoretically owed to the crown by all free men.

Vecino: A resident of a town or a *real de minas.*

Viga: A roof beam or ceiling joist.

Villa: A royally chartered settlement with certain rights to self-government; larger than a pueblo or real de minas.

Vinorama (Acacia brandegeana): A large shrub or small tree that yields the earliest crop of edible seeds that was available to the indigenous people of the peninsula.

Virrey: A viceroy; the chief administrator of a *Virreinato,* a viceroyalty, like New Spain.

Visita: The homebase of a band of Indians attached to but not resident at a mission — so named because it was visited at set intervals by the missionary; an official inspection by a *visitador,* a representative of the king, a viceroy, or, in California, a representative of the Jesuit provincial of New Spain.

Visitador: The supervising priest in a Jesuit missionary district—he got his title from one of his principal functions: the responsibility of visiting each mission twice a year to evaluate its progress; an inspector acting as a representative of and reporting to a higher authority—civilian, military, or church.

Visitador general: An inspector appointed by the Jesuit provincial to visit and report on the missions of the northwest: Nayarit, Tepehuana, Tarahumara, Sinaloa, Sonora, and California; an inspector appointed by the king and royal council to assess and act for them in a major colonial area, like New Spain.

Notes

N.B. The names of most printed sources are given in abbreviated forms. See the bibliography for full information on each. Names of source archives are abbreviated to initial letters (AGNM, etc.). See "Abbreviations Used in Appendixes and Notes" on page 394 for their full names. The recurring titles of "Padre" and "Padres" are abbreviated respectively to "P." and "PP." In most cases, no citations are provided for particular baptisms, marriages, or burials. The reader may assume that these facts were derived from the record books of the appropriate missions. Information on these mission records will be found in the bibliography.

Chapter 1: The Road to California

1. Venegas, "Empressas Apostolicas," párrafo 226.

2. Chapman, *A History of California*, pp. 44–46, 57–63. The role of popular literature in Spain's New World adventure is described in Weber, *Spanish Frontier*, pp. 23–24.

3. Clavijero, *History of California*, pp. 119–24; Chapman, *A History of California*, pp. 48–52.

4. Mathes, *La geografía mitológica de California*.

5. Chapman, *A History of California*, chaps. VII–XI.

6. Schurz, *The Manila Galleon*, pp. 232–34, 241–46.

7. The long history of efforts to open California as a Spanish domain is reviewed in Río, *A la diestra mano de las Indias*.

8. Sauer, *The Road to Cíbola*, passim. More details for the Spanish occupation of the important vicinities of Tepic and Culiacán, for example, are found in Gerhard, *North Frontier of New Spain*, pp. 138–43, 256–61; in Hu-de Hart, *Missionaries, Miners, and Indians*, p. 14. As a condition of his grant, an encomendero was charged to protect, convert, and civilize the Indians on his land. In return, he could exploit their labor and pay a share of his profit to the crown. He was required to support the priests necessary to provide spiritual and scholastic instruction to the Indians. Lockhart provides an excellent overview of the *encomienda* in Spanish America in "Encomienda and Hacienda." See also Bolton, "The Mission as a Frontier Institution," pp. 43ff.; Haring, *Spanish Empire*, p. 20.

9. Weber, *Spanish Frontier*, pp. 71–72, 95, 100; Lockhart and Schwartz, *Early Latin America*, p. 157.

10. Fray Juan Caballero Carranco, who accompanied the Lucenilla expedition to California in 1668, indicated a contemporary name for the Gulf of California in the words, ". . . we began to navigate the passage [between Sinaloa and California] which, on modern maps, is called the Vermillion Sea." Caballero, *The Pearl Hunters of 1668*, p. 38. An example of just such a map is that of the Audiencia of Guadalajara, published in 1656 and reproduced in Ibid., p. 88.

11. Spicer, *Cycles of Conquest*, pp. 46–51, 86–91, 105–7.

12. Ibid., pp. 306–7. All Jesuit missionaries attempted to shield their converts from economic

exploitation by others, but their dream was to achieve the kind of mission autonomy that had been established by their brother Jesuits in Paraguay. There, as a reaction to abuses of Indians by encomenderos, the Society of Jesus claimed vast areas — occupied by Guaraní Indians — as purely mission reductions, excluding Europeans who might wish to develop the area and claim rights to Indian labor. The case became a cause celebre; it was hailed as a veritable Utopia by some of the religious and intellectuals, but generated widespread opposition to Jesuit power and practices among entrepreneurs and bureaucrats of the royal treasury. Morner, *Jesuits in the La Plata Region.*

13. Ibid. A particularly aggravated conflict between secular and religious authority, involving the jailings of Jesuit missionaries, the excommunication of a captain, and extended acrimony came to a boil in the Sinaloa-Sonora area in the 1650s. Faría, *Apologético defensorio.*

14. The distinguishing characteristics of the Jesuit order are discussed in Lockhart and Schwartz, *Early Latin America,* pp. 156–57.

15. Some authorities contend that the title *general* began as *superior general* in which *general* served as an adjective as it does in other Jesuit titles, like *visitador general.* However, the head of the order is usually called the general or padre general, even in Jesuit writings. That usage is employed hereinafter.

16. Haring, *The Spanish Empire,* pp. 174–75, 191. A detailed picture of Jesuit influence, industry, and business acumen in New Spain — and the opposition that it engendered — is found in Konrad, *Jesuit Hacienda.*

17. Spicer, *Cycles of Conquest,* pp. 46–107. The story of the Society of Jesus in Sinaloa and Sonora is told at length from the perspective of a modern Jesuit in Dunne, *Black Robes on the West Coast.*

18. P. Provincial Luis de Bonifaz to P. Visitador of Sinaloa, 15 October 1643. Venegas, "Empressas Apostolicas," párrafo 96. As a result, Porter y Casanate's expedition included Jesuit PP. Jacinto Cortés and Andrés Báez, two Sinaloan missionaries. Ibid., párrafo 99.

19. P. Eusebio Francisco Kino has been the subject of much scholarly and popular attention. For biographical treatment, see Herbert Eugene Bolton, *Rim of Christendom,* and the introductions and footnotes to Ernest J. Burrus's several Kino-related studies (see Bibliography, under "Burrus" and "Kino").

20. Atondo, *First from the Gulf to the Pacific,* pp. 13–16.

21. Bolton, *Rim of Christendom,* p. 125–28, 171.

22. Venegas, "Empressas Apostolicas," párrafo 173. The Jesuit provincial of New Spain in 1686 was P. Luis del Canto.

23. "And should there be at times any scarcity of provisions in California, they could be imported by small craft from the productive nearby regions, namely the lands of the Seris, Guaymas, Sinaloans [Mayos], and Yaquis." P. Kino to the Duchess of Aveiro, 16 November 1686, *Kino Writes to the Duchess,* p. 198. A few months later, Kino wrote about new mines just opened at Los Frailes, Sonora, saying, "Certain it is that so great an increase of the royal revenues . . . will be obtained . . . from these new mines that it really seems that Our Lord repays abundantly all the expenses which can be incurred effecting the conversion of California. . . ." Kino felt that God had arranged that, at the very time he and his fellow Jesuits were in California at the King's expense, "such wealth should have been found right here, almost within sight of California itself. . . ." 15 February 1687., Ibid., p. 206.

24. Venegas, "Empressas Apostolicas," párrafo 174. P. Piccolo's last post in the Tarahumara was at Carichic.

25. Both men, as Italians, had early and fervent devotion to the Loretan manifestation of the Virgin. P. Kino had led a recitation of the Litanies of Our Lady of Loreto in California in 1683. Kino, *Kino Reports to Headquarters,* p. 41. While seriously ill in the late 1670s, P. Salvatierra made a vow to build a replica in Mexico City of the famous chapel or "house" of the Virgin. The Holy House of the Virgin in Nazareth, a small brick building, was believed to have been flown by angels to Loreto, Italy, in 1294. Salvatierra's eldest brother, a Jesuit in Italy, sent drawings and dimensions and P. Juan María raised the funds and supervised the reproduction. Venegas, *El apóstol,* pp. 42–52.

26. Venegas, "Empressas Apostolicas," párrafo 175. Several works, published and manuscript, eighteenth-century and modern, tell the individual or connected stories of PP. Kino and Salvatierra as they planned and achieved a Jesuit mission to California. Useful selections include the following: Venegas, "Empressas Apostolicas," párrafos 173–241; Venegas, *El apóstol,* pp. 78–123; Venegas, *Noticia,* vol. 2, abridged and rewritten by Burriel, pp. 1–21; Salvatierra, *Selected Letters,* pp. 27–33; Bolton, *Rim of Christendom,* pp. 227–28.

27. Kino, *Historical Memoir of the Pimería Alta,* vol. 1, pp. 117–21; vol. 2, p. 240.

28. Venegas, *El apóstol*, pp. 57–76; Salvatierra, *Selected Letters*, pp. 26–27.

29. Many of P. Kino's letters and petitions subsequent to his early labors in the Pimería Alta and adjoining Sonora show that he was alert to every indication that this relatively populous and rich land could support the conquest of California. For example, Kino to P. Juan Marín, 15 February 1687; Kino, *Kino Reports to Headquarters*, pp. 85–89.

30. Venegas, *Noticia*, vol. 2, abridged and rewritten by Burriel, pp. 4–6; Salvatierra, *Selected Letters*, pp. 22–33. PP. Salvatierra and Kino broke no Jesuit rules — or new ground — by planning for California's special problems. Their order had very pragmatic ideas about missionary methodology; campaigns in new areas drew on germane experiences far more than ideology.

31. P. Kino to the Duchess of Aveiro, 16 November 1686. Kino, *Kino Writes to the Duchess*, pp. 195–97.

32. Of P. Salvatierra's visit to the Pimería Alta in 1690–1691, P. Kino wrote: "In all of these journeys the father visitor and I talked together of suspended California, saying that these very fertile lands and valleys of this Pimería would be the support of the scantier and more sterile lands of California — concerning which [discussions], he made a report to Mexico." Kino, *Historical Memoir of the Pimería Alta*, vol. 1, p. 120. Kino reported, upon hearing Salvatierra's admiration for the richness of the Pimería, "I replied that it appeared to me also that these lands, so rich, might be the relief and support of the somewhat sterile and poor California . . . and we [Kino and Salvatierra] planned to return with all possible haste to continue said conquest and conversions." Ibid., II, p. 240.

33. A unique relationship between the Roman Catholic Church and the Spanish crown resulted in the institution called *patronato real* which lay behind Spain's integration of the church and its missionaries into their scheme of conquest and control. Farriss, *Crown and Clergy*, pp. 6–10.

34. Farriss, *Crown and Clergy*, pp. 1–4. Because of their mandate to form and govern missions, opponents found it easy to claim that the missionaries posed as rulers themselves and failed to make converts aware of their rightful king. Both Sonoran and Californian Jesuits were victims of such charges — made more credible by widespread reports of the independent actions of Jesuits in Paraguay.

35. Spicer, *Cycles of Conquest*, pp. 306–8.

36. In 1686, while P. Kino still believed that he was to be returned to his mission in California, he listed ideas to improve its operation; among them: "They [the missionaries] could be given an escort of a few soldiers, carefully picked and to the satisfaction of the Fathers." Kino, *Kino Writes to the Duchess*, pp. 214–15.

37. Konrad, *Jesuit Hacienda*, p. 151 and n. 1.

38. See note 12 of this chapter. Later, a California Jesuit wrote, "You have at hand the letters of our missionaries in Paraguay; they will give you an idea of how we administer our missions here in California." P. Francisco Inama to his sister, 14 October 1755. Ducrue, *Account of the Expulsion*, p. 155. The conclusions of PP. Kino and Salvatierra vis-a-vis the soldiery needed for their conquest were made concrete in the license they eventually received. Venegas, "Empressas Apostolicas," párrafos 1723–24.

39. Before leaving Sonora, P. Salvatierra suggested that P. Kino build a small bark which could carry him to California and then be used to shuttle supplies. Kino, *Historical Memoir of the Pimería Alta*, vol. 1, p. 121.

40. Venegas, "Empressas Apostolicas," párrafos 176–77. P. Provincial Ambrosio de Odón headed the Jesuit Province of New Spain at the time of P. Salvatierra's first petitions.

41. For a practical example of differences between the bureaucracies of Spain and the Society of Jesus, and a description of the efficiency of the Jesuit system, see Konrad, *Jesuit Hacienda*, pp. 120–21.

42. Gibson, *Spain in America*, p. 93. For a succinct essay on the Council of the Indies, see Haring, *The Spanish Empire*, pp. 94–109.

43. Haring, *The Spanish Empire*, pp. 110–14; Gibson, *Spain in America*, pp. 93–95.

44. "So intertwined was the Hapsburg genealogy that all four of Charles II's paternal great-grandparents and three of his maternal great-grandparents were direct descendants of Juana la Loca." Gibson, *Spain in America*, p. 161.

45. Burkholder and Chandler, *From Impotence to Authority*, p. 16; Brading in Bethell, ed. *Colonial Spanish America*, pp. 112, 113.

46. Parry, *The Spanish Seaborne Empire*, p. 280; Burkholder and Chandler, *From Impotence to Authority*, p. 18.

47. Some resistance to the plans and importunings of PP. Kino and Salvatierra, from within their order, doubtless arose because they were seen — quite accurately — as personally ambitious and unwilling to accept previous decisions by Jesuit superiors. Both these attributes flew in the face of the obedience on which the system was based. This

obedience is discussed in Konrad, *Jesuit Hacienda*, pp. 114–15.

48. Venegas, "Empressas Apostolicas," párrafos 176, 178.

49. Royally appointed officials and councils were under orders to cooperate with reasonable proposals from the clergy. Farriss, *Crown and Clergy*, pp. 1–2. But when cooperation also involved funding, the crown's usual desperate financial straits often became the overriding element in the deliberations.

50. Venegas, "Empressas Apostolicas," párrafo 177.

51. P. Jaime Bravo to Bishop of Guadalajara, November 6, 1719, BNM, AF 3/47.1.

52. Venegas, *El apóstol*, pp. 79–80.

53. José de Miranda y Villayzán was born about 1759 in Huejotzingo, near Puebla. P. Salvatierra spoke of him as the earliest benefactor of his California campaign, a man who gave generously from his modest fortune, and whose wife offered her jewels when the colony was most in need. Venegas, "Empressas Apostolicas," párrafos 1962–63.

54. "The *fiscal* was a sort of royal watchdog who defended the king's interests wherever they might appear, but especially in cases affecting the exchequer, the Church, and the rights of Indians. He also tendered legal advice to the viceroy or governor in matters of administration." C. H. Haring, *Spanish Empire*, p. 120 n. 17. Although Haring neglected to add that *fiscales* also advised *audiencias*, he makes plain in the same paragraph that they did so. This fact is evident in repeated documented activities of the Audiencia of Guadalajara during the early years of Jesuit California.

55. Burkholder and Chandler, *From Impotence to Authority*, pp. 22, 23, 59 nn. 147, 165, 197; Venegas, "Empressas Apostolicas," párrafos 531, 1963.

56. Antonio de Miranda y Villayzán corresponded with P. Salvatierra and apparently was sympathetic to the California cause. Salvatierra, *Selected Letters*, pp. 194, note 4; 197–98. At Bishop Galindo's death, Miranda y Villayzán occupied powerful positions, *juez provisor* and *vicario general*, within the cathedral chapter as it directed the affairs of the bishopric during the long process required to replace a bishop. P. Jaime Bravo to Bishop of Guadalajara, November 6, 1719, BNM, AF 3/47.1.

57. Venegas, "Empressas Apostolicas," párrafo 189; Dunne, *Black Robes*, p. 40; Río, *A la diestra mano de las Indias*, pp. 102–3.

58. Venegas, "Empressas Apostolicas," párrafo 178. P. General Tirso González's letters to P. Provincial Diego de Almonacir, dated 21 May 1695 and 28 July 1696, reflect the news and petitions he had received from PP. Kino and Salvatierra—as well as his positive responses. Kino, *Correspondencia del P. Kino con los generales*, pp. 37–39, 45–47.

59. P. Javier Saeta, in letters dated 15 and 25 March 1695, indicated that he was collecting cattle for California—despite the extreme want of his own new mission at Caborca. Kino, *Historical Memoir of the Pimería Alta*, vol. 1, pp. 136–37.

60. Venegas, "Empressas Apostolicas," párrafo 597.

61. Ibid., párrafos 190–94.

62. "Memorial que el provincial de la Compañía de Jesús, Juan de Palacios, presentó al virrey conde de Moctezuma . . . ," BNM, AF 3/42.2.

63. Venegas, "Empressas Apostolicas," párrafo 210.

64. Ibid., párrafo 213.

65. Salvatierra, *Selected Letters*, p. 31, note 49.

66. Venegas, "Empressas Apostolicas," párrafo 215.

67. Ibid., párrafos 178, 190, 201–2; Villavicencio, *Vida de Juan de Ugarte*, pp. 46–48.

68. Early in the conquest of Mexico and in its evangelization, the Catholic Church was tolerant of and interested in many aspects of native cultures—see the great work of Bernardino de Sahagún, for example. But, by the 17th century, religious leaders had largely adopted the viewpoint that all indigenous institutions were impediments that should be erased and replaced by the European and the Christian. Ricard, *Spiritual Conquest*, chap. 17. California Jesuits became aware of Rousseau (1712–1778), and at least one, the opinionated and outspoken Jacobo Baegert, left a record of his reaction: "May God . . . preserve Europe, and especially Germany, from rearing children in the Indian manner, which in part corresponds to the plan outlined by that base-minded zealot J. J. Rousseau in his *Emile*, and also to the moral teachings of some modern philosophers belonging to the same fraternity of dogs. . . ." Baegert, *Observations*, p. 76.

69. Venegas, *El apóstol*, p. 111.

70. Venegas, "Empressas Apostolicas," párrafos 203–6; Venegas, *El apóstol*, pp. 111–12. The Conde de Miravalle had ulterior motives for promoting any economic activity along the coast of northwest New Spain. He had large haciendas in the vicinity of his seat at Compostela on the road between Guadalajara and Sinaloa. He or other men of his family sold cattle, sugar, and wheat. The scope of the Miravalle fortune is sketched in Ladd, *Mexican Nobility*, pp. 28, 74, 92, 158. For some of the count's other contributions to California, see chap. 2, pp. 55–56.

71. Burrus and Zubillaga, *El noroeste*, p. 393.

72. Venegas, *El apóstol*, pp. 112–14.

73. Villavicencio, *Vida de Juan de Ugarte*, 21–22.

74. For a history of Jesuit investments in haciendas in New Spain, see Konrad, *A Jesuit Hacienda in Colonial Mexico*.

75. Venegas, "Empressas Apostolicas," párrafos 1776–84; Velázquez, *El fondo piadoso*. For the administration and uses of the Pious Fund, see chap 5, pp. 137–38.

76. Venegas, "Empressas Apostolicas," párrafo 217. As an experienced missionary, P. Salvatierra knew the necessity for a skilled mayordomo to direct a mission's daily economic activities. The mayordomo of an hacienda had similar duties and needed the same skills. Konrad, *Jesuit Hacienda*, p. 240. Salvatierra also realized that a mayordomo's skills would be invaluable in organizing and moving all the materials that he would need in California. He must have seen Esteban Rodríguez at work, heard of his reputation, and hired him to be his immediate assistant and ultimately to serve as mayordomo of his mission. Rodríguez's eventual military career, as will be seen, arose adventitiously and was foreseen by no one.

77. P. Juan Bautista Copart had accompanied P. Kino and Almirante Atondo into the mid-peninsular linguistic area that included Conchó. Copart made extensive notes from which he created a glossary. Venegas, "Empressas Apostolicas," párrafo 248.

78. Doctor Don José de Miranda y Villayzán was not only prepared to use his position on the audiencia for the benefit of Jesuit California, he also involved himself in the sometimes complicated business of procurement and transportation of supplies destined for California. His letter of 5 January 1700, to P. Procurador Juan de Ugarte indicates the broad range of support activities in which he was engaged. AGI, Guadalajara, 134.

79. Venegas, "Empressas Apostolicas," párrafos 218–20.

80. Bayle, Misión, p. 93; Salvatierra, *Selected Letters*, p. 92. Martín de Verráztegui visited Loreto in 1706, acting as a godfather on 13 June to an old woman that Capitán Rodríguez baptized *in casu necessitas*.

81. Venegas, "Empressas Apostolicas," párrafo 221; Spicer, *Cycles of Conquest*, pp. 34–35.

82. Venegas, "Empressas Apostolicas," párrafos 221–22.

83. Venegas, "Empressas Apostolicas," párrafo 226. Bartolomé de Robles was the destitute resident of Rosario that P. Salvatierra reported as a recruit but did not name. P. Salvatierra to P. Juan de Ugarte, 27 November 1697. Salvatierra, *Selected Letters*, p. 96.

84. P. Salvatierra to P. Juan de Ugarte, 27 November 1697. Salvatierra, *Selected Letters*, pp. 95–97.

85. Venegas, "Empressas Apostolicas," párrafo 225.

86. Ibid., párrafo 227; Kino, *Historical Memoir of the Pimería Alta*, vol. 2, p. 241.

87. P. Salvatierra to P. Juan de Ugarte, 27 November 1697. Salvatierra, *Selected Letters*, p. 97.

88. Venegas, "Empressas Apostolicas," párrafo 226.

89. Many converted Indians lacked Hispanic surnames; when they took positions away from their missions, they were usually called by their Christian names followed by "*de Guázabas*" (from Guázabas), or the like, to indicate their mission of origin and distinguish them from others bearing the same given name.

90. P. Salvatierra to P. Juan de Ugarte, 27 November 1697. Salvatierra, *Selected Letters*, p. 96; Venegas, "Empressas Apostolicas," párrafo 226.

91. Venegas, "Empressas Apostolicas," párrafo 228.

92. Antonio Justo, a Genovese, *Selected Letters*, p. 99. P. Salvatierra sent him ashore at San Bruno as co-leader of a shore party. Venegas, "Empressas Apostolicas," párrafo 233. In 1701, Salvatierra put Justo in charge of a California ship while it was repaired at Matanchel. AHH, leg. 281, exp. 29.

93. P. Salvatierra to P. Juan de Ugarte, Loreto, 27 November 1697. Salvatierra, *Selected Letters*, pp. 98–99.

94. Venegas, "Empressas Apostolicas," párrafo 226.

95. The seventeenth- to eighteenth-century Spanish military rank of *alférez* corresponded to a modern lieutenant, whereas *teniente* (lieutenant) stood above an *alférez* and was usually the second-in-command of a unit with a higher officer, such as a *capitán* or *general*. The term *alférez* is used here without translation because its English equivalent, "ensign," is now understood as a strictly naval term, inappropriate to this use.

96. P. Salvatierra to P. Juan de Ugarte, Loreto, 27 November 1697. Salvatierra, *Selected Letters*, pp. 100–102.

97. Francisco de Itamarra visited San Bruno and San Dionisio, the site that became Loreto, early in 1695. Venegas, "Empressas Apostolicas," párrafo

151. P. Salvatierra, in 1697, wrote, "Captain Juan Antonio Romero insisted that in another bay very close by he had taken on water two years ago, and had found the water excellent and salt free. . . ." P. Salvatierra to P. Juan de Ugarte, Loreto, 27 November 1697. Salvatierra, *Selected Letters*, p. 103.

98. P. Salvatierra to P. Juan de Ugarte, Loreto, 27 November 1697. Salvatierra, *Selected Letters*, p. 103.

99. To judge from P. Salvatierra's description of a water hole and an Indian camp, the landing place of his party was probably near the smallcraft basin constructed in 1990 as part of the development of Loreto's malecón.

100. Don Luis de Tortolero y Torres, in testifying before the Audiencia de Guadalajara on 29 April 1702, recalled that the party that landed at Conchó was met by about fifty people. AGI, Guadalajara, 134.

101. P. Salvatierra to P. Juan de Ugarte, 27 November 1697, Bayle, *Misión*, p. 43.

102. P. Salvatierra to P. Juan de Ugarte, Loreto, 27 November 1697. Salvatierra, *Selected Letters*, pp. 105–7.

Chapter 2: The Pioneer Period, 1697–1701

1. Admiral Isidro de Atondo visited Conchó on 20 February 1685 while exploring the coastal plain as far south as Chuenque and probably Ligüí. P. Eusebio Kino was not a party to this exploration, but he heard the participants' reports when they returned to San Bruno. Perhaps P. Salvatierra was not equipped with Atondo's diaries and reports, but he had discussed their contents during his many conferences with Kino. Salvatierra chose to ignore Atondo's positive contributions in his own accounts of his California adventures. Nowhere does he credit Atondo with the considerable body of geographic information that was compiled and mapped following the admiral's pioneering explorations. The report of Atondo's expedition to Conchó and beyond is in Mathes, *Californiana III*, vol. 3, pp. 587–605.

2. Ignacio del Río provides a useful overview of early reports and observations of California natives by European observers in Río, "Los Indios de Baja California (Notas Etnográficas)," *Boletín de información del Instituto de Investigaciones Históricas— UNAM*, Históricas 2, enero–abril, 1980.

3. For information about California's three distinct linguistic groups, see Index under "Cochimí," "Guaycura," and "Pericú."

4. This overview of peninsular California ethnography draws from too many sources to cite individually. The major works that preserve or derive from eyewitness accounts include the following: Aschmann, *Central Desert*; Baegert, *Observations* and *Letters*; Barco, *Historia natural y crónica*; Crosby, *The Cave Paintings of Baja California*; Río, *Conquista y aculturación*; and Venegas, "Empressas Apostolicas."

5. Baegert, *Observations*, p. 59.

6. P. Salvatierra's first attempts to use Copart's glossary for indoctrination were accompanied by spoonfuls of cooked maize, a universal language. Venegas, *El apóstol*, p. 123; Venegas, "Empressas Apostolicas," párrafo 248. P. Miguel del Barco, at the end of the Jesuit period, would look back and say, "when food was available to give the converts, the spiritual conquest prospered." Barco, *Historia natural y crónica*, p. 301.

7. For P. Juan Bautista Copart's contribution, see chap. 1, pp. 17–18, 21. In 1697, P. Salvatierra made good use of Copart's glossary and shared it, or its lessons with his followers at Conchó. Most of the men in his party seem to have learned the rudiments of the language quickly. P. Salvatierra to P. Juan de Ugarte, 27 November 1697. *Documentos para la historia de México*, Serie 2, vol. 1, p. 53. Bayle, *Misión*, includes a modern transcription of this letter, but unaccountably omits several of the middle pages. A translation to English is offered in Salvatierra, *Selected Letters*, p. 109.

8. The account of events at Conchó that led up to a battle on 13 November 1697, is taken from P. Salvatierra's letter to P. Juan de Ugarte, 27 November 1697. *Documentos para la historia de México*, Serie 2, vol. 1, p. 53; Salvatierra, *Selected Letters*, pp. 106–19; Venegas, "Empressas Apostolicas," párrafos 242–66.

9. P. Salvatierra's account of the battle on 13 November 1697, is found in Salvatierra to P. Juan de Ugarte, 27 November 1697. Salvatierra, *Selected Letters*, pp. 120–26. P. Venegas paraphrased this material and added a few items from an unidentified source, probably Esteban Rodríguez's diary. Venegas, "Empressas Apostolicas," párrafos 267–83. For references to Rodríguez's now-lost diary, see Ibid., párrafos xxviii, 217.

10. P. Salvatierra's report of the "battle" reveals that the diverse groups attacked his camp from the directions by which they habitually approached Conchó. The Monquí, subgroup of the Guaycura, ranged southward along the coastal shelf as far as Ligüí. The others, all Cochimí, lived in areas that virtually surrounded the Monquí. See p. 37.

11. P. Salvatierra to P. Juan de Ugarte, 27 November 1697. Salvatierra, *Selected Letters*, pp. 121–25.

12. Ibid., p. 123.

13. Ibid., p. 140.

14. P. Salvatierra to P. Juan de Ugarte, 27 November 1697. Salvatierra, *Selected Letters*, p. 130.

15. Polzer, *Rules and Precepts*, p. 74.

16. P. Salvatierra's report to Virrey José Sarmiento de Valladares, Conde de Moctezuma, was copied in Venegas, "Empressas Apostolicas," párrafo 313. Despite Salvatierra's naming of Luis de Tortolero as his captain immediately after the battle, it was not until 24 October 1698 that P. Juan de Ugarte, acting as Salvatierra's agent, requested that Virrey Moctezuma confirm Tortolero's appointment and issue the appropriate papers, which he did, two days later. P. Ugarte to Virrey Moctezuma, 24 October 1698 (with replies appended), AGI, Guadalajara, 134.

17. P. Salvatierra to P. Juan de Ugarte, 27 November 1697. Salvatierra, *Selected Letters*, pp. 127–28, 131–32.

18. P. Piccolo was described on his exit papers at Cádiz in 1683: "El Padre Francisco María Pícoli siciliano sacerdote natural de Palermo de veinte y siete años, Blanco, rubio, ojos azules, alto de cuerpo. . . ." AGI, Contratación, 5550.

19. "Ignacio Xavier, Indio Tarahumar, natural de Jesus Carichic: el qual havia ido con el P. Piccolo a las Californias, y lo havia acompañado en todas sus entradas y operaciones. . . ." February 1702. Venegas, "Empressas Apostolicas," párrafo 492. PP. Salvatierra and Piccolo retained their rustic companions, in part at least, to comply with a rule of their order that they be accompanied by a male escort whenever they traveled. Konrad, *Jesuit Hacienda*, p. 109.

20. P. Salvatierra to P. Juan de Ugarte, 3 July 1698. Bayle, *Misión*, pp. 62–63. *Palo blanco* grows to a height over 30 feet, is slim, often multi-trunked, and has bark as dazzling as white birch. Thick stands ornament the arroyos on the gulf side of the mid-peninsula. Padre Salvatierra's sensitivity to this and other natural beauty was remarkable, recorded as it was at the end of the seventeenth century and on the fringe of the known world where the author was leading a difficult and threatened life. His letters reflect the eye of an enthusiastic tourist, a breed rarely seen for another hundred years.

21. Many Spanish and creole families used compound surnames that persisted for generation or centuries. The second often was that of an important female ancestor. In this first report on Grumeque de Figueroa and García de Mendoza, P. Salvatierra used shortened versions, but many subsequent records show the more complete forms of the names. For clarity, complete compound surnames are used in all cases hereinafter.

22. P. Salvatierra to P. Juan de Ugarte, 3 July 1698. Bayle, *Misión*, pp. 72–73.

23. The mainland natives who came to serve the mission in California present an interesting case of cultural mobility. At home in their own missions they would have been called neophytes — despite the fact that their grandparents may have been born as Christians. But, ironically, in California they became de facto *gente de razón* — because they were the products of generations of Hispanic acculturation and had no more means to communicate with the California natives than did other members of the Spanish party. Practical logic placed them among the *gente de razón* to differentiate them from new converts.

24. Venegas, "Empressas Apostolicas," párrafos 322–23; P. Salvatierra to P. Juan de Ugarte, 3 July 1698. Bayle, *Misión*, p. 62.

25. Barco, *Historia natural y crónica*, p. 173; Taraval, *Indian Uprising*, pp. 30–32.

26. P. Salvatierra's acute awareness of the friction and enmity between the Monquí of Conchó and the Cochimí of Londó, in the second year of his California experiences, can be read plainly in Salvatierra to P. Juan de Ugarte, 9 July 1699. Bayle, *Misión*, pp. 120–25.

27. P. Salvatierra made it plain that *Monquí* was the name used by the people themselves, and that they were called *Edú* by the Cochimí. P. Kino knew them by the latter name because his base at San Bruno was in a Cochimí area. Salvatierra, *Selected Letters*, p. 172. P. Miguel del Barco explained that the Cochimí actually used the term *Edú* for all non-Cochimí speakers living to the south of them; therefore, Monquí is by far the preferred name for the people of Conchó. Barco, *Historia natural y crónica*, p. 172.

28. Kino, *Kino Reports to Headquarters*, pp. 49, 75. In the early days of P. Kino's visit to San Bruno, he recorded the names of several supposedly distinct groups — Didiúes, Noes, Imonas, Güimes, Laimones, Nebes, etc. — but as time went on, he became aware that most spoke variants of one language, that of the Didiú he met at San Bruno. P. Salvatierra came to Conchó knowing some of the names Kino had used, but in a very few years he and his associates perceived clearly the array of closely

related Cochimí dialects—and dropped the practice of recording their individual names. They also learned the Guaycuran affinity of the distinctly different Monquí language of the natives of Conchó. Several Guaycura subdivisions spoke and acted in such distinct and different ways that their identities were preserved as long as their people survived. See chap. 4, pp. 101–2.

29. Salvatierra, *Selected Letters*, p. 37.

30. P. Salvatierra included some information on the aftermath of Atondo's misadventures with peninsular natives in Salvatierra to P. Juan de Ugarte, 3 July 1698. Bayle, *Misión*, pp. 62–90; the passage in question is on pp. 74–75.

31. Barco, *Historia natural y crónica*, pp. 66, 203.

32. The account of the "Battle of Easter Sunday" that follows is taken from P. Salvatierra to P. Juan de Ugarte, 3 July 1698. Bayle, *Misión*, pp. 79–81. A much shorter eyewitness version that corroborates Salvatierra's account is given in "Testimony of Don Luis de Tortolero . . . ," Guadalajara, 29 April 1702. AGI, Guadalajara, 134.

33. P. Salvatierra referred to Grumeque de Figueroa as the *alférez* of his presidio soon after he landed in February 1698. Only on 24 October 1698, did P. Juan de Ugarte, acting as Salvatierra's agent, request that the viceroy confirm Grumeque de Figueroa's appointment and issue the appropriate papers—which he did, two days later. Ugarte to Moctezuma, 24 October 1698 (with replies appended), AGI, Guadalajara, 134.

34. P. Salvatierra to P. Juan de Ugarte, 3 July 1698. Bayle, *Misión*, p. 79.

35. P. Salvatierra to P. Juan de Ugarte, 3 July 1698. Bayle, *Misión*, p. 81. This rather casual reference to the "retreat sounded on their pipes" provides rare ethnographic data: the local Monquí had some sort of musical or signaling device that they used as a European force might use a bugle. Other Guaycurans just south of La Paz had a similar instrument described by P. Jaime Bravo during an entrada in 1720: "a pipe that serves them as a bugle in time of battle." Bravo, "Relación de Jaime Bravo," in León-Portilla, *Testimonios sudcalifornianos,*" p. 50.

36. P. Salvatierra to P. Juan de Ugarte, 3 July 1698. Bayle, *Misión*, p. 81.

37. The fruit of *pitahaya dulce* (*Lemaireocereus thurberi*), the so-called "organ-pipe cactus," was a staple crop gathered and eaten by native Californians during, at most, a month and a half each fall.

38. P. Salvatierra to P. Juan de Ugarte, 3 July 1698. Bayle, *Misión*, p. 62.

39. This mistaken assumption about "clothed Indians" induced P. Salvatierra to record an otherwise neglected bit of contact ethnography. Ibid., p. 87.

40. Chacala was the port of choice for people who lived in Compostela and for some others who plied the Sea of Cortés. Fray Juan Caballero gave pertinent reasons in explaining the choice of Chacala as a port in which to build ships for Lucenilla's 1668 expedition to California. Caballero, *Pearl Hunters of 1668*, p. 29. Admiral Atondo's 1683 expedition embarked from Chacala. Kino, *Kino Reports to Headquarters*, p. 20. Although small, Chacala offers deep water sheltered from northerly winds.

41. Loreto's privations and the arrival of Ganduzo's ship are told in P. Salvatierra to P. Juan de Ugarte, 3 July 1698. Bayle, *Misión*, pp. 86–88. The names of at least seven men from Compostela are found on a roster of Loreto's soldiers drawn up less than two years later: José Dávila y Guzmán and Felipe del Valle, relatives of the Conde de Miravalle, and Cristóbal Gutiérrez de Góngora, Francisco Rubio, Andrés Romero, Mateo Romero, and Nicolás Rodríguez de Piña. Salvatierra to the Audiencia of Mexico, 1 March 1700. BNM, AF 3/42.3. These men, or most of them, must have made up the party brought by Ganduzo in 1698.

The identities of the two relatives of the Conde de Miravalle as well as the Compostela origins of Juan Manuel Ganduzo and the other volunteer soldiers are confirmed by entries in the Compostela books of baptisms, marriages, and burials, passim., to be found on FHL microfilm, reels 654341, 654342, 652417, and 652420. In these records, the surname of José Manuel Ganduzo and his relatives is phonetically consistent, being given only as "Ganduzo," "Ganduso," or "Gandusso." In this connection, see Salvatierra, *Selected Letters*, p. 135 n. 3. But Bayle, *Misión*, p. 51 ("Ganduro"), and pp. 87–89 ("Gadaro"), offers variant forms. Bayle followed early imprint errors that were due to misreadings of Salvatierra's notoriously difficult script. Salvatierra's small, crabbed handwriting has been described as the worst ever seen in the Jesuit Order—only a small exaggeration. Since he penned several hundred historically important letters, this trait has been a burden for scholars.

42. P. Venegas's chronology for the arrival of these goods and animals is very confused, but a late summer or early fall arrival seems implicit in Venegas, "Empressas Apostolicas," párrafos 336–37, and 341. The horses mentioned in párrafo 341 were in regular use by 1 November 1698. P. Salvatierra

to P. Juan de Ugarte, 1 April 1699, Bayle, *Misión*, pp. 96–100.

43. Kino, *Kino Reports to Headquarters*, pp. 64–65, 78–79; Kino, *Kino Writes to the Duchess*, pp. 170, 174–75.

44. This and subsequent passages reporting the exploration of the route to Londó paraphrase or quote P. Salvatierra to P. Juan de Ugarte, 1 April 1699, Bayle, *Misión*, pp. 96–100. Salvatierra's description of the country does not betray any impulse to exaggerate for the amazement of a distant audience. It is accurate and restrained and justifies greater confidence in some of his other reports that are less easily substantiated. Such restraint was fairly typical of California's Jesuit writers of reports and letters — with the notable exception of P. Francisco María Piccolo's *Informe of 1702* (see p. 46 of this chapter).

45. P. Salvatierra may have been mistaken in his assumption that this trail had not been traversed by horses. In February and March of 1685, Atondo and a group under his command explored from San Bruno southward, visiting Conchó in the process. Mathes, *Californiana III*, vol. 3, pp. 587–605. Salvatierra's party first used horses for this trip to Londó in 1698. One horse came with it in 1697, but that was soon killed by local people. More had arrived during August or September of 1698. Bancroft, *North Mexican States*, vol. 1, p. 294 n. 22.

46. This difficult ascent was not named simply because of Arce's mishap. Steep grades on all regularly used trails were given names — to assist in making reports or in giving directions to travelers, etc. In an earlier letter, P. Salvatierra identified Juan de Arce as an Englishman, raised from childhood in New Spain, who had already soldiered in the presidios of Sinaloa. Salvatierra to P. Juan de Ugarte, 3 July 1698. Bayle, *Misión*, p. 73. Venegas, "Empressas Apostolicas," párrafo 325, called Arce a native of New England. Incidentally, a watercourse in the immediate area that Salvatierra described is known as Arroyo de Arce to this day.

47. P. Salvatierra to P. Juan de Ugarte, 1 April 1699. Bayle, *Misión*, pp. 101–2. In February and March of 1685, Almirante Atondo made a longer and more thorough investigation of the area south of Conchó than that of P. Piccolo — who followed roughly the same route. The later explorer was either ignorant of or chose not to emphasize his debt to his predecessor. The report of Atondo's exploration is in Mathes, *Californiana III*, vol. 3, pp. 587–605.

48. The curious double consonants that appear in early attempts to write placenames [Viggé, Ohobbé] used by native Californians appear to be due to Padre Piccolo's penchant for carrying Italian usages into Spanish. His letters abound in Italian words or Italianate spellings of Spanish.

49. Since California's discovery, the Spaniards had become more familiar with its eastern or gulf coast than with the Pacific shoreline to the west. Most members of the Jesuit colony continued to live at Loreto or near the gulf. Two popular geographic terms came into use early and persisted: *contracosta*, or "opposite coast" — meaning the Pacific shore over the mountains to the west, and *la otra banda*, "the other shore" — meaning the Sonora-Sinaloa coast lying across the gulf to the east. The latter term is still in daily use in peninsular California.

50. P. Salvatierra wrote a summary of the results of the neophytes' extraordinary excursions to mainland ports, towns, and missions. Salvatierra to P. Juan de Ugarte, 9 July 1699. Salvatierra, *Selected Letters*, pp. 155–57. The "plains" of Viggé, compared by some of these travelers to mainland grainfields, were the several prominent *playas*, or drainage basins, northwest of Biaundó. In 1683, when Atondo and P. Kino crossed the Giganta for the first time, they discovered at least two of the more northerly. They took these to be lakes since they were temporarily filled with water by recent, copious rains. Kino, *Kino Reports to Headquarters*, pp. 69–73.

51. For details of Atondo and Kino's 1684–1685 explorations and stay in the greater Loreto area, see Atondo, *First from Gulf to the Pacific*, and Mathes, *Californiana III*, vol. 3, pp. 587–605.

52. P. Salvatierra provided precise definitions of "Viggé" and "Biaundó," geographical names that have been confused in reports by subsequent missionaries and some later historians. Salvatierra to Ugarte, 9 July 1699. BNM, AF 3/40.5. A translation to English is found in Salvatierra, *Selected Letters*, pp. 152–84.

Viggé: Salvatierra (referring to the peaks near the pass crossed by Piccolo and party): "These mountain heights are called Viggé . . . the word means 'land high above the valleys.' Along the coastal areas, the term is used to designate all the high or mountainous regions [of that part] of California; and the natives on such heights are referred to as 'people of Viggé,'" Ibid., pp. 161–62.

Biaundó: "San Francisco Javier in Biaundó — the name of the valley in the province of Viggé. . . ." [The original site of Mission San Francisco Javier was Biaundó, the place discovered by P. Piccolo during the above described exploration], Ibid., p. 164.

53. In a letter to P. Salvatierra, dated 9 July 1696, Don Juan de Caballero y Ocio promised the endowment needed to found the first two missions — for which he specified the names Loreto and San Francisco Javier. He dedicated the latter to "the greater honor and glory of God and the service of my father and patron, San Francisco Javier." Caballero y Ocio thereby yielded to Salvatierra's desire that his own patroness, Nuestra Señora de Loreto, be the first honored in California, but established his choice for the patron of the second California mission. Burrus and Zubillaga, *El noroeste*, pp. 393–94.

54. P. Salvatierra wrote a detailed account of P. Piccolo's entrada to Viggé. Salvatierra to P. Juan de Ugarte, 9 July 1699. Salvatierra, *Selected Letters*, pp. 157–64. Since Salvatierra did not accompany the explorers, nor had he previously visited the region, Piccolo must have supplied all the facts — and, no doubt, many of the interpretations of the events of the trip. A composite story of this expedition is contained in Venegas, "Empressas Apostolicas," párrafos 349–59. This version drew not only upon the aforesaid Salvatierra letter, but also on another report: probably Esteban Rodríguez's lost diary from which P. Venegas took much of his information about early explorations and constructions. Venegas, "Empressas Apostolicas," párrafos xxviii, 217.

55. P. Salvatierra to P. Juan de Ugarte, 9 July 1699. Salvatierra, *Selected Letters*, p. 162; Venegas, "Empressas Apostolicas," párrafo 356.

56. P. Salvatierra made the statement that, before the entrada, he and Piccolo had discussed the possibility that captain and soldiers might be reluctant to proceed on foot into the highlands. This discussion must have resulted from concerns previously expressed by the captain. Salvatierra to P. Juan de Ugarte, 9 July 1699. Salvatierra, *Selected Letters*, pp. 157–59.

57. See pp. 58–59.

58. P. Salvatierra to P. Juan de Ugarte, 9 July 1699. Salvatierra, *Selected Letters*, p. 160. Since the California expedition led by Almirante Atondo (1683–1685) was the most recent and expensive backed by royal funds, P. Salvatierra found Atondo a particularly useful target. In his voluminous correspondence, Salvatierra made dozens of disparaging references to the small outcome of Atondo's royally financed California venture. He made few references to the involvement of P. Eusebio Kino and other Jesuits in the 1683–1685 undertaking because it suited his purposes to equate great costs and failure with the expedition's secular leadership. Salvatierra compared his own success with Atondo's failures: the admiral's expedition cost the crown a huge sum of money while Salvatierra's group was financing its own effort, etc. Such comparisons reminded royal officials of the magnitude of Jesuit contributions to colonial expansion. When Salvatierra later appealed for royal funds, such comparisons reminded officials how little they had received from their generous support for Atondo and how much they had obtained, gratis, from the Jesuit enterprise. A particularly vitriolic attack on Atondo, and one that repeats the litany of Salvatierra's charges, is found in P. Salvatierra's letter to Virrey Alburquerque, dated 25 May 1705. AGNM, Californias, vol. 63, exp. 8.

59. This may have been P. Salvatierra's earliest use of the "bad soldier" argument to assure the Jesuits' continuing control of the California presidio. He would later generalize from this incident, as in his letter to Virrey Alburquerque, 25 May 1705, "I have personally found that if I had not had that authority [to hire and fire the California captain] during the past eight years, not a single step would have been taken in California. We would still be biding our time on the beach where we first landed," etc. AGNM, Californias, vol. 63, exp. 8.

60. P. Salvatierra to José de Miranda y Villayzán, 26 October 1699. Salvatierra, *Selected Letters*, p. 200.

61. Venegas, "Empressas Apostolicas," párrafos 360–61.

62. Sale of the office of *alcalde mayor* and its use to enrich the officeholder at the expense of constituents, Indian or other, is treated at some length in Stein and Stein, *Colonial Heritage of Latin America*, pp. 78–81, and described in similar terms in Haring, *Spanish Empire*, pp. 129–33, and in Brading, "Bourbon Spain and its American Empire," (chap. 3 of Bethell, ed., *Colonial Spanish America*), p. 128.

63. Piccolo, *Informe de 1702*, pp. 38–76. A translation to English and a photographic reproduction of P. Piccolo's Mexican imprint comprise Piccolo, *Informe on the New Province of California*, 1702.

64. Piccolo's *Informe* became a nuisance as well as an embarrassment to all later California Jesuits. They were well aware of its gross inaccuracies and some had to take pains to correct the widespread misimpressions that it created. Barco, *Historia natural y crónica*, p. 345; Baegert, *Letters*, p. 127.

65. The valley of Biaundó in which P. Piccolo professed to see such agricultural promise in 1699 was an upper reach of the arroyo of San Javier, just northeast of today's Rancho Viejo. In a year of excellent rainfall, even one that followed other years of good rains, Biaundó would not merit the Sicilian padre's enthusiastic report. By 1707, a persistent lack of adequate water forced P. Juan de Ugarte, Piccolo's successor at San Javier, to move the mission more than five miles down the arroyo from Piccolo's Biaundó and its reported "groves and streams." In another seven years, Ugarte expended a very great deal of time, effort, and money to feed his mission by developing a farm system at the better-watered visita of San Miguel in another arroyo distant by more than 20 miles. Venegas, "Empressas Apostolicas," párrafos 724–32.

66. Tortolero's testimony of 29 April 1702, in Guadalajara was taken down and a copy sent to Spain. AGI, Guadalajara, 134. The Jesuits' appreciative notices of Tortolero's testimony appear in Venegas, "Empressas Apostolicas," párrafos 492, 600. Tortolero's later career is summarized in connection with Jesuit attempts to obtain retirement benefits for a later captain, Esteban Rodríguez. See chap. 10, p. 303.

67. On 23 May 1699, PP. Salvatierra and Piccolo reported to the viceroy that they had named their second-in-command, Don Antonio García de Mendoza, to the post of captain. They cited his past services in Spain and the Indies "attested to by authentic records," and his contributions at Loreto, singling out the importance of his services in the battle of 2 April 1698 — despite the fact that these were not emphasized in their original report of the skirmish (see pp. 38–39). AGI, Guadalajara, 134. Salvatierra also reported the events surrounding García de Mendoza's elevation in a letter of 9 July 1699. Bayle, *Misión*, p. 120. Virrey Moctezuma issued his official confirmation of García de Mendoza's captaincy on 9 October 1699, a few days after P. Juan de Ugarte submitted a formal request. Ugarte to Moctezuma, 6 October 1699. AGI, Guadalajara, 134.

68. Antonio García de Mendoza's birthplace can be inferred from the fact that P. Salvatierra reported that he was from Old Castile [Venegas, "Empressas Apostolicas," párrafo 325], and that he was "a Castilian from La Rioja [Salvatierra to P. Juan de Ugarte, 3 July 1698. Bayle, *Misión*, p. 73]. He also refers to García de Mendoza in connection with Fuenterrabía [Salvatierra to P. Juan de Ugarte, 9 July 1699. Ibid., p. 120] and the nearby San Sebas-

tián [Ibid., p. 73], but he clearly indicates these as places in which Mendoza had soldiered. García de Mendoza's service as adjutant in San Luis Potosí is recounted in Salvatierra to Ugarte, 9 July 1699. Ibid., p. 120. Salvatierra's reference to García de Mendoza's mining experiences in the Tarahumara are found in the same letter. Ibid., p. 125. In 1693, García de Mendoza was involved in a dispute over the use of Tarahumara Indians and the treatment of same. TBL, The Bolton Papers, item 286 (a transcript of an expediente located in the Archivo Histórico de Hidalgo del Parral).

69. P. Salvatierra to P. Juan de Ugarte, 9 July 1699. Bayle, *Misión*, pp. 125–27.

70. The third man, soldier José Machuca, may have been chosen to climb the peak precisely because he was from Querétaro. The pinnacle that was scaled was named Caballero Peak in honor of California benefactor Juan de Caballero y Ocio who lived in Querétaro. The description of this incident is based on a letter of P. Salvatierra to P. Juan de Ugarte who, as California's procurador in Mexico City, corresponded regularly with important benefactor Caballero y Ocio. Salvatierra to P. Juan de Ugarte, 9 July 1699. Bayle, *Misión*, pp. 127–28. José Machuca served in California only until 1 January 1700, when he was scheduled to be paid off. Salvatierra to P. Juan de Ugarte, 26 October 1699. UCSD, Mandeville Dept. of Special Collections, Mss. 192sc.

71. Antonio García de Mendoza to P. Juan de Ugarte, 28 June 1699. AHH, leg. 282, exp. 7. At any other presidio in New Spain, such duty letters written by military officers at the time of their appointments, would be directed to royal officials only. At Loreto, uniquely, other power and patronage was involved. By chance, we know that eleven days later Mendoza was also planning — and was probably expected and instructed — to write to Juan de Caballero y Ocio, a generous donor to the needs of Jesuit California. P. Salvatierra to Caballero y Ocio, 9 July 1699. Salvatierra, *Selected Letters*, p. 154.

72. In Mexico City, on 6 October 1699, Padre Procurador Juan de Ugarte presented Virrey Moctezuma with a formal request for the confirmation of García de Mendoza's appointment and the issuance of the official title, asking that it be in the same form accorded to the former captain, Luis de Tortolero y Torres. The request was granted on 8 October and the formal title was issued on 9 October 1699. AGI, Guadalajara, 134.

73. García de Mendoza to P. Juan de Ugarte, 28 June 1699. AHH, leg. 282, exp. 7.

74. Church construction was virtually the first priority in the establishments of Hispanic missions; a part of the desire to impress from the start the idea that the missionary valued the practice of the Catholic Christian religion over all else. Spicer, *Cycles of Conquest*, pp. 288–89.

75. For an account of the stages in the construction of Loreto's church and other buildings, see chap. 9, pp. 268–75.

76. During the early days of the California mission, before the padres had confidence in the loyalty of their converts, neophytes from Jesuit missions on the Río Yaqui were "borrowed" to act as foot soldiers during California explorations. No mention was made of their compensation, if any. See, for example, the case of 40 Yaqui warriors who came in 1708 to assist P. Juan de Ugarte in an exploration. Venegas, "Empressas Apostolicas," párrafo 798.

77. The formation of the working party, the various speeches, and the beginning of the construction are taken from Venegas, "Empressas Apostolicas," párrafos 401–5.

78. P. Venegas's source of some details of the construction must have been Esteban Rodríguez's diary [see n. 54 of this chap.] because Venegas included details not mentioned by PP. Piccolo or Salvatierra. In addition, many records attest to Rodríguez's construction skills. See, for example, Taraval, *Indian Uprising*, pp. 105–6.

79. Data on the working teams, Mendoza's labors, the numbers of adobes made, and the time required are taken from P. Piccolo's letter to P. Salvatierra, San Francisco Javier de Biaundó, 30 October 1699. Piccolo, *Informe de 1702*, pp. 144–58. There is a discrepancy between P. Venegas's account of the construction and that found in Piccolo's letter. Venegas specified that the buildings were left unroofed so that the adobe could cure while the exploration was carried out. "Empressas Apostolicas," párrafo 406. In his known letter, Piccolo described the construction and roofing as a continuous process. Since the latter account was written hurriedly, the very day the job was being completed, it may be that Piccolo compressed his portrayal of the construction, wishing to finish telling his colleague about the new buildings before he launched into a description of his journey to the contracosta. Elsewhere, in his related account, Venegas acknowledged taking information from Esteban Rodríguez's diary. This must have been the source for the many construction details found in "Empressas Apostolicas," but not in Piccolo's letter.

The modest Rodríguez was probably the boss of the second construction gang.

80. The ensuing account of exploration on the *contracosta* and of construction at San Javier de Biaundó, except where otherwise noted, was taken from P. Piccolo to P. Salvatierra, San Javier de Biaundó, 30 October 1699. Piccolo, *Informe de 1702*, pp. 144–58.

81. P. Piccolo chanced to mention these two articles of pack gear in separate letters during his long California tenure. He described items packed in "cacastles" in a letter to Hermano Jaime Bravo written on 3 April 1707. Piccolo, *Informe de 1702*, p. 160. Piccolo wrote that his soldier-companions had gone looking "*por zacate de aparejo*" (straw for stuffing aparejos) in a letter to P. Juan Manuel Basaldúa on 10 January 1717. Ibid., p. 209. These items are still in daily use and bear the same names in the remote ranches of the central and southern parts of the California peninsula. Most interesting is the fact that the crates, called *cacastles* in the mountain ranches of Baja California Sur, are widely used in other rural parts of today's Mexico, but are called *huacales* in most other places.

82. Santa Rosalía [died *c.* 1160] was a Sicilian, like P. Piccolo himself. She was named patron saint of Palermo in gratitude for her supposed role in ending a plague in 1640. In "Empressas Apostolicas," párrafo 407, P. Venegas made specific reference to Piccolo's "special devotion to this Holy Virgin."

Not satisfied to offer her a mere visiting station, Piccolo later found a site and obtained a donation that would allow a full-fledged California mission to be consecrated in her honor, Santa Rosalía de Mulegé. When this mission was founded, Piccolo's first Santa Rosalía, by then a visiting station of Mission San Javier, came to be called by the diminutive form of the name, Santa Rosalita—which its location bears to this day.

83. Explorers regularly carried water containers familiar to their horses; mules seldom require this inducement to drink at unfamiliar catchments or springs. Venegas, "Empressas Apostolicas," párrafo 809.

84. In the statement, "se ocuparon en techar la capilla, sala, y aposento con techos pajizos de tierra, como los de Loreto," the inclusion of the word "tierra" implies the sort of roof described. Ordinarily, this nearly flat roof is given an additional cover of a layer of fired tile, and that sealed with *alquitrán*, a pitch-like substance made of any available tars, greases, waxes, or plant saps, insoluble when dried. Probably these hurriedly constructed

buildings were considered temporary, or their roofs were planned to be upgraded as soon as possible. Venegas, "Empressas Apostolicas," párrafo 408.

85. "Memorial del padre Juan María de Salvatierra a la Real Audiencia de México . . . Real de Loreto Concho de las Carolinas, 1 marzo 1700." BNM, AF 3/42.3

86. P. Salvatierra's proposal to change California's name actually reiterated an idea proposed by P. Kino in support of his California venture of 1683–1685. Kino used "Carolinas" as an alternative in most of the letters and reports written during his California labors. Kino, *Kino Writes to the Duchess*, pp. 153, 170–71, 174–75, 179, 194.

87. Venegas, "Empressas Apostolicas," párrafos 577–79.

88. Ibid., párrafos 556–59, 580.

89. Virrey Moctezuma reported progress in California to Carlos II on 5 May 1698, and 20 October 1699. Venegas, "Empressas Apostolicas," párrafos 587–89.

90. Ibid., párrafo 584.

91. The copy of P. Salvatierra's "Memorial" retained by the Biblioteca Nacional de México [BNM, AF 3/42.3] was done neatly in a skillful and legible hand, but the copyist was very careless in his treatment of the signatures. Another memorial by Salvatierra, ostensibly written at Los Alamos, Sonora, four weeks later ends with exactly the same group of signatures. However, its copyist retained notations indicating that some men signed later than others, and that each group of signatures was witnessed. The set of signatures offered in the present work is an attempt to reconstruct the probable original set and remove such improbabilities as three signatories named Diego Carrasco — when the second document shows that Carrasco signed the second and third times as a witness to the signatures of others. Salvatierra to the Audiencia of Mexico, 29 March 1700. AGNM, Californias, vol. 63, exp. 4.

92. The longer version of González's name (Juan González de Tuñán) appears in P. Salvatierra to the Audiencia of Mexico, 29 March 1700. AGNM, Californias, vol. 63, exp. 4.

93. The full name Juan Alejo de Robles was written out on the draft for Robles's severance pay, 305 pesos, dated 18 October 1701. Here, as on the memorial, the soldier signed "Juan Alejo." AHH, leg. 325, exp. 1, fol. 4.

94. Capitán Diego Carrasco accompanied P. Kino on his 1698 expedition to the confluence of the Gila and Colorado rivers, and probably met P. Salvatierra during one of his visits to Sonora. He was literate. Burrus, *Kino and Manje*, pp. 104–6, 554.

95. Cristóbal Gutiérrez de Góngora, later an important man on the mainland frontier and at Compostela, was literate. This statement to the contrary either results from a copyist's error [we know this document only from copies] or because his absence from Loreto at the time of the signing made it expedient to have another sign for him. These surmises also apply to Francisco Rubio and Felipe del Valle.

96. Juan Antonio Romero had an impressive record as a captain of vessels supporting Jesuit enterprises; in addition to bringing P. Salvatierra to California, he piloted a supply vessel to the Mariana Islands, another Jesuit mission field. Kino, *Historical Memoirs of the Pimería Alta*, vol. 2, p. 140. Salvatierra made a special effort to show Juan Antonio Romero's blood relationship with Jesuit benefactor Pedro Gil de la Sierpe. On at least two occasions he wrote out the man's name in the cumbersome form of "Juan Antonio Romero de la Sierpe" no doubt for just this purpose. Salvatierra to Virrey Moctezuma, 28 November 1697. Salvatierra, *Selected Letters*, p. 87. Salvatierra to P. Juan de Ugarte, 27 November 1697. Ibid., p. 94. An even stronger and more explicit proof may be found in "Libro donde se asientan los Casamientos que se celebran en esta Ciudad de Compostela, [desde] Julio 15, 1727." FHL Microfilm #652417. In an entry dated 2 February 1730, at the marriage of one of Romero's sons, the groom's father is given as "Juan Antonio Romero Gil de la Sierpe."

Pedro Gil de la Sierpe's recruitment of men for California service is most pointedly indicated in Salvatierra's first letter to Virrey Moctezuma written in California, "I should like to let you know that our entrance into California owes very much to the zeal and generosity of the treasurer of Acapulco, Don Pedro Gil de la Sierpe. He not only left us a launch with the crew necessary to sail it, but also dispatched a well-manned galliot. *Had not some of his men been able to remain on land with me, it would not have been possible to go ashore and set up the cross.*" Salvatierra to Virrey Moctezuma, 28 November 1697. Bayle, *Misión*, p. 34.

97. "Titulo de Alcalde Mayor de la Jurisdicción de Compostela y Tepic por tiempo de un año en el Capitán Cristóbal Gutiérrez de Góngora," 22 December 1702. AIPG, Libros de Gobierno, No. 18, fols. 132–35v.

98. The source and full text of the baptismal record for the daughter Cristóbal Gutiérrez de Góngora are given in chap. 10, n. 36.

99. Some of the soldiers at Loreto had connections with more than one benefactor of California. In 1706, Cristóbal Gutiérrez de Góngora was one of the men who accompanied Gobernador Andrés de Rezábal in pursuit of Apaches who had raided Sonora and then been driven back to New Mexico. AGNM, Provincias Internas, vol. 36, exp. 2, fols. 38–55.

100. The *San Fermín* went aground at Ahome on 29 December 1699, but the news did not reach Loreto until 20 February 1700. Venegas, "Empressas Apostolicas," párrafos 413–15. A general discussion of the problems of supplying California by sea is found in chap. 5, pp. 145–49.

101. Venegas, "Empressas Apostolicas," párrafos 416–20, 581, 591.

102. Ibid., párrafo 424.

103. Ibid., párrafos 421–24. The interplay of interests over the wrecked ship *San Fermín*, the requests for a replacement, etc., are reflected in a series of reports, petitions, and opinions, dated between 9 February and 20 September 1700. AGI, Guadalajara, 134.

104. P. Salvatierra to P. Provincial Francisco de Arteaga, after 21 May 1701. Bayle, *Misión*, pp. 159–85; Venegas, *El apóstol*, p. 143.

105. P. Juan de Ugarte's transfer to Loreto was reported in Venegas, "Empressas Apostolicas," párrafos 432–37.

106. Venegas, "Empressas Apostolicas," párrafos 444–45.

107. P. Salvatierra to P. Juan de Ugarte, 27 November 1697. Bayle, *Misión*, p. 38.

108. P. Venegas had copies of García de Mendoza's complaints to the viceroy, and perhaps to others, which he quoted and paraphrased. His long passages devoted to "answering the complaints of soldiers" reveal the particulars of the captain's well-publicized grievances. Venegas, "Empressas Apostolicas," párrafos 1803–12.

109. Ibid., párrafo 444.

110. Antonio García de Mendoza's birth and death dates are unknown. However, in 1693, he had a son old enough to be party to his mining enterprise in the Tarahumara. TBL, The Bolton Papers, Item 286 (transcript of an expediente in the Archivo Histórico de Hidalgo del Parral).

111. Venegas, "Empressas Apostolicas," párrafo 443.

112. Capitán Antonio García de Mendoza's letter-writing campaign and a summary of soldiers' complaints are reported in Ibid., párrafo 444.

113. P. Sigismundo Taraval gave grudging recognition to the soldiers who saved his life by inducing him to flee from Todos Santos during the rebellion of neophytes in 1734. Taraval, *Indian Uprising*, pp. 60–61, 78.

114. García de Mendoza to Virrey Moctezuma, 22 October 1700. Venegas, "Empressas Apostolicas," párrafo 445.

115. Venegas, *Noticia*, vol. 2, abridged and rewritten by Burriel, pp. 69–70. For a modern work that follows P. Venegas's interpretation of the García de Mendoza affair, see Dunne, *Black Robes*, pp. 76, 95.

116. PP. Salvatierra and Piccolo, "Statement Concerning the Resignation of Mendoza and the Appointment of Estevan Rodriguez, Loreto, 1 September 1701." AGI, Guadalajara, 134 (transcript in TBL, Pockstaller Document 62).

117. Venegas, *Noticia*, vol. 2, abridged and rewritten by Burriel, p. 71.

Chapter 3: California Accommodates Bourbon Rule

1. Arzobispo Ortega y Montañez, viceroy from November 1701 to November 1702, betrayed his caretaker role by inactivity and poor communication with his audiencias; popular displeasure was said to have reached the point of an uprising in Mexico City. Piccolo to P. General Tirso González, 17 May 1702. Piccolo, *Informe de 1702*, pp. 100–104.

2. Burkholder and Johnson, *Colonial Latin America*, pp. 234–36.

3. D. A. Brading, "Bourbon Spain and its American Empire," in Bethell, ed., *Colonial Spanish America*, pp. 113–14.

4. Herr, *The Eighteenth Century Revolution in Spain*, pp. 8, 11–14. Felipe V's confessor was P. Guillaume Daubenton, a French Jesuit. Bangert, *A History of the Society of Jesus*, pp. 293–94.

5. P. Juan de Ugarte voiced exasperation at charges that Jesuits sought wealth in California in a letter to José de Miranda y Villayzán. Venegas, "Empressas Apostolicas," párrafo 593.

6. Susan M. Deeds documented the intense and often bitter rivalry between civilian economic interests and those of Jesuit missions in northwest New Spain. Deeds, "Rendering Unto Caesar: The Secularization of Jesuit Missions in Mid-eighteenth Century Durango," pp. 65–86. See also Spicer, *Cycles of Conquest*, pp. 285–88, 306–8.

7. D. A. Brading, "Bourbon Spain and its American Empire," in Bethell, ed., *Colonial Spanish America*, p. 133; Fisher, *Viceregal Administration*, pp. 126–28.

8. The Spanish crown exacted a tax, originally one fifth, on the production of precious stones, pearls, gold, and silver. Although the percentage was occasionally modified, the tax continued to be known as the *real quinto*, or royal fifth.

9. Spicer, *Cycles of Conquest*, pp. 306–7.

10. Most of New Spain's Indians were exposed in some degree to both mission life and that of Hispanic pueblos or camps. Spicer, *Cycles of Conquest*, pp. 285–87. Jesuit California was a rare exception; for decades, missionaries were able to exclude the usual secular presence.

11. Royal authorities were aware of the problems created by relatively uncontrolled populations of intermittently employed miners or laborers, mostly of mixed blood, who roamed the frontier to live off a succession of small mining booms that followed the establishment of Spanish power and missions. Spicer, *Cycles of Conquest*, p. 300; Stern and Jackson, "Vagabundaje and Settlement Patterns." Jesuits played on these facts as well as the prejudices of the authorities with their constant representations that their soldiery threatened to display the worst traits imagined in such vagabonds. See chap. 6, pp. 157–59, 161; chap. 7, pp. 188–89.

12. The conflicting views and actions of missionary and secular interests on the Hispanic frontier are detailed in Spicer, *Cycles of Conquest*, pp. 306–8.

13. For Jesuit ties to the elite through education, see chap. 1, pp. 6–7. For examples of their influence as confessors to the crown, court, and the upper classes, see p. 63 of this chapter; Herr, *The Eighteenth Century Revolution in Spain*, p. 16; Aveling, *The Jesuits*, p. 257. A succinct sketch of the bases and forms of Jesuit power and influence may be found in Konrad, *Jesuit Hacienda*, pp. 153–56, 173.

14. After extensive lobbying with the new Bourbon regime, the Jesuits elicited the highly favorable real cédula of 28 September 1703. A succession of virreyes, fiscales, consejos, and juntas conspired to hold all the concessions of money and privileges in abeyance until 1717 when certain provisions of the original were partially acted upon. Venegas, "Empressas Apostolicas," párrafos 607–82.

15. Venegas, *Noticia*, vol. 2, abridged & rewritten by Burriel, pp. 172–75.

16. In European and colonial capitals, elements that vied for power resorted to various charades by the necessity to operate in the same arena with absolute power. The crown was above reproach; other actors had to point fingers at each other to account for inactions or failures. See, for example, Venegas, "Empressas Apostolicas," párrafo 555.

17. Fisher, *Viceregal Administration*, p. 18.

18. Bancroft, *North Mexican States*, pp. 419–20; Dunne, *Black Robes*, pp. 114–15, 121–22.

19. Venegas, "Empressas Apostolicas," párrafo 594. Virrey Moctezuma had refused to act on Salvatierra's requests for royal funds and a ship; he claimed that he needed specific advice from His Majesty, but never forwarded Salvatierra's memorials or the support documents that were submitted to him by P. Ugarte and important Jesuit benefactors. Venegas, "Empressas Apostolicas," párrafos 583–84.

20. Copies of the *real cédula* ordering 6,000 pesos paid annually from the royal treasury to support California are found in The King, Madrid, 27 July 1701. AGI, Guadalajara, 134. (Chapman #81); Venegas, "Empressas Apostolicas," párrafos 595–97.

21. Venegas, "Empressas Apostolicas," párrafos 597–99. For more information on Alonso Fernández de la Torre's endowment of California missions, see chap. 1, p. 17.

22. The June 1701 Jesuit decision to stay in California is reported in Venegas, "Empressas Apostolicas," párrafo 441. P. Piccolo chosen as envoy, Ibid., párrafo 442. Piccolo left Loreto in December, 1701, Ibid., párrafo 468.

23. Ibid., párrafo 490.

24. Ibid., párrafo 492. P. Piccolo wrote of "my three California sons" to P. General Ambrosio Odón, 17 May 1702. Piccolo, *Informe de 1702*, pp. 100–104. Piccolo also arrange to have his California neophytes confirmed in the cathedral of Valladolid. P. Jaime Bravo to Bishop of Guadalajara, 6 November 1719, BNM, AF 3/47.1.

25. Venegas, "Empressas Apostolicas," párrafo 491. The full text of the *Informe* is transcribed in Piccolo, *Informe de 1702*, pp. 45–76. A facsimile of the original printed edition and a translation to English are presented in Piccolo, *Informe on the New Province of California, 1702*.

26. P. Piccolo's 1702 trip to New Spain to seek financial aid, Venegas, "Empressas Apostolicas," párrafos 468, 488–98. Piccolo's call for artisans and a manager of temporal affairs, Ibid., párrafo 602.

27. Ibid., párrafo 494.

28. José de la Puente Peña Castejón y Salcines, Marqués de Villapuente, was by far the most important donor to Jesuit California. During P. Pic-

colo's critical fund-raising campaign in 1702, he promised, and later delivered, 30,000 pesos—endowments for the missions of Comondú, La Purísima, and Guadalupe. Venegas, "Empressas Apostolicas," párrafos 498, 1970. By 1720, Villapuente had given 167,000 pesos to assist California missions. Gaspar Rodero, "Report to Philip V on California, 1532–1736" [1737]; Burrus, *Jesuit Relations*, p. 198. For subsequent Villapuente gifts to California, see chap. 4, p. 94, n. 9. Villapuente was also a generous donor to Jesuit missions in the orient. AHH, leg. 318, exp. 9; AHH, leg. 325, exp. 17. After Villapuente's death in 1738, Jesuits ordered and carried out 60,000 masses and 40,000 rosaries in his honor. Venegas, "Empressas Apostolicas," párrafo 1997.

29. Nicolás de Arteaga and his wife, Josefa de Vallejo, provided ten thousand pesos to found Misión de Santa Rosalía de Mulegé. Venegas, "Empressas Apostolicas," párrafos 498, 1970.

30. Gibson, *Spain in America*, pp. 82, 166.

31. Venegas, "Empressas Apostolicas," párrafos 446–50.

32. Ibid., párrafos 451–53. There is an amusing discrepancy in the reported date of Esteban Rodríguez's election to the California captaincy. In párrafo 453, P. Venegas makes this out to have been 2 September 1701. However, PP. Salvatierra and Piccolo addressed a letter to the viceroy on 1 September 1701 [see chap. 2, p. 60, n. 116], that not only announces Mendoza's resignation, but also Rodríguez's "appointment." Rather than assume that the election was a sham, it seems logical to conclude that Venegas or his source document erred by a day.

33. PP. Salvatierra and Piccolo to viceroy, 1 September 1701. AGI, Guadalajara, 134. Fiscal Doctor José Antonio de Espinosa Ocampo y Cornejo, upon being asked to advise the viceroy in the matter, concurred both with the appointment of Esteban Rodríguez and the waiving of a fee. Ibid., undated, but follows the above document in Guadalajara 134. Jesuit thrift, expressed by their request that the fee be waived, may have backfired. Within months, P. Procurador Romano was again petitioning for Rodríguez's title and confirmation. Ibid., also follows the above. No document mentions this fee in connection with the appointments of the earlier captains of the presidio of Loreto.

34. Venegas, "Empressas Apostolicas," párrafo 453. The appointments of lower level government functionaries followed a protocol that gave much room for politicking. The viceroy could confirm the appointment of an official, such as a presidial captain, and that confirmation, duly signed and delivered, would allow the appointee to assume the post, exercise authority, and receive pay. Meanwhile, in a secondary process, an application was made by the viceroy to obtain a royal appointment for the officeholder. These royal endorsements could be delayed or withheld at the pleasure of the viceroy (who might wish to make his own moves less binding), an audiencia, or royal officials in Spain. Moreover, when a new viceroy was chosen, appointments confirmed by his predecessor were sometimes not forwarded for action in Madrid until they had been reviewed by the new officeholder.

The Jesuits nominated Esteban Rodríguez for the California captaincy on two occasions. The first, in 1701, was confirmed by Arzobispo Virrey Ortega y Montañez, but he left his position as viceroy without submitting a recommendation to Madrid that Rodríguez be given an official royal appointment. Rodríguez's return to the post came in 1705 during disputes over California matters between the Jesuits and Virrey Alburquerque. The latter provided the confirmation that allowed Rodríguez to act, but neither he nor his successors chose to press for the royal appointment that should have followed. This failure probably should be attributed to tacit Bourbon disapproval of the earlier Hapsburg agreement to the creation of a religiously ruled military command.

35. Capitán Esteban Rodríguez to Arzobispo Virrey Ortega y Montañez, 18 April 1702. AGI, Guadalajara, 134. A transcription and the translation employed here are found in TBL, Pockstaller document 78. A fuller account of Rodríguez's frustrating encounter with the unlicensed pearlers (and one which corroborates the captain's letter) is found in Venegas, "Empressas Apostolicas," párrafo 1832. Rodríguez's 1704 resignation makes clear that three viceroys had stalled rather than pushing to obtain his royal appointment to the captaincy. AGI, Guadalajara, 134 (transcript in TBL, The Bolton Papers, item 294, p. 12).

36. For information on California pearling operations, see chap. 10, pp. 321–23.

37. Gerhard, "Pearl Diving in Lower California," pp. 239–49.

38. Venegas, "Empressas Apostolicas," párrafos 466, 708, 778, and 911 record some of the traffic in pearlers along California's gulf coast.

39. The final example of General Andrés de Rezábal's long and willing assistance to the California

mission came in 1721; food and other supplies needed to found the mission at Santiago were transported from Loreto to Las Palmas Bay by the general's launches. See chap. 4, p. 105.

40. [Fiscal] Dr. Joseph Antonio de Espinosa Ocampo y Cornejo to Virrey el Duque de Alburquerque [and then directed to the *junta general* by Alburquerque]. AGI, Guadalajara, 134 (transcript in TBL, The Bolton Papers, Pockstaller document 91).

41. Resolution of the Junta General, Mexico City, 27 January 1703. AGI, Guadalajara, 134 (transcript and the cited translation in TBL, The Bolton Papers, Pockstaller document 92). A Jesuit view of this entire pearling controversy, written retrospectively in the 1730s, is found in Venegas, "Empressas Apostolicas," párrafos 1833–36. In the ensuing párrafos 1837–39, P. Venegas gives the Jesuit view of the pearlers' reaction to being forced to show licenses and allow supervision by the captain at Loreto. Then, in párrafos 1840–51, Venegas used the story of those calumnies against the Jesuits to form the basis for a long essay on the growth and injustice of anti-Jesuit rumors and actions.

42. A modern analysis of mercantilism is presented in McNeill, *Atlantic Empires of France and Spain*, pp. 46–57.

43. Virrey Alburquerque to PP. Salvatierra and Piccolo, 30 January 1703. AGNM, Californias, vol. 63, exp. 11.

44. P. Salvatierra to Virrey Alburquerque, 6 February 1704. AGI, Guadalajara, 134 (transcript in TBL, The Bolton Papers, Pockstaller document 98).

45. Venegas, *El apóstol*, p. 131.

46. Examples of the California mission's involvement with pearlers are detailed on pp. 75–77 of this chap. and p. 105 of chap. 4.

47. Resolution of the Consejo Real de Indias, 2 June 1703. AGI, Guadalajara, 219 (transcript in TBL, The Bolton Papers, Pockstaller document 95). Jesuits had advance notice of the royal council's proposal to remove their control of the California military. A year earlier, P. Piccolo had written to his province's representative in Madrid, P. Procurador General Alonso Quirós, to say that if the royal council were to prevail and the king were to appoint a royal governor for California, he, Piccolo (and no doubt he spoke for P. Salvatierra), would urge Quirós to propose for the office Don Andrés Pardo de Lagos, a royal official in Mexico City known to be a logical candidate, friendly and acceptable to the Jesuits. As matters progressed, Jesuit politicking

prevailed on the basic point and they were able to continue choosing their own military captains — who also acted as governors for the crown. Piccolo to Quirós, Mexico City, 22 May 1702. Piccolo, *Informe de 1702*, pp. 108–11.

48. Real cédula, 28 September 1703. Venegas, "Empressas Apostolicas," párrafos 607–13.

49. Venegas, "Empressas Apostolicas," párrafos 607–13. Copies of this *real cédula*, as addressed on 28 September 1703, to the Audiencia of Guadalajara, the Audiencia of Mexico, and Virrey Alburquerque, are found in AGNM, Californias, vol. 64, exp. 20.

50. See Esteban Rodríguez's resignation in AGI, Guadalajara, 134 (transcript in TBL, The Bolton Papers, item 294).

51. The annual payment of 6,000 pesos to Jesuit California from the royal treasury was suspended, at least once for as many as three consecutive years, during the ongoing Wars of Spanish Succession [1702–1713]. Venegas, "Empressas Apostolicas," párrafo 866.

52. Legal and financial advisors to viceroys and audiencias had access to the archives of those offices; they made compendious records of documents that related to each of the cases on which they were asked to advise. A pertinent example is a fiscal's resumé of cédulas issued between 1700 and 1720, "Suma de algunos paresceres del Señor Fiscal, y de varias resoluciones del Real Acuerdo sobre los negocios de las Californias." AGNM, Californias, vol. 64, exp. 16, fols. 337–40.

53. Venegas, "Empressas Apostolicas," párrafos 503–5.

54. Ibid., párrafo 520.

55. For more on P. Minutili, see chap. 5, pp. 151–52, and chap. 7, p. 183.

56. Venegas, "Empressas Apostolicas," párrafos 506–7.

57. Ibid., párrafo 522, gave the exact count of horses and mules, no doubt paraphrasing his source document literally. Elsewhere, in the more narrative sections of his work, he referred to all mounts as horses, even in cases where extant letters concerning the same incidents mention both horses and mules. P. Venegas's intent must have been to simplify his text, because he proved on many occasions that he understood the distinction, made to this day, between *caballada*, a group of horses, and *bestia*, a group of mules or a mixture of horses and mules. Many communications from California missionaries throughout the 18th century show that they consistently tried to obtain as many mules as

possible. Then, as now, mules had more stamina, crossed steep rocky terrain more readily, and foraged better off the native flora.

58. Venegas, "Empressas Apostolicas," párrafos 520–24.

59. Ibid., párrafo 524.

60. Ibid., párrafos 525–26.

61. For a fuller account of P. Piccolo's activities in Sonora, see chap. 5, pp. 151–52.

62. Venegas, "Empressas Apostolicas," párrafos 530–32.

63. Ibid., párrafo 539.

64. Ibid., párrafos 539–41.

65. Ibid., párrafos 542, 551, 703. P. Juan de Ugarte's fishing program is described in the last cited passage. P. Salvatierra's reference to boating activity by Californians is in Salvatierra to Ugarte, 1 April 1699. Bayle, *Misión*, p. 94.

66. Venegas, "Empressas Apostolicas," párrafo 618. P. Pedro de Ugarte and his brother were called *parecidos* ["look-alikes"] in Villavicencio, *Vida de Juan de Ugarte*, p. 24.

67. Venegas, "Empressas Apostolicas," párrafos 618, 713–14; Venegas, *El apóstol*, pp. 197–98.

68. Venegas, "Empressas Apostolicas," párrafos 619–33.

69. Ibid., párrafo 637.

70. Venegas, *El apóstol*, pp. 151–52.

71. Venegas, "Empressas Apostolicas," párrafos 638–39.

72. Ibid., párrafo 709. P. Venegas wrote thirty years after the fact, but his sources were original Jesuit reports and letters and Esteban Rodríguez's extensive diary. Ibid., párrafos xxviii, 217.

73. Ibid., párrafo 710.

74. The resignations offered to the viceroy by Esteban Rodríguez and Isidro Grumeque de Figueroa are found in AGI, Guadalajara, 134 (transcript in TBL, The Bolton Papers, item 294).

75. Venegas, "Empressas Apostolicas," párrafo 711.

76. AGI, Guadalajara, 135 (transcript Pockstaller document 109) and photocopy in TBL, The Bolton Papers, item 24).

77. Venegas, "Empressas Apostolicas," párrafo 754–55.

78. Capitán Agustín de Encinas sent 12 cargas of dried beef to P. Salvatierra in 1700. Salvatierra to P. Provincial Francisco de Arteaga, 21 May 1700. Bayle, *Misión*, p. 149.

79. During the 1704–1705 hiatus in his captaincy, Esteban Rodríguez went courting—with important results for California history. Rodrí-

guez's marriage to Doña María de Larrea y Jiménez is described in chap. 10, p. 306.

80. Venegas, "Empressas Apostolicas," párrafo 711.

81. P. Piccolo to P. Eusebio Kino, 13 October 1704. Piccolo, *Informe de 1702*, pp. 230–31.

82. References to Juan Bautista Escalante's pre-California career are found in Almada, *Diccionario*, p. 218; Bolton, *Rim of Christendom*, pp. 307, 360; Burrus, *Kino and Manje*, pp. 341–42, 468–70, 665–66; Bancroft, *North Mexican States*, vol. 1, p. 275.

83. Juan Bautista Escalante wrote to P. Kino about his promotion to the captaincy at Loreto. Kino, *Historical Memoir of the Pimería Alta*, vol. 2, pp. 108–9.

84. Manje, "Relación . . . ," 16 April 1701. Burrus, *Kino and Manje*, pp. 468–70.

85. Venegas, "Empressas Apostolicas," párrafos 711, 715. The date of Juan Bautista Escalante's arrival at Loreto is substantiated in his letter to P. Kino. Kino, *Historical Memoir of the Pimería Alta*, vol. 2, pp. 108–9.

86. Venegas, "Empressas Apostolicas," párrafo 754–55.

87. P. Venegas made this remarkable assertion of Jesuit influence over the Sonoran presidio at Nacozari with no further explanation. Ibid., párrafos 756–58.

88. Just two days after Virrey Alburquerque approved P. Salvatierra's request that Esteban Rodríguez be allowed to return to California as captain—replacing Juan Bautista Escalante—Salvatierra, who was in Mexico City, submitted a report to the viceroy in which he argued, among other things, for continued Jesuit control of the California presidio; in it he claimed that captains performed properly only when the missionaries held power over them. Salvatierra to Virrey Alburquerque, 25 May 1705. AGNM, Californias, vol. 63, exp. 8.

89. The dates on which Juan Bautista Escalante acted as a godfather at Loreto were 24 December 1704; 1 March 1706; 17 October 1706; 18 December 1707; and 1 April 1708. In addition, he served as godfather at San Javier on 3 March 1712, with the entry signed by P. Juan de Ugarte.

90. P. Piccolo to P. Salvatierra, 24 June 1709. Piccolo, *Informe de 1702*, p. 164–78.

91. San Javier Baptisms, 3 March 1712.

92. By 1713, Juan Bautista Escalante was in Nacozari as indicated by his letters to P. Rector Daniel Januske. AHH, leg. 325, exp. 38. In 1722, Escalante retired from the presidio and became assistant alcalde mayor at San Antonio de Mote-

pori, a Sonoran mining camp then having a modest boom. Gerhard, *North Frontier of New Spain*, p. 285. Francisco Almada considered Escalante the founder of the family of that name in Sonora. Almada, *Diccionario*, p. 219. A report written by a Sonoran Jesuit in 1722 pictures Escalante as a drunk; however, the accusation appears in the context of fierce partisanship. Escalante may merely have paid the price for being an associate and perhaps friend of the officer who was contending with the missionary. "El informe de Giuseppe Maria Genovese al virrey (1722)," in González Rodríguez, *Etnología y misión en la Pimería Alta, 1715–1740*, p. 135.

93. See chap. 6, pp. 173–74.

94. Hermano Jaime Bravo had been an assistant to P. Manuel Pineiro during his brief service as padre provincial, terminated by his death. P. Salvatierra apparently fell heir to Bravo along with the provincialate. Venegas, "Empressas Apostolicas," párrafo 756. *Hermanos* were members not qualified or not yet qualified to be padres in the Jesuit order. Some were enlisted for their special skills or took training to provide needed services to the order. Many had long, useful careers, but very few became full-fledged padres—a feat that would be accomplished by Bravo. Konrad, *Jesuit Hacienda*, pp. 131–35.

95. Venegas, "Empressas Apostolicas," párrafo 760.

96. Hermano and later P. Jaime Bravo often made humorous references to his illness, as in the opening of his 21 April 1731, letter to the Marqués de Villapuente, "How do I know whether this will be my last letter to your lordship? In the natural course of things, the apparent answer is yes, for the 'thin man' is now very thin indeed by reason of a persistent hectic fever which has continued unbroken since 12 February, and which, in conjunction with his chronic stomach ailment of twenty-two years standing, is rapidly sapping his strength so that he is able only to say the Holy Mass and to hear confessions—and even this involves no small effort, because his bones are weak. But his courage is in good condition, and his spirit is as bold as ever. God's will be done in all things!" BNM, AF 4/56.3. California Jesuits and at least one visitor general worried over his wasting condition; nevertheless, Jaime Bravo lived and worked until 1744.

97. Despite Capitán Rodríguez's failures to open a land route to Mulegé in 1703, Venegas referred casually to P. Basaldúa "taking the road northward to a site called Mulegé." Apparently, either the difficult land route had by then been pioneered, or

Basaldúa was met at Bahía de la Concepción—easily reached from Loreto—by a sailing launch that could have ferried his party in increments by the sheltered water route to Mulegé. Venegas, "Empressas Apostolicas," párrafos 761–62.

Misión de Santa Rosalía de Mulegé was founded and developed with much aid and participation from men of Basque birth or descent. Its endowment came from Nicolás de Arteaga and his wife, residents of Mexico City [see p. 68, n. 29, of this chap.]. Arteaga was a Basque who had been approached in the early days of the Pious Fund by P. Juan de Ugarte, also of Basque descent. P. Basaldúa, another Basque creole, was the mission's founder. When he became ill and had to leave the post, Basaldúa left the mission in the hands of his soldier, Juan Bautista Mugazábal, also a Basque, who ran it for several months and subsequently became a Jesuit *hermano* himself, after spiritual instruction by the aforesaid P. Juan de Ugarte. In 1718, P. Sebastián de Sistiaga, yet another Basque creole, became missionary at Santa Rosalía de Mulegé. After 1728, Sistiaga and P. Juan Bautista Luyando, still another creole of Basque descent, shared the missionary posts at both Santa Rosalía and Misión de San Ignacio—founded with an endowment from Luyando himself, and named for San Ignacio de Loyola, the Basque founder of the Jesuit order. Douglass and Bilbao, *Amerikanuak: Basques in the New World*, pp. 179–80.

98. Misión de San Juan Bautista was founded at Ligüí and never relocated, but the name of its location was changed to Malibat; see explanation in chap. 4, p. 104. Problems with its endowment are discussed in chap. 7, p. 182. The steps and methods employed by Jesuits in establishing California missions are detailed in chapters 7 and 8.

99. Venegas, "Empressas Apostolicas," párrafos 811–17. While in Mexico City, P. Salvatierra arranged with the Bishop of Mexico to have his California neophytes confirmed in the church. P. Jaime Bravo to Bishop of Guadalajara, 6 November 1719, BNM, AF 3/47.1.

100. Ibid., párrafo 818.

101. Although there is no record of herd sizes in intermediate years, San Javier's cattle were numerous enough by 1719 that P. Juan de Ugarte was able to have 200 head slaughtered to be used as food by the builders of California's first ship. See chap. 4, pp. 99–100.

102. For P. Piccolo's report on "lush" Biaundó, see chap. 2, pp. 44–45.

103. Barco, *Historia natural y crónica*, p. 257. The

number of Yaquis that assisted P. Ugarte's expedition and the circumstances of their presence in California are told in Venegas, "Empressas Apostolicas," párrafos 797–98.

104. Barco, *Historia natural y crónica*, p. 258.

105. Venegas, "Empressas Apostolicas," párrafos 720–23, 819. The source and preparation of *cal* is discussed in chap. 9, p. 271.

106. P. Miguel del Barco, in an *informe* written for P. Visitador General Lizasoáin in 1762. Bayle, *Misión*, p. 227. For more on the frequent necessity to move missions, see "Sites for missions," chap. 7, pp. 193–96.

107. Barco, *Historia natural y crónica*, pp. 294–95. For information on Juan Bautista Mugazábal as *hermano coadjutor*, see chap. 5, p. 141.

108. P. Piccolo's 1709 expedition: Piccolo to P. Salvatierra, 24 June 1709; Piccolo, *Informe de 1702*, pp. 164–78. Piccolo's 1712 expedition: Venegas, "Empressas Apostolicas," párrafos 896–98.

109. Piccolo to Salvatierra, 24 June 1709. Piccolo, *Informe de 1702*, p. 175. On the mesa of Jauja, only twelve airline miles from Piccolo's 1709 route, the author in 1973 counted 200 large, well-worn metates during a forty-five minute survey that covered only a fraction of the mesa's area.

110. Venegas, "Empressas Apostolicas," párrafos 871–73.

111. Ibid., párrafos 867, 871–73.

112. Ibid., párrafos 892–93.

113. P. Piccolo and others at times referred to this man, a neophyte from Ventitán, Jalisco, as Sebastián "Martínez," apparently confusion or carelessness because, in the same letters and baptismal records, they alternatively employ the original form, "Martín," used by P. Salvatierra.

114. P. Piccolo to Hermano Jaime Bravo, 18 December 1716. Piccolo, *Informe de 1702*, pp. 181–98. The same account, with a few additional details is found in Piccolo to P. Juan Manuel de Basaldúa, 10 January 1717. Ibid., pp. 199–211.

115. Venegas, "Empressas Apostolicas," párrafos 654–57.

116. Venegas, *El apóstol*, p. 173; Venegas, "Empressas Apostolicas," párrafo 656.

Chapter 4: Missions Create Turmoil in the South

1. Venegas, "Empressas Apostolicas," párrafos 653–54.

2. Ibid., párrafo 653.

3. Ibid., párrafos 658–59.

4. Dunne, *Black Robes*, p. 156. Although it was not Dunne's source, "Empressas Apostolicas," párrafo 699, reveals the same pattern of Jesuit thought with respect to the additional presidio requested by Bravo in 1717.

5. Gerhard, *Pirates*, pp. 211–15; Schurz, *The Manila Galleon*, pp. 325–29.

6. Bancroft, *North Mexican States*, pp. 435–37; Venegas, "Empressas Apostolicas," párrafos 658–83.

7. For eyewitness descriptions of cape peoples and the perception of racial mixture, see p. 110 of this chap.

8. Beside P. Juan de Ugarte's extended efforts at exploration — detailed later in this text — he struck up a friendly correspondence with Virrey Valero and made an unprecedented gesture by sending him a sample of California silver ore so that royal officials might judge its prospects. Ugarte probably felt confident that his submission would interest Valero because the ore was collected by Don Fermín Téllez who, though only a common soldier at Loreto, came from a family with silver-mining experience at Alamos, Sonora. Ugarte to Valero, 15 March 1721, in León-Portilla, *Testimonios sudcalifornianos*, pp. 74–75.

9. The Marqués de Villapuente, long-time California benefactor (see chap. 3, p. 68, n. 116), gave 10,000 peso endowments to each of four missions to be founded in *el Sur*: La Paz, Los Dolores, Santiago, and San José del Cabo. Moreover, he influenced his sister-in-law, the Marquesa de las Torres, to fund Misión de Santa Rosa [Todos Santos] — to be named for the Marquesa's sister Rosa, wife of Villapuente. Venegas, "Empressas Apostolicas," párrafo 1971.

10. See p. 104 n. 47, of this chap.

11. Guillén, *Overland Expeditions to Bahía Magdalena and La Paz*, pp. 31–61.

12. William Strafford, "Descripcion de las Californias desde el Cavo de Sn. Lucas q. esta al sur Sus misiones Puertos Baias Plazeres Naciones Reduzidas y Gentiles . . . ," 18 January 1746. BNM, AF 4/65.1 (transcript and translation in TBL, The Bolton Papers, item 45).

13. P. Ugarte to P. Piccolo, 18 November 1719. Piccolo, *Informe de 1702*, pp. 333–45. In letters to personal friends, PP. Salvatierra, Piccolo, and Ugarte often exhibited high spirits and ready humor. No personal letters written by Sistiaga seem to be available, but, in correspondence pertaining to his duties and exercise of delegated authority, he seems uniformly serious and concerned.

Perhaps Ugarte's broad references to Sistiaga's thoughts and reactions were double entendres intended to heighten Piccolo's perception of the problems of obtaining ship timbers, and at the same time to poke a little fun at the younger Jesuit whose dour inclinations must have been well known to both his elders.

14. In 1991, a road-building crew, not made up of local men, bulldozed the remains of the stone chapel of San Patricio and used the proceeds as fill material. The road they were building passes through San Narciso, San Gabriel, and San Miguel, thus overlying or paralleling the very trail that Ugarte followed into the sierra.

15. P. Marcos Antonio Kappus, an Austrian Jesuit, was long stationed as a missionary in Sonora — at Mátape, and elsewhere. He had helped P. Salvatierra in various ways since the earliest days of the California venture. He died in 1717, but one of the oxen he had donated to California was taken on P. Ugarte's logging expedition.

16. Venegas, "Empressas Apostolicas," párrafo 972.

17. Ibid., párrafo 973.

18. Theodore Hittel had access to a document that showed El Triunfo in use bringing Yaqui volunteers to fight the rebellion in California in 1735. Hittel, *El Triunfo de la Cruz*, p. 14.

19. The Spanish marine cubit equalled about twenty-three inches. Bravo, "Entrada al Puerto de La Paz," in León-Portilla, *Testimonios sudcalifornianos*, p. 25.

20. P. Venegas devoted a very long passage to the founding and development of Misión de la Purísima because P. Tamaral was unusually diligent in recording the events and his procedures. Venegas, "Empressas Apostolicas," párrafos 925–57.

21. Hermano Jaime Bravo elevated to padre, Venegas, "Empressas Apostolicas," párrafo 686. Bravo at La Paz, Ibid., párrafos 974–84; see also p. 102 of this chap.

22. Venegas, "Empressas Apostolicas," párrafos 988–93.

23. ibid., párrafo 781. See p. 104 of this chap.

24. P. Venegas shows that this party reported reaching as far north as 28 degrees N. lat. ["Empressas Apostolicas," párrafo 1072]. But most latitudes taken by California explorers up to 1780 have proved to be too high by a degree or more. The latitude claimed by the explorers led Dunne [*Black Robes*, p. 165] to conclude that their party neared the shores of the Bahía de Sebastián Vizcaíno, but this was clearly not the case. The exploration lasted fourteen days and went south as far as the mouth of the arroyo of San Miguel de Comondú, which the explorers identified by name. The most northerly coastal point they visited was probably about 26 degrees, 30 minutes N. lat., south of Laguna San Ignacio; that striking landlocked body of water surely would have elicited some comment. P. Nicolás Tamaral's supposed exploration of the same stretch of coast is reported in Venegas, *Noticia*, vol. 2, p. 369.

25. The man captured by the English must have been in the ship's company of *Nuestra Señora de la Encarnación y Desengaño*, which was taken off Cabo de San Lucas on 22 December 1709, by Captain Woodes Rogers. This prize was taken to Guam and eventually back to England, with a stop in Holland. Schurz, *The Manila Galleon*, pp. 325–29.

26. P. Juan de Ugarte's 1721 expedition ran dangerously low on food during its return along the coast of Sonora. Although the ship had landed in a region of unconverted and dangerous Seris, Juan Miguel Montaño volunteered to go for help. In five days, he succeeded in trading some of the ship's expendable gear for over forty bushels of wheat and other foodstuffs. P. Ugarte's grateful account not only preserves the memory of the otherwise obscure Juan Miguel Montaño, but also identifies his native land by twice describing him as "the Peruvian soldier." Venegas, "Empressas Apostolicas," párrafos 1023, 1030.

27. A long, detailed account of P. Juan de Ugarte's navigation of the gulf is found in Ibid., párrafos 1008–73. The makeup of the crew is given in Ugarte to P. Procurador José de Echeverría, 12 January 1722. BNM, AF 3/53.1 (transcript and translation in TBL, The Bolton Papers, item 35). For the final Jesuit exploration of the gulf, see pp. 126–27 of this chap.

28. At least three mid-18th century writers with firsthand experience listed as distinct Guaycuran subgroups: Aripes, Callejúes, Cantiles [also known as Vinées or Periúes — not Pericúes], Catauros, Coras, Monquíes, Pecunes, and Uchitíes. Taraval, *Indian Uprising*, p. 38; Barco, *Historia natural y crónica*, pp. 245, 403–4, 404–5; Strafford, "Informe . . ." 18 January 1746. BNM, AF 4/65.1.

29. Barco, *Historia natural y crónica*, p. 171.

30. Chap. 7 describes the Jesuits' methods and practices in establishing their California missions.

31. Barco, *Historia natural y crónica*, p. 440.

32. Taraval, *Indian Uprising*, pp. 65, 74, 126; Shelvocke, *Voyage*, pp. 216, 228.

33. Early explorers and missionaries reported

that the Pericú language and customs were markedly different from those of other peninsular people. The Pericú buried the bones of their dead after painting them red with hematite and elaborately wrapping them in woven fiber bags; other peninsular people usually practiced cremation. Over a hundred Pericú graves have been excavated; anthropometrical studies show that the Pericú were strikingly dolichocephalic (long-headed). The Pericú were California's most sea-oriented people. They made balsas and canoes which they paddled and sailed. They alone inhabited the gulf islands adjacent to the peninsula and south of 25 degrees N. Latitude. Reygadas and Velázquez, *El grupo pericú*, passim.

34. The three Jesuits' descriptions of events surrounding the founding of Misión Nuestra Señora del Pilar de la Paz are found in León-Portilla, *Testimonios sudcalifornianos*.

35. Bravo, "Entrada al Puerto de La Paz," in Ibid., pp. 47–48.

36. Many documents show that California residents of the Jesuit period used the term *el Sur* to indicate the same specific geographic area; nonresidents do not seem to have understood or used it. P. Miguel del Barco (whose great work was undertaken precisely to correct errors and misunderstandings about California) emphasized the special application of *el Sur* by defining it at least three times: "For fifty leagues [125 miles], from Cabo de San Lucas northward (which is the terrain that in California is called *el Sur*) . . . "; "Traveling from south to north, a few leagues from La Paz one departs from the area that is called *Sur* and enters the territory of the Guaycura . . . ;" "Moreover, in California, the word *Sur* is applied properly to the most southern part . . . that occupies about fifty leagues or a little more ending in Cabo de San Lucas." Barco, *Historia natural y crónica*, pp. 3, 175, 395. The printed edition of Barco's manuscript does not always capitalize the "S" in *el Sur* as Barco himself did, following a practice used to distinguish it from the compass direction—which was written in lower case. See photocopy of Barco ms. in TBL, The Bolton Papers.

37. Barco, *Historia natural y crónica*, p. 245.

38. P. Jaime Bravo's belief that all the cape people south of La Paz were "Coras" is stated plainly in both Bravo to viceroy, September 1717. Venegas, "Empressas Apostolicas," párrafo 659, número 4; and in Bravo and Romano to the king, 8 April 1720. The Huntington Library, Manuscript HM 1288.

39. The Spanish name *Cantiles* was bestowed on these people in recognition of the towering pink palisades on the south flanks of Cerro Mechudo, the most striking geographic feature of their area. They were also known by the names used by neighboring bands: Vinées, Periúes (*not* Pericúes, another group), and Tepajiguetumas. Taraval, *Indian Uprising*, p. 185; Gobernador Manuel Bernal de Huidobro to Arzobispo Virrey Juan Antonio de Vizarrón y Eguiarreta, 30 April 1736. AGI, Guadalajara, 135 (Chapman document 160).

40. Barco, *Historia natural y crónica*, pp. 173–74; Taraval, *Indian Uprising*, p. 38. P. Miguel del Barco, in Ibid., p. 174, noted that the Callejúes spoke exactly the same language as the many bands of Guaycura that occupied the great area north and west of the Bay of La Paz and stretching all the way to the interface between the Guaycura and the Cochimí—just south of the missions of San Javier and San José de Comondú. In other words, Barco viewed the Callejúes simply as a branch of the greater Guaycura that competed for the La Paz area with smaller local groups that spoke different but related Guaycuran languages. P. Taraval, in the passage cited in this note, stated that the Callejúes were related to the neophytes of Misión de los Dolores, in effect, noting the same relationship described by Barco.

41. Taraval, *Indian Uprising*, pp. 60, 120–21; Strafford, "Informe . . . ," 18 January 1746. BNM, AF 4/65.1.

42. Barco, *Historia natural y crónica*, pp. 173–74; Taraval, *Indian Uprising*, p. 51.

43. Taraval, *Indian Uprising*, pp. 126, 266; Strafford, "Informe . . . ," 18 January 1746. BNM, AF 4/65.1.

44. The Callejúes and particularly the Uchitíes created a large part of the turmoil in *el Sur* by roaming not only their usual areas, but by raiding those of their neighbors as well. P. Sigismundo Taraval spent the years from 1733 to 1737 in close contact with these diverse bands, largely due to the exigencies of a major, area-wide neophyte rebellion. He perceived the diversity of those congregated at La Paz and filled the pages of a book-length memoir of the revolt with stories of the antipathies between virtually all groups. Taraval, *Indian Uprising*, pp. 38, 85, et passim.

45. See chap. 7, p. 182, "Mission endowments."

46. Venegas, *Noticia*, vol. 2, pp. 375–76.

47. "The Indians call this place by two names, which are Ligüí and Malibat. The difference arises because in the Monquí tongue it is called Ligüí and in that of the Laimón Malibat." Venegas, "Em-

pressas Apostolicas," párrafo 762. P. Venegas used the term *Laimón* rather than *Cochimí*, but numerous early references show that the Laimón were bands of Cochimí speakers who almost surrounded Loreto. For more on establishing and maintaining missions in peninsular California, see chap. 7, pp. 193–96, "Sites for missions."

48. Misión de los Dolores served Guaycura who hunted and collected food primarily on the upper parts of the plain that lies over the mountains to the west of Apaté. Apaté lacked water for agriculture. In 1734, P. Clemente Guillén decided to move to a better spring and to make his mission more accessible to plains dwellers, but the rebellion in *el Sur* interfered and the move to one of his visiting stations, called La Pasión del Señor, at a place named Tañuetía [later called Chillá] was made in 1741. The Hispanic placename La Pasión continued to be used, and the mission gradually came to be called by that name. Guillén to P. Visitador General Baltasar, 1744. TBL, Mexican Manuscripts, MM1716, doc. 70; Barco, *Historia natural y crónica*, pp. 253–54.

49. A general discussion of Loreto's problems with ships and supply will be found in chap. 5, pp. 145–49.

50. Venegas, "Empressas Apostolicas," párrafos 1074–87.

51. The relationship between the Cora and the Isleño Pericú of Isla de Cerralvo was not cultural or linguistic, but rather one of proximity and necessity. The Cora ranged through the coastal area adjacent to the island, an area to which the warrior Isleños often had to repair to escape sudden storms, obtain water, or search for food. Several early accounts refer to this alliance in rather vague terms and they appear to have strengthened the misperception that the Cora were culturally related to the Pericú. See "Santiago de los Coras" on pp. 107–8 of this chapter.

52. Venegas, "Empressas Apostolicas," párrafos 1088–92.

53. For more information on soldiers' defenses and weapons, see chap. 6, pp. 171–72.

54. Venegas, "Empressas Apostolicas," párrafos 1300–1301. This passage states that the Uchití occupied the territory midway between Santiago and La Paz. Their rampage could have been occasioned by P. Nápoli's inadvertent encroachment on their territory when he brought the Coras — for his convenience — to Santa Ana in what the Uchití probably considered their realm. Note that all later references to native Californians in the important Santa

Ana region specify that they were Uchití. [N. B. The Santiago of párrafo 1301 in this note was the site of Nápoli's final founding of the mission of the same name — the same site that bears the name today.]

55. Venegas, "Empressas Apostolicas," párrafos 1301, 987. P. Sigismundo Taraval reveals that the group evangelized by P. Bravo was related to the Uchití. Taraval, *Indian Uprising*, p. 253.

56. P. Nápoli's problems in locating a suitable site for Misión de Santiago were not unusual in the history of Jesuit California. See chap. 7, "Sites for missions," pp. 193–96.

57. P. Bravo to P. Provincial José de Arjó, 21 June 1724. BNM, AF 4/54.1.

58. Venegas, "Empressas Apostolicas," párrafos 1094–95. P. Venegas offered no comment on P. Nápoli's transfer — which probably came about as a result of P. Visitor General Juan de Guendulain's inspection tour of the Jesuit missions of California and Sonora in 1726. Historian Gerard Decorme, S. J., read this move as possibly a reproof for some shameful treatment that Nápoli might have practiced on the later-martyred P. Lorenzo Carranco, Nápoli's successor at Santiago. Decorme's tentative interpretation was based on a reading of a letter by P. Sigismundo Taraval, the Jesuit chronicler of the rebellion in which Carranco died. However, a close inspection of Taraval's account and his letter shows that he was referring to one of Carranco's neophyte antagonists — probably Domingo Botón, one-time governor of the converts at Santiago — and not to any padre. Decorme, *Jesuitas Mexicanos*, vol. 2, p. 512 n. 10.

Ten years after his transfer, Nápoli was brought back to California to try to placate the neophytes at Santiago in the aftermath of their rebellion. Nápoli's contributions to California while he was stationed in Sonora are discussed in chap. 5, pp. 150–154, "The Dependence of Jesuit California on Jesuit Sonora."

59. See pp. 107–8 and n. 38 of this chapter.

60. P. Jaime Bravo began the confusion about the extent of the land area occupied by the Cora when he reported to the viceroy in 1717 that the Cora occupied the east coast of the peninsula from La Paz to Cabo San Lucas. This was before any Jesuit exploration of the area had been made — and before a mission was founded at La Paz. Bravo was misinformed, but the misconception was still current when Padre Nápoli set out to establish Misión de Santiago. Venegas, "Empressas Apostolicas," párrafo 659, number 4. As late as 1730, P. Nicolás

Tamaral referred to his new mission at the cape as "San José de los Coras." His error reflected both the general confusion and the fact that he had been in the region only a few weeks and was not yet conversant with the Pericú language or the area's actual ethnic boundaries. P. Tamaral to P. Visitador General Echeverría, 11 December 1730. AGNM, Jesuitas, vol. 2, parte 4, exp. 39.

61. P. Venegas, in describing the peninsular native groups—distinguished largely by linguistic differences—drew on missionary reports and described the Coras as speaking the language of the Uchití but living in the land of the Pericú. However, Venegas did not perceive that this information—which is corroborated by PP. Barco and Taraval [see following note]—contradicted some of his other reports about the Cora. Venegas, "Empressas Apostolicas," párrafos 1555–56.

Reports by earlier explorers suggest somewhat different distributions of the peoples of the cape region. The Pericú seem to have once occupied a larger area than they did when the Jesuits came. That may explain why the Pericú in 1730 occupied islands as far away as Isla de San José, a hundred miles north of any area they occupied on the peninsula. It should not be assumed that any of the cape people occupied static areas; their "borders" overlapped and shifted frequently.

62. Barco, *Historia natural y crónica*, pp. 173–75, 408, 409.

63. In early 1729, José de Echeverría, then the padre procurador de Californias in Mexico City, got permission from the provincial to go to Matanchel and then to California to arrange to repair the supply ship *San José*, beached at Loreto, victim of a furious storm the previous September. While in Tepic, he bought the *San Antonio*, a small ship moored at Matanchel, to substitute for the *San José* during its renovation. Before Echeverría could embark for California, he received the news that he had been appointed visitador general of the Jesuit missions of northwest New Spain. Because of his recent post and current activities, he decided to inspect California first. He left Ahome aboard *El Triunfo de la Cruz* on 18 October 1729 and arrived at Loreto on 27 October. Despite "malignant fever," Echeverría soon left to tour the missions north of Loreto. Venegas, "Empressas Apostolicas," párrafos 1256–58.

64. Non-Spanish Jesuits used Hispanicized forms of their given names. William Gordon always signed as "Guillelmo", a variant of the usual "Guillermo."

65. Venegas, "Empressas Apostolicas," párrafos 1263–69, 1303.

66. Ibid., párrafos 1269–70.

67. Barco, *Historia natural y crónica*, p. 186 n. 28.

68. *Coyote* was a term Hispanics used to indicate a mixture of black, white, and Indian blood; *lobo*, a combination of black and Indian. New Spain's melting pot stimulated the creation and use of dozens of names supposed to identify specific racial mixtures. Most were used in imprecise ways—but they did serve to indicate the real or imagined influence of European, African, Asian, and native American ancestry in individuals or groups described by observers.

69. Venegas, "Empressas Apostolicas," párrafos 1282–83. Such complaints by missionaries followed a general pattern of behavior of men in responsible positions; when they sensed problems or opposition, they kept lists of people to blame for any failures or troubles that might result. Naylor and Polzer, *Presidio and Militia*, p. 78. People of mixed blood made ideal targets for this sort of abuse. They usually had little social status or economic clout. They were looked down upon collectively in an almost ritual fashion; white society accepted as a tenet the idea of this lower caste's untrustworthiness, rebelliousness, and general depravity. They were blamed early in the pacification and conversion of the peoples of the northwest frontier of New Spain. Naylor and Polzer, Ibid., p. 419; Stern and Jackson, "Vagabundaje," pp. 461–63.

70. Venegas, "Empressas Apostolicas," párrafos 1283.

71. Ibid., párrafo 1275.

72. Ibid., párrafos 1284–89.

73. P. Clemente Guillén to Virrey Marqués de Casafuerte, 25 September 1725. Burrus and Zubillaga, *Misiones mexicanas*, pp. 238–39.

74. Venegas, "Empressas Apostolicas," párrafo 1302. P. Sigismundo Taraval wrote of the Uchití from firsthand experience and local report, ". . . the ranchería of the Huchities . . . had always been the refuge of culprits, the annoyance of the missions, and the terror of the Indians. Within the past few years they had killed off half of the ranchería of the Pericú nation [that located at Todos Santos], had annihilated nearly the entire ranchería of the pueblo of Todos Santos during the early days of its foundation [founded 1724], and, in short, they did what they pleased, relying on their numbers and bravery and the fact that all feared them." Taraval, *Indian Uprising*, p. 85.

75. Venegas, "Empressas Apostolicas," párrafos 1303–6.

76. Rodríguez to P. Echeverría, 2 March 1731. AGNM, Historia, vol. 308, fol. 483. Echeverría left California about 1 October 1730. P. Bravo to Marqués de Villapuente, 10 October 1730. TBL, The Bolton Papers, item 32.

77. P. Sistiaga to Rodríguez, 6 March 1731. AGNM, Historia, vol. 308, fol. 488. The suggested letter from Esteban Rodríguez to the viceroy is not known to exist.

78. Venegas, "Empressas Apostolicas," párrafo 1273; Taraval, *Indian Uprising*, p. 85.

79. Changes in demographics at Todos Santos, Venegas, "Empressas Apostolicas," párrafo 1273. Crops and products, P. Gordon to P. Echeverría, "Informe de la Missⁿ. de la Paz," 26 June 1730. AGNM, Jesuitas, vol. 2, parte 4, exp. 36.

80. Señora Doña Rosa Villegas in 1730 was influenced by the Marqués de Villapuente, the great benefactor of Jesuit California, to endow Misión de Santa Rosa. Venegas, "Empressas Apostolicas," párrafo 1295. In this párrafo, P. Venegas reveals his confusion over the two Santa Rosas—which he took to be one. He described Santa Rosa as between the missions of Santiago and San José, which was the location of Santa Rosa, a pueblo of the latter mission. But he intended to indicate the proposed mission of Santa Rosa, which was always and only located at Todos Santos. This explains several mysterious passages in "Empressas Apostolicas" that locate Todos Santos, or Santa Rosa, on the gulf side rather than the Pacific side of the sierra. Years later, in 1759, P. Juan de Armesto corrected P. Andrés Marcos Burriel who had picked up P. Venegas's confusion while editing "Empressas Apostolicas" to create *Noticia de la California*. The Huntington Library, Manuscript HM 22241.

81. Barco, *Historia natural y crónica*, p. 248.

82. Venegas, "Empressas Apostolicas," párrafos 1310–20. Soldier Santiago Villalobos's commission was mentioned in P. Bravo to Villapuente, 27 June 1734. BNM, AF 4/56.5. P. Taraval confirmed this report, saying that one mission had no guard in the summer of 1734 because its soldier was absent escorting an Augustinian friar to Mexico City. Taraval, *Indian Uprising*, pp. 50–51.

83. Jesuits resisted the right of the secular church to collect tithes from them on the basis that their properties were exempt; the challenge to Virrey Vizarrón became so intense that he excommunicated several men in the Jesuit hierarchy of New Spain. Decorme, *Jesuitas mexicanos*, vol. 1, p. 361; Konrad, *Jesuit Hacienda*, pp. 95–96, 157–58.

84. The story of the first Manila ship served by a cape mission is told in Venegas, "Empressas Apostolicas," párrafos 1310–20. Testimony by officers and passengers concerning the visits of Manila ships to San Bernabé in 1734 and 1735 can be found in long expedientes in AGI, Guadalajara, 135. Additional testimony by these and other men who had visited San José del Cabo or been close to problems of the Manila trade may be found as answers to a questionnaire created by Procurador de Californias Hermano Juan Francisco de Tompes in Mexico City in 1735. Burrus and Zubillaga, *El noroeste*, pp. 413–36.

85. The following account of the neophyte rebellion at the cape missions is drawn primarily from P. Sigismundo Taraval's firsthand account, translated and published as, *Indian Uprising*. Hereinafter, this source is specifically cited only when it is quoted verbatim or serves as a source of nonchronological information. Other sources are cited wherever used.

86. Ibid., p. 114.

87. Earlier in 1734, P. Tamaral sent his soldier, Santiago Villalobos, to assist an important friar who had been left at his mission by a Manila galleon (see p. 114). But Tamaral apparently made no effort to have his escort replaced. Venegas, "Empressas Apostolicas," párrafos 1266, 1269.

88. P. Carranco may have chosen to serve without a regular soldier. Around 1725, P. Provincial José de Arjó had officially consented to requests from some missionaries that they be allowed to dispense with a soldier's protection. Dunne, *Black Robes*, p. 143.

89. P. Taraval, a witness to the early phases of the rebellion, and Miguel Venegas, working with firsthand reports, chronicled the insurrection of local neophytes and heathen in the South. Taraval offered no explanation for P. Gordon's absence from his post at La Paz. P. Venegas said that Gordon had gone off to Loreto "under certain orders." Venegas, "Empressas Apostolicas," párrafo 1328. Entries in libros de misión show unequivocally that Gordon was at Mulegé by 17 July 1733, and thereafter administered Misión de San Javier's important visita of San Miguel, probably by February of 1734, and certainly by September. In 1735, Taraval remarked casually that Gordon was assigned to San Miguel. Taraval, *Indian Uprising*, p. 150. Venegas's story fits the facts: Gordon was called north as part of the round of substitutions begun by moving P. Tamaral and then P. Taraval out of La Purísima to open the final new missions in *el Sur*.

90. It is probable that two of the soldiers at Todos

Santos at the outbreak of the rebellion were those stationed in the vicinity to herd the cattle that belonged to Capitán Rodríguez. This is supported by the fact that one of the men was Manuel de Ocio, a son-in-law of the captain. See chap. 10, pp. 303–5, 318.

91. Many Yaquis were recruited to help in California before the arrival of Governor Bernal de Huidobro; others probably accompanied him. AGNM, Californias, vol. 80, exp. 6, fols. 34–37. The experiences of the Yaqui warriors in California raise an interesting possibility. In 1740, three years after the last of these Sonorans left the peninsula, a great revolt against both mission and secular forces broke out among the Yaquis and raged in Sonora for two years. The Yaquis were a large, rather unified cultural group with an old and proud tradition of effective military actions. Yaqui men-at-arms in California saw the ineffectiveness of the Spanish against forces that the Yaquis must have thought puny. They also had a chance to evaluate the performance of Manuel Bernal de Huidobro, potentially the leader of Spanish opposition to any Sonoran rebellion. It is likely that the Yaqui veterans of the California uprising played significant roles in their own people's subsequent struggle.

92. Mainland volunteers to fight the California rebellion are listed in AGNM, Californias, vol. 80, exp. 6, fols. 34–37. Manuel Andrés Romero slain at La Paz, Venegas, "Empressas Apostolicas," párrafo 1328. Romero's age and parentage are found in "La Parroquia de Santiago de Compostela [Nayarit]," Libro de Bautismos, 3 March 1712, FHL Microfilm #654341. Juan Antonio Romero commanded the ship that brought Padre Salvatierra and his followers to Loreto in 1697. Venegas, "Empressas Apostolicas," párrafos 230, 232, 236, 242.

Inspection of parish records from many towns and villages on the western slopes of New Spain shows that men with the following surnames had come from the vicinity of Compostela: Acosta, Arroyo, Caravajal, Estrada, Gerardo, Gutiérrez de Góngora, Haro, Jacomé Induz, Morales, Peña, Pérez, Romero, Rubio Monroy, and Velasco.

93. See chap. 8, pp. 231–32.

94. Taraval, *Indian Uprising*, p. 144.

95. Venegas, *Noticia*, pp. 486–88.

96. The hearings on the Manila ship's disaster at San José del Cabo before the Audiencia of Guadalajara are in AGI, Guadalajara, 135. The Jesuit padre provincial's complaint to the crown is Joseph Barba to the King, 26 April 1735. TBL, Mexican Manuscripts, MM 1716, no. 7.

97. P. Juan Bautista María Luyando to P. Bernardo Lozano, 22 April 1737. Burrus/Zubillaga, *Misiones Mexicanas*, pp. 19–25. Anza was the father of the captain of the same name who later figured prominently in the opening of Alta California.

98. Van Young, *Hacienda and Market*, pp. 182–91.

99. A 1722 Jesuit complaint to the viceroy describes one of many soldier/settler vs. missionary disputes in Sonora. "El informe de Giuseppe Maria Genovese al virrey (1722)," in González Rodríguez, *Etnología y misión en la Pimería Alta, 1715–1740*, pp. 125–87. In his introduction and notes, González has occasion to detail many of the uses and abuses of Sonoran captaincies.

100. Hu-de Hart, *Missionaries, Miners, and Indians*, pp. 39–57.

101. Brigadier Pedro de Rivera inspected the presidios of the northwest between 1724 and 1729. His findings expose most of the stated practices and malpractices of captains. Naylor and Polzer, *Pedro de Rivera*, pp. 104–18. Rivera's only criticism — and a mild one — of Bernal de Huidobro's administration of the presidio of Sinaloa was the high prices for supplies charged to the soldiers. Ibid., pp. 82, 113.

102. Moorhead, *The Presidio*, pp. 31, 34–35.

103. Acquisition of land by soldiers, militiamen, and others, including lands near missions or claimed by missions, is a major subject in Deeds, "Mission Villages and Agrarian Patterns in a Nueva Vizcayan Heartland, 1600–1750." *Journal of the Southwest*.

104. Virrey Casafuerte appointed Manuel Bernal de Huidobro governor ["capitán del presidio de Sinaloa"], a promotion from his post as alcalde mayor of Huejotzingo [Puebla]. Bernal de Huidobro had served previously in the armies of "Castilla, Aragón y Cataluña con plazas de Alférez, Theniente, y Ayudante del Regimento de Caballería de Ordenes," and served in battles of Almansa, Sitios de Campo Mayor, and Tortosa. His appointment noted the recent death of Sinaloa's long-time governor, Andrés de Rezábal. Edict signed by the Marqués de Casafuerte, 25 May 1723. AGI, Guadalajara, 70.

105. Due to long distances and the forbidding barrier of the Sierra Madre Occidental, governors of Nueva Vizcaya and Nueva México had found it difficult to conduct needed military operations against Indians marauding in Sonora. A royal decree of 14 March 1732, combined Sonora with Sinaloa, but the bureaucracy moved so slowly that Governor Bernal de Huidobro did not assume his

enlarged office until the first days of 1734. Hu-de Hart, *Missionaries, Miners, and Indians*, p. 56; Almada, *Diccionario*, p. 111.

106. Bernal de Huidobro's orders to patrol and pacify Sonora are found in the Reglamento of 1729. Naylor and Polzer, *Pedro de Rivera*, p. 275. Although there were often discrepancies between orders and the performance of them, various references to Bernal de Huidobro's activities indicate that, prior to embarking for California, he was assiduous in his inspections of the territory over which he had command.

107. Deeds, "Rendering Unto Caesar," p. 69.

108. Navarro García, *La sublevación Yaqui de 1740*, pp. 21–22; Hu-de Hart, *Missionaries, Miners, and Indians*, pp. 61–62.

109. "Reglamento para todos los presidios de las Provincias Internas . . . Ordenanzas para el mejor Gobierno y Disciplina Militar de Gobernadores, Oficiales, y Soldados . . . México, 1729." in Naylor and Polzer, *Pedro de Rivera*, pp. 254–58.

110. Both Fiscal Vedoya and Auditor General Pedro Malo de Villavicencio, officials of the Audiencia of Mexico, made surprisingly pointed references to the viceroy's partiality in opinions submitted to that official. AGNM, Californias, vol. 80, exp. 26, fols. 178–82.

111. Bernal de Huidobro probably knew of the specific regulations against the employment of soldiers as mission servants that were contained in the recent Reglamento of 1729. Naylor and Polzer, *Pedro de Rivera*, pp. 163–64. Bernal de Huidobro probably came to California with rather inside knowledge of its presidio; ten years earlier, his cousin Juan Bernal de Huidobro had served at least two years as alférez at the presidio of Loreto. See chap. 6, p. 168.

112. An example of Bernal de Huidobro's belittling of California soldiers is found in Bernal de Huidobro to Vizarrón y Eguiarreta, 10 April 1736. AGI, Guadalajara, 135 (Chapman document 160). A Jesuit report of the governor's opinions and actions is in Taraval, *Indian Uprising*, pp. 201–2.

113. Taraval, *Indian Uprising*, p. 201.

114. Taraval's description of rebel behavior early in their uprising was echoed in his reports of rebel responses to Bernal de Huidobro's peaceful overtures. Ibid., p. 54.

115. Ibid., passim.

116. The King to Virrey Fuenclara, 2 April 1743. AGNM, Californias, vol. 64, exp. 3, fols. 91–96.

117. At the end of 1736, Bernal de Huidobro reported the California rebellion finished except

for a few remaining inhabitants of Isla de Cerralvo and the one-time converts of Misión de San José del Cabo. The ranchería of Yonaseque [Yéneca?] was killed to a man on 17 December, including the neophyte captain who had directed and assisted in the killing of P. Tamaral. Bernal de Huidobro to P. Ignacio María Nápoli [located by then at a mission on the Río Yaqui], Misión de Santiago, 28 December 1736. AGNM, Historia, vol. 392, fols. 234–35.

118. AGNM, Californias, vol. 80, exp. 50, fol. 422. Bernal de Huidobro's short-lived opposition to the establishment of a new presidio is noted in a long, retrospective *informe* submitted by Fiscal Vedoya to Virrey Vizarrón on 12 July 1739. AGNM, Californias, vol. 80, exp. 26. Vedoya's summary and opinions broadly reflect the conflicting pressures on the viceroy from royal councilors, Jesuits, and their partisans. He supports the independence of soldiers from missionaries, the promotion of California colonization, and other measures associated with Bourbon reforms, but he also cites the opinions of California Jesuits and recommends some of the actions that they wished.

119. Venegas, "Empressas Apostolicas," párrafos 1372–73; Venegas, *Noticia*, vol. 2, pp. 494–96; Ibid., vol. 3, p. 193; Barco, *Historia natural y crónica*, p. 414.

120. Hu-de Hart, *Missionaries, Miners, and Indians*, p. 61.

121. Capitán Alvarez de Acevedo excommunicated: AGNM, General de Parte, vol. 33, exp. 2. Explicit reasons for excommunication are given in AGNM, Californias, vol. 80, exp. 26, fols. 179–82. P. Agustín María de Luyando went from California to Mexico City in 1739, carrying with him an incredibly detailed list of complaints against Alvarez de Acevedo and his soldiers: working Indians on Sundays and feast days, insolence to padres, blasphemy, allowing Indians too much freedom and thereby tempting them to share their women, dance, and engage in other vices and witchcraft. He was also accused of buying the Indians' support against the padres with gifts of knives, blankets, chocolate, sugar, and panocha. A draft of his 90-page report to the archbishop-viceroy is in AGNM, Californias, vol. 64, exp. 9, fols. 172–217.

122. The dispute between Alvarez de Acevedo and Padre Antonio Tempis is minutely detailed in a series of letters between the principals. AGNM, Californias, vol. 80, exp. 27, fols. 190–203.

123. Polzer, *Rules and Precepts*, p. 23.

124. AGNM, Californias, vol. 80, exp. 27, ff. 190–203.

125. For a description of bases of Jesuit power, as well as their employment of it in dealing with adversaries, see Konrad, *Jesuit Hacienda*, pp. 153–56, 173.

126. Barco, *Historia natural y crónica*, p. 240. A large documentation of Jesuit charges and legal actions is contained in AGI, Guadalajara, leg. 89.

127. For more on the Yaqui revolt in 1740 and its relationship to California, see chap. 5, pp. 153–54.

128. These events are recounted retrospectively in The King to Virrey Fuenclara, 2 April 1743. AGNM, Californias, vol. 64, exp. 3, fol. 92v. The actual transfer of the Presidio of the South to become a subsidiary of the Presidio of Loreto took place in 1741. Barco, *Historia natural y crónica*, p. 397.

129. P. Provincial Anzaldo's accusations and arguments may be read, in an English translation, in Meredith, "The Yaqui Rebellion of 1740: A Jesuit account and its implications." *Ethnohistory*, pp. 222–61. Jesuit legal expenses were said to have been 6,000 pesos, and to have been paid by the various Jesuit mission areas; California was assessed to pay 800 pesos. P. Visitador General Baltasar to P. Provincial Escobar y Llamas, October 1744. AHH, leg. 1126, exp. 3.

130. The charged illicit trading took place in 1740, the first year in which a Manila ship landed after the fatal event of 1735. Barco, *Historia natural y crónica*, p. 248.

131. Hu-de Hart, *Missionaries, Miners, and Indians*, pp. 78–80, 86. In wildly fluctuating decisions, successive viceroys exonerated Bernal de Huidobro and reinstated him in the governorship, then rescinded the decision. Deeds, "Las relaciones entre los jesuitas y los oficiales reales . . . ," p. 99.

132. AGNM, Californias, vol. 64, exp. 3, fol. 92v.

133. The hearings and plans of the Audiencia of Guadalajara are described in chap. 10, pp. 323–24.

134. Venegas, *Noticia*, p. 502.

135. Barco, *Historia natural y crónica*, p. 235.

136. The legal case of the crown vs. Bernal de Huidobro may well have been *residencia*, a formal investigation of his activities as governor of Sinaloa. See Haring, *Spanish Empire*, pp. 138–42. His placement in Perú appears in Archivo General de Simancas, *Catálogo XX: Títulos de Indias*, p. 457.

137. Evidence has been uncovered that shows major Jesuit financial contributions or concessions to Virrey Fuenclara. Deeds, "Las relaciones entre los jesuitas y los oficiales reales . . . ," p. 99.

138. Real Cédula, 13 November 1744. AGNM, Reales Cédulas, vol. 67, exp. 32. As usual, even the royal orders that contained clauses favorable to the Jesuits had pointed references to colonization and economic development. Another, of the same date as above, called for several of the steps toward economic development that had recently been proposed by the Audiencia of Guadalajara as an outcome of the Castillo de Aysa hearings. Real Cédula directed to Virrey Conde de Fuenclara, 13 November 1744. AGNM, Reales Cédulas, vol. 64, exp. 101. For an account of the hearings, see chap. 10, pp. 323–24.

139. P. Consag's report was printed as part of the appendix to Venegas, vol. 3, abridged & rewritten by Burriel, 140–94. See also, P. Miguel del Barco's valuable additions, probably obtained in conversations with Consag. Barco, *Historia natural y crónica*, pp. 368–75.

140. Dunne, *Black Robes*, pp. 323–24. Juan and Ulloa's gratuitous error over California's peninsularity is surprising. The report on South America for which they are principally known was based on past experiences and personal observations. Juan, Jorge and Antonio de Ulloa, *Noticias secretas de América*. Madrid: Biblioteca Ayacucho 31 & 32, 1918. Antonio de Ulloa, incidentally, served later as governor of a region in Peru and of Spanish Louisiana.

141. Since P. Kino became convinced of the peninsularity of California in 1701, no local Jesuit reported any other opinion. However, through publications that reached them, those of California were aware of the ignorance of European geographers and pundits. They welcomed Consag's work and immediately considered that the issue was settled. Baegert, *Letters*, p. 127. But twenty years after the 1746 exploration, P. Miguel del Barco was well aware that their conviction was not shared by many pundits. He regretted that Consag had not put his conclusions forward more forcefully. As a result, Barco reported that P. Linck was about to mount his 1766 exploration designed to go to the mouth of the Río Colorado by land and "gather evidence that California is not an island, evidence of such a nature that the most demanding critic would not be able to object." P. Barco to P. Provincial Francisco Zeballos, 20 October 1765. Barco, *Historia natural y crónica*, p. 438.

142. For P. Jacobo Sedelmayr's 1748–1750 explorations down the Gila to the Colorado junction, see Bancroft, *North Mexican States*, vol. 1, pp. 540–41; Nentvig, *Rudo Ensayo*, pp. 15–17.

143. Regional interest in developing the west

coast, the Mar de Cortés, and California was sharpened and given direction by hearings before the Audiencia de Guadalajara, 1740–1743. See chap. 10, pp. 323–24. Royal cédulas for years after made fragmentary references to details and recommendations that came to the crown in reports of these hearings.

144. In 1749, the Marqués de Altamira, Auditor de Guerra to the Audiencia de Guadalajara, described Jesuit resistance to secular economic development in strong terms. "Dictamen del Auditor de Guerra," AGI, Guadalajara 191 (transcribed in María del Carmen Velázquez, *El Marqués de Altamira y las Provincias Internas de Nueva España*, p. 117).

145. See P. Visitador General Baltasar's diplomatic but firm letter of objection to P. Provincial Escobar y Llamas, "Sobre la entriega de la administración del presidio de Californias" [1744]. Burrus and Zubillaga, *El noroeste*, pp. 471–80. P. Visitador Sistiaga's letter to same, 19 September 1743. Ibid., pp. 437–56.

146. Clavijero, *History of California*, p. 379.

147. By 1748, only one-sixth of a Pericú population, once estimated at 3,000, survived. Barco, *Historia natural y crónica*, p. 243.

Chapter 5: The Jesuit Organization in California

1. Venegas, "Empressas Apostolicas," párrafos 1736–37. The California visitador's schedule for making the rounds of the missions apparently varied during the successive periods of the Jesuit regime. In the middle period, visitations were carried out each six months. (Esteban Rodríguez to P. Visitador General Echeverría, 2 March 1731. AGNM, Historia, vol. 308 [transcript in TBL, The Bolton Papers, item 295].) Later, P. Jacobo Baegert reported visitations at three year intervals. Baegert, *Letters*, p. 212.

2. Venegas, "Empressas Apostolicas," párrafos 1726–27.

3. Venegas, "Empressas Apostolicas," párrafos 917, 1732, 1734. After P. Salvatierra's death, California's padre visitador was appointed each three years by the provincial of New Spain—but his choices were guided by advice from senior California missionaries.

4. The central rectorate consisted of the missions of Loreto, Los Dolores, San Luis Gonzaga, La Purísima, and San Javier. The other two rectorates were made up respectively of the missions north and south of the central group. See "Visita de la provincia de Californias hecha por el padre visitador general, Juan Antonio Baltasar, a fines del año 1743 y principios de 1744," in Burrus and Zubillaga, *El noroeste*, p. 457. No available document names the many padres rectores, or records their years of service; a few instances can be reconstructed from chance references in supply lists, memoirs, or contemporary correspondences.

5. Piccolo, *Informe de 1702*, p. 13.

6. P. Clemente Guillén took over the California visitorship late in 1725. He issued a credit as padre visitador on 18 November 1725 to a mainland merchant or private procurer named Antonio Morán—perhaps the same man who taught weaving at San Javier, 1709–1712. (See chap. 7, p. 219.) Accounts of the *padre procurador en México* (under year 1727), AGNM, Californias, vol. 60 bis, exp. 6.

7. P. Sebastián de Sistiaga's tenure in this period is suggested by two letters that he wrote: one to P. Visitador General Echeverría on 27 October 1730, after Echeverría had left California, and the other to Capitán Rodríguez on 6 March 1731. In each case, Sistiaga's concerns are broader than those of a simple missionary and suggest that he was acting as the superior, the padre visitador. AGNM, Historia, vol. 308, fols. 478–79, 488.

8. See catálogo in Piccolo, *Informe de 1702*, p. 306.

9. P. Sigismundo Taraval indicated that P. Sistiaga replaced P. Guillén as California's visitador in 1736. Taraval/Wilbur, *Indian Uprising*, p. 220. Sistiaga signed as visitador in Loreto's visitation book in both 1737 and 1739. AGNM, Misiones, vol. 27, fol. 298.

10. See catálogo in Piccolo, *Informe de 1702*, p. 306.

11. P. Sebastián de Sistiaga's occupation of the visitador's post by September 1743 is verified by his own words in Sistiaga to P. Provincial Escobar y Llamas, San Ignacio, 19 September 1743. Burrus and Zubillaga, *El noroeste*, p. 438. P. Visitador General Baltasar identified Sistiaga as visitador in 1744. Baltasar, "Visita de la provincia de Californias. . . ." Ibid., p. 467. P. Miguel del Barco mentioned that Sistiaga went from the visitador's post directly into retirement in 1747. Barco, *Historia natural y crónica*, p. 272.

12. Barco, *Historia natural y crónica*, p. 291.

13. To confirm the identity of the padre visitador in 1751: AGNM, Californias, vol. 80, exp. 53, fol. 443; for 1753: AGNM, Californias, vol. 60 bis, exp. 15.

14. Catálogo in Burrus, *Misiones norteñas*, p. 99.

15. Barco, *Historia natural y crónica*, p. 291.

16. Ibid. p. 427.

17. P. Lamberto Hostell was listed as California's visitador in a 1764 Catálogo. Piccolo, *Informe de 1702*, pp. 310-11. Several documents name Hostell as the California visitador during 1766. AGNM, Provincias Internas, vol. 7, exp. 10, fols. 69-101.

18. Ducrue, *Account of the Expulsion*, p. 7 (and in numerous later autobiographical references in the same work).

19. Polzer, *Rules and Precepts*, pp. 24-25, 105-14.

20. P. Sebastián de Sistiaga responded sharply to P. Visitor General Echeverría's directions for consolidating rancherías at mission cabeceras; Sistiaga found the visitor's ideas impractical and told him why. Sistiaga to Echeverría, 27 October 1730. AGNM, Historia, vol. 308, fol. 478. For more on this incident, see Chapter 7, pp. 199-200.

21. PP. Visitadores Generales García, Baltasar, Carta, Utrera, and Lizasoáin later became provincials of New Spain, the last two in the curious circumstances of exile in Bologna, Italy. Burrus, *Jesuit Relations*, p. 64; Decorme, *Jesuitas mexicanas*, vol. 2, pp. 341, 433. PP. Guenduláin and the same García represented the province in Madrid after they had served as visitors general in New Spain. Burrus, Ibid., p. 201 n. 31.

22. Particularly extensive reports with valuable factual and statistical information were made by P. Visitadores Generales Baltasar (1744), Utrera (1755), and Lizasoáin (1762). Baltasar is found in Burrus and Zubillaga, *El noroeste*, documents LVI, LVII, LVIII, LIX, pp. 457-95. The original Utrera and Lizasoáin reports are found in the Library of the University of Texas, W. B. Stephens Collection, García Manuscripts, #47 [Lizasoáin], #66 and 67 [Utrera].

23. PP. Visitadores Generales Echeverría (1730), Baltasar (1744), and Lizasoáin requested and received reports on individual missions. Two submitted to Echeverría survive. They plus other correspondence generated because of Echeverría's visit are found in AGNM, Historia 308, fols. 469-92; in BNM, AF 4/55.1, 55.2, 56.1, 56.2; and in Venegas, "Empressas Apostolicas," párrafos 1272-81. The more numerous surviving reports from Baltasar's 1744 visit are found in TBL, MM 1716, #8, 16, 65, 66, 68, 70, 71; Burrus and Zubillaga, *El noroeste*, documents LVI, LIX; and Burrus and Zubillaga, *Misiones mexicanas*, document 32. Four surviving reports submitted to Lizasoáin are in Bayle, *Misión*, pp. 225-38.

24. Clavijero reported that visitors general were to be appointed triennially [Clavijero, *History of California*, p. 368], but they did not reach California that regularly. In July of 1742, P. Bravo had P. Miguel del Barco copy his account book (which may have been badly worn or water damaged) because his eyes were no longer up to the task. Barco headed his copy, "Razón del Primero Libro que se formó en Californias en 1 de Octubre de 1705," and then entered Bravo's original title, "Libro de entrada de generos y gasto de ellos en pagamento de la gente del Presidio." The book had been inspected and signed by every visitador general from the first in 1726 until the book was closed in 1742. AGNM, Misiones, vol. 27, fol. 298.

25. P. Visitador General Guenduláin inspected the account book at Loreto on 11 February 1726. AGNM, Misiones, vol. 27, fol. 298. P. Venegas mentions Guenduláin's visits to Comondú, La Paz, and Guadalupe in January and February of 1726. Venegas, "Empressas Apostolicas," párrafos 828, 986, 1004. Guenduláin had been P. Salvatierra's pupil at Tepozotlán in 1697; by 1737 he represented the Jesuits' Mexican Province at the court in Madrid. Venegas, *El apóstol*, p. 294; Burrus, *Jesuit Relations*, p. 201 n. 31.

26. P. José de Echeverría arrived as father visitor general in California on 27 October 1729. Venegas, "Empressas Apostolicas," párrafo 1257. He signed P. Bravo's account book eleven months later, 26 September 1730. AGNM, Misiones, vol. 27, fol. 298.

27. P. Procurador Jaime Bravo issued P. Visitador General García a draft on California funds dated 5 October 1737. AGNM, Californias, vol. 60 bis, exp. 6. García signed Bravo's account book at Loreto on 12 October 1737. AGNM, Misiones, vol. 27, fol. 298. García performed a marriage at Misión de Santa Rosalía de Mulegé on 26 July 1737. P. Miguel del Barco, who came to California in 1737, reported García's visit, and may have accompanied him as he crossed the gulf. Barco, *Historia natural y crónica*, p. 289-90.

28. P. Visitador General Lucas Luis Alvarez signed P. Bravo's account book at Loreto on 26 March 1742. AGNM, Misiones, vol. 27, fol. 298. Jesuit accounts in Mexico City record that P. Procurador Bravo gave 300 pesos to P. Visitador General Alvarez on 29 August 1742. AGNM, Californias, vol. 60 bis, exp. 6. P. Visitador General Baltasar, in reporting his 1744 inspection of California mission records, repeatedly indicated the dates of Alvarez's visits, two years before. Baltasar,

"Visita de la provincia de Californias . . . ," Burrus and Zubillaga, *El noroeste*, pp. 461–70.

29. Burrus, *Jesuit Relations*, p. 203.

30. P. Visitador General Agustín Carta's report of his visit to California is not known to exist. However, his successor, P. Visitador General José de Utrera, followed the precedent set by P. Visitador General Baltasar in 1744 and listed both the name of his predecessor, and the date of his visit to each mission. Thanks to Utrera, Carta's 1752 timetable and itinerary can be largely reconstructed: 5 November, Loreto; 12 November, San Javier; 15 November, Comondú; 17 November, La Purísima; 22 November, Mulegé; 23 November, Guadalupe; 28 November, San Ignacio; 22 December, San Luis Gonzaga; 26 December, Los Dolores. P. Utrera noted that Carta had not visited Santa Gertrudis, Todos Santos, or Santiago. P. Visitador General José de Utrera, "Nuevo estado de las Missiones de esta Provincia de la Compañía de JHS . . . ," pp. 101–219, document 67, García Mss., W. B. Stephens Collection, Library of the University of Texas.

31. P. Visitador General José de Utrera landed at Loreto at 2 P.M., 10 January 1755. His subsequent timetable and itinerary can be largely reconstructed from the dates on which he inspected the account books at each mission: 17 January, San Javier; 20 January, Comondú; 21 January, La Purísima; 25 January, Guadalupe; 28 January, San Ignacio; 31 January, Santa Gertrudis; 6 February, return to Guadalupe; 11 February, return to Comondú; 17 February, San Luis Gonzaga; 18 February, Los Dolores; 23 February, Todos Santos; 28 February, Santiago; 15 March, Loreto. "Nuevo estado de las Missiones de esta Provincia de la Compañía de JHS . . . " [unsigned manuscript in Utrera's hand], pp. 101–219, document 67, García Mss., W. B. Stephens Collection, Library of the University of Texas. Utrera also participated in California mission ceremonies: "En 11 de Febrero bautizo solemnemente. el Padre Visitador General Joseph de Utrera . . . ." Entry #881, "Libro de Bautismos, Casamientos, y Entierros . . . de Sn. Joseph Comondu" (under heading of "Año de 1755"). Utrera baptized an infant at Santa Gertrudis on the same date as his inspection of the mission's record books.

32. P. Ignacio de Lizasoáin served for over a decade as a missionary in Sonora. As visitador general, he left a valuable, detailed itinerary of his California inspection tour that virtually mapped the course of the camino real in use in 1762. Lizasoáin, Ignacio, "Noticia de la visita general de P. Ignacio Lizasoain Visitador General de esta Prov. de Nueva España q. comenzo dia quarto de Abril de 1761 AD. y se concluye a finis de Henero de 1763 . . . ," pp. 1–47, document 47, García Mss., W.B. Stevens Collection, Library of the University of Texas. Part of the California section of this itinerary is reproduced in Crosby, *The King's Highway*, p. 5.

33. P. Miguel del Barco wrote both known references to P. Carlos Rojas's visit to California. He described neophytes at Misión de Santiago, at the beginning of 1766, making written complaints to "el padre visitador general Carlos Rojas." And Barco used the same title for the visitor while describing conversations they had had over a period of months in 1766. Barco, *Historia natural y crónica*, pp. 331, 460.

34. Venegas, "Empressas Apostolicas," párrafos 1736–38.

35. Most of the Pious Fund's capital was invested in haciendas that produced profits greater than simple interest — then about 5%. Venegas, *El apóstol*, p. 157; Venegas, "Empressas Apostolicas," párrafos 1776–84. The Pious Fund is described at length in Velázquez, *El fondo piadoso*, passim; Río, "El régimen jesuitico," pp. 157–72.

36. Barco, *Historia natural y crónica*, pp. 432–33.

37. Baegert, *Letters*, p. 148.

38. AGNM, Californias, vol. 60 bis, passim. *Regalías* for typical years ranged from as little as 500 pesos [1724] to as much as 1400 [1727]. Occasionally, the account book entries indicate the specific services for which officials were compensated — such as obtaining the actual payment of funds from royal coffers that had been earmarked for California [1730].

39. Baegert, *Observations*, pp. 147–48. Most of the responsibilities of the padre procurador de Californias noted by P. Baegert are set out in more official form in Venegas, "Empressas Apostolicas," párrafos 1774–84.

40. The annual catálogos of the assignments of Jesuit mission personnel, in treating with California, placed the assistants of the procurador in Mexico City at the bottom of the list. Burrus, *Misiones norteñas*, p. 99. The very brief catálogo for 1708 places Hermano Juan Steineffer at the end of the California list, but this noted botanist actually served, then and later, only in Sonora. Piccolo, *Informe de 1702*, pp. 304–12.

41. An early and authoritative report of P. Juan de Ugarte's well documented service as *procurador de Californias* is contained in P. Salvatierra's letter to Virrey Conde de Moctezuma, 28 November 1697.

Venegas, "Empressas Apostolicas," párrafos 314, 1774.

42. Ibid., párrafos 429, 1775.

43. Ibid., párrafos 1253, 1775.

44. Ibid., párrafo 1775; Burrus, *Jesuit Relations*, p. 159. Also, during many years of his service as *procurador de Californias*, Hermano Tompes signed the pages of his account book. AGNM. Californias, vol. 60 bis, exp. 6.

45. Barco, *Historia natural y crónica*, p. 432.

46. Bayle, *Misión*, pp. 136–37. The account books of the procurador de Californias show frequent entries over a period of more than thirty years—from the 1720s to the 1750s—involving a succession of Guadalajara Jesuits, each named many times. AGNM, Californias, vol. 60 bis, exp. 6. P. Joseph Carrillo not only appears frequently in these records during the 1730s and 1740s, but he was also called *padre procurador* by P. Jaime Bravo in a letter appealing to the president of the Audiencia of Guadalajara to expedite the purchase and shipping of emergency food supplies. AGI, Guadalajara, 104 (transcript in TBL, The Bolton Papers, item 315).

47. Examples of P. Salvatierra's accounting and record-keeping practices reflect his industry, but also his carelessness, poor penmanship, and no doubt preoccupation with other matters. A *memoria* in his hand—probably from 1699 or 1700—is complete but undated [AHH, leg. 321, exp. 2]. He made out and signed, but again did not date, a payroll for the skeleton crew of the ship *San José*, beached for repairs at Matanchel—which places the document in either 1699 or 1700 [AHH, leg. 283, exp. 70]. Salvatierra wrote out drafts, payable in Mexico City, to pay for products of mainland missions: 350 pesos to P. Melchor Bartiromo of Cucurpe, 15 October 1698 [AHH, leg. 282, exp. 5], or to provide severance pay to soldiers that he released or discharged: 113 pesos to Nicolás de Gálvez, 21 November 1698 [TBL, Papeles de Jesuitas]; 250 pesos to José de Machuca, 26 October 1699 [UCSD, Mandeville Department of Special Collections, Mss. 192sc]; 340 pesos to Francisco Javier de Lima, 23 October 1700, and 305 pesos to Juan Alejo de Robles, 18 October 1701 [AHH, leg. 325, exp. 1].

48. Jaime Bravo recruited by P. Salvatierra, designated as *hermano coadjutor*. Venegas, "Empressas Apostolicas," párrafos 756, 760.

49. Ibid., párrafo 1814.

50. Ibid., párrafos 1768–70.

51. Ibid., párrafos 1771–72. The padres included a tenth point that did not relate to the procurador. They used the occasion to set out the specific right recently granted to the visitador by the viceroy. The superior of the California missionaries could appoint a person to administer civil justice in a case where the captain of the presidio was unable to serve.

52. Baegert, *Observations*, p. 148.

53. Each *padre procurador* is identified many times by title and surname in the account books kept by the *procurador de Californias* in Mexico City. AGNM, Californias, vol. 60 bis, exp. 6. In 1762, P. Procurador Lucas Ventura wrote a long report about Loreto for P. Visitador General Ignacio Lizasoáin. No doubt using Loreto's record books, he gave a circumstantial chronology of his predecessors, beginning with P. Gaspar Trujillo's replacement of P. Jaime Bravo who died in 1744. Bayle, *Misión*, pp. 228–30.

No document suggests the criteria that led to the selection of the men who served as padre procurador at Loreto. Bravo had already had fifteen years of on-the-job training when he assumed the post. Trujillo succeeded only at Bravo's death and created no record of accomplishments. His successor, P. Juan de Armesto, was so highly considered for his business and organizational skills that he was promoted directly to be procurador de Californias in Mexico City. P. Juan Javier Bischoff was moved from place to place on the peninsula as much as any California Jesuit; his service as procurador at Loreto excited little comment other than compliments for the quality of ship repairs that he oversaw. P. Lucas Ventura appears to have been competent; he probably would have held the job for many additional years had it not been for the expulsion.

54. *Hermanos coadjutores* were recruited by the Jesuits for their skills and practical experience in just such areas as bookkeeping, inventories, storage, and the like. Konrad, *Jesuit Hacienda*, pp. 109, 131–33.

55. Juan Bautista Mugazábal came to California as a soldier in 1704, was promoted to *alférez* by about 1712. See Appendix C.

56. Barco, *Historia natural y crónica*, pp. 294–95. Juan Bautista Mugazábal's activities as skipper and purchasing agent are described in: Venegas, "Empressas Apostolicas," párrafos 913–14.

57. P. Jacobo Baegert, with his Alsatian burgher's eye for the details of commerce, has left the best descriptions of Jesuit California's system for supply. In two long passages of his book, and in a letter to

his brother, Baegert outlined the duties and the interactions between the *procuradores* at Loreto and Mexico City. Baegert, *Observations*, pp. 119–20, 147–49; Baegert, *Letters*, p. 149.

58. The procurador's responsibilities with respect to ships and shipping are spelled out in Venegas, "Empressas Apostolicas," párrafo 1772.

59. Ibid., párrafos 756, 760.

60. Barco, *Historia natural y crónica*, pp. 294–95.

61. Hermano Francisco López probably worked at Loreto as early as 1752 when P. Baegert reported that two *hermanos* dispensed supplies. Baegert, *Letters*, p. 149. He was shown to be at Loreto in the catálogo compiled by P. Visitador General José de Utrera in 1755. Burrus, *Misiones norteñas*, p. 99. López was identified as *hermano* and located in California in the catálogo of 1758 [Piccolo, *Informe de 1702*, p. 310], and named and described at his work in 1759. Barco, *Historia natural y crónica*, p. 334.

62. Hermano Joaquín López y Cía first appeared in the California account books in 1760 where a sum was entered that had been allowed for his transportation and traveling expenses. His full name is given in the supply list for California personnel for 1762. See the respective years in AGNM, Californias, vol. 60 bis, exp. 15. López y Cía was also located in California by a 1764 catálogo. Piccolo, *Informe de 1702*, pp. 310–11.

63. Hermano Juan Villavieja is on the California supply list for 1766 [AGNM, Californias, vol. 60 bis, exp. 15], in a catálogo for 1767 [Piccolo, *Informe de 1702*, pp. 310–11]. A brief biography is given in Ducrue, *Account of the Expulsion*, p. 25.

64. Velázquez, *El fondo piadoso*, pp. 50–51.

65. *Memorias* for 1707–1739 [in reverse chronological order] are found in AGNM, Cárceles y Presidios, vol. 5, exp. 2, fols. 39–131. Those for 1740–1767 [in chronological order, but with 1744 misplaced at the end] are located in AGNM, Californias, vol. 60 bis, exp. 15, fols. 244–371. Additional records for the shipment in 1766 are located in the same volume, but as exp. 25, fols. 437–40. Undated *memorias*, apparently from the period of 1698–1700, are found in AHH, leg. 283, exps. 72, 76, 83; leg. 321, exp. 2 [the last in Salvatierra's hand].

66. "Memoria que remite el P. Procurador Joseph de Echeverria al Presidio de Californias en 12 de Abril de 1725 años." AGNM, Cárceles y Presidios, vol. 5, exp. 2, fols. 82–86.

67. See chap. 7, p. 219.

68. For more on the use of tobacco, see chap. 8, pp. 259, 264.

69. These loincloths ("mantas") may have been very similar to those worn until recently — or perhaps currently — by men of the Cora and Huichol groups in the Mexican state of Nayarit, an area also opened and pacified by Jesuit missions.

70. An example of fireworks used at a fiesta appears in chap. 9, pp. 289–90.

71. ". . . goods were moved overland by mules a distance of two hundred and fifty hours from Mexico [City] to Matanchel. . . ." Baegert, *Observations*, p. 120.

72. A good summary of the Spanish conquest of this region and an excellent list of sources may be found in Gerhard, *The North Frontier of New Spain*; see also Sauer, *The Road to Cíbola*, pp. 6–20.

73. Many California missionary accounts give names of way stations on the route from Guadalajara to Sonora, and refer to the high costs of transportation. An interesting description and discussion of the economics of this pack trail was written by J. Rafael Rodríguez Gallardo, the viceroy's representative sent to assess Sinaloa and Sonora in the aftermath of the great Yaqui revolt of the early 1740s. Rodríguez Gallardo, *Informe sobre Sinaloa y Sonora*, pp. 8–9.

74. Barco, *Historia natural y crónica*, p. 401.

75. Number 8 in the list of duties of the procurador at Loreto cited on p. 140 of this chap.

76. P. Bravo to Bishop of Guadalajara, 19 November 1719. AGI, Guadalajara, 134.

77. Baegert, *Observations*, p. 120.

78. The experiences of the Jesuits' California mission provides a factual counterbalance to contemporary optimism over prospects for sea trade and communication along the coast of northwest New Spain. Rodríguez Gallardo's enthusiastic 1750 arguments for bringing supplies to the northwest provinces by the use of ships rather than mules reflected the entrepreneurial viewpoint that came out of the hearings held by the president of the Audiencia of Guadalajara, the Marqués del Castillo de Aysa, from 1743 to 1745. His projections for successes would never be realized in the Spanish period. Rodríguez Gallardo, *Informe sobre Sinaloa y Sonora*, pp. 9–20. A source for numbers of ships is Barco, *Historia natural y crónica*, pp. 400–401.

79. Problems with iron in shipbuilding on the Pacific slopes of Spanish America are discussed in Clayton, *Caulkers and Carpenters*, p. 83. Pertinent aspects of practices in ship design are discussed in Ibid., pp. 61–67. For other material and technical problems, see Ibid., pp. 53–60.

80. The small town, known as Puerto de la Posesión or Realejo during the 16th to 19th centuries,

today is called Corinto. Some of the first Manila galleons were built there — prior to 1585. Gerhard, *Pirates on the West Coast of New Spain*, p. 29. In the late 1730s, efforts to buy a Realejo-built ship for the service of California created a lengthy correspondence and inquiry — as well as a review of the methods by which California was supplied. AGNM, Californias, vol. 68, exp. 1.

81. Clayton, *Caulkers and Carpenters*, p. 79.

82. Relatively poor ships built in Chile were said to have had a life expectancy of some ten years. Clayton, *Caulkers and Carpenters*, p. 81. That figure seems to have been typical for ships operating north of Colima — and even the best probably did not often serve for more than twice that span.

83. For accounts of ship repair woes during the first twenty years of the California mission, see Venegas, "Empressas Apostolicas," párrafos 336–40, 411, 773, 874–77, 966, 1255–56. These and other experiences determined the Jesuits to do more of their own repairs and even to build ships in California. See chap. 4, pp. 95–100; chap. 11, p. 347.

84. Gerhard, *Pirates*, pp. 79–80, 95.

85. As recently as 1685, English buccaneers Swan and Townley had actively raided the coast of Sinaloa and, in 1686 and 1687, a group of French pirates had lingered around the California peninsula, using La Paz and the Tres Marías Islands as bases while trying to waylay a galleon. Many shipowners were still wary ten years later. Gerhard, *Pirates*, pp. 166–73, 188–90.

86. Naylor and Polzer, *Pedro de Rivera*, pp. 153–56.

87. AGI, Guadalajara, 104 (transcript in TBL, The Bolton Papers, item 315).

88. AGNM, Californias, vol. 80, exp. 3. Almost identical transfers of responsibility were being penned at Loreto over thirty years later. AGNM, Californias, vol. 80, exp. 54.

89. PP. Baegert and Clavijero made contradictory statements about cash payments to soldiers. Baegert stated that no currency circulated. Clavijero wrote that soldiers could elect money or goods "just as they wished." The weight of other evidence favors Baegert. He spent seventeen years in the California that Clavijero never visited. Moreover, he troubled to make a further explanation of payment in kind, noting that when a discharged soldier was paid off, "he was given linen or other goods for the amount of pay still due him." Such a procedure would have made no sense had cash been available. Baegert, *Observations*, p. 148; Clavijero, *History*, p. 376.

90. The account books of the Jesuit procuradores at Loreto are not known to exist. These would have showed the materials ordered by and delivered to the missions, and the mission produce turned in for credit. Fortunately, P. Visitador General Juan Antonio Baltazar wrote two documents during his 1744 visit in which he referred to various missions' balances and, in a few cases, gave specifics of the commerce between mission and warehouse. Baltasar, "Visita de la provincia de Californias," Burrus and Zubillaga, *El noroeste*, pp. 457–70; "Sobre la entriega . . . del presidio," Ibid., pp. 471–80. A concise description of the operation of the warehouse at Loreto is given in Baegert, *Observations*, p. 148.

91. Brading, *Miners and Merchants*, p. 100.

92. An example of such price fixing is found in the Reglamento of 1729 detailed in Naylor and Polzer, *Pedro de Rivera*, pp. 282–86.

93. The practice of doubling the purchase prices is stated most explicitly in P. Visitor General Baltasar's 1744 report on the Loreto treasury. Baltasar, "Procuraduría de la misión de Loreto," Burrus and Zubillaga, *El noroeste*, pp. 490–92. The system of setting prices is confirmed in Baegert, *Observations*, p. 148.

94. California Jesuits were aware that their benefactors and some government officials knew something about captains' profiteering at most presidios. Writing primarily for that audience, P. Venegas devoted a paragraph to a very explicit statement about the difference between practices in their administration and those that California soldiers could expect under an independent captain. Venegas, "Empressas Apostolicas," párrafo 1759.

95. Loreto payroll document, 1 August 1718. AGNM, Californias, vol. 80, exp. 3.

96. Prices to be charged, presidio by presidio, were fixed by the Reglamento of 1729. Naylor and Polzer, *Pedro de Rivera*, pp. 282–86.

97. After Brigadier Pedro de Rivera's report of his inspection of the northern presidios, California Jesuits knew more about the sharp practices of captains who controlled the prices that presidial soldiers had to pay for necessities. The Jesuits added this information to their arguments against having an independent military in California. P. Juan Bautista María Luyando to P. Bernardo Lozano, 22 April 1737. Burrus/Zubillaga, *Misiones Mexicanas*, pp. 19–25.

98. Fernando de Rivera, captain of the presidio of Loreto, gave testimony in 1766 in which he identified a document, dated 7 May 1741, by which the soldiers of the Presidio of Loreto petitioned the

California Jesuits to pay them in effects rather than money (at prices that the Jesuits could justify by some undisclosed means). AGNM, Provincias Internas, vol. 7, exp. 11. There is no reason to believe that this letter was elicited by the California Jesuits by coercion, but it may have been required by them to blunt charges then being made against them by the governor of Sinaloa. Later, the troops periodically gave the procurador the power to use their pay to buy whatever he chose, declaring themselves satisfied with the form in which they received their due. AGNM, Californias, vol. 80, exp. 54, fols. 444–46.

99. During his 1683–1685 California adventures, Almirante Atondo had to send ships repeatedly to pick up food from Jesuit missions on the Yaqui River. This relief was doubtless facilitated by the presence of P. Eusebio Kino and two other Jesuits in Atondo's party. Hu-De Hart, *Missionaries, Miners, and Indians*, p. 52; Venegas, "Empressas Apostolicas," párrafos 127–28, 131.

100. López Sarrelangue, "Las misiones jesuitas de Sonora," *Estudios de historia novohispana*, vol. 2 (1967), p. 188.

101. Venegas, "Empressas Apostolicas," párrafos 250, 324, 325, 336, 338, 341; Hu-De Hart, *Missionaries, Miners, and Indians*, p. 53.

102. Kino, *Historical Memoir of the Pimería Alta*, vol. 1, pp. 58; vol. 2, p. 250, 262–64. On 25 August 1700, P. Salvatierra wrote to thank P. Kino in advance for the promised cattle. Ibid., vol. 2, p. 261.

103. P. Kino to P. General González, 8 October 1701. Kino, *Kino Reports to Headquarters*, p. 97. Kino, in a more general report to the king, wrote, ". . . I have penetrated two hundred leagues of new land on more than forty expeditions . . . these new conquests . . . are very productive and fertile lands, with which it would be possible to help California (as is actually being done) . . . with abundant supplies, flour, sheep and horses. . . ." Kino to Philip V, 10 May 1704; Ibid., pp. 117, 119.

104. P. Salvatierra to P. Provincial Francisco de Arteaga, after 21 May 1701, AGNM, Historia, vol. 21; Decorme, *Jesuitas mexicanos*, pp. 405–6.

105. P. Provincial Francisco de Arteaga to P. Eusebio Kino, 27 September 1701. Kino, *Historical Memoir of the Pimería Alta*, vol. 1, p. 356. Kino continued to stress his plan to build missions that could raise cattle for California. Kino to P. General Tirso González, 2 February 1702. Kino, *Kino Reports to Headquarters*, p. 103.

106. Salvatierra, *Selected Letters*, pp. 205–8.

107. P. Salvatierra to P. Kino, 21 September

1702. Kino, *Historical Memoir of the Pimería Alta*, vol. 1, p. 367; Venegas, "Empressas Apostolicas," párrafos 472–74, 483, 704.

108. Venegas, "Empressas Apostolicas," párrafo 1736.

109. Venegas, "Empressas Apostolicas," párrafos 527–29. P. Gerónimo Minutili was installed at Tubutama in December 1703. Bolton, *Rim of Christendom*, p. 525. Bolton reported that health was a factor in Minutili's transfer to Sonora. Kino, *Historical Memoir of the Pimería Alta*, vol. 2, pp. 84–85.

110. Decorme, *Jesuitas mexicanos*, p. 456.

111. Venegas, "Empressas Apostolicas," párrafos 472–74, 483, 704.

112. Ibid., párrafos 534, 704, 712, 753.

113. Piccolo, *Informe de 1702*, pp. 230–66.

114. Bolton, *Rim of Christendom*, p. 550.

115. January, February 1706. Bolton, *Rim of Christendom*, pp. 547–48.

116. P. Piccolo to P. Eusebio Francisco Kino, Batuc, 19 January 1706. Piccolo, *Informe de 1702*, pp. 254–55.

117. P. Kino to Hermano Juan de Iturberoaga, 7 December 1709. Bolton, *Rim of Christendom*, p. 583.

118. Venegas, "Empressas Apostolicas," párrafo 786. P. Basaldúa greeted P. Salvatierra at Guaymas on 8 October 1709, accompanied by recent converts. Venegas, "Empressas Apostolicas," párrafo 833. Jesuit historian P. Constantino Bayle, working from unspecified documents, said that Basaldúa served in Sonora with the title of procurador for California. Bayle, *Misión*, pp. 136–37.

119. P. Basaldúa went to Belem in 1709 [see previous note] and later to adjacent Ráhum where Piccolo wrote to him in 1717. Piccolo, *Informe de 1702*, pp. 199–211. P. Pedro de Ugarte was sent to Tórim about 1711. Venegas, "Empressas Apostolicas," párrafo 774. P. Francisco Peralta took Ugarte's place at Misión de San Juan Bautista de Ligüí in May 1709, but by 1711 he was sent to the mainland to oversee the repairs on a ship. Venegas, "Empressas Apostolicas," párrafo 773. By 1719, Peralta was at Ráhum and shipping food to P. Juan de Ugarte during his shipbuilding labors at Mulegé. Venegas, "Empressas Apostolicas," párrafo 972. Peralta, at Ráhum, was repaid from California coffers with over 2,800 pesos worth of supplies in 1719. AGNM, Cárceles y Presidios, vol. 5, fols. 102–3. P. Ignacio María Nápoli was sent to an unspecified Sonoran mission in 1726. Venegas, "Empressas Apostolicas," párrafo 1095. P. Francisco Osorio came to California in 1725, sub-

stituted for various ill or absent missionaries, became ill himself, and was transferred to the Sonoran mission of Mochicagui in 1727. Venegas, "Empressas Apostolicas," párrafos 1096, 1100.

120. Venegas, "Empressas Apostolicas," párrafo 774.

121. ibid., párrafo 1815.

122. For Nápoli's earlier California activities, see chap. 4, pp. 104–7.

123. P. Nápoli to P. Andrés Ignacio González, 2 September 1735. AHH, leg. 17, exp. 48.

124. P. Ignacio María Nápoli became missionary of Pótam, Ráhum, and Huírivis in November of 1736. Hu-De Hart, *Missionaries, Miners, and Indians*, p. 65.

125. A cache of forty-seven letters to or by P. Ignacio María Nápoli were assembled as part of his defense against various charges of malfeasance after the great Yaqui Revolt of 1740. AGNM, Historia, vol. 392.

126. P. Jaime Bravo to P. Procurador Ignacio María Nápoli, 15 October 1739. AGNM, Historia, vol. 392, fols. 257–58.

127. P. Sebastián de Sistiaga to P. Procurador Ignacio María Nápoli [apparently in Ráhum], Loreto, 22 November 1737. AGNM, Historia, vol. 392, fol. 247.

128. P. Jaime Bravo to P. Ignacio María Nápoli, 25 November 1739. AGNM, Historia, vol. 392, fol. 258; Testimonial by Sargento Pedro de la Riva, Pótam, [month illegible] 18, 1740. TBL, Documentos históricos mexicanos . . . de indios mayos y yaquis, Legajo primero, documento 4741, The Cowan Collection, MM 1875. Interestingly, P. Bravo, the procurador at Loreto, dispatched Sargento Riva to head the small California contingent in Sonora; Riva achieved a reputation for harsh and decisive action whenever the objectives of his command were threatened. See chap. 10, p. 315.

129. Hu-De Hart, *Missionaries, Miners, and Indians*, p. 68.

130. P. Jaime Bravo to P. Procurador Ignacio María Nápoli, 24 November 1739. AGNM, Historia, vol. 392, fols. 255–56.

131. P. Ignacio María Nápoli was the Sonoran missionary most singled out for censure by Yaquis and civil and Jesuit investigators during post-rebellion inquiries. Hu-De Hart, *Missionaries, Miners, and Indians*, p. 74. In a letter written to his provincial — and later submitted as part of his defense during a Jesuit inquest — Nápoli pointed with pride to his support for California, cited the letters

of gratitude from California missionaries, and asked his superior to contemplate what he had undergone in order to serve his brothers in California. P. Nápoli to P. Provincial Mateo Ansaldo, 20 February 1741. AGNM, Historia, vol. 392, fols. 243–44.

132. Hu-De Hart, *Missionaries, Miners, and Indians*, pp. 68–84.

133. Ibid., p. 88; Decorme, *Jesuitas mexicanos*, p. 341.

134. Barco, *Historia natural y crónica*, p. 120.

Chapter 6: The Presidio of Loreto

1. An informed but succinct essay on presidios appears in Naylor & Polzer, *Presidio and Militia*, pp. 15–29.

2. Capitán Antonio García de Mendoza; see chap. 2, pp. 57–59.

3. P. Juan María de Salvatierra's efforts to give form and substance to his California presidio are illustrated by his 1704 employment of Hermano Jaime Bravo to keep its books and handle its day-to-day affairs, and by the title and contents of Bravo's ledger, begun in 1705, "Book showing entries of goods and the distribution of same to the people of the Presidio." [For more on this account book, see chap. 5, n. 24.] The determination to employ the presidio first and foremost for Jesuit ends is expressed in Venegas, "Empressas Apostolicas," párrafos 1723–24. Explorations ostensibly carried out to find a port for Manila ships actually served Jesuit ends; they served as proof of Jesuit efforts to accommodate a royal desire, and they allowed the missionaries to assess new country and people with an eye to extending their mission chain.

4. Virrey Duque de Alburquerque to Felipe V, Mexico City, 23 March 1706. AGI, Guadalajara, 134. Alburquerque's earlier stated intent to change the basis of the California presidio is noted in Venegas, "Empressas Apostolicas," párrafo 1742. The concurrence of the Consejo Real de Indias is seen in "Resolution of the Junta, 2 June 1703," AGI, Guadalajara, 134 (transcript in TBL, The Bolton Papers, Pockstaller document 93).

5. Venegas, "Empressas Apostolicas," párrafos 637–38.

6. Venegas, in his compendious "Empressas Apostolicas," devoted twelve chapters, composed of 126 párrafos, in Libro X, to setting out and making arguments for these sets of rules that covered all aspects of the California organization.

7. Viceroys repeatedly employed a stratagem epitomized by a line attributed to the Conde de Revillagigedo, viceroy of New Spain from 1789–1794: *"Obedezco, pero no cumplo."* (I obey, but do not execute.) Haring, *Spanish Empire*, pp. 113–14.

8. Lockhart and Schwartz, *Early Latin America*, pp. 292–93.

9. In a telling passage, P. Sigismundo Taraval, writing in 1735, displayed his racial prejudice by reporting that California was conquered by only five men. He thereby discounted completely the contributions of three mainland neophytes and a Peruvian mulatto who took part in the early battles and labors of P. Salvatierra's mission. Taraval, *Indian Uprising*, p. 34.

10. Mörner, *Race Mixture*, p. 60; Lockhart and Schwartz, *Early Latin America*, pp. 129–30.

11. Lockhart and Schwartz, *Early Latin America*, pp. 293–94.

12. Gerhard, *North Frontier*, p. 250.

13. Stein and Stein, *Colonial Heritage*, p. 64. In the larger cities of New Spain, guilds effectively excluded *castas* from many skilled trades — but their actions influenced *castas* to migrate to the frontiers where shortages of skilled workers caused employers to at least partially overlook racial prejudice. Gibson, *Spain in America*, p. 127.

14. Only one man, Juan José Ceseña from Hostotipaquillo, was hired by the Jesuits to serve as a soldier in California and identified in documents of that time, or those generated during his later life, by the terms mulatto, *coyote,* or *de color quebrado* — all of which indicate a perceived black admixture. (At least two other soldiers had wives identified as partially black: Luis de Iribe and Gerónimo González.) It is probable that some others — identified one way or another as castas — had a degree of African inheritance. Few California soldiers of Jesuit times can be positively identified as mestizos, but indirect evidence based on racial identifications of spouses and children, as well as the practices of *compadrazgo*, suggest that about 25 percent of California soldiers had native American blood and operated at the social level of castas. Reasons for hiring castas are explained in Venegas, "Empressas Apostolicas," párrafo 1786. At least one long-time California soldier was an Indian, but his case was exceptional. Sebastián Martín from Ventitán, Jalisco came to Loreto in the initial party as P. Salvatierra's page. By 1701, he was a musketeer and general man-at-arms serving Salvatierra during an exploration in Sonora. Salvatierra to P. Provincial Francisco de Arteaga, after 21 May 1701. Bayle, *Misión*, p. 165. In 1716,

Sebastián Martín was one of the soldiers accompanying P. Piccolo as he explored the area that became Misión de San Ignacio. Piccolo, *Informe de 1702*, pp. 182, 184–85, 193, 202. He last appears in California documents as a signer of a Loreto payroll document in 1718 (as Martínez, a common confusion; Piccolo used both forms of his name in a single letter). AGNM, Californias, vol. 80, exp. 3.

Statistics given by Moorhead for Sonoran and Sinaloan presidios in the period ten-to-twenty years after the Jesuit period show that less than half of their soldiers were considered white (españoles). Moorhead, *The Presidio*, pp. 182–83.

15. Venegas, "Empressas Apostolicas," párrafos 1785–86.

16. See chap. 7, pp. 186–89.

17. In Sinaloa in 1741, Juan Botiller and Manuel Villavicencio were enlisted as petty officers in their respective troops. Other men enlisted at that time who had also appeared on Loreto's payroll in 1733 were Don Tomás Moscoso, Francisco de Castro, Manuel de Urbina, and Nicolás López. Don Nicolás Valdez and Juan Delgado were 1741 enlistees who had earlier appeared as employees of the presidio of Loreto. These data were taken from various lists of recruits found in Documentos Mexicanos . . . Indios Mayos y Yaquis, MM 1875, TBL.

18. Salvatierra, *Selected Letters*, pp. 149, 156.

19. The literacy reported here is estimated in large part from demonstrated ability to sign documents, many of which required reading before the soldier signed them as a witness. Most of the examples of handwriting show obvious skill and practice; a few are labored indeed. At least one soldier from Villa de Sinaloa was specified as able to read but not write: Sebastián Constantino de Arce. AHBCS, Político, document 30.

20. Jesuits regularly equated Evil or the Devil with blackness of skin, a common enough belief since medieval times — and perhaps earlier. This prejudiced view of black Africans can be seen or inferred from numerous bits of evidence found in Jesuit accounts. For another example, in 1702 an investigation was held to determine the cause of a bloody uprising among the Cochimí at San Javier. The ringleaders were questioned, and the chronicler reports that the Devil had appeared to them in the guise of a black Ethiopian and counseled them in their anti-Christian plans. Venegas, "Empressas Apostolicas," párrafo 483.

21. Ibid., párrafo 1786.

22. The 1733 Loreto payroll shows men on half-

pay who are known from other sources to have been *españoles:* Don Joseph Mariano Romero and Manuel Villavicencio. AGNM, Californias, vol. 80, exp. 3.

23. The racial composition of the forces at the mainland's frontier presidios is given in Moorhead, *The Presidio,* pp. 182–83. The California Jesuits' preference — and bias — stands out sharply in their 1739 complaint against Pedro Alvarez de Acevedo, captain of the short-lived royal presidio at San José del Cabo. The Jesuits charged that the captain interfered with their decision to replace mixed-blood soldiers, like mulatto Jacinto Caravajal, with *"otros mas decentes"* (others more upright, of better quality). It was also alleged that the captain threatened to man the new presidio with several soldiers of mixed blood. P. Luyando to the Audiencia of Guadalajara, 1739. AGNM, Californias, vol. 64, fols. 172–217.

24. The church baptismal records from Compostela [FHL microfilm 0654341], a town intimately associated with the pioneer gente de razón of the California settlement, illustrate the process in which caste was influenced by association — two concise examples are offered:

In an entry for 30 January 1701, newborn Francisco Alonzo was listed as an *español,* the legitimate son of Agustín de Vera, *español,* and María de las Nieves, *mestiza.* The child's godmother was Doña Beatriz de Chincoya, *española,* a member of the local elite class.

On August 28, 1734, a newborn was baptized as María Jacinta, *española,* legitimate daughter of Cristóbal de Soto, *coyote,* and Antonia Rodríguez, *española.* The child's godparents were Don Nicolás de la Peña and his daughter Doña Petrona Jacinta, members of the local aristocracy.

25. Venegas, "Empressas Apostolicas," párrafo 1764.

26. Ibid., párrafo 1790.

27. Ibid., párrafo 1787.

28. The Reglamento of 1729 was proclaimed about the time that P. Venegas began to write "Empressas Apostolicas"; he would have known its provisions when he made his statements about pay. The Reglamento specified pay scales at Sinaloan and Sonoran presidios in which captains received from 500 to 600 pesos a year, sergeants 415 pesos, and soldiers 400 pesos. Naylor and Polzer, *Pedro de Rivera,* pp. 153, 156. In 1733 at Loreto, Capitán Esteban Rodríguez received 880 pesos, his sergeant — and son — Bernardo Rodríguez got 330 pesos, married soldiers received 325 pesos and unmarried 300 pesos. However, at Loreto, every man

from the captain down got rations of so many pounds of grain and other foodstuffs in addition; the captain got three rations, married soldiers two, and all others one. AGNM, Californias, vol. 80, exp. 3. It must be assumed that the value of a ration was around 100 pesos in order that it fill the gap between the pay ordered by the Reglamento and that credited to soldiers at Loreto. If so, married soldiers were unusually well paid in California.

29. Venegas, "Empressas Apostolicas," párrafo 1728.

30. This quotation and the list of rules that follows are found in Ibid., párrafos 1787–88.

31. This concession, made as a compromise during bargaining with Viceroy Alburquerque, 1704–1710, would later become the basis of a fortune that allowed one California soldier to challenge the Jesuits' control of the California economy. See chap. 10, pp. 321–23.

32. Elsewhere, P. Venegas confirmed that such a school offered its services. Venegas, "Empressas Apostolicas," párrafo 1919.

33. P. Venegas drew these passages largely from reports by Hermano Jaime Bravo written in the months following P. Salvatierra's death. The requirement that a soldier personally provide two horses may be found in Bravo's report of 1 August 1718. AGNM, Californias, vol. 80, exp. 3. Various later statements by both missionaries and soldiers indicate that this requirement was soon increased to four, five, or even six mounts and/or pack animals per soldier. The latter figures were typical of the requirements at mainland presidios. Moorhead, *The Presidio,* p. 180.

34. Dobyns, *Spanish Colonial Tucson,* pp. 66–67.

35. See p. 162, and n. 31 of this chapter.

36. Venegas, "Empressas Apostolicas," párrafo 738.

37. The uses and abuses of soldiers by captains of presidios in northwest New Spain are detailed in the Reglamento de 1729 that resulted from Brigadier Pedro de Rivera's report to Virrey Casafuerte of an inspection tour carried out in the late 1720s. Naylor and Polzer, *Pedro de Rivera,* pp. 104, 109–11, 341–43. Despite the 1729 regulations to the contrary, "many of the presidio captains [of northwest New Spain] . . . continued in the time-honored practice of acquiring ranches, farms, and even mines and . . . assigning a portion of their troops to guard livestock and to labor on these private estates. This . . . reduced the soldiers to a semblance of vassalage." Moorhead, *The Presidio,* p. 35. An inspection of the northern presidios in 1766

showed that conditions had deteriorated since 1729; the abuses still abounded. Ibid., pp. 56–58.

38. Jesuit purchasing and transportation charges are discussed in chap. 5, pp. 142, 149–50. The Reglamento of 1729 revealed that most captains of mainland presidios were engaged in profiteering on supplies and goods sold to soldiers. Naylor and Polzer, *Pedro de Rivera*, pp. 109–11, 114–21. The usual practices and malpractices of mainland presidial captains in relation to providing supplies and stores to their soldiers are discussed in Vidargas, *Navegación y comercio*, pp. 109–11; Moorhead, *The Presidio*, pp. 203–4. California Jesuits knew that their benefactors, as well as government officials, were aware of these abuses. Writing primarily for those audiences, P. Venegas devoted a paragraph to a very explicit statement about the difference between practices in the Jesuit administration and those that California soldiers could expect under an independent captain. Venegas, "Empressas Apostolicas," párrafos 1758–59. At about the time Venegas was writing, an ex-California missionary was using Rivera's revelation of such exploitations by mainland captains as an argument against Arzobispo-Virrey Vizarrón's possible appointment of Manuel Bernal de Huidobro as governor of California. P. Juan Bautista María Luyando to P. Bernardo Lozano, 22 April 1737. Burrus/Zubillaga, *Misiones Mexicanas*, pp. 19–25.

39. California was "conquered" by Jesuit persuasion and a very small military support unit. Reported fatalities among all gente de razón, padres, soldiers, sailors, or servants, caused by hostilities of native Californians throughout the seventy years of Jesuit mission and civil control, added up to about a dozen.

40. Venegas, "Empressas Apostolicas," párrafo 1794.

41. Ibid., párrafo 1729.

42. Ibid., párrafo 1724.

43. Ibid., párrafo 1772.

44. Taraval and Wilbur, *Indian Uprising*, pp. 201–2.

45. The controversy over the renunciation is movingly revealed in "Sobre la entriega de la administración del presidio de Californias." P. Visitador General Baltasar to P. Provincial Escobar y Llamas, 1744. Burrus and Zubillaga, *El noroeste*, pp. 471–80; and in P. Sistiaga to P. Provincial Escobar y Llamas, 19 September 1743. Ibid., pp. 437–56. Confirmation that the renunciation was effected is found in Barco, *Historia natural y crónica*, p. 269. A similar statement in Clavijero, *History of California*, p. 379, originated as a paraphrase of the cited Barco passage.

46. Documentation for each captaincy is indicated elsewhere in this work in connection with individual captain's careers. See Index.

47. California Jesuits were aware of the criticism and occasional exposure of presidial captains who did not fill their rolls but continued to collect royal pay for the full complement. They took care to have their ranks filled. The Jesuit device of hiring soldiers at half-pay made it simple for them, if a man was lost, to promote another, on the spot, to full pay. They also hired soldiers at their own expense and put them to work first as mayordomos; they then elevated them to the presidio and royal salaries when the need arose.

48. Isidro Grumeque de Figueroa's 1698 appointment to *alférez*: Venegas, "Empressas Apostolicas," párrafo 326; his 1704 retirement and departure from California: Venegas, "Empressas Apostolicas," párrafos 711–14.

49. Nicolás Márquez was listed as "Alférez" when he acted as godfather at San Javier [1709] and Loreto [1710].

50. Juan Bautista Mugazábal was listed as "Alférez" while acting as godfather at Mission San Javier in 1714 and 1715 [San Javier Baptisms], and again in 1718 by P. Venegas as he described the soldier's final actions before becoming a Jesuit. Venegas, "Empressas Apostolicas," párrafo 913.

51. Don José de Larrea appeared as "Alférez" on Loreto's 1718 payroll document included in AGNM, Californias, vol. 80, exp. 3. He may have served several years after 1718. In 1731, P. Julián de Mayorga revealed in a letter that Larrea had been the Inquisition's California representative, called *Notario y Alguacil Mayor del Santo Tribunal*, until his death, year unspecified. Mayorga to Santo Tribunal de la Fé, 12 February 1731. AGNM, Inquisición, vol. 832, exp. 33, fols. 282–83.

52. Alférez Francisco Cortés de Monroy served intermittently in California. He seems to have pursued mining interests in Sonora when he was not employed on the peninsula. His first recorded act in California was as a witness at a Loreto wedding in December of 1717. Bancroft, *North Mexican States*, p. 438 n. 4. He was second-in-command of the first troop that explored Magdalena Bay by land in 1719. Guillén, *Overland Expeditions*, p. 41. Cortés de Monroy appears in California's account books in both February and October of 1727 as the recipient of drafts issued by P. Visitador Guillén. AGNM, Californias, vol. 60 bis, exp. 6. He returned to California from Sonora or Sinaloa in October of 1734, bringing volunteers to fight the neophyte rebellion

of that year. AGNM, Californias, vol. 80, exp. 6. P. Taraval reported on his involvement in the pacification attempts through 1735. Taraval, *Indian Uprising*, pp. 14, 213–14.

53. Several entries in the California account books in Mexico City identify Juan Bernal de Huidobro by rank and name. AGNM, Californias, vol. 60 bis, exp. 6. He was a cousin of Manuel Bernal de Huidobro, then governor of Sinaloa. Pradeau, *Expulsión de los jesuitas*, p. 145.

54. On 25 September 1725, soon after his first appointment as *padre visitador* in California, P. Clemente Guillén wrote a report to Virrey Marqués de Casafuerte in which he mentioned a recent activity of "el alférez don Juan del Valle." Burrus and Zubillaga, *Misiones mexicanas*, p. 237. Several entries in the California account books in Mexico City, dated between 1726 and 1731, identify this officer by rank and name. AGNM, Californias, vol. 60 bis, exp. 6.

55. AGNM, Californias, vol. 60 bis, exp. 6.

56. Juan Carrillo's service as an officer is known from a single source. H. H. Bancroft had access to Loreto's now lost burial records. He noted the death of "Lieut. Juan Carrillo" on 4 May 1748. It is probable that Bancroft translated *"alférez"* as "lieutenant" because José Gerardo appeared as an alférez later in the same year in which Carrillo died. Carrillo had been a California soldier since 1715. Bancroft, *North Mexican States*, p. 462 n. 67.

57. An 31 October 1749 entry in the account book of the Procurador de Californias listed "El Alferez Joseph Gerardo." AGNM, Californias, vol. 60 bis, exp. 6. A 1770 review of Jesuit California accounts showed that in 1748 "El Alferez Joseph Gerardo" owed 1,013 pesos. AGNM, Misiones, vol. 22, fol. 244.

58. Barco, *Historia natural y crónica*, pp. 238–39.

59. Pedro de la Riva was made teniente in *el Sur* when Pedro Alvarez de Acevedo was removed from the post in 1741. Barco, *Historia natural y crónica*, p. 415. Riva's last appearance in the California account books came under a 16 May 1752, notation showing that he had cashed a draft — presented after 15 March — for 482 pesos, 3 reales. It probably was paid in Guadalajara, as it appears among a series of payments made in Mexico City and Guadalajara, and was bracketed with a draft paid to P. Taraval who had retired to a post at a Jesuit *colegio* in Guadalajara in 1750. AGNM, Californias, vol. 60 bis, exp. 6, fols. 55–56.

60. By 20 October 1753, Sargento Cristóbal Gutiérrez de Góngora had received an appointment to serve in Loreto as *teniente*. AHH, Temporalidades, leg. 298, exp. 4, fol. 59. In June of 1754, Gutiérrez de Góngora gave a deposition to his captain in which he was described as "Teniente de la Provincia de California." AGNM, Provincias Internas, vol. 213, exp. 3. At Loreto, on 16 April 1755, P. Procurador Bischoff made out in his name a draft for 300 pesos. This may have been severance or travel money. His name appears no further in California records.

61. In mid-September of 1766, Teniente Blas Fernández de Somera testified that he had served in California for eight years. AGNM, Provincias Internas, vol. 7, exp. 11.

62. Eugenio de Olachea was identified as "El teniente de San Antonio" in 1766, apparently as the superior officer of the Esquadra del Sur at the same time that Blas Fernández de Somera was serving as lieutenant under Rivera at Loreto. AGNM, Provincias Internas, vol. 7, exp. 10, fols. 90–91. By chance, a report of royal officials in Guadalajara to the Council of the Indies, dated 8 October 1765, mentions that "in the government of California, the captain employs two lieutenants. . . ." AGI, Guadalajara, 250.

63. Brinckerhoff and Faulk, *Lancers for the King*, p. 43.

64. Royal regulations issued in 1772 ordered that whenever possible men employed as sergeants were to be literate. Brinckerhoff and Faulk, *Lancers for the King*, p. 29. The post of *sargento* is listed on Loreto's 1733 payroll, and the sergeant may have been the author of the document — but he is not named. AGNM, Californias, vol. 80, exp. 3. In 1751, Sargento Cristóbal Gutiérrez de Góngora was acting as company clerk. AGNM, Californias, vol. 80, exps. 53, 54.

65. Juan Antonio Hinojosa was identified as *cabo de esquadra* on 19 June 1715, in an entry in San Javier's baptismal records. The royal *reglamento* of 1772 mentions no duty of a *cabo* that would allow the post to be distinguished from that of an able and ambitious soldier; "in this manner he will make himself worthy of the billet of sergeant and for higher promotions." Brinckerhoff and Faulk, *Lancers for the King*, p. 43.

66. Venegas, "Empressas Apostolicas," párrafo 1772.

67. The 1751 muster of the Presidio of Loreto is in AGNM, Californias, vol. 80, exp. 53.

68. Guillén, "Expedición por tierra," in León-Portilla, *Testimonios sudcalifornianos*, p. 89.

69. From the account book of the procurador de

Californias in Mexico City. AGNM, Californias, vol. 60 bis, 6.

70. On the 1733 payroll of the presidio of Loreto, soldiers, including those elsewhere designated as cabos, were categorized only as married or unmarried, and on full pay or half-pay. No other distinctions were noted. AGNM, Californias, vol. 80, exp. 3, fols. 19-24. The status conferred by the post of cabo is evident in many non-military documents, like the records of baptisms and marriages in which the name of Andrés de Cota usually appears, even after his death, preceded by the title "Cabo de Escuadra." To a lesser degree, this applies to Andrés López and Fernando de la Peña.

71. Loreto's 1733 payroll lists an unnamed sergeant and is written in Robles's hand and signed by him. This duty, his previous service, and his family connection all suggest that he was the incumbent sergeant. AGNM, Californias, vol. 80, exp. 3.

72. P. Sigismundo Taraval referred to Riva as *sargento* in charge of troops at Mission Dolores in the first weeks of 1735. His elevation to the post probably took place in 1734 since he was classed as a soldier on the 1733 payroll. Taraval, *Indian Uprising*, párrafo 135. P. Miguel del Barco made two references to Riva as a sergeant prior to his commission as *teniente* in 1741. Barco, *Historia natural y crónica*, pp. 242, 415.

73. Gutiérrez de Góngora appeared in the account books of the Procurador de Californias on 31 October 1749, as "Sargento Maior Gongora." AGNM, Californias, vol. 60 bis, exp. 6. In 1751, he wrote and signed several documents as sergeant at Loreto. AGNM, Californias, vol. 80, exps. 53, 54.

74. AGNM, Californias, vol. 80, exp. 53, fol. 442.

75. AGNM, Provincias Internas, vol. 213, exp. 3.

76. Fernando de Rivera was confirmed as captain at Loreto in mid-1751. He later wrote, "When His Majesty favored me with this command, I made [Hilario] Carrillo a sergeant. He served in this post for a time and then asked to be retired." AHBCS, Económico, document 1. Godmother at a 16 September 1757 baptism at Misión de la Purísima was Doña Josefa de Pazos, wife of "el Sr. Sargento Hilario Carrillo." Mission records transcribed in Martínez, *Guía Familiar*, p. 125.

77. Archivo General de Simancas, Secretaría de Guerra (Siglo XVIII), "Hojas de Servicio de América," leg. 7278, IX, 44. On 20 December 1759, P. Lucas Ventura referred to Ortega as "el Señor Sargento Don Joseph Francisco de Ortega." Ventura to P. Procurador Juan de Armesto. AGNM, Californias, vol. 68, exp. 5.

78. Juan Antonio Hinojosa served as a godfather at San Javier on 19 June 1715, and 3 May 1716. His name was accompanied by the title, *cabo de esquadra*.

79. Bancroft reported a "Captain Andrés López" who acted as a witness to Loreto weddings in 1723-1724. Loreto had a soldier by this name, but never a captain. One of Bancroft's scholars must have misread the abbreviation "Cᵒ" (for *cabo*) as "Cⁿ" (for *capitán*). Bancroft, North Mexican States, p. 448 n. 26.

80. José Antonio de Robles was identified as *cabo de esquadra* in a 1727 entry in the California account books. AGNM, Californias, vol. 60 bis, exp. 6.

81. AGNM, Californias, vol. 80, exp. 53, fol. 442.

82. AGNM, Californias, vol. 80, exp. 53, fol. 442v.

83. AGNM, Provincias Internas, vol. 213, exp. 3.

84. Archivo General de Simancas, Secretaría de Guerra (Siglo XVIII), "Hojas de Servicio de América," leg. 7278, IX, 44.

85. The exodus of soldiers in 1701 at about the time of Capitán García de Mendoza's resignation, left only twelve on duty. However, this number was raised to eighteen in a very few months.

86. Numbers of soldiers at Loreto, 1701-1717, are estimated by adding reported recruits and subtracting discharges from the 33 men who signed the Report and Petition of 1700 [see chap. 2, pp. 54-55]. In 1718, a payroll document indicates 20 men. AGNM, Californias, vol. 80, exp. 3.

87. See chap. 4, pp. 89-91.

88. The presidio reported twenty-nine soldiers in 1730. P. Jaime Bravo to P. Visitador General José de Echeverría, 19 May 1730. AGNM, Jesuitas, vol. 2, exp. 7. In 1733, the payroll showed 32 soldiers, 5 of them on half-pay. AGNM, Californias 80, exp. 3. In 1734-1735, following the rebellion, 20 men on full pay were added, as well as 15 others paid about half as much and on a monthly rather than annual basis. AGNM, Californias, vol. 80, exp. 6.

89. The increase to two presidios of thirty men each is recorded in AGNM, Misiones, vol. 22, fols. 240-301. By 1742, the southern presidio lost its independent status and was made a division of Loreto, called the *escuadra del Sur*. A complete payroll document from 1751 naming the men of the separate musters at Loreto and in *el Sur* is located in AGNM, Californias, vol. 80, exp. 53. In 1764, Loreto was temporarily short one man at 29, and there were 30 in the South. Archivo Histórico Nacional, Madrid, Sección Estado, leg. 3882.

90. Naylor and Polzer, *Pedro de Rivera*, pp. 163-64, 341-43; a summary of the conditions that

prompted the reforms of 1729 is offered in Moorhead, *The Presidio*, pp. 25–26.

91. See chap. 4, pp. 117–21.

92. Clavijero reported, "Juan Bautista Mugazábal, the alférez of the presidio, was a man of such habits and ability that, from the time he entered California, each one of the missionaries wanted him for a companion." Clavijero, *History of California*, p. 238. P. Jacobo Baegert made several references to the advantages of having a soldier with skills—in his case, construction skills. Baegert, *Letters*, p. 172; Baegert, *Observations*, p. 127. See also references to Sebastián Manríquez.

93. A royal regulation issued in 1772 attempted to end the use of varying uniforms by mandating the style of those to be issued. Brinckerhoff and Faulk, *Lancers for the King*, pp. 18–21. By all accounts, California *soldados de cuera*, before and after this regulation, rarely wore full uniforms except during duty at the presidio.

94. Baegert, *Observations*, p. 146.

95. In 1730, P. Visitador General José de Echeverría described soldiers at his reception at Loreto as clad in ". . . long coats, hats in the Spanish fashion, shoes without ornament. . . ." Echeverría to the Marqués de Villapuente, 28 October 1729. BNM, AF 4/55.1. Thirty years later, P. Ignacio Tirsch depicted a California soldier in uniform, showing boots and a flat hat as well as a long coat with the usual military decoration. Nunis, *The Drawings of Ignacio Tirsch*, Plate XLII, p. 113. Loreto's supply orders show that men's hats and boots were imported, but do no seem to include ready-made coats. As previously noted, every supply order abounded in cloths of all sorts, most destined to be made into clothing. AGNM, Californias, vol. 60 bis, exp. 15.

96. An extended history and description of the *cuera*, and discussion of its merits, pro and con, are found in Moorhead, *The Presidio*, pp. 185–91.

97. Crosby, *Last of the Californios*, pp. 18–23.

98. Baegert, *Observations*, p. 146. The reported numbers of mounts that soldiers were required to keep varied from three to five. This may have represented the reporters' confusion of riding and pack animals, some counting riding only, and others giving the total.

99. Gobernador Gaspar de Portolá's report to Virrey Marqués de Croix, 28 December 1767, gives a newcomer's (admiring) view of California soldiers' equipment, mounts, and ability to cope with the terrain. AGNM, Californias, vol. 76, exp. 10, fols. 16–20.

100. P. José de Echeverría to the Marqués de Villapuente, 28 October 1729. BNM, AF 4/55.1. See text in chap. 9, pp. 291–92.

101. See chap. 4, pp. 120–21.

102. Baegert, *Observations*, p. 146.

103. Portolá to Croix, 28 December 1767, AGNM, Californias, vol. 76, exp. 10, fol. 17. See also chap. 12, pp. 381–82. Spanish troops deployed in northern New Spain generally performed poorly. Moorhead, *The Presidio*, p. 179.

104. In 1770, at the end of a seven-month land expedition in search of the port of Monterey, Spanish officer Miguel Costansó reported, "The soldiers of the presidio of Loreto in California . . . are men of much endurance and long-suffering under fatigue. They are obedient, resolute, agile, and we do not hesitate to say that they are the best horsemen in the world, and among those soldiers who most deserve the bread of the Majestic Monarch whom they serve." Costansó, *Diario histórico*, pp. 30–31.

105. Muster lists for the various branches of the presidio of Loreto are plainly labelled and clearly laid out in both the 1733 payroll document [AGNM, Californias, vol. 80, exp. 3, fols. 19–24] and the 1751 muster [AGNM, Californias, vol. 80, exp. 53, fols. 441–43].

106. Venegas, "Empressas Apostolicas," párrafos 1815–16.

107. In 1709, P. Pedro de Ugarte took command of the supply ship as far as Acapulco where it was to be overhauled. Ibid., párrafo 773. In 1711, P. Francisco de Peralta took the ship to Matanchel, where he proved no match for the wily and—as P. Venegas painted them—unscrupulous shipwrights. Through his inexperience and poor judgment, one ship was lost and another contracted to be built under very unfavorable terms. Ibid., párrafos 874–77. At the time, P. Salvatierra lamented that the only man in California competent to supervise repairs was Capitán Esteban Rodríguez—who could not be spared from other duties. Salvatierra to P. Procurador Romano, 11 October 1711. Salvatierra, *Selected Letters*, p. 228.

108. When Capitán Esteban Rodríguez of the presidio of Loreto in 1707 took the king's ship to collect the annual supplies—and to get married—he became the first of Loreto's "soldier-mariners." Venegas, "Empressas Apostolicas," párrafo 820.

109. In 1717, Alférez Juan Bautista Mugazábal took the ship to Chacala to repatriate shipwrecked Compostela pearlers, and went on to load supplies. Ibid., párrafo 913.

110. In 1726, the alférez of the presidio of

Loreto, Juan del Valle from Compostela, took the California ship to Acapulco for supplies. In 1730 he was back in Acapulco on the same mission; he was called *"Cabo del Barco de Californias"* (commander of the California ship). In 1732, Valle returned to Acapulco to effect repairs as well as to fetch supplies. AGNM, Californias, vol. 60 bis, exp. 6.

111. In 1734, Soldado Juan Antonio Romero, Compostelan and son and namesake of the man who sailed Salvatierra to California in 1697, took Loreto's ship to Acapulco where he was entrusted with 2,000 pesos sent down from Mexico City by the procurador de Californias. AGNM, Californias, vol. 60 bis, exp. 6.

112. Contramaestre Juan Agustín Sánchez had a long career at Loreto. He was on the 1733 payroll as an *arráez* [AGNM, Californias, vol. 80, exp. 3]; in Acapulco in command of the king's ship in 1738 [AGNM, Californias, vol. 60 bis, exp. 6]; and listed in a 1751 Loreto payroll document as *contramaestre* [AGNM, Californias, vol. 80, exp. 53, fol. 445].

113. Cristóbal Gutiérrez de Góngora was captain of Loreto's ship, the *San José*, when she was sent to Matanchel during a severe grain shortage in California in June of 1740. AGI, Guadalajara, 104 (transcript in TBL, The Bolton Papers, item 315). Gutiérrez de Góngora appears many times in the accounts of the *procurador de Californias* between 1746 and 1750 in connection with activities in obtaining supplies in Acapulco and food in Matanchel, Compostela, and Guadalajara. AGNM, Californias, vol. 60 bis, exp. 6.

114. "Capitán del Barco que vino a Acapulco Nicolás Peraza," entry on 14 April 1751 in the California account books. AGNM, Californias, vol. 60 bis, exp. 6.

115. Francisco Aguiar described his service as captain of both the *San José* and *La Concepción*, and of taking them to the other side of the gulf when supplies were needed. His testimony was taken down over twenty years after the facts, and he was not asked the dates of his experiences. TBL, California Archives, vol. 5, p. 24.

116. Ignacio Pérez de Arce was an experienced captain and entrepreneur working the Gulf of California. In 1742, he responded to a long list of questions put to him by a tribunal convened in Guadalajara by the Marqués del Castillo de Aysa to study economic development of the west coast. Pérez de Arce identified himself as captain of the ship *San Francisco* engaged in transporting California's supplies and food. He displayed an intimate knowledge of the gulf region derived not only from

shipping goods but also from extensive experience as a pearler. AGNM, Provincias Internas, vol. 87, exp. 8, fols. 181–83. Pérez de Arce appears many times in the records of the procurador de Californias between 1741 and 1746, cashing drafts on Loreto that substantiate his claims of service to that presidio. AGNM, Californias, vol. 60 bis, exp. 6.

117. In 1754, California's large ship was in Acapulco to be careened and overhauled prior to bringing the annual shipment. Its captain, in the course of his duties as overseer, signed a document, "I, Basilio de Rivera y Valle, commander of His Majesty's ship, the San José, that serves the conquest and the missions of California . . ." AHH, Temporalidades, leg. 298, exp. 4. Rivera was a native and resident of Compostela. He appears nowhere on Loreto's musters or pay records. He does appear in the records of the procurador in Mexico City as one who cashed drafts issued in Loreto between 1753 and 1756. AGNM, Californias, vol. 60 bis, exp. 6. Basilio de Rivera's final documentary appearance at Loreto was on 10 November 1756, when he witnessed a deposition by men of Loreto's marinería as to the condition at delivery of a ship supplied by the crown. AGNM, Californias, vol. 68, exp. 3.

118. Puerto Escondido offered excellent protection against all winds and served as a safe harbor when sailors had enough warning of a storm and the elements would allow boats to be moved seventeen miles to the south. But that distance was too great to tempt the Jesuits to use it as their primary California port.

119. Loreto's 1733 payroll listed two *arráeces*, but in both earlier and later years the same men, probably doing the same jobs, were called *contramaestres*. The former title was more appropriate when they had command of small craft, the latter when they acted as seconds-in-command to a captain. AGNM, Californias, vol. 80, exp. 3.

120. Venegas, "Empressas Apostolicas," párrafos 413–14, 829–31, 874–77, 879–86.

121. The number of sailors was still eighteen in 1759. Rosters for sailors of Loreto's marinería in 1733, 1751, and 1759 are found in AGNM, Californias, vol. 80, exps. 3, 53; and in AGNM, Californias, vol. 76, exp. 1. The reduction in numbers of full-time sailors working for the presidio, observed by comparing these rosters, is borne out by P. Jacobo Baegert's retrospective report (necessarily based on the years of his California experiences, 1751–1767) that the presidio employed "only about twenty" sailors. Baegert, *Observations*, p. 147.

122. The stories of the brutal murders of two *arráeces* by their neophyte crews provide the best details of the missions' arrangements to deliver their supplies by *canoa*. Barco, *Historia natural y crónica*, pp. 315–19.

123. Ibid., p. 58.

124. P. Jaime Bravo to the Audiencia of Guadalajara, 1718. AGNM, Californias, vol. 63, exp. 31.

125. Mathes, "Baja California Indians in the Spanish Maritime Service," pp. 113–26.

126. Barco, *Historia natural y crónica*, p. 386.

127. P. Francisco María Piccolo wrote to ex-California missionary P. Juan Manuel de Basaldúa, then serving at the Sonoran mission of Ráhum, asking to be sent starts of rosebushes, quinces, lemons, and oranges by way of "the contramaestre" who could be instructed to water them during the voyage. Piccolo to Basaldúa, Mulegé, 10 January 1717. Piccolo, *Informe de 1702*, p. 210.

128. See Sebastián Romero in n. 130 below.

129. Antonio Justo, native of Genoa, served as contramaestre in the flotilla of Admiral Atondo during his 1683–1685 California expedition. He held the same position on the *Santa Elvira* when it brought P. Salvatierra to Loreto in 1697. Venegas, "Empressas Apostolicas," párrafos 230, 233. He headed the group that went with the *San José* to Matanchel for repairs shortly after Salvatierra bought her from José Manuel Ganduzo in June 1698. Justo was still with her in late 1700. AHH, leg. 281, exp. 29; leg. 283, exp. 70.

130. Contramaestre Sebastián Romero had command of Loreto's launch when it made a supply run to Sinaloa in mid-October of 1698. Two California neophytes were taken along to see life in the established mainland missions. P. Salvatierra to P. Juan de Ugarte, 1 April 1699. Bayle, *Misión*, p. 93. In the fall of 1700, Romero suffered two disasters. In September he nearly lost the *San José* in a severe storm; her cargo was a total loss, due, it was said, to Romero's inept actions. In December at Ahome, he allowed the *San Fermín* to go onto a bar where she broke up. He and his assistant, Pedro Juan the Venetian, were blamed for this disaster. Venegas, "Empressas Apostolicas," párrafos 412–14.

131. Contramaestre Juan de Santo, while in Acapulco, was paid 150 pesos by order of the padre procurador in Loreto. AGNM, Californias, vol. 60 bis, exp. 6. He appeared on the 1733 Loreto payroll as "arráez" (no contramaestre was listed). AGNM, Californias, vol. 80, exp. 3.

132. Englishman Guillermo Strafford served P. Juan de Ugarte in 1721 as a shipwright and a pilot.

Ugarte to Echeverría, 12 January 1722, BNM, AF 3/53.1. On 13 June 1741, Capitán Ignacio Pérez de Arce of the barco *San Francisco* directed the procurador de Californias to pay 116 pesos to "the English contramaestre." AGNM, Californias, vol. 60 bis, exp. 6.

133. "Arráez Juan Agustín" on Loreto's 1733 payroll. AGNM, Californias, vol. 80, exp. 3. In March of 1738, Sánchez had command of the supply ship on its run to Acapulco. AGNM, Californias, vol. 60 bis, exp. 6. In 1740, he piloted the launch that crossed the gulf to get supplies at the mission of Ráhum. AGNM, Californias, vol. 60 bis, exp. 7. In a 1751 Loreto payroll document, Contramaestre Juan Agustín Sánchez headed the list of the crew of "el barco de Su Magestad." AGNM, Californias, vol. 80, exp. 53. In 1758, 150 pesos were paid out "for masses said for the wife of Juan Agustín and two deceased sailors." AGNM, Californias, vol. 60 bis, exp. 6. Sánchez wrote a good hand, judging by his signature on an affidavit for costs, materials, and work performed which he signed at Loreto in 1749. AHH, Temporalidades, leg. 298, exp. 4.

134. Pasqual Martín was *contramaestre* on Loreto's supply ship commanded by Cristóbal Gutiérrez de Góngora. AGI, Guadalajara, 104 (transcript in TBL, The Bolton Papers, item 315).

135. On 23 February 1752, "Juan de Santiago, contramaestre del Barco de este Real Presidio que vino al ya citado Puerto" [Acapulco] was given 5,000 pesos ordered by a draft issued by P. Procurador Armesto in Loreto. He is mentioned by name and title in several other bookkeeping entries dated during 1751 and 1752. AGNM, Californias, vol. 60 bis, exp. 6. Juan de Santiago was regarded as an experienced seaman by 1740 when he was sent by the Alcalde Mayor of Tepic to investigate reports of a privateer threatening shipping in the waters off Matanchel. AGI, Guadalajara, 104 (transcript in TBL, The Bolton Papers, item 315).

136. 1733 Loreto payroll [AGNM, Californias, vol. 80, exp. 3]; 1751 muster [AGNM, Californias, vol. 80, exp. 53]. Pedro Regalado de Soto's petition for a pension shows that he served until June 1774, a total of more than forty years, most of it as arráez or contramaestre. AGNM, Californias, vol. 2, parte 2, exp. 7, fols. 77–83.

137. On 5 November 1756, Manuel de los Reyes gave a deposition at Loreto in which he was identified as the presidio's contramaestre, about thirty years of age, and illiterate. AGNM, Californias, vol. 68, exp. 3. His subsequent career is known only

from retrospective testimony of Francisco Miguel de Aguiar under whom he served. That service would have been between Aguiar's enlistment at Loreto in 1750 and 1767, the last year of shipping activity in the Jesuit period. TBL, California Archives, vol. 5, p. 24.

138. José Joaquín de Robles [usually given as Joaquín de Robles] was born about 1730 and first appeared on the Loreto payroll in 1751 as a sailor. In 1756, he was listed as a caulker, and, in 1768, described as contramaestre and arráez. He was illiterate and a man of mixed blood, married to an Indian woman. AGNM, Californias, vol. 80, exp. 53; AGNM, Californias, vol. 68, exp. 3; Harvard University, Houghton Library, MS Span 4F, "Fragments of MSS. from the Mission of Loreto, Lower California, 1768–1770."

139. For more on tinglados, see chap. 9, p. 275.

140. A well-preserved bench vise of colonial style and perhaps antiquity, entirely made of mesquite and suitable for holding wooden members up to the size of rib sections used in smallcraft construction, was on display in 1990 at the INAH museum in Loreto.

141. Most of the tools and devices named in this description are mentioned by name in documents of the Jesuit period, chiefly the supply lists found in AGNM, Californias, vol. 60 bis, and in AGNM, Cárceles y Presidios, vol. 5, exp. 2.

142. See Juan Botiller, n. 149 of this chap.

143. Bayle, Misión, p. 230. Planks for these and lesser repairs were obtained regularly from Matanchel, carried by the same craft that brought the annual supply orders. Baegert, Observations, p. 147.

144. For the story of shipbuilding at Loreto, see chap. 11, p. 347.

145. Salvador Márquez (I) first appeared in California records with the baptism of his daughter María Manuela on 9 July 1708 [Loreto Baptisms]. He probably served as master caulker until c. 1740, although the last sure date is 1733, based on a payroll of that year. He was succeeded by his son, Salvador Márquez (II) who would have been about twenty-three years of age in 1733.

146. Salvador Márquez (II) had a daughter, María del Rosario, born at Loreto about 1760 — as estimated from her 1778 marriage at San Diego [San Diego Marriages]. At present, that is the latest date at which he can be placed in Loreto. Márquez signed personally and in a good hand on an affidavit of work performed at Loreto in 1749. AHH, Temporalidades, leg. 298, exp. 4.

147. Pedro Navarrete may have been brought in

to assist in the major repairs that had to be done at Loreto about 1755–1756. He gave a deposition at Loreto in November of 1756 in which he was described as a calafate, 33 years of age, and literate. AGNM, Californias, vol. 68, exp. 3.

148. Joaquín de Robles generally appeared in Loreto's records as a contramaestre or arráez. In 1756, he gave a deposition at Loreto while acting in the capacity of calafate. He was then 26 years of age and illiterate. AGNM, Californias, vol. 68, exp. 3. Robles's ability to serve in several capacities was shared with many of the presidial employees.

149. Juan Botiller was the maestro herrero listed on the 1733 payroll at Loreto. AGNM, Californias, vol. 80, exp. 3. He was the only español to work as an oficial at Jesuit Loreto. In 1741, he appeared as "Don Juan Botiller," a volunteer in a Sonoran militia company formed to resist the major Yaqui insurrection of that time. TBL, MM, #1875, "Indios Mayos y Yaquis..." He probably left Loreto around 1738–1739 when Governor Bernal de Huidobro returned to la otra banda. Several men of the presidio of Loreto traveled back and forth between service in California and work in the mines of Sonora. Botiller's son, Juan Botiller (II), who later served and died in California, was born in 1745 in the Sonoran real de minas of Baroyeca.

150. Cristóbal Ascencio was first assistant blacksmith on the Loreto payroll of 1733 [AGNM, Californias, vol. 80, exp. 3], and master blacksmith on the Loreto muster of December 1751 [AGNM, Californias, vol. 80, exp. 53].

151. Juan Murillo, son of master carpenter Manuel Murillo, was born in 1731 at Loreto. By 1768, he was Loreto's herrero y armero (smith and armorer). AHBCS, Político, doc. 7.

152. Manuel Murillo, born c. 1705, was the chief carpenter at Loreto on both the 1733 payroll [AGNM, Californias, vol. 80, exp. 3] and the 1751 muster [AGNM, Californias, vol. 80, exp. 53]. He signed himself gracefully on an affidavit of work performed at Loreto in 1749. AHH, Temporalidades, leg. 298, exp. 4. In November 1756 he signed a deposition as Loreto's chief carpenter, fifty years of age. In the same expediente, each illiterate man who gave a deposition had his testimony read back to him, gave his assent, and that was attested to by a witness who signed in his place. Murillo simply signed, which probably indicates that he was fully literate. AGNM, Californias, vol. 68, exp. 3. In the last days of 1759, he was still Loreto's chief carpenter. Rivera to Virrey Amarillas, 7 December 1759. AGNM, Californias, vol. 68, exp. 5.

153. Francisco María Murillo, born in 1728 at Loreto, son of Manuel Murillo, succeeded his father before 1766 at which time he was listed as Loreto's carpenter. Comondú Baptisms, #2148. He gave his age and birthplace during an inquiry into events of Jesuit times held at Loreto in 1797. AHBCS, Jurídico, document 47. By 1768, Murillo was assisted in his service as shipwright by his brother, Jaime Murillo, born 1740. AHBCS, Político, document 7.

154. See, for example, Moorhead, *The Presidio*.

Chapter 7: The Making of the Missions

1. The term "mission," or *"misión,"* appears in this text in both senses that were used by California Jesuits. The first and more common usage indicates a local center for evangelization of pagan or recently pagan people. In a broader usage, the entire Jesuit California venture was called a mission. In mainland Jesuit missionary usage, entities that are here called "missions" were often described by terms such as *reducción, conversión,* and *doctrina,* depending on the degree of religious advancement of their neophytes. These distinctions were never made in California, and are judged to lie beyond the scope of this work. The terms are defined and discussed in Polzer, *Rules and Precepts,* pp. 3–9.

2. In addition to exercising the powers granted to them to regulate all aspects of their California venture, Jesuits also pursued an active campaign, as expert witnesses, to discourage secular authorities from attempting to introduce colonists or entrepreneurs — other than the pearlers, some of whom were frequenting the California gulf shores before 1697. P. Salvatierra, and his successors, refused to allow casually arrived men to remain in California longer than was needed to arrange their removal. Venegas, *El apóstol,* p. 131.

3. McAlister, *Spain and Portugal in the New World,* pp. 108–9; Spicer, *Cycles of Conquest,* 281–82. In the first years of the conquest of Mexico, some compromises were made; acculturation was inhibited because influential Europeans wanted to hear about and even to see examples of the exotic cultures of the New World. Early mendicant missionaries, particularly Franciscans, in the spirit of Renaissance humanism, were interested in native ceremonial practices and in adapting them for Catholic use. Extirpation of undesirable indigenous cultural practices also went slowly because the population of heathen was immense and that of the religious was

small. Nevertheless, the philosophical decision was made, and mission practices were bent toward replacing most aspects of native culture with Christian, European elements. Ricard, *Spiritual Conquest,* pp. 34–36. Father Charles W. Polzer, S.J., saw Jesuit evangelical efforts as primarily "concerned . . . with the introduction of institutional structures that would impose acceptable cultural patterns" — in short a substitution of European culture for the indigenous. Polzer, *Rules and Precepts,* p. 39.

4. Spicer, *Cycles of Conquest,* pp. 281–83; Weber, *Spanish Frontier,* pp. 105–6.

5. Ibid., pp. 288–89. An early example of planned acculturation in California was Salvatierra's practice of sending young California men to Sonora and Sinaloa to visit missions and pueblos of gente de razón, then having them return to describe their experiences to their peers. P. Juan María de Salvatierra to P. Juan de Ugarte, 9 July 1699. BNM, AF 3/40.5; translation in Salvatierra, *Selected Letters,* pp. 155–57. Jesuit determination to restructure California's primitive societies is discussed at length in Río, *Conquista y aculturación,* pp. 101–12. A broad, informative view of Jesuit thinking and practices in missionary work in northwest New Spain is provided by Polzer, *Rules and Precepts,* Part I, "Jesuit Mission Methodology," pp. 39–58. No one imagines that all rules were followed to the letter, but the Jesuits were more meticulous than most groups that had such guidelines. *Rules and Precepts* provides a clear picture of Jesuit goals and many of the means employed in working toward them. In *The Spanish Frontier in North America,* Chapter 4, "Conquistadores of the Spirit," David J. Weber gives a useful overview of the practices of Franciscans missionaries — and missionaries in general — during the 16th through 18th centuries. A reader of *Antigua California* may wish to refer to Weber's work to find similarities and discrepancies with and between Jesuit practices in California and those of Jesuits and other orders in other places and times.

6. This discussion of peninsular cultures refers to elements that were shared to some degree between the three major groups: Cochimí, Guaycura, and Pericú. Many examples of their individual characteristics are presented elsewhere in this text. Beyond that, the reader is referred to a list of the principal sources in chap. 2, p. 28, n. 4.

7. Venegas, "Empressas Apostolicas," párrafos 1585–90, 1595–1608.

8. Ibid., párrafos 1647–50. P. Venegas's manuscript has dozens of references to *hechiceros* (shamans) consorting with the Devil, and he refers to

them as lost souls — see, for example, párrafos 942, 1647–48. However, P. Everardo Helen, an experienced California missionary, considered shamans as charlatans and opportunists. He openly doubted that they had any pact with the Devil. Venegas, "Empressas Apostolicas," párrafo 1650; Claviero, *History of California*, p. 242. In 1704, P. Juan de Ugarte converted a shaman who repented his former ways and informed Ugarte about all his shamanistic training, devices, and practices. Ugarte presumably shared this intelligence with his fellows to give them all ammunition with which to fight the common enemy. Venegas, "Empressas Apostolicas," párrafos 750–52.

9. Baegert, *Observations*, pp. 78, 89–90; Baegert, *Letters*, pp. 145, 202–3; Linck, *Reports and Letters*, pp. 46–50.

10. See, for example, Linck, *1766 Expedition*, pp. 61–64.

11. At the end of six paragraphs of misguided sophistry under the heading of "The way in which the heathen Californians governed themselves," P. Venegas presented his only facts: each ranchería had a principal chief to which all others were subject. He was not elected, nor did he inherit the office; he was elevated "by tacit consent" to govern the rest. He was honored and obeyed for his prudence, experience, and maturity. Venegas, "Empressas Apostolicas," párrafos 1660–65.

12. The most comprehensive descriptions of interband conflict are Barco, *Historia natural y crónica*, pp. 192–93, and Venegas, "Empressas Apostolicas," párrafos 1707–09. Once again, as with the institution of marriage, the Jesuits saw the Cochimí as the most civilized in their behavior of the California groups.

13. A compendium of several early accounts makes up Venegas, "Empressas Apostolicas," párrafos 1689–93.

14. See, for example, P. Helen's opinion in Ibid., párrafo 1691.

15. Adultery: Baegert, *Observations*, pp. 73–74; Baegert, *Letters*, pp. 155, 165. Abortion: Barco, *Historia natural y crónica*, pp. 191–92; Baegert, Ibid., p. 141. Infanticide: Venegas, "Empressas Apostolicas," párrafo 1695.

16. Baegert, *Observations*, p. 89.

17. Ibid., p. 79; Venegas, "Empressas Apostolicas," párrafo 1703.

18. See the various references in this work to pitahaya festivals. Some interband encounters involved athletic contests between individuals in which, as a prize, the victor passed a night with the woman of the vanquished. Venegas, "Empressas Apostolicas," párrafo 1690.

19. Baegert, *Observations*, pp. 82–83.

20. A pitahaya festival in the late summer and fall was the most important indigenous celebration witnessed by the Jesuits. P. Salvatierra to P. Provincial Arteaga, after 21 May 1701. Bayle, *Misión*, pp. 150–51; Barco, *Historia natural y crónica*, p. 192.

21. Venegas, "Empressas Apostolicas," párrafos 1777–78. Interest rates in the first decades of the 18th century were fixed at 5 percent or, at least, that figure was accepted as the norm. Ibid., párrafo 1823.

22. Ibid., párrafo 763.

23. Van Young, *Hacienda and Market*, passim.

24. For an outline of the operation of the Pious Fund, see chap. 5, p. 137.

25. Cohen, "The Fire of Tongues," pp. 218–19.

26. Bangert, *A History of the Society of Jesus*.

27. P. Benito Guisi (born Benedicto Ghisi in Venice) drowned. Venegas, "Empressas Apostolicas," párrafos 874–81.

28. P. Pedro de Ugarte, ill, left California. Venegas, *Noticia*, abridge and rewritten by Burriel, pp. 186–87.

29. P. Gerónimo Minutili transferred to Sonora. Venegas, "Empressas Apostolicas," párrafos 527–29. With this transfer, PP. Salvatierra and Kino acted to turn Minutili's zeal to the advantage of the California missions; see chap. 5, pp. 151–52.

30. Ricard, *Spiritual Conquest*, pp. 51–53.

31. "Rules for the Government of Missions, as approved by the Father Visitor Rodrigo de Cabredo, 1610." Polzer, *Rules and Precepts*, p. 63. It has been widely noted that Jesuits applied themselves successfully to the task of learning the languages of people they intended to convert. Gibson, *Spain in America*, p. 198; Río, "El régimen jesuitico," p. 32. Weber, *Spanish Frontier*, pp. 108–10, notes the declining results achieved by Franciscan missionaries of the era.

32. The order to Jesuit missionaries to create grammars appears in "Rules for the Government of Missions, as approved by the Father Visitor Rodrigo de Cabredo, 1610." Polzer, *Rules and Precepts*, p. 63.

33. Ricard, *Spiritual Conquest*, pp. 55–57.

34. Twentieth-century studies indicate Cochimí as "Proto-Yuman," that is, related to an earlier evolutionary stage of the line that later divided into the Yuman languages of historic times. See Mixco, *Cochimí and Proto-Yuman*. The Pericú and Guaycura languages remain mysterious, isolated fragments with no certain affinities.

35. Baegert, *Observations*, p. 96.

36. Baegert's essay on California languages. *Baegert, Observations*, pp. 94–104.

37. P. Sebastián de Sistiaga was P. Visitador General Baltasar's procrastinator. Baltasar, "Información de los padres de la provincia de California [1744]." Burrus and Zubillaga, *El noroeste*, p. 486. P. Jacobo Baegert carried out at least part of the study reported to be in progress in 1755 by Visitador General José de Utrera. Utrera, "Nuevo estado . . .," University of Texas, W. B. Stephens Collection, García Mss., document 67, p. 108. For Baegert's study, see n. 38 of this chap.

38. The best and most extensive study, that on Cochimí by P. Miguel del Barco, was not unearthed from its Vatican resting place until the 20th century, and not published until 1973. Barco either smuggled extensive notes safely into exile during the Jesuit expulsion, or had a better memory than his colleagues listed below. Barco, *Historia natural y crónica*, pp. 171–82, 221–29. P. Jacobo Baegert's full study—mentioned above in n. 21—was probably lost during the expulsion. His brief essay on the Guaycura language of Misión de San Luis Gonzaga was published in German in 1771. Baegert, *Observations*, pp. 94–104. In 1752, Baegert sent some useful facts about the language of the Guaycura to his brother, but this letter was not published until 1982. Baegert, *Letters*, p. 145–47. P. Benno Ducrue's linguistic studies of Cochimí, carried out for fifteen years at Misión de Guadalupe, were confiscated as he passed through Havana during the expulsion. He produced a few lines of words and phrases in 1778, after his return to Germany. Ducrue, *Account of the Expulsion*, pp. 130–39.

39. Fray Bernardino de Sahagún [*c.* 1570], quoted in Ricard, *Spiritual Conquest*, pp. 39–40.

40. Visitors to the California peninsula from the 1530s onward included fragments of ethnographical observation in reports or private letters. PP. Kino, Goñi, and Copart, the Jesuits with the Atondo expedition of 1683–1685, stayed longer, and their reports reflect their greater familiarity with the subjects. Missionaries of the permanent colony—notably PP. Salvatierra, Consag, and Linck—reported bits of ethnography as natural parts of their adventures, and probably to pique the interest of superiors, benefactors, and Spanish officials. Private letters written by PP. Jacobo Baegert and Francisco Inama include useful ethnographic observations, many of which are cited in this work.

41. Barco, *Historia natural y crónica*, pp. 171–229, contains the ethnographic essays, but many other valuable bits of ethnographic material are scattered throughout this extensive work. P. Miguel del Barco wrote out this huge manuscript, including his linguistic and ethnographic essays, either from notes or memory after being exiled to Bologna following the Jesuit expulsion in 1768. The manuscript was used, often verbatim, by Barco's younger fellow exile, P. Francisco Javier Clavijero, in writing his popular *History of California*, but then lay unused for two centuries. Baegert's contributions are less objective than Barco's, but they record his observations of Guaycura, whereas Barco's personal experiences were largely with Cochimí. Baegert, *Observations*, pp. 51–104; Baegert, *Letters*, passim.

42. P. Visitador General Baltasar's assessments of the missionaries of northwest New Spain [1743–1744] are found in Burrus and Zubillaga, *El noroeste:* the missionaries of Sinaloa in document xiii; those of Sonora in xxiv; those of California in viii. Baltasar was charged to provide the data from which crucial decisions would have to be made. That prompted him to make unusually frank and detailed reports. A good account of the complex history of this visitation, and its actual prosecution, is in Deeds, "Rendering Unto Caesar: The Secularization of Jesuit Missions in Mid-eighteenth Century Durango," pp. 65–204.

43. A voluminous compendium of Jesuit internecine complaints, accusations, and defenses covering about a century (1670–1760) is located in AGNM, Historia, vol. 392. The accusations cover a broad and inclusive range of derelictions of duty, breaches of vows, and human frailties.

44. Several Jesuit missionaries in northwest New Spain wrote serious accounts of miraculous or near-miraculous events that they had witnessed or heard reported on what they accepted as good authority. An example was provided by P. Herman Glandorff who spent forty years (1723–1763) in the Tarahumara, mostly at Tomochi. On 18 June 1752, he wrote to P. Sixtus Hasselmeier in Germany about the death of one of his neophyte women. He affirmed that, at her funeral, she sat up on the bier and gave the assembled mourners a rapturously graphic description of the House of God amongst the stars, then returned peacefully to death. TBL, The Bolton Papers, item 268 (original found in Bayerisches Staats Archiv, Jesuitica 283).

45. Venegas, *El apóstol*, pp. 131–32.

46. By ordering such get-togethers of his missionaries, P. Salvatierra was carrying out one of the oldest Jesuit rules for the missions. Polzer, *Rules and Precepts*, p. 9. The visitador of each Jesuit mission-

ary region in New Spain was instructed to hold meetings twice a year at which the padres under his supervision could renew their faith with eight days of communal study and meditation over Ignacio de Loyola's Spiritual Exercises. Each missionary, in turn, was sternly ordered not to miss more than one meeting—that is, he was ordered to attend at least once a year. Ibid., pp. 16, 64–65, 70, 81.

47. Venegas, *El apóstol*, pp. 132, 250–51.

48. For California Jesuits who experienced serious health problems, see Index and Appendix B, under headings for "Basaldúa," "Gasteiger," "Helen," "Mayorga," "Peralta," "Pedro de Ugarte," and "Wagner."

49. By the early 1730s, P. Nicolás Tamaral decided that conversion would be expedited by eliminating the threatening presence of a soldier. When Tamaral was murdered by his neophytes in 1734, the previous dependence on protection by soldiers was reinstated. Only P. Jacobo Druet, at the relatively old mission of La Purísima, is known to have purposely dispensed with this protection. Druet, "Informe y Padron de la Purissima Concepcion Mission en California & Noviembre de 1744." TBL, Mexican Manuscripts, MM 1716, #16.

50. Baegert, *Observations*, p. 145–47; Baegert, *Letters*, p. 220; Barco, *Historia Natural y Crónica*, p. 240.

51. Barco, *Historia natural y crónica*, p. 240.

52. Soldiers as role models in church ceremonies: Bayle, *Misión*, p. 138. Soldiers led chants in the local dialect: P. Salvatierra to P. Juan de Ugarte, 3 July 1698, Ibid., pp. 69–70.

53. P. Salvatierra to P. Juan de Ugarte, 1 April 1699. Bayle, *Misión*, p. 100. Two decades later, at the founding of the mission at La Paz, similar demonstrations of horses and arms were made to impress unconverted Indians. Bravo, "Entrada al puerto de la Paz," in León-Portilla, *Testimonios sudcalifornianos*, p. 44.

54. Venegas, "Empressas Apostolicas," párrafo 1808. Lesser offenders were pursued, returned, and punished by a mission's appointed neophyte officials. See p. 203.

55. Venegas, "Empressas Apostolicas," párrafo 1872.

56. Baegert, *Letters*, p. 178. The simultaneous execution of several individuals is a harsh and atypical example of mission justice as otherwise reported in Jesuit California. P. Baegert came to the peninsula in 1751 and may have confused stories about mission affairs with those of Guaycura rebels shot during the neophyte uprising in the mid-1730s. See chap. 4, p. 116.

57. Venegas, *Noticia*, vol. 2, pp. 246–47. Later uses of this stratagem are described in Barco, *Historia natural y crónica*, pp. 309, 351.

58. P. Sigismundo Taraval, no admirer of soldiers or native Californians, described an unmistakable bond between soldiers and Indian boys during the trying times of the rebellion in *el Sur*. Taraval, *Indian Uprising*, p. 45.

59. "At times he [the soldier-guard at a mission] made dinner for himself and the missionary, but at other times, the missionary made it for the two." Clavijero, *History of California*, p. 378.

60. For example, Juan Nicolás de Estrada (1743–1756) and Gerónimo González (1754–1764) at Misión de Santiago. "Mision Santiago: Fragmentos de Registro de Bautismos, desde 1739 a 1769," (manuscript in The Archives of the Archdiocese of Los Angeles).

61. Baegert, *Letters*, pp. 191–92.

62. P. Ignacio Tirsch made several references to the foolish notions of "the Sinaloas"—such as "the Sinaloas and others of a similarly foolish nature" *[los Cinaloas y otros de semejante jaez idiotas]*—in his letter to P. Rector Miguel del Barco, 16 June 1764. TBL, The Bolton Papers, item 324. Jesuit missionaries' general low esteem for the humbler gente de razón is outlined in Spicer, *Cycles of Conquest*, p. 307.

63. Venegas, *Noticia* vol. 2, abridged & rewritten by Burriel, p. 281.

64. P. Piccolo to P. Salvatierra, 24 June 1709. Piccolo, *Informe de 1702*, pp. 164–78; P. Juan de Ugarte to P. Piccolo, 18 November 1719. Ibid., pp. 333–45. P. Clemente Guillén expressed gratitude and admiration for the services of Juan Antonio Covarrubias, a soldier in his retinue on the first land journey south to La Paz, 1720. Guillén, *Overland Expeditions*, p. 69.

65. Barco, *Historia Natural y Crónica*, p. 402. P. Clavijero, who never set foot in California, took his data on Jesuit California's early years from P. Venegas, and for the later years from Barco. Yet he chose to perpetuate Venegas's negative view of soldiers as "evil-doers, bandits, and idlers taken from the dregs of the people." Ironically, Clavijero's work was published soon after its writing and influenced California history for two hundred years before P. Barco's great manuscript finally appeared in print in 1973. Clavijero, *History of California*, p. 314.

66. Prior to about 1750, Jesuit missionaries in California referred to soldiers who were serving at their missions as *sirvientes* or *compañeros*. However, it is evident that the men so designated performed the services of mayordomos, and several of them

were later called mayordomos while serving at the same jobs.

67. Venegas, "Empressas Apostolicas," párrafos 1803–13.

68. Tirsch, *The Drawings of Ignacio Tirsch*, pp. 96–97.

69. In one case, soldier Juan Bautista Mugazábal directed affairs at Misión de Santa Rosalía de Mulegé for several months. See chap. 3, p. 85. The extreme cases in which mayordomos had to assume the responsibilities for their missions occurred in 1768. When Gobernador Portolá carried out his orders to expel the Jesuits, he had no other missionaries at hand and appointed each mission's current mayordomo as its custodian. The circumstances were such that the men retained these unaccustomed responsibilities for months. Crosby, *Doomed to Fail.*

70. Manuel de la Torre Villavicencio, AGNM, Californias, vol. 80, exp. 3, and AGNM, Provincias Internas, vol. 213, exp. 3; Miguel Caravajal, AGNM, Californias, vol. 80, exp. 54; Juan Chrisóstomo de Castro, AHBCS, Económico, document 8; Joseph Gabriel de Arce, AHBCS, Político, document 29. (This last document indicates Arce's 1749 enlistment at the presidio of Loreto. Since he is not on the 1751 payroll, and since he had numerous subsequent assignments as a mayordomo, it can be presumed that he had that status in 1751. By 1752, the Santa Gertrudis Book of Baptisms shows that he was a full-fledged soldier in that mission's escort.) Sebastián de Arce, San Ignacio Book of Baptisms under date 13 September 1764, and AHBCS, Político, document 30. For more on the use of the *media plaza* by California Jesuits, see chap. 6, p. 161.

71. Barco, *Historia Natural y Crónica*, p. 402; Baegert, *Observations*, pp. 146–47.

72. See "expeditions, geographic" in Index.

73. P. Salvatierra to P. Juan de Ugarte, 3 July 1698. Bayle, *Misión*, pp. 69–70.

74. Venegas, "Empressas Apostolicas," párrafo 536. Francisco Javier Valenzuela went on to provide further crucial assistance to P. Salvatierra. In 1709, P. Salvatierra and a party of sailors and shipwrights were on the Seri coast of Sonora trying to salvage a stranded mission launch, the *San Javier.* By that time, Valenzuela was a struggling miner at the Real de Nuestra Señora de Guadalupe del Aguaje. The salvage party ran out of food and managed to get word to Valenzuela, who organized a caravan of stores and cattle to come to their aid. Ibid., párrafo 839. Valenzuela had not forgotten his California

experience. He and his men rode into the camp on the beach firing off their muskets in celebration as they came. Ibid., párrafo 849. Soon Salvatierra was again in need, and took a party on muleback eighty miles to the mining camp. Valenzuela again provided needed supplies. P. Venegas reported that the miner was rewarded for his generosity: soon after, he found a rich vein of silver and was able to pay off all his debts. Ibid., párrafos 855–57. Venegas seems to have derived most, but not all, of his information about Valenzuela's assistance to Salvatierra in Sonora from a letter that Salvatierra wrote to P. Provincial Antonio Jardón, 3 April 1710. AGNM, Historia, vol. 308, fols. 70–71. Valenzuela had further success, attested to by his appointment to the post of *alcalde mayor* in Ostimuri. Almada, *Diccionario de Sonora*, p. 42.

75. Aschmann, *Central Desert*, p. 122.

76. P. Piccolo to P. Salvatierra, 24 June 1709. Piccolo, *Informe de 1702*, pp. 165, 174; Piccolo to Bravo, 18 December 1716. Ibid., pp. 191–92. In 1721, Piccolo encouraged then inexperienced P. Clemente Guillén to make plantings at the site where he hoped to found Misión de los Dolores. P. Piccolo to P. Provincial Romano, 17 July 1721. Ibid., p. 215. This sequence suggests that the strategy had produced favorable results in former applications.

77. Venegas, "Empressas Apostolicas," párrafo 949.

78. Baegert, *Observations*, p. 56.

79. Nápoli, *Relación*, p. 14.

80. The commentary in this passage on mission site selection is based on the author's personal observations and experiences during the cumulative period of a year and a half spent in the immediate mountain and littoral areas once occupied by seven of Baja California's Jesuit missions. Much of it is based on information, traditions, and opinions supplied by ranchers whose families have lived in those areas since mission days.

81. P. Wenceslao Linck was as much responsible for this error as anyone because he was fooled by the apparent promise of an arroyo. He did learn his lesson as he demonstrated in a retrospective account. Link, *Reports and Letters, 1762–1778*, p. 59. Ironically, P. Consag explored this site in Arroyo de Calamajué years earlier when its true character was apparent. However, no adequate maps nor records were made that could inform later site seekers. See chap. 11, p. 344 and n. 47.

82. The cabeceras of missions San Javier, San José de Comondú, La Purísima Concepción, Los

Dolores, and Santiago were moved one or more times; Misión de San Juan Bautista de Ligüí was abandoned.

83. For this and much other information on Jesuit road building in California, see Venegas, "Empressas Apostolicas," libro X, capitulo xxii. A translated and annotated version of this chapter is included in Crosby, "El Camino Real," pp. 42–43. For information specifically on road building to visitas, see P. Tamaral to P. Visitador General Echeverría, 1730. Bayle, *Misión*, pp. 212–13; Baegert, *Letters*, p. 154.

84. The Spanish term *visita* has a very broad range of related meanings. One indicates the area inspected by a *visitador*. Thus, the *visita* of a Jesuit *visitador general* would be the collective mission provinces of northwest New Spain, while the *visita* of California's *padre visitador* would be the collective California missions. Polzer, *Rules and Precepts*, p. 9. But in this work, for clarity, the word *visita* is used only to describe the satellite indoctrination centers occupied permanently or seasonally by one or more rancherías assigned to a mission and, about once each month, called in to the cabecera or visited in their own area by that mission's padre. The creation of *visitas*, or satellite communities, was a standard practice of missionary orders in New Spain. Spicer, *Cycles of Conquest*, p. 292. The word *visita* appears rather infrequently in reports by California Jesuits. The original term was *pueblo de visita*, which California missionaries like P. Miguel del Barco usually shortened to *pueblo*. Wherever Barco used *pueblo* in a California context, he eventually demonstrated that he was referring to a visiting station (as, for example, with respect to the visita of San Ignacio, discussed at length in this chap.). Barco, *Historia natural y crónica*, p. 257. P. Nicolás Tamaral provided an unusually clear indication of the relationship of the terms when he wrote, *"el pueblo de San Miguel, visita de la Misión de San Javier."* Tamaral to P. Visitador General Echeverría, 1730. Bayle, *Misión*, p. 212.

85. Presumably, the *capitán* or *gobernador* chosen to lead the greater pueblo de visita was a man acceptable to the leaders of the different rancherías that formed the new unit — probably he was chosen from among them. But the new unit, formed as a convenience for evangelization, did not supplant the old arrangements for hunting and gathering. In those vital activities, bands went their ways as before.

86. Baegert, *Observations*, pp. 120–21; P. Tamaral to P. Visitador General Echeverría, 1730. Bayle,

Misión, pp. 216–18. P. Baegert's own mission of San Luis Gonzaga was so poor in food that some rancherías were brought in to the cabecera for periods of two weeks, but had to spend part of that time foraging for food in the area. Baegert, *Letters*, p. 154.

87. The name *temastián* — derived from a Nahuatl word for "teacher" — was widely used in Jesuit missions in northwest New Spain to indicate a native catechist. A number of Jesuits who had served in that area, including P. Salvatierra, spoke and wrote Nahuatl. Salvatierra, *Selected Letters*, pp. 23, 234–36; Polzer, *Rules and Precepts*, p. 57.

88. P. Tamaral to P. Visitador General Echeverría, 1730. Bayle, *Misión*, p. 218. The version of the *Alabado* used in Jesuit California opened with the words, *Bendito y Alabado sea el Santissimo Nombre de Jesus.* . . . "Blessed and praised be the Most Holy Name of Jesus. . . .", Barco, *Historia natural y crónica*, p. 268. The melody may have been that given in Engelhardt, *Missions and Missionaries*, vol. 1, p. 169.

89. Polzer, *Rules and Precepts*, p. 25.

90. Venegas, "Empressas Apostolicas," párrafos 1938–41.

91. Baegert, *Letters*, pp. 204–5, 217–30; Baegert, *Observations*, p. 74.

92. P. Salvatierra to P. Provincial Arteaga, 21 after May 1701. Bayle, *Misión*, pp. 150–51. One of "the customs of the tribe" on which Salvatierra did not elaborate here was to seize the free time provided by the easy harvest to teach the band's traditions to the young, typically a task undertaken by a shaman or shamans. These religious figures also used this opportunity to get assistance in the manufacture of the painted wooden figures on which some of their rituals depended. Venegas, "Empressas Apostolicas," párrafo 1651.

93. "The worst, however, is this: even in their last deathly sickness, when they are going to die, they are not afraid of those things of which they were not ashamed during their lifetime. I at least have not seen one who showed the least fear when he was deathly sick or was approaching death. But when I asked these sick people where they would go after death if they would not say confession, I saw and heard them answer: 'into Hell.' And this they answered, quite calm and relaxed, without a stirred up mind or emotion and without hurrying to confess their sins." Baegert, *Letters*, p. 224.

94. The verse sung by gente de razón: *Comen sin hastío, viven sin vergüenza, mueren sin temor.* Baegert, *Letters*, p. 221.

95. P. Visitador Sebastián de Sistiaga to P. Vis-

itador General José de Echeverría, 27 October 1730. AGNM, Historia, vol. 308, fol. 478 (transcript in TBL, The Bolton Papers, item 295).

96. Baegert, *Letters*, pp. 195–96.

97. Hunting: Baegert, *Letters*, p. 124. Fishing: ". . . [neophytes] do not hesitate to go out into the ocean for some hours standing on a bare, thick truss of reeds or sitting on it, and with a sharp pointed stick they pierce and catch turtles and fish." Ibid, p. 231. Taking turtles: Barco, *Historia natural y crónica*, p. 135. Neophytes at gulf coast missions also fished the adjacent waters: ". . . on calm days, Indian canoes and rafts go and come to a secure port on Isla del Carmen that lies off Loreto. . . ." P. Salvatierra to P. Juan de Ugarte, 1 April 1699. Bayle, *Misión*, p. 94.

98. Aschmann, *Central Desert*, p. 209. P. Miguel del Barco notes most of these specific items of the California natives' diet. Barco, *Historia natural y crónica*, passim. The diets of pre-contact natives of central Mexico were also better balanced than those imposed upon them by mission regimes. West and Augelli, *Middle America*, pp. 229–32.

99. Venegas, "Empressas Apostolicas," párrafo 1710.

100. McAlister, *Spain and Portugal in the New World*, pp. 174–75; Spicer, *Cycles of Conquest*, pp. 372–73.

101. P. Jaime Bravo wrote to La Paz's prime benefactor, reporting that the new mission "has already harvested its first crop of maize with which to attract the heathen." Bravo to Marqués de Villapuente, 10 October 1730. BNM, AF 4/56.2.

102. The Jesuits were not alone in their carrot-and-stick methods; a spokesman for the Franciscans who succeeded the Jesuits in California observed, ". . . the Indians pay attention to and obey only those who can give them something, and only by gifts and threats can they be attracted to prayers, the catechism, or anything that pertains to the church." Palóu, *Historical Memoirs*, vol. 1, p. 32.

103. Ricard, *Spiritual Conquest*, pp. 84–85.

104. Venegas, *El apóstol*, pp. 134–35.

105. The burial record of San José de Comondú shows that on each occasion in which a neophyte died without receiving the sacraments, the padre wrote out a relatively detailed explanation of the circumstances that had brought about the failure.

106. Baegert, *Observations*, p. 123.

107. Clavijero, *History of California*, p. 368.

108. Venegas, "Empressas Apostolicas," párrafos 1135–36.

109. Sixteenth-century use of the neophyte offices of *alcalde* and *fiscal:* Ricard, *Spiritual Conquest*, pp. 96–97. The practice continued in later times: Spicer, *Cycles of Conquest*, pp. 290–91. The Jesuits perpetuated the practice in 17th century Sinaloa: Dunne, *Black Robes*, pp. 71–74; and in Sonora: Polzer, *Rules and Precepts*, p. 49.

110. Spicer, *Cycles of Conquest*, pp. 375–76.

111. P. Tamaral to P. Visitador General Echeverría [1730]. Bayle, *Misión*, pp. 215–16.

112. Favored neophytes—usually men who had had power in their bands prior to conversion—were appointed to comparable positions in new communities of neophytes; this practice dated from the earliest years of the conquest of New Spain. The first people evangelized in New Spain were sedentary agriculturalists who had hierarchies of their own officials and were familiar with the concept of such leadership. In northwest New Spain, and particularly in California, leadership had taken very different forms; thus, the subordinate leadership roles assigned by the Jesuits in their missions were as new a phenomenon as everything else they were imposing on their converts. Lockhart and Schwartz, *Early Latin America*, pp. 114–15, 293–94.

113. Baegert, *Observations*, pp. 121–22.

114. Venegas, "Empressas Apostolicas," párrafo 1869.

115. Barco, *Historia natural y crónica*, p. 402.

116. Burrus and Zubillaga, *El noroeste*, p. 486.

117. P. Jacobo Baegert, the most negative and pessimistic of California Jesuits, said of *pajes*, "An eighteen-year-old boy . . . served in the house of the missionary from childhood on—we call them pages, and they are considered the worst by others [i.e., fellow missionaries] . . . the general opinion is that those Indians are the worst and most malicious who stay in and are in service for the mission from their early youth on." Baegert, *Letters*, pp. 225, 227. A close reading of P. Baegert reveals that his low opinion of pages was in part due to the sophistication they acquired. Another padre of Germanic extraction, Jorge Retz, brought a *paje*, Everardo Lanziegos, with him from Misión de San Ignacio when he founded Misión de Santa Gertrudis in 1752. Lanziegos served under Retz until the Jesuit expulsion in 1768, acted as a godfather at hundreds of baptisms, and as a witness at dozens of weddings. The use of pages as messengers is borne out by Lanziegos's appearances as godfather on several occasions at both San Ignacio and San Borja, Santa Gertrudis's neighboring missions.

118. An early document describing the selection

and training of especially capable boys as servants and interpreters — and the use of the term *ladino* to describe them — is Venegas, "Empressas Apostolicas," párrafo 1919.

119. Hu-de Hart, *Missionaries, Miners, and Indians*, pp. 62–63.

120. P. Sebastián de Sistiaga to P. Provincial Escobar y Llamas, 19 September 1743. Burrus and Zubillaga, *El noroeste*, p. 448.

121. The captain's empowerment to appoint neophyte officials is spelled out in Venegas, "Empressas Apostolicas," párrafo 1873. [For a translation of the pertinent passage, see the third item under powers and prerogatives of Loreto's captain, chap. 6, p. 166.] The padre visitador's actual control of the appointments of neophyte officials is stated in Venegas, *El apóstol*, p. 130. One of several cases where a padre distributed symbols and appointments without even consulting the captain is detailed in P. Piccolo to Hermano Bravo, 18 December 1716. Piccolo, *Informe de 1702*, p. 192.

122. P. Juan María de Salvatierra seems to have had a rather tolerant attitude toward pre-Christian ceremonial practices. He displayed an interest in the traditional dances of the Conchó people, encouraged his soldiers to demonstrate their own dancing capabilities in exchange, and even showed off a step or two himself. Venegas, *El apóstol*, pp. 136–37; Bayle, *Misión*, pp. 101, 139–40. However, his colleagues and successors had a darker view of many manifestations of aboriginal culture. For example, see Piccolo's description of dances performed around the time of his first visit to the San Ignacio area. Piccolo to Bravo, San Patricio, 18 December 1716. Piccolo, *Informe de 1702*, pp. 193–95.

123. Jesuit missionaries went to elaborate lengths to minimize dealings with women, and especially to avoid exposure to, or awareness of, female nudity. Even the usually urbane P. Miguel del Barco betrays a great deal of modesty in this regard — and reports others, like P. Consag, who carried this avoidance to near-comic extremes. Barco, *Historia natural y crónica*, pp. 199–201.

124. Barco, *Historia natural y crónica*, p. 215.

125. Venegas, "Empressas Apostolicas," párrafo 1142.

126. Barco, *Historia natural y crónica*, p. 299.

127. Venegas, "Empressas Apostolicas," párrafo 1657; Barco, *Historia natural y crónica*, p. 177.

128. P. Salvatierra's use of music to beguile the young — and through them, their elders: Venegas, *El apóstol*, p. 135; Bayle, *Misión*, p. 139. European

music and musical instruments had a profound impact on all peoples of the New World. From the earliest days of conversions, neophytes were trained to play and sing; their performances, incorporated into church services and festival activities, gave performers and neophytes as a whole a sense of greater and more immediate participation. Ricard, *Spiritual Conquest*, pp. 104, 168, 177–79.

129. See chap. 5, p. 144, for the 1725 importation of an organ that apparently went to San Javier. See chap. 9, p. 272, for information on Loreto's organ. San Ignacio was to receive an organ upon the completion of its church, estimated to be in 1769, but the expulsion of the Jesuits interrupted the construction and delivery of the organ. P. José Mariano Rotea to P. Procurador de Californias Juan de Armesto, 10 October 1766. AHH, Temporalidades, leg. 298, exp. 4.

130. Choirs were established as quickly as possible in new missions all over northern New Spain. Spicer, *Cycles of Conquest*, p. 290.

131. "Creditable singing . . . could be heard in some churches. Father Xavier Bischoff, from the county of Glatz in Bohemia, and Father Pietro Nascimben of Venice, Italy, were particularly responsible for introducing choral singing to California. They had trained the Californians, both men and women, with incomparable effort and patience." Baegert, *Observations*, p. 126. "To Padre Pedro Nascimbén is owed the beauty with which Indian women perform choral masses, here [Santa Rosalía de Mulegé], in Guadalupe, and in San Ignacio." José de Utrera, "Nuevo estado . . . ," University of Texas, W. B. Stephens Collection, García Mss., document 67, p. 105. It is not unlikely that Nascimbén, educated in Venice in the first quarter of the 18th century, was influenced by fellow churchman and fellow Venetian Antonio Vivaldi (1675–1741).

132. P. Francisco Escalante, [untitled, unsigned document in Escalante's handwriting, with events from 1754 to 1762; obviously the report on Santa Rosalía de Mulegé ordered in the latter year by Visitador General Lizasoáin]. AGNM, Jesuitas, vol. 3, parte 16, exp. 2.

133. Jesuit determination to institute schools at missions is stated in Clavijero, *History of California*, p. 372. Schools were installed early in the Jesuit regime at Loreto, San Javier, and San José de Comondú. Decorme, *Jesuitas mexicanos*, vol. 2, pp. 492, 495. Schools functioning at San José de Comondú and La Purísima in 1755 were described by P. Visitador General José de Utrera in "Nuevo esta-

do . . . ," University of Texas, W. B. Stephens Collection, García Mss., document 67, pp. 102, 103, 205.

134. Spicer, *Cycles of Conquest*, pp. 283–84.

135. Boys and girls stayed in school until they were married: José de Utrera, "Nuevo estado . . . ," University of Texas, W. B. Stephens Collection, García Mss., document 67, p. 103; Bayle, *Misión*, p. 236. The minimum acceptable age for a girl's marriage in Jesuit California was twelve. Baegert, *Observations*, p. 72.

136. Venegas, *El apóstol*, p. 134. Records preserved in the books of baptisms for Loreto and Santa Gertrudis illustrate the progression of godparenthood from gente de razón to neophytes. The latter, which is complete, demonstrates a sequence in which at first only soldiers served as godparents, then the newly converted were introduced to these ceremonial roles; within weeks, neophytes became the exclusive participants.

137. Bayle, *Misión*, pp. 138–39.

138. Barco, *Historia natural y crónica*, p. 314.

139. A good statement of Jesuit plans to use schools in California to indoctrinate the young is found in Venegas, "Empressas Apostolicas," párrafo 1919. Jesuit use of schooling as a fundamental tool in indoctrination after evangelization followed precedents adopted by other orders in the first years of missionary activity in the New World. Ricard, *Spiritual Conquest*, pp. 98–99. Ibid., p. 207, provides an analysis of advantages obtained by mission schooling.

140. P. Mayorga to P. Provincial Romano, 20 October 1720. BNM, AF 3/51.1; Baegert, *Observations*, passim. and *Letters* (see ensuing note).

141. Baegert, *Letters*, pp. 204–5.

142. The rebellion in *el Sur* is described in some detail in chap. 4 of this work. Attempted neophyte revolts after 1734–1737: Guaycura in 1738 [Barco, *Historia natural y crónica*, p. 239]; Pericú in 1740 [Ibid., pp. 240–42]; Coras and Aripes in 1754 [Baegert, *Letters*, p. 170].

143. Venegas, "Empressas Apostolicas," párrafo 1717.

144. Baegert, *Letters*, pp. 177–78.

145. Reports of runaways are numerous, but the most conspicuous such episode involved twenty Pericú who, in 1761, stole a dugout canoe and crossed the gulf in a desperate, quixotic attempt to carry their grievances to the viceroy. Barco, *Historia natural y crónica*, pp. 327–31; Baegert, *Letters*, p. 230.

146. Baegert, *Observations*, pp. 89–90; Barco, *Historia natural y crónica*, p. 237.

147. Baegert, *Observations*, pp. 123–24; Baegert, *Letters*, pp. 224–25.

148. Venegas, "Empressas Apostolicas," párrafos 1716–17.

149. Baegert, *Letters*, p. 220.

150. P. Baegert, in fact, lamented that parents never disciplined their children. Baegert, *Letters*, p. 218.

151. Baegert, *Observations*, p. 91.

152. Baegert, *Letters*, p. 218.

153. Native religious leaders resisted Christian evangelization in similar ways throughout New Spain and from the earliest days of the conquest. Ricard, *Spiritual Conquest*, pp. 270–71.

154. P. Juan de Ugarte converted a shaman who not only became a docile neophyte but also provided useful intelligence about shamanistic practices. Venegas, "Empressas Apostolicas," párrafos 750–52. P. Sigismundo Taraval reported a case in which an ex-shaman was converted and became an effective voice in denouncing the shams and trickeries that had once served him and his brother practitioners. Taraval, *Indian Uprising*, p. 23. Jesuit records unintentionally reveal that some padres were more tolerant of old practices and superstitions than others. This may have been a factor in the varying degrees of resistance to conversion that were encountered at different missions or by different padres.

155. Rio, "El régimen jesuítico," p. 102.

156. Venegas, "Empressas Apostolicas," párrafos 942–43, 1142–43. Early in the conversion of Sinaloa, P. Pérez de Ribas saw the burning of shamans' ceremonial paraphernalia as an appropriate parallel to Chapter 19, verse 19 of the *Acts of the Apostles* in which the magicians at Ephesus burned their books of sorcery. Polzer, *Rules and Precepts*, p. 44.

157. The padre-reporter was Nicolás Tamaral, who later died by violence during the uprising in the South — led in part by shamans. Venegas, "Empressas Apostolicas," párrafos 922–23.

158. In 1704, P. Juan de Ugarte accepted as sincere the pledges of two shamans who wished to convert. Both were baptized but died within weeks. Venegas, "Empressas Apostolicas," párrafos 750–52. As late as 1762, P. Linck reported accepting hechiceros as neophytes at the new mission of San Borja when they brought their families for instruction, promised to give up their practices as healers, and allow all their "instruments, idols, and paintings" to be publicly burned.

159. Baegert, *Observations*, pp. 89–90; Barco, *Historia natural y crónica*, p. 237. The latter source

shows that shamans still had enough influence at Comondú, thirty years after the mission was established, to threaten the padre and the system.

160. Polzer, *Rules and Precepts*, p. 44.

161. Spicer, *Cycles of Conquest*, pp. 291.

162. Barco, *Historia natural y crónica*, p. 256.

163. Baegert, *Observations*, pp. 133, 143.

164. Aschmann, *Central Desert*, pp. 213–26.

165. Baegert, *Observations*, p. 129. In 1767, when Misión de San José de Comondú had about half the population it had enjoyed during Mayordomo Caravajal's time, there were 12 fully equipped plow rigs in the tool storage area of its warehouse. Inventory of Misión de San José de Comondú, 30 December 1767. AHBCS, Religioso, document 3.

166. Barco, *Historia natural y crónica*, pp. 115–18. The translation is abridged from Barco, *Natural History*, pp. 210–11.

167. Birds, rodents: Baegert, *Observations*, pp. 129–30; locusts, blight, yields: Barco, *Historia natural y crónica*, pp. 115–18.

168. In 1719, P. Juan de Ugarte was able to order the slaughter of 200 cattle from the herd at Misión de San Javier. See chap. 4, p. 100.

169. Barco, *Historia natural y crónica*, pp. 279–81; Baegert, *Observations*, pp. 133–34.

170. Barco, *Historia natural y crónica*, pp. 217–18. San Luis Gonzaga was the mission that reported severe losses to mountain lions [in 1753–1754] despite having only small herds. Baegert, *Letters*, p. 166.

171. Barco, *Historia natural y crónica*, pp. 17, 218–19, 280–81; Baegert, *Observations*, pp. 132–34.

172. The presence and uses of dogs are revealed in several direct references: Barco, *Historia natural y crónica*, p. 13; Antonio García de Mendoza to P. Juan de Ugarte, 24 March 1699. Burrus and Zubillaga, *El noroeste de México*, pp. 409–10; P. Ignacio Tirsch to P. Rector Miguel del Barco, 16 June 1764. TBL, The Bolton Papers, item 324. P. Tirsch also included at least four dogs in his painting of Misión de San José del Cabo. Nunis, *The Drawings of Ignacio Tirsch*, Plate VIII, p. 45.

173. Barco, *Historia natural y crónica*, p. 209; Clavijero, *History of California*, p. 373; Venegas, *El apóstol*, p. 266.

174. Venegas, "Empressas Apostolicas," párrafo 1292.

175. Barco, *Historia natural y crónica*, p. 281; Baegert, *Observations*, pp. 62, 132–34; Aschmann, *Central Desert*, pp. 234–36.

176. From a eulogy written at P. Julián de Mayorga's death by P. Sigismundo Taraval. Taraval, *Indian Uprising*, p. 259.

177. Every mission eventually had its fields and irrigation system washed away. See P. José Mariano Rotea's 1762 account of the problem at Misión de San Ignacio. Rotea to P. Visitador General Lizasoáin. Bayle, *Misión*, pp. 237–38. See also brief reports of particularly destructive storms in 1717 and 1754. Ibid., pp. 203, 224.

178. A particularly explicit description of drought is found in Baegert, *Letters*, pp. 129–30.

179. Jesuit accounts bristle with anguished reports about devastation by locusts. P. Miguel del Barco's essay is an observant and thorough synthesis of the whole experience. Barco, *Historia natural y crónica*, pp. 36–46.

180. Barco, *Historia natural y crónica*, p. 71.

181. Letter from P. Francisco Inama at Misión de San José de Comondú to his Reverend Sister, a Carmelite in Cologne-on-the-Rhine, 14 October 1755. Ducrue, *Account of the Expulsion*, p. 154.

182. *Pitahaya agria* (*Machaerocereus gummosus*).

183. Taraval, *Indian Uprising*, pp. 99–100.

184. The author has personally observed, for example, that *mezcales* are absent for a distance of ten or more miles in all directions from Misión de San Borja. Also, see Aschmann, *Central Desert*, pp. 79–80.

185. Konrad, *Jesuit Hacienda*, p. 267.

186. Baegert, *Letters*, p. 145. The text of Baegert's remark shows that he unconsciously identified "Californians" only as men — and offered an apt example of women seen as sex objects.

187. Barco, *Historia natural y crónica*, p. 59.

188. Baegert, *Letters*, pp. 155, 165.

189. P. Miguel del Barco emphasized the disproportionate amounts of work and family responsibilities of women in the aboriginal Californian culture. Barco, *Historia natural y crónica*, p. 203. He also noted that, with the exception of hunting and fishing, duties virtually reserved for males, women were more diligent and more adept at basic survival skills. Ibid., p. 66. P. Taraval wrote: ". . . women in the Californias are the ones who do the work, procuring and preparing all food for their husbands." Taraval, *Indian Uprising*, p. 123.

190. Homer Aschmann emphasized the contrast of women's roles in their aboriginal culture with those of mission life. He provided a succinct essay on the division of labor at missions and, especially, the misuse or non-use of women's capabilities. Aschmann, *Central Desert*, pp. 234–35.

191. Speaking of the pitahaya season, the usually dour P. Jacobo Baegert wrote, "during this time the heaven hangs full of violins and the good Indian

thinks paradise has flown to California." Baegert, *Letters*, p. 133. P. Miguel del Barco noted that at the time of this harvest the natives were more cheerful and exhilarated than at any other time of year. Barco, *Historia natural y crónica*, p. 192.

192. See description of pitahaya festival quoted on p. 198–99 of this chapter; Barco, *Historia natural y crónica*, p. 192. P. Baegert emphasized the popularity and prevalence of traditional singing and dancing, even among "converted" Californians. Baegert, *Letters*, p. 202.

193. From the first, the Jesuits seem to have been broad-mindedly tolerant of any diversions or recreations that seemed harmless, even joining in the exercises on appropriate occasions. Venegas, "Empressas Apostolicas," párrafo 1688.

194. Barco, *Historia natural y crónica*, p. 398. The festival activities in Jesuit California derived not only from old European traditions, but also reflections and derivations of those traditions in use since the early days of Catholic missions in the New World. See Ricard, *Spiritual Conquest*, chap. 11, "Pomp and Magnificence."

195. Baegert, *Observations*, pp. 124–27.

196. Baegert, *Observations*, pp. 143–45.

197. California Jesuits perennially denied doing business with the galleon. They insisted that all stores and foodstuffs were delivered to the Manila ships as gifts. But it is well documented that officers and passengers made "gifts" to the padres in return. Barco, *Historia natural y crónica*, pp. 246–47; Baegert, *Letters*, pp. 161, 225–26. When the Jesuits were expelled inventories showed that their California missions contained porcelain and other items of commerce from the Orient. Inventory of Misión de San José de Comondú, 30 December 1767. AHBCS, Religioso, document 3.

198. Baegert, *Letters*, p. 152.

199. Missions produce for soldiers' needs: Baegert, *Observations*, pp. 151–53. Soldier builds house for missionary: Baegert, *Letters*, pp. 170–71. Soldier sells chickens to missionary: Baegert, *Observations*, p. 143.

200. P. Visitador General Echeverría wrote that "[California] wine and brandy are exchanged on the other coast for maize." Echeverría to Marqués de Villapuente, 28 October 1729. BNM, AF 4/55.1 P. Visitador Sebastián de Sistiaga wrote to P. Ignacio María Nápoli at the Jesuit mission at Ráhum, Sonora, to thank him for sending mules and pack saddles to California padres; he closed by promising to send Nápoli at least two casks of what had proved to be a very good vintage. Sistiaga to Ná-

poli, 16 October 1739. AGNM, Historia, vol. 392, fol. 260.

201. Barco, *Historia natural y crónica*, p. 359.

202. Venegas, "Empressas Apostolicas," párrafo 733.

203. P. Visitador General Utrera's report implies independent figures for the volumes of wine and brandy. It is not likely that any of the reported wine production was used in making the brandy. Utrera used the *tinaja* as a unit of measure for wine and brandy production, giving 377 *tinajas* of wine and 125 tinajas of brandy as the 1754 production. The term *tinaja* then had several possible usages. The likeliest was to describe a cask or jug containing about eleven gallons that was a standard item in the Manila trade. The Jesuits did engage in a certain amount of commerce with the Manila galleons, and those ships had many empty *tinajas* by the time they reached California. However, the term also was used to name a large earthenware jar of variable capacity—perhaps in the range of four to eight gallons. Miguel del Barco, in describing the distribution of California wine, consistently employed the term *botijas* for its containers. This also suggests an earthenware jug or bottle. If Utrera's report was based on some form of jug, the gallonages suggested in this text would be reduced by about half. Barco, *Historia natural y crónica*, p. 359.

204. P. Visitador General Utrera reported 100 tinajas of wine produced at both San Javier and La Purísima, 73 at Comondú, and 65 at San Ignacio; also 25 tinajas of brandy at San Javier, "a few" at La Purísima, and 100 at San Ignacio. It is assumed that his tinajas were the approximately 11-gallon casks in use in the Manila trade. José de Utrera, "Nuevo estado...," Univ. of Texas, W. B. Stephens Collection, García Mss., document 67, pp. 101, 102, 103, 106. Successful vineyards at San José and San Javier are described in Barco, *Historia natural y crónica*, pp. 359–60.

205. Río, *Conquista y aculturación*, pp. 148–49.

206. Descriptions of the Californians' bows, arrows, and archery skills are found in Barco, *Historia natural y crónica*, pp. 194–95; Baegert, *Observations*, pp. 64–65.

207. Barco, *Historia natural y crónica*, p. 325. The use of tanbark from *mezquitillo*: Ibid., p. 104. *Mezquitillo* was still in use for the same purpose by midpeninsular tanners in the late 20th century.

208. P. Juan Javier Bischoff, missionary at La Purísima in 1762, wrote, "Great pains have been taken that the best Indians build houses, raise sheep, and have commercial dealings among them-

selves like civilized men. . . ." Dunne, *Black Robes*, p. 390. The neophytes of Loreto were reported to have their own gardens and herds in Bayle, *Colonización*, p. 189. Neophytes at Misión de la Purísima carved and polished the beautiful dark-red heartwood of *palo blanco* into exquisite crucifixes such as all the mission converts wore suspended by cords around their necks. They went a step farther and made similar crosses close to a foot in height, which they inlaid with mother-of-pearl and engraved in intricate patterns. Unfortunately, the supply of finished products soon exceeded the demand and the craft disappeared. Barco, *Historia natural y crónica*, p. 65.

209. Baegert, *Observations*, pp. 132–34.

210. Barco, *Historia natural y crónica*, p. 135.

211. Venegas, "Empressas Apostolicas," párrafo 718. Antonio Morán's presence at San Javier is verified by the mission's book of baptisms in which the weaver appears as a godfather on several occasions in the period of 1709–1712. Morán apparently retired to his home in Tepic where he continued to assist the California colony by acting as an agent in the purchase and shipping of food and goods. See the account books of the procurador in Mexico City for the years 1722–1730. AGNM, Californias, vol. 60 bis, exp. 6.

212. Barco, *Historia natural y crónica*, p. 209.

213. Women's knitting, weaving: Ibid., p. 209; women sell or trade their products at Loreto: Ibid., pp. 325–26. Women's labor was employed in such production in missions all over northwest New Spain. In Jesuit California, shortages of raw materials severely limited the sizes of mission industries. However, San José de Comondú had four looms in 1767. "Inventory of Misión de San José de Comondú, December 30, 1767." AHBCS, Religioso, document 3. They may have been used exclusively for the mission's communal interests, or they may have been available part of the time for the neophytes' private use. P. Baegert made specific reference to missionaries who lent tools to neophytes so they could do work for themselves. Baegert, *Observations*, p. 122.

214. Baegert, *Observations*, p. 62.

215. Barco, *Historia natural y crónica*, p. 72.

216. P. Miguel del Barco so admired this form of basketry that he devoted an 800-word essay to its description. Barco, *Historia natural y crónica*, pp. 100–102. This craft was practiced by the Cochimí — and probably other peninsular people — prior to the coming of the missions. During searches for rock art in caves in the mountains of the mid-

peninsula, the author has seen dozens of basket-like fragments either in dry caves or in the hands of mountain ranchers who collected them in such caves. They show fine, tight weaving of plant materials first twisted into string-sized cordage. These must be fragments of the prevalent trays and dishes to which Barco referred, although the work seems finer than that which he described. Most specimens that I saw had also been lined with fine clay which filled all the interstices. Clay linings would have allowed the toasting of seeds by shaking them with hot coals, a process described by both Barco and Baegert.

217. Collecting and preparing *mezcal* in the traditional way is described in Barco, *Historia natural y crónica*, pp. 121–25; selling the product is in Ibid., p. 325.

218. Ibid., pp. 325–26.

219. Ibid., p. 325.

220. Ibid., pp. 325–26.

Chapter 8: Misión de San José de Comondú

1. See Bibliography for the names and locations of the surviving *libros de misión* (mission registers) for Jesuit California.

2. The cover sheet on the combined Comondú record books reads, "Libro de Bautismos, Casamientos y Entierros hechos en esta Mission de Sr. S. Joseph Comondu"; a marginal note adds, "desde el Año 1736." The originals are located in the Seminario de la Compañia de Jesús, México, D. F. Microfilm copies are held at The Bancroft Library under the title, "Asociación Histórica Americanista: Mission records of San Joseph de Comondú." Individual books cover different spans of years: Baptisms, 1736–1831 [no individual cover sheet or title]; Marriages, 1753–1826 [no individual cover sheet or title]; Burials, 1737–1826 "Catalogus Defunctorum in Missione Sn. Joseph de Comondu."

3. The first *entrada* to Londó is described in this work, chap. 2, pp. 40–41 and map 2.1. Two others were reported by P. Salvatierra in letters to P. Juan de Ugarte. Salvatierra to Ugarte, 1 April 1699. Bayle, *Misión*, pp. 109–13; Salvatierra to Ugarte, 9 July 1699. Salvatierra, *Letters*, pp. 165–74.

4. Several writers have called this visita "San Juan Bautista," perhaps confusing it with the short-lived Misión de San Juan Bautista that was founded at Ligüí in 1705 (q.v.). P. Salvatierra wrote of Londó, "the area at the foot of the Sierra de San Isidro was called San Juan de Londó in honor of our first

benefactor, Don Juan Caballero." Salvatierra to P. Juan de Ugarte, 9 July 1699. Salvatierra, *Letters*, p. 173. P. Venegas introduced an element of confusion when he wrote that the visita at Londó was "given as its patron and advocate San Juan Bautista, and called San Juan Londó." Venegas, "Empressas Apostolicas," párrafo 346. But Venegas then proceeded to follow his chief source, the letters of Salvatierra, in using "San Juan Londó" or "San Juan de Londó" — and never San Juan Bautista — in dozens of subsequent references. Miguel del Barco called this visiting station "San Juan de Londó." Barco, *Historia natural y crónica*, pp. 257, 259. Itineraries by Castillo Negrete [1853] and Alvarez y Durán [1856] show that the visita site was known as "San Juan" in the mid-19th century — as it is to this day. Castillo Negrete, "Geografía y estadística," p. 339; Alvarez y Durán, *Itinerarios y derroteros*, p. 425.

San Juan Londó was sometimes referred to as a mission, but it was never formally consecrated as such and achieved that status in practice only briefly during 1700–1703 when Salvatierra was making regular and long visits to hold services. Venegas, "Empressas Apostolicas," párrafos 715–16. San Juan's subsequent history as a visita of two missions is detailed in this chapter. A small but massive barrel-vaulted stone chapel was built at San Juan at an unknown date. Of this, the east side wall still stood in 1991.

5. The trail revealed to P. Salvatierra by his converts at Londó employed the mountain pass southwest of Canipolé. Salvatierra's reference to the difficulties encountered by Atondo's party in crossing the Sierra de la Giganta was based on incomplete knowledge of the earlier explorations. Members of the first Atondo expedition into the Giganta did indeed have a rough climb when they attacked the sierra just west of Londó. Bolton, *Rim of Christendom*, p. 145; Kino, *Kino Writes to the Duchess*, pp. 150–52. But in their second attempt, they had better guidance and crossed by the same pass used later by Salvatierra. See Atondo, *First from the Gulf to the Pacific*, pp. 19–30; frontispiece map.

6. Today the playas that P. Salvatierra described are called, as they have been since mission times, *llano redondo, llano la laguna, llano San Pedro*, and *los llanos de San Julio*. Judging from P. Kino's diary and map of 1683, he visited the first two of these playas during a 1683 climb into the sierra. Kino, *Kino Reports to Headquarters*, pp. 65–80; map on unnumbered last page of supplement.

7. The best account of this expedition and the naming of the uplands area is found in P. Sal-vatierra's long, historically important letter to P. Provincial Francisco de Arteaga, after 21 May 1701 [from internal evidence]. Bayle, *Misión*, pp. 156–57. Salvatierra gave no evidence that he was aware that Atondo and Kino had visited Comondú in 1684, but it was named in the admiral's official report. Atondo, *First from the Gulf to the Pacific*, pp. 28–29. The watercourse that passes through the original Comondú is one of the tributaries of the great arroyo, called Cadegomó downstream, followed or paralleled by Atondo as he crossed the peninsula. About 1735, the mission of La Purísima was moved, from a few miles to the north, into this important drainage.

8. Venegas, "Empressas Apostolicas," párrafo 498.

9. Both Almirante Atondo and P. Salvatierra first heard of the Comondú area from and were guided to it by people they met in Londó.

10. A letter written by P. Piccolo to P. Salvatierra, 24 June 1709, only a year after the founding of San José de Comondú, describes a request for a missionary made by a band living distant from any mission. BNM, AF 3/45.1 (transcribed in Piccolo, *Informe de 1702*, pp. 164–78).

The reaction of the isolated cultures of peninsular California to the novelty and relative material bounty that accompanied the missionaries may have been similar to that of Pacific islanders who formed "cargo cults" to invoke more of the largesse incidental to the temporary presence of the United States military during World War II.

11. Venegas, "Empressas Apostolicas," párrafo 821. This evidence of gente de razón depending on jerky as early as 1707 suggests that the habit had pre-California origins. Peninsular cattle herds had not prospered so quickly as to provide staple quantities. Sinaloan and Sonoran sister missions were doubtless the sources of meat, and their area had established the tastes and practices of California's soldier and worker recruits, most of whom were reared in those provinces.

12. The scribe's note, verbatim: "El Padre Julian de Maiorga Sacerdote natural de Villarejo de Salvanes de la Jurisdicion del orden de Santiago de hedad de treinta y seis años buen cuerpo abultado de rrostro tregueño." AGI, Contratación, 5550, (1705).

13. The parts of the vita of P. Julián de Mayorga that do not appear in AGI, Contratación, 5550 [see n. 12, above] are taken from a eulogy by fellow California missionary P. Sigismundo Taraval. Taraval, *Indian Uprising*, pp. 257–60. See also Venegas,

"Empressas Apostolicas," párrafo 821. Mayorga had special status among California Jesuits, indicated by his designation as local representative of the Inquisition and of the Bishop of Guadalajara. AGNM, Inquisición, vol. 832, exp. 33, fols. 282–83; P. Jaime Bravo to Bishop of Guadalajara, 6 November 1719, BNM, AF 3/47.1.

14. Venegas, "Empressas Apostolicas," párrafos 822–27. The combination of a sacred name with a local geographic name was standard procedure throughout the Catholic mission world. The number of suitable saints' names was limited, and multiple duplications would have been hopelessly confusing. The local name not only prevented this problem, but also, for converts, retained a familiar, comforting association with their past—most other vestiges of which the missionaries were engaged in obliterating, or at least downplaying.

15. P. Mayorga was considered safe at Comondú because many of his neophytes had been acculturated for years at Londó and Loreto. Later, when missionaries went from established peninsular missions to create new ones in little-visited areas, they took along neophytes from their former missions, both for protection and to serve as examples for the new converts. Thus, P. Taraval took at least eighteen Cochimí from Misión de San Ignacio to help him open Misión de Santa Rosa at Todos Santos. Similarly, P. Tamaral took neophytes from Misión de la Purísima to assist in founding and running Misión de San José del Cabo. Taraval, *Indian Uprising*, pp. 49–50, 62.

16. P. Mayorga to P. Provincial [Alejandro Romano], 20 October 1720. BNM, AF 3/51.1 (transcript in TBL, The Bolton Papers, Part I, item 32).

17. Venegas, "Empressas Apostolicas," párrafos 867, 871–73.

18. Ibid., párrafos 789–90. Jesuit observers did not offer any explanation for the language facility of the Mulegeños, but P. Miguel del Barco's observations about variations in the Cochimí tongue suggest an answer. Mulegé had a large, permanent supply of water near excellent sources of sea food. The place was probably a crossroads, visited by most bands that traversed adjacent lands to a distance of several days' walk. Mulegeños not only learned the variant dialects of those to the north and south of them, but would perhaps have had some traditional roles as interpreters for both. Barco, *Historia natural y crónica*, pp. 440–41.

19. Barco, *Historia natural y crónica*, p. 282.

20. Neophytes given names of benefactors and other notables: P. Salvatierra to P. Juan de Ugarte, 3 July 1698. Bayle, *Misión*, p. 90. Infants named for Jesuits: P. Piccolo to P. Salvatierra, 24 June 1709. Piccolo, *Informe de 1702*, p. 170. Because as many as several dozen converts were given the complete names of local gente de razón, researchers must be cautious. Names in books of vital records must be evaluated for other criteria before they can be said to establish the presence of specific Hispanic people at frontier missions. A single, unsupported entry may be impossible to identify unless the person's occupation, spouse, parent, or child is also identified.

21. Jesuit determination to institute schools at missions is stated in Clavijero, *History of California*, p. 372. P. Mayorga's two schools (for boys and girls) are mentioned in Decorme, *Jesuitas mexicanos*, vol. 2I, p. 495. Schools were installed early in the Jesuit regime at Loreto and San Javier. Ibid., p. 492; Venegas, "Empressas Apostolicas," párrafo 1919. Schools functioning at San José de Comondú and La Purísima in 1755 were described by P. Visitador General José de Utrera in "Nuevo estado . . . ," University of Texas, W. B. Stephens Collection, García Mss., document 67, pp. 102, 103, 205.

22. The wording of P. Miguel del Barco's report suggests that missionaries and soldiers already recognized that large stands of *carrizo* were a sure indication of a year-round spring or stream just beneath the surface. In planning explorations or in setting out for unexplored areas, they probably asked native guides to describe or take them to places with significant growths of *carrizo*. Barco, *Historia natural y crónica*, p. 254. The common giant grass seen today in Baja California and called *carrizo*, is *Arundo donax*, an introduced plant.

23. Ibid., pp. 254–55.

24. Ibid., pp. 257, 259.

25. The planting of crops and agricultural methods employed at San Ignacio undoubtedly imitated P. Juan de Ugarte's pioneer work at nearby San Miguel. Unlike P. Mayorga, the patrician Spaniard, Ugarte grew up on his family's hacienda in Honduras and, after the age of eight, worked at its chores and had a hand in supervising its affairs. Villavicencio, *Vida de Juan de Ugarte*, pp. 3–4. Ugarte's Herculean efforts at San Miguel are detailed in Venegas, "Empressas Apostolicas," párrafos 724–34.

26. See chap. 5, pp. 135–36, for a description of the Jesuit office of *padre visitador general*.

27. Venegas, "Empressas Apostolicas," párrafo 828. By 1755, Misión San José de Comondú was also pressing a significant quantity of olive oil. The

slow-growing trees must have been planted at San Ignacio during the early years of its agriculture. P. Visitador General Utrera, "Nuevo estado . . . ," Univ. of Texas, W. B. Stephens Collection, García Mss., document 67, p. 102.

28. The well-preserved remains of the church at Comondú (now Comondú Viejo) were measured, photographed, and sketched in 1990 by the author with the help of Robert Mosher and Juan Green. The entire foundation was intact and filled in with the eroded remains of adobe walls. The argument for a gable roof and thatch — rather than an adobe roof lying on *vigas* — was decided by the gable design of the later, adjacent padre's house, as well as the difficult problems of distance and terrain faced in getting mainland timbers so far inland at that early date. An unusual feature of the church is an entire floor, now much disturbed by treasure-seekers, of fired adobe bricks.

29. Venegas, "Empressas Apostolicas," párrafos 825-26.

30. Fellow-missionary P. Sigismundo Taraval described P. Mayorga's problems in rather general terms, but emphasized that they were extraordinary, even in California, "I can scarcely understand how he endured such labor and so much suffering. He united them [the local Cochimí], though he suffered much in uniting and caring for them . . . far more than did fathers stationed in other places. . . . What reward he received . . . was nothing but ingratitude, trouble, and offensive conduct . . . insults, evil acts, and ungratefulness." Taraval, *Indian Uprising*, pp. 260-61.

31. P. Mayorga to P. Provincial [Alejandro Romano], 20 October 1720. BNM, AF 3/51.1 (transcript in TBL, The Bolton Papers, item 32).

32. P. Mayorga used the name *tepetates*, derived from Nahuatl, for exposed bedrock. The term remains in universal use to the present day on the peninsula.

33. P. Mayorga to P. Provincial [Alejandro Romano], 20 October 1720. BNM, AF 3/51.1, fol. 2v.

34. Baegert, *Observations*, pp. 122-23.

35. P. Agustín María Luyando came to San Javier earlier in 1730 to assist P. Juan de Ugarte when he became ill. He baptized a few children at San Miguel in December and then P. Mayorga performed for him off and on for three years. Luyando wrote all the entries, so he must have depended on notes provided by Mayorga when the latter acted in his place. The extant pages of all these records are copies made by a later Jesuit at Comondú. See p. 257.

36. Juan Miguel Montaño was the father of a child baptized at San Miguel in December 1730.

37. "Baptismos . . . de San Miguel. . . ."

38. See chap. 4, p. 114.

39. During this same rebellion, Gobernador Manuel Bernal de Huidobro used Yaquis, recruited at Jesuit missions in Sonora, as auxiliary soldiers in California. These men had firearms, the first known to have been used by native Americans in California. Taraval, *Indian Uprising*, pp. 198, 256.

40. AGNM, Californias, vol. 80, exp. 6, fols. 34-37.

41. Taraval, *Indian Uprising*, p. 181. P. Taraval's report of low casualties among soldiers and their neophyte allies is the additive result of his accounts of many engagements rather than any single statement.

42. P. Gordon stationed at San Miguel: Taraval, *Indian Uprising*, pp. 150-51. Gordon spared exposure to the rebellion in the South: Venegas, *Noticia*, vol. 2, abridged & rewritten by Burriel, p. 461. Gordon signed his first entry in San Miguel's *libros de misión* on 12 September 1734. "Baptismos . . . de San Miguel. . . ."

43. There is no evidence that San Miguel was ever dedicated as an independent mission. But because of its economic significance and its periodic resident padre, San Miguel at times had quasi-mission status. For example, in the provincial's catálogo for 1748, San Miguel appears in the mission column as the assigned station of P. Gaspar Trujillo. Piccolo, *Informe de 1702*, p. 308. Some Jesuit writers have referred to San Miguel as a mission after 1718. Others accord it mission status for the short period between 1734 and 1737 when P. Guillermo Gordon was in residence. See Burrus, *Jesuit Relations*, p. 149.

44. Taraval, *Indian Uprising*, p. 167.

45. P. Sebastián de Sistiaga, "Informe y padrón de la mission de S. Joseph Comendú [sic] de California, en Noviembre de 1744." Burrus and Zubillaga, *Misiones mexicanas*, p. 269.

46. Three letters from P. Jaime Bravo to the Marqués de Villapuente, the benefactor who endowed Misión de San José, trace the decline in P. Mayorga's health: 10 October 1730. BNM, AF 4/56.2; 21 April 1731. BNM, AF 4/56.3; 27 June 1734. BNM, AF 4/56.5. The last letter reports Mayorga asking Bravo to come to his side; his feet were so swollen and painful that he performed the Mass with great difficulty.

47. P. Visitador General Juan Antonio Baltasar, "Información de los padres de la provincia de Cal-

ifornia." Burrus and Zubillaga, *El noroeste*, pp. 481–82.

48. Taraval, *Indian Uprising*, p. 261. This house is probably the 19 by 42 foot stone structure, 12 feet east of the portal end of the church, whose walls still stood to heights up to eight feet in 1990. See foundation plan on p. 228.

49. P. Julián de Mayorga's death and burial at San Javier rather than at San José de Comondú is revealed in the 1755 report of P. Visitador General José de Utrera who scanned the books of burials of Loreto and San Javier and recorded the deaths of Jesuits. University of Texas, W. B. Stephens Collection, García Mss., document 66, p. 390. P. Sigismundo Taraval penned a long, fulsome, but informative eulogy of Mayorga. Taraval, *Indian Uprising*, 257–62.

50. In 1720, P. Julián de Mayorga described his mission and its satellite communities at some length in a report ordered by the padre visitador. BNM, AF 3/51.1 (transcript in TBL, The Bolton Papers, item 32). P. Miguel del Barco described the mission's geography and explained why visitas of different missions were located less than two miles apart. Barco, *Historia natural y crónica*, pp. 255, 257, 259.

51. Barco, *Historia natural y crónica*, p. 384. San Pablo, the original Jesuit name for the present site of Misión de San Javier, was extinguished in a similar fashion. Ibid., p. 430.

52. The transfer of the visita of San Miguel is described in Ibid., p. 416.

53. It is possible that P. Guillermo Gordon returned to the South to help reorganize some of his former mission charges at the end of the rebellion. The idea is suggested by the fact that P. Nápoli was returned to California for that purpose after spending ten years in Sonora. However, neither Gordon nor Nápoli was again assigned to a California mission. See Appendix C for additional data on P. Gordon.

54. Dunne, *Black Robes*, pp. 303–11.

55. Misión de San Ignacio — not to be confused with San José's vanished visita of the same name — was the newest and most distant of the northerly missions, founded in 1728.

56. See pp. 229–30 and n. 33 of this chap.

57. After quelling the rebellion in California, Gobernador Bernal de Huidobro recommended that soldiers be taken out of the missions and assigned to the two presidios and to one or two strategically located bases in other areas. Barco, *Historia natural y crónica*, p. 236.

58. Ibid., p. 237. Although P. Barco's account of

this incident was written thirty-five years later, the *libros de misión* of San José de Comondú bear silent testimony to the accuracy of his memory; no entries appear between 20 May and 20 June.

59. Ibid., pp. 238–39.

60. Ibid., pp. 236–39.

61. Juan Antonio de Aguilar's 1732–1735 service at San Miguel is documented by repeated entries in the visita's baptismal record. His *media plaza* status at that time is indicated in AGNM, Californias, vol. 80, exp. 3, fols. 19–24. That he was stationed in Loreto before being returned to San Miguel/San José is indicated by the birth of his son Luis Ignacio at Loreto in 1742 — as reported in Luis Ignacio's militia enlistment. AGI Guadalajara 416, "Departamento del Sur de la California, Compañia de Dⁿ Bernardo Moreno," 7 November 1768, (Chapman Document 1112).

62. See account of Montaño's service during P. Ugarte's 1721 exploration of the gulf. Chap. 4, pp. 100–101 and n. 26. In 1730, Montaño had served as a guard at San Miguel, where another child, his daughter by wife Magdalena Miajuan, probably a neophyte, was born and baptized. In 1733, P. Visitador Clemente Guillén chose Montaño to provide testimony in a deposition to the Holy Office of the Inquisition as part of an investigation of the family background of Esteban Rodríguez's son, Manuel, who was a candidate for the priesthood. The choice of Montaño showed both the length of his service and the confidence of his employers, reiterated in the phrase, "a soldier, resident of this royal presidio, an upright, substantial man. . . ." P. Guillén to Dr. Don Nicolás Carlos Gómez de Cervantes, et al., 27 September 1733. Archivo de la Sagrada Mitra, Guadalajara, ramo Ordenes. FHL Film #0 168 724.

63. "Baptismos . . . de San Miguel . . ."; "Libro de Bautismos, Casamientos y Entierros . . . de Sn. Joseph Comondu."

64. Barco, *Historia natural y crónica*, p. 402.

65. "The total number of natives . . . is 513": Sebastián de Sistiaga, "Informe y padrón de la misión de S. Joseph Comendú [sic] de California, en Noviembre de 1744." Burrus and Zubillaga, *Misiones mexicanas*, p. 268. "150 families live . . . among the several settlements [of Misión de San José]." P. Visitador General Baltasar, "Visita de la provincia de Californias" [1744]. Burrus and Zubillaga, *El noroeste*, p. 465.

66. Since few maps were made and the locations of the headquarters of the rancherías were seldom described, most of the places associated with rancherías can no longer be located geographically. Their

names, like looted artifacts of unknown provenance, linger on as tantalizing evidence of an essentially lost culture.

67. Polzer, *Rules and Precepts*, passim.

68. For two years, P. Nicolás Tamaral operated the visita at San Miguel; he then founded Misión de la Purísima Concepción, the next step northward in the expanding Jesuit chain. Venegas, "Empressas Apostolicas," párrafos 298–304. In 1730, in response to a request by P. Visitador General Echeverría, Tamaral submitted a thorough report on his mission. AGNM, Historia, vol. 21, fol. 171 (transcription in Bayle, *Misión*, pp. 212–19). That report contains Tamaral's outline of a day at his mission. The day described in the present work is based on Tamaral — for sequence and certain activities — and on the libros de misión of San José de Comondú for the specific names and occupations of neophytes. These sources are not cited piecemeal; other sources are individually cited.

69. Barco, *Historia natural y crónica*, p. 268. The training of neophyte singers to augment church services long had been an important part of the conversion plans in Hispanic missions. Spicer, *Cycles of Conquest*, p. 290.

70. Barco, *Historia natural y crónica*, p. 403.

71. Soldiers' duties, contributions in supervising mission labors: Ibid., p. 403.

72. See the case of weaver Antonio Morán, brought from Tepic to San Javier to teach his craft to women, chap. 7, p. 219.

73. Pottery making unknown to native Californians: Barco, *Historia natural y crónica*, p. 190. Women spin, weave, knit: Ibid., p. 209.

74. Bayle, *Misión*, pp. 216–17.

75. P. Sebastián de Sistiaga, "Informe y padrón de la mission de S. Joseph Comendú [sic] de California, en Noviembre de 1744." Burrus and Zubillaga, *Misiones mexicanas*, p. 268.

76. Occasionally, the missionaries betrayed more than a hint that they perceived some positive influence by gente de razón. In that connection, P. Miguel del Barco compared neophytes to gentiles, ". . . those who were baptized in their infancy have gained more cultivated minds and better manners by their exposure to missionaries, soldiers, and others. . . ." Barco, *Historia natural y crónica*, p. 209.

77. Muster rolls or their equivalents for the years 1718 and 1733 are found in AGNM, Californias, vol. 80, exp 3, fols. 19–24. A muster for 1751 is located in AGNM, Californias, vol. 80, exp. 53.

78. See discussion of *memorias*, as these supply lists were called, in chap. 5, pp. 137, 141–42, 149.

79. Salvatierra's request for a master mason is quoted in chap. 9, p. 269.

80. Barco, *Historia natural y crónica*, p. 430.

81. Baegert, *Observations*, pp. 126–27.

82. Juan Clemente Padilla's role as a visitor, not a part of the usual staff at Comondú, was emphasized by P. Wagner in the book of baptisms; in six of the eleven entries in which Padilla or his wife appear, he is identified as "*el albañil*" or she is called "the wife of the mason." Wagner seldom used the equivalent designations for his soldier, his mayordomo, or the members of their families.

83. It is unlikely that Comondú's carpenters were simply local neophytes with special skills or training. P. Baegert made pointed mention of converts trained as stoneworkers, but made no reference to native carpenters. No neophytes are identified as carpenters in the vital records of other California Jesuit missions, and, even in the Comondú books, these are the only carpenters identified between the opening of the books and the mid-1750s — when a well-known presidial carpenter was assigned for a larger project. See pp. 259–61 of this chap.

84. Barco, *Historia natural y crónica*, pp. 276–77.

85. P. Tamaral to P. Visitador General Echeverría, 1730. Bayle, *Misión*, p. 217; Barco, *Historia natural y crónica*, pp. 276–77.

86. Barco, *Historia natural y crónica*, pp. 277–78. Mid-20th century variants of these structures — all built within a few miles of California Jesuit mission sites, and by descendants of 18th-century soldiers and mission servants — appear in photographs in Crosby, *Last of the Californios*, pp. 5, 15, 93, 105, 139, 141, 179.

87. Jesuit descriptions of the construction and use of irrigation ditches a half mile or more in length are found in Barco, *Historia natural y crónica*, p. 283; Baegert, *Observations*, p. 129.

88. Venegas, "Empressas Apostolicas," párrafo 731.

89. Barco, *Historia natural y crónica*, pp. 256, 260; P. Sebastián de Sistiaga, "Informe y padrón de la mission de S. Joseph Comendu [sic] de California, en Noviembre de 1744." Burrus and Zubillaga, *Misiones mexicanas*, pp. 268–69.

90. The only quantitative report of Misión de San José's livestock and produce is found in P. Visitador General José de Utrera's 1755 informe that lists 2,000 cattle, mostly running wild, 166 horses, 90 burras [with which to breed mules], 842 sheep, and 272 goats. Crops for 1753 included 2,400 bushels of wheat, 1,250 bushels of corn, and 800 gallons of wine. The concurrent population of the

mission was 387 people of all ages. Utrera, "Nuevo estado. . . ." University of Texas, W. B. Stephens Collection, García Mss., document 67, pp. 102, 205. The assumption that these quantities of the grains represented a small surplus is based on 400 people receiving 1,600 calories per day from that source — on average, perhaps 80 percent of their total energy intake.

91. Venegas, "Empressas Apostolicas," párrafos 732-33.

92. Barco, *Historia natural y crónica*, p. 424.

93. Ibid., pp. 75-76. "Four small vineyards" at Comondú in 1744: Baltasar, "Visita de la provincia de Californias." Burrus and Zubillaga, *El noroeste*, p. 465.

94. Inventory of Misión de San José de Comondú, 30 December 1767. AHBCS, Religioso, document 3.

95. Barco, *Historia natural y crónica*, pp. 68-69.

96. Ibid., pp. 392-93. Alférez Mugazábal later became a California Jesuit himself; see chap. 3, p. 85; chap. 5, p. 141.

97. A photograph of such a press, handmade in 19th century Baja California, may be seen in Crosby, *Last of the Californios*, p. 91.

98. Venegas, "Empressas Apostolicas," párrafo 828.

99. P. Visitador General Utrera, the source of the most detailed report on Comondú's agriculture, mentions only 6 fanegas — about 16 bushels — of beans as minor crops. Utrera, "Nuevo estado . . . ," University of Texas, W. B. Stephens Collection, García Mss., document 67, p. 102.

100. This section of the present work — devoted to mission organization and particular neophytes — is largely derived from hundreds of entries in "Baptismos . . . de San Miguel . . . ," and "Libro de Bautismos, Casamientos y Entierros . . . de Sn. Joseph Comondu." Data obtained from these *libros de misión* has no further citation — separate notes indicate data from other sources.

101. The appointments of Indian officials at missions are discussed in detail in chap. 7, pp. 202-4.

102. P. Sebastián de Sistiaga, "Informe y padrón de la mission de S. Joseph Comendú [sic] de California, en Noviembre de 1744." Burrus and Zubillaga, *Misiones mexicanas*, p. 268.

103. The full quotation is in chap. 7, p. 199.

104. The peninsular Carrillos, sons and grandsons of Juan Carrillo, were pioneer soldiers and settlers in most parts of Spanish and Mexican Alta California. Several thousand descendants trace their lineage to Juan Carrillo. The Zamorano Index to H. H. Bancroft's *History of California* lists 38 Carrillos that appear in that pioneer work.

105. Juan Carrillo and Ifigenia Millán had other children who do not appear in Comondú records by 1742, but who, because of their ages, must have been present. All were born after 1730, so they would have been younger than Ignacia, Micaela, and Josefa. Sons included Guillermo, Hilario, Raymundo, and Mariano; additional daughters were Isabel and Antonia Victoria. Most of the Carrillo children went on to have significant roles in California history and genealogy.

106. The most extreme case of this common California missionary practice may be found in the baptismal record of Misión de San Fernando de Velicatá. Between 1779 and 1785, P. Pedro Gandiaga presided over more than one hundred baptisms of neophyte infants in which either María Concepción Arce or María Gertrudis Arce served as a godmother — each about fifty times. These girls, daughters of the mayordomo, José Gabriel de Arce, were aged 9 to 15 as these events transpired. "Mision de San Fernando de Velicata Bautismos, 1769-1818," Saint Albert's College, Oakland, California.

107. Polzer, *Rules and Precepts*, pp. 27, 29, 112, 116, 119, 123.

108. All the padres — Luyando, Gordon, Wagner, and Druet — who made entries in the vital records at San Miguel and San José between 1731 and 1746, were unusually erratic record keepers in entering, or not entering, surnames for Hispanic people who resided there. This conclusion is based on comparisons with contemporary libros de misión, those of Todos Santos and Santiago, and with those written during the following decade at the missions of San Ignacio, Santa Gertrudis, and San José de Comondú itself.

109. Baltasar, "Visita de la provincia de Californias." Burrus and Zubillaga, *El noroeste*, p. 464.

110. P. Baltasar was a shrewd and experienced visitor general; his report was highly confidential and based on his own observations; it can be accepted as more frank than the hyperbole common in eulogies of those times. Baltasar, "Información de los padres de la provincia de California." Burrus and Zubillaga, *El noroeste*, p. 485.

111. AGNM, Californias, vol. 80, exp. 53, fols. 17-18; AGNM, Californias, vol. 60 bis, exp. 6.

112. Profesiones. AHH, leg. 16, fol. 55.

113. By chance, the child baptized by P. Barco on this occasion would be one of very few Cochimí neophytes born at Comondú who had significant

later histories. Juliana Bustamante matured and married a casta, jack-of-all-trades Sebastián Manríquez, and became a significant forebear of California people. See p. 261 of this chapter.

114. P. Visitador General Baltasar, "Información de los padres de la provincia de California." Burrus and Zubillaga, *El noroeste*, p. 485. P. Barco operated a facility at San Javier that was referred to in contemporary literature as a hospital. Venegas, *Noticia*, vol. 2, abridged & rewritten by Burriel, p. 194.

115. Ducrue, *Account of the Expulsion*, p. 160; Barco, *Historia natural y crónica*, p. 262.

116. The circumstances surrounding P. Francisco Javier Wagner's last illness and death were strikingly similar to those of his predecessor, P. Julián de Mayorga, who also was taken from Comondú to San Javier to be nursed and subsequently to die. Wagner's death came eight years after that of Mayorga. The date of death is given in P. Sebastián de Sistiaga, "Informe y padrón de la mission de S. Joseph de Comendú [sic] de California, en Noviembre de 1744"; Burrus and Zubillaga, *Misiones mexicanas*, p. 269. Wagner's death in San Javier (like that of Mayorga) is revealed in notes on burials of Jesuits at the missions of Loreto and San Javier made by P. Visitador General José de Utrera in 1755. University of Texas, W. B. Stephens Collection, García Mss., document 66, p. 390.

117. Barco, *Historia natural y crónica*, p. 262. (N. B., León-Portilla, Barco's editor, read the date for this catastrophe as November, 1744, but Utrera, upon hearing about it in 1755, recorded it as an event of 1749. Utrera, "Nuevo estado . . . ," Univ. of Texas, W. B. Stephens Collection, García Mss., document 67, pp. 104, 193.) In 1744, Misión de Guadalupe had a population of 701: P. Gasteiger's "Informe y padron dela Mission de Na. Sa. de Guadalupe en la California a 21 de Nove. de 1744," located in TBL, MM 1716, Papeles relativos a los Jesuitas en Baja California y otras regiones septentrionales de la Nueva España, 1686–1793, number 65.

118. P. Sebastián de Sistiaga, "Informe y padrón de la mission de S. Joseph de Comendú [sic] de California, en Noviembre de 1744." Burrus and Zubillaga, *Misiones mexicanas*, p. 269; P. Visitador General Baltasar, "Visita de la provincia de Californias . . . 1743 y . . . 1744" in Burrus and Zubillaga, *El noroeste*, p. 466; Baltasar, "Información de los padres de la provincia de California." Ibid., pp. 485–86; Baegert, *Observations*, p. 122–23. In his report to P. Visitador Baltasar, Druet pointedly referred to the fact that he administered his mission

without the help of a soldier or servant. "Informe y Padron de la Purissima Concepcion Mission en California & Noviembre de 1744." TBL, Mexican Manuscripts, MM 1716, #16. P. Visitador General José de Utrera, inspecting Misión de la Purísima a few months after Druet's death, recorded observations and anecdotes to illustrate the deceased padre's eccentricities. Utrera, "Nuevo estado . . . ," University of Texas, W. B. Stephens Collection, García Mss., document 67, pp. 103, 206. Druet's entries in San José's record books are terse and in a crude, poorly legible hand.

119. Padilla's move to Santa Ana is revealed in his son Juan Francisco Padilla's statement recorded at San Diego, 20 May 1782, that he was thirty-three years of age and born at Santa Ana, Antigua California. On the garrison list at San Diego, Padilla was identified as a mestizo and illiterate. Mason, "Garrisons of San Diego Presidio," pp. 399–424.

120. Studies of population decline in Baja California are found in Cook, *Disease among the Indians of Baja California*; Jackson, "Demographic Patterns in the Missions of Central Baja California."

121. The 1744 census is given in P. Sebastián de Sistiaga, "Informe y padron de la mission de S. Joseph Comendú [sic] de California, en Noviembre de 1744." Burrus and Zubillaga, *Misiones mexicanas*, pp. 267–69. The 1754 census is given in Utrera, "Nuevo estado . . . ," Univ. of Texas, W. B. Stephens Collection, García Mss., document 67, p. 162.

122. Baegert, *Observations*, pp. 120, 122.

123. Burrus and Zubillaga, *Misiones mexicanas*, p. 269.

124. The people of Comondú Viejo and Londó relocated to the cabecera of Misión de San José de Comondú because of its reduced population: Barco, *Historia natural y crónica*, p. 260. P. Visitador General Utrera's 1755 informe shows that by then Loreto had reclaimed Londó to use as a cattle ranch to supply food for the presidio. Utrera, "Nuevo estado . . . ," University of Texas, W. B. Stephens Collection, García Mss., document 67, pp. 112, 163.

125. For a more extended account of the Robles family, see chap. 10, pp. 307–8.

126. From 1745 to 1746, P. Francisco Domínguez was a missionary at Navojoa and Caamoa on the Río Mayo in Sonora. In 1747, his missions did not operate because they received no supplies. Somehow Domínguez was invited to San José de Comondú where he performed and recorded baptisms in April and September, 1747. In 1749, he was moved from the Sonoran missions to those of

Nayarit. AGNM, Misiones, vol. 22, fols. 24–24v, 103, 105v, 107, 111, 120.

127. By the late 18th century, and markedly during the 19th century, Comondú was a place favored by Baja California gente de razón as a village of residence or a place to spend summers away from Loreto's heat. By the mid-19th century, after the territorial capital was moved from Loreto to La Paz, Comondú was larger than Loreto and the political headquarters of the mid-peninsula.

128. The births in Compostela (now in the Mexican state of Nayarit) of the siblings Cristóbal de Pazos, soldier of the presidio of Loreto; Josefa de Pazos, wife of Hilario Carrillo; and Catarina de Pazos, wife of Antonio Patrón, are found in the baptismal register of the Parroquia of Compostela, FHL Microfilm #654341.

129. "El Alférez Joseph Gerardo" appears in the accounts of the Jesuit procurador in Mexico City in an entry dated 31 October 1749. AGNM, Californias, vol. 60 bis, exp. 6.

130. Estrada and his wife were also from the Tepic-Compostela area; their son José María Estrada was born in Tepic in 1740. 1768 Milicias, Departamento del Sur de Californias, AGI, Guadalajara, 416.

131. At Loreto, P. Rondero was given a draft for 250 pesos as a *viático* (travel expenses). AGNM, Californias, vol. 60 bis, exp. 6.

132. Ducrue, *Account of the Expulsion*, p. 17.

133. One of P. Inama's early entries — early also in his Spanish-speaking career — indicated that Juan Peraza, a Guaycura, had died without the holy sacraments "because, having gone to bed well, he awoke dead" [". . . habiéndose acostado bueno, amaneció muerto"].

134. 7 March 1750. AGI, Contratación, 5550 (transcript in TBL, The Bolton Papers, item 276).

135. Letter from P. Inama to his Reverend Sister, a Carmelite nun in Cologne, 14 October 1755. Ducrue, *Account of the Expulsion*, pp. 150–58.

136. P. Tirsch admitted that some ideas of the ancient natural scientists confused him, but declared that the theories of contemporary scientists left him unconvinced. P. Ignacio Tirsch to P. Rector Miguel del Barco, 16 June 1764. TBL, The Bolton Papers, item 324. Tirsch's general interest in "the animal and vegetable kingdoms" was remarked by Barco in a letter to a visitador general. Barco, *Historia natural y crónica*, pp. 431–32. Today, Tirsch's paintings are the only eyewitness visual renditions of plant, animal, and human life in Jesuit California. Nunis, *The Drawings of Ignacio Tirsch*.

137. Apart from his original research, P. Inama had a well-developed understanding of man's blood circulation, pressure points, and the use of tourniquets. Perhaps his studies had included medicine. P. Barco, in writing about California reptiles, devoted most of the space in his manuscript concerning snakes to Inama's letter and to enthusiastic words about Inama's methods. Barco, *Historia natural y crónica*, pp. 24–33. Inama seems to have been quite fascinated by dangerous and poisonous animals. In his above-cited letter to his sister, he described scorpions, pumas, and alligators. Ducrue, *Account of the Expulsion*, pp. 152–53.

138. Profesiones. AHH, leg. 16, fol. 113.

139. Utrera, "Nuevo estado . . . ," University of Texas, W. B. Stephens Collection, García Mss., document 67. P. Visitador General Utrera's daybook reveals that the last visitador general who preceded him in California was the Sardinian, P. Agustín Carta, who arrived toward the end of 1752. P. Carta's report of his inspection tour was never made public and is now lost.

140. P. Visitador General Agustín Carta omitted Santa Gertrudis from his 1752 visitation of peninsular missions. Utrera wrote in his report that Santa Gertrudis had not been founded at the time of Carta's visit, but the libros de misión show that many baptisms had taken place before Carta set foot on the peninsula. This apparent riddle was caused by P. Jorge Retz's unusual approach to the founding of his mission. In 1751, he and several soldiers made repeated visits to the site to make preparations. On 16 July 1751, Retz began to baptize the people who were there and who would be attached to his mission. Although the mission was a year away from its formal founding, Retz opened Santa Gertrudis's libros de misión to record these baptisms.

141. A *visitador general* was recorded as a participant in California ceremonial life on only one previous occasion. On 26 July 1737, P. Visitador General Andrés Javier García performed a wedding at Santa Rosalía de Mulegé.

142. P. Juan Javier Bischoff to Hermano Josef Goebel, La Purísima, 11 October 1759. British Museum, Additional Documents 13,986, Papeles Varios de Indias, Tomo III, #28. Eight years earlier, P. Fernando Consag, from San Ignacio, 17 April 1751, thanked Goebel for much the same service; Ibid., #25.

143. With the coming of Bourbon rule, foreign literature was increasingly sought and available in New Spain, even in remoter provinces. After 1730,

French and English socio-political tracts were so popular that they were a concern for the Holy Office of the Inquisition. Greenleaf, *Roman Catholic Church*, pp. 164–76.

144. P. Barco, in a letter to the provincial written in 1765, shows that he was familiar with Venegas, *Noticia*, published in Madrid in 1757, abridged & rewritten by Burriel, and recent works of various middle-European geographers.

145. Barco, *Historia natural y crónica*, pp. 432–33.

146. Utrera, "Nuevo estado . . . ," University of Texas, W. B. Stephens Collection, García Mss., document 67, pp. 102, 103, 205.

147. San Miguel's original record books could have deteriorated from excessive handling as they were packed back and forth from cabecera to visita, or from water damage caused by a leaking roof, etc., if they were stored at the visita. P. Francisco Inama's copies of several older Comondú records provide a welcome bonus. Inama had the unique—among California Jesuits—habit of writing appropriate accents on indigenous names, particularly place-names. Thanks to him, the accents on many ultimate syllables can be written with confidence rather than merely being deduced from the few surviving examples, e.g., Comondú and Mulegé.

148. The 1762 census showed small numbers of widowed neophytes (11 men and 7 women), but those figures can be deceptive. Missionaries exerted constant pressure on all who had lost mates to remarry; in the record books, widowed people can no longer be distinguished after they remarried. Lizasoáin, "Noticia . . . ," University of Texas, W. B. Stephens Collection, García Mss., document 47, p. 4.

149. 1755 census: Utrera, "Nuevo estado . . . ," University of Texas, W. B. Stephens Collection, García Mss., document 67, p. 102. 1762 census: Lizasoáin, "Noticia . . . ," University of Texas, W. B. Stephens Collection, García Mss., document 47, p. 4.

150. Cattle escaped from captivity at Loreto as early as 1700—and doubtless thereafter wherever they were raised. P. Salvatierra to P. Provincial Arteaga, 1701. Bayle, *Misión*, pp. 141–42.

151. In 1762, P. Visitador General Lizasoáin wrote out the last census of livestock in Jesuit California. Lizasoáin, "Noticia . . . ," University of Texas, W. B. Stephens Collection, García Mss., document 47, p. 2. All counts of livestock made in 1762 represented increases of 25 percent or more above the figures reported by the previous visitor general in 1755. Utrera, "Nuevo estado . . . ,"

University of Texas, W. B. Stephens Collection, García Mss., document 67, p. 102.

152. Fernando de Rivera y Moncada, captain of the presidio of Loreto, described the circumstances at Comondú in 1767, "There is a sufficient herd of cattle, but because they are wild [*bronco*], and because of the mortality caused by shortages of fodder and water in the last few years, there is no way to know their numbers." Inventory of Misión de San José de Comondú, 30 December 1767. AHBCS, Religioso, document 3. Earlier the same year, P. Visitador Benno Ducrue reported that the missions as a whole had suffered a loss of half their herds of cattle, sheep, and goats due to both the drought and four consecutive years of locust plagues. P. Ducrue to P. Provincial Salvador Gándara, 25 September 1767. BNM, AF 4/70.2.

153. Utrera, "Nuevo estado . . . ," University of Texas, W. B. Stephens Collection, García Mss., document 67, p. 102.

154. Barco, *Historia natural y crónica*, p. 423.

155. By 1744, some thought was being given to establishing a mission for Guaycura between San Luis and San Javier. Barco, *Historia natural y crónica*, p. 423. This plan was never implemented and the people were allowed to gravitate to Misión de San José.

156. P. Inama to his sister, 15 October 1755. Ducrue, *Account of the Expulsion*, p. 156. Inama's shock at the Guaycura appetite for carrion shows the degree of acculturation that had been reached by the longer-missionized Cochimí that he had inherited at Misión de San José. In the early days of the conquest, all California people were described as having such eating habits.

157. San José's 1744 population of 513 is given in P. Sistiaga, "Informe y padrón de la mission de S. Joseph Comendú [sic] de Californias, en Noviembre de 1744." Burrus and Zubillaga, *Misiones mexicanas*, p. 268; its 1762 population of 350 in Lizasoáin, "Noticia," Univ. of Texas, W. B. Stephens Collection, García Mss., document 47, p. 2.

158. Baegert, *Observations*, p. 122. The Californians smoked wild tobacco (probably *Nicotiana glauca*) before the coming of the Jesuits [Clavijero, *History of California*, p. 46], but preferred the domesticated product, which was imported to California to the extent of some 800 pounds a year. AGNM, Californias, vol. 60 bis, exp. 15.

159. Baegert, *Observations*, p. 122.

160. Barco, *Historia natural y crónica*, p. 260.

161. Ibid., pp. 120, 260. The "Inventory of Misión de San José de Comondú, 30 December 1767."

[AHBCS, Religioso, document 3.] shows that the mission was prepared to deliver some of its occasional surplus to the warehouse at Loreto or a sister mission. The storehouse inventory showed 46 aparejos, the pack saddles for mules, 75 leather bags of the type used for hauling grain, and ten [number uncertain due to document damage] saddles, bridles, and sets of spurs.

162. P. Barco's own report on the construction of his church is found in Bayle, *Misión*, pp. 226-27. Barco's elegant little essay on *tezontle* is in Barco, *Historia natural y crónica*, pp. 163-65. When P. Visitador General Utrera inspected San Javier in January 1755, he found Barco's stone church completed up to the cornices — that is, the point from which the *tezontle* vaults would be sprung. Utrera, "Nuevo estado . . . ," University of Texas, W. B. Stephens Collection, García Mss., document 67, p. 101.

163. Some curious trait of Manríquez, a whimsicality perhaps, caused him at times to give different surnames to the padres entering his many appearances as a father, godfather, and husband into the mission records. Beside Sebastián Manríquez — and that was the form most commonly given — he appeared as "Sebastián de Arias," "Sebastián Matías de Arias," "Sebastián Madrano," etc. In the case of each variant, a positive identification can be made because of his constant given name, his listing as a carpenter, or because his wife's name is included.

164. "[A church], which in its size and artistic beauty to surpass all others, was about to receive a vault when the architect, a native-born Mexican missionary and builder, was expelled and forced to depart for Europe." Baegert, *Observations*, p. 125. P. Rotea was the only Mexican among the expelled Jesuits. His church finally received its vaulted roof in 1789, the work supervised by San Ignacio's longtime Dominican missionary, Juan Crisóstomo Gómez.

165. Inventory of Misión de San José de Comondú, 30 December 1767. AHBCS, Religioso, document 3.

166. People who herd cattle or goats or hunt deer in the environs of Baja California missions often can point out the sources of stone used in their construction. Blocks of *cantera*, a relatively soft volcanic agglomerate, were quarried from exposed rock faces. A good example can be seen less than a mile from Santa Gertrudis, upstream in the same arroyo. Useful pieces of basalt, or the related *tezontle* were found in tumbled flows or slides. They were dressed on the spot, then hauled to the construction site. Such a source for the *tezontle* used in building Misión de San Ignacio is found on a mesa at the southeastern end of the Sierra de San Francisco.

167. Utrera, "Nuevo estado . . . ," University of Texas, W. B. Stephens Collection, García Mss., document 67, p. 102; Lizasoáin, "Noticia . . . ," University of Texas, W. B. Stephens Collection, García Mss., document 47, p. 2; Clavijero, *History of California*, p. 370.

168. This elegant altarpiece for Misión de San José was included on the manifest for the California *memoria* in 1761. AGNM, Californias, vol. 60 bis, exp. 6.

169. Coronado, *Descripción e inventarios*, pp. 77-79. San José de Comondú lost at least one bell — and perhaps as many as three — when the Franciscans removed peninsular mission goods to outfit the new establishments in Alta California. P. Baegert noted San José as one of three missions that, before the Jesuit expulsion, had seven to nine bells. Baegert, *Observations*, p. 125.

170. See p. 251 and n. 113 of this chap.

171. Within the mission system, a neophyte who wished to be married elsewhere than at his home mission needed a permit from his missionary. The padre who would perform the service had to have the permit in hand before he officiated.

172. Josefa Manríquez married Salvador Mayoral, son of Pablo Regino Mayoral, a Filipino sailor at the presidio of Loreto. Salvador became mayordomo at Comondú, where he met and married Josefa. Their sons Pedro and Raymundo were the progenitors of the extended Mayoral family in the areas of Sierra de Guadalupe, La Purísima, and Mulegé.

Pasquala Manríquez married José María Higuera. Their son Juan Serafín soldiered at Loreto, received a disciplinary discharge, and became a rancher near La Paz.

Luis Gonzaga Manríquez enlisted at the presidio of San Diego, Alta California, in 1790, and married María Juliana Alanís. Their six children contributed to many Alta California families.

In Alta California, Luis Gonzaga displayed one of his father's odd tendencies when he gave his mother's name as "Juliana de Astorga," thereby using a surname never recorded at her native Comondú.

173. Mason, "Garrisons of San Diego Presidio," pp. 399-424.

174. For Aguilar's birth, see p. 250 of this chap.; early service is summarized in his re-enlistment

paper: AHBCS, Político, document 33; later service in hoja de servicio: AGNM, Provincias Internas, vol. 200, fol. 335.

175. Bancroft, *History of California*, vol. 2, p. 540–41 n. 3.

176. H. H. Bancroft, who had access to Loreto's libros de misión, reported that Juan Carrillo was buried on 4 May 1748. Bancroft, *North Mexican States*, vol. 1, p. 462 n. 67.

177. A succinct outline of the family of José Francisco Ortega and Antonia Victoria Carrillo and its impact on Alta California may be found in Bancroft, *Pioneer Register and Index*, pp. 268–69.

178. San José de Comondú baptism #918, under "Año de 1756": "On the 6th of March I solemnly baptized Francisco Javier, son of my companion, Martín de Olivera, and of Micaela Carrillo, his wife. The godparents were my companion, Juan María Ruiz, and his wife, Isabel Carrillo. JHS Francisco Inama." (P. Inama regularly used *el compañero* to describe his soldier-escort.)

179. P. Inama probably used the word *cacique*, a generalized New World term for a native leader, as local color for his German-speaking sister, rather than giving the actual terms usual in mission documents: *gobernador, fiscal, alcalde* (q.v.).

180. P. Inama to his sister, 14 October 1755. Ducrue, *Account of the Expulsion*, pp. 154–55.

181. P. Hostell to his father, 17 January 1758. Ibid., pp. 173–74.

182. P. Juan de Armesto to P. Andrés Marcos Burriel, 14 April 1759. The Huntington Library, HM 22241.

183. Barco, *Historia natural y crónica*, p. 260. No doubt the valuable terraced fields and groves of San Miguel continued to be worked.

184. P. Piccolo ordered rosebushes from Sonora. Piccolo, *Informe de 1702*, p. 210. In 1748, PP. Consag and Gasteiger personally ordered 15 different kinds of seeds. In 1750, P. Neumayer ordered 11 packets of seeds as well as the aforesaid firearms. AGNM, Californias, vol. 60 bis, exp. 15.

185. Inventory of Misión de San José de Comondú, 30 December 1767. AHBCS, Religioso, document 3.

186. A photograph of a traditional bed-frame and a chair of colonial design — examples made from local materials a few miles from Misión de Guadalupe in the early 1900s — appear in Crosby, *Last of the Californios*, p. 131.

187. The California missionary-chroniclers, PP. Barco and Baegert, each made several references to goods from the Manila ships that found their way to missions distant from the cape. Barco, *Historia natural y crónica*, pp. 246–47; Baegert, *Letters*, pp. 161, 225–26.

188. P. Visitador General Lizasoáin's visit: Lizasoáin, "Noticia . . . ," University of Texas, W. B. Stephens Collection, García Mss., document 47, p. 2. Brandy, tobacco used by padres: Baegert, *Letters*, p. 153; widespread use of chocolate by missionaries, gente de razón: Baegert, *Observations*, p. 120.

189. 1751 Loreto muster: AGNM, Californias, vol. 80, exp. 53, fols. 441–43.

190. In recording the wedding, P. Inama noted that, as required, he was in possession of a royal permit for Camacho's marriage, probably the result of a simple request from Fernando de Rivera, captain of the presidio of Loreto, to an appropriate functionary in the viceroy's office.

191. P. Visitador Benno Ducrue to P. Provincial Salvador Gándara, 25 September 1767. BNM, AF 4/70.2.

192. Aschmann, *Central Desert*, pp. 207–8.

193. P. Inama to his sister, 14 October 1755. Ducrue, *Account of the Expulsion*, p. 156. By 1761, California Jesuit P. Jacobo Baegert was openly speculating about the Jesuit role in an expansion to "Cape Mendocino and beyond." Baegert, *Letters*, p. 233.

Chapter 9: The Pueblo of Loreto

1. P. Salvatierra to José de Miranda y Villayzán, 25 December 1698. Salvatierra, *Selected Letters*, p. 147.

2. In the early days of their California evangelism, Jesuit missionaries reported few counts of families and individuals that could yield precise statistics on family sizes. In 1744, such counts were made in Loreto and the remaining missions. Those figures yield family sizes that ranged from as low as 3.1 at San Javier to as high as 4.0 at San Ignacio, the newest mission at the time. In any event, families were reported to be small when the Jesuits arrived. The missionaries found widespread practice of abortion and infanticide, now known to have been recourses of many other hunting-gathering peoples. P. Lamberto Hostell to P. Josef Burscheid, 17 January 1750. Ducrue, *Account of the Expulsion*, p. 179.

3. By the end of 1700, 35 deaths had been registered in Loreto's book of burials, "a few being of gente de razón." Bancroft, *North Mexican States*, vol. 1, p. 304.

4. P. Jaime Bravo to P. Visitador General José de Echeverría, 19 May 1730. AGNM, Jesuitas, vol. 2, fols. 1–4. Four years later, P. Sigismundo Taraval referred to "the small and almost extinct tribe of Loreto." Taraval, *Indian Uprising*, p. 62.

5. P. Gaspar de Trujillo to P. Visitador General Juan de Baltasar, 1744. TBL, Mexican Manuscripts, MM 1716, document 68. Trujillo also noted that a total of 1199 people had been baptized at Loreto since its founding in 1697. Four hundred of these were the original converts; six to seven hundred would have been children born to neophytes at Loreto; the balance probably included a few additional converts and children of gente de razón.

6. 1755: Utrera, "Nuevo estado . . . ," Univ. of Texas, W. B. Stephens Collection, García Mss, document 67, pp. 112, 163; 1762: Lizasoáin, "Noticia . . . ," Univ. of Texas, W. B. Stephens Collection, García Mss., document 47, fol. 1; 1767: Baegert, *Observations*, p. 117.

7. "El estado de la Misión del Real Presidio de Nuestra Señora de Loreto lo manifiesta el siguiente informe de un padre jesuita misionero [P. Lucas Ventura] al padre visitador [P. Ignacio Lizasoáin] este mismo año [1762, indicated by the dates of previous and subsequent documents in a series of reports]." Bayle, *Misión*, p. 233.

8. See chap. 6, pp. 170–173, "Common *soldados* in California." Thirty positions often meant 32 or 33 soldiers because of the Jesuit practice of employing *medias plazas* (q.v.).

9. Baegert, *Observations*, p. 117.

10. See "California *marineros*," chap. 6, pp. 174–75.

11. See *"Oficiales de rivera,"* chap. 6, p. 176.

12. P. Jaime Bravo to P. Visitador General José de Echeverría, 19 May 1730. AGNM, Jesuitas II, exp. 7.

13. P. Visitador General Ignacio de Lizasoáin, "Noticia . . . ," Univ. of Texas, W. B. Stephens Collection, García Mss., document 47, fol. 1.

14. Clavijero, *History of California*, p. 367. Clavijero's figure of about four hundred inhabitants for Loreto in 1768 agrees well with the numbers reported by Lizasoáin in 1762: 120 neophytes and 274 gente de razón. A visitor to the peninsula just after the expulsion reported that California had a total gente de razón population of about 400. A hundred therefore lived elsewhere than Loreto. Costansó, *Diario Historico*, p. 6 [of the original imprint]; p. 80 [of the translation].

15. P. Salvatierra to P. Juan de Ugarte, 27 November 1697. Salvatierra, *Selected Letters*, p. 104.

The story of the first days of Salvatierra's mission to California is told more fully in chap. 2 of this work.

16. Venegas, "Empressas Apostolicas," párrafos 238–40.

17. Ibid., párrafo 322.

18. Testimony of Don Luis de Tortolero y Torres, Guadalajara, 29 April 1702. AGI, Guadalajara, 134. Also Venegas, "Empressas Apostolicas," párrafo 323.

19. Venegas, "Empressas Apostolicas," párrafo 323. In a letter to Virrey Moctezuma, 31 December 1697, P. Salvatierra specified that *carrizo (Phragmites communis)*, a large reed grass, was used in this construction; this must have been the material for the roofs described by P. Venegas (who was paraphrasing another Salvatierra letter) as "thatched." AGI, Guadalajara, 134.

20. Venegas, "Empressas Apostolicas," párrafos 322–23.

21. The construction of a *ramada* is described on pp. 274–75, 282 of this chap.

22. "Several times we drank out of a hole which we dug in a waterless riverbed. . . . This kind of waterhole provides the entire supply of water . . . in the mission of Loreto." Baegert, *Letters*, pp. 120–21. "The beneficial arroyo that washes at the foundations of Loreto runs only a few times in the rainy season — and then only two or three days after the heaviest rains . . . and is then dry all the rest of the year. But Divine Providence wished that we should encounter a stream two varas underground that yields the water needed by the real and the pueblo . . . when one opens little wells. . . ." "El estado de la Mision del Real Presidio de Loreto lo manifiesta el siguiente informe de un padre jesuita misionero [Lucas Ventura], dirigido al padre visitador [Ignacio Lizasoáin] este mismo año [1762]," in Bayle, *Misión*, pp. 227–28.

23. Ricard, *Spiritual Conquest*, pp. 173–76.

24. TBL, Mexican Manuscripts, "Papeles de Jesuitas, 1649–1769," No. 27.

25. Venegas, "Empressas Apostolicas," párrafos 387–91. P. Venegas's account of church construction at Loreto, although taken from original documents, was written thirty-five years after the facts; the Jesuit historian probably simplified his account so as to aggrandize the legends of the two pioneer missionaries. It is unlikely that Antonio García de Mendoza, an experienced mason, helped to lay out the buildings — as specified in this same passage — yet was not involved in the construction. The same chronicler mentions a few paragraphs later that P. Piccolo had García de Mendoza take a

crew to San Javier to build an adobe chapel and roof it "in the same manner as that of Loreto." Esteban Rodríguez was also present at Loreto and Biaundó. This ex-hacienda mayordomo was an experienced adobe mason as he would prove on many subsequent occasions. The subsequent work at San Javier Biaundó is described in this work, chap. 2, pp. 49–50, 53.

26. Venegas, "Empressas Apostolicas," párrafos 387–91. The missionaries and their chroniclers left only few and fragmentary written indications — and no drawings — of the site plan of Loreto. The church that survives occupies the approximate location of the 1699 construction, a valuable reference point because the supposed remains of the presidio are more difficult to authenticate. P. Venegas has the distance between the structures as *dos cuadras*. A *cuadra* was generally accepted as a square 100 *varas* on a side; the *dos cuadras* therefore represented 550 feet. P. Salvatierra also wrote that the new chapel "se halla menos de un tiro de arcabuz del presidio," ["is found less than a harquebus shot from the presidio"] useful because it allows an estimate of the value of his oft-used "*tiro de arcabuz*" at about 600 to 700 feet. Salvatierra to Miranda y Villayzán, 12 September 1700. Bayle, *Misión*, p. 140.

27. Several contemporary, or near-contemporary, California church constructions have foundations about three feet across, and apparently had walls of a similar thickness. The reported width of this church, 16½ feet, therefore must have been measured inside. If outside, an entirely inadequate interior width of about ten feet would have resulted. Venegas, "Empressas Apostolicas," párrafo 391.

28. Ibid., párrafo 391. Although some use of Indian labor for more modest constructions must have preceded it, this project begun in 1699 marks the beginning of the long process of teaching Hispanic technology to California natives.

29. P. Taraval, in describing a construction supervised by Esteban Rodríguez, mentioned this common Mexican method of making lintels and doorframes. Taraval, *Indian Uprising*, pp. 105–6.

30. Carrizo is the probable material indicated by repeated references to *techo pajizo*, a straw roof. The giant grass was found in most arroyos that had subsoil moisture. Carrizo was specified as the thatching material of the first church built at San José del Cabo. Palm fronds, the preferred thatch of later times, were readily available at both Loreto and San José del Cabo, but would not have elicited the description "pajizo." P. José de Echeverría to

Marqués de Villapuente, 12 July 1730. BNM, AF 4/55.2

31. Venegas, "Empressas Apostolicas," párrafos 393–94; also, P. Salvatierra to José de Miranda y Villayzán, 12 September 1700. Salvatierra, *Selected Letters*, p. 201.

32. Venegas, "Empressas Apostolicas," párrafo 395.

33. The five padres present for the church dedication in Loreto were Salvatierra, Piccolo, Juan and Pedro Ugarte, and Basaldúa. Ibid., párrafos 395, 397–99, 530–34. Although Juan de Ugarte and crew would later find and fell enough of California's giant poplars to build a sixty-foot ship, these trees were too rare and too remote to be used routinely for large structures. Barco, *Historia natural y crónica*, p. 61.

34. Venegas, "Empressas Apostolicas," párrafos 397–400.

35. Ibid., párrafo 400.

36. Ibid., párrafo 399.

37. Baegert, *Observations*, p. 117.

38. Knowledge of this *pozo*, or well, resulted from a bit of informal archaeology performed around 1950 when some pipes were laid and a streetway was cleared and widened. My 1990 informant was Francisco Barreño, a local man then employed as supervisor of the state museum associated with the Loreto church and mission site.

39. Barco, *Historia natural y crónica*, pp. 325–26, 398–99.

40. Ibid., pp. 157–58.

41. Venegas, "Empressas Apostolicas," párrafos 909, 1253–54.

42. P. Visitador General Baltasar's choice of structures with which to compare Bravo's work probably suggested his opinion of its artistry. The building was, and is, plain. Others did not hesitate to say so. The quote is taken from Baltasar's "Informe de los padres de la provincia de California." Burrus and Zubillaga, *El noroeste*, p. 484.

43. Barco, *Historia natural y crónica*, p. 60.

44. The dimensions of Loreto's church are taken from Coronado, *Descripción e inventarios de las misiones de Baja California*, 1773, p. 31.

45. No document consulted mentions moving the site of the church, a major event in any small town — and one usually brought about by necessity rather than by choice. Local inquiry, beginning in 1969, has produced the unfailing response that no foundations or other indications of an earlier church have been reported.

46. P. Procurador Lucas Ventura's report on the

Loreto mission, written for P. Visitador General Ignacio de Lizasoáin, 1762. Bayle, *Misión*, p. 228.

47. Church towers were built in part from light, strong vesicular basalt, called in Mexico *tezontle*. The nearest source of this volcanic material was in the environs of San Javier, a long haul from Loreto. P. Miguel del Barco, longtime missionary at San Javier, left an admirable description of this material and of its architectural uses. Barco, *Historia natural y crónica*, pp. 163–65.

48. In addition to the remarks quoted above, P. Visitador General Baltasar made reference to the funding for both constructions, "[Bravo] as pastor and minister of Loreto had to draw on profits [of the presidio] in order to construct his church and residence." Baltasar, "Procuraduría de la misión de Loreto en Californias." Burrus and Zubillaga, *El noroeste*, p. 491. P. Clavijero, no doubt on the basis of information supplied by P. Barco, wrote, "Father Jaime Bravo . . . built a large church in Loreto, [also] the house of the missionary-procurator, and a good boat that served the colony for twenty-five years. He died May 13, 1744, at the Mission of San Javier. . . . His body was taken to Loreto and buried in the church which he himself built." Clavijero, *History of California*, p. 321. P. Baegert later described the procurador's residence as "a small, square, flat-roofed, one-story structure of adobe brick thinly coated with lime." The apparent disagreement between this and other reports as to the building's size can probably be explained by the different yardsticks used. One of Baegert's objectives was to deflate myths about California that were circulating among his sophisticated, urban, central European audience. He minimized every aspect of California. The statement that the house was built of adobe was probably due to the ignorance of one who never lived or stayed at Loreto for more than a day or two at a time. Baegert made the same error with respect to the guardhouse (q.v.) that was elsewhere documented as a stone-and-mortar building. Baegert, *Observations*, p. 117.

49. P. Visitador General Baltasar, "Procuraduría de la mission de Loreto." Burrus and Zubillaga, *El noroeste*, p. 491.

50. P. Visitador General Baltasar's opinion as to the condition of soldiers' homes was echoed a quarter of a century later by P. Jacobo Baegert. See "Homes for gente de razón," pp. 282–83 of this chap.

51. Baegert, *Observations*, pp. 116–18.

52. P. Bischoff started work on the *muralla* at Loreto: Bayle, *Misión*, p. 230. The remains of this dike were still visible (but very ruinous) in 1826. Hardy, *Travels in Mexico*, p. 244. P. Rotea's account of muralla building at San Ignacio is in Bayle, *Misión*, pp. 237–38. For a view of San Ignacio's *muralla* in 1971, see Crosby, *The King's Highway*, p. 105.

53. During the 20th century, the beachline in front of Loreto has encroached into the land, as evidenced by a comparison of Ing. Ferrer's carefully surveyed mapping in 1900 (AHBCS, Ferrer, Ernesto, "Plano del Fundo del Pueblo de Loreto," Municipio de Comondú, 12 September 1900) with measurements made in 1987, and by observing that the base of a late 19th century lighthouse, once on the beach, by 1987 stood about fifty yards offshore. It is possible that Loreto, in the 18th century, was as much as a hundred yards farther from the beach than it is today.

54. Piccolo, *Informe*, p. 8.

55. Venegas, "Empressas Apostolicas," párrafos 398–99. P. Juan de Ugarte's constructions may have been a few dozen yards south of the original site. The location that the presidio seems to have occupied in later times is somewhat more than P. Salvatierra's estimated distance of easy musket range from the water holes — or, as is likely, the water holes were farther down the watercourse in those times.

56. P. Barco specifies the use of selected *palo blanco* trunks as *horcones*, or forked supports — a practice that still persists in the mid-peninsula, and will continue as long as this type of construction is employed. *Palo blanco* is the only relatively straight-trunked tree available — and its wood is strong and durable. Barco, *Historia natural y crónica*, p. 65.

57. This description of building a *ramada* paraphrases P. Barco's somewhat longer version — and closely matches the practices of present-day ranchers in the mountains of Baja California. Ibid., p. 277.

58. P. Jacobo Baegert's personal recollection of Loreto included an unmistakable reference to *tinglados*: ". . . a few poles thatched with rushes make up the armory, or the shipyard." Baegert, *Observations*, p. 117.

59. AGNM, Californias, vol. 80, exp. 55, fol. 448.

60. Baegert, *Observations*, p. 117.

61. Barco, *Historia natural y crónica*, pp. 64, 67–68. The younger branches of dipúa and mesquite to this day are cut as food for riding and pack animals on trails all over the mid-peninsula.

62. This plan is based on AHBCS, Ferrer, Ernesto, "Plano del Fundo del Pueblo de Loreto," Municipio de Comondú, 12 September 1900. The

Presidio structures may have actually been a diameter or two south of the location shown here and stood on what was then part of the mesa. Watercourses, particularly the more southerly of those shown, may have been established in the present location by the great chubasco of 1829 which rerouted watercourses on the floodplain and destroyed much of Loreto. Today, the mission compound, padre's house, and parts of the muralla survive and can be seen and measured. The pozo has been uncovered and inspected within the past fifty years. The locations and dimensions of other constructions are conjectured from specific statements in documents cited elsewhere in this text. The agricultural plots are based on those shown by Ferrer.

63. In their earlier homes, mainland women may have had contact with or even employed Indian women as servants. But those Indians were already somewhat acculturated by long contact with missions or Hispanic pueblos near their own villages.

64. P. Ignacio Tirsch made paintings of California neophyte women in clothing that appears to have been a simpler counterpart of that worn — in his depictions — by Hispanic women. Tirsch, *The Drawings of Ignacio Tirsch*, pp. 87, 101, 117.

65. The Monquí of Conchó were adept at languages and learned Spanish readily. Barco, *Historia natural y crónica*, p. 176. They were a numerically small group whose habitat formed an interface between areas occupied by speakers of other Guaycuran idioms, on the south, and Cochimí, to the north and west. The Monquí probably understood the languages of both their larger neighbors and had experience as go-betweens and translators.

66. Venegas, "Empressas Apostolicas," párrafos 1787, 1919. P. Venegas uses the word "niños" to describe the children included in schooling. There is no sure way to decide whether this means boys, or is a collective term for all children.

67. Bayle, *Misión*, p. 229. An extensive examination of 18th-century California documents shows a greater percentage of apparently literate men, or at least men who could sign themselves expertly, among those who matured in the Jesuit period than among those raised at any time in the ensuing century.

68. Report on the state of Loreto both as mission and presidio, submitted by P. Procurador Jaime Bravo to P. Visitador General José de Echeverría, 20 May 1730. AGNM, Jesuitas, vol. 2, parte 7. Only a few officers, or soldiers from well-to-do mainland families, had the means to employ house servants. These servants, like the typical mission servants, were castas from Sinaloa.

69. A comparison of records that identify gente de razón by name and condition, or allow those facts to be deduced, indicates that all Hispanic women present in Jesuit California before 1750 were members of the families of employees of the presidio or missions.

70. Loreto's 1733 payroll shows that, of 32 soldiers, 13 were unmarried. AGNM, Californias, vol. 80, exp. 3. The newest recruit, Don Juan de Santiago Romero, had been married three years. Compostela Marriages, FHL Microfilm #0652417.

71. The 1733 payroll for the presidio of Loreto shows the unusually high number of bachelors or men whose families were not in California; of 32 soldiers, only 14 drew family rations, and of 39 sailors, only 12 did so. AGNM, Californias, vol. 80, exp. 3.

72. The careers of individual soldiers are difficult or impossible to trace due to the very limited numbers of payroll or muster documents for the presidio of Loreto, coupled with the padres' disinclination to record personal data related to their employees. Nevertheless, several soldiers were commended for exceptional service or efforts, or were given large responsibilities and trusted with large sums of money yet had short careers in California. Such cases suggest voluntary retirement, although imponderables, such as health, could have been the cause in any particular case.

73. Jesuit writings abound with references to their right to terminate contracts with employees who misbehaved. An example of this practice is provided by a report that P. Juan Bischoff, while padre and procurador at Loreto (1752–1757), "rooted out scandals among the soldiers and sailors by picking out the troublemakers and sending them back to the mainland." Bayle, *Misión*, p. 229.

74. Venegas, "Empressas Apostolicas," párrafos 1760, 1788; Venegas, *El apóstol*, pp. 129–30. Whereas Sonoran Jesuits complained incessantly about the bad examples that both soldiers and civilians set for Indians, for a number of years the California padres were able to use gente de razón as positive role models. This situation was reported in various ways, often rather obliquely, at intervals from 1697 to 1767 despite the fact that virtually simultaneous reports to higher Jesuit authorities, benefactors, and royal officials accused soldiers of many kinds of wrongdoing. See P. Salvatierra to P. Juan de Ugarte, 3 July 1698. Bayle, *Misión*, pp. 81–82.

75. P. Bravo to P. Visitador General Echeverría, 19 May 1730. AGNM, Jesuitas, vol. 2, parte 7, fols. 1–4.

76. Bayle, *Misión*, p. 231.

77. Venegas, "Empressas Apostolicas," párrafo 1919.

78. Despite other interpretations that have been printed, the term *chino*, in 18th-century California, indicated a man from the Philippine Islands. P. Salvatierra mentioned five *pampangos*, natives of Manila Bay, as sailors at Loreto in 1700. Salvatierra to Audiencia of Mexico, 1 March 1700. BNM, AF 3/42.3. Gaspar Molina, a Filipino, was prominent as a sailor and ship builder between 1746 and 1764 — see chap. 11, p. 347. In 1768, Geronimo "Chino" was granted land near San José del Cabo to serve as a colonist "after many years of service to the presidio of Loreto." AHBCS, Económico, document 5. Also in 1768, María Gertrudis, daughter of Pablo Regino Mayoral, *chino marinero*, was baptized at Loreto. This man appears to be an ancestor of most of the people named Mayoral in Baja California today.

79. In a community like Rosario, Sinaloa, whose baptismal records are virtually complete from 1667 to 1814, and whose marriage investigations cover 1760–1831, much of the social structure could be plotted, along with its changes over the years.

80. The survival of a few sheets from Loreto's early baptismal records only makes the loss of the greater part more poignant — not to mention the books of marriages and burials that have been lost in their entirety. All were in existence and in the private collection of Owen Livermore at the close of the nineteenth century when Hubert Howe Bancroft referred to them in writing his standard California history. Unfortunately, Bancroft made no copy of the works. The originals, with the exception of a few scattered sheets, have disappeared, the greatest single documentary loss in the history of Antigua California. If accessible, these pages would provide important data for the study of California's demographics and social history. Surviving sources are various: a few marriages were solemnized at missions whose registers still exist; less direct reports of marriages come from the enlistment and service records of sons, the marriage records of children, and a small number of miscellaneous documents that contain direct or indirect references to married couples.

81. This social ranking of Loreto's community, while based on California documents, corresponds very closely with the generalized rankings of people of different racial background in the greater Spanish New World — as reported in Lockhart and Schwartz, *Early Latin America*, p. 130.

82. Master craftsmen and soldiers were paid identical or similar salaries [AGNM, Californias, vol. 80, exp. 3], but the maestros, with one exception, were castas, and therefore ranked socially below any español. However, as compared to the average mestizo soldier, master craftsmen were older, typically had much longer service, and probably enjoyed more community esteem.

83. See Appendix D.

84. In the New World, Germanic or other non-Spanish European names are far more frequently encountered in areas with Jesuit missions. Of the various missionary orders, only the Jesuits brought substantial numbers of non-Spanish padres. Both Sonora and California had high percentages of middle-European Jesuits, hence the popularity of Saint John of Nepomuk, the patron saint of Bohemia, and Saint Gertrude the Great, important in Saxony and its environs.

85. P. Baegert's facetious reference to "the one and a half carpenters and equally numerous blacksmiths" almost certainly indicates that, in 1767, each trade had one full-time practitioner, and that a third man divided his time between them. Baegert, *Observations*, p. 117.

86. Ramadas of similar construction are found in most regions of Mexico. However, personal observation in the mid-20th century has demonstrated that those of rural Sinaloa and the isolated sierra ranches of Baja California Sur were virtually identical both in materials and design. William Redmond Ryan's sketch made in Baja California *c.* 1848 shows a ranch house in this idiom and that sketch could have been made in the same area today. Ryan, *Adventures in Upper and Lower California*, facing p. 138. Ryan's drawing is reproduced and compared to a photograph of a mid-twentieth century ranch in Crosby, *Last of the Californios*, p. 93.

87. Baegert, *Observations*, p. 143.

88. Barco, *Historia natural y crónica*, pp. 21–22.

89. Goatherding dogs were in use at Loreto by early 1699 — and, by inference, earlier. Antonio García de Mendoza to P. Juan de Ugarte, 24 March 1699. Burrus and Zubillaga, *El noroeste*, pp. 409–10.

90. P. Ignacio Tirsch to P. Rector Miguel del Barco, 16 June 1764. TBL, The Bolton Papers, item 324.

91. P. Miguel del Barco reported that güéribo was an exception to the rule that all California woods were too hard and cross-grained to be work-

able; it was a local wood suitable for all sorts of carpentry. But he also noted that it was scarce, difficult to bring from the sierras, and that it never came into common use. Barco, *Historia natural y crónica*, p. 61.

92. See Sebastián Manríquez, chap. 8, pp. 259–61.

93. No document written in Jesuit times records any sort of innovation. Collections of household, workshop, military, and riding or packing gear, such as that at the state museum in Loreto, or smaller assemblages in private hands, show no variation from counterpart equipment used on the neighboring mainland.

94. P. Fernando Consag, upon encountering pottery in use by Yumans in the northern gulf region, remarked that those people understood pot making well, "a business unknown to the peninsular Californians farther to the south, neither heathen nor Christian, until they were taught by people from *la otra banda* at the instigation of the California missionaries." Venegas, *Noticia*, vol. 4, abridged & rewritten by Burriel, p. 170.

95. Baegert, *Observations*, p. 132.

96. Barco, *Historia natural y crónica*, p. 64.

97. Clavijero, *History of California*, p. 42.

98. Size of Loreto's herds: Utrera, "Nuevo estado . . . ," Univ. of Texas, W. B. Stephens Collection, García Mss., document 67, pp. 112, 163. By the time P. Baegert came to California (1751), Loreto's diet-of-necessity had become entrenched, a fact that he recognized when he wrote, ". . . the españoles . . . do not know anything else but corn, tortillas, and *tasajo*, as they call beef dried in the sun." Baegert, *Letters*, p. 188.

99. P. Baegert referred to *alforjas*, the large "saddle-boxes" in which most materials or goods were stored during trips on pack-animals. He was mistaken in listing them as items made of tanned leather; they were, and still are, made from rawhide.

100. Baegert, *Observations*, p. 132.

101. The quotation used in the text was given to the author orally by Elías Villavicencio, born 1886, of Rancho El Rosario, near the site of Misión de Guadalupe. The 18th-century version remembered by P. Jacobo Baegert reads as follows: *No hay cosa mayor, que un tassajo bien salado. Se bebe agua encima, que es horror.* Baegert, *Letters*, p. 188. Perhaps two centuries of oral transmission worked the small change; perhaps the German-speaking Baegert did not get it quite right in the beginning.

102. Venegas, "Empressas Apostolicas," párrafo 659, número 9. There is no evidence that the Jesuits got a monopoly on salt from Isla del Carmen or were able to profit from it beyond filling their own immediate — and important — needs for salt. In 1727, P. Juan Francisco de Castaneda, S. J., Procurador General de Indias, requested that the Council of the Indies grant the California missions the use of Isla del Carmen as a secure place to raise cattle. Since the island had very little water, this may have been another, more veiled effort to get control of the salt. AGI, Guadalajara, 134 (Chapman document 121).

103. Barco, *Historia natural y crónica*, p. 135.

104. The story of a poisonous fish liver, told on p. 294 of this chap., illustrates how little gente de razón knew about local fish.

105. Although several of the items indicated in this passage as imports for men or women do not appear on the 1725 *memoria* described earlier, all were listed as contents of shipments in other years. AGNM, Californias, vol. 60 bis, exp. 15.

106. See chap. 5, p. 143.

107. See P. Visitador General Echeverría's description of Loreto neophytes' clothing in 1730 on p. 292.

108. Baegert, *Letters*, p. 122. P. Baegert, in his letters and his book, displays more interest and attention to worldly matters than any of his colleagues who left records of their thoughts.

109. P. Ignacio Tirsch depicted the clothing and hairstyles of gente de razón men and women in California in drawings made during the years 1762–1767. These seem to emphasize everyone's "Sunday Best" garb. Tirsch, *The Drawings of Ignacio Tirsch*, pp. 101, 111, 113 [and probably p. 115 as well; note its obvious relationship with p. 117 in which the Indians are identified as Californians]. Tirsch also sketched California Indians in their traditional garb — or lack of same — and as they appeared in a later, acculturated state, probably at Loreto, the most sophisticated center in California. His neophytes appear so Hispanicized — due in part, perhaps, to the artist's ineptitude — that only the captions identify them as Indians. Tirsch, Ibid., pp. 87–95, 101, 117.

110. Shoe making in California is described in chap. 6, p. 171.

111. Women's scarfs: Tirsch, *The Drawings of Ignacio Tirsch*, pp. 85, 101, 113. Hats: Ibid., pp. 41, 45, 95, 97, 111, 113; Faulk, *The Leather Jacket Soldier*, p. 61.

112. See P. Visitador General Echeverría's eyewitness description on pp. 291–92.

113. P. Jaime Bravo, "Entrada al puerto de la

Paz," in León-Portilla, *Testimonios sudcalifornianos,* p. 40.

114. Tirsch, *The Drawings of Ignacio Tirsch,* pp. 85–113.

115. Ibid., pp. 99, 105, 111, 113.

116. See, for example, the extreme modesty of Hermano Mugazábal in the presence of women noted in P. Lucas Ventura to P. Visitador General Lizasoáin, 1762. Bayle, *Misión,* p. 232. P. Baegert, as remarked in note 108 of this chapter, was a conspicuous exception to the rule.

117. Very few gente de razón appear in the surviving burial records of the Jesuit missions. Loreto—whose records are lost—probably saw more deaths because those who were ill for protracted periods would have been brought there for care. Health conditions relative to other places were reported subjectively by various California Jesuits who were offering opinions based on their own observations. Baegert, *Letters,* pp. 158, 184, 198, 209; P. Hostell to his father, 17 January 1750. Ducrue, *Ducrue's Account,* p. 177.

118. In 1709–1710, a great epidemic of smallpox killed half of all California natives. Loreto buried six or seven a day, a great labor—as was feeding all those too sick to forage. Venegas, "Empressas Apostolicas," párrafos 871–73.

119. The first such surgeon in Jesuit California was José Murguía who arrived in 1698; see chap. 2, pp. 35–36.

120. P. Salvatierra wrote of an Indian with a scalp wound severe enough "that several stitches were needed to make the wound heal." Salvatierra to P. Juan de Ugarte, 1 April 1699. Bayle, *Misión,* p. 104.

121. Venegas, "Empressas Apostolicas," párrafos 1327, 1329. P. Clemente Guillén also wrote to P. Jaime Bravo to ask for a leech for himself, and Bravo dispatched the man—obviously from Loreto. Bravo to Marqués de Villapuente, 27 June 1734. BNM, AF 4/56.5. These appear to be the last references to bleeding as a medical practice in Jesuit California. (P. Venegas was writing in 1737 or 1738.)

122. Bravo, "Entrada al puerto de la Paz," in León-Portilla, *Testimonios sudcalifornianos,* p. 41.

123. Venegas, "Empressas Apostolicas," párrafo 871.

124. See chap. 8, p. 256.

125. Barco, *Historia natural y crónica,* pp. 112–13.

126. Tirsch, *The Drawings of Ignacio Tirsch,* pp. 30–31.

127. *Tabardillo:* Barco, *Historia natural y crónica,*

pp. 102–3; *palo blanco:* Ibid., p. 66; *jojoba,* Ibid., pp. 96–98; *cardón:* Ibid., p. 84.

128. PP. Juan María de Salvatierra, Francisco María Piccolo, Juan de Ugarte, and Jaime Bravo sent personal letters, all or part of which displayed marked jocularity. On occasion at least, Salvatierra, Pedro de Ugarte, and Pedro María Nascimbén displayed a sense of fun shared with fellow padres or neophytes.

129. The observance of fiestas at purely mission centers is discussed in chap. 7, pp. 215–16.

130. P. Salvatierra to P. Juan de Ugarte, 1 April 1699. Bayle, *Misión,* pp. 100–101.

131. Ibid., pp. 99–100.

132. P. Bravo to P. Visitador General Echeverría, 19 May 1730. AGNM, Jesuitas, vol. 2, fols. 1–4.

133. P. José de Echeverría to the Marqués de Villapuente, 28 October 1729. BNM, AF 4/55.1.

134. Crosby, *Last of the Californios,* pp. 134–40, 143–44, 173–76.

135. This heightened anticipation of, and intense interest in, locally significant news—and the men who carried it—survived into the late 20th century among the people of Baja California's mountain ranches. Crosby, *Last of the Californios,* pp. 143–44.

136. A list of capable ship captains among the soldiery at the presidio of Loreto is located in chap. 6, pp. 173–74.

137. Documentation by year: 1700, Venegas, "Empressas Apostolicas," párrafos 413–14; 1709, Ibid., párrafos 829–31; 1713, Ibid., párrafos 870, 879–86; 1715, Ibid., párrafos 869, 891; 1740, AGNM, Californias, vol. 60 bis, exp. 6.

138. 1717: Venegas, "Empressas Apostolicas," párrafos 909–11; 1728: Ibid., párrafos 1253–54.

139. P. Salvatierra to José de Miranda y Villayzán, 15 September 1702. Bayle, *Misión,* p. 188.

140. Venegas, "Empressas Apostolicas," párrafos 791–96. Miguel del Barco was familiar with P. Venegas's report of this incident and he knew and described *botete,* noting that although the liver was the only poisonous part of the fish, people feared it so that they picked out the many they caught and threw them on the beach to die rather than use any part for food. Barco, *Historia natural y crónica,* pp. 132–33.

141. For more on the affair of the murdered skipper of a canoa, see chap. 10, p. 315.

142. P. Juan de Armesto to P. Andrés Burriel, 14 April 1759. The Huntington Library, HM 22241. Armesto's use of the anecdote a dozen years later—to enliven a story about neophyte resistance to mission rule—indicates the longevity and presumed

listener interest that such stories had. The unclad hero of the tale was very probably Gaspar de Pisón, an Andalucian then employed in opening a mine in the area described, and recently a soldier in the southern troop. See chap. 11, pp. 364–65.

143. The story of Juan María Ruiz's death is told quite graphically by P. Miguel del Barco, but, since it is in the section that he devoted to natural history, the chronicler omitted the man's name. That detail is provided by H. H. Bancroft (who probably got it from Thomas Savage), who in turn interviewed members of the Ruiz family). Barco, *Historia natural y crónica*, p. 18; Bancroft, *History of California*, vol. 2, p. 540 n. 3; TBL, Cal. Ms. B93–6, Savage, "Documentos para la historia de California," vol. 2.

144. Tobacco was a regular item on Loreto's annual supply list. Baegert reported that the standard container (size not given) was sold in California at the fixed price of ten reales. When mainland prices went up, this agreed on price resulted in a loss to the missions. Baegert, *Observations*, p. 148. P. Venegas casually mentions a soldier lighting a *cigarro* on the coals of an abandoned Indian cookfire. Venegas, "Empressas Apostolicas," párrafo 793. P. Ignacio Tirsch depicted a California soldier, astride his horse and dressed in his *cuera*, holding a lighted cigar. Tirsch, *The Drawings of Ignacio Tirsch*, p. 111. In a letter to his brother, also a religious, P. Jacobo Baegert noted, "After dinner I have some drops of brandy and a pipe of tobacco; that is the fashion." Baegert, *Letters*, p. 153. Earlier, in describing his passage to California through New Spain, Baegert wrote, "our people of this province are strong smokers, however not pipe smokers, but they roll up the dry leaves into little stalks." Ibid., p. 105.

145. Baegert, *Observations*, p. 131.

146. P. Sistiaga to Capitán Esteban Rodríguez, 6 March 1731. AGNM, Historia, vol. 308 (transcript in TBL, The Bolton Papers, item 295).

147. P. Salvatierra to P. Juan de Ugarte, 3 July 1698. Bayle, *Misión*, p. 89.

148. Kino, *Kino Writes to the Duchess*, p. 137.

149. For an example of Loreto's soldiers on duty in Sonora, see chap. 5, p. 153.

150. On 9 July 1708, María Manuela, daughter of Salvador Márquez, mulatto caulker, and his wife, María de la Cruz, probably Indian, was baptized by P. Salvatierra with Hermano Jaime Bravo as godfather. On 30 August 1708, María Rosa, daughter of skipper Juan de León and his wife, Juana María Jaramillo, was baptized at Loreto by P. Julián de Mayorga, with Esteban Rodríguez and his wife as godparents. These baptismal entries record the first children known to have been born to gente de razón in California.

151. Venegas, "Empressas Apostolicas," párrafos 1834–36.

152. The pearlers' tragedy is described in chap. 3, pp. 75–77.

153. In 1704, after being stranded shipless at Loreto for some months, P. Salvatierra, Esteban Rodríguez, and Isidro Grumeque de Figueroa obtained passage to Matanchel from a pearler. Venegas, "Empressas Apostolicas," párrafos 708–11. In 1714 and 1715, persistent food shortages were alleviated only with the help of pearling craft. Ibid., párrafo 891.

154. P. Echeverría to Marqués de Villapuente, 28 October 1729. BNM, AF 4/55.1

155. Utrera, "Nuevo estado . . . ," Univ. of Texas, W. B. Stephens Collection, García Mss., document 67, pp. 112.

156. P. Jaime Bravo reported that Loreto's neophytes were being trained in many crafts and skills by 1712. Bayle, *Colonización*, p. 181.

Chapter 10: A Challenge from Within

1. Although Ulloa, Alarcón, Kino, and Ugarte had previously offered compelling evidence for the peninsularity of California, their reports and opinions were not widely accepted. The complete text of Consag's report on his 1746 explorations of the Gulf of California and the mouth of the Colorado River is found in Venegas, *Noticia*, vol. 3, abridged & rewritten by Burriel, pp. 140–94.

2. P. Jaime Bravo recorded Esteban Rodríguez's birthplace and parentage in a 1731 letter attesting that the captain's son Manuel, a candidate for the priesthood, was a legitimate child and of unmixed European blood, ". . . el S^r. Cap^n. es Español Europeo nacido en Los Algarves a la Ziudad de Tavira Obispado de Faro hijo lejitimo de Gaspar Rodrigues y D^a. Beatriz de Laysa Hidalgos Conocidos y Christianos Viejos." Bravo certification, 18 December 1731. Archivo de la Sagrada Mitra [Guadalajara, México], Ramo: Ordenes (FHL Film #0,168,724).

3. Esteban Rodríguez arrived in New Spain in 1688: P. Bravo's certification, 18 December 1731. Archivo de la Sagrada Mitra, Ramo: Ordenes. Rodríguez served as mayordomo at Tepotzotlán: Barco, *Historia natural y crónica*, p. 267.

4. The longest and most specific appreciation of

Esteban Rodríguez's contributions as a craftsman is that accorded by P. Sigismundo Taraval, around 1735, near the end of the captain's active career. Taraval, *Indian Uprising*, p. 105.

5. In fact, Esteban Rodríguez had no crime or dispute involving gente de razón known to have been reported to higher authorities or to have required formal legal proceedings. His successors were less fortunate. See chap. 11, Capitán Rivera's extended controversies with Manuel de Ocio.

6. Venegas, "Empressas Apostolicas," párrafos 508–19.

7. See discussions of Esteban Rodríguez's problems with viceroys, chap. 3, pp. 69–72, and the process by which the crown came to pay his salary, chap. 4, pp. 89–91.

8. Barco, *Historia natural y crónica*, pp. 268–69.

9. P. Salvatierra to Miranda y Villayzán, 26 October 1699. Salvatierra, *Selected Letters*, p. 200; Venegas, "Empressas Apostolicas," párrafo 361. These events are detailed in chap. 2, pp. 45–47.

10. Venegas, "Empressas Apostolicas," párrafos 360–61.

11. Luis de Tortolero y Torres served as *alcalde mayor* of Compostela in 1702: Everardo Peña Navarro, *Estudio histórico del estado de Nayarit*. Tepic: El Gobierno del Estado de Nayarit, 1946, pp. 242–43.

12. Luis de Tortolero's marriage, presence as a landowner in the Tepic area, and longevity are indicated by entries dated between 1710 and 1729 in the books of baptisms and marriage investigations [title pages missing] from La Parroquia de San Cayetán de Jalisco, FHL Microfilms #707085, 707102. His death in 1730 is indicated by an entry in the baptismal record, dated 2 January 1731, in which the godparents were "Francisco Xavier de la Cruz y Thereza de Jesus, mulatos esclabos de los bienes de Dn. Luis Thortolero, difunto."

13. See chap. 4, pp. 106–7.

14. No official record of Jesuit concessions to Esteban Rodríguez appears to have been kept — the details came out thirty years later during a lawsuit involving Rodríguez's heirs. Manuel Villavicencio testified that, about 1731, he and Cayetano Rodríguez were assigned to tend the captain's private herd of cattle. AGNM, Provincias Internas, vol. 213, exp. 3.

15. Cattle go wild during rebellion of 1734–1738: AGNM, Provincias Internas, vol. 213, exp 3.

16. Significance of wild cattle by the early 19th century: Combier, *Voyage au Golfe de Californie*, p. 303.

17. Don Esteban used the Portuguese form of his surname, "Rodrigues." His full signature, "Estevan Rodrigues Lorenso," may be seen in AGNM, Californias, vol. 80, exp. 3. fol. 20. Subsequent family members employed the standard Spanish version, "Rodríguez." See, for example, the signature of his son, "Bernardo Rodriguez," beneath that of the captain on the above cited document.

18. Loreta Rodríguez's return to California: "Libro de Bautismos . . . de Sn. Joseph Comondu," 21 December 1745; children raised in California: AHBCS, Jurídico, leg. 13, document 47, testimony of Raymundo Carrillo.

19. Esteban Rodríguez sold his rights to cattle: AGNM, Provincias Internas, vol. 213, exp 3.

20. Barco, *Historia natural y crónica*, p. 268.

21. AGNM, Provincias Internas, vol. 213, exp 3.

22. Venegas, "Empressas Apostolicas," párrafos 709–14, 754–57. For the events surrounding Esteban Rodríguez's resignation from and restoration to the captaincy, see chap. 3, pp. 78–82.

23. María de Larrea born in Magdalena: AHBCS, Jurídico, leg. 13, document 47, testimony of Raymundo Carrillo.

24. María de Larrea's parents were Don Roque de Larrea and Doña Josefa Jiménez; two of her brothers were priests. Bravo certification, 18 December 1731. Archivo de la Sagrada Mitra, Ramo: Ordenes. P. Bravo testified to the nobility of her family, resident in Nueva Galicia, in Jaime Bravo's report to Virrey Valero, 1717, copied out in Venegas, "Empressas Apostolicas," párrafo 659, número 8. P. Venegas referred to her, as of 1707, as a resident of Nueva Vizcaya. This difference may represent neither a contradiction nor an error, but rather the changing boundaries of these two provinces at about that time. María de Larrea's family may have included either of two men whose names appear in documents related to the opening of California: Don Domingo de Larrea, in 1696, promised Salvatierra 300 pesos annually to support his cause. Salvatierra to P. Provincial Juan de Palacios, 10 October 1696. Burrus and Zubillaga, *El noroeste*, p. 396. Don Juan Bautista Larrea joined General Andrés de Rezábal in 1699 in reviewing the performance of troops who put down the revolt of neophytes in the Jesuit mission region of the Tarahumara. Archivo Histórico Municipal de Hidalgo del Parral, 1699, document 127.

25. Venegas, "Empressas Apostolicas," párrafo 820.

26. P. Bravo to Virrey Valero, 1717. Venegas, "Empressas Apostolicas," párrafo 659.

27. P. Piccolo to P. Provincial Romano, 17 July 1721. Piccolo, *Informe de 1702*, pp. 216–18.

28. Chocolate imported to California, popular with gente de razón: Baegert, *Observations*, p. 120. Wine, brandy, tobacco available to California missionaries (and presumably their captain): Baegert, *Letters*, p. 153.

29. José de Larrea alférez at Loreto in 1718: AGNM, Californias, vol. 80, exp. 3, fol. 24.

30. José Antonio Robles served as alférez at Loreto in 1733: see chap. 6, p. 168. José Antonio de Robles was the husband of Loreta Rodríguez: see pp. 307–8.

31. Numerous documents attest that each of these people was a child of Esteban Rodríguez and María de Larrea. However, evidence for their birth order and birth dates is fragmentary; neither statistic is firmly established for any child. The probabilities, as listed, are based on a wide variety of references involving military service, education, marriage, and the like. In perhaps the simplest and most explicit case, Loreta's age and position can be deduced from her parents' wedding in 1707 and her marriage in 1724, reported by Bancroft who had access to the now lost Loreto Book of Marriages. Bancroft, *North Mexican States*, vol. 1, p. 448 n. 26. Josefa's birth can be confidently placed after 1717, because P. Jaime Bravo in that year told the viceroy that Rodríguez had six children. Bravo to Virrey Valero, 1717. Venegas, "Empressas Apostolicas," párrafo 659, número 8.

32. At a hearing held in Loreto in 1797 to establish the fitness of one of Robles's grandsons for the priesthood, witness Francisco de Aguiar attested that José Antonio de Robles was reputed to be descended from a judge of the audiencia, in context, probably that of Mexico. All witnesses reported that Robles left a spotless personal reputation in California. AHBCS, Jurídico, document 47.

33. AGNM, Californias, vol. 80, exp. 8, fol. 45v.

34. Testimony concerning Esteban Rodríguez's difficulties in supporting his family, particularly daughter Loreta and her sons, is found in AGNM, Provincias Internas, vol. 213, exp. 3., and AHBCS, Jurídico, document 47.

35. Three of the Robles sons were on the 1751 muster of the presidio of Loreto. Their ranking on the list probably corresponds to their ages. José (7), Francisco (14), and Pantaleón (18) must have been born in Loreto prior to the family's departure. AGNM, Californias, vol. 80, exp 53. Manuel Mariano was born in Valladolid: AHBCS, Jurídico, document 47. His first known appearance as a Califor-

nia soldier was in 1761. "Libro de los Bautismos del Norte de Santa Gertrudis de Cadacaman, Desde el Año de 1751," entry for 30 September 1761.

36. Cristóbal Gutiérrez de Góngora's presence in California: Salvatierra, "Memorial . . ." BNM, AF 3/42.3. The following entry, indicates Gutiérrez de Góngora's status with Miravalles: 9 July 1712 ". . . en la Capilla de el Condado de Miraballes . . . [there was baptized] M^{za}. Isabel española . . . hija leg^a. de el Capp^n. D. Xp^{al}. de Gongora y de D^a. Rossa de la Torre y Redondo fueron sus pp^{o}s. D. Joseph Antt^o. de Abalos y Espinossa Caballero de el Orden de S.tiago y D^a. Isabel de la Torre y Redondo . . . fueron tt^{o}s. D. Xp^l. de Ribera y Mendossa Alferez Real de esta Ciudad y D. Ju. Antt^o. Romero Alcalde ordinario de dha Ciudad. . . ." This from the book of baptisms (title page missing) from La Parroquia de Compostela [FHL Microfilm #654341]. Nearly all the people listed in this brief entry have some direct or indirect connection with Jesuit California. Dávalos y Espinosa was a younger son of the Conde de Miravalle. Romero was the man who captained the *Santa Elvira*, the ship that brought Salvatierra's band to California in 1697; he was also a cousin of another prominent benefactor of the Jesuits, Pedro Gil de la Sierpe of Acapulco. Salvatierra, *Selected Letters*, p. 87. Proof that the Compostela Juan Antonio Romero was indeed the California pioneer and not another man of the same name is found in "Libro donde se asientan los Casamientos que se celebran en esta Ciudad de Compostela [desde] Julio 15, 1727" [FHL Microfilm #652417] in an entry, dated 2 February 1730, for the marriage of one of Romero's sons. The surname given for the father of the groom is "Romero Gil de la Sierpe." Rivera y Mendoza was the father of Fernando de Rivera y Moncada, later to be California's captain under the Jesuits (1751–1767), and territorial governor — after being a central figure in the opening of Alta California. Gutiérrez de Góngora's wife — mother of the child Isabel — was sister to the godmother, Isabel de la Torre y Redondo. She, in turn, was the wife of Luis de Tortolero y Torres, first captain of the presidio of Loreto (1697–1699). The people who supported and manned Jesuit California moved in very small circles.

37. "Titulo de Alcalde Mayor de la Jurisdicción de Compostela y Tepic por tiempo de un año en el Capitán Cristóbal Gutiérrez de Góngora," 22 December 1702. AIPG, Libros de Gobierno, No. 18, fols. 132–35v.

38. Gutiérrez de Góngora's marriage established: Compostela baptisms, 16 December 1706. [FHL

Microfilm #654341]. Son *Cristóbal María* baptized: Compostela baptisms, 23 September 1708 [FHL Microfilm #654341]. Additional sons:

Francisco María Blas was baptized on 20 February 1711, at San Cayetán de Jalisco, the church of a pueblo ten miles south of Tepic that was then the place of worship and ceremony favored by the well-to-do of Tepic. He was educated and later ordained a priest and served in the church where he was baptized. His baptism and entries as a priest: San Cayetan de Xalisco baptisms [FHL Microfilm #707085].

Ignacio Antonio is known from entries dated 21 October 1729, and thereafter for several years in: San Cayetan de Xalisco books of baptisms and marriages [FHL Microfilms #707085, 707102].

Juan Luis acted as a godfather on 30 May 1729, at San Cayetán de Jalisco [FHL Microfilms #707085]. He later served in California, or at least visited; he acted as a godfather at San José de Comondú on 7 September 1739. Comondú baptisms #448.

39. See n. 12 of this chap.

40. AGNM, Californias, vol. 80, exp. 6, fols. 34–37.

41. AGNM, Californias, vol. 60 bis, exp. 6.

42. Cristóbal Gutiérrez de Góngora's son, José María, became a pioneer in opening Alta California. He dropped "Gutierrez" from his name and signed himself: "Joseph Maria de Gongora." His parentage was recorded in: San Diego Marriages #117, 16 May 1776.

43. The circumstances surrounding the birth of Cristóbal Gutiérrez de Góngora's daughter Francisca Javiera (on 22 August 1747, Comondú Baptisms #663) are discussed in chap. 8, pp. 253–54.

44. Marriage record of Francisco Javier Gutiérrez de Góngora at the Sagrario of Tepic, 2 March 1772. FHL Microfilm #654–320.

45. Cristóbal Gutiérrez de Góngora's handwriting may be seen in a Loreto payroll document dated 5 April 1751. AGNM, Californias, vol. 80, exp 54. His signature to that document can be seen in Fig. 6.1, p. 160 of this work.

46. AHH, leg. 284, exp. 31.

47. P. Bravo to Marqués de Villapuente, 12 July 1730. BNM, AF 4/56.1.

48. Certifications by P. Jaime Bravo and Capitán Esteban Rodríguez, 18 December 1731. Archivo de la Sagrada Mitra [Guadalajara, Jalisco, México], Ramo: Ordenes [FHL Film # 0,168,724].

49. A Manuel Rodríguez appeared as an *escribano real* (royal notary public) in Mexico City, notarizing documents involved in various Jesuit transactions.

If this was Esteban Rodríguez's son, his employment as a notary by the Jesuits was probably a further sign of the religious order's determination to assist the family of their valued ex-captain. Examples include 1746: AGNM, Provincias Internas, vol. 7, expediente 12, fols. 134, 136, 138, 144, 147; 1751: Velázquez, *El fondo piadoso*, p. 238.

50. P. Sistiaga to P. Provincial Escobar y Llamas, 19 September 1743. Burrus and Zubillaga, *El noroeste*, p. 450. For Manuel's role in a disputed Rodríguez inheritance, see chap. 11, pp. 340–42.

51. P. Piccolo to P. Provincial Romano, 17 July 1721. Piccolo, *Informe de 1702*, pp. 216–18.

52. AGNM, Inquisición, vol. 832, exp. 33, fols. 282–83.

53. AGNM, Californias, vol. 80, exp. 3, fol. 20.

54. The story of the presidio in *el Sur* of California and Bernardo Rodríguez's involvement are told in chap. 4, pp. 122–23.

55. See chap. 8, pp. 234–35. In Jesuit California, sentences of death or exile were unusually harsh measures. It is probable that the recent rebellion in the South had convinced the Jesuits that stern reactions were needed to discourage further flare-ups.

56. Bernardo Rodríguez served as captain at Loreto for three years before his royal appointment was signed. "Presidio de Loreto; patentes de Capitanes y nombramientos de Subos. Oficiales de Guerra, 1746–1782," 15 June 1746. AGI, Guadalajara, 506 (Chapman document 269).

57. Barco, *Historia natural y crónica*, p. 269. For several years, California Jesuits and their superiors in Mexico City had been debating the pros and cons of retaining the power to hire and fire soldiers. Burrus, *Jesuit Relations*, pp. 112, 226–33. The renunciation of the treasured right to select soldiers depended on timing and political pressure as well as the character of the two captains, father and son. "Sobre la entriega de la administración del presidio de Californias." P. Visitador General Baltasar to P. Provincial Escobar y Llamas, 1744. Burrus and Zubillaga, *El noroeste*, pp. 471–80; P. Sistiaga to Provincial Escobar y Llamas, 19 September 1743. Ibid., pp. 437–56.

58. In 1745, Bernardo Rodríguez ordered, on his personal account, silver-trimmed statues of San José and San Rafael. AGNM, Californias, vol. 60 bis, exp. 15.

59. Venegas, *Noticia*, vol. 2, abridged & rewritten by Burriel, p. 551; vol. 3, p. 193.

60. Account books of the California Procurador in Mexico City. AGNM, Californias, vol. 60 bis, exp 6.

61. AGNM, Californias, vol. 80, exp 50, fols. 420–33.

62. Barco, *Historia natural y crónica*, p. 243.

63. Pedro de la Riva gave his age as forty-six years on 27 February 1747. Dispensa matrimonial, Archivo de la Sagrada Mitra [en el Archivo de Guadalajara, México, 2341 (II)].

64. Kino, *Historical Memoir*, vol. 2, pp. 195–96.

65. P. Ugarte to P. Procurador de Californias José de Echeverría, 12 January 1722. BNM, AF 3/53.1.

66. Juan de la Riva was listed as "adjutant" in the military company of General Domingo Jironza in 1695. Naylor and Polzer, *Presidio and Militia*, p. 602. On 5 June 1710, Riva testified in writing that Agustín, aged ten or eleven, in no way resembled P. Agustín de Campos and was wholly and purely Pima. This document identifies Riva as a native of Parral and "Capitán de Guerra y teniente de Alcalde Mayor." AGNM, Historia, vol. 333, fols. 12–13. Riva signed himself "Juan de la Riva Salazar." In 1721, Juan de la Riva provided mules and muleteers to take much-needed food and other supplies to Juan de Ugarte when he had to put in on the Sonoran coast during his exploration of the gulf. Ugarte to Echeverría, 12 January 1722. BNM, AF 3/53.1 (transcript in TBL, The Bolton Papers, item 35). Pedro de la Riva's enlistment and acceptance at Loreto was probably influenced by these contacts.

67. P. Tamaral to Capitán Esteban Rodríguez, 16 January 1731. AGNM, Historia, vol. 308, fols. 481–82.

68. Loreto payroll for 1733: AGNM, Californias, vol. 80, exp. 3, fol. 22. It is strange to find Pedro de la Riva, a man married into Esteban Rodríguez's family, not addressed as *don* on this payroll. The omission appears to be a copyist's error; in most subsequent documents, Riva was accorded the title. Riva and his sons usually signed themselves as "de la Riva," but other writers, on occasion, gave their surname as "Rivas" or "Ribas."

69. José Jacobo and Mariano José Rivas gave their parents as Pedro [Rivas] and Maria Rodríguez when they enlisted in a California militia company in 1768. The alférez of the company was their brother, Joaquín Rivas. "Departamento del Sur de la California. Compa. de d. Antonio Ocio." AGI, Guadalajara, 416.

70. P. Visitador General Juan Antonio Baltasar stated in 1744 that "the lieutenant who is at the presidio of San Lucas is the son-in-law of the old captain." Burrus and Zubillaga, *El noroeste*, p. 474.

71. Taraval, *Indian Uprising*, pp. 130–34.

72. P. Jaime Bravo to P. Ignacio María Nápoli, 25 November 1739. AGNM, Historia, vol. 392, fol. 258; Testimonial by Sargento Pedro de la Riva, Pótam, [month illegible] 18, 1740. TBL, Documentos históricos mexicanos . . . de indios mayos y yaquis, Legajo primero, documento 4741, The Cowan Collection, MM 1875.

73. The story of California's dependence on Sonoran missions for food, and the 1740 revolt by Yaqui neophytes may be found in chap. 5, pp. 150–54.

74. Virrey Vizarrón acts on advice of attorney general and auditor: AGNM, Californias, vol. 80, exp. 26, fols. 179–182.

75. Barco, *Historia natural y crónica*, p. 242.

76. AGNM, General de Parte, vol. 33, exp. 42. The modern military term "lieutenant" does not exactly fit the rank to which Pedro de la Riva was raised as commander of a unit, but subsidiary to the captain of the presidio of Loreto. He was actually a *teniente de capitán*, an assistant captain.

77. AGNM General de Parte, vol. 33, exp. 38. Pedro de la Riva's promotion was not put into effect until about August 1741, its delivery perhaps having been delayed by political maneuverings. Barco, *Historia natural y crónica*, p. 242.

78. AGNM, General de Parte, vol. 33, exp. 38. The use of Pedro de la Riva's full surname, Riva Salazar, in this appointment provides further evidence that Pedro was the son of Don Juan de la Riva Salazar; see n. 66 of this chap.

79. P. Sistiaga to P. Provincial Escobar y Llamas, 19 September 1743. Burrus and Zubillaga, *El noroeste*, pp. 450–51. P. Visitador General Juan Antonio Baltasar in 1744 speculates aloud about evil consequences in case of Bernardo Rodríguez's demise and Riva's promotion: Ibid, pp. 474–75.

80. P. Sistiaga to P. Provincial Escobar y Llamas, 19 September 1743. Burrus and Zubillaga, *El noroeste*, pp. 450–51.

81. Mariano José de la Riva gave his age as 30 years when he enlisted in a militia company of Antonio de Ocio at the Real de Santa Ana on 6 November 1768. AGI, Guadalajara, leg. 416.

82. Dispensa matrimonial, 27 February 1747, Archivo de la Sagrada Mitra [en el Archivo de Guadalajara, México, 2341 (II)]. The Real de Santa Bárbara de las Mojarras and Chimaltitlán lay 5 miles apart and some 20 miles east of Tepic.

83. Doña María Teresa de Liñán y Mejía appeared as a co-godparent on 10 April 1752, in Tequila with "Don Joseph Joachin de Rivas," her stepson, and one of the three sons of the California

lieutenant. Tequila baptisms, libro 5, fol. 61. FHL Film #228–374. José Joaquín de la Riva would have been twelve when his father married this third wife.

84. Barco, *Historia natural y crónica*, pp. 316–17.

85. Ibid., p. 243.

86. Ibid., pp. 243–44.

87. AGNM, Californias, vol. 80, exp. 50, fol. 423.

88. This Santa Rosa, about two and a half miles north of San José del Cabo should not be confused with Misión de Santa Rosa, established in 1734 in the arroyo of Todos Santos near the Pacific shore.

89. Pedro de la Riva's use of land at Santa Rosa came to light in a statement by Fernando de Rivera recalling the years [1742–1748] in which he served under Riva at San José del Cabo. AHBCS, Económico, document 1. The story of Alvarez de Acevedo's attempts to claim watered land for his presidio is told in chap. 4, pp. 123–24.

90. Barco, *Historia natural y crónica*, pp. 244–45. Placenames involved in this move can be confusing. Misión de Santa Rosa, which had been reduced to a visita of the La Paz mission after the rebellion, was located at the place consistently called Todos Santos, before and since. The name Santa Rosa virtually disappeared from use after its people were sent to Santiago and its site occupied by the mission formerly at La Paz. The long and awkward title, "Nuestra Señora del Pilar de la Paz," had long since been shortened to La Paz. When that mission moved, it acquired Todos Santos as its popular title — and eventually its official name. Meanwhile, the name, "La Paz," remained permanently attached to the mission's original site — the excellent harbor which eventually became the capital, successively, of the territory and then the state of Baja California Sur. Nevertheless, in a variety of letters, reports, and libros de misión, a few missionaries continued to employ the old names of the missions for many years after the changes were made. *Caveat lector.*

91. P. Antonio Tempis to P. Visitador General Baltasar, 1744. TBL, Mexican Manuscripts, MM 1716, #66.

92. No explanation — other than coincidence — has been advanced for the simultaneous presence in California of Scotch missionary William Gordon (1730–1739), English pilot William Strafford (1719–1746), and English soldier Joseph Harris (before 1739–1744). All were accepted members of local establishments.

93. Harris stationed at Todos Santos and Ignacio Arriz reputed to be his child: AHBCS, Económico, leg. 9, document 3 [in which the name is given as Arris and Harris]. Harris stationed at Todos Santos and married to a Pericú: "Mision Santiago, Fragmentos de Registro de Bautismos," 3 May 1742. [All pages in this sheaf of records with dates between 1739 and 1748 were signed by P. Bernardo Zumziel and belong to a lost book of Todos Santos baptisms.]

94. AHBCS, Económico, document 3.

95. AHBCS, Económico, document 3. Ignacio Arriz accompanied Capitán Rivera to Alta California in 1769 and spent the rest of his life there, or on the peninsula's northern frontier. His career is sketched in Crosby, *Doomed to Fail*, pp. 7–10, 22–23.

96. Jacobo and Mariano, sons of Pedro de la Riva, described as tall: "Departamento del Sur de la California, Compa. de d. Antonio Ocio." AGI, Guadalajara, 416.

97. Riva ordered personal adornment, luxuries, etc.: AGNM, Californias, vol. 60 bis, exp. 15, in years 1748 and 1750.

98. AGNM, Californias, vol. 60 bis, exp. 15.

99. On 10 November 1750, Riva was charged for 6 months of schooling, board and supervision at the Colegio de San Ildefonso, Mexico City: AGNM, Californias, vol. 60 bis, exp. 6. Jacobo Rivas's letter of 21 April 1763 vis-a-vis a debt incurred while attending the Colegio de San Juan: AHH, leg. 286, exp. 14. All three sons of Pedro de la Riva and María Rodríguez were literate.

100. Material in this section that pertains to the rebellion in the South is taken from Taraval, *Indian Uprising*, pp. 34–66, unless a separate footnote indicates another source.

101. See pp. 303–5.

102. P. Guillermo Gordon was the missionary nominally assigned to La Paz, but he was actually serving at San Miguel at this time. See chap. 4, p. 113, and chap. 8, pp. 232–34. For more on Manuel Andrés Romero, see chap. 4, pp. 115–16.

103. Taraval, *Indian Uprising*, p. 60.

104. Ibid., p. 61.

105. AGNM, Californias, vol. 80, exp. 3.

106. The society of New Spain practiced a universal and often exaggerated deference to all peninsular Spaniards, no matter what their previous status or occupation. Brading, *Miners and Merchants*, p. 109.

107. In 1766, Manuel de Ocio gave his age as 66 years: AGNM, Provincias Internas, vol. 7, exp. 10, fol. 71.

108. P. Baegert called Manuel de Ocio an Andalucian, reports that he was trained as a black-

smith: Baegert, *Observations*, p. 46. P. Taraval stated that Ocio came from Old Castile: Taraval, *Indian Uprising*, p. 55.

109. AGNM, Provincias Internas, vol. 120, exp. 1.

110. AGNM, Provincias Internas, vol. 7, Exp. 6, fol. 44.

111. Manuel de Ocio's marriage to Rosalía Rodríguez and her death before 1754: AGNM, Provincias Internas, vol. 213, exp. 3; AGNM, Provincias Internas, vol. 120, exp. 1, fol. 11.

112. The beach described by Barco is actually closer to 27 30' N. Lat. Latitude calculations in 18th-century California regularly ran between half a degree and a full degree too high. The great die-off of pearl bearing bivalves may have been due to a storm, but it may also have been related to the fact that this very area lay near the northern edge of the pearl oyster's range and the southern margin of that of a clam that also forms pearls. Rodríguez, *Descripción y toponimia*, p. 18; Gerhard, "Pearl Fishing in Lower California, 1533–1830," p. 239.

113. Barco, *Historia natural y crónica*, p. 137. The present description of Manuel de Ocio's pearling activities paraphrases or quotes Ibid., pp. 136–42.

114. Ibid., pp. 141–42.

115. Ibid, p. 142.

116. Rodríguez, *Descripción y toponimia*, passim; William Strafford, "Descripcion de las Californias desde el Cavo de Sn. Lucas q. esta al sur Sus misiones Puertos Baias Plazeres Naciones Reduzidas y Gentiles . . . ," 18 January 1746. BNM, AF 4/65.1 (transcript and translation in TBL, The Bolton Papers, item 45); Esteva, *Memoria sobre la pesca de la perla*, pp. 11–14 (see also pocketed maps); Gerhard, "Pearl Fishing in Lower California, 1533–1830."

117. Barco, *Historia natural y crónica*, pp. 137.

118. Gerhard, "Pearl Fishing in Lower California, 1533–1830."

119. Yaqui Indians were identified as the principal pearl divers in the Mar de Cortés in testimony given at the 1740–1742 hearings, held in Guadalajara by the Marqués del Castillo de Aysa and described on pp. 323–24. AGNM, Provincias Internas, vol. 87, exp. 8, fols. 151–62.

120. Barco, *Historia natural y crónica*, pp. 137–39, 144.

121. Ibid., p. 142.

122. Most pearls imperfect: Ibid., p. 142.

123. Pearls the true basis of Manuel de Ocio's fortune: Ibid., p. 153; Baegert, *Observations*, p. 46.

124. A record of Aysa's hearings, 1740–1742: "Testimonio de los Autos formados por el M Ille. Sr

Dn Franco de Aisa Marqués del Castillo de Aysa del Consejo de S. M. su Presidente Governador, y Cappn. Gral de este Reino. Sobre los Puertos de la California, y demas Parajes de Pesqueria de Perlas, Abrigo de Embarcaciones, y demas como adentro se expresa. Año de 1742." AGNM, Provincias Internas, vol. 87, exp. 8, fols. 151–97v.

125. Francisco de Aysa to the King, 3 June 1740; testimony about events in California, 19 July–19 September 1740, AGI, Guadalajara, 135. For Gobernador Bernal de Huidobro's anti-Jesuit stance, see chap. 4, pp. 117–21.

126. Mota y Padilla, Matías de la. *Historia de la conquista de Nueva Galicia*. Guadalajara: Talleres gráficos de Gallardo y Alvarez del Castillo, 1920 (Original edition in 1742).

127. Vidargas del Moral, "Navegación y comercio en el Golfo de California," pp. 33–46.

128. Sánchez Leñero family origins, commercial network: Van Young, *Hacienda and Market*, pp. 145, 155–56.

129. Manuel de Ocio and Juan Manuel Sánchez Leñero buy the right to collect the royal fifth: AHH, leg. 334, exp. 6.

130. Although Manuel de Ocio may have come from a family with no distinction, had little education, and worked only as a soldier, he had been born a peninsular Spaniard. This advantage overcame most social obstacles and gave Ocio an entree with merchants, most of whom were also Spaniards. Brading, *Miners and Merchants*, pp. 104, 109. For a view of typical relationships between Guadalajara merchant creditors and their clients, see Greenow, *Credit and Socioeconomic Change*, passim.

131. "Meritos de Dn. Antonio Ygnacio de Mena, Theniente Coronel de Milicias Provinciales . . ." AGI, Guadalajara, 311 (tira 1).

132. AIPG, Protocolos de Manuel Mena (mayor), tomo XXVI, fols. 204–8.

133. In typical fashion, the purchase agreement for property in Guadalajara listed the names of the four adjacent property owners. AIPG, Protocolos de Manuel Mena (mayor), tomo XXVI, fols. 527–29.

134. Purchase in May 1744: AIPG, Protocolos de Manuel Mena (mayor), tomo XXVII, fols. 219–21. Purchase in March 1745: AIPG, Protocolos de Alejo de Santa María Maraver, tomo X, fols. 122–24, 125–26. Total number of house purchases indicated: AIPG, Protocolos de Manuel Francisco Nogueras, tomo IV, fols. 14–16.

135. Barco, *Historia natural y crónica*, pp. 141, 153.

136. Manuel de Ocio's early success in the southern *placeres* resulted in part from events that had slowed or halted pearling in the area during the previous decade. In 1730, storms destroyed or damaged many pearling craft. P. Bravo to Marqués de Villapuente, 10 October 1730. BNM, AF 4/56.2. From 1734 to 1738, the neophyte rebellion in *el Sur* stopped most pearling activity and, in 1740 and 1741, the Yaqui rebellion in Sonora disrupted the supply of divers and supplies. Thus, for a dozen years, the bivalves that produced the pearls had at least a partial respite from the annual assaults of pearl-seekers.

137. The proposed relationship between Manuel de Ocio and Antonio Ignacio de Mena, miner and merchant, was typical in the development of mines on the northwest frontier of New Spain. Brading, *Miners and Merchants*, pp. 149–52; Van Young, *Hacienda and Market*, p. 146; Kicza, *Colonial Entrepreneurs*, p. 56.

138. Real Cédula of 13 November 1744. AGNM, Misiones, tomo 22, fols. 196–210.

139. "Meritos de Antonio Ygnacio de Mena," AGI, Guadalajara, 311 (tira 1). In this listing of *meritos*, it was claimed that Mena started this company with Ocio in 1743. It seems likely that the earliness of the date was exaggerated for effect; the climate for such a venture—and Ocio's actions—suggest 1745–1746 as a more probable time.

140. P. Juan de Ugarte to Virrey Baltasar de Zúñiga y Guzmán, Marqués de Valero Ayamonte, 15 March 1721. BNM, AF 3/48.4. Ugarte reported sending Don Fermín Téllez (who was from the silver-mining center of Alamos, Sonora) to collect ore from the area that later became the modern [1890–1950] copper mines at Santa Rosalía. Ugarte to Virrey Valero, 15 March 1721. León-Portilla, *Testimonios sudcalifornianos*, pp. 74–80.

141. Rodríguez, *Descripción y toponimia indígena de California, 1740*, p. 12.

142. See chap. 4, p. 105.

143. See chap. 4, pp. 122–24.

144. A business relationship between Manuel de Ocio and Pedro de la Riva is suggested by several documents in which Ocio designated Riva to receive property that he had claimed, or, vice versa, where Ocio represented that he could act as Riva's agent. See AHH, Temporalidades, leg. 298, exp. 4, and AGNM, General de Parte, vol. 39, exp. 144.

145. Significantly, Antonio Ignacio de Mena later said that a primary purpose of his venture with Manuel de Ocio was "to civilize the warlike nations that infested the land," and he mentioned the Uchití by name. "Meritos de Antonio Ygnacio de Mena," AGI, Guadalajara, 311 (tira 1).

146. See the account of Pedro de la Riva's campaign against the Uchití on p. 315.

147. *Nuestra Señora del Carmen* wrecked: AGNM, Californias, vol. 68, exp. 2, fols. 44–53. Jesuits rent use of Ocio's new ships: AGNM, Californias, vol. 60 bis, exp 6.

148. Although no known records list the names or places of origin of Manuel de Ocio's employees, there is other evidence. When a militia was formed in that locale less than twenty years later, about a hundred of the men who were enlisted gave birthplaces off the peninsula. Thirty of those were born in such mining centers as Guanajuato, Zacatecas, San Luis Potosí, Parral, Hostotipaquillo, Cosalá, Rosario, Río Chico, Baroyeca, and Alamos. Lists of the 1768 militia companies are found in AGI, Guadalajara, 416. By 1768, and probably from their inception, Yaquis and Mayos from Sonora were being hired to work in California mines. Navarro García, *Don José de Gálvez*, p. 177.

149. Mineworkers at Santa Ana in the early years had wives and children with them. Barco, *Historia natural y crónica*, pp. 319–20; Baegert, *Observations*, p. 47. Therefore, it is not likely that a majority were mainland neophytes, who usually left their families at home. Later, when families had proved to be difficult to sustain and when no one retained hopes for raising Santa Ana's status to that of a *villa*, the less encumbered and less expensive Yaqui workers were sought.

150. AGNM, General de Parte, vol. 39, exp. 144.

151. Barco, *Historia natural y crónica*, pp. 319–20; Baegert, *Observations*, p. 47.

152. P. Sistiaga to P. Provincial Escobar y Llamas, 19 September 1743. Burrus and Zubillaga, *El noroeste*, pp. 437–56; Baltasar, "Sobre la entrega de la administración del presidio de Californias," Ibid., pp. 471–80.

153. P. Sistiaga to P. Procurador General Pedro Ignacio Altamirano, 20 April 1747. The Bancroft Library Collection "The Society of Jesus: Letters and Reports relating to Jesuits in Lower California, Sinaloa, Sonora, and Arizona." MM 1716, vol. 45.

154. Pedro de la Riva was the acting commandant at Loreto in early 1751: AGNM, Californias, vol. 80, exp. 54.

155. Pedro de la Riva orders personal adornment: AGNM, Californias, vol. 60 bis, exp. 15.

156. The California Jesuits had renounced this power in 1744. Barco, *Historia natural y crónica*, p. 269.

157. See pp. 323–24.

158. The padre visitador's role in electing a captain is spelled out in P. Sistiaga to P. Provincial Escobar y Llamas, 19 September 1743. Burrus and Zubillaga, *El noroeste*, p. 446. Bernardo Rodríguez's death is recalled in Barco, *Historia natural y crónica*, p. 269.

159. Virrey Sr. Conde de Revillagigedo to P. Procurador Juan de Armesto, "Nombramiento de Rivera y Moncada" [as captain of the Presidio of Loreto], 27 March 1751, in Aguirre, *Documentos para la historia de Baja California*, documento número 4, p. 41.

160. AGNM, Californias, vol. 80, exp. 54.

161. Temporary ratings are discussed in chap. 6, p. 169.

162. Rivera y Moncada, *Diario*, p. xli.

Chapter 11: The Mission Yields a Share of California

1. Barco, *Historia natural y crónica*, pp. 269–70.

2. Fernando de Rivera receives the *bastón* as the token of his command: "Cargo los costos del despacho del nuevo Capitan que fueren 90 pesos, y 20 pesos mas de un Baston con puño de plata que de orden del Padre Armesto remito para el mismo." 31 March 1751, Accounts of the Procurador for the Californias in Mexico City, AGNM, Californias, vol. 60 bis, exp. 6. This ancient symbol accounts for the Spanish expression, *empuñar el bastón*, "to take the command."

3. In 1741, the galleon's pilot died at San José del Cabo, leaving several thousand pesos in Esteban Rodríguez's care. The captain notified authorities and awaited instructions. The funds proved to belong to a partnership; the pilot's executors and the courts made a long business of concluding the case. Before it was settled, Rodríguez had died and the Jesuits had become caretakers of the money—which was finally awarded to claimants and taken off Jesuit books. AGNM, Provincias Internas, vol. 7, exp. 12; AGNM, Californias, vol. 60 bis, exp. 6 (entry dated 8 October 1741).

4. Different authorities assign different dates for the "founding" of Misión de Santa Gertrudis. P. Jorge Retz opened the book of baptisms with entry #1 on 16 July 1751.

5. P. Bischoff's reforms were recounted by P. Lucas Ventura in his 1762 report for Visitador General Lizasoáin. They betray the interesting fact that, although the captain by that time nominally had the power to hire and fire soldiers, the padre

was unequivocally reported to have identified the culprits, and seen to their banishment to *la otra banda*. Bayle, *Misión*, p. 229. Bischoff's power, and his success in these reforms, also cast some doubt on the performances of his two predecessors, PP. Gaspar de Trujillo and Juan de Armesto. Had they been diligent, it would seem that matters at Loreto would not have gotten so out of hand.

6. Francisco Javier de Ochoa born at El Fuerte, enlisted at Loreto on 5 September 1751: TBL, The Eldredge Papers.

7. Ostimuri was a jurisdiction, sometimes independent, sometimes subordinate to Sonora, located between the Ríos Mayo and Yaqui and bounded on the west by the gulf and on the east by the heights of the Sierra Madre Occidental. Gerhard, *North Frontier of New Spain*, p. 264.

8. AHBCS, Político, document 47.

9. Joseph Velazquez (as he signed as a witness: AGNM, Provincias Internas, vol. 211, exp. 15, fol. 252), born 1721 in San Ildefonso de Ostimuri, enlisted in California in 1751—as shown in his military service record, AGI, Guadalajara, 286 (Chapman document number 4909). His daughter Francisca was born in La Cienega, Sonora, in 1746; that data taken from her death notice, transcribed in Pablo L. Martinez, *Guía Familiar*, México, D.F.: Editorial Baja California, 1965, p. 483.

10. The data given on Francisco de Aguiar y Manzano, plus information that he was born in 1727 and enlisted by Rivera at Loreto on 10 January 1752, is taken from the document by which he was re-enlisted in 1775. AHBCS, Político, document 32.

11. Fernando de Rivera testified in early September, 1766, that he had come to California twenty-four years and some months previously. AGNM, Provincias Internas, vol. 7, exp. 11.

12. Cristóbal de Rivera y Mendoza was probably the son of a Spaniard of the same name, born in the village of Chillón, Estremadura, and resident in New Spain after 1680. No record of this immigrant's first wife is available, but he remarried in 1689 in Mexico City to a *criolla* of that city, María Francisca Durán y Zamora. Rubio Mañe, "Gente de España en la Ciudad de México: año de 1689."

13. Cristóbal de Rivera y Mendoza held the post of *escribano público y real* by 21 February 1707: Biblioteca de Jalisco, Ramo Judicial Civil, C23–11–317. He had ascended to the position of *alcalde ordinario* at Compostela by 18 December 1709: Baptismal record of La Parroquia de la Ciudad de Compostela [FHL Film #654341]. Rivera y Mendoza's bid to

retain the position of *alférez real* is found in "Testimonio sobre la venta de oficios ... de Alferez de Compostela a D. Xbal de Rivera y Mendoza ... año de 1723," AGI, Guadalajara, 93. Multiple entries between 7 March 1711 and 14 November 1724 in the vital records of La Parroquia de la Ciudad de Compostela show that he had obtained the post before the earlier date and served during the intervening years. [FHL Films #654341, 652417.]

14. Fisher, *Viceregal Administration*, pp. 74–75.

15. Entry of 2 February 1723, Compostela Baptisms, FHL film #654341.

16. Rivera y Mendoza's marriage to Inez de Guzmán y Valle [often given as Valle y Guzmán] is proved by multiple entries between 18 December 1709 and 11 October 1717 in the vital records of La Parroquia de la Ciudad de Compostela [FHL Microfilms #654341, 652417]. Rivera y Mendoza's marriage to Josefa Ramón de Moncada is shown in a baptismal entry on 17 April 1718, La Parroquia de la Ciudad de Compostela [FHL Film #654341].

17. Fernando de Rivera y Moncada's baptism on 14 November 1724 appears in the record book of La Parroquia de la Ciudad de Compostela [FHL Film #654341]. Fernando de Rivera's godfather, Basilio Ramos, apparently was the man for whom the infant's older half-brother Basilio had been named. Fernando de Rivera's uncle, Fernando Ramón de Moncada, was the brother of Josefa Ramón de Moncada and the husband of Micaela de Guzmán y Valle, sister of the deceased Inez de Guzmán y Valle, as shown in a baptism of 10 August and 9 November 1718 in the same book.

18. The death of Fernando de Rivera's father is indicated in Compostela marriages, entry on 24 February 1733 [FHL Film #652417].

19. Three of several instances in which Fernando de Rivera sent money to his mother: 200 pesos on 16 May 1752; 132 pesos in late 1753; 125 pesos on 15 March 1754. AGNM, Californias, vol. 60 bis, exp. 6.

20. No contemporary documents attest to Fernando de Rivera's pre-captaincy career in California. All the information for this section is taken from retrospective writings, largely by Rivera himself, such as AHBCS, Económico, document 3.

21. AGNM, Provincias Internas, vol. 7, exp. 10.

22. AHBCS, Económico, document 3.

23. For details of the Pericú attack on a Manila ship, see chap. 4, pp. 116–17.

24. Schurz, *The Manila Galleon*, pp. 330–36.

25. Unless otherwise noted, all information on the visit of the *Hervating* to California is taken from

Gerhard, "A Dutch Trade Mission to New Spain," pp. 221–26.

26. Less than five years before the *Hervating* incident, Virrey Fuenclara was urged to take active measures, even of his own invention and on his own initiative, to combat contraband commerce. Fisher, *Viceregal Administration*, p. 19.

27. "Debe 50 pesos pagados a Juan de Estrada ... con la que occurrio a Mexico dicho Estrada, en 13 de Abril de 1747. ..." Accounts of the Procurador de Californias in Mexico City. AGNM, Californias, vol. 60 bis, exp. 6.

28. Testimony of José de Robles and Fernando de Rivera in AGNM, Provincias Internas, vol. 7, exp. 11.

29. The relationship between miners and battles with Indians is explained in chap. 10, pp. 325–27.

30. For the text of Fernando de Rivera's preliminary appointment, see chap. 10, pp. 331.

31. AGNM, General de Parte, vol. 38, exp. 91.

32. AHH Temporalidades, leg. 298, exp. 4, fol. 57.

33. In reporting to a viceroy, minor officials, such as presidial captains, were accustomed—and, no doubt, expected—to express themselves in highly deferential terms. But there were degrees of conformity. In 1742, Bernardo Rodríguez was asked to submit written testimony about California's economic resources for hearings called by the Marqués del Castillo de Aysa, president of the Audiencia de Guadalajara. Rodríguez followed his testimony with a passage urging his lordship to consult others so that they might offset the failings of his unworthy report. He closed by apologizing that he was but a poor, California-born soldier ["... y asimismo el disculparme con que soy un pobre Soldado rustico y Californio"]. AGNM, Provincias Internas, vol. 87, exp. 8, fol. 189v. In 1748, Rodríguez again employed a more subservient style than that of his father or his successor when he signed an informe directed to the viceroy, "Your faithful servant Bernardo Rodríguez de la Rea kisses the hands and feet of Your Excellency. ..." Rodríguez to Virrey Revillagigedo, 1 October 1748. AGNM, Californias, vol. 80, exp. 50, fol. 420.

34. There is no indication of the person or persons who appraised Bernardo Rodríguez's estate. It is probable that the figure at which they arrived represented replacement value, not liquidation value—two very different figures on a cash-poor frontier.

35. AHH, Temporalidades, leg. 298, exp. 4. This

material is repeated with slight variations in AGNM, General de Parte, vol. 39, exp. 70.

36. AGNM, Californias, vol. 60 bis, exp. 6.

37. AHH, Temporalidades, leg. 298, exp. 4.

38. See P. Fernando Consag's 1753 exploration, p. 344.

39. For more on Manuel Rodríguez, see chap. 10, p. 309.

40. AHH, leg. 284, exp. 31 (AGNM, General de Parte, vol. 39, exp. 70 copies this document—with a few minor differences and omissions).

41. Rivera to P. Juan de Armesto, 5 December 1753. AHH, Temporalidades, leg. 298, exp. 4.

42. Virrey Revillagigedo's advisor is specified as an *auditor de guerra* in this expediente. AHH, leg. 284, exp. 31. Haring notes that the viceroy "had full charge of military justice, and sat as a court of appeal in civil and criminal cases concerning persons who enjoyed the military *fuero* . . . on such occasions he was advised by a legal counsel, generally a judge of the audiencia, called the *auditor de guerra*." Haring, *Spanish Empire*, p. 115.

43. There is no evidence of Don José Bon's arrival in California or of a further resolution of the inheritance controversy.

44. AHH, leg. 284, exp. 31.

45. For examples, in 1754: AGNM, Provincias Internas, vol. 213, exp. 3; in 1766: AGNM, Provincias Internas, vol. 7, exp. 10.

46. Barco, *Historia natural y crónica*, pp. 372, 376–78.

47. Ibid., pp. 284–86. P. Consag had found the arroyo of Calamajué and correctly judged its potential. Unfortunately, his maps and geographic accounts were inexact and ambiguous. Only twelve years later, the arroyo was rediscovered during a season of heavy rains. Temporarily, the water ran sweet and the Jesuits innocently constructed a mission that would depend upon it. In one season, normal conditions returned and the mission in Arroyo de Calamajué died even as it was being born. Ibid., pp. 346–47.

48. The complete record of Fernando de Rivera y Moncada's wedding:

[Left marginal entry] "Dⁿ. Fernando de Rivera y Moncada, por poder, con Dᵃ. Theresa Davalos y Patron."

[Body of entry] "En la Yglesia Parrocˡ. de Compostela en dies y nuebe dias del mes de Henero de mil setᵒˢ. cinqᵗᵃ. y cinco años como lugar Thenᵗᵉ. de Cura por poder de Dⁿ. Fernando de Rivera y Moncada Capⁿ. del Rˡ. de Loreto de California, conferido a Dⁿ. Basilio de Rivera, su hermano, en dho

Rˡ. en ocho dias del mes de Noviembre de mil setᵒˢ. cinqᵗᵃ. y quatro años; segun orden Nra Sta Mᵉ. Yglesia, case, y vele a dho Dⁿ. Fernando de Rivera y Moncada hijo legᵐᵒ. de Dⁿ. Xptoval de Rivera y Mendoza, y de Dᵃ. Josepha de Moncada; substituiendo su persona el referido Dⁿ. Basilio de Rivera; con Dᵃ. Maria Theresa Davalos y Patron, origᵃ. y vezᵃ. de esta Ciuᵗ. hija legᵐᵃ. de Dⁿ. Diego Davalos, y de Dᵃ. Antonia Patron y Romero se amonestaron en tres dias festivos *inter missarum solemnia*, y precedieron todas las demas diligencias que ordena, y dispone el Santo Concilio de Trento, de que no resulto impedimento algᵒ. fueron testigos al veer, contraher y celebrar dho matrimonio Dⁿ Jᵘ de Sea, Dⁿ Manuel de la Peña, Pedro de la Peña, y otros, y para que conste de firme, con el Cura Benefᵗᵒ.

Bʳ Pedro Fernandez de los Rios
Antonio Lopez de Zalazar"
[Cura Beneficiado]
[Teniente Cura]

[During the 17th and 18th centuries, baptismal and marriage records for the parochial church of Compostela were entered on pages of bound volumes, each including some twenty to thirty years. Most of these volumes are now damaged and a few pages, usually the first and last, are lost or scattered. At the time that FHL Microfilm #0654341 was made, the entry for Rivera's wedding was on a loose sheet that had become mixed with unbound pages of baptismal entries from the 1710 period. It is possible that the page with Rivera's entry once was part of the incomplete book found on FHL Film #0652417, "LIBRO DONDE SE ASIENTAN LOS CASAMIENTOS QUE SE CELEBRAN EN ESTA CIUDAD DE COMPOSTELA [begun] Julio 15, 1727."]

49. The protocol by which the California captain applied for a leave of absence is suggested by letters written by Rivera to two different viceroys. In each case, he proclaimed the country at peace and his lieutenant prepared to handle any eventuality, then stated that he had private matters that required his presence on the mainland. Rivera to Marqués de Amarillas, 12 April 1759. AGNM, Californias, vol. 76, exp. 1; Rivera to Marqués de Cruillas, 25 October 1761. AGNM, Californias, vol. 76, exp. 3.

50. Basilio de Rivera was given drafts at Loreto for sums up to 500 pesos on three occasions during 1753 and 1754. At the time, his home was in Compostela, as church records show. He was carrying on a long tradition in which men from Compostela captained Loreto's ships. (See chap. 6, p. 173.)

The marriage record detailed in n. 47, above, implies that Basilio personally received his half-brother's proxy. This interpretation is supported by the account books of the California procurador in Mexico City. They show that both Basilio de Rivera and his full brother, Cristóbal Gregorio de Rivera y Valle, received drafts written in Loreto on 11 November 1754. AGNM, Californias, vol. 60 bis, exp. 6.

51. Information about the family of Teresa Dávalos y Patrón is derived from the books of baptisms, marriages, and burials for Compostela, passim. FHL Microfilms #0654341, 0654342, 0652417, 0652420.

52. Compostela was a relatively small place and its elite class was heavily inter-related by marriage and *compadrazgo*. For example, in 1727, Fernando de Rivera's parents served as godparents at the baptism of an aunt of Teresa Dávalos y Patrón. FHL Microfilm #0654341.

53. Teresa's father, Don Diego Dávalos y Valle, signed as a witness to a deposition at Loreto on 5 November 1756. AGNM, Californias, vol. 68, exp. 3.

54. Martínez, *Guía Familiar*, p. 31.

55. Bancroft, *North Mexican States*, vol. 1, p. 468.

56. Pedro de la Riva was last documented on the rolls of the presidio of Loreto on 13 October 1751, when he was still *teniente* of the Escuadra del Sur. AGNM, Californias, vol. 80, exp. 53. Riva's last appearance in the California account books came under a 16 May 1752, notation showing that he had cashed a draft — presented after 15 March — for 482 pesos, 3 reales. This credit was probably redeemed in Guadalajara, as it appears among a series of drafts paid there or in Mexico City, and was bracketed with a draft paid to P. Taraval who had retired to a post at a Jesuit *colegio* in Guadalajara in 1750. AGNM, Californias, vol. 60 bis, exp. 6, fols. 55–56. On 10 April 1753, the active Riva was appointed alcalde mayor of Santa María del Oro de Tequepexpa, the same post near Tepic and Compostela that Luis de Tortolero, Loreto's first captain obtained when he was retired from California. The appointment made pointed and repeated references to Riva's command of the "Presidio of the South of California." On 10 December 1753, an assistant to the alcalde mayor reported to the president of the Audiencia of Guadalajara that Don Pedro de la Riva had died suddenly two days before. AIPG, Libros de Tierras y Aguas, No. 54. Riva's third wife, Doña María Teresa de Liñan y Mejía, was pregnant at his death and subsequently bore their son, Agustín de la Riva y Liñan, progenitor of a family today widespread. Tequila baptisms, FHL Film #228-374.

57. The last California document that mentions Cristóbal Gutiérrez de Góngora is a *libranza* for 300 pesos from P. Visitador Hostell, a sum and mode of payment that suggests severance pay; the only purpose of a libranza issued in California was to allow it to be cashed elsewhere. 16 April 1755, AGNM, Californias, Vol. 60 bis. Gutiérrez de Góngora and wife had several additional children, as evidenced in parish records. When the Loreto-born son, Francisco Javier, married, the church record indicated the places of his birth and upbringing, and also that his parents were still alive. Marriage records of the Sagrario of Tepic, 2 March 1772. FHL Microfilm #654-320.

58. Blas Fernández de Somera was the brother of Jesuit P. Miguel Fernández de Somera: Barco, *Historia natural y crónica*, p. 439. P. Somera served at Ocoroni: Decorme, *Jesuitas Mexicanos*, vol. 1, p. 480. Nepotism was common in New Spain's frontier military units, but only in Jesuit-dominated California would the relative of a missionary have had such preference.

59. Rivera to Marqués de Amarillas (the first request for leave), 12 April 1759. AGNM, Californias, vol. 76, exp. 1. His second request, AGNM, Californias, vol. 76, exp. 3. The death of Josefa Ramón de Moncada y de la Peña is revealed in the procurador's accounts, "200 pesos que por una libranza de el Bachiller Don Ambrosio Miguel Rivera, pague para los Gastos de Entierro y Funerales de la Madre del Señor Capitan a quien se les avisara." AGNM, Californias, vol. 60 bis, exp. 6. Ambrosio was Fernando's full brother, and a priest.

60. In keeping with a custom of the times, most ships had "official" names, often of religious provenance, and entirely different popular names by which they were presumably known to their crews and to those who depended on them. Thus, the ship wrecked in 1759 was officially the *San Francisco Xavier*, and popularly *El Aguila*. Correspondence relative to *El Aguila* is found in AGNM, Provincias Internas, vol. 213, exps. 7, 8; AGNM, Californias, vol. 68, exps. 5–8; AGNM, Californias, vol. 76, exp. 2. The wreck took place off a place then called Purum, apparently near the rocks known today as Los Frailes. This information and a report of the wreck's aftermath appear in Barco, *Historia natural y crónica*, pp. 332–36.

61. See chap. 4, pp. 95–100.

62. Barco, *Historia natural y crónica*, pp. 334–36.

63. For information on the *marinería* at the presidio of Loreto, see chap. 6, pp. 173–77.

64. Barco, *Historia natural y crónica*, pp. 64–65.

65. Ibid., pp. 335–36. For *La Concepción's* role in the expulsion, see chap. 12, p. 385.

66. Ibid., pp. 287, 295–312.

67. Ibid., pp. 287–304.

68. Ibid., p. 304.

69. Ibid., pp. 337–39.

70. Linck, *Reports & Letters*, p. 32.

71. Linck, *Diary of 1766 Expedition to Northern Baja California*, pp. 56–58.

72. Barco, *Historia natural y crónica*, p. 353.

73. AGNM, General de Parte, vol. 39, exp 144. See chap. 10, pp. 315, 327, for an account of battles with the Uchití in 1747–1748.

74. See Appendix C for the unusual story of P. Dominguez's brief visit to California.

75. María de Larrea participated in baptisms at San José on 22 August, 30 September, 8 October, and 20 October 1747. Book of Baptisms of San José de Comondú. Mariano de Ocio's burial is recorded in "Catalogus Defunctorum in Missione Sⁿ. Joseph de Comondu."

76. AGNM, Provincias Internas, vol. 213, exp. 3.

77. Barco, *Historia natural y crónica*, p. 153. The general description of early mining activities is based on personal inspection of the Santa Ana area and its artifacts, and on Amao, *Minas y Mineros en Baja California*, pp. 100–104.

78. Blasting powder was used during these same years in excavating rock for the foundation of a new church at Misión de Guadalupe. Barco, *Historia natural y crónica*, p. 262. Although no document mentions its use at Santa Ana, the probability is good for such employment.

79. Manuel de Ocio claimed to have refined silver ore by both smelting and amalgamation: AGNM General de Parte, vol. 39, exp. 144. Santa Ana does not display the remains of the substantial constructions required by the *patio* process, a more efficient form of amalgamation. Beside large structures, the *patio* process made use of larger equipment and was limited to areas with much larger water supplies, better transportation, and miners with larger capital. Descriptions of 18th-century Mexican silver smelting and the *cazo* process are based on Brading, *Miners and Merchants in Bourbon Mexico*, pp. 137–39; West, *Mining Community*, pp. 25–35; Bargalló, *La minería y metalurgia*, pp. 91–95, 160–66.

80. AGNM General de Parte, vol. 39, exp. 144.

81. Velázquez de León, *Descripción de la Antigua California: 1768*, pp. 36–37.

82. P. Sistiaga to P. Provincial Escobar y Llamas, 19 September 1743. Burrus and Zubillaga, *El noroeste*, pp. 443–44. Baegert, *Letters*, pp. 191–92.

83. Barco, *Historia natural y crónica*, pp. 319–21; Baegert, *Observations*, pp. 46–47.

84. Stern and Jackson, "Vagabundaje and Settlement Patterns" provides descriptions of the prevailing conditions in small mining centers on the northwest frontier of New Spain in the same period of time.

85. An example of the baptism of an obviously illegitimate child is found in "Mission Santiago, Fragmentos de Registro de Bautismos," entry #271, "On the first of September, I applied the holy oils and performed other ceremonies for Joseph de la Luz, baptized earlier by Joseph Gabriel Ojeda [the mission's soldier]. He is the son of Estefana Urias, a single woman, the daughter of Francisca Perez, wife of [Diego Joseph de] Garate, neighbors from the mining village of [page damaged; the *real de minas* was either Santa Ana or San Antonio] . . . JHS Julian Joseph Salazar [the missionary incumbent at Santiago]."

86. Barco, *Historia natural y crónica*, pp. 323–25. When the peninsular natives were attracted to the mines, they merely repeated the actions of most North American natives who were faced with similar temptations; see, for example, the actions of Yaquis, in Sonora and elsewhere, in Hu-de Hart, *Missionaries, Miners, and Indians*, pp. 41–42.

87 AGNM, General de Parte, vol. 39, exp. 144.

88. Barco, *Historia natural y crónica*, pp. 319–20; Baegert, *Observations*, p. 47. P. Francisco Badillo can be identified as the missionary at Santiago by reference to the Santiago book of baptisms. P. Carlos Neumayer is placed at Todos Santos by various documents in AGNM, Provincias Internas, vol. 213, exp. 3.

89. AGNM, General de Parte, vol. 39, exp. 144. In this document, the lieutenant is given as "Pedro de la Torre," but there can be no doubt that it was actually Riva. The AGNM *ramo* of General de Parte consists of secretaries' copies, not original documents. Loreto's muster of that same year shows that Manuel de la Torre Villavicencio was Riva's sergeant and second-in-command *en el Sur.* AGNM, Californias, vol. 80, exp. 53. Villavicencio wrote out "de la Torre" as part of his signature (as can be seen in AGNM Provincias Internas 213, exp. 3). It is apparent that, in creating the General de Parte document, the copyist confused two signatures that, on the original, were adjacent. All such documents were signed by witnesses, which doubtless was Villavicencio's role.

90. This land dispute between a military captain and a missionary is detailed in chap. 4, pp. 122–24.

91. The Santa Rosa affair is recalled rather obliquely in AGNM, Provincias Internas, vol. 7, exp. 10, fol. 97. The viceroy's decree was dated 26 October 1753.

92. AGNM, General de Parte, vol. 39, exp. 144.

93. AGNM, General de Parte, vol. 39, exp. 144.

94. AIPG, Protocolos de Manuel Francisco Nogueras, vol. 4, fols. 14–16. The priest's surname was also given in various documents as Falemboc, Talenbock, Talembock, etc.

95. AGNM, General de Parte, vol. 39, exp. 144 (dated 18 May 1753)

96. AGNM, General de Parte, vol. 39, exp. 144.

97. Virrey Revillagigedo's words of warning to his officials in Acapulco were most emphatic—and no doubt intended also for Ocio's eyes and consideration, "... *esten a la mira, colen y velen el que en manera alguna el prenotado Don Manuel. . . .*" AGNM, General de Parte, vol. 39, exp. 144.

98. Baegert, *Observations*, p. 46.

99. Barco, *Historia natural y crónica*, p. 153.

100. Bishko, "The Peninsular Background of Latin American Cattle Ranching," pp. 491–515.

101. West, *The Mining Community*, p. 57.

102. AGNM, Provincias Internas, vol. 7, exp. 6, fols. 44, 47.

103. AGNM, Provincias Internas, vol. 7, exp. 10.

104. AGNM, Provincias Internas, vol. 213, exp. 3.

105. AGNM, Provincias Internas, vol. 7, exp. 10, fol. 97.

106. The two most prominent examples of contests for land and cattle between Manuel de Ocio and the California Jesuits are found in: AGNM, Provincias Internas, vol. 213, exp. 3; AGNM, Provincias Internas, vol. 7, exp. 10.

107. Ocio and his men seem to have been particularly active in the arroyos of Las Gallinas and Valle Perdido and in their flood plain to the southwest. By about 1760, Ocio had a house at Las Gallinas and apparently was treating the area as his property.

108. AGNM, Provincias Internas, vol. 213, exp. 3.

109. AGNM, Provincias Internas, vol. 7, exp. 10.

110. AGNM, Provincias Internas, vol. 7, exp. 6.

111. Baegert, *Observations*, p. 47; P. Lamberto Hostell in AGNM, Provincias Internas, vol. 7, exp. 10, fol. 96.

112. AHBCS, Aspecto Económico, document 131. Baegert, *Observations*, p. 182.

113. Baegert, *Observations*, p. 46.

114. AIPG, Protocolos de Antonio de Berroa, tomo X, fols. 228–29.

115. Lindley, "Kinship and Credit in Guadalajara's Oligarchy," passim.

116. AIPG, Protocolos de Antonio de Berroa, tomo X, fol. 228. Other testimony on the subject of Ocio's cattle: In 1766, P. Visitador Lamberto Hostell reported that Ocio was branding over 1,000 a year. AGNM, Provincias Internas, vol. 7, exp. 10, fol. 93v.; Ignacio Acevedo testified that around 1767 Ocio branded 1,200 a year. AGNM, Provincias Internas, vol. 7, exp. 6, fol. 45v.

117. Lindley, "Kinship and Credit," passim.

118. All known Rodríguez grandsons, except the wealthy Antonio de Ocio, stayed to enjoy Jesuit employment. These included all four sons of José Antonio de Robles, the three of Pedro de la Riva, and the only son of Cristóbal Gutiérrez de Góngora. Beside the matter of employment, this determination to stay in California suggests the closeness of the Rodríguez clan and the local advantages that membership conferred.

119. Pre-Hispanic rock paintings at hundreds of sites attest to the antiquity of deer hunting in peninsular California. Crosby, *Cave Paintings of Baja California*. Deer hunted by neophytes: Baegert, *Letters*, p. 124.

120. Evidence of gente de razón trading with the galleon is provided by one of the first of King's Visitor José de Gálvez's edicts after his arrival in 1768. He forbade "the residents of this part of the South of California from bringing gamuzas of deer skin, or other products of the land down to San José del Cabo and trading with the *nao de Filipinas* for supplies or other merchandise . . ." TBL, California Archives, tomo I, p. 7.

121. AGNM, Provincias Internas, vol. 211, exp. 15, fol. 258.

122. Gaspar Pisón's presence in Tepic in 1745 and the birth of his daughter (20 January 1746) is recorded in the book of baptisms from La Parroquia de la Ciudad de Tepic [FHL Film #654236]. His presence in California in 1745: AGNM, Californias, vol. 27, exp. 6, fols. 53–55. In addition, the padre procurador's accounts show a payment to Pisón in 1746. AGNM, Californias, vol. 60 bis, exp. 6.

123. AGNM, Provincias Internas, vol. 211, exp. 15, fol. 258. Gaspar Pisón was probably the Andalucian who lost his weapons and clothing during the Indian attack described in chap. 9, pp. 294–95.

124. Manuel de Ocio had an assistant: Barco, *Historia natural y crónica*, p. 153.

125. AGNM, Provincias Internas, vol. 211, exp. 15, fol. 258.

126. Simón Rodríguez founds San Antonio: Baegert, *Observations*, p. 46. General references to the opening of San Antonio are found in Barco, *Historia natural y crónica*, pp. 154, 319.

127. The dramatic decline in the take of pearls, noted by most chroniclers, is borne out by the fees collected each five years from those who rented the collection of the *real quinto*. Ocio and Sánchez Lleñero paid 1,400 pesos in 1749. In 1754, Manuel de Ocio and a Guadalajara business partner, Don Diego Sánchez de Peñahermosa, were successful in bidding to collect the quinto for another five years for 420 pesos. In 1759, they were chosen again, even with a bid reduced to 200 pesos to compensate for alleged smaller profits. In 1764, Pisón must have paid even less. Gerhard, "Pearl Diving in Lower California," p. 247; Baegert, *Observations*, pp. 45, 182.

128. AGNM, Provincias Internas, vol. 211, exp. 15, fol. 228–333.

129. See p. 360.

130. See pp. 340–42.

131. Baegert, *Observations*, p. 46.

132. Utrera, "Nuevo estado . . . ," University of Texas, W. B. Stephens Collection, García Mss., document 67, p. 391.

133. Barco, *Historia natural y crónica*, p. 319. This cleric, unnamed by Barco, was Mateo Adolfo Falembock, the man requested in Ocio's original petition to the bishop of Guadalajara. See p. 357.

134. Barco, *Historia natural y crónica*, pp. 319–20.

135. Decorme, *Jesuitas Mexicanos*, vol. 2, p. 543.

136. Loreto's 1733 muster: AGNM, Californias, vol. 80, exp. 3, fols. 19–24.

137. Juan Nicolás de Estrada married to Juana Morillo and this couple given as parents of José María and José Bonifacio: "Departamento del Sur de la California. Compañía de D. Antonio Ocio." 7 November 1768. AGI, Guadalajara, 416.

138. "Misión de Santiago, Fragmentos de Registro de Bautismos," entry #215, 28 February 1754.

139. For example, soldier Juan Nicolás de Estrada signed as witness at Santa Ana on 8 October 1754. AGNM, Provincias Internas, vol. 213, exp. 3.

140. Juan Nicolás de Estrada listed as a soldier *en el Sur*: AGNM, Californias, vol. 80, exp. 53. Noted as soldier and cabo at Misión de Santiago: "Misión de Santiago, Fragmentos de Registro de Bautismos," entries #197, 8 June 1753, and #255, 5 March 1756.

141. AIPG, Protocolos de Antonio de Berroa, tomo IV, fols. 219v–20v.

142. AIPG, Protocolos de Antonio de Berroa, tomo V, fols. 231v–32v.

143. AIPG, Protocolos de Antonio de Berroa, tomo V, fols. 258v–60. José María de Estrada's career at the presidio of Loreto is summarized on pp. 390.

A note for social historians: Juan Nicolás de Estrada had a brother named José Marcelino de Estrada, also a California soldier who served in the South. He was married to Rosalía Heras and they too had a son named José María, born at Tepic in 1740. Moreover, Juan Estrada, a mulato mineworker from Ahome, Sonora, came to the Santa Ana/San Antonio area, *c.* 1768. He and his wife, María Gutiérrez, also had a son named José María. These three men, each named José María Estrada, served either in the militia, or at the presidio of Loreto during the 1768–1790 period.

144. AIPG, Protocolos de Antonio de Berroa, tomo VII, fols. 245–46.

145. AGNM, Californias, vol. 60 bis, exp. 6. The sale of the launch in itself tells little about José María Estrada's fortunes; it only demonstrates that he owned such a craft. He might have bought the launch to resell at a profit, or he may have had to sell it to pay for his annual supplies.

146. AGNM, Provincias Internas, vol. 7, exp. 10.

147. Actually, by 1762, the California Jesuits had been ordered by Virrey Cruillas to put their dealings with the galleons on a businesslike basis, to put prices on the stores and foodstuffs that galleons needed, and to collect payment before they sailed. Barco, *Historia natural y crónica*, pp. 248–49.

148. AGNM, Provincias Internas, vol. 7, exp. 11.

149. The civil officials who had visited California, Governors Rezábal and Bernal de Huidobro of Sinaloa, were military men with only provincial appointments and with no experience in the central government—a description that would also fit Gaspar de Portolá when he came to California.

150. P. Visitador Benno Ducrue to P. Provincial Salvador Gándara, 15 September 1767. BNM, AF 4/70.2.

151. Barco, *Historia natural y crónica*, p. 363. Similar, usually stronger criticism of Jesuit practices was putting pressure on the order and its missions all over the northwest of New Spain. The offer to renounce California establishments was matched by similar offers covering over twenty missions in Nayarit, Sinaloa, the Tarahumara, and Chinipas. Some Jesuit offers to the viceroy bracketed the Cal-

ifornia renunciation with the others. P. Provincial Salvador Gándara to unspecified viceroy, [no date, but 1766]. AHH, leg. 325, exp. 12. For these matters and a broader discussion of the political problems of Jesuit missions in New Spain, see Deeds, "Rendering Unto Caesar," pp. 37–38.

152. AGNM, Provincias Internas, vol. 7, exp. 11.

Chapter 12: The Expulsion

1. Priestley, *José de Gálvez*, pp. 133–34.
2. Ibid., p. 135.
3. ibid., pp. 54, 142–55, 210–11.
4. Ibid., p. 216.
5. ibid., pp. 156–65.
6. Hu-de Hart, *Missionaries, Miners, and Indians*, pp. 49–50; "El informe de Giuseppe Maria Genovese al virrey (1722)," in González Rodríguez, *Etnología y misión en la Pimería Alta, 1715–1740*, pp. 125–87.
7. Lockhart and Schwartz, *Early Latin America*, pp. 350–51.
8. Priestley, *José de Gálvez*, pp. 210–30.
9. Boneu, *Gaspar de Portolá*, p. 117.
10. Virrey Croix decided to replace the California Jesuits with missionaries from the small Franciscan College of San Fernando, whose headquarters were located handily in the city of Mexico. That college assembled twelve of its missionaries — called *Fernandinos* — under the direction of Fray Junípero Serra, and sent them to California. Palóu, *Historical Memoirs of New California*, pp. 3–5.
11. Palóu, *Historical Memoirs*, p. 9; Baegert, *Observations*, pp. 167–68.
12. Palóu, *Historical Memoirs*, pp. 9–10. The Fernandinos and Jesuits actually met each other on the road from Tepic to San Blas as the former headed for California and the latter for exile. Palóu wrote this passage as if he had first hand information — or he may have had this information from Gobernador Portolá.
13. The problems and woes of California Jesuits in 1767 are reported and discussed at length in P. Visitador Benno Ducrue to P. Provincial Salvador Gándara, 25 September 1767. BNM, AF 4/70.2.
14. Gaspar de Portolá's arrival in California on 30 November 1767, is given by Barco, *Historia natural y crónica*, p. 362; Baegert, *Observations*, p. 168; Ducrue, *Account of the Expulsion*, p. 42. Portolá arrived on *La Lauretana*: Portolá to Croix, 28 December 1767. Palóu, *Historical Memoirs*, pp. 17–18.
15. Barco, *Historia natural y crónica*, pp. 246, 276.

16. The extent and nature of local people's trade with the Manila galleon can be gauged by the vehement and specific proscriptions proclaimed by José de Gálvez less than a year after Portolá's arrival in California. TBL, California Archives, tomo 1, pp. 7–14. This contraband commerce continued, as is indicated by reiterations of the Gálvez doctrine by subsequent governors Barri, Neve, and Rivera. The Manila galleon did put into San Bernabé in January 1768, a little over a month after Portolá's landing. Barco, *Historia natural y crónica*, p. 248.
17. Baegert, *Observations*, p. 168; Barco, *Historia natural y crónica*, pp. 361–62.
18. Palóu, *Historical Memoirs*, pp. 17–18. When Virrey Croix decided to replace the California Jesuits with missionaries from the College of San Fernando, leaders of the Province of Jalisco, a larger Franciscan missionary organization with headquarters in Guadalajara, exerted their influence to have their group named to occupy California. Higher Franciscan authorities advised that the Fernandinos be sent to take over ex-Jesuit missions in Sonora, and that the Jaliscans be sent to California. The viceroy acceded to this request and ordered the change. Serra and his superiors reacted quickly with concerted arguments and pressures from their well-connected supporters. The orders for change were withdrawn and the College of San Fernando was once again awarded California.

But the Jaliscans crossed the storm-tossed gulf while they still held valid orders to occupy the peninsula. Like Portolá, they landed near the cape and had to make their way northward. However, since the governor and his men monopolized the available riding animals, two months passed before mounts were delivered and they were able to complete their journey. A few days after they had reached Loreto and headed out to their individual mission assignments, the Jaliscans received orders from the viceroy to quit California and go to Sonora. The Fernandinos under Junípero Serra arrived on the peninsula on 1 April 1768. As they journeyed to their designated missions, some Fernandinos passed recalled Jaliscans straggling back to Loreto.
19. Barco, *Historia natural y crónica*, p. 362. Baegert, *Observations*, p. 168.
20. Ducrue, *Account of the Expulsion*, pp. 42, 44.
21. Sailors on ships and boats that plied the Mar de Cortés were predominantly Yaquis and California natives. Palóu tells us that the crew of the launch that put in at Puerto Escondido and La Paz was primarily made up of California neophytes.

Palóu, *Historical Memoirs of New California*, p. 9. Ocio's other craft were similarly manned. Furthermore, Yaqui sailors would also have been familiar with the California coast, from the cape to Loreto, and would have known a good deal about day-to-day life in Jesuit California both from long sea trips with California mates and frequent layovers in California ports. See also Mathes, "Baja California Indians in the Spanish Maritime Service," pp. 113-26.

22. The three Jesuit accounts of the expulsion contain brief accounts of Portolá's coming. Although they do not contradict each other in any way, each has a slightly different list of facts which add up to the present account. Barco, *Historia natural y crónica*, p. 361-62; Baegert, *Observations*, p. 168; Ducrue, *Account of the Expulsion*, pp. 42, 44.

23. Barco, *Historia natural y crónica*, p. 362.

24. Ducrue, *Account of the Expulsion*, pp. 42, 44.

25. Portolá's background and career are presented and the lack of particulars concerning his appointment as governor of California are noted in Boneu Companys, *Gaspar de Portolá*, pp. 107-17.

26. Ducrue, *Account of the Expulsion*, pp. 42, 44.

27. See chap. 11, pp. 368-70.

28. Baegert, *Observations*, pp. 168-69.

29. Barco, *Historia natural y crónica*, p. 363.

30. Ibid., p. 363.

31. Palóu, *Historical Memoirs*, pp. 23-24. For a detailed scrutiny of Portolá's *comisionados*, see Crosby, *Doomed to Fail*.

32. Baegert, *Observations*, p. 169.

33. Ibid., p. 169.

34. Portolá's grateful reference to Rivera's efforts on his behalf is contained in the governor's first report to the viceroy (described on pp. 381-82). Portolá to Croix, 28 December 1767. AGNM, Californias, vol. 76, exp. 10, fols. 16-20.

35. Portolá's actual words were "hallo por conveniente y preciso se quedan los muchos de los soldados, si puede ser, de dicha Compañía, y aun los dos officiales que son el Capitan y el Theniente por el pronto, . . ." Portolá to Croix, 28 December 1767, AGNM, Californias, vol. 76, exp. 10, fol. 17. Fernando de Rivera's later career and his relations with Spanish officers are best understood in the context of his creole background and the stigma of his service under the Jesuits.

36. Portolá to Croix, 28 December 1767, AGNM, Californias, vol. 76, exp. 10, fols. 16-20.

37. Ducrue, *Account of the Expulsion*, pp. 44, 46, 58. The date of Portolá's arrival at Loreto is given in Barco, *Historia natural y crónica*, p. 364.

38. Fernández de Somera sent to the South: Portolá to Croix, 3 February 1768, AGNM, Californias, vol. 76, exp. 11, fols. 21-28. Rivera inventoried the northern missions: Portolá to Croix, 28 December 1767, AGNM, Californias, vol. 76, exp. 10, fols. 16-20; also, "Inventario de la mission de San Joseph de Comondu," 30 December 1767, AHBCS, leg. 12,3, and "Inventario de la mision de Santa Gertrudis," 16 January 1768, AHBCS, leg. 12,5.

39. Barco, *Historia natural y crónica*, p. 364.

40. Ducrue, *Account of the Expulsion*, p. 58.

41. Portolá to Croix, 28 December 1767, AGNM, Californias, vol. 76.

42. Ducrue, *Account of the Expulsion*, p. 58. From other sources it is known that Portolá's alférez was José Lasso, but, since the signed document can not be found, the names of his secretary and sergeant are unknown.

43. Ibid., pp. 58, 60.

44. The scarcity of supplies in California and the dire need for new stocks is a recurrent, pressing theme in Portolá's successive letters to Virrey Croix, dated 28 December 1767; 3 February 1768; 18 February 1768; 22 March 1768; and 9 April 1768. AGNM, Californias, vol. 76.

45. Inventories ordered: Barco, *Historia natural y crónica*, p. 364; Baegert, *Observations*, pp. 169-70. Inventories apparently could not be completed at all missions prior to the Jesuits' departure, but were left to the *comisionados* to complete—probably counts of livestock, and possibly lists of items stored at visitas. On 3 February 1768, as he embarked the Jesuits for their trip to Matanchel, Portolá wrote, "Because the commissioners have not finished inventories at all missions, I cannot send the originals to Your Excellency . . . but I will do so as soon as the task is completed." Portolá to Croix, 28 December 1767, AGNM, Californias, vol. 76. Epidemic at San Borja: Ducrue, *Account of the Expulsion*, pp. 62, 64. P. Retz overweight, infirm: Barco, *Historia natural y crónica*, p. 439. Retz with injured foot, unable to walk or ride: Ducrue, Ibid., pp. 52, 54.

46. Ducrue, *Account of the Expulsion*, pp. 66, 68.

47. Portolá to Croix, 3 February 1768, AGNM, Californias, vol. 76, exp. 12, fols. 29-31; Baegert, *Observations*, p. 168. In contrast to those of California, Sonoran Jesuits were sent to Mexico City on foot after long periods of cruel incarceration. On the way, they were transferred into the custody of a succession of local government officials. They suffered much mistreatment and many died. Pradeau, *Expulsión de los jesuitas*, passim.

48. Ducrue, *Account of the Expulsion*, p. 72. The identification of the ship that carried the Jesuits away appears in Palóu, *Historical Memoirs of New California*, p. 19.

49. Ducrue's work provides a circumstantial account of the California Jesuits' experiences as they were transported successively to New Spain and Spain. He described the trip of the northern Europeans to Ostend — from which port they returned to their native provinces. Burrus, in his introduction to *Ducrue's Account of the Expulsion*, relates briefly the fate of each California *expulso*.

Epilogue: The Aftermath

1. Navarro García, *Gálvez*, pp. 164, 168; Palóu, *Historical Memoirs*, p. 30. A useful account and interpretation of Gálvez's plans for peninsular California is Río, "Utopia in Baja California: The Dreams of José de Gálvez."

2. Navarro García, *Gálvez*, pp. 163, 168–69.

3. Crosby, *Doomed to Fail.*

4. Jackson, "Demographic Patterns in the Missions of Central Baja California," p. 111.

5. Haring, *Spanish Empire*, p. 186. Some negative outcomes of mission practice might have been anticipated from the 1755 comments of Comondú's Padre Francisco Inama who saw in the neophytes "a blind obedience and a child-like confidence" in the missionaries, and reported that the padres worked so hard because their charges had recourse to "no other help, counsel, guidance, or care." See chap. 8, p. 263.

6. Polzer, *Rules and Precepts*, p. 58. Ignacio del Río summed up the results of the Jesuit mission period in similar if more detailed and specific terms than those used by Polzer. Río, "El régimen jesuítico," p. 70.

7. Several of the Gálvez-ordered land grants, with the visitor's signature, are found among the early entries in AHBCS, ramo Económico.

8. "Instrucción de 12 de Agosto de 1768 en el Real de Santa Ana de la Peninsula de la Baja California por el visitador general del Reino de la Nueva España Conde D. José de Gálvez para la enajenación de terrenos realengos," AGNM, Provincias Internas, tomo 166, exp. 3.

9. Navarro García, *Gálvez*, p. 169; Bancroft, *North Mexican States*, vol. 1, pp. 484–86, 692–93.

10. A recent study of some of Gálvez's other activities in New Spain shows that his reputation as a reformer and organizer generally outran his actual accomplishments. Salvucci, "Costumbres viejas, 'hombres nuevos': José de Gálvez y la burocracia fiscal novohispana."

11. The discovery of Velicatá is described in Chapter 11, p. 350.

12. For Spanish engineer Miguel Costanso's eyewitness assessment of the performance of the California soldiers, see chap. 6, p. 173 n. 104.

13. The term Baja California did not come into common use until 1800.

Bibliography

A Preliminary Note

Although based on many dozens of different sources, this work necessarily rests on the foundation of writings by three eighteenth-century Jesuits. The first was Miguel Venegas, a historian who depended almost exclusively on eyewitness reports from California. The second and third, Miguel del Barco and Jacobo Baegert, were California missionaries, veterans of years of toil in the milieu about which I write. By chance, the work of the first dealt with the opening half of the Jesuits' tenure in California, and the experiences of the two others covered the remaining years.

Mexican Jesuit Padre Miguel Venegas, resident in Mexico City, collected information on California during his research for other projects, but about 1730 he began to work on a history of the Jesuit mission in California. He was eventually able to consult a large percentage of the reports and letters that had reached Jesuit archives from the padres working in the field. In 1739 he completed the epic manuscript, "Empressas Apostolicas," 683 pages in his own beautiful and compact hand. For various reasons, including security concerns by the rulers of Spain, this work was never published. Later, the Mexican Jesuits sent the manuscript to Spain where it was given to a distinguished Jesuit scholar, Padre Andrés Marcos Burriel, who reduced and shaped it to the work that was published as *Noticias de la California* in 1757. The latter work is better organized, more succinct, and therefore more readable than "Empressas Apostolicas," but it is also one step farther from the original documents and contains many fewer incidents and much less detail.

The quality of Venegas's work can be assessed since several dozen of his hundreds of source documents are extant and can be compared with his history. They demonstrate that, in his own work, Venegas simply paraphrased his sources, accurately and often to the smallest details. As a result, although I have used the originals wherever possible, I cite "Empressas Apostolicas" as an invaluable substitute for all the material that he saw and that we cannot. The complicated story of Venegas's works is well told by W. Michael Mathes in a supplement to his omnibus edition, *Obras californianas del Padre Miguel Venegas, S.J.*

The history of Padre Miguel del Barco's *Historia natural y crónica de la Antigua California [Adiciones y correcciones a la Noticia de Miguel Venegas]* is very different. After thirty years of service in California, Barco was exiled to Bologna where he drew on his own memory and those of several of his fellows from the California mission to create a monumental appendix to the published Venegas/Burriel work. As in the case of "Empressas Apostolicas," many original documents cover small aspects of Barco's chosen ground and can be compared with his composition. Under the most intense scrutiny, Barco's work proves to be remarkable in its scope, detail, accuracy, and objectivity.

The third author, Johann Jakob (Jacobo) Baegert, like Barco, was expelled from California in 1768. After returning to Europe, Baegert wrote his *Observations in Lower California* to provide an eyewitness commentary on Venegas/Burriel and to relate his own impressions and ideas. Baegert also wrote five long letters to his brother that were published recently (Baegert, *The Letters of Jacob Baegert, 1749–1761*). Baegert was not as thorough as Barco, nor did he cover as much ground. He was less objective, often taking passionate positions on the issues of the times, but he provides a valuable supplement. He did his work among the Guaycura, whereas Barco worked almost exclusively with the Cochimí, and Baegert's very lack of objectivity is useful because it does contrast with Barco and provides a different perception of the realities of Jesuit California.

In general, manuscript sources related to California in this period are exceptionally scattered and incomplete. Taken together, Venegas, Barco, and Baegert provide more data and insights than the sum of all other documentation.

Primary Sources

DOCUMENTS (ORIGINAL, TRANSCRIPT, AND MICROFILM)

Bracketed initials are the abbreviations used in notes throughout the work.

Archivo General de Indias, Sevilla [AGI]
Audiencia de Guadalajara, legajos 70, 93, 104, 134, 135, 219, 250, 286, 311, 400, 416, 506
Contratación, legajo 5550.
Archivo General de la Nación, México, D. F. [AGNM]
    Californias, volumes 2 bis, 27, 60 bis, 63, 64, 68, 76, 80
    Cárceles y Presidios, volume 5
    General de Parte, volumes 33, 38, 39
    Historia, volumes 21, 308, 333, 392
    Inquisición, volume 832
    Jesuitas, volumes 2, 3
    Misiones, volumes 12, 22, 27
    Provincias Internas, volumes 7, 36, 87, 120, 200, 211, 213
    Reales Cédulas, volumes 64, 67

Archivo General de Simancas, Simancas
    Secretaria de Guerra (Siglo XVIII)

Archivo Histórico de Baja California Sur, La Paz [AHBCS]
    Ramo I, La Colonia, 1744–1821

Archivo Histórico de Hacienda, México, D. F. [AHH]
    Legajos 17, 281, 282, 283, 284, 286, 295, 298, 321, 325, 334

Archivo de Instrumentos Públicos de Guadalajara [AIPG]
    Protocolos de notarios públicos

The Bancroft Library [TBL]
    The Bolton Papers
    California Archives
    Mexican Manuscripts
    Microfilm of mission registers not otherwise available [see p. 00]

Biblioteca Nacional de México, México, D. F. [BNM]
Archivo Franciscano, volumes 1–4.

The Family History Library of The Church of Jesus Christ of Latter-day Saints [FHL]
The Mexican Collection of Colonial Parish Registers

The Huntington Library
Gálvez Papers
Huntington Manuscripts

The University of Texas Library
W. B. Stephens Collection, García Manuscripts

Extant Mission Registers from Jesuit California

Much information for this work was gleaned from *libros de misión*, but they are rarely cited. Instead, in most instances, the pertinent mission and the type of entry (baptism, marriage, or burial) are indicated in the text so that the source can be found in the list below.

LORETO

Baptisms:
23 November 1701 to 23 July 1703
1 July 1704 to 2 March 1717

SAN JAVIER (SAN FRANCISCO JAVIER DE BIAUNDÓ)

Baptisms:
26 May 1709 to 28 May 1711 [#618–791]
11 January 1712 to 3 May 1716 [#820–1122]

SAN MIGUEL (A VISITA OF MISIÓN SAN JAVIER)

Baptisms:
3 December 1730 to 15 September 1737

SAN JOSÉ DE COMONDÚ

Baptisms:
7 December 1736 to 29 November 1767 [#1373–2176]
Marriages:
1 January 1753 to 12 January 1768
Burials:
2 March 1737 to 13 January 1749
April 28, 1751 to April 9, 1767
Fragments of the four sets of records listed above are held by the Seminario de la Compañía de Jesús, México, D.F. The Bancroft Library has a film of these holdings—in which the pages containing the noted fragmentary records from Loreto, San Javier, and San Miguel are somewhat mingled with those from the more complete books from San José de Comondú.

SAN IGNACIO

Baptisms:
25 July 1743 to 1 November 1743 [#150–179]

April 1744 to 31 May 1744 [#268–338]
7 September 1744 to 25 December 1744 [#378–462][1]
20 February 1745 to 4 June 1745 [#502–587]
16 December 1746 to 9 August 1747 [#733–876]
4 February 1747 to 9 June 1747 [#982–1013]
21 June 1748 to 14 December 1748 [#1351–1527]
15 December 1740 to 2 May 1750 [#1662–1731]
29 April 1759 to 16 April 1765 [#2280–2555]8 November 8, 1766 to 16 May 1767 [#2616–2635]
Marriages:
3 July 1748 to 26 August 1750 [#885–967]
14 September 1750 to 5 March 1757 [#998–1148]
9 March 1757 to 24 January 1768 [#1179–1917][2]

LA PURÍSIMA

Baptisms:[3]
Burials:
20 January 1757 to 16 September 1759 [#1–66]
Books of both missions held by the Archivo Episcopal, La Paz, Baja California Sur.

SANTA ROSALÍA DE MULEGÉ

Marriages:
22 October 1718 to 25 January 1767
Burials:
October 1718 to 24 December 1766
Held in The Gleason Library of The University of San Francisco.

TODOS SANTOS (SANTA ROSA)

Baptisms:
24 March 1739 to 13 October 1744
14 March 1746 to 2 March 1748

SANTIAGO

Baptisms:
1 March 1753 to 21 December 1754
7 December 1755 to 14 July 1756
21 March 1762 to 2 January 1768
Books of both missions held by the Archive of the Archdiocese, Los Angeles, California.
[The Todos Santos baptismal pages are misidentified in their present repository as belonging to the baptismal register from Misión de Santiago.]

---

1. One small sheet of San Ignacio baptisms is located among the San Borja Burials; it covers seven baptisms on 25 December 1744 [#458–462].
2. In the middle of a page, Padre Consag unaccountably skipped from #1197 to #1138 and then to #1739—after which he proceeded with consecutive numbers.
3. Pablo L. Martínez transcribed about fifty Jesuit entries from this incomplete libro. Martínez, *Guía Familiar*, pp. 125–28.

SANTA GERTRUDIS

Baptisms:
16 July 1751 to 23 January 1768 [#1–2701]
Marriages:
9 January 1752 to 6 January 1768 [#1–826]
Burials:
25 January 1752 to 7 January 1768 [#1–1654]
The book of baptisms is held by the Museo del Estado, Mexicali, Baja California; that of marriages by St. Johns's Seminary, Camarillo, California; that of burials by the Archivo Episcopal, La Paz, Baja California Sur.

SAN BORJA

Baptisms:
28 August 1762 to 17 January 1768 [#1–2092]
Marriages:
3 September 1762 to 25 November 1767 [#1–677]
Burials:
18 September 1762 to 5 January 1768 [#1–526][4]
The book of baptisms is held by the Archivo Episcopal, La Paz, Baja California Sur; that of marriages by The Gleason Library of The University of San Francisco; that of burials by the Museo del Estado, Mexicali, Baja California.

DOCUMENTS (TRANSCRIBED AND PRINTED)

Aguirre, Amado, ed. *Documentos para la historia de Baja California* (Recopilación dispuesta por el Ingeniero Amado Aguirre . . .) Instituto de Investigaciones Históricas, Universidad Nacional Autónoma de México/Universidad Autónoma de Baja California, México, D.F./ Tijuana, Baja California, 1977.

Alvarez, José J. y Rafael Durán, eds. *Itinerarios y derroteros de la República Mexicana.* Mexico, D. F.: Imprenta de José A. Godoy, 1856.

Barco, Miguel del. *Historia natural y crónica de la Antigua California [Adiciones y correcciones a la Noticia de Miguel Venegas].* Edición, estudio preliminar, notas y apéndices: Miguel León-Portilla. México, D.F.: Universidad Nacional Autónoma de México, 1973.

Bayle, Constantino. *Misión de la Baja California.* [Transcriptions of Salvatierra letters and later documents from Jesuit California]. Madrid: La Editorial Católica, 1946.

Bravo, Jaime. "Razón de la entrada al Puerto de la Paz: conquista de la nación Guaycura, y fundación de la Misión de Nuestra Señora del Pilar en California, Año de 1720." See León-Portilla, *Testimonios sudcalifornianos.*

Burrus, Ernest J. *Kino and Manje, Explorers of Sonora and Arizona . . . A Study of Their Expeditions and Plans.* [With 30 additional documents in Spanish by Juan Mateo Manje and others.] Rome: Jesuit Historical Institute, 1971.

———. *Misiones norteñas mexicanas de la Compañía de Jesús, 1751–1757.* México: Antigua Librería Robredo de José Porrúa e Hijos, Sucs., 1963.

Burrus, Ernest J., and Félix Zubillaga, eds. *Misiones mexicanas de la Compañía de Jesús, 1618–1745* [Cartas e informes conservadas en la "Colección Mateu"]. Madrid: Ediciones José Porrúa Turanzas, 1982.

---

4. Many pages are so badly stained as to be in part unreadable.

————. *El noroeste de México; documentos sobre las misiones Jesuíticas, 1600–1769.* México, D.F.: Universidad Nacional Autónoma de México, 1986.

Castillo Negrete, Francisco. "Geografía y Estadística de la Baja California, 1853." *Boletín de la Sociedad Mexicana de Geografía y Estadística*, 1 serie, 7 (1859), pp. 338–59.

Coronado, Eligio M. *Descripción e inventarios de las misiones de Baja California, 1773.* [AGNM, Misiones, tomo 12, exp. 10 transcribed and printed]. Palma de Mallorca: Institut d'Estudis Baleárics, 1987.

Costansó, Miguel. *Diario Historico.* [A facsimile of the 1771 original reproduced in] *The Costansó Narrative of the Portolá Expedition: First Chronicle of the Spanish Conquest of Alta California.* Translated and edited by Ray Brandes. Newhall, California: Hogarth Press, 1970.

Documentos para la historia de México. 20 vols. México: Imprenta de F. Escalante, 1853–1857. Series 2, 4.

Ducrue, Benno. *Ducrue's Account of the Expulsion of the Jesuits from Lower California.* [In the original Latin and in English]. Translated and edited by Ernest J. Burrus, S.J. Rome: Jesuit Historical Institute, 1967.

Faría, Francisco Javier de. *Apologético defensorio y puntual manifiesto.* Versión paleográfica de Gilberto López Alanis. Culiacán: Universidad Autónoma de Sinaloa, 1981.

González Rodríguez, Luis, ed. *Etnología y misión en la Pimería Alta, 1715–1740: Informes de Luis Javier Velarde, Giuseppe Maria Genovese, Daniel Januske, José Agustín de Campos y Cristóbal de Cañas.* México. D. F.: Universidad Nacional Autónoma de México, 1977.

Guillén, Clemente. "Expedición por tierra desde la Misión de San Juan Malibat a la Bahía de la Paz en el Seno Californico, Año de 1720." See León-Portilla, *Testimonios sudcalifor-nianos.*

Kino, Eusebio Francisco. *Correspondencia del P. Kino con los Generales de la Compañia de Jesús.* México, D.F.: Editorial Jus, 1961.

León-Portilla, Miguel, ed. *Testimonios sudcalifornianos; nueva entrada y establecimiento en el puerto de La Paz, 1720.* [Informes by Jaime Bravo, Juan de Ugarte, and Clemente Guillén, introduced, edited, and annotated by León-Portilla]. México, D.F.: Universidad Nacional Autónoma de México, 1970.

Mathes, W. Michael, ed. *Californiana III: Documentos para la historia de la transformación colonizadora de California, 1679–1686.* 3 vols. Madrid: Ediciones José Porrúa Turanzas, 1970.

Nápoli, Padre Ignacio María, S.J. *Relación del Padre Ignacio María Nápoli acerca de la California, hecha el año de 1721.* Ed. Roberto Ramos. México, D.F.: Editorial Jus, 1958.

Naylor, Thomas H., and Charles W. Polzer, eds. *The Presidio and Militia on the Northern Frontier of New Spain.* Tucson: The University of Arizona Press, 1986. [Presents original versions of all documents as well as translations.]

————. *Pedro de Rivera and the Military Regulations for Northern New Spain, 1724–1729.* Tucson: The University of Arizona Press, 1988. [Presents original versions of all documents as well as translations.]

Nentvig, Juan, S.J. *Descripción geografica, natural, y curiosa dela Prov*. de Sonora por un amigo de el Servicio de Dios y el Rey Nro Señor.* Edición preparada, con una introducción histórica, notas, apéndice e índice analítico, por Germán Viveros. México, D. F.: Archivo General de la Nación, Segunda Serie, Número I, n.d.

Piccolo, Francisco María, S.J. "Descubrimiento por tierra de la contracosta y otros parajes de tierra . . . cuya es esta carta escrita al Padre Juan María Salvatierra, el 30 de Octubre de 1699." See Ramos, *Tres Documentos.*

————. *Informe del estado de la Nueva Cristianidad de California, 1702* [y otros documentos]. Edición, estudio y notas por Ernest J. Burrus, S.J. Madrid: Ediciones José Porrúa Turanzas, 1962.

————. *Informe on the New Province of California, 1702* [contains photographic facsimile of the 1702 imprint]. Translated and edited by George P. Hammond. Los Angeles: Dawson's Book Shop, 1967.

Ramos, Roberto, ed. *Tres Documentos sobre el descubrimiento y exploración de Baja California por Francisco María Piccolo, Juan de Ugarte y Guillermo Stratford.* México, D.F.: Editorial Jus, 1958.

Rivera y Moncada, Fernando de. *Diario de Fernando de Rivera y Moncada.* Edición, Prólogo, y Notas por Ernest J. Burrus, S.J. Madrid: Ediciones José Porrúa Turanzas, 1967.

Rodríguez Gallardo, J. Rafael. *Informe sobre Sinaloa y Sonora, año de 1750.* Edición, introducción, notas, apéndice e índices per Germán Viveros. México, D.F.: Archivo General de la Nación, 1975.

Rodríguez Lorenzo, Esteban [attributed]. *Descripción y toponimia indígena de California, 1740.* Informe atribuido a Esteban Rodríguez Lorenzo. Introducción, Edición y Notas de Miguel León-Portilla. La Paz, Baja California: Gobierno del Territorio de Baja California, Cuaderno de Divulgación, Número 44, n.d.

Ugarte, Juan de. "Carta del Padre Visitador Juan de Ugarte al Excelentísimo Señor Marqués de Valero, Virrey. Fundación de la Misión de Nuestra Señora del Pilar, en el Puerto de la Paz. Marzo 15 de 1721." [See León-Portilla, *Testimonios sudcalifornianos.*]

———. "Relación del descubrimiento del Golfo de California o Mar Lauretano . . . en el Año de 1722." [See Ramos, *Tres Documentos.*]

Velázquez de León, Joaquín. *Descripción de la Antigua California: 1768.* Transcripción, presentación y notas de Ignacio del Río. La Paz: Edición del H. Ayuntamiento de La Paz (Colección Cabildo, 2), 1975.

Documents (translated and printed)

Atondo y Antillón, Isidro. *First from Gulf to Pacific; the* [Atondo] *diary of the Kino-Atondo Peninsular Expedition.* Translated and edited by W. Michael Mathes. Los Angeles: Dawson's Book Shop, 1969.

Baegert, Johann Jakob. *Observations in Lower California.* Translation, Introduction, and Notes by M. M. Brandenberg and Carl L. Baumann. Berkeley and Los Angeles: University of California Press, 1952.

———. *The Letters of Jacob Baegert 1749–1761.* Introduced and edited by Doyce B. Nunis, Jr. Translated by Elsbeth Schulz-Bischof. Los Angeles: Dawson's Book Shop, 1982.

Burrus, Ernest, ed. and trans. *Jesuit Relations: Baja California, 1716–1762.* Los Angeles: Dawson's Book Shop, 1984.

———. *Kino and Manje, Explorers of Sonora and Arizona . . . A study of their expeditions and plans.* Rome: Jesuit Historical Institute, 1971.

Caballero Carranco, Juan. *The Pearl Hunters in the Gulf of California, 1668. Summary Report of the Voyage made to the Californias by Captain Francisco de Lucenilla.* Introduced, translated, and edited by W. Michael Mathes. Los Angeles: Dawson's Book Shop, 1966.

Costansó, Miguel. *The Costansó Narrative of the Portolá Expedition: First Chronicle of the Spanish Conquest of Alta California.* [Contains a facsimile of the 1771 Mexican imprint.] Translated and edited by Ray Brandes. Newhall, California: Hogarth Press, 1970.

Ducrue, Benno. *Ducrue's Account of the Expulsion of the Jesuits from Lower California.* Translated and edited by Ernest J. Burrus, S.J. Rome: Jesuit Historical Institute, 1967.

Guillén, Clemente. *Clemente Guillén, Explorer of the South. Diaries of the Overland Expeditions to Bahía Magdalena and La Paz, 1719, 1720–1721.* Introduced, translated, and edited by W. Michael Mathes. Los Angeles: Dawson's Book Shop, 1979.

Kino, Eusebio Francisco. *Kino Reports to Headquarters: Correspondence of Eusebio F. Kino from New Spain with Rome.* Translation and notes by Ernest J. Burrus. Rome: Jesuit Historical Institute, 1954.

———. *Kino Writes to the Duchess. Letters of Eusebio Francisco Kino to the Duchess of Aveiro.* Translated and edited by Ernest J. Burrus. Rome: Jesuit Historical Institute, 1965.

———. *Kino's Historical Memoir of the Pimería Alta: A Contemporary Account of the Beginnings of California, Sonora, and Arizona.* Translated and edited by Herbert E. Bolton. 2 vols. Berkeley and Los Angeles: University of California Press, 1948.

Linck, Wenceslaus. *Wenceslaus Linck's Diary of His 1766 Expedition to Northern Baja California.* Translated and edited by Ernest J. Burrus. Los Angeles: Dawson's Book Shop, 1966.

———. *Wenceslaus Linck's Reports & Letters, 1762–1778*. Translated and edited by Ernest J. Burrus. Los Angeles: Dawson's Book Shop, 1967.

Palóu, Francisco. *Historical Memoirs of New California*. Edited by Herbert Eugene Bolton. 4 vols. Berkeley: University of California Press, 1926.

Piccolo, Francisco María, S.J. *Informe on the New Province of California, 1702* [contains photographic facsimile of the 1702 Mexican imprint]. Translated and edited by George P. Hammond. Los Angeles: Dawson's Book Shop, 1967.

Salvatierra, Juan María de. *Juan María de Salvatierra. Selected Letters about Lower California*. Translated and annotated by Ernest J. Burrus. Los Angeles: Dawson's Book Shop, 1971.

Taraval, Sigismundo. *The Indian Uprising in Lower California, 1734–1737*. Translated with introduction and notes by Marguerite Eyer Wilbur. Los Angeles: The Quivira Society, 1931.

Tirsch, Ignacio. *The Drawings of Ignacio Tirsch, A Jesuit Missionary in Baja California*. Introduced and edited by Doyce B. Nunis, Jr. Translated by Elsbeth Schulz-Bischof. Los Angeles: Dawson's Book Shop, 1972.

Secondary Sources

BOOKS AND MONOGRAPHS

Almada, Francisco R. *Diccionario de historia, geografía y biografía sonorenses*. Chihuahua: Ruiz Sandoval, 1952.

Amao, Jorge Luis. *Minas y mineros en Baja California, 1748–1790*. Tesis. México, D.F.: Universidad Nacional Autónoma de México, 1981.

Aschmann, Homer. *The Central Desert of Baja California: Demography and Ecology*. Berkeley and Los Angeles: University of California Press, 1959.

Aveling, J. C. H. *The Jesuits*. New York: Stein and Day, 1981.

Bancroft, Hubert Howe. *History of California*. Vol. 1, 1542–1800. San Francisco: The History Company, 1886.

———. *History of the North Mexican States*. Vol. 1. San Francisco: A.L. Bancroft & Co., 1884.

———. *California Pioneer Register and Index, Including Inhabitants of California, 1769–1800, and List of Pioneers*. [Extracted from *The History of California*]. Baltimore: Regional Publishing Co., 1964

Bangert, William V. *A History of the Society of Jesus*. St. Louis: The Institute of Jesuit Sources, 1972.

Bargalló, Modesto. *La minería y metalurgia en la América española durante la epoca colonial*. México-Buenos Aires: Fondo de Cultura Económica, 1955.

Bayle, Constantino. *Historia de los descubrimientos y colonización de los padres de la Compañía de Jesús en la Baja California*. Madrid: Librería General de Victoriano Suárez, 1933.

Bethell, Leslie, ed. *Colonial Spanish America*. New York: Cambridge University Press, 1987.

Bolton, Herbert Eugene. *Rim of Christendom, a biography of Eusebio Francisco Kino, Pacific Coast pioneer*. 1936. Reprint. Tucson: University of Arizona Press, 1984.

Boneu Companys, Fernando. *Gaspar de Portolá, Explorer and Founder of California*. Translated and revised by Alan K. Brown. Lérida: Instituto de Estudios Ilerdenses, 1983.

Brading, D. A. *Miners and Merchants in Bourbon Mexico, 1763–1810*. Cambridge: Cambridge University Press, 1971.

Brinckerhoff, Sydney B., and Odie B. Faulk. *Lancers for the King: A Study of the Frontier Military System of Northern New Spain, with a Translation of the Royal Regulations of 1772*. Phoenix: Arizona Historical Foundation, 1965.

Burkholder, Mark A., and D. S. Chandler. *From Impotence to Authority, The Spanish Crown and the American Audiencias, 1687–1808*. Columbia & London: University of Missouri Press, 1977.

Burkholder, Mark A., and Lyman L. Johnson. *Colonial Latin America*. New York & Oxford: Oxford University Press, 1990.

Chapman, Charles E. *A History of California: The Spanish Period.* New York: The Macmillan Company, 1921.

Clavijero, Francisco Javier. *The History of [Lower] California.* Translated from Italian and edited by Sara E. Lake and A. A. Gray. Palo Alto: Stanford University Press, 1937.

Clayton, Lawrence A. *Caulkers and Carpenters in a New World: the shipyards of colonial Guayaquil.* Athens: Ohio University, Center for International Studies, 1980.

Cohen, Thomas. "The Fire of Tongues: Antonio Vieira and the Christian Mission in Brazil." [Doctoral dissertation, Stanford University 1990] Ann Arbor: University Microfilms, 1990.

Combier, Cyprien. *Voyage au Golfe de Californie. . . .* Paris: A. Bertrand, 1864.

Cook, Sherburne F. *The Extent and Significance of Disease among the Indians of Baja California, 1697–1773.* Berkeley: University of California Press, Ibero-Americana 12, 1937.

Crosby, Harry W. *The Cave Paintings of Baja California.* San Diego: Copley Books, 1975. Revised edition. 1984.

———. *Doomed to Fail: Gaspar de Portolá's First California Appointees.* San Diego: Institute for Regional Studies of the Californias, Border Studies Series #2, 1989.

———. *The King's Highway in Baja California.* San Diego: Copley Books, 1974.

———. *Last of the Californios.* San Diego: Copley Books, 1981.

Decorme, Gerard, S.J. *La obra de los jesuitas mexicanos durante la epoca colonial, 1572–1767.* 2 vols. México, D.F.: Antigua Librería Robredo de José Porrúa e Hijos, 1941.

Deeds, Susan McClymont. "Rendering Unto Caesar: The Secularization of Jesuit Missions in Mid-eighteenth Century Durango." Ph.D. diss., University of Arizona, 1981.

Dobyns, Henry F. *Spanish Colonial Tucson: A Demographic History.* Tucson: University of Arizona Press, 1976.

Douglass, William A., and Jon Bilbao. *Amerikanuak: Basques in the New World.* Reno: University of Nevada Press, 1975.

Dunne, Peter Masten. *Black Robes in Lower California.* Berkeley and Los Angeles: University of California Press, 1952.

———. *Pioneer Black Robes on the West Coast.* Berkeley: University of California Press, 1940.

———. *Juan Antonio Baltasar, Padre Visitador to the Sonora Frontier, 1744–1745.* Tucson: Arizona Pioneers' Historical Society, 1957.

Engelhardt, Zephyrin. *Missions and Missionaries of California.* Vol. 1. Santa Barbara: Mission Santa Barbara, 1929.

Esteva, José María. *Memoria sobre la pesca de la perla en la Baja California.* Mexico City: Imprenta de A. Boix, a cargo de Miguel Zornoza, 1865.

Farriss, N. M. *Crown and Clergy in Colonial Mexico, 1759–1821: The Crisis of Ecclesiastical Privilege.* London: Athlone, 1968.

Faulk, Odie B. *The Leather Jacket Soldier: Spanish Military Equipment and Institutions of the late 18th Century.* Pasadena: Socio-Technical Press, 1971.

Fisher, Lillian E. *Viceregal Administration in the Spanish-American Colonies.* Vol. 15. Berkeley: University of California Publications in History, 1926.

Gerhard, Peter. *The North Frontier of New Spain.* Princeton: Princeton University Press, 1982.

———. *Pirates on the West Coast of New Spain.* Glendale: The Arthur H. Clark Co., 1960.

Gibson, Charles. *Spain in America.* New York: Harper & Row, 1966.

Greenleaf, Richard E. *The Roman Catholic Church in Colonial Latin America.* New York: Knopf, 1971.

Greenow, Linda. *Credit and Socioeconomic Change in Colonial Mexico: Loans and Mortgages in Guadalajara, 1720–1820.* Dellplain Latin American Studies, No. 12. Boulder, Colorado: Westview Press, 1983.

Hardy, Robert W. H. *Travels in the interior of Mexico, in 1825, 1826, 1827, & 1828.* London: Bentley, 1829.

Haring, Clarence H. *The Spanish Empire in America.* New York: Harcourt, Brace, and World, 1947.

Herr, Richard. *The Eighteenth Century Revolution in Spain*. Princeton: Princeton University Press, 1958.

Hinojosa, Salvador. *Arquitectura misional de Baja California Sur*. La Paz: Gobierno del Estado de Baja California Sur, 1988.

Hittel, Theodore H. *El Triunfo de la Cruz: The first ship built in the Californias*. [Reprint of article in *The Californian*, vol. 1, no. 1, pp. 15–18, January 1880.] San Francisco: California Historical Society, n.d.

Hu-De Hart, Evelyn. *Missionaries, Miners, and Indians: Spanish Contact with the Yaqui Nation of Northwestern New Spain, 1533–1820*. Tucson: The University of Arizona Press, 1981.

Kicza, John E. *Colonial Entrepreneurs: Family and Business in Bourbon Mexico City*. Albuquerque: University of New Mexico Press, 1983.

Konrad, Herman W. *A Jesuit Hacienda in Colonial Mexico: Santa Lucía, 1576–1767*. Stanford: Stanford University Press, 1980.

Ladd, Doris M. *The Mexican Nobility at Independence 1780–1826*. Austin: Institute of Latin American Studies, The University of Texas, 1976.

Lindley, Richard. "Kinship and Credit in the Structure of Guadalajara's Oligarchy, 1800–1830." Ph.D. diss., University of Texas at Austin, 1976.

Lockhart, James, and Stuart B. Schwartz. *Early Latin America*. Cambridge and New York: Cambridge University Press, 1983.

Martínez, Pablo L. *Guía Familiar de Baja California, 1700–1900*. México, D. F.: Editorial Baja California, 1965.

Mathes, W. Michael. *Las misiones de Baja California*. La Paz: Gobierno del Estado de Baja California Sur/Editorial Aristos, 1977.

——. *La geografía mitológica de California: orígenes, desarrollo, concreción y desaparición*. Guadalajara: Academia Mexicana de la Historia, 1985.

McAlister, Lyle N. *Spain and Portugal in the New World, 1492–1700*. Minneapolis: University of Minnesota Press, 1984.

McNeill, John Robert. *Atlantic Empires of France and Spain: Louisbourg and Havana, 1700–1763*. Chapel Hill and London: The University of North Carolina Press, 1985.

Mixco, Mauricio J. *Cochimí and Proto-Yuman: Lexical and Syntactic Evidence for a New Language Family in Lower California*. University of Utah Anthropological Papers, Number 101, Salt Lake City: University of Utah Press, 1978.

Moorhead, Max L. *The Presidio, Bastion of the Spanish Borderlands*. Norman: University of Oklahoma Press, 1975.

Mörner, Magnus. *The Political and Economic Activities of the Jesuits in the La Plata Region*. Stockholm: Library and Institute of Ibero-American Studies, 1953.

——. *Race Mixture in the History of Latin America*. Boston: Little, Brown and Company, 1967.

Navarro García, Luis. *Don José de Gálvez y la comandancia general de las provincias internas del norte de Nueva España*. Sevilla: Escuela de Estudios Hispano-Americanos, 1964.

——. *La sublevación Yaqui de 1740*. Sevilla: Escuela de Estudios Hispano-Americanos, 1966.

Nunn, Charles F. *Foreign Immigrants in Early Bourbon Mexico, 1700–1760*. Cambridge: Cambridge University Press, 1979.

Parry, J. H. *The Spanish Seaborne Empire*. New York: Alfred A. Knopf, 1966.

Peña Navarro, Everardo. *Estudio histórico del estado de Nayarit*. Tepic: El Gobierno del Estado de Nayarit, 1946.

Polzer, Charles W. *Rules and Precepts of the Jesuit Missions of Northwestern New Spain*. Tucson: University of Arizona Press, 1976.

Pradeau, Alberto Francisco. *La expulsión de los Jesuitas de las provincias de Sonora, Ostimuri y Sinaloa en 1767*. México, D.F.: Antigua Librería Robredo, de José Porrúa e Hijos, Sucs., 1959.

Reygadas Dahl, Fermín, and Guillermo Velázquez Ramírez. *El grupo pericú de Baja California*. La Paz: Fonapas, 1983.

Ricard, Robert. *The Spiritual Conquest of Mexico*. Translated by Lesley Byrd Simpson. Berkeley: University of California Press, 1966.

Río, Ignacio del. *A la diestra mano de las Indias: Descubrimiento y ocupación colonial de la Baja California.* La Paz: Gobierno del Estado de Baja California Sur—Dirección de Cultura, 1985.

——. *Conquista y aculturación en la California jesuítica, 1697–1768.* México, D.F.: Universidad Nacional Autónoma de México, 1984.

——. *Guía del Archivo Franciscano de la Biblioteca Nacional de México.* México, D.F.: Universidad Nacional Autónoma de México, 1975.

——. "El régimen jesuítico de la antigua California." Tesis. México, D.F.: Universidad Nacional Autónoma de México, 1971.

Roca, Paul M. *Spanish Jesuit Churches in Mexico's Tarahumara.* Tuscon: The University of Arizona Press, 1979.

Ryan, William Redmond. *Personal Adventures in Upper and Lower California, in 1848–1849.* London: William Shoberl, 1850.

Sauer, Carl Ortwin. *The Road to Cíbola.* Ibero-Americana, No. 3. Berkeley: University of California Press, 1932.

Schurz, William Lytle. *The Manila Galleon.* New York: E.P. Dutton & Co., 1939.

Shelvocke, George. *A Voyage Round the World by Way of the Great South Sea. . . .* 2d ed. Revised and republished by George Shelvocke. London: W. Innys, J. Richardson, M. T. Longman, 1757.

Spicer, Edward H. *Cycles of Conquest: The Impact of Spain, Mexico, and the United States on the Indians of the Southwest, 1533–1960.* Tucson: The University of Arizona Press, 1962.

Stein, Stanley J., and Barbara H. Stein. *The Colonial Heritage of Latin America: Essays on Economic Dependence in Perspective.* New York: Oxford University Press, 1970.

Van Young, Eric. *Hacienda and Market in Eighteenth-Century Mexico.* Berkeley, Los Angeles and London: University of California Press, 1981.

Velázquez, María del Carmen. *El Fondo Piadoso de las misiones de Californias.* México, D.F.: Secretaría de Relaciones Exteriores, 1985.

——. *El Marqués de Altamira y las provincias internas de Nueva España.* Mexico City: El Colegio de México, 1976.

Venegas, Miguel. *El Apóstol Mariano representado en la vida del V. P. Juan Maria de Salvatierra. . . .* Mexico: Imprenta de Doña Maria de Ribera, 1754. [An indexed facsimile of this work makes up vol. 5 of *Obras Californianas del Padre Miguel Venegas;* vide infra.]

——. "Empressas Apostolicas de los PP. Missioneros de la Compania de Jesus, de la Provincia de Nueva España, Obradas en la Conquista de Californias Debida y Consagradas al Patrocinio de Maria Santissima, Conquistadora de Nuevas Gentes en Su Sagrada Imagen de Loreto." (1737) Manuscript in collection of The Bancroft Library, Berkeley; Microfilm MM 1701 from the same source. [An indexed facsimile of this work forms vol. 4 of *Obras Californianas del Padre Miguel Venegas.*]

——. *Obras californianas del Padre Miguel Venegas, S.J.* Edición y Estudios por Dr. W. Michael Mathes; Bibliografías e Indices por Profra. Vivian C. Fisher y Profr. Moisés Coronado. 5 vols. La Paz: Universidad Autónoma de Baja California Sur, 1979.

——. *Noticia de la California y su conquista temporal y espiritual. . . .* (Abridged and rewritten by P. Andrés Marcos Burriel from: Venegas, "Empressas Apostolicas"; with appended documents). Madrid: En la imprenta de la viuda de M. Fernandez, 1757. [An indexed facsimile of this work is found in Mathes, Fisher, and Coronado, *Obras Californianas de . . . Miguel Venegas,* vols. 1–3.]

Vidargas del Moral, Juan Domingo. "Navegación y comercio en el golfo de California, 1740–1824." Tesis. México, D.F.: Universidad Nacional Autónoma de México, 1982.

Villavicencio, Juan Joseph de. *Vida y virtudes de el venerable y apostolico Padre Juan de Ugarte de la Compañia de Jesus, missionero de las Islas Californias, y uno de sus primeros conquistadores.* Mexico: Imprenta del real, y mas antiguo Colegio de San Ildefonso, 1752.

Weber, David J. *The Spanish Frontier in North America.* New Haven and London: Yale University Press, 1992.

West, Robert C., and John C. Augelli. *Middle America, Its Lands and Peoples.* 2d ed. Englewood, New Jersey: Prentice Hall, 1976.

Zamorano Club. *The Zamorano Index to History of California by Hubert Howe Bancroft*. Los Angeles: University of Southern California, 1985.

PERIODICAL ARTICLES

Bishko, Charles Julian. "The Peninsular Background of Latin American Cattle Ranching." *Hispanic American Historical Review* 32 (1952): 491–515.

Bolton, Herbert Eugene. "The Mission as a Frontier Institution in the Spanish-American Colonies." *American Historical Review* 23 (October 1917): 42–61.

Crosby, Harry. "El Camino Real in Baja California: Loreto to San Diego." *The Journal of San Diego History* 23, no. 1 (Winter 1977): 1–45.

Deeds, Susan McClymont. "Las relaciones entre los jesuitas y los oficiales reales . . . ," *Memoria del IV Simposio de Historia de Sonora*, Hermosillo, Mexico: Instituto de Investigaciones Históricas, 1979, pp. 94–108.

———. "Mission Villages and Agrarian Patterns in a Nueva Vizcayan Heartland, 1600–1750." *Journal of the Southwest* 33, no. 3 (Autumn 1991): 345–65.

Gerhard, Peter. "A Dutch Trade Mission to New Spain, 1746–1747." *Pacific Historical Review* 23 (1954): 221–26.

———. "Pearl Diving in Lower California, 1533–1830." *Pacific Historical Review* 25 (1956): 239–49.

Jackson, Robert H. "Demographic Patterns in the Missions of Central Baja California." *Journal of California and Great Basin Anthropology* 6, no. 1 (1984): 91–112.

Lockhart, James. "Encomienda and Hacienda: The Evolution of the Great Estate in the Spanish Indies." *Hispanic American Historical Review* 49 (1969): 411–29.

López Sarrelangue, Delfina. "Las misiones jesuitas de Sonora y Sinaloa, base de colonización de la Baja California." *Estudios de Historia Novohispana*, Instituto de Investigaciones Históricas de la UNAM, 2 (1967): 149–202.

Mason, William M. "The Garrisons of San Diego Presidio: 1770–1794." *The Journal of San Diego History* 24, no. 4 (Fall 1978): 399–424.

Mathes, W. Michael. "Baja California Indians in the Spanish Maritime Service, 1720–1821." *Southern California Quarterly*, 62, no. 2, (Summer 1980): 113–26.

Meredith, John D. "The Yaqui Rebellion of 1740: A Jesuit account and its implications." *Ethnohistory* 22, no. 3 (Summer 1975): 222–61.

Río, Ignacio del. "Los Indios de Baja California (Notas Etnográficas)." *Boletín de Información del Instituto de Investigaciones Históricas — UNAM*, Históricas 2, enero–abril, 1980.

———. "Utopia in Baja California: The Dreams of José de Gálvez." Translated by Arturo Jiménez-Vera. *The Journal of San Diego History* 18, no. 4 (Fall 1972): 1–13.

Rubio Mañé, Ignacio. "Gente de España en la Ciudad de México: año de 1689." Sobretiro del *Boletín del Archivo General de la Nación* Segunda Serie, Tomo VII, Números 1–2. Mexico City, 1966: 5–406.

Salvucci, Linda Kerrigan. "Costumbres viejas, 'hombres nuevos': José de Gálvez y la burocracia fiscal novohispana, 1754–1800." *Historia Mexicana* 33, no. 2 (1983): 224–64.

Stern, Peter, and Robert H. Jackson. "Vagabundaje and Settlement Patterns in Colonial Northern Sonora." *The Americas* 44 (April 1988): 461–81.

Index

Italicized words in headings will also be found in the Glossary; names of ships are exceptions, but they are labelled as ships. Botanical names of indigenous plants are given in the Glossary as well as with their first appearances in the text. The names of Jesuit padres are preceded by P.; titles of other churchmen are written out.

Acapulco 56, 162, 166, 359
   as American terminal of trans-Pacific trade 5, 114, 117, 148, 336
   as shipping port for California supplies 22, 99, 147, 169, 173, 292
   ship construction and repair at 148, 176, 217
Acevedo, Gertrudis 253, 421
Acevedo, Ignacio de 112
   biog. data for 413
Acevedo, Rosa Francisca de 364
Acosta, Teresa de 418
Adac (mission site) 179, 348–49,
Adobe construction
   of churches 49–50, 225, 227–29, 241, 269–70
   of dwellings 242, 271, 274, 282, 284
Agriculture at missions 209
   included inappropriate crops 209
   irrigation systems for 84, 194, 209, 212, 227, 242
   coconuts 285
   corn (maize) 242
   figs, oranges, pomegranates 113
   rice 227
   wheat 209–10, 242
   see also Cattle, Locusts, Wine
Aguiar, Francisco Miguel de 174, 335
   biog. data for 414
Aguilar, Francisco Javier 250, 262

Aguilar, Juan Antonio de 262
   as soldier guard at San Miguel 235–36, 247, 250–52
   as soldier guard at San José de Comondú 231, 248, 249
   biog. data for 414
Aguilar, María Josefa 414
Aguirre, Clara 418
Ahome (Sinaloan port and mission) 57, 146 map, 153, 293
Aiñiní (mission site) 108, 179
Airapí (mission site) 179
Alabado (a hymn) 197, 238–39
Alamos (Sonoran mining town) 9 map, 21 map, 145, 146 map
   photograph of following 110
Alarcón, Hernando de 4, 101, 127
Alburquerque, Duque de (viceroy) 395
   brings Bourbon policies to New Spain (1702) 61, 68, 72
   contests Jesuit powers in California 73–74, 78, 156
   feels pressure from Jesuits 78
Alcoholic drinks 295
   brandy 100, 217, 244, 264, 307
   see also Wine
Alférez (military rank) 432n. 95